A Handbook of Leisure Studies

A Handbook
of Leisure Studies

Edited by

Chris Rojek
Faculty of Law and Social Science, Brunel University, West London, UK

Susan M. Shaw
Department of Recreation and Leisure Studies, University of Waterloo, Ontario, Canada

A. J. Veal
School of Leisure, Sport and Tourism, University of Technology, Sydney, Australia

First published in hardback 2006
First published in paperback 2007 by
PALGRAVE MACMILLAN
Houndmills, Basingstoke, Hampshire RG21 6XS and
175 Fifth Avenue, New York, N.Y. 10010
Companies and representatives throughout the world

PALGRAVE MACMILLAN is the global academic imprint of the Palgrave
Macmillan division of St Martin's Press LLC and of Palgrave Macmillan Ltd.
Macmillan® is a registered trademark in the United States, United Kingdom
and other countries. Palgrave is a registered trademark in the European
Union and other countries.

ISBN-13 978–1–4039–0278 8 hardback
ISBN-10 1–4039–0278 X hardback
ISBN-13 978–1–4039–0279 5 paperback
ISBN-10 1–4039–0279 8 paperback

This book is printed on paper suitable for recycling and made from fully
managed and sustained forest sources. Logging, pulping and manufacturing
processes are expected to conform to the environmental regulations of the
country of origin.

A catalogue record for this book is available from the British Library.

Library of Congress Cataloging-in-Publication Data
A handbook of leisure studies / edited by Chris Rojek, Susan M. Shaw, A.J. Veal.
       p. cm.
   Includes bibliographical references and index.
   ISBN 1–4039–0278–X (cloth : alk. paper)   1–4039–0279–8 (pbk)
    1. Leisure—Research. I. Rojek, Chris. II. Shaw, Susan M., 1946–   III. Veal,
Anthony James.

   GV14.5.H245 2006
   790.107'2—dc22

                                                                          2006043215

10   9   8   7   6   5   4   3   2   1
16   15   14   13   12   11   10   09   08   07

Printed and bound in Great Britain by
Antony Rowe Ltd, Chippenham, Wiltshire

Contents

Notes on Contributors

Chris Barker is Associate Professor in the Communications and Cultural Studies Program at the University of Wollongong, Australia. He has written extensively in the field of media and cultural studies and his books include: *Television, Globalization and Cultural Identities* (1999); *Cultural Studies: Theory and Practice* (2000); *Making Sense of Cultural Studies: Central Problems and Critical Debates* (2002); and *The Sage Dictionary of Cultural Studies* (2004). He is currently conducting research concerned with the intersection of culture, identity and emotion.

Kumkum Bhattacharya is Professor in the Department of Social Work, Visva-Bharati University, India, founded by Rabindranath Tagore. She has conducted research among the Santals, the third largest tribe in India and among minority groups. She has published research in the field of culture and personality studies.

Susan Birrell is a Professor in the Departments of Health and Sport Studies, Women's Studies, and American Studies at the University of Iowa, USA. She studies sport and cultural reproduction from a critical cultural studies perspective. She co-edited *Reading Sport* (2000) with Mary McDonald and *Women, Sport and Culture* (1994) with Cheryl Cole. Her current research project explores the cultural meanings of mountaineering by focusing on narratives about Mt Everest.

Garry Chick is Professor in the Department of Recreation, Park and Tourism Management at the Pennsylvania State University, USA. He holds a PhD in anthropology from the University of Pittsburgh and is a past-president of the Society for Cross-Cultural Research and the Association for the Study of Play. His recent publications include: *The Encyclopedia of Leisure and Recreation in America* (co-editor, 2004) and a chapter on cultural constraints on leisure (with Erwei Dong) in *Constraints on Leisure* (ed. E. Jackson, 2005).

Fred Coalter is Professor of Sports Policy in the Centre for Sports Research, University of Stirling, Scotland, and was formerly Director of the Centre for Leisure Research at the University of Edinburgh (1990–2003) and Director of the Centre for Leisure and Tourism Studies at the Polytechnic of North London (1986–1990). He is an Honorary Fellow of the Institute of Leisure and Amenity Management and a Fellow of the Academy of Leisure Sciences. He has published widely in the area of sport and leisure policy, including *Recreational Welfare* (1988), and *Freedom and Constraint: The Paradoxes of Leisure* (ed., 1989).

Daniel Thomas Cook is Associate Professor of advertising and communications at the University of Illinois, USA. He is the author of *The Commodification of Childhood*

(2004), which explores the rise of children as consumers, and editor of *Symbolic Childhood* (2002), a compendium of original research addressing the politics of representation of children. His articles have appeared in academic journals such as *Leisure Sciences, Sociological Quarterly* and the *Journal of Consumer Culture* and in more popular publications like *Global Agenda* (2006) and *LiP Magazine*.

Chas Critcher is Professor of Communications and Head of the Humanities Research Centre at Sheffield Hallam University, UK. He is author/editor of *The Devil Makes Work* (1985); *Sociology of Leisure: A Reader* (1995); *Out of the Ashes? Decline and Regeneration in Britain's Mining Communities* (2001); and *Moral Panics and the Media* (2003).

David Crouch is Professor of Cultural Geography, Tourism and Leisure, and Director of The Culture, Lifestyle and Landscape Research Centre at the University of Derby. He is author/editor of: *Leisure/ Tourism Geographies* (1999); *Visual Culture and Tourism* (2003); and *The Media and the Tourist Imagination: Convergent Cultures* (2005). He is co-editor of *Leisure Studies* and has published numerous articles and chapters on cultural geography, leisure, tourism, space and performance and research methods.

Joanne Finkelstein is Executive Dean and Professor in the Faculty of Arts, Education, Human Development, Victoria University, Australia. She is author of: *The Sociological Bent : Inside Metro Culture* (with Susan Goodwin, 2005); *After a Fashion* (1996); *Slaves of Chic: An A-Z of Consumer Pleasures* (1994); The Fashioned Self (1991); and *Dining Out: A Sociology of Modern Manners* (1989).

Adrian Franklin is Professor of Sociology in the School of Sociology and Social Work, University of Tasmania, Australia. His current interests include tourism theory, place making and the wider ordering effects of tourism. He is Editor of *Tourist Studies* and author of: *Animals and Modern Cultures* (1999); *Nature and Social Theory* (2002); *Tourism: An Introduction* (2003); and *Animals Nation: The True Story of Animals and Australia* (2006).

Valeria J. Freysinger is Associate Professor in the Department of Physical Education, Health, and Sport Studies at Miami University of Ohio, USA. Her scholarly interests include leisure and life course development/ageing and social (in)equality in leisure (specifically, gender, race and age inequalities). She is a co-author of *Both Gains and Gaps: Feminist Perspectives on Women's Leisure* (1995) and *21st Century Leisure: Current Issues* (2000) and author of a number of book chapters and articles on leisure and life course development/ageing.

Yvonne Harahousou is a Professor in the Department of Physical Education and Sports Sciences in Democritus University of Thrace, Greece. Her research interests are in the area of sports sociology, leisure and physical activity. She is a board member of the Women Sport International Association, Chair of the World Leisure Committee on Leisure in Later Life and President of the Hellenic Association for Advancing

Women and Sport. She has published a number of research papers on women and sport and leisure and the elderly. Her current projects explore the 'ageing well' issue cross-culturally and ageing and physical activity.

Maureen Harrington is Senior Lecturer in the Department of Tourism, Leisure, Hotel and Sport Management, and team leader of the Work and Life Balance stream of the Centre for Work, Leisure and Community Research at Griffith University, Australia. Her most recent publication, 'Sport and Leisure as Contexts for Fathering in Australian Families', appeared in a special issue of *Leisure Studies* on Fathering through Leisure (2006).

David Harris is Senior Lecturer in the School of Sport, Physical Education and Leisure, College of St Mark and St John, UK. He is the author of several textbooks, including *From Class Struggle to the Politics of Pleasure* (1992), *Teaching Yourself Social Theory* (2003) and *Key Concepts in Leisure Studies* (2005), and has contributed to the UK Higher Education Academy's website on Leisure, Hospitality and Tourism Education. He has his own website at <http://www.arasite.org>.

Othello Harris is Associate Professor in the Departments of Physical Education, Health and Sport Studies and Black World Studies at Miami University, Ohio, USA. His research interests include race relations, social stratification and race and sport involvement. He is co-editor of two books: *Encyclopedia of Ethnicity and Sports in the United States* (2000) and *Impacts of Incarceration on the African American Family* (2002). His work has been published in journals such as: *The Black Scholar; Sociology of Sport Journal; Journal of Social and Behavioral Sciences; Journal of African American Men; Masculinities;* and *Sociological Focus.*

Lawrence Haworth is Distinguished Professor Emeritus at the University of Waterloo, Canada, and is a Fellow of the Royal Society of Canada. He is the author of books on work and leisure, the idea of autonomy, risk assessment and the philosophy of the city, among others. Most recently he co-authored *A Textured Life: Empowerment and Adults with Developmental Disabilities* (1999).

Karla A. Henderson is Professor in the Department of Parks, Recreation and Tourism Management at North Carolina State University, USA. She has been active in many professional organizations, including President of the Academy of Leisure Sciences and the Society of Park and Recreation Educators, has published in a number of professional journals and is currently co-editor of *Leisure Sciences*. She has been co-author of several books including *Both Gains and Gaps: Feminist Perspectives on Women's Leisure* (1995); *Introduction to Recreation and Leisure Services;* and *Evaluating Leisure Services: Making Enlightened Decisions* (1996). Her research interests include gender and diversity, physical activity and active living, youth development and camping, and qualitative research approaches.

Benjamin K. Hunnicutt is Professor in the Department of Leisure Studies at the University of Iowa, USA. He received his MA and PhD in American history from the University of North Carolina Chapel Hill. He is a member of the Academy of Leisure Sciences and is author of several books, book chapters and articles, including: *Kellogg's Six-Hour Day* (1996); *Work Without End: Abandoning Shorter Hours for the Right to Work* (1988); 'The Economic Constraints of Leisure', in *The Constraints of Leisure* (2004); and 'The New Deal: The Salvation of Work and the End of the Shorter Hour Movement', in *Worktime and Industrialization: An International History* (1989).

John M. Jenkins is Associate Professor of Leisure and Tourism Studies and Research Associate at the Centre for Full Employment and Equity, University of Newcastle, Australia. He has written more than 50 book chapters and journal articles on issues concerning leisure, outdoor recreation and tourism policy and planning and is co-author and editor of several books, including: *The Encyclopedia of Leisure and Outdoor Recreation* (2004); *Outdoor Recreation Management* (1999); *Tourism and Recreation in Rural Areas* (1997); and *Tourism and Public Policy* (1995).

Chris Jenks is Professor of Sociology and Vice-Chancellor at Brunel University, UK. His most recent books are: *Cultural Reproduction* (1993); *Visual Culture* (1995); *Core Sociological Dichotomies* (1998); *Theorizing Childhood* (1999); *Images of Community: Durkheim, Social Systems and the Sociology of Art* (2000); *Aspects of Urban Culture* (2001); *Culture* (2002); *Transgression* (2003); *Subculture: The Fragmentation of the Social* (2004); *Culture* (2nd edn, 2004); *Childhood* (2nd edn, 2004); *Urban Culture* (2004); *Qualitative Complexity* (2006); and *Transgression* (2006).

Douglas A. Kleiber is Professor of Recreation and Leisure Studies in the Department of Counseling and Human Development Services at the University of Georgia, USA. He holds academic degrees in psychology and educational psychology from Cornell University and the University of Texas, respectively, and is a Charter member of the American Psychological Society and past President of the Academy of Leisure Sciences. His book *Leisure Experience and Human Development* (1999) reflects most of his research interests.

Rob Lynch is Professor of Leisure and Tourism Studies and Dean of the Faculty of Business, University of Technology, Sydney, Australia. He was founding chair of the Australian and New Zealand Association for Leisure Studies and founding Managing Editor of *Annals of Leisure Research* and is co-author of: *Dynamics of Collective Conflict* (1989); *Leisure and Change: Implications for Museums in the 21st Century*; and *Australian Leisure* (3rd edn, 2006).

Roger C. Mannell is a psychologist and Professor of Leisure Studies, Health Studies and Gerontology at the University of Waterloo, Canada. His research deals with factors that influence leisure and lifestyle choices and their impact on health and well-being. He has authored numerous publications and co-authored the book, *A Social Psychology of Leisure* (1997), which has been translated into Japanese and

Chinese. He was elected a Fellow of the US Academy of Leisure Sciences in 1986 and he was 1989 recipient of the Allen V. Sapora Research Award and the 1991 National Parks and Recreation Association's Theodore and Franklin Roosevelt Research Excellence Award.

Alison Pedlar is Professor in the Department of Recreation and Leisure Studies, University of Waterloo, Canada, and a member of the Academy of Leisure Sciences. Her work has principally focused on community development and quality of community life for individuals with disabilities and other marginalized populations. Recent publications include: 'Moving Beyond Individualism in Leisure Theory: A Critical Analysis of Concepts of Community, and Social Engagement' (*Leisure Studies*, 2003); and *A Textured Life: Empowerment and Adults with Developmental Disabilities* (1999).

John J. Pigram is Adjunct Professor attached to the Centre for Ecological Economics and Water Policy Research, University of New England, Australia. He has long-standing research and teaching interests in outdoor recreation and tourism and is co-author of several books including: *Outdoor Recreation Management* (1999), and the *Encyclopedia of Leisure and Outdoor Recreation* (co-editor, 2005).

Chris Rojek is Professor of Sociology and Culture, Brunel University, UK. He is author/editor of: *Capitalism and Leisure Theory* (1985); *Leisure for Leisure* (1989); *Sport and Leisure in the Civilizing Process* (1992); *Ways of Escape* (1993); *Decentring Leisure* (Sage, 1995); *Leisure and Culture* (Macmillan, 2000); *Celebrity* (2001); *Stuart Hall* (2003); *Frank Sinatra* (2004); *Leisure Theory: Principles and Practice* (2005); and *Cultural Studies* (2006).

David Rowe is Director and Professor, Centre for Cultural Research at the University of Western Sydney, Australia, and was formerly Director of the Cultural Industries and Practices Research Centre at the University of Newcastle, Australia. His books include: *Popular Cultures: Rock Music, Sport and the Politics of Pleasure* (1995); *Tourism, Leisure, Sport: Critical Perspectives* (1998); *Globalization and Sport: Playing the World* (2001); *Sport, Culture and the Media* (2nd edn, 2004); and *Critical Readings: Sport, Culture and the Media* (2004).

Juliet B. Schor is Professor in the Department of Sociology, Boston College, USA and was formerly at Harvard University and the UN World Institute for Development Economics Research. She is author of: *The Overworked American: The Unexpected Decline of Leisure* (1991); *The Overspent American: Why we Want What we Don't Need* (1999); and *Born to Buy: The Commercialized Child and the New Consumer Culture* (2004). She is a co-founder of the Center for a New American Dream (http://www.newdream.org).

Susan M. Shaw is a Sociologist and Professor in the Department of Recreation and Leisure Studies at the University of Waterloo, Ontario, Canada. She is past president of the Academy of Leisure Sciences and the Canadian Association for Leisure Studies. Her research publications, which include *Both Gains and Gaps: Feminist Perspectives on Women's Leisure* (co-author 1995), have focused on leisure and gender, time use, the intersection of work, family and leisure, and the implications of leisure for social and cultural change.

Atara Sivan is Professor in the Department of Education Studies, Hong Kong Baptist University, Hong Kong. She has been investigating the area of leisure education and serves as scientific adviser for the development of leisure education curricula. She is author of numerous articles, book chapters and books, including: *Leisure Eduction Towards the 21st Century* (1993); *Leisure Education, Community Development and Populations with Special Needs* (2000); and *Leisure Education in School Systems* (2002).

Marianne Staempfli is Assistant Professor in the Department of Recreation and Leisure Studies at Brock University, Canada. Her research interests include safe risks and youth development, the interrelationship between personality and environmental stressors, as well as gender constraints/stereotypes in outdoor recreation for youth and young adults. She received her PhD in leisure behaviour from the University of Waterloo where she examined the role of playfulness in the perception of environmental stressors during adolescent leisure. She has worked nationally and internationally with youth and young adults in different capacities.

Robert A. Stebbins is Faculty Professor in the Department of Sociology at the University of Calgary, Canada, and Visiting Professor at the University of Luton, UK. He received his PhD in 1964 from the University of Minnesota and has written over 160 articles and chapters and written or edited 32 books, including: *Between Work and Leisure* (2004), and *Challenging Mountain Nature: Risk, Motive, and Lifestyle in Three Hobbyist Sports* (2005). He is a Fellow of the Academy of Leisure Sciences and a Fellow of the Royal Society of Canada.

Deborah Stevenson is Associate Professor and Director of the Cultural Industries and Practices Research Centre in the School of Humanities and Social Science, University of Newcastle, NSW, Australia. She is author of: *Agendas in Place: Cultural Planning for Cities and Regions* (1998); *Art and Organisation: Making Australian Cultural Policy* (2000); and *Cities and Urban Cultures* (2003).

Hugo van der Poel is Educational Director of leisure studies curricula in the Department of Social-cultural Sciences, Tilburg University, Netherlands, lecturer in Leisure and Sport Management, NHTV University of Applied Sciences, Breda, Netherlands, and member of the Board of the W. J. H. Mulier Institute (the Dutch Social Scientific Centre for Sport and Society). He is author of *Tijd voor vrijheid (An Introduction to Leisure Studies*, 3rd edn, 2004). His research interests and publications are in the field of leisure theory and leisure and sport policy.

A. J. (Tony) Veal is past President of the Australian and New Zealand Association for Leisure Studies and former Chair of the Leisure Studies Association (UK). He is Adjunct Professor at the School of Leisure, Sport and Tourism at the University of Technology, Sydney, Australia, and is author/editor of: *Leisure and the Future* (1987); *The Olympic Games: A Social Science Perspective* (2000); *Australian Leisure* (3rd edn, 2006); *Leisure and Tourism Policy and Planning* (2nd edn, 2002); *Work and Leisure* (2004); *Free Time and Leisure Participation: International Perspectives* (2006); and *Research Methods for Leisure and Tourism* (3rd edn, 2006).

Jiri Zuzanek is Distinguished Professor Emeritus at the University of Waterloo, Canada, and formerly held appointments in the University of Lund, Sweden, Queen's University, New York, and the University of Western Ontario, Canada, and was Research Director of the UNESCO European Centre for Leisure and Education, Prague. He has researched and written extensively on the sociology of leisure and popular culture and time-use, time-pressure, stress and health. He is author of: *Social Research and Cultural Policy* (1979); *Work and Leisure in the Soviet Union* (1980); *World Leisure Participation* (co-editor, 1996); *The Effects of Time Use and Time Pressure on Child–Parent Relationships* (2000); and *Free Time and Leisure Participation: International Perspectives* (co-editor, 2005).

1

Introduction: Process and Context

Chris Rojek, Susan M. Shaw and A. J. Veal

This Handbook is designed to provide a cadastral survey of the various and diverse ways in which leisure forms and practice are situated and develop and the contribution of Leisure Studies in elucidating these processes. In the last 20 years, Leisure Studies has matured. Throughout the world, student numbers in higher education institutions have expanded. The 1991 *International Directory of Academic Institutions in Leisure, Recreation and Related Fields* (D'Amours, 1991) listed some 1,400 institutions in 60 countries offering tertiary education in the field. Institutionally, in the universities, the subject has been subjected to the buffetings of higher education reform. Departments of Parks and Recreation in North America and leisure and recreation elsewhere, have been combined with a variety of other disciplines or fields, including tourism, hospitality, marketing and sport (Mommaas, 1997). Despite its changing form and location in universities, the subject, formerly recognized as marginal, even in some eyes, *eccentric*, is now acknowledged to be a key part of the social science and Management Studies canon.

Nor is it just a matter of growing academic numbers throughout the West, Southeast Asia and South America. Simultaneously, the significance of leisure and the professional, vocational, market and state resources assigned to leisure forms and practice, is more accentuated in everyday culture. There is a sharper appreciation of the role of leisure in a range of quality of life issues. For example, the causal links between popular leisure activities such as smoking tobacco, alcohol consumption, eating food with high cholesterol content and low fibre, and illness and mortality are now widely understood. Similarly, the role of play in stress release and tension management and the role of physical exercise in promoting health, are broadly acknowledged. Likewise, the expansion of consumer culture together with the development of the casualization of work, the expansion of part-time work, fixed term and flexitime work contracts and the growing numbers of the retired, combine to magnify the centrality of leisure in contemporary Western lifestyle.

Contra the Victorian precedent, the American 'New Deal' and the British welfare state philosophy of William Beveridge, paid labour is now commonly viewed as the means to finance leisure choice and practice rather than the proverbial 'central life interest'.[1] These developments have posed important new dilemmas for students of leisure. For example, while casualization is prominent, it may also represent a loss of power for workers and trade unions who want full-time work. Similarly, the shift to part-time work is not evenly distributed between the sexes. Women are over-represented, a fact which reflects continuing structural inequality in the labour market and concerns about balancing work and family. Nonetheless, most commentators would agree that the cultural prominence of leisure has risen dramatically over the last quarter of a century.

In view of these considerations, it is perhaps surprising to note that this is the first Handbook of Leisure Studies to be published. Pioneering collaborative studies, such as *Mass Leisure* (Larrabee and Meyersohn, 1958) and *Leisure and Society in Britain* (Smith et al., 1973) offered valuable accounts of the field. But both are now rather long in the tooth and each was descriptive rather than producing a coherent field of study. More recently, Jackson and Burton's (1999) *Leisure Studies: Prospects for the Twenty First Century*, provided a stimulating and instructive collection, which built upon their interesting earlier collaboration (Jackson and Burton, 1989) to clarify several matters concerning methodology, individual experience, delivery and key debates in Leisure Studies. These books represent a survey of research accomplishments, but they neglected to develop a deep conceptual or theoretical basis for understanding leisure. In particular, their contribution to clarifying the place of power, identity, representation and change in leisure is disappointing. In addition, 26 of the 32 chapters were written by contributors based in North America. This is perhaps a fair reflection of the academic division of labour and power in the field. Conversely, the bias towards North American perspectives raises concerns about the balance and breadth of the volume.

While the majority of contributors to this Handbook are based in the US, Canada and the UK, we made it a matter of policy to commission chapters from elsewhere. Accordingly, the Handbook includes chapters from scholars living and working in Japan, India, the Netherlands, Greece, Hong Kong and Australia. We can hardly be said to have eliminated the problem of Western bias. But we have made an effort to recognize that there are serious problems in placing Western perspectives at the centre of analysis. This is a direct response to what was already emerging as a signal theme in academic and everyday life when the Jackson and Burton (1999) collection appeared, and has since been more pronounced, namely globalization. Indeed, although globalization is a key theme in this volume, it is part of a fivefold category of key themes that are presented as offering a firm focus for the discipline of Leisure Studies:

1. *Globalization*, the growing economic, cultural and political inter-connectedness and interdependence of human relations.
2. *Interdisciplinarity*, the hybrid, yet self sustaining character of the discipline, which draws on the theories and methods of the established Social Sciences, especially Sociology, Geography, Psychology, Economics and Political Science, but which has reached a level of disciplinary maturity.

3. *Power*, the positioning of leisure forms and practice in relations of power.
4. *Process*, the recognition that leisure activity is sensuous, variable and multidimensional and mobile rather than simply the expression of economic, cultural and social reproduction.
5. *Context*, the location of leisure forms and practice in the central questions of individualistic citizenship, especially issues of moral tolerance, social inclusion and distributive justice.

The rest of the Introduction elaborates on this fivefold category, expanding upon the significance of each, and relating each directly to leisure forms and practice. The relation of the chapters in each of the five parts of the Handbook to the elucidation of the key themes that structure the volume is addressed at the end of each section below.

Globalization

Prima facie, to nominate globalization as a prominent theme in contemporary Leisure Studies is innocuous. Everybody is aware that we live in an interconnected world in which events in one place may have rapid repercussions elsewhere. Arguably, because leisure is so powerfully rendered in cultural terms as a positive social status and lifestyle value, there is a tendency for leisure professionals and students to tilt towards upbeat evaluations of globalization. For example, the Sao Paulo Declaration, issued by the World Leisure and Recreation Association in 1998, while recognizing the 'increasing threats and opportunities' presented by globalization, nonetheless included Articles among its provisions that state:

> All governments and institutions should preserve and create barrier free environments, e.g. cultural, technological, natural and built, where people have time, space, facilities and opportunity to express, celebrate and share leisure.

> All private and public sectors consider the threats to diversity and quality of leisure experiences caused by local, national and international consequences of globalization. (World Leisure, 1998)

Scarcely anyone would oppose the sentiment behind these demands, for it seeks to promote the widening of access to leisure resources and increasing participation. However, both beg many thorny questions. Roughly speaking, these can be divided into issues relating to the mechanics of international strategy and the dangers of conflating globalization with a new version of Westernization.[2]

To take the subject of the mechanics of international strategy first, structured bilateralism and multilateralism can be positive forces in international relations. For example, bilateral and multilateral agreements exist to try to control illegal leisure activities supplied by global drug cartels and prostitution rings. They can scarcely be judged to be an unqualified success. Still, at least they constitute a basis for principled international policing. However, the power of foreign governments to interfere in the affairs of sovereign states is heavily conditioned. Bilateral and multilateral agreements usually rely upon economic and moral force. They seldom involve physical force. Rogue states have a relatively wide berth to ignore collective agreements. In addition, states, of course, have the option of unilaterally revoking agreements. In these incidents the moral and economic authority of bilateralism and multilateralism is frequently seriously compromised. For example, the 2001 decision by President George W. Bush not to participate in the Kyoto (1997) treaty on global warming presented a challenge to international efforts to prevent the attrition of the environment. The US is estimated to account for approximately 25 per cent of greenhouse gas emissions (Alterman and Green, 2004: 200). This is of direct concern to leisure professionals since a major cause of pollution is vehicle exhaust fumes, and driving for pleasure has been celebrated as a long-standing right of the American consumer (Gartman, 1994). In this regard, international resolve has found it very difficult to oppose American exceptionalism. The result is that the threat to the global environment has intensified. Similarly, the failure of China to enforce multilateral intellectual property agreements is said to adversely affect Western music and film industries.

A different range of problems is raised by the conflation of globalization with Westernization. The economic and military preponderance of Western interests in global affairs means that most international issues in leisure forms and practice are stamped with a Western seal of approval. Indeed, in much of the post-war era, the Western model of leisure was assumed to constitute the destination for all societies bent upon progress. This followed theories of modernity which held that the Western example was of revolutionary significance in approaches to social and economic development. Different theories placed greater or lesser emphasis upon what constitutes the core components in the Western model. But all pointed to the significance of individualism, secularism, nationalism, rationalization, urbanization, science, technology, pluralism, the market and the development of a public sphere of debate which Karl Popper (1950) labelled, somewhat tendentiously, 'the open society'.[3]

The model of leisure attached to this theory of modernity was quite specific. It presupposed that work is the central life interest, that rational individualism had replaced traditional society, that pluralism had succeeded tribal, courtly and colonial political structures, large-scale Fordist forms of industry had supplanted small, local businesses and that the nation-state was the primary unit of analysis in relation to social, economic, cultural and political processes. In the last 20 years all of these assumptions have been destabilized. The single evolutionary view of modernity has been supplanted by a perspective which recognizes that a variety of mixtures between traditional and modern elements is compatible with the notion of progress. The emphasis is now upon 'different modernities' (Gaonkar, 2001; Pieterse, 2003).

Part and parcel of this is the recognition that the Western version of modernization possesses limitations which prevent it from being simply exported to the rest of the world. While some continue to emulate the Western commodification of sexuality and youth culture, the preference for secular over religious celebration in leisure practice, the liberal tolerance shown to alcohol use, the privatization and compartmentalization of leisure from community life, the standardization and regulation of consumer culture, have been vigorously resisted and condemned in many countries as examples of Western decadence rather than progress. In the 1970s and 1980s, the deplored example of the West was a profound stimulant to the revival of Islamic fundamentalism.

Part 1 of the Handbook aims to demonstrate the dangers in conflating Westernization with globalization.

Rojek explores the role of culture in resisting the juggernaut of Westernization. His discussion uses the concepts of *kultur* and *zivilization* to sketch how the poliltics of resistance and opposition operates in leisure practice. The resistance of local traditions to sweeping global processes is highlighted and a case is made that the focus for Leisure Studies should not be either culture or civilization, but the interplay between the two. Chick despatches the important, and frequently ignored, task of examining the anthropology and pre-history of leisure. Arguably, a bias in historical work in Leisure Studies is to present leisure as a product of industrialization (Cunningham, 1980; Cross, 1993; Kammen, 1999). Perhaps this reflects the wider, traditional subservience to evolutionary theories of modernity that, until recently, prevailed in Leisure Studies. Be that as it may, Chick's chapter goes some way towards redressing the balance by producing a compelling case for the significance of pre-industrial play forms and practices.

Hunnicutt then disentangles the historical roots of the Western case and elucidates the seminal processes behind Western leisure forms and practices. Bhattacharya further exposes the ethnocentricity of Western modernity and correlative models of leisure, by considering non-Western traditions. Using India as a case study, her chapter contributes to a more acute understanding of globalization by addressing the textured, multilayered character of leisure forms and practice throughout the world.

Interdisciplinarity

The antecedents of Leisure Studies are mixed in convoluted ways, which have always complicated the task of defining the subject. We can safely say that the question of the meaning and purpose of free time has interested philosophers and educators since ancient times. It is also a constant in all of the major world religions, since many leisure practices were, and are, seen to have moral dimensions, as did 'non-work' in the West after ascetic Protestantism introduced the notions of religious 'calling' and the work ethic (Weber, 1936; DeLisle, 2003). However, while the question of free time is obviously present in these traditions, it tends to be addressed narrowly in terms of private subjective or specific community interests. As such, much of it is conventionally the subject of control and prohibition while 'permitted' areas of activity, such as the arts and sport, are presented in either positive or aspirational terms relating to the individual, with 'freedom' the preponderant mooted quality of leisure forms and practice or in religious, collectivist terms in which leisure is the expression of social order and cultural reproduction.

At the present juncture, our concern is to maintain that the question of leisure in Western urban-industrial society commenced as an adjunct of a much larger agenda in moral philosophy and political economy relating to the nature of private duties, public responsibilities, distributive justice and the shifting, restless topic of improving personal and social life. Historically speaking, with respect to the design of public life, these issues were articulated in leisure forms and practice developed first and foremost through vocational-professional means rather than the Academy. With the exception of Veblen (1899) and some pioneering but isolated American work in the 1920s and 1930s (Lundberg et al., 1934; Neumeyer and Neumeyer, 1936) and speculative British essays (Russell and Russell, 1923; Keynes, 1931), there was scant academic interest in leisure until the late 1950s. From the outset, in the urban-industrial age, the question of leisure was interrelated with professional and practical concerns having to do with the control and regulation of populations. The subject of the uses of free time was initially addressed in relation to six problem areas in urban-industrial life: housing, city planning, child development, physical and mental health, family and community life and crime. The professional and vocational grid of power that emerged to manage these issues was located among specialists in architecture, town planning, education, medical practice, social work and policing. This professional grid played the principal role in defining the nature of 'respectable' leisure forms and practices, and assigning resources through the privileged monitoring and advisory partnership it possessed with the legislative state apparatus. It was also central in defining the ways in which leisure and recreation were officially applied to improve the human condition.

The move towards the interventionist state in the West after the 1880s provided a fillip to the influence of this grid because it posed new questions of national heritage (including the criteria of preservation for places of outstanding natural beauty and wildlife reserves) and the provision of public leisure resources.[4] These distributive considerations overlaid the connotations of freedom and constraint from the Puritan period. Questions of leisure were now debated in relation to scientific and technological productivity and the issues of moral and social progress attached to them. Throughout, the old Puritan anxiety about the dangers of unregulated leisure for health and social order remained. But it was eclipsed by the enormous productivity of the industrial age that expanded access to leisure resources through the provision of paid holiday time and the growth in levels of real disposable income.

The key academic disciplines that forged Leisure Studies were themselves influenced by the central questions of regulation and improvement produced by the urban-industrial age. Sociology, Psychology, Social Psychology, Geography, Economics and Political Science drew upon an analysis of state and market solutions to questions of urban-industrial resource allocation, especially issues relating to maintaining order and managing change. However, the question of leisure did not emerge as a topic of concern within these disciplines as they emerged in the nineteenth century and the first half of the twentieth century. Leisure Studies did not appear on the map until after the Second World War. It emerged partly as a by-product of policy concerns – for example, the substantial research work of the US Outdoor

Recreation Resources Review Commission (1962) arose from concerns about how the outdoor environment was to be managed to cater for the massive growth in demand generated by expansion of 'Parks and Recreation' in American Universities. Other academics relatively detached from the managerial and administrative theatre began to explore a series of important hermeneutic questions about the meaning of leisure, leisure values, social inclusion, social exclusion, affluence, deprivation and distributive justice.

Part 2 of the Handbook investigates these interdisciplinary roots. Van der Poel considers the contribution of Sociology and Cultural Studies to the study of leisure. The opposition to common-sense views of leisure as mere voluntarism by a variety of sociological arguments concerning the structural influences on leisure choice and action, is cogently expressed. Mannell, Kleiber and Staempfli provide an account of the influences of Psychology and Social Psychology to the development of the discipline. This provides a useful counterpoint to that form of sociological reasoning which erases individual autonomy and choice by a version, or more often an *implication*, of structural determinism. The contribution of Psychology and Social Psychology provides a vital function in reminding us that the choices and actions of individuals occupy the fulcrum of the discipline. Leisure Studies has done much to elucidate the ways in which choice and action are positioned. But Mannell, Kleiber and Staempfli remind us that the psychological dilemma of individual choice and action is a constant in personal and group trajectories of leisure. Crouch investigates the influence of Geography. Spatial culture and the distribution of human resources are fundamental in the organization of leisure forms and practices. Crouch shows how geography clarifies the location principles behind leisure choices and actions. Veal's chapter on Economics considers the relation of choice and action in leisure in relation to the distribution and access to the fruits of production. Play may be a universal in human society. But leisure forms and practices were dependent upon the production of an economic surplus. This produced a surplus of time and a culture of luxury which was initially monopolized by ruling strata, but which later spread throughout society. Veal's chapter analyses the contribution of Economics in the planning and prediction of resource distribution and the widening of access to leisure assets. Coalter's chapter investigates the contribution of Political Science and Public Policy. Leisure is sometimes understood as involving a continuous balance between freedom and constraint. The management and reconciliation of these polarities is a political process. Coalter provides a guide to central political questions in the allocation of leisure resources. He clarifies the processes by which the competing themes of individualism and collectivism are reconciled and also the pressure points that elicit change in the relationship between them.

The subtext behind all of the chapters in Part 2 of the Handbook is that Leisure Studies has matured to assimilate elements from the social sciences to create viable disciplinary boundaries which demarcate the field as distinctive. It is no longer satisfactory to consider it as some kind of Johnny-come-lately appendix to older, established traditions of theory and research. In the last 20 years Leisure Studies has come of age. This doesn't mean ejecting the social sciences from the premises. After all, the discipline is organically related to the social sciences. However, just as an organism changes and grows in novel and challenging ways, the discipline of Leisure Studies is innovating new methodologies, concepts and theories in relation to traditional questions of the work–leisure balance, access to and the distribution of leisure resources and the relation of leisure to lifestyle and power. This section of the Handbook is designed to show the academic origins of the field, but also to maintain that interdisciplinarity has created a vigorous generative discipline which is moving beyond the established social sciences in elucidating questions of leisure.

Power

All societies depend upon the production of surplus to maintain order, govern change and secure growth. Leisure Studies is distinctively focused upon issues relating to the distribution of surplus and access to leisure resources. The term 'leisure resources' refers not merely to economic assets, but also to the honorific properties associated with access and restraint. Veblen's (1899) study of the leisure class, arguably the first genuine modern classic work in the study of leisure, potently demonstrates how the representation of leisure functioned to convey status and power in industrial society in ways that gradually became independent of economic power. One of the central arguments of the study is that conspicuous consumption is destined to popularize the values of excess and waste to a degree that threatens the viability of the economy.

Leisure is continuously and has ever been, positioned within power relations. Society has devised a variety of formal institutions and informal mechanisms to regulate access to leisure resources. In some cases, these have produced prohibitions on the uses of free-time behaviour. For example, over many years, the Church, the state and the law combined to regulate or prohibit a range of activities including drinking, gambling, theatre and Sunday leisure.[5] Gradually, a mantle of stigmas and taboos settled upon these activities and significant political mobilization was required to achieve liberalization. More prosaically, institutions like work, class, gender, race, the state, the corporation and the various branches of mass communications operate to distribute leisure resources and regulate access.

We call this set of formal and informal institutions the *axial constructs* around which leisure forms and practices emerge and develop. They are *axial* in the sense of being fundamental to the leisure actions and choices that individuals make and the leisure trajectories which they follow. They are *constructs* in two senses. First, they provide what the late French sociologist, Pierre Bourdieu (1977, 1984) called *habitus*. Habitus refers to the generative principles and structures through which distinctive traditions of behaviour and social values are embodied. Through our ways of speaking, accents, fashion choices, work and leisure activities, we reveal how we are positioned in relation to luxury and privation, inclusion and exclusion, power and subordination. Axial constructs are central to *habitus* because they regulate distribution and access to leisure resources.

Second, they are fundamental in representing the perspectives of justice, inequality, rights, responsibilities, social inclusion and exclusion in leisure forms and practice. In this sense they *manufacture* our view of the world and facilitate orientation. While they cannot, except in highly unusual circumstances, *determine* our individual perspective they can encourage preferred options and readings of social and economic circumstances which incline our behaviour to follow certain trajectories.[6]

The third part of the Handbook explores the central axial constructs in Western leisure. Zuzanek's chapter investigates how individuals and groups are positioned in relation to the resource of time. The common-sense view of time is that everyone has the same access to it. But as soon as the question of economic and cultural inequality is addressed this common-sense view collapses. To Bill Gates, chairman of Microsoft and one of the world's richest people, and one of his shopfloor employees, the access to leisure resources in a minute or an hour are very different things. Zuzanek clarifies the various complexities involved in the relation between leisure choice, action and time. Schor, builds upon her (1991) influential approach to work and leisure to examine how orientations and experiences of work impact upon leisure trajectories. The focus here is not merely upon economic inequality, but also upon the motivations that individuals bring to work and leisure choices. Axiomatic to the analysis is the proposition that consumer culture positions individuals in distinctive ways in relation to the work–leisure balance. Henderson and Shaw consider the axial construct of gender. The feminist contribution to Leisure Studies has been enormously important in demonstrating how identity is constructed through relations of power and representation. This chapter provides a critical assessment of how gender operates to channel leisure resources and mould leisure identities. Harahousou fastens upon a subject that is emerging as a key challenge for affluent societies, namely ageing. While questions relating to the lifecycle have been a focal concern in the discipline, they have usually concentrated upon youth cultures and subcultures. As life expectancy in the West has grown, the subject of leisure and old age has become more pressing. Harahousou's chapter demonstrates how leisure choice and action is influenced by the lifecycle and elucidates the various challenges to the allocation of state resources, through extended provision of pension entitlement, posed by large cross-sections of the population living longer.

Another key institution in society that has been peculiarly neglected by most leisure researchers is race. Freysinger and Harris's chapter provides some restitution, by examining the place of race and racism in leisure. They show how race persists as a key factor in the unequal allocation of leisure resources and how connotations of race influence the entire culture of Western leisure. Critcher's chapter investigates the institution of class in relation to leisure forms and practice. The emphasis upon the significance of class is stronger in the European and Australian traditions of Leisure Studies than in its North American counterpart. However, the collapse of the communist alternative in Eastern Europe in the 1980s and the advocacy of 'Third Way' politics in the European Union has raised questions about the continuing relevance of class in the analysis of leisure. Critcher's chapter defends the importance of class in understanding leisure forms and practice. He demonstrates the salience of class inequality in the distribution of leisure resources and types of participant leisure practice. Jenks shows the complex ways in which identity is tied with subcultural constructions of collectivity and difference. Cook's chapter tackles the crucial question of leisure and consumer culture. The historical trend in commodified culture is for voluntary, free leisure practices to be co-opted by the leisure industry and transformed into a source of revenue. In turn, this raises important questions of how free leisure practice really is in contemporary consumer culture. Cook provides a penetrating critical guide to these issues which demonstrates how far 'voluntary' choice in leisure has been colonized by the criteria of the leisure industry. Rowe's chapter reminds us of the vital importance of mass communication in contemporary leisure choice and practice. In mass society, leisure choices are not simply given through the individual's relationship with the community, they are coded and themed by the machinery of mass communications. The representation of leisure is an essential component in individual leisure choice. In traditional communities the key institutions of representation are the family and community. In modern societies, these institutions still play a significant role, as Stebbins's (1992) study of serious leisure practice verifies. But increasingly, the mass media equip us with data relating to leisure options and positive and stigmatized leisure forms. Rowe's chapter illuminates the central role of mass communications in contemporary leisure practice and cogently stresses the fundamental importance of the media in shaping leisure choice and identity.

Process

For most people, in most circumstances, leisure is desired; passionately so in the majority of cases. Leisure is usually presented as an unequivocal good. Yet this presupposes a variety of preconditions, among the most important of which are that we possess the health to enjoy leisure and that we have the financial means to access leisure resources. For someone in the advanced stages of multiple sclerosis or Parkinson's disease, limitless leisure may be a dreadful prospect. How are you to fill the minutes and hours pleasantly if your body has ceased to obey your will? Likewise, the man or woman who plays golf or tennis on Saturday and who is made redundant on Monday is apt to rapidly become an object of concern, if not pity. How will they manage? What will they do when the severance money runs out? Do they have any private assets to tide them over in the immediate or long term? Where will the money come from to look after the children? Leisure is generally desired, but its quality comes with many strings attached. To participate in it with pleasure presupposes that we occupy quite secure status positions that are prior to leisure choice and inform leisure practice. Health, ownership or use of sufficient capital and paid employment are pivotal. Once these are eliminated, once we become physically ill, homeless, or suffer a significant fall in income, leisure often ceases to be valued as a self-evident good. It may swiftly become our prison.

To allude to the status preconditions of leisure is to submit, in other words, that a political economy surrounds leisure forms and practice. Leisure practice is *positioned* in wider fields of influence and power. This *positioning* reflects the struggle of individuals and collectivities to gain access to leisure resources and the unintended consequences that result from the outcome of this struggle. For a variety of historical reasons, our culture typically conflates leisure with voluntarism. Yet once we examine leisure agents and leisure practice the sinews that govern access and participation are quickly exposed. Individual choice is *situated* and freedom *conditioned* by social, cultural, political and economic variables. We may select leisure activities, but we do so in *patterned* ways that reflect, among other things, nationality, culture, tradition, sexuality, wealth, income, ethnicity, religion, health and age as well as individual taste and personality. In addition, the *representation* of leisure practice is also situated and patterned. That is, the portrayal and meaning of freedom, choice and self-determination is culturally coded and socially themed. Our prosaic sense of personal autonomy and freedom of choice in leisure practice is therefore deceptive. We act in conditions under which personal autonomy is supported and shaped by many social, cultural and economic factors. Similarly, our leisure choices are made in a context in which representations of preferred and stigmatized options are culturally textured.

There have been many attempts in Leisure Studies to expose the allocative mechanisms and structures of power which distribute, code and theme leisure practice. This is of course at the core of economic analysis (Gratton and Taylor, 2000). Some approaches, like the functionalist perspective associated with the work of Stanley Parker (1983) and the Systems approach propounded by Cheek and Burch (1976), produce powerful accounts of the order of leisure relations and patterns of practice. One may take issue with some of their theoretical assumptions and their failure to incorporate an adequate dimension of power into the analysis. Yet at least they are clear about the structure of certain aspects of leisure relations. When it comes to the issue of social change, they are much weaker. Functionalist and Systems approaches struggle to illuminate why catalysts and takeoff points emerge in leisure forms and practice that change the quality and experience of leisure. Even so, those perspectives that fasten upon the importance of division and change, like the Marxist approach, tend to get frozen in inflexible propositions. Clarke and Critcher (1985) noted the difficulties that cultural Marxists had in the 1970s in coming to terms with feminism. Their own study, while constituting perhaps the leading neo-Marxist contribution in the field, nonetheless exaggerated class as an explanatory variable and equates positive leisure experience with false consciousness.

This does not seem to get to grips with an obvious and taken-for-granted aspect of leisure experience, namely that it is a source of pleasure. That is why the majority desire leisure so ardently and why they assign so many resources to it. While it is correct to submit that leisure practice is a relation of power and that this conditions leisure experience, we should be cautious about proceeding on the basis that experience can be analytically *predetermined* by the position of individuals in relation to leisure resources. Theories of leisure are indispensable in helping us to map the terrain, but human behaviour is sensuous and innovative. Ethnography and qualitative research must be at the heart of Leisure Studies because they contribute to our knowledge of the diversity of leisure experience and the processes through which this experience develops. Leisure practice *is* process.

Accordingly, the fourth section of the Handbook focuses on questions of diversity and process in leisure experience. Birrell examines the significance of sport in trajectories of leisure behaviour. The cultural prominence of sport has grown massively in the post-war period. It is now a major source of investment in personal leisure time and it has become a leading industry in contemporary capitalism. Birrell examines the relationship between sport and leisure and provides an assessment of the significance of sport in modern culture. Stevenson's chapter addresses the topic of the arts, entertainment and the mass media. These are the key mechanisms of mass representation in culture. They provide us with a continuous flow of data relating to the quality and range of leisure choices that are available to us. Stevenson investigates the relationship between these means of representation and the experience of leisure. Jenkins and Pigram's chapter considers the motivations and types of experience associated with the allocation of leisure resources to nature and outdoor recreation. They contrast the experience of outdoor recreation with the frustrations and limitations of urban existence. The chapter clarifies the yearning that many leisure seekers have in going back to nature as a source of escape. Franklin's chapter turns to the subject of tourism. Tourism is now the world's fourth biggest industry. More people are travelling for pleasure than ever before. But what do they hope to find on their travels? And how is their experience patterned? Franklin's chapter illuminates the contradictions in tourist experience and demonstrates why tourism has developed into a staple of modern leisure practice. Finkelstein and Lynch provide a penetrating guide to the social objectives and rituals involved in eating out. Restaurant dining is one of the most popular types of leisure practice. Finkelstein and Lynch show why eating out is an important form of display and positioning in leisure practice. Harrington's chapter probes into the subject of family leisure. She elucidates the division of labour in family leisure practice and considers the role of family leisure in developing identity and solidarity. Sivan's chapter explores the use of leisure experience in education and self-development. Play and recreation are pivotal mechanisms in acquiring meaning and belonging. Sivan clarifies the relationship between leisure, personal learning and social integration. Stebbins developed the influential distinction between serious and casual leisure. In this chapter he sets out his latest thinking on the subject, clarifying the experience involved in each leisure form and expanding on their respective social consequences.

Context

In the West, the philosophy of modern public leisure strategies and private civil leisure trajectories were born in the seventeenth century, with Locke's (1690) liberal philosophy of the duties of individualism in relation to religion and the state and Hobbes's (1601) contract theory as a pre-emptive strategy to avoid the 'war of all against all'. Both Locke and Hobbes heralded a version of individualistic citizenship that submitted that men and women are rational managers of their destinies. Both also outlined strategies to construct solidarity out of the universal human dilemma of natural scarcity. Individualistic citizenship implied new levels of personal responsibility, mutual respect and tolerance in the form and conduct of public life. In addition, it suggested a pretext for curbing or weeding out behaviour deemed to produce negative consequences. The Puritans were hostile to free expression and mistrusted emotion and 'natural' feelings. Instead they opted for a programme of moral regulation that acknowledged the value of leisure practice but defined it characteristically, in terms of 'sober mirth' (Daniels, 1995). Leisure acquired connotations of respectability, self-control and constraint. The old association with freedom and licence was hardly erased by this development. Even today most of us strongly associate leisure with personal choice and responsible freedom. At the same time, notions of citizenship, especially the idea of 'respectable leisure', and moral regulation inhibit the practical expression of individual choice and freedom. The seventeenth-century philosophy of individualistic citizenship was instrumental in laying the foundations for the balance between freedom and constraint in leisure forms and practice that continues to this day.

The causes behind this development were various. The accumulation of fiscal powers in the hands of the state, initially, chiefly for the purposes of war, exploration and the maintenance of Empire, was important since it raised the question of the proper use of public resources. But so were the development of constitutionalism; the separation of the state from the Church; the growth of science, industry, business and technology in producing regular, dependable economic surplus; the philosophy of individualism; the expansion of public education and health services, and the transference of populations from the country to urban-industrial centres. Leisure became a central issue in public life when the rights and responsibilities of the individual to engage in programmes of self-determination became generalized.

By the late eighteenth century in Western Europe and the British colonies of the Eastern American seaboard this condition was clearly under way. The American (1776) and French (1789) revolutions were conducted in the name of the rejection of monarchical law and precedence and the advocacy of public rights and duties. This itself presupposes three huge structural shifts in the constitution of society. First, the decline in religious power which conventionally presented individual action as fate. Secularism and science are closely interrelated. By the late eighteenth century, the effect of both was to make individuals seek this-worldly solutions for their condition and the social, economic and political contexts in which they found themselves to be located.

Second, the transference of power from the monarch and court society to a body of representatives elected by the public and a correlative standing salaried staff complement of civil servants charged with the task of impersonally translating Parliamentary decisions into policy. The decentring of monarchical power was paralleled by loss of sovereignty of colonial powers over colonized territories. By democratizing accountability, these political developments increased the requirement for ordinary citizens to reflect upon their own aspirations for better forms of leisure and superior types of society.

Third, and underwriting each of the two developments mentioned above, the emergence of the 'public sphere' (Habermas, 1962) in which matters of private and public duty, virtue and aspiration are legitimately and exhaustively debated in the press, literature, science and the various branches of the media. The public sphere takes duty, virtue and aspiration as an object not only of reflection but also of action. By the late eighteenth century, Jefferson, Franklin, Paine, Rousseau, Ferguson and Adam Smith were openly debating the rights of 'Man' as central parts of a programme of civil renewal and moral enrichment. Although it hardly proceeded at pell-mell pace, and was uneven and dilatory in incorporating women, ethnic minorities and unskilled workers, the next two centuries witnessed a clear trend in Western society to increase the democratization of the public sphere by enlarging popular participation in the debate around care for the self and care for the other. In the course of this, diverse issues of private and public leisure were articulated.

We make these points in order to hold that there is value in exploring what we call *indexical thematics* in leisure practice. By this we mean an approach that commences with analysing the immediate context of leisure practice, but tracks action back to the reference points of the institutional structure of power and discourses of citizenship and subjectivity.

This submission is important because we wish to combat the common-sense view that leisure forms and practice possess autonomy, flexibility and self-determination. We have already made the point that leisure forms and practice are *positioned*. It follows that a primary task of students of leisure is to explore the chain of causality and dynamics relevant to this positioning and try and produce objective knowledge about them. In introducing the concept of indexical thematics we mean to deepen what is meant by the concept of positioning to include rights and responsibilities that are either manifest or latent in the concept of individualistic citizenship.

The term 'indexical' is borrowed from Harold Garfinkel's (1967) ethnomethodology.[7] Garfinkel applied it to maintain that the immediacy and particularity of social accounts and practices militate against generalized sociological accounts. The critical emphasis here is aimed against the structural functionalism of Talcott Parsons that, in the discipline of Leisure Studies, is most fully realized in the work of Cheek and Burch (1976). Garfinkel wanted to insist on the uniqueness of exchange and the aridity of social theories which 'read off' action from predetermined propositions relating to socialization and the development of identity. We share the same preference. However, we also wish to maintain that individual actions and exchanges draw on generative rules and resources which are independent of personal will. Personal leisure choice draws on an index of options that are structurally conditioned. Marxist and feminist accounts in the study of leisure have done much to clarify the cultural and economic dimensions of this index. They elucidate how class and gender theme leisure conduct. We wish to produce a more inclusive, differentiated approach to indexical thematics by proposing that leisure practice raises three continuous sets of questions relating to, *distributive justice, social exclusion* and *moral tolerance*.

The final part of the Handbook is designed to elucidate some of the paradoxes that these present for the discipline. Rojek examines the topic of representation. Our orientation to questions of distributive justice, social inclusion and moral tolerance partly reflects our *habitus*, but also the many ways in which leisure forms are constructed in society. Representation is crucial for the practice of individualistic citizenship because it constitutes the foundation for rational judgement. In this chapter Rojek explores the mechanics of representation. He analyses the leisure practice of smoking to demonstrate the interplay between positive and negative connotations of leisure practice. In a subsequent chapter, Rojek investigates how identity coagulates around types of representation, particularly the commodity form. Using the case studies of the automobile and the Apple Mac computer, he shows how leisure choice in commodity culture extends beyond the possession of a leisure commodity to enunciate a statement about lifestyle and inner worth. In sum, leisure choice is about constructing and strategically placing our identities in relation to others. While structural forces propel us in certain directions and compel us to make what might be called 'preferred choices and readings' in leisure action, Rojek insists on the reality of individual conscience and the capacity of leisure actors to make rational judgements about their actions. Indeed, the latter may be taken as a core identifying characteristic of individualistic citizenship. Barker's chapter focuses on the role of praxis in leisure forms and behaviour. Praxis relates individual choice to wider structural questions of resource allocation, morality and the balance between social inclusion and social exclusion. Barker helps students of leisure to appreciate the centrality of this concept in exploring questions of identity and trajectories of leisure practice. Harris's chapter moves on to address the important subject of how leisure practice articulates social and civil rules and resources. Articulation is a neo-Marxist concept, associated with the sociology of Antonio Gramsci, but elaborated, and to some extent codified, in contemporary culture by Stuart Hall and his colleagues in the Birmingham School approach to contemporary culture. Harris shows how beliefs and values penetrate leisure choice and practice and further how individual forms of behaviour reflect historically and socially constructed rules and resources. Pedlar and Haworth focus on leisure and the community. Most commentators on modern society argue that community life has been replaced by privatization and disembedding.[8] Pedlar and Haworth consider the continuing relevance of the concept of community for Leisure Studies. Their chapter raises key issues of autonomy and solidarity in leisure forms and practice. Shaw's chapter reminds us that leisure is not merely a basis for integration and harmony. It is also a mechanism of resistance and a source of conflict. A sign of the increasing maturity of the discipline is that students of leisure are now more willing to entertain the notion that the old critical slogan that 'the personal is political' also applies to leisure relations. Gender, class, race and status influence the grain of leisure patterns. Shaw demonstrates that the dimension of resistance is fundamental in the concept of leisure and the discipline must do more to illuminate its operation and history.

Leisure Studies: the agenda

This Handbook can be read and used as a survey of the discipline. The chapters also constitute topics in an agenda for future research. The backcloth to this is the central social and economic transformations that are occurring in everyday life. If leisure is to be seen as integral to these processes, then those engaged in Leisure Studies must engage with the central social, economic, cultural and political questions of the time. They will need to avoid the temptation of regarding leisure to be an enchanted glade wherein the logic of practice is independent of the gravity of social, economic, cultural and political forces that inform everyday experience and orientation. Which of these questions are most pertinent to Leisure Studies today?

1. The revolution in science and technology associated with genetic engineering, cloning and replacement surgery constitutes a profound challenge, not merely to the concept of ageing as it has been traditionally understood, but also to orthodox thinking about the lifecycle. These developments offer exciting new opportunities for humankind. Extending life and reducing suffering have long been dreamt of, and modern science and technology is making huge strides in both fields. But they also present deep challenges to conventional thought on marriage, family life and the work ethic. The extension of the period of retirement implies new fiscal challenges for the state and occupational pension schemes. These in turn have consequences for economic growth and international competition. If more resources have to be set aside to cover old age, they can only come from greater borrowing, higher growth or reducing resource distribution at earlier stages in the lifecycle. Analogously, if each stage of the lifecycle is to be substantially prolonged, what are the consequences for our understanding of the breaks between adolescence, youth, adult and old age subcultures? The relation between parents and children? The gendered nature of the institution of marriage, the restrictive definition of marriage in many parts of the world and the lack of access to divorce in some societies? These questions have a direct bearing upon leisure choice and leisure form. Students of leisure will need to keep abreast of these developments in natural science and associated policies to produce meaningful accounts of leisure in the social sciences.

2. The emergence of the US as the world's only genuine superpower raises a series of questions about the Americanization of global society. American television, film, music, literature, social science, computer systems, sport, restaurant chains, systems of education, beer, clothing, sports equipment, automobiles and countless other commodities constitute a strong basis for technological convergence. Whether convergence at the cultural level will follow suit is one of the pressing topics of our time.

   Likewise, American ascendancy is regarded to be oppressive and threatening by large sections of the world's population. 9/11 showed the level of disenchantment and antagonism outside America for 'the American way', particularly in the Muslim world. The ascent of China and India as opposing economic and military powers to American hegemony and the counterveiling example of the European Union, where traditions of welfarism and intervention are more deeply entrenched, suggests a series of difficult counterpoints for the conduct of international relations. The old polarities of the Cold War have given way to a more complex picture of global cross currents and frictions which impact upon trajectories of leisure. Leisure has always been an expression of culture (Rojek, 2000). To date in human history cultural identity has been based first on tribe and subsequently on nation, with religion and Empire providing overlays for some of the time. To what extent will the emerging world order change this pattern?

3. Globalization underlines how far the leisure of the West relies upon output from the developing world. Many of the West's foremost leisure multinationals, such as Nike, Adidas, Starbucks and Armani, source their production from Third World labour in the Philippines, Taiwan, Indonesia, Thailand and Mexico. While Japan in the 1970s, and Malaysia and Singapore more recently, have managed to build booming economies with – eventually – rising wages on the back of low-wage, export-oriented economies, and China currently seems set to repeat the pattern, this has not been true of all developing countries. Western consumers enjoy unparalleled exposure to leisure commodities and services. But it comes on the back of an organized global system of low wages, the use of child labour, unacceptable levels of illiteracy and high rates of disease and mortality. While there is a considerable literature on these issues in other branches of the social sciences, and some attention has been given to the issues in Tourism Studies, Leisure Studies has generally failed to engage with the moral and practical issues presented by the development gap. The interrelationship between Western leisure forms and Third World oppression need to be illuminated. Only then will leisure professionals be in a position to combat the individualistic credo that individuals can do whatever they like in their free time provided they obey the limits of the law.

4. Within the social sciences there is a persistent tendency to postulate strategies of reform and improvement at either the level of the responsible citizen or the enlightened state. What this ignores is the obvious fact of multinational corporate power. The global reach of multinationals enable them to be highly effective in processes of flexible accumulation. Precisely because of this they have the potential to be equally effective in flexible distribution, especially in the area of leisure forms. Leisure professionals should pay more attention to the multinational sector as a third force in the globalization of leisure. The potential for alliances and partnerships with global charities is enormous and largely untapped. Of course, the citizen and the state remain crucial in effective strategy. But creative thought about the third force in leisure practice is an area of great fruitfulness in theory and research.

5. The degradation of the environment through the burning of fossil fuels poses enormous global risks. Leisure forms constructed around the automobile and jet travel are significant net contributors to the physical processes that enhance global warming. Perhaps it is time to shift Veblen's concept of conspicuous consumption from a focus on the commodity form to the global destruction of natural resources. Leisure professionals need to address the relationship between the pursuit of pleasure and environmental attrition. They must devise ways of curtailing abuse and excess before a global physical crisis forces people to change their behaviour. This is partly a question of research, but it also requires the development of suitable pedagogies at the levels of schools, universities and community education.

6. The freedom, choice and flexibility that leisure practice is held to deliver has been so strong that leisure is often read as one of the principal expressions of the ideology of Western superiority. The discipline has reached a stage of maturity

in which a more scientific understanding of leisure forms and practice should be accomplished. Basic to this, is widening our understanding of how leisure contributes to various types of individual and group pathology. Leisure practice is not always personally and culturally enriching. It can be the transmission belt for gender, racial, homophobic and religious stereotypes that breed intolerance and insensitivity. For many people, leisure is experienced as disempowering and dehumanizing. Leisure professionals and students need to address the causal links between bullying, persecution, terrorism and leisure forms. Our aim must be to understand more objectively, how leisure is practiced. We cannot assume, on *a priori* grounds, improving, integrating effects for leisure.

The relevance of studying leisure behaviour has never been greater. The move towards mass systems of tertiary education and the revolution in mass communication produced by satellite broadcasting has exposed the limitations of representative, elected government. One sign of this is the resources that most contemporary democratic governments devote to demonstrating that they are 'in touch' with the people through focus groups, the development of special public missions and Quangos. In the 1960s and 70s social movements like feminism, gay and lesbian rights and anti-racism established and popularized the principle that 'the personal is political'. The influence of this transformation in civil society provides the context for the political, economic and cultural processes in which government and everyday life operate today. Settings of serious leisure were and remain catalysts in developing these movements. Individuals were energized and politicized in meetings in clubs, pubs, coffee bars and lecture halls. What emerged at this time was a powerful mass renewal of voluntarism which, in turn, extended cultural privatization and individualism.

However, by overemphasizing the decline of community, critics of modern civic life like David Putnam (2001) may have missed a recent shift in citizenship: the rise of the active citizen. Campaigning for the protection of the environment, stopping bullying in schools, educating people about the effects of diet, alcohol consumption and secondary smoking, promoting awareness of institutionalized racism and sexism, opposing the psychology of 'logo' brand-culture and a variety of other cultural and social concerns are arguably significantly more prominent than 50 years ago. Significantly, much active citizenship occurs informally, where people develop concepts of neighbourliness and social responsibility more routinely and collectively than critics like Putnam allow. The sense of solidarity that people develop is sometimes based around face-to-face meetings, but more often it takes the form of developing recognition and belonging through television, radio, newspapers and the internet. Harris (2004: 62–7, 251–6) provides an interesting analysis of how the internet has shifted educative and political functions of leisure to more decentred and non-hierarchical forms of practice. The use of mass communications in leisure is creating spaces for engagement and exchange in which the boundaries separating people by age, gender, race and physical distance have either frayed or collapsed. All of this is hard to analyse because much of it occurs in privatized settings and it is, moreover, somewhat fragmented.[9] Action may be issue specific. It may be cultivated in the midst of relatively passive and even conformist attitudes to many aspects of life. But perhaps the ethic of involvement and making a difference is more ordinary and stronger in daily life than most realize. Leisure is, perhaps, the primary setting for the active citizen. One of the most valuable challenges facing students and professionals in Leisure Studies is to elucidate the connections between leisure forms and practice and the dynamics of personal transformation and civil action.

Leisure will never be life's primary activity, because labour remains the source of all value. However, leisure is the means through which cultural, political, ethical and spiritual existence can be enhanced and refined for the betterment of life in general. We believe that the study of leisure should be guided by this ambition. It is the best reason one can give for doing Leisure Studies in the complex, challenging, difficult, but always exciting, 'local–global balance' of the world in which we live today.

Notes

1. The notion that work is the central life interest is the Victorian deformation of Puritan thought. The Puritans believed that work was dedicated to expanding God's glory. The urban-industrial age ushered in by the Victorians transformed this into the sober work ethic.
2. Practically speaking, the issue of Westernization today is dominated by the question of Americanization, since the US is the only genuine superpower. One of the main challenges of students and professionals in Leisure Studies in the twenty-first century is to develop a reflexive understanding of US power in the commodification and acculturation of leisure forms and practice.
3. It is tendentious because class, gender, race and status differences raise obvious difficulties with the notion of liberalism and social openness. Popper was perhaps too uncritical of the formal political equality achieved under the liberal democracies.
4. These questions were of course formulated and perpetuated in the context of major inequalities of power, in which differences of class, race, gender, religion and status were paramount.
5. These activities survived in what might be called the subterranean economy of leisure in which they were conflated with a culture in which illicit pleasure was a source of attraction.
6. The notion of 'preferred option' implies that we are positioned in relation to leisure resources and options so that some forms of conduct become 'natural' and 'obvious' while others are neutralized.
7. Ethnomethodology is an approach in sociology dedicated to uncovering the members' methods and forms of social competence used in constructing a sense of collective reality. Ethnomethodologists attack orthodox sociology for failing to acknowledge that social reality is constructed by the micro-actions of individuals and treating subjects as 'cultural dopes'.
8. Privatization simply means that tendency for social experience to be conducted in domestic settings or settings sequestered from public view. One aspect of this is the interiorization of experience, that is, the tendency to promote personal experience as the best guide to reality. Disembedding is a product of modernity and refers to the tendency for individuals to be plucked from their family of origins and places of birth by the labour process.
9. Of course, Harris also recognizes that the internet produces new opportunities for manipulation and exploitation. However, his discussion cogently demonstrates the structural shift in leisure practice and form that the new technology offers.

Bibliography

Alterman, E. and Green, M. (2004) *The Book on Bush*, New York, Penguin.

Bourdieu, P. (1977) *Outline of a Theory of Practice*, Cambridge, Cambridge University Press.

Bourdieu, P. (1984) *Distinction*, London, Routledge

Cheek, N. and Burch, W. (1976) *The Social Organization of Leisure in Human Society*, New York, Harper & Row.

Clarke, J. and Critcher, C. (1985) *The Devil Makes Work*, London, Macmillan.

Cross, G. (1993) *Time and Money*, London, Routledge.

Cunningham, H. (1980) *Leisure in the Industrial Revolution*, Beckenham, Croom Helm.

D'Amours, M. (1991) *International Directory of Academic Institutions in Leisure, Recreation and Related Fields*, Trois Riviers, Quebec, World Leisure and Recreation Association/Presses de Université du Québec.

Daniels, B. C. (1995) *Puritans At Play*, New York, St Martin's Press.

DeLisle, L. (2003) 'Keys to the Kingdom or the Devil's Playground? The Impact of Institutionalized Religion on the Perception and Use of Leisure, *Annals of Leisure Research* 6(2): 83–102.

Gaonkar, D. (2001) *Alternative Modernities*, Durham, Duke University Press.

Garfinkel, H. (1967) *Studies in Ethnomethodology*, Engelwood Cliffs, Prentice Hall.

Gartman, D. (1994) *Auto-Opium*, London, Routledge.

Gratton, C. and Taylor, P. (2000) *Economics of Sport and Recreation*, London, E & FN Spon.

Habermas, J. (1962) *The Structural Transformation of the Public Sphere*, Cambridge, Polity Press.

Harris, D. (2004) *Key Concepts in Leisure Studies*, London, Sage.

Hobbes, T. (1601) *Leviathan*, Harmondsworth, Penguin.

Jackson, E. and Burton, T. (eds) (1989) *Understanding Leisure and Recreation: Mapping the Past, Charting the Future*, State College, PA, Venture Publishing.

Jackson, E. and Burton, T. (eds) (1999) *Leisure Studies: Prospects for the Twenty First Century*, State College, PA, Venture Publishing.

Kammen, M. (1999) *American Culture, American Tastes*, New York, Basic Books.

Keynes, J. M. (1931) 'Economic Possibilities for Our Grandchildren', in *The Collected Writings of John Maynard Keynes, Vol. 9, Essays in Persuasion* (1972 edn), London, Macmillan, pp. 321–32.

Larrabee, E. and Meyersohn, R. (eds) (1958) *Mass Leisure*, Glencoe, Free Press.

Locke, J. (1690) *Two Treatises of Government*, Cambridge, Cambridge University Press.

Lundberg, G., Komarovsky, M. and McInery, M. A. (1934) *Leisure: A Suburban Study*, New York, Columbia University Press.

Mommaas, H. (1997) 'European Leisure Studies at the Crossroads? A History of Leisure Research in Europe', *Leisure Sciences* 19(4): 241–54.

Neumeyer, M. and Neumeyer, E. (1936) *Leisure and Recreation*, New York, A. S. Barnes & Co.

Outdoor Recreation Resources Review Commission (1962) *Outodoor Recreation for America*. Washington, DC, ORRRC.

Parker, S. (1983) *Leisure and Work*, London, Allen & Unwin.

Pieterse, J. (2003) *Globalization and Culture*, Boston, Rowman and Littlefield.

Popper, K. (1950) *The Open Society and its Enemies*, 2 Vols, London, Routledge.

Putnam, D. (2001) *Bowling Alone*, New York, Touchstone.

Rojek, C. (2000) *Leisure and Culture*, Basingstoke, Palgrave Macmillan.

Russell, B. and Russell, D. (1923) *In Praise of Idleness and Other Essays*, London, Allen & Unwin.

Schor, J. (1991) *The Over-Worked American*, New York, Basic Books.

Smith, M., Parker, S. and Smith, C. (eds) (1973) *Leisure and Society in Britain*, London, Allen Lane.

Stebbins, R. (1992) *Amateurs, Professionals and Serious Leisure*, Montreal, McGill University Press.

Veblen, T. (1899) *The Theory of the Leisure Class*, London, Allen & Unwin.

Weber, M. (1936) *The Protestant Ethic and the Spirit Of Capitalism*, London, Penguin.

World Leisure (1998) São Paulo Declaration, Cedar Falls, IA, World Leisure; available at <www.worldleisure.org/pdfs/saopaulo.pdf>.

Part 1
Origins

2
Leisure, Culture and Civilization
Chris Rojek

Culture or civilization? What is the most suitable context in which to locate leisure forms and practice? For some readers it may seem a peculiar brace of questions to address. In everyday speech, culture and civilization are often presented as interchangeable, with nothing but the thinness of a halfpenny to choose between them. Both terms signify distinctive continuities in collective patterns of behaviour. Continuities are understood as both enabling and constraining influences upon individual behaviour. Culture refers to localized continuities having to do with deep-rooted, customary principles and practices of inclusion and exclusion. For this reason, it is often most readily applied in respect of community, race, religion and the nation-state. Weber (2002: 67–98) emphasized the significance of the idea of 'calling' in the culture of Protestantism. He argued that it distinguished Protestants from other religions and provided the basis for continuity and solidarity upon which the roots of culture were established. Daniels's (1995) study of leisure practice among Puritans in Colonial New England demonstrates powerfully how the Puritan critique of Roman and Anglican theology produced leisure forms organized around the doctrine of 'sober mirth' that was designed to cement cultural solidarity and automatically represent standards of cultural inclusion and exclusion. A corollary of the migration of people is the migration of cultures. The resultant cultural exchange between migrant and host cultures is a major resource in the development of civilization. Among the customary practices of a particular people at a particular time and place, it is possible to differentiate between high and low culture. But the crux of the differentiation refers to practices that are customary, local and embedded.

In contrast, the term 'civilization', which derives from the Latin *civilis*, meaning 'referring to the citizen', denotes levels of self-consciousness and reflexivity which are more mixed. Civilization is constructed from cultural and cross-cultural materials that permit levels of government, culture and ways of life that are rationally evaluated as 'higher' or 'superior'. Because civilization is constituted from cultural and cross-cultural resources there is some confusion about where civilization starts and culture ends. Huntington (1993, 1996) deals with the problem by approaching civilization as the highest cultural grouping and broadest level of cultural identity organized around what he calls 'common objective elements'. Among the 'common objective elements' he has in mind are language, history, religion, customs and institutions. Civilization, then, possesses an attachment to progress in the name of common objective elements that provide solidarity and the claim of superiority over other civilizations. Other definitions of civilization rely upon technical criteria. V. Gordon Childe (1936) identified civilization with technological mastery and the means of recording communication through writing. Among the preconditions of civilization that he lists are the plough, the wheeled cart, sailing ships, the smelting of copper and bronze, solar calendars, standards of measurement, irrigation, specialized craftsmanship, urban centres and surplus food. While particular cultures developed some of these characteristics their crystallization as the foundation of civilization depended upon cultural exchange through war, trade and travel. Civilization thus has a more dynamic connotation than culture. It implies advancement beyond a primitive stage, the refinement of interests, tastes, the elaboration of standards of sophisticated behaviour and self-control, through cross-cultural communication and exchange.

If anything, nowadays the term 'civilization' possesses a degree of stigma, certainly for liberals. Generally, commentators are more relaxed with the term 'culture'. This undoubtedly reflects the influence of post-colonial criticism, in which 'Western civilization' is often conflated with 'imperialism'.[1] This criticism stresses the role of Empire in subduing Native populations in various ways and planting settler communities. The Native is coralled into a subaltern relationship in which the imperialist is the dominant partner, as the 'barbarian' is subordinate to the 'civilized agent'. There is, then, palpable bad conscience in Western academic circles about 'Western civilization' since what might be called its 'pre-post-colonial' application is deemed to have gone hand in glove with imperialism.

As a result, it is all the more important to emphasize the contradictory nature of Western civilization. The Native and his advocates have every right to point to genocide, torture, rape, pillage and systematic subordination as elements in the imperial project to spread Western civilization globally. The other side of the coin is the application of legal-rational law, public education, an organized system of health and what Ernest Gellner (1998) called 'the ethic of cognition' which permitted various forms of positive technological and moral innovations and underpinned the principles of freedom of thought and freedom of speech.[2]

Since the late 1980s, the turn towards globalization in cultural and social theory has revived interest in the contradictory character of Western civilization. In the hands of commentators like Samuel P. Huntington (1993, 1996) globalization has replaced the ideological and political struggle of the Cold War and is instrumental in precipitating 'the clash of civilizations' as the various leading non-Western forms – Confucian, Japanese, Islamic, Slavo-Orthodox and Latin American – confront Western hegemony and particularly the superpower status of the United States. Other writers are more sanguine, and regard globalization as presenting new opportunities for tolerance, reciprocity and cosmopolitan citizenship (Beck, 1999;

Beck and Beck, 2001; Pieterse, 2004). We shall return to Huntington's thesis in the conclusion of the chapter.

Leisure professionals have tended to support diffuse opportunity-based perspectives of building unity and widening access through globalization rather than a centralized programme of political and economic action. For example, the Sao Paulo Declaration (1998) and the Charter for Leisure (2000), issued by the World Leisure and Recreation Association, define various general global rights of leisure and identify a proselytizing and political role for leisure professionals in refining and disseminating them. Broadly speaking, these rights have to do with dismantling cultural, technological and political barriers, facilitating the spread of diversity and pluralism, investing in public provision of leisure and recreation and widening access. However, they are expressed at a high level of generality. In particular, the transnational mechanisms to achieve their ends are unparticularized. While the intent of the World Leisure and Recreation Association is manifestly not to underwrite a global campaign for Westernization, the rights that they advocate are strongly reminiscent of the core values of Western liberal democracy. This again raises the thorny question of the equilibrium between non-Western cultural integrity and the encompassing regime of Western civilization.

Culture and culturalism

In the modern period, leisure has been understood as a transmission belt for both representing and disseminating cultural values. Tylor (1874: 1) defined culture as 'That complex whole which includes knowledge, belief, art, morals, law, custom and other capabilities and habits acquired by man as a member of society.'[3] However, secluded inside this definition is an evolutionary distinction borrowed from Matthew Arnold (1869) that identifies culture with the highest expressions and aspirations of society pursuant to progress and human perfection. This was quite typical of nineteenth-century social and cultural thought. As Tylor clarified:

> The educated world of Europe and America practically settles a standard by simply placing its own nations at one end of the social series and savage tribes at the other, arranging the rest of mankind between these limits ... as they correspond more closely to savage or cultured life. (Tylor, 1874: 26)

There is not much room for hybridity, mutuality or reciprocity here. Instead, high culture is presented as the inevitable future for societies that are defined as being lower down the chain of evolution and also for strata that exemplify the traits of low culture within societies where high culture has flourished. Cultural elitism of this sort carried over well into the twentieth century. For example, T. S. Eliot's (1948) famous contribution to cultural theory, clearly envisaged the achievements of the West as the pinnacle of culture, and implied that other cultures subsist at lower stages in the ladder of progress.

In the discipline of Leisure Studies, cultural elitism has seldom been overtly expressed. Although it is true that many of the contributions from the most powerful country in the academic division of labour in the discipline, namely the US, in the 1970s and 1980s, operated on the presumption that the institutions and values of American leisure systems offer the best hope for the rest of humanity (Kaplan, 1975; Cheek and Burch, 1976; Kraus, 1984). Early contributions to the European sociology of leisure made the same mistake (Dumazedier, 1974; Roberts, 1978; Parker, 1983). In studying the relationship between leisure and culture we must be wary of arguments that presuppose cultural superiority or imply cultural inferiority. One thing that post-colonialism has unequivocally accomplished is to reveal the partiality of cultural perspectives and the genie of ethnocentricism that lurks behind much research and writing on comparative culture and leisure. Now, the emphasis in anthropology and comparative research is upon difference rather than hierarchy.

It fell to Pieper (1952) to give the most systematic formulation of the relationship between leisure and culture. He defined leisure famously as the *basis* of culture. In part he was intent on rebutting the slavish dependence on the work ethic in liberal democracies by reclaiming aspects of the Aristotelian view of leisure that identified it with the contemplative life. According to Pieper (1952: 21), this was also consistent with the meaning of leisure in Christian thought. To be sure, his discussion of leisure explicitly invested the concept with ecumenical overtones. He submitted that leisure provides 'the affirmation of man's true nature' and 'the power to overstep the boundaries of the workaday world and reach out to superhuman, life-giving existential forces that refresh and renew us' (ibid.: 43, 44). This is an idealist, metaphysical perspective on the subject. In identifying leisure as the basis of culture Pieper abstracted leisure forms and practice from history and material conditions. He assigned to it an eternal, spiritual function of divine renewal. His entire discussion was couched in a tacit disapproval of secularism and the regimentation and fragmentation of industrial culture. Yet it is precisely this culture that students of leisure must get to grips with if we are to understand the relationship between culture and contemporary leisure forms and practice. Pieper's account flees from the messy, conflictual substructure of leisure in industrial culture. It endeavours to reinstate the meaning of leisure that applied in a vanished world. This severely limits its use in the social scientific analysis of culture.

Pieper's account places leisure before culture. He argues that it is through contemplation in the unhindered, free time of people that the building blocks of culture are assembled and mortised. But this is to abstract the power of the mind from its cultural context. Jack Kelly attempts to remedy this error by declaring that culture is 'the stuff out of which all leisure experiences are made' (Kelly, 1987: 165–6). In elaboration, he holds that leisure forms and meanings are always ethnically patterned by culture. Leisure practice may dialectically transform culture, but the latter is regarded to have precedent. In both Pieper and Kelly, the concept of culture is curiously abstract. While Kelly's sociological approach incorporates a power dimension in explaining inequalities of resource distribution and access, it does not fully address the role of economics and politics in structuring leisure forms and practice. Pieper's work is somewhat less nuanced, relying chiefly on undifferentiated categories of 'Man' and 'leisure experience'.

An alternative perspective, developed in the context of Cultural Studies, but which has been cogently applied to Leisure Studies (Clarke and Critcher, 1985), focuses squarely upon issues of power, influence and inequality in respect of questions of access and distribution. Raymond Williams's (1963, 1965, 1979) famous exhortation to study culture as 'the whole way of life of a people' is generally accepted to be a seminal contribution to *cultural materialism* (Milner, 1993). Several features distinguish this perspective. Most obviously, it focuses upon the institutions, values, beliefs and patterns of cultural inclusion and exclusion. Cultures are distinguished from one another by the *continuity* of these features and, moreover, by the persistence of coding and representation that is characteristic to them. The *material* element in cultural materialism involves relating these features and characteristics systematically to economic, cultural and political inequality. This approach emphasizes the *situated* character of culture in relation to power, influence and other cultures. There is no place for idealism or metaphysics here. Rather, culture is understood to be the reflection of identifiable historical processes that condition access and distribution.

Arguably, to date, the fullest contribution of this perspective to the field of Leisure Studies was Clarke and Critcher's (1985) study of class and leisure in Britain. Their work locates leisure forms and practices in historical processes. It addresses class inequalities in the distribution of access to resources of leisure, notably leisure time, technology and space. But it is also stamped with the criticisms made of Williams's work by Stuart Hall (1980). Hall maintained that Williams's 'culturalist' approach is fallible because it is over-reliant upon a literary mode of analysis that is inattentive to economic and political processes. Williams was held to have replaced the 'abstract' approach to culture with a 'descriptive' alternative. While this was acknowledged to be a significant improvement, it was also regarded to be incapable of sustaining a genuinely 'analytic' approach to culture. To do that required the addition of theoretical insights from 'structuralism'. Drawing from the continental tradition of Western Marxism, especially as exemplified in the work of Antonio Gramsci and Louis Althusser, Hall submitted that the insights of 'culturalism' must be alloyed with 'structuralism'. By the latter term, he meant a tradition in social and cultural analysis that paid heed to the 'complex unity' of the various processes of hegemony, representation and resistance underwriting the dominant power bloc.

Evidence of this exists in Clarke and Critcher's (1985: 100–44) accent on the commodification of leisure and the centrality of the state apparatus in regulating access to leisure resources and constructing the identity category of 'respectable leisure'. The market and the state are presented as making strategic incursions into popular culture in order to maintain hegemony and engineer consent. In particular, they extend divisive notions of private interest and consumerism into the pelt of culture, fraying traditional continuities of practice, belief and representation in the process, and fomenting possessive individualism.

What can local cultures do against the capitalist state and the onslaught of global consumer culture? Later approaches imply that the options for effective resistance are negligible (Ritzer, 2004). Clarke and Critcher are more optimistic as befits their roots within the tradition of cultural materialism. As they put it:

It is too easy to interpret leisure as wholly determined by political, economic and social institutions and interests, as if its meanings can be simply derived from their workings. Human conduct is rarely so pliable, least of all where, as in leisure, it cannot be directly supervised. The meanings expressed through leisure may be 'received' from the way society is organised but they can be constructed into unique patterns, given particular slants, even on occasions usurped by the activation of meanings other than those which are socially 'approved'. (Clarke and Critcher, 1985: 226–7)

The possibility of cultural resistance is therefore defended, although remarkably scant attention is paid to the social movements and institutions that might accomplish it. An alliance between elements of class and gender is advocated throughout the book, and the state is identified as the key lever of social change.[4] But the relationship between this preferred alliance and the political programme designed to seize control of the state is only lightly sketched.

Elsewhere, at the level of theory, Williams (1977: 122–3) categorized the options of counter-hegemony. *Emergent* forms refer to novel meanings, values, practices and relationships which are detached from, or oppose hegemonic codes of behaviour. *Residual* forms refer to cultural elements that have not been fully co-opted by hegemony. This is consistent with the theoretical and political foundation of cultural materialism which insists that hegemonic culture is never one dimensional.[5] Even groups adversely positioned in relation to access to economic, cultural and political resources possess powers of resistance. However, as with the analysis of Clarke and Critcher (1985) it is not readily apparent how resistance is to be realized in practice. Willis's (1978, 1979) ethnographic work richly demonstrates the construction of counter-cultures constructed around lifestyle and leisure practice. What diminishes their oppositional power is a philosophy of resistance styled as basically latent opposition and governed by opportunism. Because they are unable to generate a coherent alternative political programme they exist largely as symbolic resources of antagonism. Their diversity and political incoherence mean that the system can co-opt them without surrendering the fundamentals of hegemonic control.

Because cultural materialism was pioneered in the Marxist tradition of social analysis it has always wrestled with the salience of class in accounting for leisure choice and practice. The tension is evident in Clarke and Critcher's (1985) work. It simultaneously tries to defend the centrality of class while noting the contrasting significance of gender, race and subculture. Many commentators submit that culture is distinct from class and the attempt to code the former in terms of the latter is unsatisfactory. For example, although Bourdieu (1977) maintains that class remains central, he insists on significant levels of cultural variation within class categories. His concept of *habitus* (Bourdieu, 1977: 95) refers to the acquired system of generative schemes rooted in locality. By the term 'generative schemes' Bourdieu means, *inter alia*, sociolinguistic forms, values, beliefs, myths, collective insignia and traditions. Through these mechanisms culture is constituted and reproduced. They generate the *cultural capital* that distinguishes cultural formations from each other. Bourdieu (1984) elaborated this approach in his analysis of social distinction and taste cultures. This recognizes a more prominent role in consumer culture for divisions around leisure practice within social classes than Clarke and Critcher (1985) muster. In Bourdieu's approach, taste cultures organized around commodities are acknowledged to be a significant source of identity and solidarity. Conversely, Clarke and Critcher (1985) tend to regard them in orthodox Marxist terms as expressions of false consciousness that obscure the underlying predicament and opportunities posed by class membership. By insisting on the significance of taste cultures in consumer society and leisure practice, Bourdieu highlighted the difficulties faced by Marxists in maintaining the conventional wisdom of the inevitability of class revolution.

Thornton's (1995) study of youth culture seized upon many elements in Bourdieu's approach. She demonstrated how youth leisure practice ritualized membership of taste cultures as a way of representing difference, vitality and solidarity. The cultivation of philosophies of 'living for the moment' are developed as strategies for avoiding confronting directly relations of economic, cultural and political dependence. Blackshaw's (2003) analysis of working-class youth subcultures elucidates a parallel strategy in the emphasis on displays of excess in leisure practice. By throwing their money away on drink, drugs, nightclubs and foreign holidays, his 'lads' articulated their social distance from the culture of respectability and parsimony in which they were enmeshed. However, as the lads grew older and embraced the treadmill of paid labour and family life, their leisure culture replaced motifs and practices of excess with nostalgia for the 'good old days' of their youth, when they were without responsibilities, and when everything seemed, momentarily, to be possible. The burden of this work is that youth cultures based around taste are powerful sources of identity and solidarity, but their fate is to succumb to a politics of resignation as the sheer weight of class dependencies are progressively unveiled. Of course, there are exceptions to the rule. Escape and upward mobility are possibilities for individuals and groups. But the balance of analysis emphasizes the *intractable* character of cultural reproduction.

All of these studies illustrate the persistence of cultural forms. But they also reveal the main weakness in cultural analysis. The study of culture tends to privilege the nation-state as the principal unit of analysis. Class struggle and cultural formation are analysed first and foremost in terms of the national-popular (Gramsci, 1971). That is, the conditions that prevail in a territorially bounded unit of population. This was evident in the influential Birmingham School of Contemporary Cultural Studies which focused overwhelmingly on British experience (Hall et al., 1978; CCCS, 1982). Later work in this tradition acknowledged the importance of globalization (Hall, 1991; Hall and Jacques, 1989). However, this did not translate into a renewal of interest in the meaning of civilization.

Globalization raises new doubts about the meaningfulness of cultural isolation. Today, it is more plausible to hold that the flow of information and entertainment produced by modern systems of mass communications necessarily overrides cultural and political barriers. Both the Soviet system and Islamic fundamentalism have been unsuccessful in imposing a moratorium on communication precisely because it is now practically impossible to prevent the electronic circulation of news and ideas. It is tempting to point only to the positive effects of this process in breaking down cultural barriers, expanding tolerance and widening access. But the process is not one-sided.

For example, globalization has improved the mechanisms used by drug cartels to distribute illegal narcotics and prostitution networks. In this way illegal leisure activity is more globalized than ever before. It has also produced new environmental and financial risks as national environments and economies have become more interlinked. In addition, it has produced new levels of stratification, especially in respect of Third World labour in which questions of poverty, hunger and illiteracy are effectively insulated from the West. Castells (1998: 344) calls the bottom stratum in the international division of labour, 'generic, expendable labour'. That is, workers located principally in the Third World, but also in some declining industrial centres in the advanced core economies, who are effectively irrelevant as producers or consumers in capital accumulation. The concept is similar to the old Marxian concept of the 'reserve army of labour', that is, the workforce that is surplus to the needs of the system. The Marxian concept implied that the growth of this surplus would create momentum for radicalizing labour and revolution. However, because generic expendable labour is dispersed globally today, the prospect for collective reaction has diminished. For the most part they are either invisible or marginalized in *barrios*, *favellas*, shanty towns or slum districts where they are left to their fate in the context of declining resources from the welfare state.

The globalization of generic expendable labour raises important questions of global leisure and welfare for workers and consumers in the advanced industrial core countries, not least in respect of care for the other and promoting access. Leisure professionals have recognized new obligations. For example, the World Leisure and Recreation Association issued the Sao Paulo Declaration in 1998 which, among other things, declared that:

> All persons have the right to leisure through economic, political and social policies that are equitable and sustainable.

> All governments and institutions should preserve and create barrier free environments e.g. cultural, technological, natural and built, where people have time, space, facilities and opportunity to express, celebrate and share leisure.

> All Governments will enact and enforce laws and policies designed to provide leisure for all.

> Efforts be made to understand better the consequences of globalization for leisure through a coherent programme of ongoing research.

> Efforts be made to disseminate information on the costs and benefits to leisure from the several and profound forces of globalization. (www.worldleisure.org)

These Articles seem to tacitly acknowledge the emergence of cosmopolitan citizenship and urge the accommodation of cultures to global processes that recognize diversity, widen access and encourage participation. The revival of interest in cross-cultural communication and exchange, and the rational improvement of culture by these means, suggest that it is a timely moment to re-examine the relevance of the concept of civilization for the study of leisure.

Civilization

At the turn of the nineteenth century, after being a term associated overwhelmingly with progress and refinement, the concept of 'civilization' started to be handled with critical circumspection. In the words of Terry Eagleton (2000: 11), 'civilization was abstract, alienated, fragmented, mechanistic, utilitarian, in thrall to a crass faith in material progress; culture was holistic, organic, sensuous, autotelic, recollective'. The primary source for this observation is Norbert Elias's (1978, 1982) study of the civilizing process. As I noted at the beginning of the chapter, civilization is a multidimensional term referring, *inter alia*, to the level of technology, the type of manners, the development of scientific knowledge, the refinement of architecture, relations between the sexes, forms of judicial punishment, religious ideas and customs forms and practices of leisure, and types of agriculture. However, for Elias there is one common denominator behind all of these dimensions which allows for the scientific study of the concept:

> Civilization ... expresses the self-consciousness of the West ... It sums up everything in which Western society of the last two or three centuries believes itself superior to earlier societies or 'more primitive' contemporary ones. By this term Western society seeks to describe what constitutes its special character and what it is proud of: the level of *its* technology, the nature of *its* manners, the development of *its* scientific knowledge or view of the world and much more. (Elias, 1978: 3–4, emphasis in the original)

The criticism of civilization which, in the twentieth century climaxed with Oswald Spengler's (1926) diatribe, *The Decline of the West*, focused on the rational engulfment of culture by civilization. Much as today, many pundits abhor the spread of the McDonald's food chain or Western reality TV shows globally, in the 200 years between the Enlightenment and the Holocaust, there was a cultural reaction in Europe against 'civilized' values. In part this reflected the belief that the concept of civilization carried authoritarian overtones. By the early nineteenth century, instead of being represented as a process, civilization was proselytized as a *project* that could be applied for the purpose of individual self-improvement and social progress. The leisure practices and sports activities of the West were utilized as a central component in civilization-building on colonized territory (Mangan, 1992; Cannadine, 2001). Western civilization was presented as the highest achievement of what has been thought and done in human affairs. Consider the rational recreation movement, which began to be influential after the 1880s.

In Western Europe the rational recreation movement was a strategy of class control and Imperial civilization-building that employed motifs from Christianity, Science and Naturism to engineer convergence between the leisure practices of the aspiring, industrious working class, loyal colonials and the values of 'respectable society' (Bailey, 1978; Cunningham, 1980). Borzello's (1987) study of the use of art exhibitions in the East End of London to 'elevate' the public clearly shows how paintings with moral, 'improving' themes were applied, in the words of Lord Rosebery, to 'civilize a rough'. Long before Fordism, the public arts were applied to extend the social control that respectable society exerted over labour in the workplace to leisure relations. Cross (1993: 107–8) refers to the 'pedagogical', 'salvationist' language of American leisure and recreation professionals that deliberately tried to uproot practices that were perceived to be 'primitive' or 'uncivilized' and replace them with values of 'respectability' and 'civilization'. This language carried over into the ideology of the American leisure and recreation profession.

Yet in both the lower classes and colonized territories, the project of civilization was far from being welcomed with open arms. This is what Eagleton (2000: 11) was driving at in using words like 'abstract', 'alienated', 'fragmented', 'mechanistic', 'utilitarian' and 'crass' to describe the cultural reaction to the onslaught of civilization. Resistance to Western civilization took several forms. Elias's (1978, 1982) work concentrates upon the reaction of German *kultur* to civilization. The latter term was given moral buoyancy by the French Physiocrats and other bourgeois reformers in eighteenth-century France who portrayed the term as a fixed condition for 'uncivilized' people to emulate. This derivation owed much to the use of the term *civilité* used by French courtiers in the sixteenth century to signify refinement and polished manners.

In Germany the term *zivilization* acquired a somewhat different meaning. The absence of a strong central state or political centre meant that the nation was divided between many courts, all of them French speaking in the seventeenth and eighteenth centuries, and each of them relatively closed and hostile to outsiders. The aristocratic disdain for the German language intensified a preoccupation with national identity, especially among the rising circles of the bourgeoisie. They acknowledged the validity of *zivilization* but regarded it as secondary to German *kultur*. The latter term signified depth of feeling, integrity, development of the individual personality and all that was natural, real and authentic in domestic culture. *Kultur* developed as the self-consciousness of the German bourgeoisie symbolizing their accomplishments, identity and distinction from other ranks in German society. In particular, it was used to differentiate the bourgeoisie from the Francophile German courts. Louis XIV and Napoleon both invaded Germany, thus reinforcing the antithesis to civilization, expressed in the French form. The tension between *kultur* and *zivilization* was to have fateful consequences. To some extent the First World War was waged in the name of civilization. The defeat of Germany reinvigorated the preoccupation with *kultur* and its foundational significance in national identity. Spengler (1926), drawing on the philosophy of Nietzsche, condemned Western civilization for generating alienation, brutalization and superficiality. Although the book was misunderstood by Nazi ideologues, as was the philosophy of Nietzsche, both figured in the Nazi appropriation of the concept of *kultur* and the rise of the Third Reich.

Civilization and cultural convergence

I have spent some time on Elias's comparison between the concepts of *zivilization* and *kultur* because I want to convey the latent and manifest tensions embedded in the two concepts. The former has roots in the Enlightenment project of social and economic progress that identified Western Europe as the summit of human development. These roots stretched back further to sixteenth-century ideals of *civilité*, in which refinement, bearing and manners were cultivated as symbols of honour and prestige. Cannadine (2001) demonstrated powerfully how the codification and extension of the honours system was central to the development of the British Empire. Titular distinctions, such as barons, viscountcies, earldoms, marquessates and dukedoms were manufactured to both reward white colonizers and co-opt native princes and potentates.[6] English parliamentarianism, individualism, constitutionalism, human rights, equality, liberty, rule of law, separation of Church and state, leisure forms and sports were transported to the colonies as part of a calculated strategy of cultural convergence. This was largely a strategy in which British institutions and hierarchy were portrayed as the quintessence of Western civilization. However, fundamental errors are made in presenting it as exclusively so. For example, Cannadine (2001: 41) shows convincingly that after the Indian Mutiny of 1857, the Bentnick-Macauly-Dalhouise policy of undermining the corrupt, despotic regimes that were thought to govern India, was reversed. It was acknowledged to be a superficial and unhelpful stereotype. What replaced it was much more complex and subtle. The alternative policy officially *revered* many of the 'traditional' and 'timeless' cultural forms and structures of Southeast Asia. The pageantry of the Maharajas, Moguls, Sultans and Nabobs was selectively co-opted and imitated by the British. In some cases, colonial artists and sportsmen, like the cricketer Ranjit-singhi, the Maharaja jam saheb of Nawanger, were celebrated as ambassadors of co-operation and goodwill. Of course, racism deeply permeated the British attitude to Empire. However, *contra* the argument of many post-colonial critics, it was not *ubiquitous*. As Cannadine puts it:

> When, as they usually did, the British thought of the inhabitants of their empire (as they usually thought about the inhabitants of their metropolis) in *individual* terms rather than in collective categories, they were more likely to be concerned with rank than with race, and with the appreciation of status similarities based on perceptions of affinity. From one perspective, the British may indeed have seen the peoples of their empire as alien, as other, as beneath them – to be lorded over and condescended to. But from another, they also saw them as analogous, as equal, and sometimes even *better* than they were themselves. (Cannadine, 2001: 123, emphasis in the original)

Should this surprise us? Critics of the concept of civilization often highlight its *pulverizing* effect on native cultures, but that was never its only function. It also *allows* for cultural accommodation. At its best, it seeks to combine the highest cultural elements from the midst of a politically and territorially bounded population.

Moreover, cultures are very resistant to co-option by civilization. Elias's (1978, 1982) study showed clearly that German *kultur* reacted against the Francophile precedent of civilization practised in German court society. *Kultur* as exemplified through poetry, literature, philosophy and the arts and physical leisure activities in gymnasia and combat sports like duelling, became a prominent ingredient in the German nation-building programme.

American foreign policy in the post-war reconstruction of Western Europe and Southeast Asia illustrates the tenacity of culture further. US Foreign policy in post-war reconstruction in Western Europe and Southeast Asia gave credence to consumerism in producing cultural convergence. It applied what might be called a 'Baseball plus Coca-Cola' model in spreading common cultural values in Japan and Germany. As with British Empire building in the nineteenth century, the American system was presented as the highest expression of what Western Civilization had to offer to mankind. Leisure choice was central to the strategy of cultural convergence. By making Western Europeans and Southeast Asians absorb American leisure and sport forms, Americans sought to create a 'one system' model of civilization that would defeat the Soviet alternative by extending individual leisure choice and pluralism. Although the Soviet system did eventually collapse, it had more to do with an inability to resolve internal contradictions than convergence to the American consumerist ideal. 'Baseball plus Coca-Cola' produced superficial cultural convergence, but Western shopping centres, sports grounds and medicine did not erase cultural difference.

Issues of cultural accommodation, hybridization and cultural imperialism are central to the global model of leisure presented by the World Leisure Organization in the Sao Paulo Declaration (1998) and the Charter for Leisure (2000). They need to be handled sensitively, not merely in relation to the developing world but also with respect to the nations that possess more economic and political power in setting the agenda for the globalization of leisure. The end of the Cold War has been rightly celebrated as eliminating a dangerous political instability in global affairs. However, it has resulted in the domination of international relations by one superpower, namely the United States. The European Union, China, Japan and India provide a measure of counterveiling power. But none possess the economic, military and political power of the US. This is a situation holding both positives and negatives. Great power is a blessing if it is handled with the recognition of difference. It becomes a curse if it rides roughshod over traditional and elected differences in pursuit of a set of compelling ideals of civilization.

The clash of civilizations

Samuel Huntington (1993, 1996) coined the term 'the clash of civilizations'. He meant it to refocus the epochal struggle between tradition and innovation, half-buried in the decaying political ideology of the Cold War. Arguably, it unintentionally exposes the American dilemma in the twenty-first century, which is how to act globally in a context in which there are no credible opponents to American superpower status. Huntington's thesis is brutally simple: symbolically, and in terms of *realpolitik*, the US is the leading power in the West. Its foreign policy objectives drive the deliberations of international bodies, most notably the International Monetary Fund and the United Nations Security Council. But US superpower status is resented by many weaker players in the world order. Huntington's analysis proceeds on the basis that civilizations are like tectonic plates divided by fault-lines. Modernization creates superficial convergence in, for example, urban-industrial form, medical services, leisure and sport practices and commodity culture. However, underlying this are immutable differences having to do, *inter alia*, with questions of faith, sexual relations, family structures, beliefs and values. Given the military, economic and science development gap between the West and other civilizations, Huntington predicts major instability around 'the West versus the Rest' fault-line. His thesis is that the clash between civilizations will replace the ideology of the Cold War producing a new front of potential crisis and bloodshed.

The Manichaean elements in Huntington's thesis have been widely challenged (Rashid, 1997; Camilleri and Muzaffar, 1998; Pieterse, 2004). In particular, the geophysical motif of fault-lines is regarded to be inappropriate since it exaggerates the incommensurate character of contrasting beliefs and values between civilizations. In Huntington's thesis culture is portrayed as territorially defined which raises immediate issues of barriers and boundaries. Yet as the anthropologists Ulf Hannerz (1992) and James Clifford (1992) observe, under globalization it is misleading to posit civilizations as hermetic, culturally sealed territories. Cultures travel and cultural exchange is fluid and open-ended, and only in perverse forms does it freeze into static, closed postures. Huntington's view of Confucian-Islamic culture in particular, is regarded to be too monolithic. It overstates the trait of religious fundamentalism and underscores liberalism as merely a superficial by-product of modernization. Against this, Huntington's critics point to the many forms of interweaving and hybridity between civilizations.

Huntingdon tends to treat the persistence of cultural, religious and ideological difference between civilizations as the triumph of traditionalism. He implies that the West has developed mature modernization, while 'the Rest', especially Confucian and Islamic types of civilization, have adopted a more primitive mixed model of cultural traditionalism and technological, military and scientific progress. The question is, why should one version of modernity be regarded to be 'mature' and others 'traditional'? We are dealing with an ideological judgement here which elides the subject of 'different modernities'. By the latter term is meant the recognition that modern technology, science, medicine, industry, urban forms, leisure types and military hardware can be combined through different cultural types of mediation. In the Caribbean and North America, creolization means a mixture of African and European elements, while in Latin America it refers to those of European descent born on the continent. The term stands in opposition to doctrines of the negative racial effects of miscegenation by highlighting the value of mixture and combination. 'By stressing and foregrounding the *mestizo* factor, the mixed and in-between,' writes Pieterse, 'creolization highlights what has been hidden and valorizes boundary crossing. It also implies an argument with westernization:

the West itself may be viewed as a mixture and western culture as Creole culture' (Pieterse, 2004: 70).

Conversely, Huntington's thesis successfully highlights the depth of antipathy to the model of Western civilization by oppositional groups. The religious fundamentalist movement that arguably is currently most potently represented on the world stage by the Islamic version, regards many aspects of Western life as corrupt and immoral. At this level, the civilizations do indeed clash, with communication and education being the best long-term hopes to achieve mutual reciprocity. Providing financial aid from the West to build prosperity is a necessary strategy because it recognizes the divide of economic inequality and helps to ameliorate it. But by itself it is likely to belong to the category of 'degrading compassion' that Richard Sennett (2003) elucidates in his critique of 'cod welfarism'. The West needs to recognize cultural difference and promote tolerance and mutual understanding as central values of civilization. Leisure forms offer many opportunities to assist this process. The Arts, Sport and Volunteering have high potential to assist the development of mutuality and respect because they involve voluntary co-operation and the building of common goals. Putnam's (2000: 223–4, 411–12) influential book acknowledges the role of leisure in expanding civic engagement and adding to social capital. Here the argument may be expanded to apply to the relations between civilization. Leisure professionals committed to globalization should pursue a twin policy of education through play within the cultures in which they are situated and cross-cultural exchange in the Arts, Sport, Education and Volunteering. Engaging together in leisure pursuits provides one means of transcending our ethnic, professional and ideological identities to build common social capital.

The answer to the question posed at the start of this chapter, then, is that *both* culture and civilization are the most suitable context to locate leisure forms and practice. For it is in the interplay between the two that patterns of resource allocation and action are reproduced and develop. Leisure professionals who conflate globalization with the spread of Western civilization are likely to unintentionally store up a mass of analytic and policy problems. Programmes of innovation and reform based upon abstract appeals in the name of progress are unlikely to curry favour. Globalization may give the world more mobile telephones, more television sets, more internet connections and more tourism, but these technological and cultural elements cannot produce common civilization. Local traditions and interests have cultural roots and elective distinctions. Leisure professionals who are committed to widening global access need to respect cultural difference and seek to work with them rather than subordinate them to the so-called imperatives of progress. At the same time, they cannot be anything other than the carriers of the cultures and civilizations in which they are located. Professional responsibility requires the leisure professional to be reflexive, not merely about other cultures but also about the culture and civilization to which he or she is attached. In this way Huntington's severe, militaristic metaphor of the clash between civilizations can be counterposed by the more expansive and productive idea of civilizational *interplay*.

Notes

1. The post-colonial conflation of Western civilization with Imperialism distorts the internal contradictions in Western civilization and polarizes the West from 'the colonized'. A more nuanced analysis of the relations of exchange and domination is required. The concept of 'hybridity' does this, but it tends to be associated with the post-colonial moment. In contrast, one needs to insist that hybridity was an original and consistent feature in the development of Western civilization.
2. Gellner elucidates the ethic of cognition thus: 'People were not atoms to begin with, nor did they from the start atomize their world. They began as docile members of communities, and their perceptions begin as *Gestalten*. But it was when they began to think as individuals, and to break up their world, as an intellectual exercise, that they also burst through the erstwhile limits of cognition and production. It was then that the great scientific and economic revolutions took place. It was then that cognitive and productive growth, which are *essential* not contingent elements of our world, became possible. The separation of issues and data, the imposition of a standard and symmetrical descriptive idiom, the exclusion of claims to specialized and privileged status (either for sacred data or sacred sources of information) – all this is almost certainly an important element in any genuine understanding of the distinctive world to which we belong' (Gellner, 1998: 182).
3. Interestingly, Tylor (1874: 1) treats culture and civilization as equivalent terms in his discussion.
4. One enormous gap in the Birmingham School approach to leisure and culture is the absence of any serious engagement with the corporation. The approach fails to detect differences and nuances between corporations and instead presents them as unitary. Social change is understood in conventional Gramscian terms as involving the state to facilitate progressive social transformation over the (territorially bounded) national popular. Globalization implies that different strategies of change are relevant today and that levering progress through the multinational corporation is a viable option in the reconstruction of a more ethical, equal global order.
5. The emphasis on negotiation, movement and tension in hegemony contrasts pointedly with the monolithic society 'without opposition' mode of analysis that prevailed at the high-water mark of the Frankfurt School (Marcuse, 1964).
6. Cannadine's (2001) argument is in part an attack on the post-colonial turn. He seeks to argue that Western civilization was not exclusively or preponderantly about the construction of 'Otherness' or the presumption of cultural inferiority. He calls for a more layered analysis of Western civilization that recognizes that the 'construction of affinities' was at the heart of the Western project.

Bibliography

Arnold, M. (1869) *Culture and Anarchy*, New York, Bobbs-Merrill.
Bailey, P. (1978) *Leisure and Class in Victorian England*, London, Methuen.
Beck, U. (1999) *What is Globalization?*, Cambridge, Polity Press.
Beck, U. and Beck, E. (2001) *Individualization*, London, Sage.
Blackshaw, T. (2003) *Leisurelife*, London, Routledge.
Borzello, F. (1987) *Civilizing Caliban*, London, Routledge & Kegan Paul.
Bourdieu, P. (1977) *Outline of a Theory of Practice*, Cambridge, Cambridge University Press.
Bourdieu, P. (1984) *Distinction*, London, Routledge.
Camilleri, J. and Muzaffar, C. (eds) (1998) *Globalization*, Petaling Jaya, International Movement for a Just World.
Cannadine, D. (2001) *Ornamentalism*, London, Penguin.
Castells, M. (1998) *End of Millennium*, Oxford, Blackwell.
Centre for Contemporary Cultural Studies (1982) *The Empire Strikes Back*, London, Birmingham, Hutchinson.

Cheek, N. and Burch, W. (1976) *The Social Organization of Leisure in Human Society*, New York, Harper & Row.

Childe, V. Gordon (1936) *Man Makes Himself*, New York, New American Library.

Clarke, J. and Critcher, C. (1985) *The Devil Makes Work*, London, Macmillan.

Clifford, J. (1992) 'Travelling Cultures', in L. Grossberg, C. Nelson and P. Treichler (eds) *Cultural Studies*, London, Routledge.

Cross, G. (1993) *Time and Money*, London, Routledge.

Cunningham, H. (1980) *Leisure in the Industrial Revolution*, Beckenham, Croom Helm.

Daniels, B. (1995) *Puritans at Play*, New York, St Martin's Press.

Dumazedier, J. (1974) *The Sociology of Leisure*, Amsterdam, Elsevier.

Eagleton, T. (2000) *The Idea of Culture*, Oxford, Blackwell.

Elias, N. (1978) *The Civilizing Process Vol. 1: The History of Manners*, Oxford, Blackwell.

Elias, N. (1982) *The Civilizing Process Vol. 2: State Formation and Civilization*, Oxford, Blackwell.

Eliot, T. S. (1948) *Notes Towards the Definition of Culture*, London, Faber.

Gellner, E. (1998) *Language and Solitude*, Cambridge, Cambridge University Press.

Gramsci, A. (1971) *Selections From Prison Writings*, London, Lawrence & Wishart.

Hall, S. (1980) 'Cultural Studies: Two Paradigms', *Media, Culture & Society* 2: 57–72.

Hall, S. (1991) 'Old and New Identities, Old and New Ethnicities', in A. King (ed.) *Culture, Globalization and the World System*, Basingstoke, Macmillan, pp. 41–68.

Hall, S. et al. (1978) *Policing the Crisis*, London, Macmillan.

Hall, S. and Jacques, M. (eds) (1989) *New Times*, London, Lawrence & Wishart.

Hannerz, U. (1987) 'The World in Creolisation', *Africa* 57(4): 546–59.

Hannerz, U. (1992) *Cultural Complexity*, New York, Columbia University Press.

Huntington, S. P. (1993) 'The Clash of Civilizations', *Foreign Affairs* 72(3): 22–49.

Huntington, S. P. (1996) *The Clash of Civilizations and the Remaking of World Order*, New York, Simon & Schuster.

Kaplan, M. (1975) *Leisure: Theory & Policy*, New York, Wiley.

Kelly, J. (1987) *Freedom To Be*, New York, Macmillan.

Kraus, R. (1984) *Recreation and Leisure in Modern Society*, London, Longman.

Mangan, J. (1992) (ed.) *The Cultural Bond*, London, Cass.

Marcuse, H. (1964) *One Dimensional Man*, London, Abacus.

Milner, A. (1993) *Cultural Materialism*, Melbourne, Melbourne University Press.

Parker, S. (1983) *Leisure and Work*, London, Allen & Unwin.

Pieper, J. (1952) *Leisure: The Basis of Culture*, New York, Pantheon.

Pieterse, J. (2004) *Globalization & Culture*, Lanham, Rowman & Littlefield.

Putnam, D. (2000) *Bowling Alone*, New York, Simon & Schuster.

Rashid, S. (1997) (ed.) *The Clash of Civilizations? Asian Responses*, Karachi, Oxford University Press.

Ritzer, G. (2004) *The Globalization of Nothing*, Thousand Oaks, Pine Forge.

Roberts, K. (1978) *Contemporary Society and the Growth of Leisure*, London, Longman.

Sennett, R. (2003) *Respect*, New York, Norton.

Spengler, O. (1926) *The Decline of the West*, Oxford, Oxford University Press.

Thornton, S. (1995) *Club Cultures*, Cambridge, Cambridge University Press.

Tylor, E. B. (1874) *Primitive Culture*, Boston, Estes and Lauriat.

Weber, M. (2002) *The Protestant Ethic and the Spirit of Capitalism*, London, Penguin.

Williams, R. (1963) *Culture and Society 1780–1950*, Harmondsworth, Penguin.

Williams, R. (1965) *The Long Revolution*, Harmondsworth, Penguin.

Williams, R. (1977) *Marxism and Literature*, Oxford, Oxford University Press.

Williams, R. (1979) *Politics and Letters*, London, New Left Books.

Willis, P. (1978) *Learning to Labour*, London, Saxon House.

Willis, P. (1979) *Profane Culture*, London, Routledge & Kegan Paul.

3
Anthropology/Pre-history of Leisure

Garry Chick

Edward Burnett Tylor, widely regarded as the founder of anthropology, titled Chapter XII in his 1881 text, *Anthropology*, 'The Arts of Pleasure'. In that chapter, Tylor described aspects of poetry and rhyme, music and musical instruments, dance, drama, art, play, and games among ancient and tribal cultures. The chapter contrasted with the four previous chapters in his book, each of which he titled 'The Arts of Living' (noting chapters IX through XI as '*continued*' as each addressed a somewhat different set of topics). Tylor's separation of the Arts of Life and the Arts of Pleasure foreshadowed the later division of human culture by anthropologists into its utilitarian aspects and its expressive aspects. In a very general sense, the former relates to the ways in which we make our livings and raise our families while the latter addresses how we imbue our lives with meaning. Tylor is better known, however, for providing one of the first, and most influential, English-language definitions of culture in his 1871 book, *Primitive Culture*:

> Culture, or civilization, taken in its wide ethnographic sense, is that complex whole which includes knowledge, belief, art, morals, law, customs, and any other capabilities and habits acquired by man as a member of society. (Tylor, 1871: 1)

Culture is the unifying concept of anthropology and Tylor's definition remains influential as it makes explicit the notion that culture is something that is shared and is learned, rather than innate. Although there are many definitions of culture, most can be grouped into four primary types (Chick, 1997). First, culture has often been defined as the knowledge, beliefs and values held by those who share a culture. Keesing (1976: 139) indicated that culture refers to 'systems of shared ideas, to the conceptual designs, the shared systems of meaning, that underlie the ways in which a people live'. In the second type, distinctive behaviour or behaviour patterns are added. Ember and Ember (1988: 167), for example, define culture as 'the set of learned values, behaviors, and beliefs, that are characteristics of a particular

41

society or population'. Third, some authors have added artefacts to the definition. Brown (1991: 40) provides an example: '[Culture is] the conventional patterns of thought, activity, and artifact that are passed on from generation to generation in a manner that is generally assumed to involve learning rather than specific genetic programming.' Finally, Roberts (1964: 438) offered an encompassing definition: 'It is possible to regard all culture as information and to view any single culture as an "information economy" in which information is received or created, retrieved, transmitted, and even lost.' In this definition, information could be stored in heads, behaviours or artefacts but the information is what is important, not the means of storage.

Utilitarian and expressive culture

The division of culture into utilitarian and expressive components or aspects is not hard and fast but it is a useful heuristic. Nor should the utilitarian and expressive aspects of cultural information be thought of as the ends of a continuum but, instead, as qualities of separate continua on which cultural items often, but not always, vary inversely. A painting, for example, usually has little in the way of utility for a buyer but is largely expressive. For the artist, however, her painting will be both highly expressive and highly utilitarian if she makes her living by selling her works. A Rolex watch and a Timex watch may be similarly utilitarian but the Rolex is surely more expressive.

Leisure and expressive culture, more generally, are commonly held to be non-utilitarian and 'intrinsically motivated'. However, the apparent non-utilitarian and non-survival relatedness of expressive culture may be deeply misleading. The kinds of expressive and leisure activities engaged in by different societies do not appear to vary randomly, as might be expected if expression and leisure were truly irrelevant to survival and reproductive success. These observations are directly relevant to two of the abiding concerns of anthropologists and other social scientists, that is, the nature of cultural evolution and change and the nature of culture as an adaptive system. In addition, leisure and expressive culture seem to offer fertile arenas for creativity. In the first half of the twentieth century, the well-known anthropologists Bronislaw Malinowski (1931) and Alfred L. Kroeber (1948) described leisure as a creative domain wherein cultural innovation and progress may take place.

Expressive culture can be separated into the arts, which encompass the plastic and graphic arts, music, dance, drama, literature, myth, legend, and so on, and entertainment, which includes play, games, sport, leisure and recreation. Like the division of culture into its utilitarian and its expressive aspects, the separation of expressive culture into the arts and entertainment is best regarded as a useful heuristic. Particular activities may be both very artistic and very much entertainment for consumers (for example, a ballet) while others may be more art than entertainment for producers (a painting, for example). Some activities may be highly entertaining but not very artistic (such as a pick-up softball game). Unfortunately, just as anthropologists have overwhelmingly studied utilitarian culture rather than expressive culture, when they have examined expressive culture, they have overwhelmingly focused on the arts rather than entertainment. Nevertheless, some advances have been made in the anthropology of entertainment. The goal of this chapter is to review the contributions that anthropologists have made to that part of expressive culture.

The fields of anthropology

As anthropology developed during the latter third of the nineteenth century through the first third of the twentieth century, it took on a distinct division of labour. Four fields developed within the discipline. Biological anthropologists direct their attention to human physical differences, adaptations, evolution and relationships to other primates. Archaeologists maintain culture as their focus but direct their attention to its description over long time-periods via the analysis of the remnants of past human groups. Anthropological linguists deal with the relationship of language to culture and society, its historical development and language structure. Finally, cultural anthropologists (usually called social anthropologists in Europe) try to understand the cultures of people of the recent past and today as well as how cultures change and evolve. Each of these subfields of anthropology is relevant to the study of leisure although, as might be expected, the degree to which each has contributed to date differs markedly.

Leisure and biological anthropology

Research on play among animals, especially mammals, is substantial and has a long history (Fagen, 1981; Bekoff and Byers, 1998; see Chick, 2001, for a review). Recent studies suggest that play is essentially a juvenile activity and that the retention of neonatal characteristics into adulthood results in playful behaviour throughout the adult lifespan. The adaptive values of play are frequently discussed (for example, Chick, 2001; Smith, 1982).

Veblen (1899) and Huizinga (1955) claimed that leisure was born in the play and rituals of pre-history. Indeed, Huizinga claimed that play was the foundation of culture itself. However, animal play surely existed long before humans, so the origins of leisure and culture may be older still. Recent research suggests that non-human mammals such as chimpanzees, orangutans, dolphins, whales, elephants, some birds, and possibly even rats, have rudimentary cultures (for example, de Waal, 2001; Whiten et al., 1999). Despite the growing body of evidence for culture among non-human animals, the study of leisure has, thus far, been restricted to humans. The observation of some animals, such as dogs, monkeys, or apes, suggests that they frequently engage in activities that seem to be distinct from play but, yet, are not overtly utilitarian in nature, such as eating, fleeing from danger or chasing prey. Studies of primates engaged in grooming or in idle play with infants or juveniles seem to demonstrate the existence of a number of leisure-like qualities in those activities. Dog owners are aware of the leisurely qualities of the chewing of a real or rawhide bone by their pet. Any nutritional, teeth cleaning or other utilitarian values of such behaviour seem to be incidental.

At least two theoretical issues are important with respect to leisure and animals. First, research on leisure among animals may tell us something about its development, motivation and function in humans. Animal leisure, if it can be claimed to exist, may help clarify some of our conceptual and definitional difficulties with leisure, recreation and related concepts. For example, the concepts of intrinsic motivation and perceived freedom are central to many current definitions of leisure. These qualities seem to occur in certain forms of animal behaviour, such as those mentioned above. Conceptualizing leisure as a state of mind, involving intrinsic motivation and perceived freedom, seems to imply consciousness yet the nature of consciousness remains controversial. Yet leisure researchers appear to uncritically use concepts such as intrinsic motivation, perceived freedom, and other implied aspects of consciousness, including Csikszentmihalyi's (1975) familiar notion of 'flow', without first giving due regard to the nature of consciousness itself, either in humans or in animals.

Second, leisure, or leisure-like behaviour, may play a significant role in the social organization of animals and in social and behavioural evolution. Primates, including humans, are extremely social animals and a major portion of the learning of social behaviour, including communication skills and other species-typical adult behaviours, occurs in the context of play and leisure-like activities. Critical learning about social hierarchy and the ability to predict the behaviour of others is learned in the rough-and-tumble play of infants and juveniles, the casual play of infants, juveniles and adults, and in social leisure-like activities such as grooming among monkeys and apes. The possibility that leisure confers some selective or adaptive advantage has rarely been explored (but see Rubin et al., 1986; Chick, 1995).

Leisure may well be rooted in mammalian biological and behavioural repertoires. If the concept of leisure can be meaningfully applied to animals, especially higher mammals, knowledge about leisure among humans might be advanced much in the same way that knowledge of human learning, language and other psychological processes has been advanced through the study of such behavioural systems in various animals. In particular, it may be necessary to rethink some of the definitional characteristics that we ascribe to the term 'leisure' based on studies of animal consciousness. Although Smith (1985) claimed that animals cannot receive pleasure through creative thought and symbolic processes, implying that animals cannot exhibit consciousness, there is tangible evidence to the contrary. As has been found to be the case in so many other arenas, the difference between leisure among higher mammals and humans may be one of degree rather than one of kind (Chick and Barnett-Morris, 1987).

Leisure and anthropological linguistics

The contributions of anthropological linguistics to the study of leisure are greater in potential than in reality. The potential lies in whether or not the long-standing theoretical positions relating language and worldview have merit. According to the Sapir-Whorf Hypothesis, the way in which we perceive and experience the world is determined or, at least, influenced by our language (Kay and Kempton, 1984). That is, in its strong form, the Sapir-Whorf Hypothesis predicts that the nature of reality is created by the grammatical and semantic characteristics of language. Hence, speakers of different languages do not simply see the same reality with different labels attached but literally see different realities. Do speakers of English, for example, who have the word 'leisure' therefore see the world differently than speakers of German who have only the term *'freizeit'*, whose direct translation to English is 'free time'? Informal studies suggest that only about 10 per cent of languages have lexemes (that is, single words) that translate directly to the English 'leisure', while about 90 per cent of languages have lexemes that translate directly to the English word 'play' (Chick et al., 2001). Does this mean that 90 per cent of non-English-speakers cannot understand, or possibly not even experience, leisure, while 90 per cent can understand, and experience, play? Such a claim seems preposterous but no research exists to directly refute it. While some linguists dispute even the weak form of the Sapir-Whorf Hypothesis, that our perceptions of reality are only influenced rather than determined by our language, others maintain its validity in one form or another.

Leisure and archaeology

Because archaeologists base their inferences about past cultures on analyses of artefacts including, in some cases, writings, art and sculpture left by those cultures, their data sources do not include behaviour that leaves no traces. No permanent artefacts are necessarily associated with resting or chatting with friends, for example, while both of these were surely important recreations for people of the past everywhere. However, some leisure and recreational activities do involve artefacts. Sites around the world have yielded balls, javelins, darts, hoops, marbles, dice, game boards, board game pieces, playing cards and numerous other devices used in recreational games and sports. The development of sporting games, including track and field, wrestling, boxing and archery, among the ancient Greeks and Romans are well known from archaeological, artistic and narrative sources. Ancient art forms, such as painting and sculpture, often depict game and sports.

The natives of present-day Mexico and Central America played a rubber-ball game, often on monumental urban courts, from as early as 1400 BCE until it was suppressed by the Spanish in the sixteenth century. Frescoes, stone carvings, painted pottery and clay figurines depict the game and its play among the Maya and Aztecs. The largest ball court is at Chichén Itzá in the northern Yucatan. Built between 900 and 1100 CE, it measures some 70 by 168 metres (Chick, 1996). The labour effort necessary to construct such massive stone courts reflects the importance of the game in pre-Hispanic Mesoamerican life. Simplified versions of the Mesoamerican ball game are still played in some areas of northwestern Mexico.

Game boards carved into temple roofs in the ancient Egyptian ruins at Memphis, Thebes and Luxor indicate that mancala, the classic African game of strategy, was played there prior to 1400 BCE. Chess boards and pieces found in India suggest that it developed there and diffused to Persia by the sixth century CE. The game reached the Arab kingdoms, Greece and Medina by about 650 CE and was probably brought to Europe by Crusaders. It became popular in southern Europe by the fifteenth century and thereafter spread throughout the continent.

Dice are among the most commonly found recreational artefacts in archaeological sites. 'Knucklebones' (usually bones from the ankles of sheep or pigs) that were marked on several sides were often used for dice, but antlers, pebbles, walnut shells, peach or plum stones, pottery disks, walrus ivory, and beaver or woodchuck teeth, were used as well. Greek and Roman dice were most often made of bone or ivory, but amber, marble and porcelain, and other materials were also used. Cubical dice are the most common, but pyramidal, rectangular, pentahedral and octahedral dice are also found.

Abundant archaeological evidence exists for the sports, games and other recreational activities of past cultures (see, for example, Howell, 1971). Unfortunately, in the field of Leisure Studies, we have tended to concentrate on the historical and archaeological accounts of the spectacular (for example, the Olympics) and the lurid (such as the Roman games). As Kelly (1982) has pointed out, we know little about the recreation of the common folk of the past. This is an area where archaeology can make contributions to the study of leisure and recreation, but only if such contributions are recognized as important by archaeologists.

Leisure and cultural anthropology

Ethnography, the description of the ways in which others live, has traditionally been the foundation of cultural anthropology. Describing the ways in which different cultural groups experience leisure and manifest their expressive cultures has always been a small but important part of the ethnographic enterprise. Among ancient writers, travellers and chroniclers such as Herodotus (484–425 BC) described games and other recreations in Lydia and Egypt and Tacitus (55–120 CE) wrote about dice games among the Germanic tribes. Spanish clerics and soldiers, such as Sahagún, Motolinía and Durán, left descriptions of games, art, music and rituals among the Aztecs, Mayas and other native peoples of Mesoamerica. Lafitau, a French Jesuit missionary, described games and pastimes of Native North Americans (Chick, 1984). In 1851, New York attorney Lewis Henry Morgan published *League of the Iroquois*, one of the first ethnographies in the modern sense of the term and therein described games, sports and other recreations in a Native American tribe.

Ethnographic treatments of kinds of leisure and expressive culture have only occasionally received book-length treatment in anthropology. Examples include Stuart Culin's (1907) *Games of the North American Indians*, Theodore Stern's (1948) *The Rubber Ball Games of the Americas*, and Kendall Blanchard's (1981) *The Mississippi Choctaws at Play: The Serious Side of Leisure*. Much more often, leisure and expressive culture have been addressed as chapters or parts of book-length ethnographies or as articles in journals or edited volumes. Descriptions of leisure, recreational and expressive activities provide cross-cultural researchers with data for comparative studies. Tylor produced the first cross-cultural comparative study of recreational activities in 1879 when he compared the Aztec game of patolli with the Indian game, pachisi, in an effort to demonstrate that Mesoamerican civilization had been influenced by Asian civilization. Early comparative studies, such as those of Tylor and Stuart Culin (1895), who claimed that games originated in magical rites and exist now as survivals from primitive conditions, reflected the theories of culture that prevailed at the time, including unilinear evolutionism and diffusionism, and were soon rejected by most anthropologists.

Functionalism, the idea that social institutions operate to meet the needs of society members and to maintain social equilibrium, developed early in the twentieth century and provided a way of explaining social organization and social structures. Under the sway of functionalism, anthropological descriptions and analyses of leisure and other expressive activities, with the exception of religion, magic, taboo, witchcraft and related topics, waned as such activities were thought to be relatively inconsequential for cultural maintenance. A few physical educators conducted functional analyses of recreational activities in other cultures, however. Dunlap (1951) examined the functions of physical recreations in Samoa, suggesting that they were tied to social organization, religion, economic pursuits and warfare. Stumpf and Cozens (1947, 1949) suggested that sports, games and recreation among the Maori and the Fijians served as training for war, the acquisition of skill and grace, as a means for promoting tribal solidarity, and as an outlet for healthy competitive urges in otherwise co-operative societies. Anthropological studies of play, games and other expressive activities declined significantly between 1900 and 1990, however (Chick and Donlon, 1992).

John M. Roberts, Malcolm J. Arth and Robert R. Bush gave the anthropological study of leisure and expressive activities a new beginning in 1959 with their publication, 'Games in Culture'. This paper initiated a long series of studies wherein Roberts and his colleagues examined games and other recreational and expressive activities, including arts and crafts, tourism, folk tales, poems, riddles, music, recreational driving and flying, and trap shooting, from either cross-cultural comparative or intracultural perspectives. Roberts proposed that many leisure and recreational activities provide 'cultural models' of important real-world activities and that these models provide safe arenas for learning. Roberts and Sutton-Smith (1962) also suggested that recreational and expressive models might assuage psychological conflicts that naturally arise as a part of enculturation or social life. For example, the board game Monopoly became immensely popular during the Great Depression of the 1930s, as it allowed people who may have had little money to behave, in a play world, like tycoons.

Leisure may also have other functions. Franz Boas (1940), who is generally acknowledged as the founder of American anthropology, and V. Gordon Childe (1951), the great British archaeologist, held that leisure has a major role in cultural evolution. They felt that the adoption of sedentary agriculture provided an increase in the food supply that permitted larger settlements, craft specialization and extra leisure that could be devoted to invention. In turn, the technological developments that resulted from this newfound leisure provided increased agricultural productivity, even larger settlements, greater craft specialization and more leisure. This 'surplus theory' of cultural evolution and change was important in anthropology through the 1950s and is still cited in other fields, including leisure studies. In the late 1950s, however, anthropologists working among the Bushmen of the Kalahari Desert of southwest Africa found, contrary to expectations, that the people living even in this harsh environment spent relatively little time in the food quest and consequently had abundant free time. Other research suggested that sedentary agriculture does not, in fact, provide either a more dependable or a more nutritious diet than food collecting and that increases in free time are used mostly for rest, rather than thinking and invention (Just, 1980). Anthropologist Lauriston Sharp had already published similar information about the Yir Yiront, an Australian Aboriginal group in 1952. He wrote that 'Any leisure time the Yir Yiront might gain by using steel axes or other Western tools was invested, not in "improving the conditions of life," and certainly not in developing aesthetic activities, but in sleep, an art they had thoroughly mastered' (Sharp, 1952: 82). More recently, Johnson (1978) compared time-use patterns of the French with those of the Machiguenga, a hunting, gathering and simple horticultural society of the upper Amazon River basin, finding that Machiguenga men and women had more free time than French men and women. It is also clear that there is little merit for food collectors to acquire resources beyond their immediate needs if they have no way of storing or transporting them. Hence, even if technologically simple folk have few possessions, many seem to have abundant time left over after the food quest is satisfied, a situation that anthropologist Marshall Sahlins (1968) referred to as 'Zen affluence'.

This led Just (1980) to speculate that leisure might be instrumental in cultural elaboration and evolution opposite to the way indicated by the surplus theory. If, as cultures become more complex, the amount of free time available decreases, then free time takes on economic value as a scarce commodity. Since things that have economic value are to be used wisely, free time would be better directed to work on technological advances that would create more free time. Like the surplus theory, this 'time scarcity' theory proposes a system of positive feedback, but one where cultural evolution results from efforts to better utilize constantly declining, rather than increasing, free time.

The difficulty with the time scarcity theory is not that it is based upon incorrect data but that the data used in its formulation were incomplete. The comparison of the French and the Machiguenga (Johnson, 1978), cited above, is an example of a study that looks at societies located at nearly opposite ends of the scale of cultural complexity (which is commonly used as a measure of degree of cultural evolution) while disregarding those in between. In contrast, in a cross-cultural study of time spent in productive labour for !Kung San, Machiguenga, Canchino, Kikuyu, Logoli and American women, Munroe et al. (1983) found that the amount of time spent in productive labour for the three horticultural societies (the Canchino, Kikuyu and Logoli) was considerably higher than that for the hunter-gatherers (the !Kung San and the Machiguenga) or the urban-industrial group (the Americans). Munroe et al. suggested that the relationship between cultural complexity and the amount of time spent working is curvilinear, with cultures of low and high complexity having relatively more time free from work than those of medium complexity.

Others have indicated that there is no relationship between patterns of time use and cultural complexity. Hawkes and O'Connell (1981) and Hill et al. (1985) maintain that when time spent in food processing and miscellaneous chores is added to the time spent in food acquisition, estimates of the total amount of time spent working by hunter-gatherers increases sharply. They concluded that no significant differences could be found between hunter-gatherers and subsistence horticulturalists in the amount of time spent on subsistence work.

Chick (1993) conducted a cross-cultural sample of 55 different societies in order to test these perspectives on time use and availability empirically. Since leisure itself could not be coded due to the lack of information on the topic, Chick operationalized it as the time left over after work. Societies in the Standard Cross-Cultural Sample (Murdock and White, 1969) were coded for hours of productive labour per day (for males only) and these data were compared with previously coded data on cultural complexity (Murdock and Provost, 1973). The relationship between hours of labour and cultural complexity was assessed through the use of second-order polynomial regression in order to determine whether the data were best fit by a straight line or a parabola. Though societies at the lower ranges of cultural complexity seemed to have somewhat fewer hours of labour than those at the upper range, the data were fit nearly as well by a straight line as a parabola. Hence, societies of mid-range cultural complexity did not exhibit significantly longer hours of work than those of either lower or higher complexity. Additional research is clearly needed on this topic.

Leisure itself changes as culture changes. Technological changes since the Industrial Revolution such as the automobile, the radio, the television and the personal computer have brought about revolutionary changes in the way many people experience their leisure. Chick (1991) showed that the festival sponsorship system (the *fiesta* system) in rural Mexico traditionally has both religious and recreational aspects. Because the small, rural communities are acculturating to the national culture of Mexico due to the media and increased access to the outside due to modern transportation, these systems are in the process of disappearing. Their loss has forced many residents of these communities to seek recreational opportunities outside of their villages. On the other hand, other, larger, communities have secularized their festivals. By doing so, they have attempted to create attractions for tourists in order to further economic development. These secular festivals are no longer organized and administered by lay community members but by local political and business figures.

Belgian anthropologist/historian Arnold van Gennep's (1909) study of rites of passage foreshadowed an approach to the anthropology of leisure that differs from the presumably objective and scientific studies reviewed above. Van Gennep claimed that rites of passage, which he defined as rituals that celebrate the transition of individuals or groups of individuals from one life state to another, are cultural universals that apply, minimally, to birth, marriage and death. Moreover, all rites of passage have three characteristic stages. First, individuals go through rites of separation that mark their severance from a previous life-stage. Second, individuals pass through a stage marked by rites of transition. Finally, they are established in their new status by rites of incorporation. The three stages are not equally emphasized in all life transitions, however. Rites of separation are emphasized in funerary rituals while rites of transition are prominent in initiation ceremonies. Marriage emphasizes rites of incorporation. Many, although not all, rites of passage are accompanied by recreational activities such as feasting, dancing, music, games, play and the production of art, although most of these have symbolic features as well.

The anthropologist Victor Turner (1967) characterized the transitional stage as especially symbol-laden and often troublesome. He referred to this stage as 'liminal' (from the Latin *limen*, meaning 'threshold'). Indeed, many rituals associated with this stage involve passing through some sort of threshold, door, or archway, as in the practice where, in some cultures, grooms carry their brides over the threshold of their new homes. Initiates often develop a feeling of both separation from the everyday world, but also of togetherness with other initiates, that Turner (1969) called 'communitas'. He emphasized the importance of rituals, including their recreational aspects, in the examination of 'how people think and feel about relationships and about the natural and social environments in which they operate' (Turner, 1969: 6). Further, Turner claimed that communitas is the basis for religious experiences such as those encountered by pilgrims to sacred places and shrines, a perspective that he and Edith Turner (1978) later applied to tourism. The Turners viewed tourism as a ritual escape from normal life similar to the rituals of holy days. Graburn (1983) claimed that tourism falls into two types: one, that is part of the normal annual cycle such as holiday get-togethers; the other, a sort of rites-of-passage tourism associated with events such as graduating from high school (for example, the senior trip), marriage (the honeymoon), or retiring. More recently, Cohen (2003) discussed backpacking as both a form of tourism and as a rite of passage wherein backpacking youths leave their normal life and enter a liminal state, having to fend for themselves in an alien situation.

In one of the foundational pieces of symbolic anthropology, Clifford Geertz (1973) described the Balinese cockfight as a form of what he called 'deep play', that is, play in which the stakes are so high that it is irrational to engage in it at all. He described cockfighting in Bali thusly because it is both illegal and involves wagering large sums of money on a very chancy activity. This article, aside from its merits as ethnography or a theoretical contribution, contributed substantially to the legitimacy of cultural interpretation and the study of cultural meaning. While Geertz has not pursued research in expressive culture, others, such as Bruner (1996), Clifford (1997) and Kirshenblatt-Gimblett (1998) extended his interpretive enterprise into the expressive arena, particularly tourism. These authors have concerned themselves with how both Western and non-Western arts and cultures are displayed and interpreted, especially for tourists.

The future of the anthropology of leisure

Leisure, however defined, is a cross-cultural universal (though having a word, such as 'leisure', as a general descriptor for it is by no means universal). All known human groups have art, music, body decoration, play, games and other activities that appear to be done for their own sake (Brown, 1991). Nevertheless, as indicated earlier, anthropologists have devoted far more attention to the utilitarian than the expressive aspects of culture and, when they have studied expressive culture, they have focused on the arts rather than leisure. Hence, anthropologists have largely ignored the place of leisure in the processes of socialization, enculturation, culture change, cultural evolution and cultural adaptation. They have been more successful in addressing expressive culture as a symbolic system or system of meanings. For their part, leisure researchers have largely focused on North Americans and Europeans, although there are exceptions (for example, Ibrahim, 1981; Gihring, 1983; Florian and Har-Even, 1984; Khan, 1997; McDonald and McAvoy, 1997).

There are positive signs, however. Efforts to explain leisure behaviour by reference to culture, although long implicit in ethnographies, are only recently making their explicit appearance in the anthropological literature (for example, Chick, 1981, 2002; Dressler and Bindon, 2000). Moreover, cultures both prescribe 'appropriate' forms of leisure and proscribe 'inappropriate' forms (Chick and Dong, 2004). Dressler and his colleagues (for example, Dressler et al., 1996; Dressler and Bindon, 2000) found that members of cultural communities share understandings of what constitutes a 'successful lifestyle', operationalized as material possessions and leisure activities. Moreover, the degree to which individuals can actually participate in this consensus lifestyle correlates positively with measures of physical and mental health, including arterial blood pressure, symptoms of depression and perceived stress. Anthropologists working in the humanistic and symbolic tradition led by Geertz and Turner are also making advances, particularly with respect to tourism in terms of the relationship of cultural authenticity to the commodification of culture (for example, Bruner, 1989, 1996; Clifford, 1997). The awareness of leisure as a significant part of culture, greater efforts to ethnographically document leisure and expressive behaviours and cross-cultural comparative studies of leisure should enhance understandings of both leisure and culture in the future.

Bibliography

Bekoff, M. and Byers, J. A. (eds) (1998) *Animal Play: Evolutionary, Comparative, and Ecological Perspectives*, Cambridge, Cambridge University Press.

Blanchard, K. (1981) *The Mississippi Choctaws at Play: The Serious Side of Leisure*, Urbana, IL, University of Illinois Press.

Boas, F. (1940) *Race, Language and Culture*, New York, Macmillan.

Brown, D. E. (1991) *Human Universals*, Philadelphia, Temple University Press.

Bruner, E. M. (1989) 'Of Cannibals, Tourists, and Ethnographers', *Cultural Anthropology* 4: 439–46.

Bruner, E. M. (1996) 'Tourism in the Balinese Borderzone', in S. Lavie and T. Swedenburg (eds) *Displacement, Diaspora, and Geographies of Identity*, Durham, NC, Duke University Press, pp. 157–79.

Chick, G. (1981) 'Concept and Behavior in a Tlaxcalan *Cargo* Hierarchy', *Ethnology* 20: 217–28.

Chick, G. (1984) 'The Cross-cultural Study of Games', *Exercise and Sport Sciences Reviews* 12: 307–37.

Chick, G. (1986) 'Leisure, Labor, and the Complexity of Culture: An Anthropological Perspective', *Journal of Leisure Research* 18: 154–68.

Chick, G. (1991) 'Acculturation and Community Recreation in Rural Mexico', *Play & Culture* 4: 185–93.

Chick, G. (1993) 'Leisure and the Evolution of Culture: Cross-cultural Tests of Several Hypotheses', in G. Cushman, P. Jonson and A. J. Veal (eds) *Leisure and Tourism: Social and Environmental Change*, Sydney, WLRA/University of Technology, pp. 293–300.

Chick, G. (1995) 'The Adaptive Qualities of Leisure: A Cross-Cultural Survey', in C. Simpson and B. Gidlow (eds) *Proceedings of the ANZALS Conference, 1995*, Canterbury, New Zealand, Australian and New Zealand Association for Leisure Studies, pp. 158–63.

Chick, G. (1996) 'The Mesoamerican Ball Game', in D. Levinson and K. Christensen (eds) *Encyclopedia of World Sport: From Ancient Times to the Present*, Santa Barbara, CA, ABC-CLIO, pp. 636–40.

Chick, G. (1997) 'Cultural Complexity: The Nature and Measurement of the Concept', *Cross-Cultural Research* 31: 275–307.

Chick, G. (1998) 'Leisure and Culture: Issues for an Anthropology of Leisure', *Leisure Sciences* 20: 111–33.

Chick, G. (2001) 'What is Play For? Sexual Selection and the Evolution of Play', in S. Reifel (ed.) *Theory in Context and Out: Play & Culture Studies, Vol. 3*, Westport, CT, Ablex Publishing, pp. 3–25.

Chick, G. (2002) 'Cultural and Behavioral Consonance in a Tlaxcalan Festival System', *Field Methods* 14: 26–45.

Chick, G. and Barnett-Morris, L. (1987) 'The Hairy Leisure Class: A Consideration of Leisure Among Nonhuman Higher Mammals.' Paper presented at the Leisure Research Symposium, National Recreation and Park Association Congress for Recreation and Parks, New Orleans, LA, September.

Chick, G. and Donlon, J. (1992) 'Going Out on a Limn: Geertz's "Deep Play: Notes on the Balinese Cockfight" and the Anthropological Study of Play', *Play & Culture* 5: 233–45.

Chick, G., Makopondo, R. and Winneshiek, W. (2001) 'Lexicons for Leisure: Cross-Cultural Comparisons'. Paper presented at the annual meeting of the Society for Cross-Cultural Research, San Diego, CA, 21–25 February.

Chick, G. and Dong, E. (2004) 'Cultural Constraints on Leisure', in E. Jackson (ed.) *Constraints on Leisure*, State College, PA, Venture Publishing (forthcoming).

Childe, V. Gordon (1951) *Man Makes Himself*, New York, Mentor Books.

Clifford, J. (1997) *Routes: Travel and Translation in the Late Twentieth Century*, Cambridge, MA, Harvard University Press.

Cohen, E. (2003) 'Backpacking: Diversity and Change', *Tourism and Culture Change* 1: 95–110.

Csikszentmihalyi, M. (1975) *Beyond Boredom and Anxiety*, San Francisco, Jossey-Bass.

Culin, S. (1895) *Korean Games, with Notes on the Corresponding Games of China and Japan*, Philadelphia, University of Pennsylvania Press.

Culin, S. (1907) *Games of the North American Indians*, Washington, DC, US Government Printing Office.

de Waal, F. B. M. (2001) *The Ape and the Sushi Master*, New York, Basic Books.

Dressler, W. W., Dos Santos, J. E. and Campos Balieiro, M. (1996) 'Studying Diversity and Sharing in Culture: An Example of Lifestyle in Brazil', *Journal of Anthropological Research*, 52: 331–54.

Dressler, W. W. and Bindon, J. R. (2000) 'The Health Consequences of Cultural Consonance: Cultural Dimensions of Lifestyle, Social Support, and Arterial Blood Pressure in an African American Community', *American Anthropologist* 102: 244–60.

Dunlap, H. L. (1951) 'Games, Sports, and Other Vigorous Recreational Activities and Their Function in Samoan Culture', *Research Quarterly* 22: 298–311.

Ember, C. R. and Ember, M. (1988) *Anthropology* (5th edn), Englewood Cliffs, NJ, Prentice-Hall.

Fagen, R. M. (1981) *Animal Play Behavior*, New York, Oxford University Press.

Florian, V. and Har-Even, D. (1984) 'Cultural Patterns in the Choice of Leisure Time Activity Frameworks: A Study of Jewish and Arab Youth in Israel', *Journal of Leisure Research* 16: 330–7.

Geertz, C. (1973) 'Deep Play: Notes on the Balinese Cockfight', in C. Geertz (ed.) *The Interpretation of Cultures*, New York, Basic Books, pp. 87–125.

Gihring, T. A. (1983) 'Leisure-time Activities in an Urban Nigerian Setting: Attitudes and Experience', *Journal of Leisure Research* 15: 108–24.

Graburn, N. H. H. (1983) 'The Anthropology of Tourism', *Annals of Tourism Research* 10: 9–33.

Hawkes, K. and O'Connell, J. F. (1981) 'Affluent Hunters? Some Comments in Light of the Alyawara Case', *American Anthropologist* 83: 622–6.

Hill, K., Kaplan, H., Hawkes, K. and Hurtado, A. M. (1985) 'Men's Time Allocation to Subsistence Work among the Ache of Eastern Paraguay', *Human Ecology* 13: 29–47.

Howell, M. L. (1971) 'Archaeological Evidence of Sports and Games in Ancient Civilizations', *Canadian Journal of the History of Sport and Physical Education* 11: 14–30.

Huizinga, J. (1955) *Homo Ludens: A Study of the Play-Element in Culture*, New York, Basic Books.

Ibrahim, H. (1981) 'Leisure Behavior Among Contemporary Egyptians', *Journal of Leisure Research* 13: 89–104.

Johnson, A. (1978) 'In Search of the Affluent Society', *Human Nature* 1: 50–9.

Just, P. (1980) 'Time and Leisure in the Elaboration of Culture', *Journal of Anthropological Research* 36: 105–15.

Kay, P. and Kempton, W. (1984) 'What is the Sapir-Whorf Hypothesis?' *American Anthropologist* 86: 65–79.

Keesing, R. M. (1976) *Cultural Anthropology: A Contemporary Perspective*, New York, Holt, Rinehart & Winston.

Kelly, J. R. (1982) *Leisure*, Englewood Cliffs, NJ, Prentice-Hall, Inc.

Khan, N. A. (1997) 'Leisure and Recreation Among Women of Selected Hill-farming Families in Bangladesh', *Journal of Leisure Research* 29: 5–20.

Kirshenblatt-Gimblett, B. (1998) *Destination Culture: Tourism, Museums, and Heritage*, Berkeley, University of California Press.

Kroeber, A. L. (1948) *Anthropology*, New York, Harcourt Brace.

Malinowski, B. (1931) 'Culture', in E. R. A. Seligman (ed.) *Encyclopedia of the Social Sciences, Vol. 2*, New York, Macmillan, pp. 621–46.

McDonald, D. and McAvoy, L. (1997) 'Native Americans and Leisure: State of the Research and Future Directions', *Journal of Leisure Research* 29: 145–66.

Morgan, L. H. (1851) *League of the Iroquois*, New York, Corinth Books, 1962.

Munroe, R. H., Munroe, R. L., Michelson, C., Koel, A., Bolton, R. and Bolton C. (1983) 'Time Allocation in Four Societies', *Ethnology* 12: 355–70.

Murdock, G. P. and Provost, C. (1973) 'Measurement of Cultural Complexity', *Ethnology* 11: 254–95.

Murdock, G. P. and White, D. R. (1969) 'Standard Cross-cultural Sample', *Ethnology* 8: 329–69.

Roberts, J. M. (1964) 'The Self Management of Cultures', in W. H. Goodenough (ed.) *Explorations in Cultural Anthropology*, New York, McGraw-Hill, pp. 433–54.

Roberts, J. M., Arth, M. J. and Bush, R. R. (1959) 'Games in Culture', *American Anthropologist* 61: 597–605.

Roberts, J. M. and Brian Sutton-Smith, B. (1962) 'Child Training and Game Involvement', *Ethnology* 1:166–85.

Rubin, J., Flowers, N. M. and Gross, D. R. (1986) 'The Adaptive Dimensions of Leisure', *American Ethnologist* 13: 524–36.

Sahlins, M. (1968) 'Notes on the Original Affluent Society', in R. B. Lee and I. DeVore (eds) *Man the Hunter*, Chicago, Aldine, pp. 85–9.

Sharp, L. (1952) 'Steel Axes for Stone Age Australians', in E. H. Spicer (ed.) *Human Problems in Technological Change: A Casebook*, New York, Russell Sage, pp. 69–90.

Smith, P. K. (1982) 'Does Play Matter? Functional and Evolutionary Aspects of Animal and Human Play', *Behavioral and Brain Sciences* 5: 139–84.

Smith, S. L. J. (1985) 'On the Biological Basis of Pleasure. Some Implications for Leisure Policy', in T. L. Goodale and P. A. Witt (eds) *Recreation and Leisure: Issues in an Era of Change*, revised edn, State College, PA, Venture Publishing, pp. 56–68.

Stern, T. (1948) *The Rubber Ball Games of the Americas*, Seattle, University of Washington Press.

Stumpf, F. and Cozens, F. W. (1947) 'Some Aspects of the Role of Games, Sports, and Recreational Activities in the Culture of Modern Primitive Peoples: The New Zealand Maoris', *Research Quarterly* 18: 198–218.

Stumpf, F. and Cozens, F. W. (1949) 'Some Aspects of the Role of Games, Sports, and Recreational Activities in the Culture of Modern Primitive Peoples: The Fijians', *Research Quarterly* 20: 2–20.

Turner, V. (1967) *The Forest of Symbols*, Ithaca, NY, Cornell University Press.

Turner, V. (1969) *The Ritual Process: Structure and Anti-Structure*, Ithaca, NY, Cornell University Press.

Turner, V. and Turner, E. (1978) *Image and Pilgrimage in Christian Culture: Anthropological Perspectives*, Oxford, Blackwell.

Tylor, E. B. (1871) *Primitive Culture: Researches into the Development of Mythology, Philosophy, Religion, Language, Art, and Custom*, London, John Murray, 1903.

Tylor, E. B. (1879) 'On the Game of Patolli in Ancient Mexico and its Probable Asiatic Origin', *Journal of the Royal Anthropological Institute of Great Britain and Ireland* 8: 116–31.

Tylor, E. B. (1881) *Anthropology: An Introduction to the Study of Man and Civilization*, New York, D. Appleton.

van Gennep, A. (1909) *The Rites of Passage*, (trans. M. B. Vizedom and G. B. Caffee) Chicago, University of Chicago Press, 1960.

Veblen, T. (1899) *The Theory of the Leisure Class*, London, Allen & Unwin, 1925.

Whiten, A., Goodall, J., McGrew, W. C., Nishida, T., Reynolds, V., Sugiyama, Y., Tutin, C. E. G., Wrangham, R. W. and Boesch, C. (1999) 'Cultures in Chimpanzees', *Nature* 399: 682–85.

4

The History of Western Leisure

Benjamin K. Hunnicutt

Beginning with Classical Greece and Rome, via Medieval Europe, the Reformation and the Industrial Revolution, there is a rich historiography of the development of leisure in the West. Leisure has reflected, and continues to reflect, patterns of social, cultural, religious, political, economic and technological change and difference. Rival schools have developed descriptive traditions and critical/neo-Marxist approaches to historical analysis. This chapter reviews and evaluates these traditions and raises questions concerning the future development of historical studies of leisure.

Definitions

Few have argued that leisure is an essential, unchanging part of human nature. Leisure for everyone may be desirable, but humans are human regardless of whether they have leisure. Moreover, humans have thrived without a concept of or word for leisure historically and into the present. However, in order for leisure to exist, some human awareness of being at or having leisure is essential; still fewer writers have maintained that animals have leisure or that people can have leisure and not know about it.

The major texts in leisure studies have long agreed that leisure is an historical product; that there was a time (for example, among hunter-gatherer peoples) when leisure was unknown, and that at some point leisure emerged as a cultural category, initially identified by new words and in institutions, rituals, myths, and so on. Sebastian de Grazia begins *Of Time, Work and Leisure* (1962: 3) with 'The discovery [of leisure] took place in the Mediterranean world some time after Creto-Mycenaean civilization ... Leisure never existed before ...'

Furthermore, over time leisure developed and changed, sometimes radically. There were, and remain considerable variations between cultures as to what constitutes 'leisure', what may be understood as a leisure activity, or what value leisure has. The challenge for the historian who tries to write about this topic, then, is to follow faithfully the historical trace of the words for, cultural concepts of, and institutional forms for leisure as they developed and changed over time. As tempting as it may be to impose seemingly stable modern definitions on history, and to use modern concepts to describe historical subjects, such an approach is fundamentally misleading as it fails to appreciate the historical complexity such a topic as leisure displays.

Arguably the primary and perhaps only way that leisure has been consistently identified through history is by contrast with work. Without the 'figure', work, the 'ground', leisure, is historically indistinct and vague at best – perhaps indistinguishable. Without work, leisure is an incoherent historical subject. Work and leisure developed together historically, gradually defining more and more activities in terms of this basic word/concept pair. Over time, work and leisure have also been valued in different ways, and that valuing often determined by contrasting the one as more valuable with the other as less valuable.

Certainly there have always been 'grey areas', activities between work and leisure that are hard to fit into either category. However, such areas, like the colour, depend on the fundamental distinction between contrasting opposites.

The origin of leisure, then, is inextricably connected with the emergence of work as a coherent cultural and language category. Moreover, leisure's multiform historical manifestations are inseparable from work and its various representations through time. As work changed, leisure changed as well.

The birth of leisure as σχολή→ in the Greek Classical Age

Whereas scholars have agreed for decades that hunter-gatherers living today have no word for or concept of leisure (or idleness, or laziness), perhaps even more surprising is their finding that most ancient peoples have no one word for or general concept of work as we moderns understand it.

For example, cultural anthropologists agree that within existing hunter-gatherer cultures, there is not the clear separation between work and the rest of life we take for granted. 'Work' is so blended with other kinds of social activities that it is virtually unrecognizable, not only for pre-industrial people themselves, but for cultural anthropologists who visit them (Thomas, 1964: 51–2). As Sahlins (1968: 80) explained, 'Work is not divorced from life. There is no "job," no time or place one spends most of one's time not being oneself.'

Of course, humans have always had words for a panoply of subsistence activities such as farming, weaving, and so on, that we subsume today under the general category 'work'. Just as in the case of leisure, however, what has been lacking historically is a covering noun for or concept of 'work' as a general set of activities related together by some defining group of common traits or specific qualities.

The first of what Karl Marx (1859) called the modern 'specific qualit[ies] ... common to many [work activities], or common to all', to emerge historically, beginning the long process of work's articulation, was undoubtedly control; control of nature and/or control of people. Summing up the social anthropologist's view, Sandra Wallman (1979: 1–2) writes: '[Work] makes no sociological sense without reference to control ... work is "about" control.'

Whereas one may find earlier examples of 'work' associated with slavery and understood as human control over other humans, 'leisure', even 'freedom', as specific words or explicit concepts are rare in the ancient world before the emergence of the Greek city-states. It is only with the evolution of Greek Civilization that humans first recognize and identify leisure as a clear cultural category, value it as a cultural good, contrast it unambiguously with 'work', and begin to build institutional forms (such as schools) around the new reality.[1]

Instead of one covering term, 'work', the Greeks used a variety of words for a variety of subsistence activities during the Archaic period (800–500 BCE).[2] Moreover, they understood several of these activities to be parts of religious observances. For example, ἔργον, farming, was a noble, even sacred undertaking. However, the value the Greeks placed on the independent yeoman farmer and the creative craftsman Aeschylus honoured in *Prometheus Bound*, faded by the fifth century.

Increasingly, the Greek city-states developed as slave societies during and after the Archaic period. As slavery increased, larger estates absorbed the smaller free farms and tenancy spread (Vernant, 1983: 266; Godelier, 1980).

Vernant notes that once farming lost its religious sanction, once tilling the land was conceived less as a service to the gods and understood more as a service to humans, it lost its status and virtue. Instead, farm 'work' began to be understood as an act of servility, requiring the overseer's lash rather than the pious practice of daily sacrifice. After the fifth century, little was left of 'work' other than manual effort. 'Work', reduced to forced labour and redefined as the services of underlings, then spread as a general category to other kinds of activities such as crafts and manufacturing. Godelier (1980: 834) concludes: 'This simultaneous evolution of, and representations of, farming and the crafts and of the [declining] status of those performing them is a reflection of the evolution of the economies of antiquity in the direction of more and more extensive use of slave labor.' Contempt the Greeks held for labour, crafts and the manual arts resulted from the spread of slavery and servitude in the city-states (Toynbee, 1955), emerged as one of the most important Greek words now translated as 'work' or 'toil'. The word captured manual and servant/forced labour as the new distinguishing features of 'work', understood as a general category. Before the Hellenistic period, πόνος conveyed a sense of pain, suffering, stress or trouble associated with war or other extreme trials.[3]

The new understanding of 'work' and the spread of various conditions of servitude in Greece further distinguished two classes of peoples and two kinds of activities: free versus controlled. However, except for women, whose roles were clearly limited to households and whose activities were largely controlled by a patriarchy, the two classes of people and activities were opposed in a continuum rather than a dichotomy: grey areas abounded (Wiedemann, 1981: 3).

In Classical Greece, the conditions of servitude and freedom were mixed together in complex and confusing ways. While it is impossible to categorize precisely the various grades of servitude, nevertheless the language allowed comparisons: less free versus more free, as well as various specific pairs.[4] Together with numerous Classical writers, Plato and Aristotle employed such comparatives when discussing activities suitable for those who served, contrasted with activities appropriate for those who were served.

The social continuum, slave to free, opened a new general cultural and language continuum, differentiating work from leisure by contrast, and establishing the basis for a more modern-sounding definition of the two terms. Relatively empty and fluid at first, through time these newly opening cultural categories were articulated.[5] Gradually the vacuum they initially represented filled with activities understood to be more appropriate for servants and women, on the one hand, and masters, on the other; with activities that were understood to be more controlled, or necessary, versus those that were freer; with activities that were understood more as 'means' to others that were understood to be more important 'ends'.

Since that original conception, the specific contents of work or leisure have varied through time. Nevertheless, the establishment of this new contrasting continuum, based on the effective and systematic control of some humans over others, laid the foundation for the gradual build-up of modern concepts of work and leisure in the Western World.

Such considerations support de Grazia's (1962) claim that the Greeks 'discovered' leisure. Part of the discovery lay in a new valuation of leisure vis-à-vis 'work'. The virtue the Greeks assigned to ἔργον and their disapproval of ἀεργός (not-work, or idleness) in the Archaic period were reversed after the fifth century as leisure was newly valued as the time for some humans to realize their full humanity. Through the same process, work was degraded as a subservient role.

Bernarde Bosanquet concluded that 'the value we put on liberty... comes from the contrast with slavery ... [Slavery] is the practical starting point in the notion of freedom' (quoted in Patterson, 1991: 9). Something similar may be said about leisure. The Greeks began to value leisure when the spread of slavery redefined work.

Leisure's questions

The Greeks discovered leisure as a new cultural arena in which vital questions of human means and ends, of purpose and hence of meaning, have been addressed down through the ages. Such questions were the practical results of new power to control humans, and the opportunities power brings. By relating work to leisure as means to ends in their language, institutions and written texts, the Greeks founded a discourse that continues today, implicitly asking leisure's enduring questions: 'What are the powerful able to do when they control others?' (the older form), or 'What is there to do when there is no work left to do?' (the more modern technological concern). Other ways of restating this historical question include 'What is worth doing in and for itself?' (the more philosophical, autotelic question, 'ending' the continuum, means to ends) and 'Why do something rather than nothing?' (the more desperate existential question).

Such questions rival in importance Heidegger's (1927) famous query that revolutionized modern philosophy, 'Why is there something and not nothing?' However, leisure's questions are as direct and down to earth as Heidegger's are formal and technical. Ordinary humans confront leisure's questions daily. Through time, answers to leisure's questions have proven to be the practical, culture-generating expressions of freedom.

Such considerations also lend support to Joseph Pieper's (1952) claims about 'leisure, the basis of culture'. Beginning with the Greeks, leisure has provided an arena in which cultures were played out; in which humans were able to engage each other in public, creating fine arts, playing sports, making music, doing politics, having conversations, and performing free activities that constituted the very bone and sinew of their cultures. Leisure provided an opening to engage in what Jürgen Habermas (1985) called 'communicative action'; a seedbed in which 'social capital' (Putnam, 2000) formed through the ages. Leisure, rather than work, was the medium (or glue, to use Emile Durkheim's (1984) metaphor) that held societies together.

Moreover, the problem of what to do with leisure's practical freedoms has long challenged humans to continue a search for meaning even in seemingly stable cultures. However problematic it may be to pin down 'human nature' once and for all, undoubtedly the human creature is at least in part the meaning-seeking creature that Giambattista Vico described in the eighteenth century. More recently, Clifford Geertz (1973: 140) observed that 'man [*sic*] as a symbolizing, conceptualizing, meaning-seeking animal ... has become an increasingly popular [theoretical construct] both in the social sciences and in philosophy over the past several years'.[6] An example of Geertz's claim may be found in Thomas Goodale and Geoffrey Godbey's (1988: introduction) excellent history of leisure that begins with 'Leisure, historically, has been the arena in which one developed a point of view in which to take in the world.'

Leisure has remained an enduring cultural opening in which humans, having temporarily managed life's means, have pursued life's ends, perennially struggling with purpose and hence meaning. Meaning, beckoning beyond the chain of means and ends, becomes accessible in history, even a pressing concern, when purpose is fulfilled or exhausted. Historically, the procession of 'what is this for?' has led regularly to the realization of or a confrontation with 'the thing for itself'.

Leisure's darker side: control for the sake of control

The popular historian Arnold Toynbee concluded, however, that the uses of leisure for the creation of culture, or a serious search for meaning, were far from leisure's primary historical expressions.

> [Even though] the progress of civilization during the short period of 5000 years can been seen to have been the work of ... this leisured minority ... the individual creators of civilization have been only a minority of the ... [leisured] minority. A majority of the privileged minority have probably been drones, always and everywhere. (Toynbee, 1955: 89)

Undoubtedly one of the first uses of leisure was the exercise of power and control for the sakes of power and control. Patterson's (1991) examples of the uses of archaic 'freedom' present a chilling insight into the emergence of 'leisure'. His list includes the ritual slaughter of captives, exploitation of women, the toying with and torture of slaves, peasants and animals as common amusements.

Human brutality, sexual exploitation and excess, blood 'sports', public spectacles, executions and torture, political and family intrigues and power struggles, overindulgence in food and drink, mind-numbing idleness, and the simple pleasure of dominating and bossing others around, are among the first activities that humans, newly empowered, discovered and enjoyed for their own sakes, and which remain among the most familiar leisure pursuits.

Opposition to allowing such disreputable activities to be parts of leisure has long existed among modern scholars such as de Grazia, Habermas and Hemingway who want to distinguish mere free time from more socially important leisure. However, strong etymological evidence exists supporting the claims that control for the sake of control is found at the birth of modern 'leisure', and that leisure originally formed vis-à-vis work as control.

The best-known Greek word for leisure, σχολή, representing the explicit discovery of leisure by Western Civilization, is derived from a Proto-Indo-European root, *seĝh*. The etymological sense of *seĝh* as leisure in the Greek word σχολή is directly related to a victory and to the ability to dominate others, which provides leisure's peace/opportunity. The first articulate word for leisure, then, is suggestive by its cognates and in its origins, of the cultural arena opened by work as control.[7]

'Leisure for all': free from service

As slavery spread, and work clearly defined by the emergence of various conditions of servitude, servants and women as well as masters must have understood and experienced leisure. Undoubtedly servants and women held in whatever degree of bondage, were able to understand the difference between the times in their lives when service was required of them, and other times when they were free to do more of what they wished. Indeed, these must have been central concerns of their lives each day; when the master was looking the other way, when he was gone for the day, when they retired to their quarters.

Moreover, they must have experienced a significant amount of such time free from the master's gaze since the control and direction of servants tended to be inefficient, even haphazard before the Industrial Revolution. Everyday 'theft' of their own time was probably the most common form of slave and servant resistance. Modern writers have made a strong case that the work of servants and slaves in the Classical and medieval worlds was much less demanding than modern jobs precisely because it was much less structured, supervised, regulated and regular.

However, few historical records exist to support this *prima facie* case and to discern more exactly what servants and slaves did with their 'free time'. Just as they have done with the excesses of the wealthy, modern scholars have tended to dismiss the 'free time' of lower or working classes as relatively unimportant, as departing from the ideal leisure was supposed to have represented.

What little evidence that does exist suggests that most slaves, servants, women and peasants probably followed the example of wealthy drones, giving in to idleness, abandon and licentiousness in their free time. For example, the land of Cockaigne, (Bonner, 1910), where all of life's necessities grow on trees, rivers flow with wine, no one works and excesses of all kinds are practised, is perhaps the most ancient and certainly the most widely known folk legend, dating back to before the ninth century BCE.[8]

Pieter Bruegel the Elder, 'The Land of Cockaigne' (1567)

However, ordinary people were as likely to have employed their free time in positive uses as cultural elites. Indeed, one might speculate that to the degree that servant or folk subcultures existed outside dominant cultures in any age, they must have depended at least in part on leisure; that is, on some release of time from the controls of dominant cultures. Down through the ages, festivals, feasts, rituals, ceremonies, fairs, and so on, existing on the margins of societies and to some degree in opposition to the sanctions of civil authority and dominant institutions, were vital for the preservation of the alternate subcultures, such as the Helot, peasant and working classes in Europe and Asia.

To the extent that activities such as fairs and festivals, funerals and marriages, were set apart from and contrasted with work as control and with other expressions of socioeconomic power, and to the extent that humans held in various conditions of servitude looked forward to having time off from their duties to do things with their family and friends, such times may be considered leisure by the historian and counted as part of the creation, practice and endurance of folk subcultures.

The Quotidian

After the Second World War, French writers began to recognize the historical significance of everyday life, of what Foucault called the patient grey detail of daily

Pieter Bruegel the Elder, 'Battle Between Carnival and Lent' (1559)[9]

lived experiences. The 'Quotidian' or 'Everydayness' originated with Georg Lukàcs, but Henri Lefebvre (1947: 87) expanded on the theory, proposing 'a rehabilitation of everyday life ... and its positive content' based on a 'concept of everydayness [which can] reveal the extraordinary in the ordinary'.[10]

From its beginning, leisure has been filled largely with vital everyday experiences. The simple pleasures of table, bed and nature, the body as lived experience in and of itself, the daily flow of sensations, living through the fundamentals of human existence; play, sleep, breath, digestion, sex, light, have long provided daily sources of significance and awareness.

Just as carnivals, festivals and fairs may be counted as leisure to the extent they were set in contrast with and opposition to dominant cultures, so the experience of the 'Quotidian' may be counted as leisure when daily life is experienced against the backdrop of social domination. The slave in the Antebellum American South, pausing at the end of the row he was ploughing to enjoy the breeze on his face, then yearning for release and feeling his oppression intensely, is an image familiar to all held in bondage to whatever degree. Even though it may be somewhat unfamiliar today, it is also an image of leisure.

The experience of women, claiming occasional moments for themselves and defining parts of their lives in opposition to dominant male controls and institutions, promises to be a vital leisure history yet to be uncovered.

Leisure the basis of culture

Dominant historical cultures that left historical records present a panoply of responses to the challenge of leisure. Such a bewildering variety of philosophies, cultural forms, activities and institutions grew from the cultural interstices opened by the extensions of power over human beings that only a sampling of some of the best known is possible, even in the most extensive history of leisure.

One of the historical hallmarks of leisure is diversity. Unlike technology, the marketplace and work, leisure shows little historical development in the sense that it displays some sort of natural evolution, or progress from more primitive to more advanced and complex forms. Indeed, scholars such as de Grazia have frequently claimed the reverse: that leisure has regressed through the centuries, losing its richness and potential.

In addition to a narrative, then, a complete history of leisure will include a catalogue of the various ways in which individual cultures filled the cultural opening made possible by the spread of work as control.

The Great Chain of Being: leisure to be all that you can be

In the *Great Chain of Being*, Arthur Lovejoy (1936) described a worldview, common to the educated elites of classical age as well as the Medieval world. The Great Chain of Being provided a framework within which 'leisure', along with other parts of life, was understood for well over a thousand years.

A number of the Greeks in the Classical Age, for example, saw the universe as hierarchically ordered, depending on a Perfect Being from whom all creation emanated. Those beings closer to Being-In-Itself, because of their proximity to perfection, were themselves more perfect, more peaceful and contented in their own being than the creatures below them. Further away, creatures were less perfect, less content, more subject to the chaos into which God projected His essence. Nevertheless, all creatures had a niche, a special place in the Great Chain to call their own. Their place determined their essence (or their virtues), and was *given* to them by their Creator.

Humans had a unique place. Below them, animals, plants and minerals were destined to decline into chaos, being too far away from God to hope for something better. Above, more perfect beings were within God's orbit, and ineluctably attracted toward perfection. Only humans had a choice, to move up toward perfection or down toward chaos. Our place on the Great Chain determined our essence, our human nature; freedom.

Virtue lay in making *right* choices. Other beings had their virtues given them outright. Fish were born swimming, birds soon learned to fly. No choice was involved. However, other than freedom, humans did not have their other virtues, their other essential qualities, given them outright. Gods only proffered what humans could really be. Humans had to use their freedom rightly, moving up the chain, realizing their potential to become fully human, turning from 'necessity' and the temptation to sink to subhuman existence.

Plato and Aristotle

For both Plato and Aristotle, leisure was the freedom to move up the Chain toward human potential and authenticity. Plato founded the first institution of higher learning, the direct ancestor of the modern university, to teach people about the right use of leisure's freedom. Reflecting this heritage, the Greek word for leisure, σχολή is the etymological source of many modern words for 'school' and 'scholarship'. Directly contrasting leisure (σχολή) with work (ἀσχολίαν), Plato taught that working too much was unwise – indeed, this was one of the primary teachings of the Academy. In working more than necessary, taking excessive care of business, chasing after unnecessary wealth, excessive reputation and pleasures and so on, people made bad use of their freedom, choosing to become 'voluntary slaves' to their baser nature. Idleness was equally unwise. Leisure was not simply 'free time' for excessive sleep, woolgathering or inactivity. The sign of an educated person was active leisure; *playing* sports and music, *engaging* in public debate, *doing* philosophy. The closer one came to one's essential self and the Truth, the more energized the soul became. Education meant 'turning the eye of the soul' upward, toward a person's authentic nature and toward Truth. Acquiring the discipline and skills necessary to do the Liberal Arts was difficult. Students had to work at their lessons. Nevertheless, the goal of academic work was freedom. The Liberal Arts (rhetoric, sciences, music, sports and gymnastics) were the free arts. They were free because God had *given* them to humans – at least the potential had been given. Virtue lay in achieving human potential. Thus humans had to work to be free. We have to practise and train to *play* music and sports and do other liberal activities. Work was for leisure (Hunnicutt, 1990).

After school, Plato's students found an abundance of opportunities to practise what they had learned. Ancient Athens, for example, contained an extensive public sector, a leisure infrastructure where free people did free things, remnants of which we see today in our libraries and parks. The famous *agora* was more an open space for daily religious, political, judicial and social activities than a marketplace for commerce. However, for both Plato and Aristotle even the Liberal Arts did not reach the heights of human potential. For Plato, doing philosophy represented the pinnacle of human achievement and the best use of leisure. Philosophy was the freest, most human, most engaging, and the most fun (most playful) of all leisure activities. Describing philosophy, he used a sports metaphor of hunting – of chasing after Truth that always eludes.

Doing philosophy was not confined to a small group of academics as it is today. Philosophy was an everyday 'democratic' activity, available to all (educated) citizens. It was a practical search for meaning, and for answers to the questions about life, love, justice, beauty, that all humans had the potential to do. Moreover, failure to do philosophy was failure to become fully human. As Plato put it, 'an unexamined life is not worth living'.

Nevertheless, according to Plato, humans were always 'at the beginning of wisdom'. They never possess Truth that endures, only truths (mere opinions) that wear away with time. Catching a glimpse of transcendent Truth will sustain human needs for meaning and significance for the day, but will not provide for the future. Chasing after Truth and meaning must be ever new activities, enduring leisure pursuits necessary for authentic living (Hunnicutt, 1990).

Moreover, doing philosophy, like hunting, is a team effort. Individuals must engage in dialogue with their fellows, searching with their words for the truth about their lives; trying to answer, 'What is justice or love?', 'What is the best way to live together and enjoy life?', and so on. Contemplation had its place, but did not substitute for active, public discourse. The joint search for meaning was the key to the good life.

Leisure: the glue of societies

The 'communicative action' leisure ideal is even clearer in Aristotle. Aristotle is best known for his often repeated quote: 'war must be for the sake of peace, business for the sake of leisure' ('Politics', 1333a, 30–35). However, John Hemingway redirected our attention to the importance Aristotle and the Greeks of his day placed on leisure as an opportunity for civic engagement rather than passive contemplation. Aristotle conceived of human nature as the potential to become the social animals and the thinking beings we are meant to be (Hemingway, 1988).

Leisure represented a Greek ideal and involved a moral quality because it was the opportunity to choose and move toward better things. Emphasizing the civic character of Greek leisure, Hemingway concluded that for Aristotle the right use of leisure was life's highest calling in 'The direction of human reason and virtue to the creation of a cohesive community bound by the principles of civility' (Hemingway, 1988: 190). Aristotle illustrated this point with a cautionary tale. Without the ability to live together, practising and creating their culture in leisure as did the Athenians, the Spartans, who thrived in war, collapsed as a society in time of peace.

Leisure rather than work or war was the glue that held societies together in the ancient world. The division of labour did supply some order and interdependence among the serving classes. In the *Republic*, Plato presented an early version of Durkheim's famous argument that societies are held together by divisions of labour that created webs of marketplace interdependencies; the tailor depending on the farmer for food, the farmer depending on the tailor for clothes, and so on (*Republic*, 369ff).

But for Plato and Aristotle, and the many who agreed with them through the ages, such economic interdependencies were not enough to keep people living together peaceably. Instead, the Polis required civility. According to Aristotle, the city depended on the virtues of courage, temperance, wisdom and justice. Recent interpretations of ancient civility have emphasized the more general virtue of *tolerance* as an aggregation of these four virtues in modern dress; attentiveness, openness, veracity and responsibility. Each of these virtues promoted the joint search for 'truth as a bond between human beings'; each, done in freedom and done for its own sake, was an appropriate use of leisure (Hemingway, 1988: 183).[11]

Rome and the Middle Ages: leisure and nature

Until the Protestant Reformation, dominant cultures in Europe valued many of the same uses of leisure as did the Greeks, so much so that scholars have long referred to a millennia-old 'leisure tradition'. The Liberal Arts curriculum endured as the foundation of universities through the Middle Ages. The distinctions between work and leisure in language persisted. For example, in Latin, as in Greek, work (*negotim*) was defined by contrast with leisure (*otium*). Similarly, the Liberal Arts (*artes liberales*) continued to be distinguished from utilitarian endeavours (*artes serviles*). Leisure continued to be understood as representing the opportunity for ends (what Pieper called the *Summa bona*) for which work was the means. Leisure continued to pose freedom's questions.

Variations on these older themes emerged, however. In Rome, writers such as Virgil and Horace placed a new emphasis on nature. Virgil, like Aristotle, viewed both war and work as necessary means to achieve their opposites, peace and leisure. However, Virgil expected that Roman victory in war would pacify the known world. The blessings of *Pax romana* would then make the world safe for leisure and for a recovery of the Golden Age Hesiod described.

With the establishment of *Pax romana*, the Roman victors could return to the land and take up the rural arts once again, but now in freedom. Slaves and servants, being compelled to farm, had degraded agriculture. But by returning to farming in leisure, Virgil expected to re-ennoble both the act and the land, 'setting vines in rows and grafting pears'. Leisure transformed and redeemed farm 'work'. Leisure even elevated and re-ennobled the Roman soil, transforming it into Place in and for itself. As a gentleman farmer living close to the land and to its fructifying influence, Virgil considered his life and the lives of those around him enriched, nearer to realizing authentic human potential because they were nearer human origins and Mother Nature (O'Loughlin, 1978: 62).

Horace represented a more extreme version of the Roman 'pastoral tradition'. Accepting the same distinctions between work and leisure as means to ends as had the Greeks and Virgil, Horace yearned for an even deeper immersion in the natural world in leisure. Withdrawing from the corrupt city that he felt could never redeem itself by victory in war, Horace retired to his country estate far from city life, getting as close as possible to the natural world.

Leisure for simplicity, tranquillity and self-sufficiency: the kingdom within

In the country, Horace delighted in the frugal, simple life. Perhaps his most famous poem, 'Carpe Diem' advises us to live in the moment and to 'pluck the day, putting as little trust as possible in tomorrow'. Another of Horace's Odes (II–XVI), entitled 'Otium' (Leisure) notes that humans of all sorts naturally desire leisure and peace. He advises:

He lives happily on a little ... whose soft slumbers are not carried away by fear or sordid greed.

Why do we strive so hard in our brief lives for great possessions?

Joyful let the soul be in the present, let it disdain to trouble about what is beyond and temper bitterness with a laugh.

With Horace, the Classical schools of philosophy, the Stoic, Epicurean and, one might argue, the Sceptic and the neo-Platonist mystics, emphasized the importance of leisure as the opportunity to escape the madding crowd to find *tranquillity*, *simplicity* and *self-sufficiency*.

For example, Epicurus, a Greek philosopher whom Horace admired, advised that those who could should live a life of absolute contemplation: 'Live retired ... The greatest fruit of self-sufficiency is freedom' (O'Loughlin, 1978: 42). He and his followers valued leisure primarily because it allowed for the soul's tranquillity. A simple, uncomplicated life paid off, allowing a person to redirect their attention to the pleasures of the mind (philosophy) and to the simple enjoyments of conversation and friendship.[12]

For many of the Stoics, Epicureans, Sceptics and neo-Platonists, leisure was the arena that opened access to the kingdom within. They valued new kinds of privacy and individualism that required self-sufficiency (αὐτάρκεια), imperturbability (ἀταραξία) rather than civic engagement. Representing an elite version of the 'Quotidian', followers of these schools also valued access to the beauty and wonder of nature and everyday experiences that leisure provided (O'Laughlin, 1978: 40). The modern associations of leisure with private acts, personal motives and enjoyment have roots in these Classical schools.

Leisure in the Middle Ages: contemplation

As Joseph Pieper pointed out, the leisure tradition established by the Greeks continued through the Middle Ages. The Liberal Arts taught in the universities, the understanding of work and leisure as means to ends, endured. As with the Romans, however, one may make distinctions.

New groups, cloistered in monasteries, were the particular beneficiaries of the time freed from work by new kinds of state and institutional controls; feudalism and the hegemony of the Catholic Church. The coming of the clergy and monastic orders presents one of the most striking divisions of work and leisure in history. Not only were these new classes initially exempt from ordinary work, they often separated themselves from everyday civil life, retreating to monasteries and convents. The divisions between work and leisure were drawn even more sharply within the monasteries, members of which distinguished the *Vita activa* (activities that were directed toward meeting human needs such as acts of charity and public duties, as well as necessary work in the monasteries) from the *Vita contemplativa* (activities of the mind and spirit directed toward God; that is, prayer, contemplation, study, worship, celebration).

Reflecting this distinction, the daily schedule within the monasteries required periods of prayer and celebration to be interspersed with regular periods of business, including manual work, administration, works of charity, and so on. Both kinds of pursuits were necessary parts of the overall leisure of the monasteries. Lingering too much in *Vita activa*, one was liable to run out of spiritual energy and lose purpose. Too long spent in the *Vita contemplativa* meant that charity was being neglected. True leisure was a balancing act between the two (Pieper, 1952). Thus the monastic tradition, particularly the Benedictine Orders, began to place a new spiritual value on 'work' that influenced the coming of the Protestant work ethic.

The great reversal: the rise of work and fall of leisure

Leisure was once a cultural opening, long available for various peoples to pursue various *Summa bona* as understood through the ages; from Greek civic engagement to Roman *tranquillitas* to Christian *Vita contemplativa*. But the litany was interrupted. In the historical account, the catalogue of leisure's uses as the basis of culture must give way to narrative when the Reformation and the coming of capitalism transformed work and leisure.

Other than the joint origins of work and leisure, this transformation is the salient event in the history of these two centrally important cultural realities. Adriano Tilgher (Tilgher and Fisher, 1930), Joseph Pieper (1952) and Jacques Ellul (1980) described a 'revolution', a 'metamorphosis', a 'great reversal', a 'trans-valuation' in beliefs about and understandings of work and leisure that turned the world upside down. Dorothy Canfield Fisher characterized the change as 'a tremendous revolution in men's outlook which has transformed human life a thousand times more than any of our mere mechanical inventions' (Tilgher and Fisher, 1930: vii).

The foundation for this 'world turned upside down' interpretation dates back to the original critical analysis of modern work, Max Weber's *Protestant Ethic and the Spirit of Capitalism* (1930). It was he who recognized that modern beliefs about work are unique and fundamentally 'irrational'. It was he who first proposed that the modern valuing of work in and for itself, summed up as 'one does not work to live; one lives to work', represented a revolution in human history (Pieper, 1952: 40).[13]

The revolution began within Christianity during the late Middle Ages, with the Benedictine Orders' emphasis on the manual work and the *Vita activa* as practical methods to advance spiritual discipline. However, the theology behind the modern valuation of work originated in the convoluted arguments of John Calvin, in his tortured logic of predestination (God decided who was saved before time began), sin (because of Original Sin, all humans deserve damnation) and redemption (God saves only whom He wants – good works are never enough).

Following this train of thought, Calvin and his Puritan followers placed primary importance on work as a spiritual *end in itself*. Even though humans could never save themselves by their own efforts, and were entirely dependent on the Grace of God, nevertheless, God called everyone to work. All had a 'vocation', a calling.

Working hard and consistently, people could at least demonstrate that they had a chance, and were not undoubtedly among the damned who were not diligently working. Accordingly, work was for more work, and did not culminate either in some reward or in better kinds of non-work activities. Work was as good as it gets, on earth at least.

In the Puritan world, not-working was idleness, one of the most grievous of the Protestant panoply of sins. Instead of providing an opportunity for human creativity and expression, or for pursuit of the *Summum bonum*, time free from work was an opening, a fertile ground for all the other sins: drink, profligacy, licentiousness, perversion, despair. Leisure was the Devil's workshop because Original Sin predisposed *all* humans to misuse freedom. Such was the human condition that a liberal education would never change, and only the discipline of work would control.

In this new worldview, work and leisure reversed in value and priorities, and as means to ends. Work began to answer leisure's question, 'What is worth doing in and for itself?' Leisure began to assume a subservient role in the modern world, becoming the means to accomplish and support the higher, better purpose, work.

The Puritans led the way to the modern understanding that time off work was important primarily as a preparation for work; merely a time to rest and recuperate for more work, and, if time permitted, pray and raise the next generation of workers. Other leisure uses were trivial at best, but very likely disreputable.

As Jacques Ellul and Max Weber pointed out, capitalism's everlasting economic activity and endorsement of unlimited acquisition depended on the more fundamental valuing of work as an end in itself. It was not greed for gain that spurred the Industrial Revolution. Greed and envy did not begin with capitalism. They are timeless. At the bourgeois centre of capitalism were true *believers*, a middle class leading the way for all people by their own example of devotion to constant working. Such believers did not seek to exploit the work of others, desiring release from work for something better, as had generations before them. They envisioned work without end for all. The religious energy that Protestants imparted to work during the sixteenth, seventeenth and eighteenth centuries endured and influenced the modern world profoundly. During the nineteenth century, the work ethic's theological superstructure, the complex of theological arguments supporting work as the central cultural value sloughed away. The giants of finance and captains of industry in the United States, for example, were careful to separate their religious life from their business while supporting work as the primary cultural value. To use Weber's words, the 'Protestant work ethic' became the 'spirit of capitalism' as work, in and for itself, became the wellspring of Western values, the reservoir of modern meaning and the channel for social solidarity.

Work emerged out of the nineteenth century both as the basis of modern culture and as the glue that held societies together. Emile Durkheim, lifting directly from Plato's *Republic*, concluded that divisions of labour provided social solidarity. But for Durkheim, webs of economic interdependence were enough. Unlike Plato and Aristotle, he and the social scientists who followed him had little use for leisure and the free civic engagement that leisure once provided.

Building on what Ellul called the new 'ideology of work', the industrial world elevated work as it subordinated leisure. Work now sat squarely at the centre of the Modern Age; the enduring economic imperative, social reality, cultural focus and political touchstone.

Work's centrality has been a recurring theme for scholars for much of the twentieth century. Among the more important statements of the thesis is Hannah Arendt's: 'The Modern Age has carried with it a theoretical glorification of labor and has resulted in the factual transformation of the whole of society into a laboring society ... [and in the] glorification of labor as the source of all values' (Arendt, 1958: 4, 85). Arguably the primary point of *The Human Condition* is Arendt's critique of the Modern Age for its 'glorification of labor' (ibid.: 92) and neglect of all other 'human conditions'.

Daniel Bell observed that 'as *homo faber*, man [*sic*] could seek to master nature and discipline himself. Work ... [is] the chief means of binding an individual to reality' (Bell, 1960: 262). Nels Anderson (1961) began his book by observing that 'Industrial urbanism is largely a work culture ... It is a culture that judges man [*sic*] by his will to work.'

People in the industrial nations, led by the United States, have come to answer traditional religious questions ('Who am I?', 'Where am I going?', 'How do I make sense of the world?', 'What do I need to do to get out of the mess I am in?', 'What is there to do today?') more in terms of their work/job/profession/career than in terms of traditional religions. The new work ethic is no longer Protestant, there is little or no God-talk associated with it. It is a distinctively modern and secular work ethic/religion growing to fill the void left by the retreat of the traditional faiths and the fading of the ancient challenge of leisure.

Following in the train of the spread of the modern work-based worldview, *Homo faber* has embarked on a campaign to colonize leisure and all regions of human existence historically free from the marketplace and work. The Western world has extended the marketplace and work's hegemony over more and more of life, inundating previously free places and activities, obscuring leisure as a primary cultural value (Gorz, 1990: introduction). The boundary of work and leisure has constantly been thrust back in a process Pieper described as the 'rise of the world of total work'.

Leisure has endured, however, continuing to stand in relation to work as figure to ground. As such, leisure has emerged as a challenge to work's hegemony, offering more traditional, humane and democratic alternatives.

Internationally, for example, one of the labour movement's prime achievements has been the reduction of work hours. The American Federation of Labor (AFL) often reminds Americans that workers 'gave us the weekend'. Part of labour's centuries-long shorter-hours campaign involved a vision of a world in which work would be reduced to a minimum, and ordinary humans would spend the best part of their lives as only the wealthy had before, in leisure.

In some of the first examples of the emergence of the labour movement in the United States, this democratic leisure vision was present. In 1827, in what Commons (1966: Vol. 1, 185–6) called 'the earliest evidence of [labour] unrest' in the United

States, Philadelphia journeymen carpenters, striking for ten hours, resolved that 'all men have a just right, derived from their Creator, to have sufficient time each day for the cultivation of their mind and for self-improvement'. Giving voice to the carpenters' sentiment, William Heighton in 'An Address to the Members of Trade Societies and to the Working Class Generally' envisioned American progress as the reduction of working hours from '12 to 10, to 8, to 6, and so on' until 'the development and progress of science have reduced human labor to its lowest terms' (ibid.: 186).[14]

Other labour leaders and supporters, people such as Dorothy Canfield Fisher and Joseph Pieper, explicitly recommended recovery of the Classical 'leisure tradition' that began with the Greeks. In the Modern Age, however, in a process Pieper (1952) called 'deproletarianization', workers would make use of *'machine* slaves' to join the privileged, practising the liberal arts and actively engaging in the search for community and for meaning that were historically the defining traits of humanity. However, the ending of the shorter hours movement early in the twentieth century, the 60-year stabilization of leisure time and the recent *decline* of leisure hours coincided with the fading of the nineteenth- and early twentieth-century leisure vision. In its place stand utopian visions of eternal economic growth, commodified and devitalized leisure and 'good jobs' – of work that is its own reward.

Part of the modern 'false consciousness' that Lefebvre described consists of the loss of the leisure vision shared by generations of Americans and Europeans and the adoption of a competing view; that more work forever more is the answer to leisure's historical question 'What is work for?' Alienation now fills our leisure as much as our work. Lefebvre described a suburban businessman commuting home, momentarily aware of his alienation, seeing though the mystification of modern life that reverses authentic relationships between human values such as work and leisure, then awaking to his 'false consciousness'. In his 'concept of moment', Lefebvre (1947: 134) reveals vital roles that leisure might still play in the modern world. Leisure still opens access to the 'Quotidian', to the valuing of everyday experiences of life outside work and the marketplace. Leisure still provides a contrast to modern work and as such offers an effective critique of inauthentic work existence and ideology.

Leisure may also present a challenge to the dominant religion of work and market-based world view. The leisure experience of peasants, working classes and women, who formed subcultures and carved out experiences in opposition to dominant cultural forms throughout history, may serve as examples of how leisure might mount a critique of the 'world of total work' and represent and promote alternative values and ways of life.

In the preface to *Eros and Civilization*, Herbert Marcuse (1962) summed up leisure's modern potential as an enduring threat to work as an end in itself.

Automation threatens to render possible the reversal of the relation between free time and working time: the possibility of working time becoming marginal and free time becoming full time. The result would be a radical transvaluation of values, and a mode of existence incompatible with the traditional culture. Advanced industrial society is in permanent mobilization against this possibility.

Notes

1. Perry Anderson (1988: 34) maintained that '[t]he Sumerian, Babylonian, Assyrian and Egyptian Empires ... were not slave economies, and their legal systems lacked any sharply separate conception of chattel property. It was the Greek city-states that first rendered slavery absolute in form and dominant in extent, thereby transforming it from an ancillary facility into a systematic mode of production.'

2. For example, τεχνη (cf. technology) was used for crafts and manufacturing; ἔργον for farming (mainly for the cultivation of cereal grains) and war; ἤμερος (contrasted with ἔργον) for cultivating trees or vines or taming animals; ποιεῖν for manufacture and making things; θεραπεύω (cf. therapeutic) primarily for serving the gods, but also for cultivating trees and land and for training animals; ἀρόω for ploughing or tilling (metaphorically, an assigned task, cf. 'row to hoe'); ἐπιχειρ-έω for putting one's hand to, or attempting, setting to work on, and so on.

3. πόνος evolved after the Archaic period, referring more and more to work of servants. Manual and servant labour, by definition, had to be controlled and directed in useful directions by those in power. Plato represented the dominant view of those in power in the fifth and fourth centuries BCE when he judged servants unworthy of the fellowship of free men who naturally devoted themselves to the business of directing the work of menials (ασχολια) and, most importantly, to opportunities for leisure.

    ἔργον as farm work was also degraded as it came to be associated more with the day labourer, the half-free, half-slave Helot (serf), and the country bumpkin than with the noble yeoman. Crafts and even the fine arts fell into similar disrepute as masters, commissioners and retainers assigned underlings and Metics (free, non-citizens of Athens) to perform them. τεχνίτης came to mean nothing more than a mere technician, a hack who followed rules of the trade slavishly.

4. In his *Works on Socrates*, Xenophon (c.430–355 BCE) ('Economics', 21.9) (see Perseus at <http://www.perseus.tufts.edu/cgi-bin/ptext?doc=Perseus%3Atext%3A1999.01.0211> discusses how best to exercise command over various forms of business (πρᾶξις such as farming, running a household, conducting a war, and so on. Concluding that specific tasks needed specific direction, he proposed various pairs and chains of commands: Boatswains/seamen; generals/troops/private solider; 'a bailiff or manager – who can make the workers keen, industrious and persevering', master-in-the-field/workmen. The work or specific function (ἔργον) of the master/overseer, and so on, was to direct the work of underlings.

5. A good example of Orlando Patterson's (1991: *passim*) claim that slavery disrupts established cultures may be found in the extensions of servitude in Classical Greece. This expansion created new, mutually defining cultural categories, work and leisure.

6. Geertz (1973: 14–15) goes on to observe: 'The concept of culture I espouse ... is essentially a semiotic one. Believing, with Max Weber, that man is an animal suspended in webs of significance he himself has spun, I take culture to be those webs, and the analysis of it to be therefore not an experimental science in search of law but an interpretative one in search of meaning ...'

7. *Seĝh* is related in origin to the common Greek word εχειν, which means to have, hold, restrain, possess (cf. eunuch), and the Latin (from *seĝh -wer*) *severus* (cf. severe), meaning stern, as well as the Greek σθένος, strength, might and power. The Old High German *sigu*, meaning victory (from Germanic *sigiz*, victory as 'a holding or conquest in battle'), is also derived from *seĝh*, hence Siegfried. *Seĝh*'s O-grade form, *sogh*, is associated with the Greek ἐποχή, meaning 'a holding back', pause or cessation, and thus 'leisure', and the verb ἐπέχω, meaning in part to enjoin or impose a task, to have power over, occupy a country, prevail or dominate.

8. Hesiod's Golden Age was probably based on such a folktale, dating back into the dim regions of the Greek 'Dark Ages'.

9. Bruegel was able to capture leisure and work as contrasting cultural realities during the Middle Ages in this picture. He portrays leisure activities (frolicking about, acting the fool, dancing, playing, and so on) by contrasting them with one of the most important forms of constraint and control imposed by the Church, the season of Lent. He also pictured leisure activities against the backdrop of other kinds of the work-like pursuits of merchants, labourers, and so on.

   Moreover, Bruegel represents some of the leisure as mocking and parodying the surrounding serious pursuits. This picture is one of the best visuals showing work and leisure together as mutually defining cultural categories – as figure and ground. Whereas Lefebvre (1947) and E. P. Thompson (1967) may well have been right that, for the most part, life and work were blended for the peasant before the Industrial Revolution, one can see the distinction between the two occasionally and quite vividly, as in this rendering by Bruegel.

   Mikhail Bakhtin (1968: introduction) remarked: 'The carnival crowd in the marketplace or in the streets is not merely a crowd. It is the people as a whole, but organized in their own way, the way of the people. It is outside of and contrary to all existing forms of coercive socioeconomic and political organization, which is suspended for the time of festivity.'

   Bakhtin continued: 'Man experiences this flow of time in the festive marketplace, in the carnival crowd, as he comes into contact with other bodies of varying age and social caste. He is aware of being a member of a continually growing and renewed people. This is why for festive folk laughter presents an element of victory … the defeat of power, of earthly kings, of the earthly upper classes, of all that oppresses and restricts' (ibid.: 92).

10. Second quote found at <http://www.bard.edu/ccs/exhibitions/museum/10thanniversary/refuse/>.

11. In a less rigorous presentation, Plato makes some of Aristotle's points when he has old Protagoras retell one of the best known of the Greek fables, Prometheus' theft of fire from the gods. At the beginning of creation, Epimetheus, charged by the gods to allocate the gifts the gods had provided for all creatures, botches the job, giving out everything to brute animals before humans arrived on the scene. Prometheus, pitying the poor, barefoot, defenceless and naked human lot, steals technical skills (fire stands for these) from Hephaestus and Athena so humans could make a living. But soon they find they cannot live together. They try to come together to avoid being attacked by wild beasts, exchanging the products of their labour, but find they 'injured each other for want of political skill' (πολιτικὴν γὰρ τέχνην) (322c). Zeus, afraid that the human race would destroy itself, dispatches Hermes to give humans their last, best gifts; respect for others (αἰδώς) and a sense of justice (δίκη) that brought order to the cities and a 'bond of friendship (φιλίας) and union'.

12. The central doctrine of the Stoics was similar to the Epicureans: 'live according to Nature'. Certainly there were major differences between and within these Classical schools. But they did agree about the importance of leisure for the exercise of the mind in the search for meaning.

13. The quote is Pieper's paraphrase of Weber's text, 'a man exists for the sake of his business, instead of the reverse' (Weber, 1930: chapter II, 'The Spirit of Capitalism').

14. In 1926, the AFL recommitted itself to continuous work reduction, resolving to fight for the 'progressive shortening of the hours and days per week' (Wright, 1926).

Bibliography

Anderson, N. (1961) *Work and Leisure*, New York, Free Press of Glencoe.

Anderson, P. (1988) *Passages from Antiquity to Feudalism*, London and New York, Verso.

Arendt, H. (1958) *The Human Condition*, Chicago, University of Chicago Press.

Bakhtin, M. M. (1968) *Rabelais and His World*, Cambridge, MA, MIT Press.

Bell, D. (1960) *The End of Ideology: On the Exhaustion of Political Ideas in the Fifties*, Glencoe, IL, Free Press.

Bonner, C. (1910) 'Dionysiac Magic and the Greek Land of Cockaign', *Transactions and Proceedings of the American Philological Association* 41(179): 175–85.

Commons, J. (1966) *History of Labor in the United States*, 4 vols, New York, A. M. Kelly.

de Grazia, S. (1962) *Of Time, Work and Leisure*, Garden City, NY Anchor Books.

Durkheim, E. (1964) *The Division of Labor in Society*, New York, Free Press of Glencoe.

Ellul, J. (1980) 'Ideology of Work', *Foi et Vie* (July).

Gardiner, M. (2000) *Critiques of Everyday Life*, New York and London, Routledge.

Geertz, C. (1973) *The Interpretation of Cultures*, New York, Basic Books.

Godelier, M. (1980) 'Aide-Mémoire for a Survey of Work and its Representations', *Current Anthropology* 21 (6 December): 831–35.

Goodale, T. and Godbey, G. (1988) *The Evolution of Leisure*, State College, PA, Venture Publishing.

Gorz, A. (1990) *Critique of Economic Reason*, New York, Verso.

Habermas, J. (1985) *The Theory of Communicative Action: Reason and the Rationalization of Society*, New York, Beacon Press.

Heidegger, M. (1927) *Sein und Zeit*, Frankfurt am Main, Klostermann.

Hemingway, J. (1988) 'Leisure and Civility: Reflections on a Greek Ideal', *Leisure Sciences* 10: 179–91.

Hunnicutt, B. (1990) 'Plato on Leisure, Play, and Learning', *Leisure Sciences* 12: 211–27.

Lefebvre, H. (1947) *Critique of Everyday Life*, Vol. 1, trans. John Moore, London; New York, Verso, 1991.

Lovejoy, A. O. (1936) *The Great Chain of Being: A Study of the History of an Idea*, Cambridge, MA, Harvard University Press.

Marcuse, H. (1962) *Eros and Civilization*, New York, Vintage Books.

Marx, K. (1859) *A Contribution to the Critique of Political Economy*. Part I, 'The Commodity', trans. S. Ryazanskay, online at <http://csf.colorado.edu/mirrors/marxists.org/archive/marx/works/1850/pol-econ/ch01.htm->.

O'Loughlin, M. (1978) *The Garlands of Repose: The Literary Celebration of Civic and Retired Leisure: The Traditions of Homer and Vergil, Horace and Montaigne*, Chicago, University of Chicago Press.

Patterson, O. (1991) *Freedom in the Making of Western Culture*, New York, Basic Books.

Pieper, J. (1952) *Leisure, the Basis of Culture*, New York, Pantheon Books.

Putnam, R. D. (2000) *Bowling Alone: The Collapse and Revival of American Community*, New York, Simon & Schuster.

Sahlins, M. (1968) *Tribesmen*, Englewood Cliffs, NJ, Prentice-Hall.

Thomas, K. (1964) 'Work and Leisure in Pre-industrial Society', *Past and Present* 29 (December): 50–61.

Thompson, E. P. (1967) 'Time, Work Discipline, and Industrial Capitalism', *Past and Present* 38 (December): 56–97.

Tilgher, A. and Fisher, D. C. (1930) *Work, What it has Meant to Men Through the Ages (Homo Faber)*, New York, Harcourt Brace and company.

Toynbee, A. (1955) 'Man at Work in God's World in the Light of History', *Vital Speeches of the Day* 22 (15 November): 87–95.

Vernant, J. P. (1983) *Myth and Thought among the Greeks*, London and Boston, Routledge.

Wallman, S. (ed.) (1979) *Social Anthropology of Work*, New York, Academic Press.

Weber, M. (1930) *The Protestant Ethic and the Spirit of Capitalism*, New York, Allen & Unwin.

Wiedemann, T. (1981) *Greek and Roman Slavery*, Baltimore, Johns Hopkins University Press.

Wright, C. (1926) 'Epoch-making Decision in the Great American Federation of Labor Convention at Detroit', *American Labor World*: 22–4.

Xenophon, *Works on Socrates*, 'Economics', 21.9.

5

Non-Western Traditions: Leisure in India

Kumkum Bhattacharya

Introduction

Indian civilization is ancient, having a rich cultural heritage. Two of the broad parameters of this heritage are classical and folk that can be further qualified by the dimension of modernity. Ideas about leisure and leisure activities in India perforce have evolved under the combined influence of classical and folk heritage. In fact, it may not be wrong to say that the two enjoy a symbiotic relationship of give and take. In the case of India, it is difficult to resolve whether the folk form predates the classical or if the folk form feeds the classical; both have a long history of independent existence and both have distinct contemporary forms. Descriptions of leisure activities as found in the epics and accounts of social history (Vatsayana's *Kama Sutra*, Kalidasa's *Abhijnanam Sakuntalam* and *Meghdootam*, and Banbhatta's *Kadamvari* are some of the examples in which leisure of various classes of individuals have been described) often demarcate between the 'mundane' and the 'high', taking the 'mundane' as folk and the 'high' as classical. In India there is another category that could be classified under neither the folk nor the classical, that of the forms of culture found among the tribes. The organic link between the folk and the classical cannot be extended to the culture of the tribes, which can be described in Durkheimian terms as being segmentary in nature. Thus social-cultural distinctions and their implications for leisure seem to have been always there. Ethnicity, class and parameters of heritage (the ways in which heritage is perceived and valued; in consequence, the efforts that go in its preservation and conservation) are some of the social-cultural features that are being discussed here. Also, there existed distinctions between rural and urban or more exactly, village-centric and town-centric practices of leisure. More important than the distinctions is the influence these broad forms of leisure have had on people of more contemporary times. The influences are experienced in the economic sphere, emergence of class, social structure and secular ideals in the context of nation-state. In India, it is difficult to unravel the strands of intercultural influences on people for the reason that its ethos has for millennia been shaped by outsiders from diverse backgrounds. In fact it is difficult to separate or identify the indigene. This is in some contrast to nations that are composed of settlers and the indigenous people. In India it is difficult to knit leisure activities within any identifiable or uniform pattern. This is not to suggest that there are no common strands in observable behaviour or in the ways of thinking, it is important to keep the diversity of the population as one of the dimensions of analysis.

India has as long a history of Christian influence as in the new world; Islam too came to India early. Thus if we assume that Hinduism was the single system in operation before these two ways of thinking, then we shall be missing the wood for the trees as there have been influences of every tradition on ways of life that has come to shore. Each phase of the course of evolution and development of new religions, their encounter with the prevailing traditions and ways of thinking, left their impression on society. The accent on religion and its impact on various aspects of life are very important in the case of India. Religion has been a powerful patron of leisure, including its experiences (ranging from community to mass), its activities and the variety of intangible and tangible cultural products which it generates. In contemporary times, religion has been made to gel with polity in extending patronage as well as appropriate 'control' to the products of cultures in which leisure is included. This has been possible because of the transformations that have taken place providing scope to the traditional institutions to play other roles relevant to the times (Beteille, 1970; Kothari, 1970; Bhattacharya, 1998).

Unlike other religions, it is difficult for Hinduism to claim an egalitarian view of man, partly because of its hierarchical caste system and partly because of the distinctions it makes in the social spheres of people controlled to a great extent by the economic choices that they have access to. The distinctions in social spheres of life are created by a combination of many related and unrelated factors, of which undoubtedly economy is one. Settlement pattern, dominant regional cultures, the enduring traditions of location and community, the opportunities available and the means of resource mobilization are some other significant factors. Hinduism has also had to continually encounter the idealized egalitarian approach of the great traditions as well as the lesser-known homogeneous traditions of the tribes who are considered as the autochthones of India. Even if we assume that the tribal people are the indigenous population of India, we have to counter their impact with the fact of their marginalization even in the remote past from some other more mainstream social groups or with the fact of their isolation in terms of geography. There is prehistorical evidence to suggest that diverse populations were coexistent. It follows that some sort of hierarchy or distinction between man and man has existed since as long as one can go back in the history of India though it is also abundantly clear that non-hierarchical traditions were also in existence, though they did not create that much of an impact and there is not much evidence to show that there was any interaction between the two traditions (hierarchic and egalitarian). However, it may explain how, from within Hinduism, there arose the traditions of Buddhism, Jainism and Vaishnavism, providing strong impetus to non-hierarchical structures in secular life, with implications for leisure activities. It may do well to remember the regional variations in the practices of Hinduism that play an important role in the organization of leisure activities.

Industrialization is seen as one of the strongest influences on leisure, including ideas about leisure and ways of utilizing leisure time. It has also greatly contributed to making leisure into an industry providing a livelihood for many. (In fact, and this is tongue in cheek, it has transformed leisure into work!) In the case of India, industrialization has not had a uniform impact, like other forces (various empires, different traditions, religions, and so on) industrialization has also been variously experienced and adjusted to. Industrialization has been subject to many of the forces outlined earlier. It has contributed to the contrast that can be drawn between time spent on work and the time that is free from work and this is most apparent in the urbanized parts of the country. Rural India is still largely agriculture based where the crop cycles regulate time available to people. Globalization seems to exert greater impact, albeit differentially on aspects of life that are accessed through mass media of communication; this impact seems to be riding roughshod over tradition and heritage.

It would be a better idea to think of India as having a population with a long history of migration from other parts, exporting and encountering diversity in varying degrees. However, there is a common thread of mutual acceptance that knits the people of this country and integrates the diversities and it is from these points of view, that the forces that shape the many paradigms of leisure have to be seen. Starting from the backdrop of the folk or 'mundane' and the classical or 'high' forms of culture, it can be mentioned very briefly that the folk forms generally evolving in rural areas are nurtured and patronized by rural people while the classical, possibly having strong rural roots, is patronized by the urban populations and institutions. Patronage is very closely related to leisure activities; traditional arts and crafts that have now been reinvented as hobbies and pastimes in urban centres earlier depended entirely on patronage for their nurturance. This in turn sustained the relationship between caste and occupation. In the Hindu tradition, some castes had definite occupations and in this vein, there are some castes whose occupation is akin to professional entertainment such as: professions of itinerant bards, scroll makers, painters, drummers, singers and dancers, and so on, which are still pursued by particular castes and communities. Another feature of traditional patronage hinges on attitudes of deference and respect for practitioners of arts and crafts leading in some cases to the development of schools or *gharana*. This is highly developed in the cases of classical music, dance and art as well as in some folk forms like wall paintings (Madhubani district, Bihar), iconoclastic sculpture (south India) and scroll paintings (Rajasthan, Orissa, Gujarat, West Bengal). These are some of the sectors in which the sobriquet of 'master' or *ustad* is appended to distinguish the skilled practitioner and teacher or *guru*. Traditional providers of entertainment for the labour-free elite have for some time been brought under government patronage in many cases, which has helped in taking their product out of the original context and making it palatable to urban audiences or the changed tastes of their clients. In this way, activities that were not considered leisure activities but ways of life and livelihood have been transformed into leisure activities for the modern amorphous mass. Reference can be made to the brilliant description of the staging of truncated *kathakali* (a dance form of south India) pandering to the limited time and attention span of the urbanite in Arundhati Roy's *God of Small Things* (1997).

The other social category, tribe, is fairly widespread in India. There are 400-odd tribes spread across the length and breadth of the country. Their relationship with the non-tribes is segmentary in nature and they are generally located in the cultural periphery of Indian tradition and heritage. An account of the experience and nature of leisure among the tribes is important in order to understand various aspects of non-Western traditions of leisure and also to appreciate how diversities are integrated into a gestalt or composite whole. The usual definitions of leisure are not adequate to explain the nature and experience of leisure of the tribes or those who dwell in the villages of India. There is much to be said for the need to transcend the traditional meanings of leisure, especially the one that is more universally held – leisure being a product of industrialization (Dumazedier, 1967).

Most available literature assumes that leisure perforce is to be contrasted with work, with the idea of time that is not spent in work, with activities that are away from the scene of work, and so on. That there is a close link between industrialization and organized leisure goes without saying. However, communities which are yet to be inducted into the mindset that goes with industrialization cannot draw distinctions between work and non-work or work time and free time in their daily lives. With the concentration on the many beneficial aspects of meanings and forms of leisure and wide variety of homogenized leisure activities, research focusing on leisure in other societies gets sidetracked or ignored (Sharma, 1990). Leisure has assumed the dimensions of an industry in which leisure services are conceived and provided following commercial considerations of profit and loss.

Issues relevant in the context of India

There were and are, at least in certain parts of the country, traditional entertainers for whom entertainment was occupation and vocation. They were usually itinerant in the plying of their trade, going from one village to another, often in the same region or in those villages in which there existed a *jajmani* relationship (Wiser, 1936).[1] The entertainment provided by these itinerant entertainers was traditional fare, more or less known to the people. The time of the visiting of the players was also more or less fixed. Some of the traditional forms of such entertainment are singing the stories of the *Ramayana*, the *Mahabharata*, the legends of Radha-Krishna and other stories from mythology. Acting and dancing were a part of the entertainment; there were many forms of dancing. Some dances originated in the temples (the *devdasi* tradition of south India), some in the courts (*kathak* of north India) and some forms in the fairs (*nachni* of Bengal). These are only a few of the examples; there are many more forms spread across the length and breadth of the country. There are many forms of drama, some of which are *jatra*, *nautanki*, *gatha*, *alkap*, *tamasha* and *kathakali*. N. K. Bose argued that urbanization has led to personalized leisure diverse in character and there is decay of the traditional modes of transmission of culture (Bose, 1957: 2, 9). In his study he has shown that urbanization urges people to take upon themselves the responsibility of providing entertainment, the chief form of leisure, and as a result the traditional entertainers for whom entertaining was employment are left without a vocation. This personalized leisure is then moulded according to personal preferences. In a rejoinder to Bose, Ray-Burman (1957) has pointed out that leisure was always personal, both in industrial and pre-industrial societies, and it is society that made available leisure to individuals or groups of individuals in significant forms. There is little doubt that the experience of leisure is personal, but what has changed is the fading of the social institutions that used to provide the means of leisure (Kaplan, 1970), as a result of which anything could be leisure for an individual, thus expanding the ambit of leisure. What has resulted is that individuals have personalized the means of leisure for which they now depend on commercial institutions that have made the means of leisure (not the ideas) their business concern, in contrast to more altruistic involvement of social institutions in this aspect. The role of civil society in participating in leisure on a non-profit basis is restricted to very few aspects of leisure. Museums, art galleries, cultural academies, craft fairs, cultural functions, free parks, infrastructure and amenities for tourists, and so on, are a few of the instances that point to the involvement of civil society in aspects of leisure either through the provision of public space or allowing people the scope and opportunity to engage in the public sphere (Dutta, 2004).

Roberts (1970, 1978, 1999) has stressed the productive power of industrialization that has provided the population with time and money to cultivate leisure interests on an unprecedented scale and that it has also created a new awareness of leisure. Personalization of leisure has been catalysed by industrialization that created the salaried classes with the means not only to spend for leisure but also to have time off from work to indulge their interests; that is, to experience leisure. Individual leisure is vested with exclusivity, used as a marker of individual identity and a means of expressing freedom of choice, however illusionary that may be! Of the many paradigms (see Veal and Lynch, 2001: 87–104) within which leisure is viewed, the functionalist (Parsons, 1951; Parker, 1971; Clarke and Critcher, 1985) and the interpretive (Denzin, 1978; Henderson, 1991) paradigms seem more relevant in the context of India. Following the first paradigm, class and operating systems that could be social or civil in nature determine experience and activities of leisure. Following the interpretive paradigm, analysis of leisure among the tribes is largely a matter of interpretation.

Concerns of gender in understanding leisure are fraught with contradictions and confusions – bypassing the time-tested model of role differentiations delineated by economic capacities would indeed be difficult. Traditionally, certain leisure activities were earmarked for women, who were categorized, following the principles of lifecycle stages, as child, young girl, maiden, wife (including mother) and widow. Religion with its rites and rituals played a great role in this, as did social structures and patterns of culture that in some measure went beyond mere economic capacities. Obviously, in contemporary times the traditional no longer continues to provide sustenance, especially in the plethora of role–leisure options and economic empowerment that have been brought about through education. What makes the picture confusing is the fact that women belonging to the tribes and some of the lower castes always seem to enjoy greater freedom in exercising their agency in leisure ungoverned by social compulsions, and this to some extent is related to their relative economic freedom. However, their means of leisure may not always appeal to women of other social strata, compounding the contradictions that are woven into designing intervention strategies when working in the area of leisure for women.

It is clear that leisure is being predominantly viewed as entertainment, and indeed, searching for the appropriate semantics of leisure in the Indian languages, it is difficult to find words that echo the various shades of meaning that are associated with leisure. Even in Sanskrit, the source language for a large number of Indian languages, leisure is signified by entertainment and relaxation. The Sanskrit word for leisure is *vinoda*, synonymous with pleasure, entertainment, enjoyment, and so on. In order to be a true connoisseur of *vinoda* one had to be a *rasika*, or an aesthete who is appreciative of music, poetry, arts, beauty and wine. In contrast, according to Chanakyaniti (fifth- to sixth-century text) one would be considered 'low' if one only slept, quarrelled and indulged in base things. Contemporary ideas about leisure in India are a mix of the traditional and the Western concepts and modes. The problem with not having culture-free terminology for leisure leads to a tendency to impose the dominant meanings, ideas and, by implication, the means of leisure on all people. This further leads to a skewed focus on differences rather than an appreciation of variety.

The various ministerial portfolios on culture, education, rights and welfare, youth affairs, and women, on one hand, and tourism and sports, on the other, could be clustered under culture policy. The government of India has a long list of public holidays to celebrate festivals of various religions, and even takes the responsibility of being the chief organizer of some of the more important religious festivals as they involve large numbers which necessitates the maintenance of law and order. Sponsorship of sports, film festivals, television channels, theatre, the arts, crafts and cottage industries is perceived to be an important function of national government. The various forms of government-sponsored cultural academies that have been established are witness to the concern for institutionalizing cultural policy. Post-liberalization of the economy has brought about a spurt in the growth of private enterprise and non-government organizations that have come forward to participate in the various sectors of cultural policy planning and execution. In some ways there is a shift from policies that are targeted at the lowest common denominator to more attention being paid to demographic age structures and age-based institutionally defined role structures, differences in economic status and the symbolically coded, cultural representation of the diversity of the population (Koch-Weser, 1990).

Possession of leisure was and is a marker for the distinctions in social class, separating the elite from the non-elite (Dressler and Willis, 1969). As mentioned earlier, vernacular literature contains significant material on the class distinctions in the nature of leisure if not the possession of leisure.

Modern or more contemporary writings do not seem to be concerned about raising the issue of the distinctions between industrial and pre-industrial societies in the ways in which they may perceive leisure; rather, they are focused on the variety of leisure activities and the importance of the role of the state in providing for non-work time. It is assumed that pre-industrial societies will find themselves eventually in the same predicament of having more time than before on their hands. There is also the apprehension that more and more leisure activities will involve others in the provision of the services but actually be more and more individualized.

Non-Western traditions

As a special focus on the non-Western tradition of leisure, the experience and nature of leisure among the tribes of India are described in this section. This is not because there is any conflict with the traditional meaning of leisure or with the fact that leisure is a product associated with industrialization through which work and non-work became crystallized and the differences became more sharpened. In this context the concept of leisure sharpened, in contrast to the more overlapping areas of work and leisure found in non-industrial societies. There is need to transcend this traditional meaning as it is not quite adequate to account for either the experience of leisure or the ideas that the tribes associate with leisure.

We will have to suspend some of the ideas of leisure that we have ourselves as well as what is suggested in the literature. In this section two tribes are described: the Santals, a settled peasant community in eastern India (see Archer, 1974), and the Jarawas, a hunter-gatherer tribe of the Andaman Islands, India. Very briefly, the former are for the most part settled agriculturists, but with a vibrant tradition of migration. They do not own much land, for which reason they have to employ themselves on the lands of others on a daily wage-earning basis. This obvious dependence on availability of work implies often unequal work, thereby unequal free time every day, as well as there being seasonal variation. There is another important factor, that of time spent in actual work, which is dependent on the employer, and this is not always consistent with the payment for labour done.

In one heavy work day the Santal men and women may be seen taking short rests as pauses in work without disturbing the overall tempo. During this time the men may smoke, sit in a comfortable position or take out a sling to catch birds. Women doing construction work are usually engaged in brick-carrying or supplying materials to the mason. They too stop work periodically, sitting to chat with the other women who may still be working at their own pace, or to pick up and feed the baby they may have left under a tree. Actual work may be conducted at a slow pace without hurry, but no work is left unfinished. It is fascinating to watch them arranging the bricks, preparing them for use. Most Santal women use a rather artistic arrangement that women of other communities working in the same place do not. This input of art is not at all a requirement of the work that is assigned to them.

When there are visitors at home, their arrival does not upset the tempo of work that the householders may be engaged in, formalities of welcome are not rushed and conversations are carried on during engagement in work. Then there may be a long time that may be spent with the visitor away even from routine household duties. After a hard day's work or on the days when the men may have no work or may have stayed away from work, they may drink rice beer that they brew themselves or just sit still weaving a net or in quietude, sitting side by side with other men on the roadside outside their homes. There is not much talk, but silent communication takes place. Sometimes women may spend their free time in singing songs in unison; they can be heard doing this in their place of work. Their festivals are great times for leisure – not so much the rites and rituals, but the dancing, the singing and the playing of musical instruments. Leisure consists in visiting fairs and having something to eat or going on rides. In the traditional Indian fairs the exhibits that draw a large section of the rural crowds are not material things on sale but strange and freakish things or displays of nerve, such as the circus acts. For patronizing or enjoying these activities a certain amount of surplus generation is required and it is found that these activities peak in the seasons after harvest.

However, what is more important than these observations from field situations is how the Santals perceive what has been described as leisure. Do they also see these and other such activities as leisure, or do they have their own semantics? The question 'What is leisure?' evoked a general response: 'There is no time for leisure as all time is spent in work.' In the absence of ideas of gainful work or prescribed-time work, the idea of leisure time does not develop. When asked what a person was doing sitting in the sun, the answer was 'nothing', an answer that they rarely made about their own individual inactivity. This seems, paradoxically, a case of double standards for which it has not yet been possible to come up with an acceptable and logical reason. A few possible lines of thinking may be that it is very difficult to differentiate between work and leisure or non-work in everyday life, though there may be an ideal distinction between the two without any one being value-loaded or the two being compartmentalized; also, a person who is inactive is not stigmatized as an idler, thus a person described as 'doing nothing' is not in any way specially marked out. Idlers are not denigrated as long as the persons so described are not dependent on others for economic sustenance and are not a nuisance to society. There is much tolerance for inaction. The question remains whether we can consider non-work as leisure in the case of the Santals. This is a difficult question, but it is the integration of work and leisure among them that distinguishes their quality of life even to a lay observer.

There is a word in the Santal language, *raska*, that means 'fun' or 'joy' (Culshaw, 1949). In all that they do, they expect that it should have the quality of evoking *raska*, and it is not uncommon to observe that they sometimes even leave a particular employment because of the lack of this spirit. They work because there is *raska* and they sing and dance because there is *raska*. This is not age-specific; Santals of all ages appreciate *raska*. Nobody disturbs another's experience of *raska*, be they parents in the case of their children or vice versa. The age groups have their own ways of experiencing *raska* and it is for this reason that, as one grows older in this society, there exists scope for the old to derive their own sense of *raska*. These are not the antecedent features of having to reorient their leisure activities.

In contrast, the Jarawas are hunter-gatherers who work for a maximum of four or five hours on the days that they work, because they work only when they need to. They are not dependent on any employer, nor are they dependent on modern resources. Thus a large part of their day is without work. It is obvious why work hours are distinguished from non-work hours; this is in acceptance of the fact that leisure is surely associated with the time spent away from work. Among the Jarawas, there seems to be a form of pure leisure that they experience, because of their complete dependence on resources that are not available through commercial means. This is in sharp contrast to what the contemporary industrialized person experiences, the need to generate 'enough' wealth in order to enjoy 'quality' leisure. There is also a qualitative difference in expectations of leisure that can be analysed in terms of cross-cultural variations.

This little known tribe of the Andaman Islands spends very little time in actual work. They spend long stretches of time every day in relative inactivity, lying down in the communal hut; sitting at the opening of the hut; beading a shell necklace or weaving a basket, neither for exchange with other goods nor for sale. One could say that these were all economic activities of one sort or the other, but why should these be seen as different from some of the things that we do in fashioning objects according to our interests without any pecuniary considerations? After the day's hunt is done, there is hectic activity cleaning and cooking the kill, and once the meal is over, the other activities could be termed as activities of relaxation or leisure (Mukhopadhyaya et al., 2002; Sreenathan, 2001). There is a lesson for us here; we have come to confuse leisure and economics (at various levels: status, prestige, turning hobbies and interests into sources of economic sustenance, and so on) and forgotten the reason for getting involved in leisure activities.

Anxiety and leisure

The above section brought into focus the relationship between anxiety and leisure. From the description of the tribes, it emerges that they have somehow succeeded in striking a balance between work and leisure – not by sharp distinction but through interspersing work and leisure in the cycle of the day. Also, the experience of leisure assumes a pure quality because of the sustenance it receives from intangible aspects of their own culture and way of life.

Bogardus (1960) and Eldridge et al. (1950) strike a somewhat sombre note. Bogardus says that the development of increased leisure time does not necessarily give people more time for solving social problems or exercising social control. In fact many of them use this extra time in a restless search for excitement and in avoiding social responsibilities. Such people rush away from social responsibility. Eldridge et al. bemoan the fact that 'more and more leisure hours of the masses are being pre-empted by the commercialized forms of recreation ... and we have a peculiar philosophy of leisure along with the commercialisation of leisure and that we have an impoverishment of life during leisure hours'. Jules Karlin (1967) asks how the newly won leisure hours available due to industrialization are to be used. He asks if there will be 'a great cultural revival in the arts', though the rush for a 'fun oriented future foretells that the teen-age subculture of today may be tomorrow's adult life in automated society'. Obviously this will be a departure from the earnestness with which the Greeks took their leisure, meaning as time spent in non-necessitous exercise of the creative faculties. The Greek term for leisure is *schole*, from which the word 'school' is derived. The object of leisure was the pursuit of excellence, unrelated to the necessity of earning one's living.

However, what is missing in most writings is the relation between stress and leisure. Leisure is seen as a means of working out the tensions created by work experiences or conditions. In our societies, leisure becomes a pursuit, and sometimes, like the ancient Greeks, a serious one. Among the tribes leisure is not seen as something 'elusive' that has to be worked for, it comes naturally through work and life experience. For us, pursuit of leisure in order to reduce stress has created its own vicious cycle: we use leisure to reduce tension, but we sometimes carry our tensions over into our leisure activities. One of the reasons is that our leisure is more artefacted than that of the tribes.

Time and leisure

In reading the novels written in the mid-to-late nineteenth century, especially in Bengal, it is interesting to note that the elite, without doing a bit of work in the morning, make elaborate preparations for the evening's leisure, either an evening of classical music, or a game of cards with friends interlaced with absorbing conversation – *adda* as it is called in Bengali. In fact this has been showcased as a mark of a true urban Bengali, with some *adda* sessions being recorded as texts and being used as treatise on social questions. These chat sessions were used by the leading intellectuals and academicians as sounding boards for their ideas, and this is true to a great extent even today. There are also stories of the poor farmer, his back bent with the burden of work and tax, finding no time even to say his daily prayers (which could have been means of relaxation, if not exactly leisure). There are very few emic accounts (anthropological or otherwise) of how people who earn their livelihood by labour spend their time away from work. Whatever accounts there are tinged by the bias of the writer.

The Indian tradition is blessed with many social and religious festivals and occasions and participation in them is a form of leisure. In fact the timings of the festivals and occasions tell us about the rhythm of agriculture activities that used to prevail. The festivals and occasions to a large extent coincided with post-harvest or provided relief from the monotony of the lean seasons. Economy and time are so closely linked with leisure in most societies, and this is also borne out by history which tells us that the same relationship is extended in the case of hunter-gatherer communities. In such communities, where they still exist, it is difficult to establish this direct relationship. It is indeed difficult to demarcate the activities that are related to the economic sector from the other activities, including leisure. This applies to the Jarawas, discussed above, who are one of the few hunter-gatherer communities in the world, who inhabit the west coastline of the Andaman Islands, on whom some recent works are available (Mukhopadhyaya et al., 2002; Sarkar, 1990). Similar parallels can be drawn with other hunter-gatherer communities in terms of the difficulties encountered in differentiating between economic and other activities, very much in the vein of today's executive golfer who strikes a business deal during a round of golf or one who makes a happy compromise between business and leisure.

For peasant societies, the rhythm of time is patterned; activities are organized as well as punctuated with regular breaks. It is during these breaks that festivals and social occasions are observed and there is a clearer demarcation between economic and other activities. However, among these communities also, utilization of time outside work may have some economic implications; this is with reference to the arts and crafts produced by these communities. Creating things possessing aesthetic attributes surely must provide a sense of creative pleasure. An in-depth study of the many folk-level arts and crafts that can be found in India reveals a deep creative joy being manifest in the artefacts: one can imagine the labour that must have gone into them and the time that must have been devoted to them, and considerations other than economic that must have been in the forefront. From a functional point of view, the arts and crafts had a limited use, mainly in rites and rituals.

Turning our attention to pastoral communities, India is host to quite a few communities who travel with their animals for pasture in deserts, both inland and mountainous, by no means easy terrain. These semi-nomadic communities find their pleasures in the most unlikely of places. For the mountain pastorals, the summer months are spent in work while part of the winter too may be spent in travelling to warmer reaches at lower altitudes, thus the relationship between time and leisure does not follow the general principles. The writings that are available on the pastorals provide information about their customs, rites and rituals; there is very little information about how they spend their time outside of work. The assumption quite correctly may be that social festivity is leisure where pleasure is guaranteed!

Activities and leisure

Visiting centres of pilgrimage, visiting tourist spots and sightseeing, playing games, visiting family and friends, participating in social and religious festivals, singing and dancing, attending cultural functions or political rallies, pursuing hobbies and interests, going to the movies, picnics, eating out, and just lazing are some of the activities that are earmarked as leisure activities. It has to be remembered that the list is by no means universally applicable nor exhaustive. Age, social position, economic status, education, location, gender, community identity, and so on, are some of the factors that influence preference for and participation in activities.

Going on a pilgrimage is an ancient tradition in India. Pilgrimages to places associated with great Indian personalities are almost as popular as those to holy places. A person who has visited all the pilgrimage sites in the four corners of the country is revered among the rural Hindus; the Muslim who has visited Mecca assumes the title 'Haji'. There are many spots in the country that are connected with Islam, but there is not much known about the Christian pilgrimage spots, though an opportunity for Christians to participate in the Christian conferences held all over the world is considered very prestigious. For the Buddhists, a visit to Bodhgaya, where Buddha attained the status of the all-knowing, and the caves at Ajanta and Ellora, famous for wall murals and statues of Buddha, is a must; the Jains visit the beautiful carved Jain temples; the Bahais, followers of a Sufi faith, have their Lotus Temple; and the Parsis, who are Zoroastrians, have their designated places of worship and pilgrimage. Pilgrimage in India is a flourishing industry and the government is entering into partnerships with the non-government sector so that facilities can be improved and revenue earned. It might be of interest to know that the Government of India provides a subsidy to the Haj pilgrims. And it would be interesting to study the demographic features of the pilgrims – the older generation predominates though there are quite a number of young people visiting the pilgrimage centres in the higher reaches of the Himalayas. The visitors are a mix of rural and urban, with the rural preferring pilgrimage to traditional sites, while the urban prefer combining a visit to a religious site with visits to tourist spots.

Tourism as a leisure activity has gained in popularity and this has been helped by the existing railway network, airlines and the hotel and hospitality industry. In fact, if one randomly searches the websites on leisure in India, the majority are found devoted to tourism and hospitality – not so much sports as could be expected in industrialized nations or even the other activities like crafts, music and dance that India is famous for. In this context, tourism is found to be confined to the urban salaried classes whose children attend regular schools and have school vacations. Certain times of the year are marked for certain communities. For example, autumn, the time of year in which Bengalis have a long official break, is called the Bengali tourist season and it is indeed remarkable that most of the destinations have eating places that cater to the Bengali palate; somewhat anachronistic to the notion of travel and broadening one's mind! Shopping goes hand in hand with tourism and this has given a tremendous boost to the arts and crafts of regions, with some places depending entirely on tourism for their economy. India is rich in a wide variety of tourist spots, some of which are historically important. It is obvious that there is a very direct link with tourism and one's economic standing.

There are a variety of games played in India, some of which could be described as sports. Board games, of which there are many, are of social significance in some communities. Among sports, football, alley cricket, wrestling, playing with sticks and stones, and other team games are played, as are tennis, badminton, snooker, golf, billiards, table tennis, and so on. Sport in India is still trying to find its feet, as most sports are beyond the means of many. Preferred games are those that do not require too much expenditure. Sports academies are town-centric and expensive. The children in villages make do with their own variations of the games that are recognized as sport. With the spread of television and the cable network, people are becoming aware of the world of sports and the world players. David Beckham is as much a star in India as the native-born Sachin Tendulkar (of cricketing fame, comparable to the great Donald Bradman). Football is the most played sport in the country. Jumping into the village pond is a favourite activity for young boys; however, swimming is not considered a sport. In urban cities, swimming has become a part of the curriculum (almost) with parents investing time, effort and money in giving their children swimming lessons. Among the traditional sports, wrestling is quite popular in north India and training in martial arts is found in Kerala, a southern state on the west coast and in Manipur, a state of the northeast. In Kerala, the annual regatta attracts hordes of spectators and the festival takes on the features of a carnival.

There are many local games that children play with crudely fashioned toys of clay and wood. A favourite with the children of most villages across India is a wheel that is sped along with a long piece of hard wire held in the hands. Fishing and catching snails from ponds and rivers can occupy a young boy for a large part of the day, as can going on a fruit-gathering mission from the gardens and orchards of the big landowners. Such games are naturally denied to the city or urban children who find the Western model of field and parlour games more to their taste.

Visiting fairs and shows, known as *mela*, is a very popular leisure activity. Many fairs are held throughout the year in various places all over the country, and the festival almanac of India lists the fairs to which people from far and near are drawn. Most fairs are rural-based and are associated with various occasions or are specialized in terms of goods sold. Fairs spawn a carnivalesque ambience in which there is a happy blend of commerce and merriment. Fairs have a long tradition and are a means by which people can obtain everyday goods and at the same time rejuvenate themselves from the exertions of hard labour. India had an agriculture-based pattern of life involving routine and monotonous labour, from which these fairs provided a much-needed break. Rabindranath Tagore, Nobel Laureate (1913) and founder of a school and university (Visva-Bharati) based on his unique philosophy of education (see O'Connell, 2002), understood the importance of fairs as a means of entertainment, interaction and learning. The tradition of holding annual fairs with goods from rural and urban India being exhibited and traded continues even today and is a unique feature of the university. It would be appropriate here to mention that the involvement of the masses in the country's freedom struggle was often mobilized through fairs (Hindumela, first organized in 1867 to propagate indigenous art, literature and music as a means of generating national pride under colonial rule). The cities and towns organize their special fairs, in many of which the arts, crafts, textiles and cultures of the varied population of the country are showcased. The winter months see many of these fairs being organized in permanent fairgrounds. The annual Book Fair is very successful in terms of the sheer number of visitors (even if it is not matched in terms of sales!). The fairs organize interactive poetry and prose-reading sessions, debates on pertinent issues, pavilions commemorating a particular writer/philosopher, as well as providing space for impromptu musical performances and art displays by the younger people. Food stalls are as much a draw as the book stalls. Some cities have built up quite a high-profile image of their residents being book lovers (Kolkata and Kolkatans being so described). The circus is another winter event that is a popular means of entertainment. It is not particularly indigenous in nature but the Indian circus has survived due to sustained audience demand. The Indian film industry is second only to Hollywood; Hindi films dominate, with a sizeable number of regional-language films being released. Parallel cinema and docu-films are fast emerging as a genre of alternate cinema. Television is expanding and FM radio has flooded the cities.

Conclusion

Leisure in India reflects the dynamics of class and economics of its people, further defined by geographical location, education and the tradition in which they have been socialized. Traditional providers and means of entertainment are constantly being expropriated and reshaped in contemporary times, as are ideas of leisure. Leisure is more personalized, and this has contributed to the development of a still nascent leisure industry. Networking, maintaining contacts and investment of time and money seem to be directly proportional to the 'sum total' of the experience of leisure and the value ascribed to it. Nevertheless, there exists a vibrant baseline of niche cocooned leisure, as found among the tribes, rural populations and some other categories (religious, linguistic or ethnic) that are integrally connected with festivals and occasions that are celebrated or observed with community participation and involvement. It is not so much about drawing a distinction between work time and leisure time or other time; rather, it is the ability to recognize and analyse the differential experience of leisure that would make for a more complete understanding of leisure in India.

Note

1. *Jajmani* is a system of interrelatedness in service within the community. The service provider receives patronage from the person or family to which the service is provided – and the relationship between the two is often hereditary. A *jajmani* system of patronage often existed in the sphere of leisure, too.

Bibliography

Classical Indian texts

Banbhatta's *Kadamvari*
Kalidasa's *Abhijnanam Sakuntalam* and *Meghdootam*
Vatsayana's *Kama Sutra*

Other sources

Archer, W. G. (1974) *A Hill of Flutes: Life, Love and Poetry in Tribal India. A Portrait of the Santals*, London, George Allen & Unwin.
Beteille, A. (1970) 'Caste and Political Group Formation in Tamilnad', in R. Kothari (ed.) *Caste in Indian Politics*, Delhi, Orient Longman Ltd.
Bhattacharya, K. (1998) 'History, Reality and Relevance: A Study of Indian Villages', *Visva-Bharati Quarterly* 7(2): 57–64.
Bogardus, E. R. (1960) *The Development of Social Thought*, Bombay, Vakils.
Bose, N. K. (1957) 'The Effect of Urbanization on Work and Leisure', *Man in India* 37(1): 2–9.
Clarke, J. and Critcher, C. (1985) *The Devil Makes Work: Leisure in Capitalist Britain*, London, Macmillan.
Culshaw, W. J. (1949) *Tribal Heritage*, London, Lutterworth Press.
Denzin, N. K. (1978) *The Research Act* (2nd edn), New York, McGraw-Hill.
Dressler, D. and Willis, N. M. (1969) *The Study of Human Interaction*, New York, Alfred A. Knopf.
Dumazedier, J. (1967) *Towards a Society of Leisure*, London, Collier Macmillan.
Dutta, P. (2004) 'Public Sphere and Civil Society', in M. D. Kaushal (eds) *Folklore, Public Sphere and Civil Society*, Chennai, IGNCA, and New Delhi, NFSC.
Eldridge, S., Gibbard, H. A. and Rosenquist, C. M. (1950) *Fundamentals of Sociology: A Situational Analysis*, New York, Thomas Y. Cromwell.

Henderson, K. A. (1991) *Dimensions of Choice: A Qualitative Approach to Recreation, Parks and Leisure Research*, State College, PA, Venture Publishing.

Kaplan, M. (1970) *Leisure Theory and Policy*, New York, John Wiley.

Karlin, J. (1967) *Man's Behaviour: An Introduction to Social Science*, New York, Macmillan.

Koch-Weser, E. (1990) 'Trends in Leisure and Communication: A Challenge for Social Research and Policy Planning', in K. Mahajan (ed.) *Communication and Society*, New Delhi, Classical Publishing Company.

Kothari, R. (ed.) (1970) *Caste in Indian Politics*, Delhi, Orient Longman Ltd.

Mukhopadhyaya, K., Bhattacharya, R. K. and Sarkar, B. (2002) *Jarawa Contact: Us with Them and Theirs with Us*, Kolkata, Anthropological Survey of India, Government of India.

O'Connell, Kathleen M. (2002) *Rabindranath Tagore: The Poet as Educator*, Kolkata, Visva-Bharati.

Parker, S. (1971) *The Future of Work and Leisure*, London, MacGibbon & Kee.

Parsons, T. (1951) *The Social System*, London, Routledge & Kegan.

Ray-Burman, B. K. (1957) 'Observations on "The Effect of Urbanization on Work and Leisure"', *Man in India* 37(2): 217–29.

Roberts, K. (1970) *Leisure*, London, Longman.

Roberts, K. (1978) *Contemporary Society and Growth of Leisure*, London, Longman.

Roberts, K. (1999) *Leisure in Contemporary Society*, Wallingford, CABI International.

Roy, A. (1997) *God of Small Things*, New Delhi, IndiaInk.

Sarkar, J. K. (1990) *The Jarawas*, Calcutta, Seagull Books.

Sharma, P. (1990) *Sociology of Leisure: Themes and Perspectives*, New Delhi, Bahri Publications.

Sreenathan, M. (2001) *The Jarawas: Language and Culture*, Calcutta, Anthropological Survey of India, Government of India.

Veal, A. J. and Lynch, R. (2001) *Australian Leisure* (2nd edn), Sydney, Longman.

Wiser, W. H. (1936) *The Hindu Jajmani System*, Lucknow, Lucknow Publishing House.

Part 2
Key Disciplines

6
Sociology and Cultural Studies

Hugo van der Poel

In order to survive people need to do things. They have to eat and drink, protect themselves from heat and cold, violence and illnesses. These activities take time. There are great differences in the amount of time individuals, groups and societies spend on necessary activities, but most people, particularly among the wealthier groups and societies, will not have to spend all their time on these activities. Apart from time to rest and sleep, they will have some spare time, time not burdened with more or less unavoidable or obligated tasks. In societies where civil rights and freedoms are somehow (constitutionally) guaranteed, this spare time, if not wholly needed for rest and recuperation, can be experienced as relatively free time, time in which one feels free – and often actually is free – to pursue goals and undertake activities of one's own choosing. Roughly speaking, leisure encompasses the goals and activities people choose freely to fill their least obligated time.

However, for sociologists it is obvious that – paraphrasing Marx – people may spend part of their time freely, but not under conditions of their own choosing. Or, as Berger put it in one of the early articles on the sociology of leisure,

> the very idea of free time belongs to a presociological age. If sociology has taught us anything it has taught us that no time is free of normative constraints, what is work for some, is leisure for others, it is said, and of course this is right. Is work work if I love it? Is leisure leisure if I feel it is burdensome or boring? These are the kind of questions which make students of leisure tear their hair and in despair reach for the operational definition. Any normative distinction between work and leisure as action should be a distinction between the kinds of norms which constrain them or a distinction regarding the extent to which norms have been internalized. (Berger, 1963: 29)

Paramount in the (sociological) study of leisure therefore is the 'conditioning of freedom'. The sociology of leisure studies the conditions that people have to deal with at a particular point in time and space, that limit the range of options from which they can make a choice to fill their time. These conditions may be called constraints, obligations, (non-)availability, (non-)accessibility or norms, but what they have in common is that they somehow make it impossible to pursue certain goals or undertake certain activities. At some times we 'have to' perform tasks such as work or taking care of the children, at other times we are 'free' from this type of necessary tasks, but still cannot choose to enjoy particular activities because the facilities are not available, are too expensive, are against the law or local custom or not accessible or permissible for persons with a specific social identity (for example, youngsters that are not allowed to enter bars or buy cigarettes). It should be stressed, however, that most conditions have a double-faced nature. That is, rather than simply making action impossible altogether, they select options for action. By definition, acting means doing something and the possibility of doing it otherwise (Giddens, 1976). For instance, labour laws made it mandatory to limit working hours per week, thus at the same time creating a significant amount of free time. Sunday laws forbid all sorts of activities on Sunday, thus setting Sunday apart from the other days in the week and opening the opportunity to experience a weekly rhythm, quietness in the otherwise bustling city and time to spend with the family.

In terms of research, this focus has lead to a distinction between independent variables (the conditions) and dependent variables (the activities and forms of action chosen) and trying to detect how and to what extent the independent variables 'determine' what we do in and with our free time. This distinction between 'independent' and 'dependent' variables suggests that 'conditions' and 'freedom of choice' should be understood as an opposition between pre-given and unalterable structures and variable action or agency. As such, this is an expression of the so-called agency–structure dualism that has haunted the social sciences from their inception (Giddens, 1976). It should be clear, however, that most conditions, and certainly the conditions which are studied by social sciences, are (wo-)man-made, change over time and vary by place. What appears as 'independent' in any particular piece of research is no more than a snapshot, a frozen image taken out of a process of permanent change. These societal changes, such as secularization, individualization and globalization, are mostly unintended and occur as unforeseen, unwanted and/or unplanned 'by-products' of the choices we continuously make in our daily lives. Sometimes, however, this type of change is wanted, if not deliberately planned and brought about. Examples of the latter are the emancipation of the labour class and women and the increase of the educational level of the population at large in welfare states. So (social) scientists dealing with leisure look not only at the explanation or determination of differences in leisure behaviour by independent variables, but also at the origins of and changes in these independent variables. They study the origins of constraints, norms and differences in accessibility in leisure, seek to explain the continuity of the conditions for leisure behaviour and their susceptibility to change, the acceptance of and the resistance to these conditions and will contribute to the articulation of alternatives for and the modes of (deliberate) change of these conditions.

Writing a chapter on the sociology of leisure in a Handbook of Leisure Studies is a conditioned activity just as any other activity. It is more or less 'determined' to provide an overview of what the sociology of leisure has hitherto produced in terms of books and articles; definitions, theories and research methods; research findings, confirmed knowledge and remaining research questions. All of this in a few pages and with the young student in mind. Such a chapter would necessarily resemble similar chapters in other handbooks and reinforce the conditions that exist for new students that enter the field of the sociology of leisure. Interestingly, the American leisure sociologist Kelly (1999), in his last of many overviews of the sociology of leisure, has chosen to present the material in the form of a 'dialectical model', allowing him to present the 'common wisdoms' as theses, the critiques on these common wisdoms as antitheses, and his ideas and suggestions for the future of the sociology of leisure as syntheses. In doing so he is able to present both the 'traditional' overview, mainly reporting of research that has aimed to ascertain the determining factors of leisure behaviour, and critical studies, that have questioned the legitimacy and self-evidence of these determining factors.

This chapter will depart from a different angle. Because most substantive issues will be dealt with elsewhere in this Handbook, this particular chapter is focused on the sociological perspective itself. What do sociologists 'see' when looking at leisure, what sort of questions do they typically ask? To begin with, we will pay attention to the conditioning of the sociology of leisure itself. If the sociology of leisure provides a certain perspective to study leisure, where does this perspective come from, whose perspective is it, what do you see with this perspective and what not? Second, we will look at 'society', or more precise, the societal embeddedness of leisure. What are important societal changes and how do these changes impact on leisure? Third, we want to look at the effects of these societal developments, such as globalization and individualization, on the organization of daily life, and thus at the (changes in the) conditioning of leisure in the context of the intensifying 'battle for time'. The last section of this chapter will ask questions about a separate 'sociology of leisure', alongside 'cultural studies' and amidst multi-, inter- or transdisciplinary leisure studies.

Perspectives, contingencies and alternatives

A sociology of leisure typically starts with the ideas of the Ancient Greeks and Romans on leisure. Then there is a hop to industrial Britain of the nineteenth century and the reduction of working hours in Western societies since the First World War. Furthermore, one may expect to find sections on 'leisure and work' (the influence of work on leisure and vice versa), 'leisure and the family/the community' (including class and gender differences in leisure), 'leisure in the lifecycle' (including topics such as socialization, leisure education and changes in leisure preferences and behaviour due to ageing) and a concluding section on leisure policy and provision. The more recent sociologies of leisure will also explicitly cover cultural aspects of leisure (such as lifestyles, identities and consumption) and perhaps be somewhat more specific on leisure as a form of social relationship (see, for instance, Parker, 1976; Parry, 1983; Horna, 1994; Critcher et al., 1995; Roberts, 1970, 1978, 1999; Kelly, 1999). Some of these topics will be addressed in some more detail in the next section and all of them will be extensively dealt with in later chapters of this Handbook.

The fact that it is relatively easy to point out topics that are 'naturally' covered in a sociology of leisure indicates some form of 'discipline'. The discipline organizes a particular group of academics by giving them a common ground of definitions, theories, methodologies and topics they all are familiar with and can have knowledgeable debates about. Handbooks and overviews and the lectures in which these are used introduce new students to this particular academic field, where you can become an insider by knowing about the aforementioned definitions, theories, and so on. However, it should be borne in mind that there is nothing 'natural' about scientific disciplines, that what is included in and excluded by the discipline is to a large extent contingent and heavily influenced by the time and place of its formation and later development. The 'disciplining' by the discipline should not prevent us from asking questions about its central themes, theories, definitions and approaches. There are at least three good reasons to ask such questions: other perspectives, changes in time/space, and alternatives.

Who made the discipline into a discipline? To what extent does 'the' sociology of leisure contain generalizable knowledge, and to what extent does it reflect the preoccupations of a particular group of persons? Does the sociology of leisure as we know it fit the people living in India, China or Africa, or is its meaning restricted to the Anglo-Saxon world with all together less than 10 per cent of the world population within its borders? What has the sociology of leisure to say about the majority of the people who – in most Western countries – do not work (children, elderly, inmates, people with chronic illnesses or disabilities, or the unemployed)? Apart from the influences of work and the family on leisure, what does the sociology of leisure have to say about the influences of the market, advertising and the media on the ways we spend our free time? So the first thing to be aware of when reading a sociology of leisure is the perspective from which it is written. Lanfant's *Les théories du loisir* (1972), Rojek's *Capitalism and Leisure Theory* (1985) or Aitchison's *Gender and Leisure: Social and Cultural Perspectives* (2003) are good examples that different perspectives are possible and lead to different sociologies of leisure.

A second question to ask is whether a particular sociology of leisure reflects the preoccupations of a person or group of people situated in a particular time and place. Is it possible to write a sociology of leisure in Chad, Liberia or Nepal, dealing with leisure in those societies? Would it have been possible to write a sociology of leisure, even in Britain or France, during the nineteenth century? Will it be possible in the twenty-second century? This question obviously follows from the historicity of sociology as a science and leisure as a modern phenomenon. Both have roots in the nineteenth century, but only after the Second World War did sociology become a full blown academic discipline in the Western welfare states and leisure become a mass phenomenon, partly as an effect of this same welfare state. If today the welfare states are being 'reorganized' and under severe pressure in a globalizing world, where will that leave both sociology and leisure? The least one can say is that topics such as work and leisure, leisure and the family, leisure and education, and leisure policy and provision are themes that were particularly important in the context of the welfare states and reflect the role sociologists thought they could play as 'legislators' and 'social planners' in these welfare states (Bauman, 1987; Mommaas, 1996; Mommaas et al., 1996a).

The third and perhaps most critical question to ask is whether there are, could be or should be (better) alternatives. Alternatives for the society we live in at large, alternatives for the influences from work or family on our leisure and/or alternative forms of work or family. We do not have to take the world system of liberal democracies-cum-capitalism for granted. After the fall of the Iron Curtain in the early 1990s there still remain immense problems of poverty, pollution, depletion of resources, war and diseases that may raise questions about the superiority of the 'Western' way of organizing societies, including the role of labour and families within those societies. Is the way we spend our leisure today the best way to spend our leisure? Does it make us happier? If so, does it do so in an efficient manner, with the fewest negative side-effects for others, future generations and/or the environment? Do we know what makes us happier, do we have experiences to prove that? Do we learn anything at school that helps us to spend our leisure in a satisfying way?

To conclude, the sociology of leisure today is an identifiable subdiscipline that has been around for at least half a century. For instance, the World Leisure and Recreation Association (WLRA) and the predecessor of Research Committee 13 (Leisure) of the International Sociological Association (ISA) were both founded in 1956. Since then a lot of research has been done, theories developed and hypotheses tested. The subdiscipline thus developed historically and contingently, in the context of the expanding welfare states. Its contingent nature implies that it could have been and can be developed in alternative ways.

Modernity and leisure

Sand, water, grass and sunlight are things that do not require human beings around. They are material and have an existence of their 'own'. Cars, pizzas, violins and CD players could not have existed without the people who invented, developed and produced these things. However, being made, they also have a material existence and a 'lifecycle' relatively independent from human action. Society, the 'free market', friendship, clubs and leisure do not have a material existence. These entities exist virtually. We know them because we can witness their effects in human actions, in what we think and do. As researchers we cannot put these entities under a microscope. We can only 'see' and study these entities by studying human behaviour and the (material) effects of human behaviour, most often by identifying regularities in this behaviour. Once regularities appear, it is assumed that a certain rule or rule-set explains this regularity. This rule or rule-set is, or is part of, one of these virtual entities such as the free market, friendship or leisure.

'Sociology', 'modernity' and 'leisure' are all virtual entities. Sociology is a particular rule-set (a 'discipline') that prescribes how to study its object, which in this case is another virtual entity, that is, society. Looking back in history it is clear that this particular way of thinking about society was developed in a time of tremendous societal changes in nineteenth-century Britain, France and Germany. 'Founding fathers' such as Saint Simon, Marx, Weber, Durkheim and Simmel studied the contemporaneous changes in people's behaviour, and trying to make sense of these changes, they 'invented' the social world and disciplined the ways to study this (virtual!) social world separately from either the natural or the religious world. With the knowledge of hindsight one can say they actually invented 'modernity' as a particular set of social conditions that, developing since the Renaissance, unfolded in the late nineteenth century. Most notably, these changing conditions were the industrialization of production and war, mobilization (trains, bikes, trams, steamships), urbanization, imperialism and the formation of a world-covering system of nation-states ('societies') and colonies, the instrumentalization of science and the democratization of secondary and higher education, the advent of socialism, freedom of press and organization and the coming into existence of civil society, including unions and political parties.

Did these early sociologists, or at least the 'big three' – Marx, Weber, Durkheim – have a theory or sociology of leisure? In 1985 Rojek wrote of these big three – plus Freud – as representing 'a submerged tradition in leisure theory' (Rojek, 1985: 3). He did so in an attempt to overcome the failure of 'social formalism', up till then the 'dominant research tradition in the sociology of leisure, ... to situate leisure relations in the context of the history and general power structure of capitalist society' (Rojek, 1985: 3). Although Rojek overlooked important studies that had appeared in non-English languages, in which, for instance, Marx had been thoroughly discussed (see, among others, Lanfant, 1972; Nahrstedt, 1972; see also Corijn, 1998), he had a point as far as the Anglo-Saxon perspective seemed to dominate the subdiscipline. Although Rojek may have overstated his case that these authors did have a theory of leisure (in the case of Marx, see Corijn, 1998: 244–6), his intervention has been important to show that their writings do indeed contain concepts, theories, perspectives and themes that still have a bearing on understanding leisure, its social roots and its societal importance.

Paradoxically, the sociology of leisure did not really develop out of the analyses of the founding fathers, but rather more out of the mundane worries of politicians and policy-makers about what the working class would do with its free time. When, after the First World War, most industrial societies – within the framework of the newly established International Labour Organization (ILO) – agreed to bring back working hours to eight hours per working day, this question was the central theme of a series of surveys held in those countries where the new labour laws were introduced. It was particularly important to learn whether this new free time had led to more abusive forms of leisure, such as drinking and gambling. Others had high hopes of more union, educational and cultural activities. However, most research in the interwar period showed that the labour class used their leisure for rest and recuperation on the one hand, and indulging in new forms of consumption, such as listening to the radio, going to the cinema and playing sports on the other hand (Beckers and Mommaas, 1996; Cross, 1993). An important instrument developed in this time was the time-budget study, which became a defining instrument for the discipline of leisure studies (see, among others, Lanfant, 1972; Szalaï, 1972; Mommaas et al., 1996b; Cushman et al., 1996; Robinson and Godbey, 1997; Pentland et al., 1999).

After the Second World War, Western countries developed into welfare states. Within these welfare states, sociology established itself as an academic discipline with the task to deliver the 'social engineers', that the welfare state needed for the agencies set up to deal methodically with most, if not all society's problems. The period of 1950–80/90 is also referred to as the heyday of 'the social compromise' between the interests of capitalism and the working class (Corijn, 1998: 194). The working class in the Western world no longer sought the 'communist revolution', by which it was to take over control of the means of production (capital, factories, and so on) and thus control over society. In turn, the capitalist class agreed with the skimming of the surplus value (the profits made in the production process and on capital investments) by way of taxes and insurance contributions. With these monies the state could pay for education, pensions, infrastructure, and so on, and indeed also for leisure provisions. In most countries the sociology of leisure came into being because the welfare state was in need of research and officials for a scientifically underpinned planning of sport, cultural, youth and recreational facilities. In the Netherlands, Wippler's *Sociale determinanten van het vrijetijdsgedrag (Social Determinants of Leisure Behaviour)* (1968) provides a perfect example of this type of research. It was one of the first studies in this field to use factor analysis, hoping to find the 'determinants' that would help to predict leisure behaviour. The study grew out of contract research as part of the planning of recreational facilities in the northern part of the Netherlands. At the time this type of research had some urgency because many social scientists thought that the 'leisure society' was at hand (see, among others, Friedmann, 1950; Dumazedier, 1962; Fourastié, 1965), that people had to be prepared and educated to be able to spend this free time in a responsible and edifying way and that the state had to play a steering and stimulating part in this development.

Rojek's critical intervention is one among others that reflected both internal academic developments as well as shifting societal conditions in the 1980s (for example, van Moorst, 1982; Clarke and Critcher, 1985; Deem, 1986; Mommaas and van der Poel, 1987). From today's vantage point this period indicated the beginning of the shift from Modernity 1 to Modernity 2 (Rojek, 1995) or First Modernity to Second Modernity (Beck and Willms, 2004), although at the time it was more fashionable to talk about the advent of postmodernity. Here we will focus on these latter societal shifts. In the last section of this chapter we will return to the more internal academic developments and their consequences for the study of leisure.

Comparing the first decade of the twenty-first century with 20–30 years ago, some of the most fundamental changes marking a 'global shift' (Dicken, 1998), with far-reaching consequences for leisure and the study of leisure, can be summed up as follows.

First, we've seen an enormous acceleration in the globalization of the economy, politics, culture and environmental risks. Goods (such as televisions and sport shoes), services (credit card facilities, car rentals), information (the internet), risks (plane crashes, SARS), capital and labour move around the globe far more quickly and can hardly be stopped at a nation-state's border any more (see, for example, Maguire, 1999; Castells, 2001; Ritzer, 2004).

Second, the globalized economy comes with a 'dematerialization' and 'digitalization' of the economy in the West, and the shift of the 'material' (industrial) economy to low-wage countries, mostly in Asia. The often cited example is Nike, that earns its money by activities such as research and development, marketing and distribution in the US, and contracts out the production of sport shoes to factories in Southeast Asia, paying workers US$2 per pair (Goldman and Papson, 1998; Maguire, 1999). More and more economists tell us that today we live in an 'entertainment economy' (Wolf, 1999) or 'experience economy' (Pine and Gilmore 1999), in which an increasing part of the 'added' or 'surplus value' is created by the commodification of time, experiences, emotions and/or relations, and less by the commodification of material products. Competitive advantages are gained by (being faster in) product innovation, creativity, exclusive access to copyrights and better marketing, while fixed capital (real estate, material supplies, machinery) and physical infrastructure (for instance, a distribution system) diminish in importance as sources of added or surplus value.

Third, in the global world the major part is played by transnational corporations forming 'webs' or 'networks' of internal and external relationships between enterprises around the globe (Castells, 1996–98; Shapiro and Varian, 1999). Prime examples in the leisure economy are Disney, Fininvest, Bertelsmann and McDonald's.

Fourth, nation-states also have to 'network' in organizations such as the UN, the WTO, NAFTA and the EU and to co-ordinate their policies with other nation-states. Because of that, and because they have agreed to open up their borders, they have lost much of their independence in their control on what happens within their territory (for some interesting examples with respect to leisure activities such as binge drinking and smoking marijuana, see Kurzer, 2001). With the liberalization of the economy and the increased volatility of capital they have fewer possibilities to steer the national economy. More and more states have to compete among each other to be attractive for capital investments, leading to an increasing pressure on tax levels and thus the overall state budget, on the one hand, and willingness to accommodate investors, on the other, by cheap loans, limiting the powers of unions, being pliable with labour and environmental regulations, and so on. We can also witness an increasing interest in 'state' and 'city marketing', for instance, leading to higher budgets for elite sport, museums like the Guggenheim in Bilbao and flagship events and facilities such as the London Eye (see Ward, 1998; Gratton and Henry, 2001).

Fifth, we have witnessed an enormous time–space compression in all areas of life, due to the opening of borders, the expansion of the different modes of relatively cheap high speed transport (particularly cars and planes) and the explosion of (commercial) media, including the internet. Everything is available or within reach everywhere, be it in a virtual or non-virtual way, 24 hours a day.

Sixth, citizens/employees/consumers are now more mobile, inventive, educated, matured and demanding than ever, at least those that are connected with or have access to the network society (Rifkin, 2000). Old categories and divides between rich and poor, capital and labour, man and woman lose their explanatory power with regard to differences in leisure behaviour, because now often people have multiple identities (they do household tasks in combination with work on the labour market and following courses, thus amassing in themselves a form of cultural capital) and have become mobile physically and socially. Concepts such as 'labour', 'household' and '(wo)man' tend to become 'zombie concepts' (Beck and Willms, 2004) as a result of their internal differentiation. How useful is a concept like 'labour' in explaining differences in leisure behaviour, when it formally encompasses the paid work of farmers and artists, tanker cleaners and butchers, CEOs and traders at a stock market, nurses and taxi-drivers? Our society increasingly has become an 'individualized society' (Bauman, 2001).

Seventh, because 'opposing' categories such as 'labour' and 'leisure' have become internally differentiated and fragmented, the distinctions between these categories are blurred or 'de-differentiated' (Rojek, 1995). There are now large grey areas between labour and leisure (lounging or playing golf with business relations, working at home, doing work related voluntary work, following courses to get one's cultural capital up to date), but also between 'labour' and 'capital' (see, for example, Florida, 2002, on the 'creative class'), between man and woman (transsexuality, the 'houseman', the 'metroman', the 'power girl'), and so on. Within the field of leisure we also see more 'hybrid' activities, such as between sport and tourism (walking, cycling or diving while on holiday, visiting the Olympic Games as part of the holiday), shopping and entertainment ('retailtainment'), cultural participation and holidaying ('cultural vacations', city trips, visiting the 'Cultural Capital of the Year').

Eighth, work, household tasks, taking care of the children, following some form of education, volunteering, shopping, doing sports, holidaying – it is all possible now for most people in the 'connected world'. In fact, people become more and more forced to make choices from the growing abundance of possible ways to spend the always limited number of 24 hours a day. The organization of daily life is no longer prescribed by traditions and fixed roles, but is a matter of co-ordination and negotiation between the members of the household, the other networks one participates in, and all the things that could or should be done and vie with each other for the attention of the individual.

It must be clear that these major societal shifts have not left leisure unaffected. Part of the contribution of sociologists to the study of leisure is to monitor these major changes and discuss their possible impacts on leisure. This can be done from a historical-sociological perspective (see, for example, 'figurational sociology': Elias and Dunning, 1986; Jary and Horne, 1987; Rojek, 1985) as well as by a more 'prospective sociology' that surveys (possible) future developments and brings into discussion alternative strategies to deal with these futures. However, it looks as if the sociology of leisure is ashamed that the prospect of a leisure society never appeared to come around and since feels it should be silent about the future. Nevertheless, there still is a need for a sociology of leisure that discusses why the leisure society has never come around. Which assumptions have proven to be wrong? What can we learn about leisure and society from this future that did not materialize? Today, one would expect fierce debates among leisure sociologists about the possible impacts of the emergent experience economy, the internet and/or ecological risks on leisure (behaviour). And the more daring sociologists of leisure to be discussing possible impacts of possible futures. What will happen if hydrogen replaces oil as our main source of energy and hydrogen cells will allow for a wholly decentralized energy production, similar to the decentralization of communication with the introduction of personal computers and mobile phones? How will tourism be affected by climate change and rising sea levels? What will be the impact of the greying of the population in most Western countries, for example, in combination with developments in medicine, robotics, genome technology, xeno transplantation and the like, making it possible to live healthy and be mobile – if somewhat 'assisted' by science – well into our eighties or even nineties?

Leisure and the organization of daily life

Leisure is not a stand alone affair. It is part and parcel of the organization of daily life. It is influenced by the other things we do during the day, the week and the year, and it has its own impacts on these other daily activities. If the organization of daily life and all the components in it is affected by societal changes, so is leisure itself and its place within the daily string of activities.

As a virtual quality of daily life, leisure is not directly visible or discernable by particular activities. Put otherwise, there are no inherent or intrinsic leisure activities. Playing chess, gardening or watching television may at first hand appear to be straightforward leisure activities, but we need to know more about the context in which these activities take place before we can conclude that these activities really are leisure activities. For instance, the aforementioned activities can all be done by prisoners, they can be part of work or they may be the effect of an almost unavoidable social obligation. Leisure is not self-evident, but instantiated or articulated in the course of daily life and its constitutive (behavioural) components. The various activities that make up daily life vary in their 'leisure character' or degree of leisure. What then characterizes activities as leisure activities to a greater or lesser extent?

First of all, the less related to matters of subsistence that activities are, the more they may be perceived as leisure activities. As a corporeal human being, everybody has to provide for – or to be provided with – the means for sustaining life. This fact of life, this unavoidable necessity leads to obligated activities in daily life, to activities that are necessary to keep the source of these means flowing. A social position is a set of rights and obligations that an actor, who is accorded a certain social identity, may activate or carry out. A social identity most often is based on a specific, culturally relevant criterion or criteria, such as gender, kin, age, ethnicity or occupation (van der Poel, 1997). Connected with our source of income there is a particular social identity and related social position, that is, a particular set of rights and obligations. If we fulfil the obligations by spending time on the necessary activities that follow from these obligations, we are allowed to spend the rest of the time on other activities. Remember that 'leisure' comes from the Latin *licere*, meaning 'to be allowed to'. There are many different types of social positions related to the various ways one can provide for or can be provided with the means of sustaining life, such as factory labourer, professor, person of independent means, housewife, student, pensioner or unemployed. In each case, what activities one has to do in daily life in order to safeguard the flow of income or other forms of life provision will differ, as will the activities one cannot do in order not to endanger this flow of income, and the activities one is allowed to do. Leisure thus is by no means a monolithic free time space, but on the contrary is highly differentiated by the social positions people occupy and the distribution of these positions across the population. Accordingly, the leisurely character of activities is always dependent on the social position of the person who performs these activities and thus, indirectly, on the societal changes that impact on the content and distribution of these social positions.

Second, to the extent people are allowed to spend their time more or less according to their own wishes, we expect to see in the 'free' choice of their activities something of people's ideals and desires. Activities that fit a pursued self-identity or self-narrative and/or appear to give them pleasure. Or perhaps 'activities whose normative content renders them most important to us, those things we want to do for their own sake or those things that we feel ethically (as distinguished from expediently) constrained to do' (Berger, 1963: 29). At this point, sociology meets other disciplines contributing to the study of leisure, such as psychology, the discipline most likely to be able to say more about what activities lead to 'optimal experiences' or 'flow' (Csikszentmihalyi, 1990), what makes people choose and stick to certain activities and shy away from others. A bridging concept that may be useful here is 'serious leisure', as developed by Stebbins (see elsewhere in this Handbook). However, this is not to say that sociologists have nothing to say about pleasure, identity or desire. A century ago nobody 'desired' to have a television or being an 'idol', simply because these phenomena did not yet exist. It may be a matter of biology and psychology that people have desires and can experience pleasures, the actual content of these desires and pleasures appears to vary with the conditions in which people live. A desire refers to something missing. New things to have and new possibilities to spend time potentially create new desires, because the individual can now miss – and thus desire – more things and pastimes than before. Paradoxically, the growing abundance of possibilities to consume may thus lead to an increase in desires. If desire is (also) about the relationship between individuals and (missing) 'objects', it becomes important to ask whether there are differences between individuals in what they are allowed to or can desire, what the social character of the object is (friends, status, acceptance, and so on) and how the supply of objects is organized (why is there a growing supply, in whose interest does this supply grow, to what extent are desires deliberately aroused?).

To sum up, activities have a higher leisure content the less they have to do with the provision of the means of sustaining life and the more they belong to the range of activities one is allowed to pursue at will. Subsequently, it is expected that the leisure content is higher if activities fit people's self-identity and are expressive of what people feel is important, meaningful and/or desirable in their life. For sociologists of leisure this leads to the following questions. First, what types of leisure ('leisurescapes': see van der Poel, 1997) are generated by the various social positions (here understood as sets of rights and obligations, particularly with regard to the use of time) people occupy, and why, how and to what extent these sets of rights and obligations change (substantially) over time? Second, how are the various social positions distributed across society, which forces exert an influence on this distribution and how do we expect the distribution will change as a result of the aforementioned societal developments? Third, who decides which (pleasurable) activities are allowed, and which not (see also Rojek, 1995: 173ff)? What rule-systems do exist, what makes these systems change? Fourth, what do the 'free choices' people make in their most 'leisurable' time tell us about the ideals of people, their ideas of happiness, their desires (Corijn, 1998), what it is that makes life worthwhile for them?

Sociology of leisure, cultural studies and leisure studies

It is no point of discussion that leisure is a multifaceted phenomenon, including aspects such as time and space, scarce resources, environmental risks and power relations and leads to questions about meaningfulness, morality, accessibility, emancipation, personal growth and well-being. No single discipline is able to encompass all this and thus there is a need for a plurality of 'leisure studies'. This is not the place to dwell on the question whether this plurality should be understood as an inter-, multi- or transdisciplinary Leisure Studies (see, for example, Corijn 1998; Jackson and Burton, 1999). However, at the end of this chapter there remains the question of what the sociology of leisure and cultural studies contribute to leisure studies, or might or should contribute to this more overarching approach of leisure.

In an attempt to provide an answer to this last question, something else needs discussion before that. Why do we find 'cultural studies' in the title of this chapter? Is there a more close relation between the sociology of leisure and cultural studies than say between cultural studies and the psychology of leisure or leisure history?

Passing over the questions one may raise about the relation between the 'sociology of culture' (or 'cultural sociology'?) and 'cultural studies', one could give two sketches of the relationship between the sociology of leisure and cultural studies. The first sketch portrays this relation as a short-lived intervention of cultural studies in the field of leisure studies during the (early) 1980s, reminding the sociology of leisure of its own roots, potentialities and tasks. Clarke and Critcher's *The Devil Makes Work: Leisure in Capitalist Britain* (1985) is perhaps the most clear, worked-out and explicit example of this intervention. The intervention berated the contemporary sociology of leisure for its uncritical acceptance of capitalism, its lack of theory and overemphasis of quantitative surveys, its unwillingness to discuss power (and class) relations in leisure and the paternalism with regard to non-elite pastimes. After this intervention, both cultural studies and the sociology of leisure went their own separate ways again, with very few sociologists of leisure publishing in journals or handbooks in the field of cultural studies, and vice versa. This is not to say that this intervention left the sociology of leisure unaffected. To some extent the criticisms were accepted and have led to a 're-rooting' and broadening of the scope of and methods and theories used in the sociology of leisure. In this sketch cultural studies have stirred up and enriched the sociology of leisure and thus, indirectly, leisure studies.

The second sketch would portray the intervention in the sociology of leisure as just a side-step in the contribution of cultural studies to the study of leisure. It would show that there is a wealth of research on the use of media, on fashion, music and Madonna, on fandom, soccer and McDonald's; in short, on all aspects of popular culture that is or could be of importance in trying to understand what people do in their free time. Although such a sketch could be made – and perhaps should be made in the next edition of this Handbook – it has to be borne in mind that most of the authors writing on these topics from a cultural studies perspective seldom if ever refer to leisure, and/or do so from a sociological perspective. Of course there are exceptions, such as Willis, who notes:

> There is now a necessity in leisure, the necessary symbolic work of modern cultural survival, of developing identity and connecting its powers actively to the cultural world. (…) In many ways most people's lives are just being awakened after being deadened at work, boxed in, bored or worn out at home. Young people are in the vanguard of seeking pleasure, fun, autonomy and self-direction – and this quest is increasingly focused in and on leisure, in and on the hidden continent of the informal. They seek possibilities there, in their own way, which have formerly been open only in the more glamorous public worlds of artists, writers and the truly 'leisured' classes. (Willis, 1990: 16)

The above quote not only articulates in contemporary vocabulary the received idea that leisure, play and culture are closely linked, it also gives this idea a sense of urgency by underlining that now more than ever it is outside the world of work and the family that identities are developed and given direction. And it also points to the question of – when work and family (and religion!) no longer provide the ideals to strive at, no longer arouse the desires that steer identity building activities – what are the icons, the ideals, the examples, the new objects of desire? If (young) people 'are in the vanguard of seeking … self-direction', what and where are the signposts they use or can use to find the direction themselves? This question obviously can be asked as an ethical question, but it is also an empirical question, open to sociological research. If indeed people seek 'self-direction', then where do they prefer to go and how do they find their way in that direction? What are the signposts? What they see on television or in the movies? What they hear listening to rap or hip hop music? What they read in the newspaper or learn in school? What they experience in their sports team or on the street? What they see from the lives of their parents or today's icons such as David Beckham and Britney Spears?

Both sketches do not mutually exclude each other. Cultural studies intervened in the development of the sociology of leisure as well as made a contribution to leisure studies on their own. This latter contribution focuses on processes of signification in and through leisure, on the meaning people themselves give to their leisure activities, the (explanation of the) differences therein, and the power relations embedded in the language we use to give meaning to what we do. The contribution of the sociology of leisure to leisure studies is found in situating leisure in a continuously changing societal context. It stresses leisure's instantaneous and recursive character in the social relationships that produce and reproduce it. Particularly, the sociology of leisure focuses on the (differences in) the permissibility of activities corresponding to the variety in social positions individuals may occupy. Where do these differences come from, how are they reproduced and how and why do they change in time and space?

Conclusion

Being a multifaceted phenomenon, leisure is difficult to grasp from a single disciplinary perspective. The previous section might suggest that we can develop a more encompassing understanding of leisure when we simply add up the strong points of the various disciplines that have the distinct facets of leisure as their main focus. This was the general idea behind the formation of leisure studies in the 1950s and 1960s, expressing the modern confidence in the growth of society with the help of rational knowledge.

The modern project contained a paradoxical element. If leisure studies had succeeded in understanding *all* determinants of leisure behaviour, would that not have meant that leisure behaviour had become completely predictable and hence 'steerable'? Then who would be steering, and what would this imply for the 'free' character of leisure? Before someone starts worrying about this it has to be conceded that leisure studies have nowhere come close to this goal. (But perhaps marketing has?) Still, it is an intriguing question. Does freedom expand, or does it shrink, the more we know about the influences on what we do? To what extent does this depend on who has access to that knowledge and also, given the necessary complicated nature of that knowledge, who can handle it? Are rule-breaking, resistance, 'transgression' (see, for example, Rojek, 1995) or 'controlled de-controlling' (Elias and Dunning, 1986) examples of 'freedom', and if so, permissible forms of freedom? Is it possible that there is and always will be some 'undetermined' aspect of our behaviour to provide the basis for acting 'freely' (Corijn, 1998)? Or does that idea date back to Berger's 'presociological age' and should we understand freedom and free time not as being defined by the absence of rules, but on the contrary, by their presence, as a product of social relationships by which people are allowed to act freely (Mommaas and van der Poel, 1987)?

What is clear is that the sociology of leisure has to start with understanding how it is that certain parts of daily life are less constrained and filled with necessary activities than others. This is the 'negative idea' of freedom ('freedom of': see Berlin, 1982), but an intriguing one in a time that more and more people in Western countries feel pressed for time and have the feeling that they have not enough time to do everything they want. People have so much 'positive freedoms' ('freedom to') that they cannot choose or are stressed by the choices they make. On societal level the puzzle is why the leisure society does not come about, in spite of the sharp increase in labour productivity. On the level of the organization of daily life the question is what conditions need to be met in order to be able to enjoy leisure. Perhaps we have to be free not only from the constraints and obligations related to the provision for the means to sustain life, but also from most of the desires we are free to pursue in our free time.

Bibliography

Aitchison, C. C. (2003) *Gender and Leisure: Social and Cultural Perspectives*, London and New York, Routledge.

Bauman, Z. (1987) *Legislators and Interpreters: On Modernity, Post-modernity and Intellectuals*, Cambridge, Polity Press.

Bauman, Z. (2001) *The Individualized Society*, Cambridge, Polity Press.

Beck, U. and Willms, J. (2004) *Conversations with Ulrich Beck*, Cambridge, Polity Press.

Beckers, T. and Mommaas, H. (1996) 'The International Perspective in Leisure Research: Cross-National Contacts and Comparisons', in H. Mommaas, H. van der Poel, P. Bramham and I. P. Henry (eds) *Leisure Research in Europe: Methods and Traditions*, Wallingford: CAB International, pp. 209–44.

Berger, B. M. (1963) 'The Sociology of Leisure: Some Suggestions', in E. O. Smigel (ed.) *Work and Leisure: A Contemporary Social Problem*, New Haven, CT, College and University Press, pp. 21–40.

Berlin, I. (1982) *Four Essays on Liberty*, Oxford, Oxford University Press.

Castells, M. (1996–98) *The Information Age: Economy, Society and Culture* (3 vols), Oxford, Blackwell.

Castells, M. (2001) *The Internet Galaxy*, Oxford, Oxford University Press.

Clarke, J. and Critcher C. (1985) *The Devil Makes Work: Leisure in Capitalist Britain*, London, Macmillan.

Corijn, C. (1998) *De onmogelijke geboorte van een wetenschap. Verkenningen in de ontwikkeling van de studie van de vrijetijd*, Brussels, VubPress.

Critcher, C., Bramham, P. and Tomlinson, A. (eds) (1995) *Sociology of Leisure. A Reader*, London, E. & F. N. Spon.

Cross, G. (1993) *Time and Money: The Making of Consumer Culture*, London and New York, Routledge.

Csikszentmihalyi, M. (1990) *Flow: The Psychology of Optimal Experience*, New York, HarperCollins.

Cushman, G., Veal, A. J. and Zuzanek, J. (eds) (1996) *World Leisure Participation: Free Time in the Global Village*, Wallingford, CAB International.

Deem, R. (1986) *All Work and No Play? The Sociology of Women and Leisure*, Milton Keynes, Open University Press.

Dicken, P. (1998) *Global Shift: Transforming the World Economy*, London, Paul Chapman.

Dumazedier, J. (1962) *Vers une civilisation du loisir*, Paris, Le Seuil.

Elias, N. and Dunning, E. (1986) *Quest for Excitement: Sport and Leisure in the Civilising Process*, Oxford, Blackwell.

Florida, R. (2002) *The Rise of the Creative Class: And How it's Transforming Work, Leisure, Community and Everyday Life*, New York, Basic Books.

Fourastié, J. (1965) *Les 40.000 heures: Inventaire de l'avenir*, Paris, Laffont-Ganthiers.

Friedmann, G. (1950) *Ou va le travail humain?* Paris, Gallimard, 1970.

Giddens, A. (1976) *New Rules of Sociological Method*, Cambridge, Polity Press, 1993.

Goldman, R. and Papson, S. (1998) *Nike Culture: The Sign of the Swoosh*, London, Sage.

Gratton, C. and Henry, I. P. (eds) (2001) *Sport in the City: The Role of Sport in the Economic and Social Regeneration*, London and New York, Routledge.

Horna, J. (1994) *The Study of Leisure: An Introduction*, Toronto, Oxford University Press.

Jackson, E. L. and Burton T. L. (eds) (1999) *Leisure Studies: Prospects for the Twenty-First Century*, State College, PA, Venture Publishing.

Jary, D. and Horne, J. (1987) 'The Figurational Sociology of Sport and Leisure of Elias and Dunning and its Alternatives', *Loisir et Société/Society and Leisure* 10(2): 177–94.

Kelly, J. R. (1999) 'Leisure and Society: A Dialectical Analysis', in E. L. Jackson and T. L. Burton (eds) *Leisure Studies: Prospects for the Twenty-First Century*, State College, PA, Venture Publishing, pp. 53–68.

Kurzer, P. (2001) *Markets and Moral Regulation: Cultural Change in the European Union*, Cambridge, Cambridge University Press.

Lanfant, M-F. (1972) *Les théories du loisir*, Paris, Presses Universitaires de France.

Maguire, J. (1999) *Global Sport: Identities, Societies, Civilizations*, Cambridge: Polity Press.

Mommaas, H. (1996) 'The Study of Free Time and Pleasure in the Netherlands: The End of the Legislator', in H. Mommaas, H. van der Poel, P. Bramham and I. P. Henry (eds) *Leisure Research in Europe: Methods and Traditions*, Wallingford, CAB International, pp. 63–106.

Mommaas, H., van der Poel, H., Bramham, P. and Henry, I. (1996a) 'Leisure Research in Europe: Trajectories of Cultural Modernity', in H. Mommaas, H. van der Poel, P. Bramham and I. P. Henry (eds) *Leisure Research in Europe: Methods and Traditions*, Wallingford, CAB International, pp. 245–84.

Mommaas, H., van der Poel, H., Bramham, P. and Henry, I. (eds) (1996b) *Leisure Research in Europe: Methods and Traditions*, Wallingford, CAB International.

Mommaas, H. and van der Poel, H. (1987) 'New Perspectives on Theorizing Leisure', *Loisir et Société/Society and Leisure* 10(2): 161–76.

Nahrstedt, W. (1972) *Die Entstehung der Freizeit*, Göttingen, Vandenhoeck & Ruprecht.

Parker, S. (1976) *The Sociology of Leisure*, London, George Allen & Unwin.

Parry, N. C. A. (1983) 'Sociological Contributions to the Study of Leisure', *Leisure Studies* 2(1): 57–81.

Pentland, W. E., Harvey, A. S., Lawton, M. P. and McColl, M. A. (eds) (1999) *Time Use Research in the Social Sciences*, New York, Kluwer Academic/Plenum Publishers.

Pine, B. J. and Gilmore, J. H. (1999) *The Experience Economy*, Boston, Harvard Business School Press.

Rifkin, J. (2000) *The Age of Access: How the Shift from Ownership to Access is Transforming Modern Life*, London, Penguin.

Ritzer, G. (2004) *The Globalization of Nothing*, Thousand Oaks, CA, Pine Forge Press.

Roberts, K. (1970) *Leisure*, London, Longman.

Roberts, K. (1978) *Contemporary Society and the Growth of Leisure*, London, Longman.

Roberts, K. (1999) *Leisure in Contemporary Society*, Wallingford, CAB International.

Robinson, J. P. and Godbey, G. (1997) *Time for Life: The Surprising Ways Americans Use Their Time*, University Park, PA, Pennsylvania State University Press.

Rojek, C. (1985) *Capitalism and Leisure Theory*, London, Tavistock.

Rojek, C. (1995) *Decentring Leisure: Rethinking Leisure Theory*, London, Sage.

Shapiro, C. and Varian, H. R. (1999) *Information Rules: A Strategic Guide to the Network Economy*, Boston, Harvard Business School Press.

Szalaï, A. (ed.) (1972) *The Use of Time: Daily Activities of Urban and Suburban Populations in Twelve Countries*, The Hague, Mouton.

van der Poel, H. (1997) 'Leisure and the Modularization of Daily Life', *Time & Society* 6(2/3): 171–94.

van Moorst, H. (1982) 'Leisure and Social Theory', *Leisure Studies* 1(2): 157–69.

Ward, S. V. (1998) *Selling Places: The Marketing and Promotion of Towns and Cities 1850–2000*, London, E. & F. N. Spon.

Willis, P. (1990) *Common Culture: Symbolic Work at Play in the Everyday Cultures of the Young*, Milton Keynes, Open University Press.

Wippler, R. (1968) *Sociale determinanten van het vrijetijdsgedrag*, Assen, van Gorcum.

Wolf, M. J. (1999) *The Entertainment Economy: How Mega-media Forces are Transforming Our Lives*, London, Penguin.

7

Psychology and Social Psychology and the Study of Leisure

Roger C. Mannell, Douglas A. Kleiber and Marianne Staempfli

Various social science traditions have influenced theory and research on leisure. In this chapter, we describe psychological perspectives, and these perspectives are primarily those of social psychology with some influences from personality and developmental psychology. Advocates of the development of a social psychology of leisure have generally championed post-positivist *psychological* social psychological approaches, but interpretive or constructionist *sociological* social psychologies have contributed as well. These influences are discussed along with other factors that have shaped the social psychological tradition in leisure studies. The frequent claim that leisure research, particularly North American research, is predominantly psychological is also examined. Though clearly focused on individual-level phenomena, we question whether it is substantially grounded in psychological epistemology, methodology and theory. The future of psychological approaches to the study of leisure is explored, including the cross-cultural and international diversity of efforts to understand leisure from social psychological perspectives. We find little evidence that indigenous social psychologies of leisure have emerged in other cultural contexts. However, there are promising social psychological efforts emerging to explore and explain cross-cultural differences and similarities in leisure behaviour and experience. Finally, the growth of interest in leisure as a psychological variable outside of leisure studies and implications for the future are discussed.

Leisure services and the focus on individual leisure experience and behaviour

In North America during the past three or four decades, there has been growing interest in the use of psychological, particularly *social psychological*, theory and research methods for understanding leisure. There seems to have been less enthusiasm in other jurisdictions. Consistent with the social psychological approach in the field of psychology, the focus has been on the *leisure experience and behaviour of the individual*. Consistent with this perspective, researchers have looked to two sources for explanations. Leisure behaviour and experience are seen to be a function of the interplay of *internal psychological dispositions* (for example, perceptions, feelings, emotions, beliefs, attitudes, needs, personality) and *situational influences* that are part of the immediate social environment (for example, other people, group norms, human artefacts, media).

Advocates of a social psychology of leisure have been primarily North American (see Neulinger, 1974, 1981; Iso-Ahola, 1980a; Mannell and Kleiber, 1997) and to a lesser extent British (see Haworth, 1979; Ingham, 1986, 1987; Argyle, 1996). Also, leisure researchers from Australia and New Zealand have made significant contributions to specific areas of enquiry such as leisure and health (for example, Coleman, 1993). The adoption of social psychological approaches has been influenced by the view that leisure is both a highly individual experience while at the same time typically engaged in with other people, and that it is linked in a very significant way to psychological health. In North America, the social psychological approach has also come to be favoured because of the 'professionalization' of leisure services as a helping profession that deals with the leisure problems of individuals as well as the enhancement of individual leisure, lifestyle and health. Consequently, leisure studies and the development of a social psychology of leisure in North America has been strongly influenced by an overriding concern by many researchers for generating knowledge for those who plan, manage and provide recreation and leisure interventions and services for individuals (Mannell, 1984; Ingham, 1986). This concern has been reinforced by the location of leisure studies in university parks and recreation departments that have a primary role in educating and training students to become practitioners (Burdge, 1991).

Identifying the boundaries and terrain of a social psychology of leisure

One of the major challenges in providing an overview of the social psychology of leisure is distinguishing what actually constitutes this subfield of leisure studies, that is, where to draw the boundaries for the area of enquiry and whose work to include. The social psychology of leisure is not a recognized subfield of either psychology or sociology; it is the offspring of leisure studies itself. Scholars in leisure studies whose work could be considered psychological or social psychological might not label it as such themselves, and much of the individual-level research found in leisure studies is not psychological or social psychological based on the theory and research methods employed.

Kuhn (1962) argued that the textbooks used in the education of new scholars provide a blueprint for the way in which a field sees itself. Four books, if we count Neulinger's first and second editions as one, have been published and provide varying descriptions of the psychology and social psychology of leisure as a field of study – *The Psychology of Leisure* (Neulinger, 1974, 1981), *The Social Psychology of Leisure and Recreation* (Iso-Ahola, 1980a), *The Social Psychology of Leisure*

(Argyle, 1996) and *A Social Psychology of Leisure* (Mannell and Kleiber, 1997). It is apparent that the social psychology of leisure continues to be a work in progress and that there are significant gaps in knowledge that the authors bridge with mainstream social psychological theory and research that is untested in leisure contexts. Also, the stories told by these books about the social psychology of leisure are predominantly based on both the tenets and theories of *psychological* social psychology and its primarily post-positivist epistemology and characteristic use of quantitative methodologies. This characteristic is not too surprising given that all of the authors were educated in the psychological tradition, and with the exception of Argyle, a British psychologist, are North American. Though the psychological approach has stimulated a considerable amount of informative research, it would be inaccurate to characterize the social psychological theory and research on leisure as being homogeneously post-positivist and psychological. Mannell and Kleiber noted that 'there are, however, social psychologies that are qualitative and interpretive ... and recently leisure research from these perspectives has been increasing ... [and] ... we have ... drawn on qualitative leisure research in this book' (Mannell and Kleiber, 1997: 28).

Psychological and sociological social psychologies and the study of leisure

Psychology as a scientific field of study emerged in the last quarter of the nineteenth century and had its roots in Western Europe and North America. Psychology is the science of mental processes and behaviour and their interaction with the environment, and psychologists study the processes of sense perception, thinking, learning, cognition, emotions and motivations, personality, abnormal behaviour, interactions between individuals, and interactions with the environment. The field is allied with the physical sciences in the study of perception and brain-behaviour relationships and anthropology and sociology in the study of social influences on behaviour. Social psychology emerged out of this latter 'alliance'. Triplett (1897–98) published the first research article in social psychology at the end of the nineteenth century. Interestingly, the recreational and sporting activity of cycling was the subject of this first published social psychological study though the focus was on the performance of the rider rather than the experience or meaning of the activity. Given that social psychology is located at the peripheries and intersection of the fields of psychology and sociology, it also has a sociological counterpart. Broadly speaking, sociologists devote their efforts to understanding social phenomena that have effects on individuals and psychologists specialize in identifying the mechanisms or mental processes through which social phenomena have their effects (Thoits, 1995).

From a psychological perspective, social psychologists attempt to understand how the actual, imagined, or implied presence of others influences the thoughts, feelings and behaviours of individuals (Allport, 1968) and this approach has been called 'psychological social psychology' (Stryker, 1997). While there are advocates in the psychological community for the development of a constructionist social psychology (for example, Gergen, 1999), mainstream *psychological* social psychology has been and continues to be primarily post-positivist and concerned with individuals' perceptions or construal of their social environment, recognizing that individuals can misperceive social and physical realities and that it is these perceptions, mistaken or not, that influence behaviour and experience (Ross and Nisbett, 1991). Experimental and quasi-experimental research designs are widely used by psychological researchers though other field research methods have grown in popularity during the past 25 years. Many leisure researchers have adopted the epistemology but only rarely used the research methods and contemporary theories.

Psychological social psychology is considered a cognitive science and various theories have passed in and out of popularity. Theories about *attitudes and attitude change* were developed and tested in the 1950s. In the 1960s *consistency or balance* theories dominated. They were developed to explain when inconsistencies among a person's cognitions (that is, beliefs, attitudes and values) or between cognitions and actions would motivate her or him to change either beliefs or behaviour. *Attribution* theory emerged in the 1970s and helps explain the kinds of causal explanations people give for the events they encounter and the effects these inferences have on their social behaviour. Beginning in the late 1970s and continuing to the present, *social cognition*, the study of how we perceive, remember and interpret information about ourselves and others, has proven very influential.

Sociological social psychology includes research on social structure and personality, small groups research and symbolic interactionism (Thoits, 1995). In the first two social psychologies, post-positivist approaches are common. Interpretivist or constructionist perspectives such as symbolic interactionism and phenomenology, which have much in common, and grounded theory, which evolved from symbolic interactionism (Robrecht, 1995), have been the sociological social psychological approaches most commonly adopted in the study of leisure. For example, with symbolic interactionism, the ways in which people define reality, and how beliefs are related to actions are explored. Reality is viewed as being created by people through attaching meaning to situations. These meanings are expressed by symbols such as words, objects and events, and these symbolic meanings are the basis for actions and interactions. Symbolic meanings are different for each individual, though through these they may be shared by groups and transferred to new members by socialization (Fine, 1993). Most interactionists advocate the systematic collection of data, whether through in-depth interviewing, ethnography or introspection.

The two social psychologies often seem to exist as two solitudes, divided more by their different epistemological assumptions than the aspects of human social behaviour in which their practitioners are interested (Matalon, 1999). Factors such as disciplinary egocentrism and institutional barriers have also limited communication between psychological and sociological social psychologies (see Stephan et al., 1991). However, in leisure studies, the two social psychologies appear to co-exist reasonably well.

Treatment of leisure in social psychology

As noted earlier, the social psychology of leisure does not exist as a subfield in either the discipline of psychology or sociology. In fact, leisure has all but been ignored by social psychologists in the field of *psychology* during the past 100 years (Mannell and Kleiber, 1997). A few exceptions exist. For example, Allport (1924) in his book on social psychology argued that leisure serves as a form of need compensation – compensation for oppressive work. Also, leisure settings have provided useful testing grounds for studies of basic social psychological processes. Sherif et al. (1961) carried out a number of studies in the leisure setting of children's summer camps to study general social psychological principles dealing with the role of group membership on the development of leadership and stereotypes. The first major study of intrinsic motivation and the factors that undermine it, involved studying children playing with magic markers in a 'playroom' (Lepper et al., 1973). Diener et al. (1984) serendipitously found that people's personalities were more likely to influence their behaviour and experience in settings characterized by opportunities for free choice. Extroverts were more likely to choose social activities and introverts solitary activities in recreational situations than they were in work settings. These types of studies, however, were not carried out to further our knowledge of leisure behaviour *per se*.

There has been some limited interest in leisure phenomena by *sociological* social psychologists, particularly those espousing symbolic interactionist and grounded theory perspectives. Like psychologists, sociological researchers have typically been interested in more basic social psychological phenomena such as social roles, self-presentation and socialization. However, this research has provided rich detail about specific leisure activities and the groups of individuals who participate in them. For example, in his classic study, *Street Corner Society*, William Foote White (1943) 'hung out' with a gang of young Italian men as a participant observer and made many of his observations during the gang's free-time activities. From among these observations, he noted that group structure and status in the gang influenced leisure behaviour. On several occasions, he observed that when the members of the gang bowled competitively against one another, their scores matched their structural positions in the gang regardless of their actual bowling skills and, in turn, their bowling scores reinforced and maintained their gang status. The research and theorizing of Gary Alan Fine is another example of symbolic interactionism or sociological social psychological research on leisure. Following extensive fieldwork involving participant observation and informal interviews, Fine (1987) published a fascinating account of a group of pre-adolescents playing summer Little League baseball and the shared meanings they developed about girls, morality and adult control in their lives. He also studied a group of older youth who developed a subculture around role-playing fantasy games such as Dungeons and Dragons (Fine, 1983). The extensive research on amateurs and the rewards and costs of engagement in various types of serious leisure by sociologist Robert Stebbins (2001) is another good example of this type of sociological social psychology.

Development of a social psychology of leisure in leisure studies

From the mid-1960s to the early 1970s research studies using psychological social psychological concepts began to appear in the North American leisure studies literature. However, little formal psychological thinking about leisure was occurring elsewhere. European leisure studies was and continues to be predominantly sociological. In 1979, John Haworth, a British psychologist, argued for the need to develop a better understanding of the role of the individual as an active agent in creating his or her 'existence and future' within the 'leisure sphere' (Haworth, 1979: 53). He appeared to be reacting to what he saw as a preference for sociological analysis and 'structural-functionalist models emphasising the importance of institutional and societal forces' (ibid.) for understanding leisure behaviour. A later review of psychological contributions to the study of leisure by another British psychologist (Ingham, 1986, 1987) suggests that 'the major thrust of psychological contributions to the study of leisure has come from the United States' and that 'few psychologists in the United Kingdom profess to an interest' (Ingham, 1986: 256). He notes, however, that the little psychological attention given to leisure was social psychological and would likely evolve to increasingly 'overlap with micro-level approaches within sociology (ibid.: 255–6).

Systematic efforts to develop a psychological social psychology of leisure as a distinct field began in North America in the mid to late 1970s. Of the social sciences, sociology had been the major contributor internationally of both theory and research on the role and nature of leisure in modern industrial society. The recognition of the importance of person factors and the immediate social context in understanding leisure can be found in the writings of a number of early leisure scholars. Many texts and influential writings on leisure speculated about the psychological effects of leisure on the individual, in particular personality development (see Iso-Ahola, 1980a). However, though leisure philosophers and writers acknowledged the importance of social psychological variables, little theory development and research were carried out.

Some of the earliest empirical work that can be labelled psychological or social psychological was done by researchers in the United States interested in understanding why people participate in outdoor recreation and interest in studying motivation emerged in the 1960s, blossomed in the 1970s, and continues to flourish today along with issues of crowding, activity specialization and development of a sense of place (see Manning, 1999). The founding of the *Journal of Leisure Research* in 1969 gave an important push to the development of the social psychology of leisure. Although it was not exclusively psychologically oriented, the journal did provide an outlet for early contributions in this area (Iso-Ahola, 1995). This published research on leisure incorporated such psychological social psychological concepts as attitudes, motivation and satisfaction, social contextual influences and moods.

In the 1970s, a more systematic social psychological foundation was developed for outdoor recreation motivational research with the goal being to ultimately improve management strategies. A psychological approach was proposed where recreation was defined as 'an experience that results from recreation engagements' (Driver and Tocher, 1970: 10). An expectancy-valence approach to motivation, an approach also found in psychological analyses of work behaviour, served as a theoretical basis for this research. Neulinger (1974) also argued for the importance of psychological theory and methods for understanding the subjective nature of leisure but he was more concerned with its implications for quality of life. He felt that social psychological concepts such as *locus of control, perceived freedom and intrinsic motivation* might prove useful for understanding leisure. He also advocated a 'person–environment' interaction approach (Neulinger, 1974: 110), and for the use of laboratory experiments (ibid.: 132–3). Many of these suggestions were subsequently picked up and explored by leisure researchers working in the psychological tradition. In 1978, the first Psychology/Social Psychology of Leisure Research Session was held at the annual conference of the US-based National Recreation and Parks Association. This session has since become a major gathering place for researchers working in the social psychology of leisure area. Also, other sessions such as management and therapeutic recreation have become 'psychologized' with the frequent reporting of studies focusing on social psychological variables (Iso-Ahola, 1995).

In addition to the four books on the social psychology of leisure mentioned earlier and the steady increase of psychologically-oriented research published in journals such as *Leisure Sciences, Society and Leisure*, and *Leisure Studies*, a great deal of social psychological leisure theory and research has been published in books and special journal issues. In 1980, two books on the psychology and social psychology of leisure were published (Iso-Ahola, 1980b; Ibrahim and Crandall, 1980). Ouellet (1984) edited a special issue of the journal *Society and Leisure* on selected psychological and social psychological topics. Most of the chapters in Wade's (1985) book, *Constraints on Leisure*, were social psychological analyses of leisure, as were many of those in Jackson and Burton's 1989 and 1999 books. The major journals in the field of leisure studies continue to publish special issues dealing with benefits, constraints, ethnicity, discrimination, family and health, and much of this work has a social psychological focus.

Today research on leisure motivation and satisfaction continues in the outdoor recreation and resource management area and has been applied to many other types of leisure behaviour (see Manning, 1999; Mannell, 1999). While survey research methods continue to be overused, some researchers have employed laboratory, field and quasi-experiments, and others have used modified time diaries, the experiential sampling method, single-subject designs and visual methods that have led to advances in our ability to conceptualize, measure and examine leisure experience and behaviour from a psychological perspective. Individual and personality differences in leisure behaviour were barely addressed in the early years with a few exceptions but with the development of leisure-specific personality constructs such as intrinsic leisure motivation, leisure boredom and the self-as-entertainment orientation, it has become an active area of study. Early interest in measuring leisure attitudes cooled, and resurfaced in the early 1990s with an interest in how to influence and change leisure attitudes (Mannell and Kleiber, 1997). Interest in leisure socialization and the influence of lifecycle changes on leisure (and vice versa) have continued to grow (Kleiber, 1999) and greater attention is starting to be given to the role of leisure in childhood and adolescent development (Hutchinson et al., 2003a). The concern about the relationship between work and leisure has evolved beyond examining the impact of work on leisure, and now research is being done on how people organize and balance the work, leisure and family domains of their lives as well as the influence of leisure on work and job satisfaction (Mannell and Reid, 1999).

There has also been a substantial growth of research on gender and leisure in the past decade (Henderson et al., 2002), and an interest in the socio-cultural and cross-cultural dimensions of leisure and ethnicity as they affect leisure is starting to mature (Stodolska and Yi, 2003; Walker et al., 2005). Early interest in the role of leisure in health has become a major area for leisure theory development (Iwasaki and Mannell, 2000; Kleiber et al., 2002) as has the impact of life events such as caregiving (Dupuis, 2000) and disability (Hutchinson et al., 2003b) on leisure and health.

In North American leisure studies, frameworks such as *leisure benefits* (Driver and Bruns, 1999) and *leisure constraints* (Jackson, 2005) have provided a means of organizing thinking about whole areas of social psychological research as they apply to leisure services. In the case of constraints research, the focus of the research has expanded to include the identification of factors that encourage leisure involvement (that is, affordances and facilitators) and the negotiation strategies employed by people to overcome constraints. Constraints models are becoming more *social cognitive* and the psychological mechanisms of negotiation and motivation are being tested with more sophisticated statistical modelling approaches. Interpretive social psychological approaches have been useful in identifying the meanings and context of constraints (see Jackson, 2005).

An increasing number of leisure researchers have utilized interpretive sociological social psychological approaches and there appears to be wide acceptance of their use (Weissinger et al., 1997). Theory and research emerging from this perspective have added insights in traditional areas of enquiry and expanded the areas of interest to include research on the leisure behaviour and experience of individuals in the context of women's health (Parry and Shinew, 2004), romantic relationships (Herridge et al., 2003), resistance and empowerment (Green, 1998) and body image and identity (Frederick and Shaw, 1995).

Social psychology of leisure as an international field of study

Based on our discussion of the psychology and social psychology of leisure thus far, most references to early contributions to this subfield are primarily North American and to a lesser extent British. To what extent has the social psychological study of leisure become an international enterprise? There are several ways to look at this issue. Debates within the mainstream of American social psychology itself, what we have been calling psychological social psychology, are instructive. Over half a century ago, after the Second World War, there began what has been called an American 'colonization' of Western European social psychology and its influence has spread to many other countries as their scholars have become interested in studying social influences on individual behaviour (van Strien, 1997). The sheer volume of American research has been almost overwhelming and the primary theories and approaches used have been American. This globalization of social psychology within the discipline of psychology is reflected by an increasing proportion of authors from outside the United States publishing in the premier US journals (Quiñones-

Vidal et al., 2004). However, there has been some recent interest in the extent to which different regions or localities are developing their own indigenous social psychologies that reflect their values and traditions. Some analysts have suggested that a 'decolonization' has been occurring that involves an effort to achieve a cross-fertilization of American and non-American perspectives. There have been substantial efforts to make social psychology texts relevant outside of North America in Britain, Europe and Australia by including data from these countries (Demitrakis, 1997; Vaughan and Hogg, 1995) though it is not clear that this strategy has led to new perspectives or theories. There has been some advocacy for the development of indigenous social psychologies. For example, in a recent volume, the simple transference of social psychological ideas and research findings from the American-European to Asian contexts is questioned (Yang et al., 2003). There appears to be growing recognition that the development of indigenous social psychologies might help researchers identify cultural bias and better adapt social psychology to the international and multicultural community. For example, Sinha (2003) suggests that the field of social psychology in India is moving toward indigenization by integrating ancient Indian wisdom and more contemporary folkways with the Western psychological tradition, which may contribute to a better understanding of Indian realities. He argues that the international community of social psychologists (psychological) can facilitate this integration by being constructive in its critique of the process. However, at the present time, there would appear to be no recognized coherent and well-articulated indigenous psychological social psychologies, nor have these developments influenced mainstream social psychology. While the nature of constructionist sociological social psychological research is such that it is less likely to inhibit the emergence of unique local social psychological perspectives, Cook (2000) suggests that sociological social psychologies have not addressed the challenge of becoming more cross-cultural.

With respect to the social psychology of leisure, there is very little evidence that alternative indigenous non-Western leisure social psychologies are emerging at the present time, either psychological or sociological. However, some interest is being shown in the psychological study of leisure by scholars in other countries where the tradition has not previously been established. For example, Murray and Nakajima (1999) and Santos et al. (2003) have adapted standardized measures of leisure motivation and leisure stress coping developed by North American researchers for use in Japan and Portugal respectively. Also, Mannell and Kleiber's (1997) book on the social psychology of leisure was translated into Japanese in 2004.

Cross-cultural social psychological explanations of leisure

A related issue is the extent to which there is a comprehensive social psychology of cultural differences in leisure. In a 1997 review of the social psychology of leisure literature, we concluded that there were no such developments (Mannell and Kleiber, 1997, p. 27). This state of affairs was not surprising. Theory and research in the field of cross-cultural social psychology, itself, has until quite recently remained on the periphery of mainstream social psychology (Matsumoto, 2000), and this is certainly the case in the study of leisure. However, the contributions of cross-cultural social psychological analysis are gaining in recognition in mainstream social psychology and this type of thinking is making its way into the field of leisure studies (Mannell, 2005). In a recent article, Walker et al. (2005) provide an example of how a central social psychologically-based leisure construct, intrinsic motivation, might operate as a basic psychological process across cultures but affect experiential and behavioural outcomes, including leisure, differently depending on cultural context.

Though there has been a steady increase in interest in the ethnic and cultural dimensions of leisure in the last decade, until recently research has been largely descriptive of differences among various cultural, ethnic and racial groups (Floyd, 1998). Researchers have focused on identifying differences in leisure constraints, meanings, needs and motives, preferences, and behaviours, and how these vary according to the recreational setting. Though some theory has been developed and tested to explain and predict these differences in leisure behaviour, basic research on the actual social psychological mechanisms underlying ethnic and cultural differences in leisure remains to be done (Hutchison, 2000). Walker et al. (2005) illustrate how cross-cultural analysis can be used to acquire a detailed picture of not only how but why the meaning of leisure and people's reaction to it might differ from one culture to another. This development is significant for two reasons. First, it is important to move beyond a description of differences to an understanding of why these differences exist. Second, this type of analysis and research is a way of determining the extent to which various social psychological processes, including those involved in leisure, are culturally universal or culturally relative. Ultimately, researchers need to go beyond the surface of cultural differences in leisure behaviour and vigorously examine the cultural factors that produce them.

'Leisure' as a social psychological variable outside of leisure studies

As we noted earlier in this chapter, historically, leisure-related phenomena have been incorporated from time to time as 'variables' or 'contexts' in social psychological studies by researchers outside of leisure studies, that is, those who have primary allegiance to other fields of study. There are also several areas of study in which researchers have traditionally shown more interest in leisure. In gerontology and fields concerned with persons with disabilities, leisure has been examined as an important lifestyle influence and as an explanatory factor in successful ageing or coping and life satisfaction. More recently 'non-leisure' psychological researchers interested in adolescence have shown substantial interest in the role of leisure in socialization, developmental processes, participation in risky behaviours and health (for example, Hansen et al., 2003).

In addition to these areas of enquiry, a perusal of the social science literature of the last decade suggests that there is a modestly growing interest in leisure-related phenomena among psychologically-oriented researchers outside of leisure studies. Many studies have been reported in which some aspect of leisure, usually participation, is incorporated as an independent or dependent variable. Not withstanding this development, there is little evidence of interest in leisure as a phenomenon in and of itself; however, there appears to be a growing recognition that leisure-related phenomena are important for understanding other behavioural and experiential phenomena of interest to researchers. Researchers, who have included leisure as a variable in their studies, show varying degrees of awareness of the leisure studies literature, particularly the social psychology of leisure literature. Some draw extensively on it and others not at all. Samdahl and Kelly (1999) completed a citation analysis of the *Journal of Leisure Research* and *Leisure Sciences* and found that sources outside of leisure studies seldom cited articles from these journals. Conversely, leisure researchers publishing in these journals rarely cited outside sources. The authors concluded that these major leisure research journals were intellectually isolated from important and relevant bodies of literature.

This neglect of outside research by researchers in leisure studies may in part be related to the extent to which leisure is treated as a meaningful and central construct in these other research literatures. In many cases, leisure is simply one of a number of behavioural or attitudinal dimensions examined, often as a dependent variable, or it serves only as a convenient context or setting for the study. There are, however, a few social psychologists outside of leisure studies who have developed 'leisure theory'. For example, Aron and Aron (1986) have developed the *leisure expansion theory of marital satisfaction*. The theory is based on the idea that marital satisfaction will be enhanced by leisure participation only when the partners engage in joint activities that are 'expanding', that is, activities that are exciting and stimulating and lead to mutual personal and relationship growth. This type of development is all too rare.

A final note

The social psychology of leisure is not recognized as a distinct subfield in either the fields of psychology or sociology. It is a child of leisure studies. In spite of a growing body of literature, the maturing of theory and research in some areas, and the increase in the number of issues being addressed by researchers, the social psychology of leisure is an immature field of study. Though it appears that leisure as a phenomenon is being discovered by researchers in mainstream disciplines as well as other multidisciplinary fields, this research is scattered and the findings are not cumulative, nor likely to coalesce into a coherent body of knowledge in the near future. Consequently, neither leisure researchers nor researchers from other fields who use leisure as a 'variable' in their research are benefiting from the increased interest among social scientists in leisure as a psychological and social psychological phenomenon.

Much of the quantitative and post-positivist research that has been reported on individual leisure behaviour is not truly social psychological from any disciplinary perspective in terms of the use of psychological paradigms, theory and research methods. Much of the social science done in leisure studies has been descriptive and based on survey research with little theoretical or methodological foundation in any particular type of social psychology. Much of the individual-level published research is social psychological in only the most rudimentary sense. Though the collection of data on attitudes, needs and satisfactions has been common, and these psychological phenomena have their beginnings in the individual's interactions with his or her social environment, their use by leisure researchers typically provides few insights for explaining how the underlying social psychological processes involved actually work.

There is also a continuing reluctance by social psychological leisure researchers to use the full range of methods available – on the one hand, psychologically oriented research continues to rely too much on survey research methods and avoid other methods that have proven useful to inquiry such as laboratory and field experiments, activity logs, time diaries, and the experiential sampling method. On the other, those researchers using sociological interpretive social psychological approaches have relied almost exclusively on the semistructured interview and very little research has been reported using participant observation, case studies, ethnography and other qualitative methods. There is still a serious lack of use and application of social psychological theory to develop research questions and explanations that probe beyond the surface of leisure-related phenomena. Finally, little social psychological research on leisure has been reported in countries other than the United States, Britain, Australia and New Zealand and there is little evidence that social psychologies indigenous to non-Western cultures are emerging.

The psychology and social psychology of leisure as a field of study has often been caught in the cross-fire of debates about the field of leisure studies itself being too focused on individual-level analysis, too positivist, and not sufficiently critical of the status quo. There appears to be a general consensus in leisure studies that psychological and social psychological approaches to the study of leisure have come to dominate and that there is a need to reinstate the more macro-level social sciences such as sociology, economics, political science and cultural studies. There have been periodic calls to study social structural factors such as social class, gender and race as they influence leisure behaviour and experience and the social contexts in which they occur. There have also been suggestions that analyses be undertaken to better articulate the interplay between structure and agency by linking an understanding of the individual with macro-sociological, economic and political processes. Sociological social psychologies such as symbolic interactionism have been more interested in this link and the agency–structure dynamic. For example, Denzin suggested that symbolic 'interactionism is both a theory of experience and a theory of social structure' (Denzin, 1992: 2). Only a few psychological social psychologists have been concerned with this issue (for example, Ross and Nisbett, 1991) and it is rarely an issue in analyses and discussions of leisure by psychologically-oriented leisure researchers.

Associated with this criticism is the assertion that contemporary social psychological research on leisure is too positivist and conservative in its goal of establishing knowledge about various aspects of the social world, and not enough attention is given to critical analysis and normative social science with a concern about how things 'ought to be' (for example, Coalter, 1999; Hemingway, 1999). This state of affairs may in part be a result of the strong link, at least in North America, between recreation practice and services, and leisure studies. Practitioners have not typically seen themselves as agents of social or political change and, consequently, have been rather uncritical of social, economical and political issues as they relate to social structural influences on leisure (Reid, 1995).

While these types of concerns and criticisms may be justified, they are not criticisms of psychological approaches to the study of leisure *per se*. They are criticisms of the field of leisure studies as a whole and suggest that other approaches need to be valued and applied by leisure scholars. The psychological enterprise has useful insights to contribute but approaches that consider more macro- or societal-level factors need to be pursued as well. For example, the question of how a society can reorganize its economy and sociopolitical institutions to better deal with the growth of automation, 'forced' leisure and the asynchronous work schedules in families requires sociological, political and economic analyses. This concern does not invalidate the social psychological approach. It should remind us, however, that many of the factors that influence our attitudes, needs and beliefs as well as the social situations we encounter during the course of our daily lives are themselves influenced by broader social, political and economic forces – forces that require the perspectives of other social sciences if they are to be better understood.

The psychological study of leisure is primarily social psychological and includes post-positivist psychological and constructionist sociological social psychological approaches. This pluralism appears to be healthy and researchers using these perspectives often study similar phenomena resulting in a profitable cross-fertilization of insights and understanding. For example, multiple perspectives and mixed methods have been particularly valuable in the development of theory and research on leisure constraints. As well, there has been substantial growth in studies of gender and, in particular, the discovery of differences in the meaning of leisure for women and its potential role in resisting cultural stereotypes and constraints on various aspects of life. Researchers are also giving more attention to ethnic and cultural diversity in leisure behaviour and experience and are moving beyond simple descriptions of differences and similarities to developing improved understanding and explanations. The growth in the use of mainstream social psychological constructs, theory and sensitizing concepts, though modest, and the development of some social psychological theory indigenous to leisure studies itself, is encouraging.

Bibliography

Allport, F. H. (1924) *Social Psychology*, Boston, MA, Houghton Mifflin.

Allport, G. W. (1968) *The Person in Psychology: Selected Essays*, Boston, MA, Beacon Press.

Argyle, M. (1996) *The Social Psychology of Leisure*, London, Penguin Books.

Aron, A. and Aron, E. N. (1986) *Love and the Expansion of Self: Understanding Attraction and Satisfaction*, New York, Hemisphere.

Burdge, R. J. (1991) 'Leisure Research and Park and Recreation Education: Compatible or Not?', in T. L. Goodale and P. A. Witt (eds), *Issues in an Era of Change* (3rd edn), State College, PA, Venture Publishing, pp. 359–66.

Coalter, F. (1999) 'Leisure Sciences and Leisure Studies: The Challenge of Meaning', in E. L. Jackson and T. L. Burton (eds) *Leisure Studies: Prospects for the Twenty-first Century*, State College, PA, Venture Publishing, pp. 507–19.

Coleman, D. (1993) 'Leisure Based Social Support, Leisure Dispositions and Health', *Journal of Leisure Research* 25: 350–61.

Cook, K. S. (2000), 'Advances in the Microfoundations of Sociology: Recent Developments and New Challenges for Social Psychology', *Contemporary Sociology* 29(5): 685–92.

Demitrakis, K. M. (1997) 'Social Psychology: Different Perspectives and Presentations', *Contemporary Psychology* 42: 896–7.

Denzin, N. K. (1992) *Symbolic Interactionism and Cultural Studies: The Politics of Interpretation*, Oxford, Blackwell.

Diener, E., Larsen, R. J. and Emmons, R. A. (1984) 'Person X Situation Interactions: Choice of Situations and Congruence Response Models', *Journal of Personality and Social Psychology* 47: 580–92.

Driver, B. L. and Bruns, D. H. (1999) 'Concepts and Uses of the Benefits Approach to Leisure', in E. L. Jackson and T. L. Burton (eds) *Leisure Studies: Prospects for the Twenty-first Century*, State College, PA, Venture Publishing, pp. 349–69.

Driver, B. L. and Tocher, S. R. (1970) 'Toward a Behavioral Interpretation of Recreational Engagements, with Implications for Planning', in B. L. Driver (ed.) *Elements of Outdoor Recreation Planning*, Ann Arbor, MI, University of Michigan Press, pp. 9–31.

Dupuis, S. (2000) 'Institution-based Caregiving as a Container for Leisure', *Leisure Sciences* 22: 259–80.

Fine, G. A. (1983) *Shared Fantasy*, Chicago, IL, University of Chicago Press.

Fine, G. A. (1987) *With the Boys*, Chicago, IL, University of Chicago Press.

Fine, G. A. (1993) 'The Sad Demise, Mysterious Disappearance, and Glorious Triumph of Symbolic Interactionism', *Annual Review of Sociology* 19: 61–87.

Floyd, M. F. (1998) 'Getting Beyond Marginality and Ethnicity: The Challenge for Race and Ethnic Studies in Leisure Research', *Journal of Leisure Research* 30: 3–22.

Foote White, W. (1943) *Street Corner Society*, Chicago, IL, University of Chicago Press.

Frederick, C. J. and Shaw, S. M. (1995) 'Body Image as a Leisure Constraint: Examining the Experience of Aerobic Exercise Classes for Young Women', *Leisure Sciences* 17: 57–73.

Gergen, K. (1999) *An Invitation to Social Construction*, Thousand Oaks, CA, Sage.

Green, F. (1998) '"Women Doing Friendship": An Analysis of Women's Leisure as a Site of Identity Construction, Empowerment and Resistance', *Leisure Studies* 17: 171–85.

Hansen, D. M., Larson, R. W. and Dworkin, J. B. (2003) 'What Adolescents Learn in Organized Youth Activities: A Survey of Self-Reported Developmental Experiences', *Journal of Research on Adolescence* 13: 25–55.

Haworth, J. T. (1979) 'Leisure and the Individual', *Society and Leisure* 1: 53–61.

Hemingway, J. L. (1999) 'Critique and Emancipation: Toward a Critical Theory of Leisure', in E. L. Jackson and T. L. Burton (eds) *Leisure Studies: Prospects for the Twenty-first Century*, State College, PA, Venture Publishing, pp. 487–506.

Henderson, K. A., Hodges, S. and Kivel, B. D. (2002) 'Context and Dialogue in Research on Women and Leisure', *Journal of Leisure Research* 34: 253–71.

Herridge, K. L., Shaw, S. M. and Mannell, R. C. (2003) 'An Exploration of Women's Leisure Within Heterosexual Romantic Relationships', *Journal of Leisure Research* 35: 274–91.

Hutchison, R. (2000) 'Race and Ethnicity in Leisure Studies', in W. C. Gartner and D. W. Lime (eds) *Trends in Outdoor Recreation, Leisure and Tourism*, New York, CABI.

Hutchinson, S. L., Baldwin, C. K. and Caldwell, L. L. (2003a) 'Differentiating Parent Practices Related to Adolescent Behavior in the Free Time Context', *Journal of Leisure Research* 35: 396–422.

Hutchinson, S. L., Loy, D. P., Kleiber, D. A. and Dattilo, J. (2003b) 'Leisure as a Coping Resource: Variations in Coping with Traumatic Injury and Illness', *Leisure Sciences (Special Issue: Leisure, Stress, and Coping)* 25: 143–61.

Ibrahim, H. and Crandall, R. (1980) *Leisure: A Psychological Approach*, Los Angeles, CA, Hwong Publishing.

Ingham, R. (1986) 'Psychological Contributions to the Study of Leisure, Part One', *Leisure Studies* 5: 255–79.

Ingham, R. (1987) 'Psychological Contributions to the Study of Leisure, Part Two. *Leisure Studies* 6: 1–14.

Iso-Ahola, S. E. (1980a) *The Social Psychology of Leisure and Recreation*, Dubuque, IA, Wm. C. Brown Company Publishers.

Iso-Ahola, S. E. (1980b) *Social Psychological Perspectives on Leisure and Recreation*, Springfield, IL, Charles C. Thomas.

Iso-Ahola, S. E. (1995) 'The Social Psychology of Leisure: Past, Present, and Future Research', in L. A. Barnett (ed.) *Research About Leisure: Past, Present, and Future Research* (2nd edn), Champaign, IL, Sagamore, pp. 65–96.

Iwasaki, Y. and Mannell, R. C. (2000) 'Hierarchical Dimensions of Leisure Stress Coping', *Leisure Sciences* 22: 163–81.

Jackson, E. L. (ed.) (2005) *Leisure Constraints*, State College, PA, Venture Publishing.

Jackson, E. L. and Burton, T. L. (eds) (1989) *Understanding Leisure and Recreation: Mapping the Past, Charting the Future*, State College, PA, Venture Publishing.

Jackson, E. L. and Burton, T. L. (eds) (1999) *Leisure Studies: Prospects for the Twenty-first Century*, State College, PA, Venture Publishing.

Kleiber, D. A. (1999) *Leisure Experience and Human Development*, New York, Basic Books.

Kleiber, D. A., Hutchinson, S. L. and Williams, R. (2002) 'Leisure as a Resource in Transcending Negative Life Events: Self-protection, Self-restoration, and Personal Transformation', *Leisure Sciences* 24: 219–35.

Kuhn, T. (1962) *The Structure of Scientific Revolutions*, Chicago, IL, University of Chicago Press.

Lepper, M. R., Greene, D. and Nisbett, R. E. (1973) 'Undermining Children's Intrinsic Interest with Extrinsic Reward: A Test of the "Overjustification" Hypothesis', *Journal of Personality and Social Psychology* 28: 129–37.

Mannell, R. C. (1984) 'A Psychology for Leisure Research', *Society and Leisure* 7(1): 13–21.

Mannell, R. C. (1999) 'Leisure Experience and Satisfaction', in E. L. Jackson and T. L. Burton (eds) *Leisure Studies: Prospects for the Twenty-first Century*, State College, PA, Venture Publishing, pp. 235–51.

Mannell, R. C. (2005) 'Evolution of Cross-cultural Analysis in the Study of Leisure: Commentary on "Culture, Self-construal, and Leisure Theory and Practice"', *Journal of Leisure Research* 37: 100–5.

Mannell, R. C. and Kleiber, D. A. (1997) *A Social Psychology of Leisure*, State College, PA, Venture Publishing.

Mannell, R. C. and Reid, D. G. (1999) 'Work and Leisure', in E. L. Jackson and T. L. Burton (eds) *Leisure Studies: Prospects for the Twenty-first Century*, State College, PA, Venture Publishing, pp. 151–65.

Manning, R. E. (1999) *Studies in Outdoor Recreation: A Review and Synthesis of the Social Science Literature in Outdoor Recreation*, Covallis, OR, Oregon State University Press.

Matalon, B. (1999) 'The Individual and the Social: Some Reflections on the Range and Limits of Social Psychology', *Psychologie Francaise* 44: 221–6.

Matsumoto, D. (2000) *Culture and Psychology: People Around the World*, Belmont, CA: Wadsworth/Thompson Learning.

Murray, C. and Nakajima, I. (1999) 'The Leisure Motivation of Japanese Managers: A Research Note on Scale Development', *Leisure Studies* 18(1): 57–65.

Neulinger, J. (1974) *The Psychology of Leisure: Research Approaches to the Study of Leisure*, Springfield, IL, Charles C. Thomas.

Neulinger, J. (1981) *The Psychology of Leisure* (2nd edn), Springfield, IL, Charles C. Thomas.

Ouellet, G. (Guest ed.) (1984) 'Psychological Studies of the Leisure Experience', special issue of *Society and Leisure* 7.

Parry, D. C. and Shinew, K. J. (2004) 'The Constraining Impact of Infertility on Women's Leisure Lifestyles', *Leisure Sciences* 26: 295–308.

Quiñones-Vidal, E., Lozpez-García, J., Peñaranda-Ortega, M. and Tortosa-Gil, F. (2004) 'The Nature of Social and Personality Psychology as Reflected in JPSP, 1965–2000', *Journal of Personality and Social Psychology* 86: 435–52.

Reid, D. G. (1995) *Work and Leisure in the 21st Century*, Toronto, Wall and Emerson.

Robrecht, L. C. (1995) 'Grounded Theory: Evolving Methods', *Qualitative Health Research* 5: 169–77.

Ross, L. and Nisbett, R. (1991) *The Person and the Situation: Perspectives of Social Psychology*, New York: McGraw-Hill.

Samdahl, D. M. and Kelly, J. J. (1999) 'Speaking Only to Ourselves? Citation Analysis of Journal of Leisure Research and Leisure Sciences', *Journal of Leisure Research* 31: 171–80.

Santos, L. R, Ribeira, J. P. and Guimarães, L. (2003) 'Study of a Scale for Children and Strategies of Coping through Leisure Activity'/'Estudo de uma escala de crenças e de estrategias de coping através do lazer', *Analise Psicologica* 21: 441–51.

Sherif, M., Harvey, O. J., White, B., Hood, W. R. and Sherif, C. W. (1961) *Intergroup Conflict and Cooperation: The Robbers Caves Experiment*, Norman, OK, Institute of Groups Relations, University of Oklahoma.

Sinha, J. B. P. (2003) 'Trends Toward Indigenization of Psychology in India', in K. Yang, K. Hwang, P. B. Pedersen and I. Daibo (eds), *Progress in Asian Social Psychology: Conceptual and Empirical Contributions*, Westport, CT, Praeger, pp. 11–27.

Stebbins, R. A. (2001) *New Directions in the Theory and Research of Serious Leisure*, New York, Edwin Mellen.

Stephan, C. W., Stephan, W. G. and Pettigrew, T. F. (eds) (1991) *The Future of Social Psychology: Defining the Relationship between Sociology and Psychology*, New York, Springer-Verlag.

Stodolska, M. and Yi, J. (2003) 'Impacts of Immigration on Ethnic Identity and Leisure Behavior of Adolescent Immigrants from Korea, Mexico and Poland', *Journal of Leisure Research* 35: 49–79.

Stryker, S. (1997) '"In the Beginning There is Society": Lessons from a Sociological Social Psychology', in C. McGarty and S. A. Haslam (eds) *The Message of Social Psychology: Perspectives on Mind in Society*, Malden, MA: Blackwell, pp. 315–27.

Thoits, P. A. (1995) 'Social Psychology: The Interplay between Sociology and Psychology', *Social Forces* 73: 1231–43.

Triplett, N. (1897–98) 'The Dynamogenic Factors in Pacemaking and Competition', *American Journal of Psychology* 9: 507–33.

van Strien, P. J. (1997) 'The American "Colonization" of Northwest European Social Psychology after World War II', *Journal of the History of the Behavioral Sciences* 33: 349–63.

Vaughan, G. M. and Hogg, M. A. (1995) *Introduction to Social Psychology*, Upper Saddle River, NJ, Prentice-Hall.

Wade, M. G. (ed.) (1985) *Constraints on Leisure*, Springfield, IL, Charles C. Thomas.

Walker, G. J., Deng, J. and Dieser, R. B. (2005) 'Culture, Self-construal, and Leisure Theory and Practice', *Journal of Leisure Research* 37: 77–99.

Weissinger, E., Henderson, K. A. and Bowling, C. P. (1997) 'Toward an Expanding Methodological Base in Leisure Studies: Researchers' Knowledge, Attitudes and Practices Concerning Qualitative Research', *Society and Leisure* 20: 435–51.

Yang, K., Hwang, K., Pedersen, P. B. and Daibo, I. (eds) (2003) *Progress in Asian Social Psychology: Conceptual and Empirical Contributions*, Westport, CT, Praeger/Greenwood.

Zuzanek, J. (1991) 'Leisure Research in North America: A Critical Retrospective', *Society and Leisure* 14: 587–96.

8
Geographies of Leisure

David Crouch

This chapter rapidly shifts from acknowledging the more traditional arenas of geographical work in leisure studies to engage in a fuller discussion of new orientations and contributions that geography is making to leisure studies. Once understood as a support to much of leisure studies, an objective framework or reference for other disciplines, geography has developed, first through wider connections with a range of social sciences and humanities, a pivotal contribution to advances in leisure studies, in both conceptual insight and significant added value for application to.

Geography has a creditable record in objective and positivist contributions to understanding leisure; issues of location, physical accessibility, participation and distributions; the understanding of demographics in lifestyle and life choices, often informing institutional intervention and stakeholder investment. Space and spaces have been important features of leisure studies for a long time. Geography can be considered as distance, location, distribution, accessibility, kinds of places and their attraction to users and consumers for leisure. In other ways space has been informative in terms of city and country, urban and rural, as distinctive geographies, landscapes, and thereby informative in terms of delivery, provision, and so on, connected with concerns of spatial policy regarding regeneration, leisure development and provision, and promotion of accessibility.

Space is evidently significant in leisure in a number of obvious ways: leisure phenomena 'happen' in particular locations (some also virtual). Buildings, for example, where leisure happens may be built in one place rather than another; there are variations in the distribution of leisure activities, provisions, opportunities, and so on. The character of leisure supply and demand relates to geographically distributed economic, social and environmental, and cultural components. Leisure sites are geographically situated: the park, the club, the pub, the home, the tennis court, the stadium, the footpath and the theme park, the cinema, and so on. Leisure activities also involve mobility, whether Urry's automobility (2000) or on foot, getting to and ambling around a site. The reshaping of the geography of leisure over recent decades is profound, as exemplified in the case of Britain (Crouch, 2000a).

Cities have become reshaped and given new significance and meanings by the reconstruction of centres and shopping areas and the relocation of stadia alongside the investment in new provision, alongside disinvestment of a range of leisure activities as a result of work by private, public and voluntary sectors, including components of the so-called 24-hour city and the decline of public parks. In rural areas commodification has revitalized leisure spaces and their diversity, including the development of theme parks and the loss of footpaths, and measures to improve access to other areas. Facilities have been relocated, offering respectively improved or deteriorated access and provision. Themed heritage sites and city trails add further changes to the spatial configuration of leisure. These changes are accompanied by the often powerful repositioning of sites as they are wrapped in new visual culture.

In yet other ways geography has been an organizing framework, as an area descriptor through which to explore any aspect of leisure studies, or through which to identify enactions of policy, as a 'policy parcel'. In these and other ways space was conceptualized as a matter of location and a convergence of material conditions of supply and demand, of economic, social and environmental components acting on particular geographical intersections in individual places. Leisure geography has provided a rational tool, an ordering mechanism for investment, supply and management decisions. These apparently 'objective' elements of leisure geography remain available and useful.

Through more recent critical investigations of the geography or geographies of leisure, a more fruitful explanation of how these identified changes and site categorizations work can be found: what provision and production of leisure sites, spaces and facilities means in terms of the distribution of life chances and choices, access and value, and what these mean in relation to the leisure experiences of users, consumers and individuals. Significant shifts over the last decade engage us fruitfully in a critical debate on representations, via cultural studies and critical theory, in the study of leisure processes. This work contributes to the interpretation of meanings and their construction and constitution, the role and significance of place and space, in arguments concerning leisure in complex cultural change and cultural changes in leisure, disrupting borders of gender, ethnicity, age and social and cultural capital. Traditional categories of leisure and their operation have been increasingly problematized. These developments lead to a more subjective development of geography's value in leisure studies, concerned with the contemporary complexity of agencies, ideologies and 'users' or consumers of leisure, and contingent flows of events and networks. Geography's newer contributions in this mode have been informed in particular by critical work in cultural geography.

These several threads of geography's contribution are increasingly acknowledged as diverse and contested, as the work of cultural geography in particular becomes more reflexive, with significant consequences for its investigative methodologies. The emerging debate engages concerns of cultural identities, power and distribution, meaning and knowledge processes, along various strands of postmodern interpretation contributing to 'making sense' of leisure. These contributions emerge not only as intellectually exciting but also as valued contributions to policy and professional work.

Leisure happens, is produced and consumed, in spaces. These spaces may be material, and relate to concrete locations. Yet the spaces, and therefore geographies, of leisure may be metaphorical, even imaginative. Imaginative spaces are not merely in the virtual space of contemporary leisure but also in the imagination of the consumer and the representations of the agencies providing and producing leisure sites: visual culture and other narratives of communication (Crouch and Lubbren, 2003). Metaphorical spaces include popular and promoted abstractions of city and countryside; nature and city downtown. City and country, and numerous smaller, imagined intimate spaces of production and consumption, are also practised spaces of encounter, as we will see. Space, then, can be important in metaphorically 'shaping', contextualizing leisure, and the commercial and public policy pre-figuring of the meaning of leisure sites and the leisure experience may be transformed by the ways in which individuals encounter those spaces and activities. Lefebvre's (1981) categorization of space may be translated into material and metaphorical spaces, and spaces of action and practice (Shields, 1991).

In particular, recent geographical and other social science debates have conferred in unpacking the complexity of the leisure experience through empirical investigations of the encounter (Crouch, 1999a), taking us beyond the limit of an instrumental, empiricist view of space in leisure as merely 'located'. In turn, an understanding of the experience of leisure in spaces of its engagement and use, informs the work of production and provision. An important component of this revisiting of geographical interpretations of leisure, there is a revitalization of the consideration of the body. The body remains an important feature of the representation of leisure spaces, where the body is inscribed, as in sport, in terms of particular values and significance, yet the body is also active, and a component of the individual user/ consumer's subjectivities (Featherstone and Turner, 1995; Crouch, 2001).

A critical presentation is made of the contemporary debates of these recent geographies of leisure, concerning consumption and production/provision, practice and performance, identity and the significance of consuming spaces in negotiating contemporary life. Emerging conceptualizations of space enable new insights concerning the value, use and ideologies and identities surrounding distinctive spaces; neighbourhoods, virtual spaces, open spaces, public and private spaces, clubbing; so-called 'cool spaces' of youth leisure; relations between leisure and tourism, and so on, which emerge as opportunities to cross-fertilize with familiarly bounded intellectual concerns. So-called distinctions of 'city' and 'country', ideas of 'nature' and 'landscape', malls and car boot sales, even gardening in leisure become refigured. Spaces of leisure are understood to be more diverse and less easily typologized than earlier work defined (Crouch, 2000a). Geographies of leisure have moved more closely to discussions and conceptualizations of process, processes of leisure, where geography is seen as relational and dynamic, as explored in terms of its representations and contexts, and the production and the consumption of spaces (Crouch, 1999a, 2000b). This chapter explores these themes with reference to both conceptual debates and to empirically-informed interpretations, including those that demonstrate the interdisciplinary contributions of geography to leisure studies.

Moving towards complexity

However, in this chapter geography is discussed in terms of leisure from standpoints of recent research and critical debate, in particular in terms of evaluations of leisure provision, promotion, communication and experience. Thus emerging geographies of complexity, process, uncertainty and subjectivity render profound insights into diverse geographies of leisure, and inform policy too in terms of understanding the dynamics of provision, the diversity of production, the consequences of commodification and the diversities of consumption. This has prompted new discourses on lifestyle and space that engage issues of gender, cultural diversity and the wider package of postmodern thinking. Critical geographies have developed interventions concerning complexity, fluidity and the active consumer; complexities of the exercise of power in the production of space; increasingly diverse forms of contestation and debates about the body in leisure. A number of these issues are considered in this chapter through notes on a wide range of investigations from spaces of wilderness, home, city parks to cultural quarters, caving and the virtual site; sites of food to clubbing and car boot sales; of music making, caravanning, dancing, cinema attendance, sailing and gardening (Bale, 1993, 1999; Bassett and Wilbert, 1999; Cant, 2003; Cloke and Perkins, 1998; Crang, 1999; Crouch, 1999a, 2000a; Edensor, 2001; Finnegan, 1989; Gregson and Crewe, 1997; Groening and Sheider, 1999; Hubbard, 2003; Laurier, 1999; Lee, 2003; Malbon, 1999; Miller et al., 1998; Neilsen, 1995; Thrift, 1997; Valentine, 1999; Zukin 1995).

This list of investigative sources includes those traditionally ghettoized as tourism. Boundaries between leisure and tourism are dissolving fast, too, in terms of the value and quality of the emerging insights that overlap what leisure and tourism mean (Crouch, 1999a; Urry, 2002). This emerges partly as a result of the growing refusal to conceptualize and explain leisure and tourism from separate, commercial and public policy driven agendas. In this emerging way of conceptualizing what happens in leisure, why leisure works as it does, these institutionally-informed categories of leisure and tourism dissolve. Moreover, distinctions between leisure and tourism in terms of respective commercialization and commodification, a night spent away from home, and distance from location (destination) are hardly significant any more, if ever they were, in terms of the experience, the production, consumption and practice of leisure; key themes taken further in this chapter. These newer geographies augur for shifts in research methodologies, often combining methods, taking forward traditional distributional and other quantitative frameworks into the more diverse and often qualitative methods noted towards the end of this chapter.

Places as sites of leisure provision, production and practice can be itemized as presented above, in terms of themed heritage sites, theme parks, landscapes and Centre Parcs, regenerated shopping areas and 'cultural zones' and those in decline; major new stadia and clublands, produce a new geography of layout of parts of towns and rural places (Crouch, 2000a). However, these may be better conceptualized in terms of processes rather than categories, the emerging insight more useful for professional application and enactment. Thus we may explain a series of processes more hermeneutically: processes of different lifestyles, of their connections with redesign and marketing; provision, underinvestment and so-called 'McDisneyfication', accessibility and gendering; identity, inclusivity and cultural diversity.

Space is a component of cultural phenomena, interactive and processual. A key insight that cultural geography has contributed to leisure studies in recent years concerns the ways in which leisure is valued through the encounter the individual makes with space, and how this is part of an ongoing process of self-realization, lay knowledge and identity (Crouch, 2000b).

The power of the location and design of leisure sites was evident in the discussion by Clarke and Critcher in terms of city parks (1985), identified, structured and presented in terms of, for example, social taste and accessibility. Bale argued the ways in which meaning and cultural position of sports stadia can be embedded in their landscape and so help to contextualize the attraction and meaning of particular sites and project their cultural power and their use for particular groups (Bale, 1993). The power of the leisure gaze again confers power on the visual communication of the configuration of particular sites, as now familiarly exemplified in Urry's discourses on leisure in contemporary society (2002), as these sights/sites inform the experience of leisure visits. The power of the shopping mall has been identified as a framing of consumer engagement that contextualizes expectations for the shopper. In both visited sights/sites and shopping areas, and many more diverse spaces, these may be understood to enhance the leisure experience by the power of commodification over recent decades (Crouch, 2000b). Sites have become increasingly re-presented by a semiotics used in a conscious visual culture in the media and in the material framework of the site itself, including the promotion of sites for health and leisure and in such branding as Sport for All.

There remain many sites and situations where leisure is self-generated, where the meanings and semiotics of sites are configured, contextualized and constituted almost wholly by the participants themselves (Crouch and Tomlinson, 1994), often, but not only, amongst what we may call 'enthusiasms'. Yet they may equally be, for example, young people making their leisure informally; talking, walking together, even using vacant land in ways that may conflict with other moral geographies of leisure (Willatts, 1985). Moreover, the diversities of consumption in commodified sites make them increasingly constituted amongst the consumers, in such as the fuzzily-bounded consumption experience of the car boot sale, both enthusiasm and straight retailing for both buyers and sellers (Gregson and Crewe, 1997). However, increasing investigation of leisure use demonstrates that the meanings of leisure sites more widely, indeed of any leisure sites, may be constructed, at least in part, by the individuals (Miller et al., 1998). Identifying the 'work' of the consumer, Miller argues that consumption is an active process where the act of purchase, for example, in a shopping street, is merely one stage in a longer and more complex process. Arguing the limits of representation in the denotation and connotation of cultural value amongst sites and products, Miller identifies much of this to be a process of individual cultural contextualization, identifying the limits too of prefiguring in terms of the reasons things matter, and why people do things (Miller, 1998). Consumption is, of course, not limited to acts of purchase.

Of course, it remains evident that regulations and official rationalizations; market packaging and promotion of sites and their activities for leisure remain very real; they are a focus of cultural significance and political power. Making sense, however, of the interaction between prescribed meanings and values and their engagement in relation to individual acts is complex, iterative and contingent. Translating insights like these into a consideration of the work of agencies, policy, producers and promoters produces a challenge. Each culture holds a stock of cultural value and meanings and moralities that it projects and invests in distinctive places; gendered, racialized, socialized in diverse ways. Projected contextualized cultural positioning remains 'real' (Bourdieu, 1984; Young, 1990), and, inserted into the availability/ provision, location, design and representation of leisure sites, these influence and can restrain the individual and consumer, in terms of both physical and cultural accessibility which colours the ways in which individuals participate, and the contingent meanings and values of those actions and the spaces in which they occur (Nash, 2000). Projected leisure meanings can be offered through the decay, promotion or education associated with particular locations as well as by wider association. Yet the power of these spatial cultural contexts is, at least, incomplete. The individual leisure user or consumer is a participant in the production of these spaces and what they mean. As Bassett and Wilbert have argued with regard to the so-called virtual spaces of the web, there is an active engagement of the user (Bassett and Wilbert, 1999). Using the website, the individual occupies and practises a non-virtual site – the bedroom, the cybercafe – with which their experience resonates in multiple time/space, and through which other concrete and imagined spaces of other uses can be engaged. So-called virtual leisure is not enacted outside space/time.

The production by the individual or consumer of meaning and value is more than an act of resistance. In any leisure situation there may be limits to the power of contexts, and so the presentation and representation of a site has its limits on its influence over its use. In a consideration of activities beyond resistance, Thrift (1997) turns attention, in a critical consideration of dancing, to the practice of the individual/consumer in refiguring space. Malbon (1999) has explored club dancing with a particular interest in self-identification. Whilst in dancing the individual may perform to particular 'givens' of choreography and the distinctive cultural contextualizations of the place where it happens, the individual enacts more diverse self-provisioned codes in the engagement of the space, and in that space, in interaction with others (Malbon, 1999). Malbon argues that through this interplay of context and individual action, the meaning and significance of the event may be negotiated in ways very different from the familiar production, or provision and consumption model may suggest.

Thrift, and similarly Malbon, amongst others, offer an intervention into debates concerning the significance of leisure activities and in particular locations or spaces in terms of the working of cultural and social identities. Thereby identities may be produced and reproduced, not merely along prefigured lines of expectation or provision and proscription. Moreover, the working of identities is not merely understood in terms of mental reflexivity. Understanding the engagement the individual makes with space, and in the activity of doing leisure, is an important informing component of this process. The body is important in this process, and may not act merely as inscribed with meaning and significance in a particular cultural circumstance. The body is active, leisure practice is embodied. Thrift and others have explored the several grounds of this embodied encounter (Crouch, 2001; Thrift, 1997). This investigation often involves attention to the close-up experience that individuals have of leisure spaces, in a way informed by Bachelard's (1994) discussions of the poetics of space, and thus how these may be constituted by the individual.

Tim Ingold (2000) progresses an interpretation of the individual acting in the world as engaged, working their sense of life from, as well as through, their experience, in addition to their circumstances and in relation to contexts. As individuals work their lives through, they may work some of its components out for themselves. The individual is engaged in an act of negotiation, ongoing, not temporally bounded and signified in terms of the relative intensities of events (Crouch, 2003a; Crang, 1999). Leisure and the spaces in which it happens are part of these acts, and informative of this process. Leisure acts, or practices, happening in spaces, demonstrate the spatial interaction and, through that spatial interaction or encounter, the temporal, contingent process of making sense, partly through the character of bodily encounter with place. Shotter (1993) called this a practical ontology of active and physical engagement in the world. The individual works not only in an abstract mental process but also in physical action. Physical action informs feeling and thinking; physical action expresses attitude and feeling. These are processes of making sense of the world; of figuring and refiguring what is there, what is imagined, what is prefigured and proscribed in material objects and available cultural metaphors through doing leisure, through an encounter made with leisure spaces.

Merleau-Ponty's (1962) interpretations of the relation between space and the individual offers a way of rethinking how individuals engage and encounter their surroundings in terms of the embodied character of what they do (Radley, 1995; Crossley, 1995, 1996). In the late 1990s the work of Merleau-Ponty was reappraised from an apparently marginal contribution in philosophy on limited individualism, significant in humanistic geography in the early 1980s in trying to engage and situate the individual in terms of spaces of activities (Ley and Olds, 1988), to an active rapprochement with the complex cultural world of power, mediation and the construction and constitution of meaning iterative with the world inscribed through cultural mediation (Nash, 2000). Important in this reappraisal has been this development of the active engagement by the individual with flows of cultural contexts.

The notion of embodied practice as expressive provides a useful orientation for thinking through relations between touch, gesture, haptic vision and other sensualities and their mobilization in *feelings of doing* (Harre, 1993). The word 'doing' distinguishes what people may do without particular practical outcome from that oriented around tasking. Expressively encountering, the individual engages in body-practice as an everyday activity of living (Radley, 1995). Neilsen (1995) has explored the intersubjective components of embodied experience in the encounter of attending a football match and arriving at the ground. Ideologies of sport, he demonstrates, do not limit the meaning of this experience. Prefigured representations of club allegiance and, perhaps, of masculinity are transformed by the engagement in diverse enthusiasms the attenders make, and the feeling of being in a crowd. In a very different context, the experience, value and attraction of negotiating a river in white water rafting extends significantly beyond the limits of commodified wrapping, as the participant engages with the multidimensionality of their experience, as Cant has argued with regard to caving (Cloke and Perkins, 1998; Cant, 2003). Just as tourists at the Taj Mahal encounter its spaces in diverse ways in some alignment with their own cultural inclinations and the ways in which they move around a site, so we may reason that leisure visitors may do the same (Edensor, 1998).

Engaging with friends and the feeling of safety of a suburban or out-of-town location can be significant components in the valuing of a trip to the cinema (Hubbard, 1993). Feelings of security seemed important to mothers with children walking in New York public parks following the introduction of CCTV, contributing important new dimensions to the culture of cities (Zukin, 1995). Walking the uplands of northern England, Anne Game (1991) identified the ways in which she constituted the value of her leisure through a multiplicity of sensual encounters, of touching (knowing a place with two feet as well as informed by prior reading reinforced by her gaze). She felt, turned and experienced the climate bodily as she explored ground she had read about in the literature. The imaginative and poetic capacity of individuals in their encounter with spaces is also highly significant in the ways in which activities and the spaces in which they occur are made sense of. Visits to gambling places and open country offer ways of escape (Cohen and Taylor, 1993).

The extension of commodification into many previously more self-generated leisure forms has potentially changed the parameters of meaning this leisure has. Yet it may not be presumed that this effect is overwhelming. In several recent studies of gardening – a fairly pervasive site of 'home' leisure – a range of discourses has developed. Commodification of gardening through highly professionalized garden centre representations and associated media coverage may establish certain significance of this leisure activity, including the commodification of ideologies of the home (Church and Bhatti, 2001; Miller, 2000). However, it is evident that a much wider range of meanings and values is engaged amongst individuals gardening, and this extends to the purchase and also exchange of garden commodities, as Lee (2003) identifies in his work on the circulation of knowledge in what he calls the 'alternative economies' of such as the hardy plant enthusiasts. Partly this complexity of meaning is negotiated by the individual in his or her embodied encounter with the material content and self-constituted metaphor made in gardening (Groening and Sheider, 1999).

The active process of making sense of places through leisure encounters may be termed *spacing* (Crouch, 2001, 2003a). The individual in leisure produces his or her own lay geography; through what they do in leisure and where they do leisure, making sense of the world thereby, as in Shotter's ontological knowledge, including the reworking of given codes. These ideas can be mobilized towards thinking of space in terms of spacing as negotiating life in the act of spacing. It is in recent debates on performance and its performativities that the possible constituents of spacing offer a further step. In particular, Deleuze and Guattari's (1988) attention to the uncertainties of flows and momentary character of performativity elaborate the uncertainties and complexities of spacing, and its potential, as part of performativity, to reconstitute life (Grosz, 1999). There are resemblances between performativity and embodied practice that are briefly considered in the following summary of certain themes of performativity.

Leisure activities tend to have protocols along which individuals act and are understood to pursue particular leisure meanings and values. Yet this may not be the limits of how we may understand the meaning and value of different leisure pursuits and the significance of the geographies in which they occur. The literature on performance and performativity is informative for the elucidation of the ways in which protocols may work. Whilst performance can emphasize the framework of everyday protocols, the performative can err to the potential of openness.

Cultural mediation provides, like the frameworks Taussig describes identified in anthropology, frameworks through which the individual in relation to the world is inscribed. In the contemporary period this occurs through official and institutional protocols. Performativity, like embodied practice, is profoundly bodily (Dewesbury, 2000), and the body is expressive (Tulloch, 2000). Performance is theorized in ways that provide ground for the active working of the individual in her or his life. The individual's performance is proscribed by protocol, in ritualized practice, working to pre-given codes, habitually repeated, conservative (Butler, 1997; Carlsen, 1996). Yet inherent in performance is the possibility whereby relations with contexts may be reconfigured, broken, adjusted or negotiated (Lloyd, 1996; Thrift and Dewesbury, 2000), thus affecting as well as being the affect of context. This resonates with Young's (1990) reinterpretation of gendered sport participation.

The reconfigurative or reconstitutive potential of performance is increasingly cited in terms of performativity, as modulating life and discovering the new, the unexpected, in ways that may reconfigure the self, in a process of 'what life (duration, memory, consciousness) brings to the world: the new, the movement of actualisation of the virtual, expansiveness, opening up': enabling the unexpected (Grosz, 1999: 25). Like practice, performance, in this more innovative form of performativity, is a 'cultural act, critical perspective, a political intervention', and so may contain the transformative (Roach, 1995: 46). Radley (1995: 14) argues that individuals create a potential space in which they can evolve imaginary powers of feeling. Performativity articulates practices (Schieffelin, 1998: 195, quoted in Tulloch, 2000: 4), and enables closer interrogation of practice. Performativity opens up the individual as engaged in a process of 'becoming' in ways that are only incompletely proscribed. These ideas share character with Ingold's (2000) notion of doing in terms of 'dwelling'. He distinguishes between ideas for things, space, and so on, as prefigured and determinate; and the motor of 'dwelling' that sustains the present and future, from which contemplation and new possibilities of reconfiguring the world, in flows, can occur.

Both the performative and embodied practice are characterized in doing, and in particular spaces. Each is articulated for the individual in terms of doing as constituting, refiguring, their own significations, as material or embodied semiotics of space, and may respond to other representations of the world (Game, 1991; Crouch, 2001). We may take from Anne Game the idea of processual semiotics, or embodied semiotics, constituted through practice and its space encounter, engaging diverse contextual devices along the way. Performance as performativity is taken further as ongoing and multiple interrelations of things, space and time in a process of becoming, in engaging the new that may be, like Radley's consideration of embodied practice, unexpected and unconsidered, not only prefigured, suggestive of a similar performative shift beyond mundane, routine habituality. That 'going further' may emerge from exactly those apparently momentary things (Dewesbury, 2000). Moreover, the borders between 'being' as a state reached and becoming are indistinct and constantly in flow (Grosz, 1999), although they may be focused in *the event* (Dewesbury, 2000: 487–9). In the present discussion, becoming is distinguished from being in the sense of Grosz's *becoming* as 'unexpected', where performance's performativities may open up new, reconstitutive possibilities. It is in the notion of multiple routes of 'becoming' that the discourse on performativity is particularly powerful. Thus ways in which individuals are drawn to and encounter leisure spaces may be affected by aspirations of holding onto their life, or trying to take that life further, or emerging as such through, or in, the performance (Crouch, 2003a/b).

Furthermore, this multisensual, personally expressive and intersubjective character of encountering spaces through leisure offers a discourse that demonstrates the limits of the power of contextualizations in the ways in which leisure may be commodified, or selectively provided, in pursuit of proscribed objectives, ideologies, the extension of values and anticipated proscriptions made by leisure professionals and industries rather than in linear, rational ways. The embodied practice the individual leisure 'user' or performer makes are of interest not only in terms of the ways in which the space is engaged in action, but in making sense of life, individual self-identification and relations to the world, through a process of practical ontology. In Shotter's discussion of cultural politics in everyday life, or as Domosh (1998) termed it, micro-politics, there is an attention drawn to the significance of the apparent minutiae of the mundane that may actually be of much greater felt importance. Partly through prior contexts and their representations, engaged through and in relation to the lay knowledge of the encounter, activities and sites of action are made sense, given value, in individuals' lives. This is a crucial process of interaction between contexts and practices rather than linear consumption, and instead occurs in complex multiple flows.

These flows of knowledge present important issues of power in the use of leisure spaces. Whilst, for example, leisure spaces as leisure practices may be gendered and culturally distinguished by wider culture, their enactment in the encounter can disrupt these pre-givens, as Iris Marion Young (1990) argued on observing her daughter's sport engagement. Gill Valentine's acute (1999) observation of 'eating out' demonstrates the unsettling power of practised meanings through the negotiation that occurs in the act of consumption, as individuals intersubjectively construct their own strategies of making sense of the spaces and practices of leisure sites. Prevailing ideologies of landscape and spaces of nature can be profoundly reconstructed by leisure practices, as diverse distinctive agendas may be worked in the doing (Crouch, 2003b). It may be argued that meaning in the way identified in this chapter pertains most significantly to focused leisure, purposeful, through which the individual committedly pursues their life. Such a position would follow the recent debates in leisure studies on so-called serious leisure (Stebbins, 2001). Yet the argument presented in this chapter is very different. Indeed, arguing the parameters of 'seriousness' is bedevilling and collides with too many issues of 'leisure moralities' anyway. These processes of embodied consumption (and indeed, in diverse ways, their respective seriousness *and* playfulness) are workable in any situation (play can be serious too). Spending time on a piece of vacant land might be a very valuable part of young people's life negotiation.

As Maffesoli has argued, leisure spaces may be important material sites of contemporary cultural encounter and cultural processes. Whilst traditional sites of cultural identity – the neighbourhood, the workplace – may be less powerful in the reproduction of cultural identity and distinction, the pub, the club, the golf course and the shopping mall, often habitual but also vicarious, can provide the spatial ingredients of proximity that become endowed with significance through habitual use (Maffesoli, 1995). Ruth Finnegan (1989) demonstrated this significance of sites in relation to amateur music-making in the English new town of Milton Keynes, from chapel choirs to jamming, rock and blues. Space has not evaporated in the contemporary world, and leisure spaces remains significant sites of identity and identification, however fluid and contingent those identities may be.

Burkitt (1999) discussed the taking up of these components of practical, embodied action as informing of not only the meaning of things, but the meaning of our place in the world, in negotiating our own identity. Burkitt (1999) has drawn together ideas of body-practice and the social constructionist notions of identity and in particular Shotter's notion of ontological knowledge to argue that embodied practice may be important in working identity. Similarly Ingold's (2000) process of *dwelling*, whereby encounters with objects, individuals, space and the self-progression of life, including the way it gains meaning. Thus the individual 'fills' the space with meaning through their encounter, iteratively and chaotically in relation with the contextual and wider culturally pre-given components available.

A way of thinking through this process of negotiation is explored below in terms of the individual in action, as a participant in leisure, working out how he or she finds him- or herself in the world and in relation to the world, as an identity; in particular through the ideas, developed from these discourses on performance, of 'holding on' and 'going further' (Crouch, 2003a). Working our lives out through doing leisure – and from having encounters with leisure spaces – can make new knowledge, can refigure what is there through agendas of performance, and the emerging knowledge can contribute to the popular discourses of everyday life, through which ideas, feelings and events in the world may be renegotiated.

Conclusions

Emerging from these discussions of the spaces of leisure it is evident that it is necessary to speak of new geographies of leisure – not only in terms of diverse academic geographical interpretations, but also in the sense of the multiple and temporal geographies that individuals make of spaces, and also how these lay geographies can be influential in their constitution of what leisure means, and the significance of leisure enacted in distinctive spaces, in their identities.

In many of the empirical investigations that have driven this re-evaluation of the geographies of leisure, distinctive new tools of research methods have been used. Leisure geography research activities can extend over a range of activities and spaces, including pubs, barbecues, going for walks (with the informants) or playing games. This can enable a flow of conversation between groups of varying size, different exchanges, and some checking of narrative. Making these encounters as researchers is a varied experience, given our respective (in)competences and differences in an activity we may be investigating, and being especially careful to sustain critical, reflexive objectivity. These may not be spaces we have encountered, yet we may feel able to translate and transfer encounters in other leisure spaces. We may feel what Katz (1994) has called the 'in between' character of the researcher, joining in socially, and yet being also semi-detached.

What we feel ourselves in the moments of our own encounters with these spaces, then, may not necessarily be equated with our subjects. In any case, as researchers, we have a distinctive 'learnt' as well as experienced set of ideas of what particular kinds of places and their events might signify. Moreover, our subjects usually have not asked us to do the work, yet *we* seek to encounter *them*. We may both *other* ourselves and feel *othered* by our informants. We can feel difficulty in encountering because our subjects are doing what they may want to do, enjoying themselves (or not). This kind of intervention as research practice can inevitably disrupt, detract, formalize. Our subjects can have distinctive responses to us. Some may feel that we are to understand site designs, destination images, efficiency of performance of professionals or clubs – we may not; but talk on such subjects, responsively and reflexively used, can open further areas of exploration. Some individuals seek to use the interviews to promote their organization. Most subjects tend to make us feel comfortable and welcome; others tend not to do so. In one project, a researcher sitting calmly in a deckchair talking and drinking tea was approached by another individual wearing many decorative chains and pulled by a dog 'trained for man-work' and was asked what he was doing. On hearing his reply, the man said: 'You must be fucking mad' (Crouch, 2001). We too act as human beings, feel discomfort, have fun, experience human relations and behave practically.

As noted earlier, the traditional linear, rational and positivist interpretations of space events in geographical thinking remain useful. Structuring analysis to score institutional categories is an important task, although these often need to be decontextualized and decentred, in the emerging comprehension of complexity and embodied action-knowledge in the world (Ingold, 2000). The developments discussed in this chapter offer complementary insights and frames of the world. Challenges for the geographies of leisure include the further critical engagement of more rational objective geographies and the more reflexive, critical stances emphasized in this chapter.

Thinking geographically in these emerging ways helps to deliver a wider rethinking in leisure studies, too. The old distributions of leisure-work cease to apply in the situation of the multiplicity of identity formation processes and their mutual contingency. Inside leisure the issues of power, allocation and commodification can be explored in terms of negotiations, opportunities and tensions, and still in terms of conflicts. The shaping of leisure is not one-sided in terms of production and provision, or even voluntarism on the one 'side', consumption on the other, but instead more complex in the production of a structure of feeling (Harrison, 2000). Understanding leisure in this way demands a much more integrative investigation and analysis that can acknowledge complexity, and complexity does not reside only with production.

Bibliography

Bachelard, G. (1994) *The Dialectics of Duration*, Clinamen Press, Manchester.

Bale, J. (1993) *Landscapes of Sport*, London, Routledge.

Bale, J. (1999) 'Parks and Gardens: Metaphors for the Modern Places of Sport', in D. Crouch (ed.) *Leisure Tourism Geographies*, London, Routledge.

Bassett, C. and Wilbert, C. (1999) 'Where You Want to Go Today (Like It or Not): Leisure Practices in Hyperspace', in D. Crouch (ed.) *Leisure Tourism Geographies*, London, Routledge.

Bourdieu, P. (1984) *Distinction: A Social Critique of the Judgment of Taste*, London, Routledge.

Burkitt, I. (1999) *Bodies of Thought: Embodiment, Identity and Modernity*, London, Sage.

Butler, J. (1997) *Excitable Speech: A Politics of Performance*, London, Routledge.

Cant, S. (2003) '"The Tug of Danger with the Magnetism of Mystery": Descents into "the Comprehensive, Poetic-Sensuous Appeal of Cave"', *Tourist Studies* 3(1): 67–82.

Carlsen, M. (1996) *Performance: A Critical Introduction*, London, Routledge.

Church, A. and Bhatti, M. (2001) 'I Never Promised You a Rose Garden': Gender, Leisure and Home-making', *Leisure Studies* 19(3): 183–97.

Clarke, J. and Critcher, C. (1985) *The Devil Makes Work: Leisure in Capitalist Britain*, London, Macmillan.

Cloke, P. and Perkins, H. S. (1998) 'Cracking the Canyon with the Awesome Foursome', *Environment and Planning D: Society and Space* 16: 185–218.

Cohen, N. and Taylor, L. (1993) *Escape Attempts*, London, Routledge.

Crang, M. (1999) 'Rhythms of the City: Temporalised Space and Motion', in J. May and N. Thrift (eds) *Time/Space: Geographies of Temporality*, London, Routledge, pp. 187–203.

Crossley, N. (1995) 'Merleau-Ponty, the Elusory Body and Carnal Sociology', *Body and Society* 1: 43–61.

Crossley, N. (1996) *Intersubjectivity: The Fabric of Social Becoming*, London, Sage.

Crouch, D. (1999a) *Leisure/Tourism Geographies*, London, Routledge.

Crouch, D. (1999b) 'The Intimacy and Expansion of Space', in D. Crouch (ed.) *Leisure/Tourism Geographies*, London, Routledge, pp. 257–76.

Crouch, D. (2000a) 'Leisure and Consumption', in H. Matthews and V. Gardiner (eds) *The Changing Geography of the United Kingdom*, London, Routledge, pp. 261–75.

Crouch, D. (2000b) 'Places Around Us: Embodied Lay Geographies in Leisure and Tourism', *Leisure Studies* 19(2): 63–76.

Crouch, D. (2001) 'Spatialities and the Feeling of Doing', *Social and Cultural Geography* 2(1): 61–75.

Crouch, D. (2003a) 'Spacing, Performing, Becoming: Tangles of the Mundane', *Environment and Planning A* 35: 1945–60.

Crouch, D. (2003b) 'The Performance of Geographical Knowledges', in B. Szersinski et al. (eds) *Nature Performed*, Oxford, Blackwell.

Crouch, D. and Lubbren, N. (eds) (2003) *Visual Culture and Tourism*, London, Berg.

Crouch, D. and Tomlinson, A. (1994) 'Leisure, Space and Lifestyle: Modernity, Postmodernity and Identity in Self-generated Leisure', in I. Henry (ed.) *Modernity, Postmodernity and Identity*, Brighton, Leisure Studies Association.

De Certeau, M. (1984) *The Practice of Everyday Life*, Berkeley, University of California Press.

Dewesbury, J-D. (2000) 'Performativity and the Event', *Environment and Planning D: Society and Space* 18: 473–96.

Domosh, M. (1998) *'Those Gorgeous Incongruities': Polite Politics and Public Space on the Streets of Nineteenth-century New York*, New York, Annals of the Association of American Geographers 88: 209–26.

Edensor, T. (1998) *Tourists at the Taj*, London, Routledge.

Edensor, T. (2001) 'Performing Tourism, Staging Tourism: (Re)Producing Tourist Space and Practice', *Tourist Studies* 1(1): 59–82.

Featherstone, M. and Turner, B. S. (1995) 'Body and Society: An Introduction', *Body and Society* 1(1): 1–12.

Finnegan, R. (1989) *The Hidden Musicians: Music Making in an English Town*, Buckingham, Open University Press.

Game, A. (1991) *Undoing Sociology*, Buckingham, Open University Press.

Gregson, N. and Crewe, L. (1997) 'The Bargain, the Knowledge and the Spectacle: Making Sense of Consumption in the Space of the Car-Boot Sale', *Environment and Planning D: Society and Space* 15: 87–112.

Groening, G. and Sheider, U. (1999) 'Design versus Leisure', in D. Crouch (ed.) *Leisure/Tourism Geographies*, London, Routledge.

Grosz, E. (1999) 'Thinking the New: Of Futures Yet Unthought', in E. Grosz (ed.) *Becomings: Explorations in Time, Memory and Futures,* Ithaca, NY, Cornell University Press.

Harre, R. (1993) *The Discursive Mind*, Cambridge, Polity Press.

Harrison, P. (2000) 'Making Sense: Embodiment and the Sensibilities of the Everyday', *Environment and Planning D: Society and Space* 18: 497–517.

Hubbard, P. (2003) 'A Good Night Out? Multiplex Cinemas as Sites of Embodied Leisure', *Leisure Studies* 22(3): 255–72.

Ingold, T. (2000) *The Perception of the Environment: Essays in Livelihood, Dwelling and Skill*, London, Routledge.

Katz, C. (1994) 'Playing the Field: Questions of Fieldwork in Geography', *Professional Geographer* 46: 67–72.

Laurier, E. (1999) 'That Sinking Feeling: Elitism, Working Leisure and Yachting', in D. Crouch (ed.) *Leisure/Tourism Geographies*, London, Routledge.

Lee, R. (2003) (with A. Layshon and C. Williams, eds) *Alternative Economic Spaces*, London, Sage.

Lefebvre, H. (1981) *La production de l'espace*, 2nd edn, Paris, Editions anthropos.

Ley, D. and Olds, K. (1988) 'Landscape as Spectacle', *Environment and Planning D: Society and Space* 6: 191–212.

Lloyd, M. (1996) 'Performativity, Parody and Politics', in V. Bell (ed.) *Performativity and Belonging*, London, Sage, 195–214.

Maffesoli, M. (1995) *The Time of Tribes*, London, Sage.

Malbon, B. (1999) *Clubbing: Dancing, Ecstasy Vitality*, London, Routledge.

Merleau-Ponty, M. (1962) *The Phenomenology of Perception*, London, Routledge.

Miller, D. (ed.) (1998) *Material Culture: Why Some Things Matter*, London, Routledge.

Miller, D. (2000) 'Virtualism: The Culture of Political Economy', in I. Cook, D. Crouch, S. Naylor and J. Ryan (eds) *Cultural Turns, Geographical Turns*, London, Longman.

Miller, D. et al. (1998) *Shopping, Space and Identity*, London, Routledge.

Nash, C. (2000) 'Performativity in Practice: Some Recent Work in Cultural Geography', *Progress in Human Geography* 24(4): 653–64.

Neilsen, N. K. (1995) 'The Stadium and the City', in J. Bale (ed.) *The Stadium and the City*, Keele, Keele University Press.

Radley, A. (1995) 'The Elusory Body and Social Constructionist Theory', *Body and Society* 1(2): 3–23.

Roach, J. (1995) 'Culture and Performance in the Circum-Atlantic World', in A. Parker and E. Sidgewick (eds) *Performativity and Performance*, New York, Routledge, pp. 45–63.

Rojek, C. (1995) *Decentring Leisure*, London, Sage.

Rojek, C. and Urry, J. (1997) *Touring Cultures*, London, Routledge.

Schieffelin, E. L. (1998) 'Problematising Performance', in F. Hughes-Freeland (ed.) *Ritual, Performance, Media*, London, Routledge, pp. 194–207.

Shields, R. (1991) *Places on the Margins*, London, Routledge.

Shotter, J. (1993) *The Politics of Everyday Life*, Cambridge, Polity Press.

Stebbins, R. (2001) 'The Costs and Benefits of Hedonism: Some Consequences for Taking Casual Leisure Seriously', *Leisure Studies* 20(4): 305–10.

Taussig, M. (1992) *The Nervous System*, London, Routledge.

Thrift, N. (1997) 'The Still Point: Resistance, Expressive Embodiment and Dance', in S. Pile and M. Keith (eds) *Geographies of Resistance*, London, Routledge, pp. 124–54.

Thrift, N. and Dewesbury, J-D. (2000) 'Dead Geographies – and How to Make Them Live', *Environment and Planning D: Society and Space* 18: 411–32.

Tulloch, J. (2000) *Performing Culture*, London, Sage.

Urry, J. (1995) *Consuming Places*, London, Routledge.

Urry, J. (2000) *Sociology Beyond Societies*, London, Routledge.

Urry, J. (2002) *The Tourist Gaze*, 2nd edn, London, Sage.

Urry, J. (2003) *An Introduction to Global Complexity*, London, Sage.

Valentine, G. (1999) 'Consuming Pleasures: Food, Leisure and the Negotiation of Sexual Relations', in D. Crouch (ed.) *Leisure/Tourism Geographies*, London, Routledge.

Willatts, S. (1985) *The New Reality*, Belfast, Orchard Gallery.

Young, I. M. (1990) *Throwing Like a Girl and Other Essays in Feminist Philosophy and Social Theory*, Bloomington, IN, Indiana University Press.

Zukin, S. (1995) *The Culture of Cities*, London, Routledge.

9

Economics of Leisure

A. J. Veal

Economists were among the first to analyse leisure, foremost among them being Thorstein Veblen, whose *Theory of the Leisure Class*, published in 1899, was subtitled *An Economic Study of Institutions*. It is one measure of Veblen's originality that it was another 60 years before the economics of leisure was substantially addressed again, with the beginning of the modern era of leisure studies and the publication of the seminal *Economics of Outdoor Recreation*, by Marion Clawson and Jack Knetsch, in 1966. However, it is arguable that Veblen's was both the first and last book published in English on the economics of *leisure* since subsequent books have typically focused on just one sector of leisure only. Table 9.1 lists the major books in the field arranged according to major focus and date of publication. It can be seen that, since the 1980s, there has been a drift towards books on specific sectors, notably the arts, sport and tourism. Of course books do not represent the totality of intellectual activity in a field of study; journals and conference papers are also relevant. In the social sciences, however, books are a useful indicator and frequently consist of consolidating statements and/or reprinting of research which has previously been promulgated in other media.

The economics of leisure

While most of the references to Veblen's work in the leisure studies literature tend to refer to his conception of 'conspicuous consumption' as a sociological phenomenon, in fact this is equally an economic concept and the book itself is fundamentally about economics. Veblen set out to explore the historical – and indeed pre-historical – development of societies to the state where they were able to produce a *surplus* of material goods over and above the requirements for subsistence and then to examine how this surplus was controlled, distributed and used. In hunter-gatherer societies, even in times of abundance, very little by way of a material surplus was produced – instead, when sufficient food, clothing and shelter for immediate needs had been secured, work stopped, resulting, in some cases, in abundant time for extensive

140

Table 9.1 Books on the economics of leisure, 1899–2004

Year	Work-leisure	Outdoor recreation	Arts and entertainment	Sport	Tourism	Events
2004						Preuss, Economics of Staging the Olympic Games
2003		Hanley et al., New Economics of Outdoor Rec'n; Harmon & Putney, Full Value of Parks		Fort & Fizel, International Sports Economics Comparisons		
2001			Throsby, Economics & Culture	Zimbalist, Economics of Sport; Dobson & Goddard, Economics of Football	Tisdell, Tourism Economics	
2000			Frey, Arts & Economics	Gratton & Taylor, Economics of Sport & Rec'n	Vogel, Travel Industry Economics; Tisdell, Economics of Tourism	
1999			Wolf, The Entertainment Economy			
1998			O'Hagan, The State and the Arts			
1997			Towse, Cultural Economics	Noll & Zimbalist, Sports, Jobs & Taxes	Sinclair & Stabler, Economics of Tourism	
1996			Towse, Baumol's Cost Disease; Klamer, The Value of Culture; Casey et al., Culture as Commodity?			
1995					Lundberg et al. Tourism Economics; Tribe, Economics of Leisure & Tourism	
1994			Peacock & Rizzo, Cultural Economics & Cultural Policy; Heilbrun & Gray, Economics of Art & Culture; Feldstein, Economics of Art Museums; Pearce, Museum Economics and the Community	Cooke, Economics of Leisure and Sport		
1993				Bull, Economics of Travel & Tourism; Gratton & Taylor, Government and the Economics of Sport		
1991	Schor, The Overworked American					
1989			Frey & Pommerehne, Muses and Markets			Syme et al., Planning & Evaluation of Hallmark Events
1988			Myerscough, Economic Importance of the Arts in UK			
1986		Walsh, Recreation Economic Decisions				Burns et al., Adelaide Grand Prix
1985	Kelly, Recreation Business			Gratton & Taylor, Sport and Recreation: An Economic Analysis		
1983			Hendon & Shanahan, Economics of Cultural Decisions			
1980			Hendon et al. Economic Policy for the Arts	Sloane, Sport in the Market?		
1979			Throsby & Withers, Economics of the Performing Arts			
1978			Netzer, The Subsidized Muse			
1977					Archer, Tourism Multipliers	
1976			Blaug, The Economics of the Arts			
1975	Searle, Rec. Economics & Analysis; Vickerman, Economics of Leisure & Recreation		Peacock & Weir, The Composer in the Market Place			
1969	Owen, The Price of Leisure					
1966	Clawson & Knetsch, Economics of Outdoor Recreation		Baumol & Bowen, Performing Arts – The Economic Dilemma			
1899	Veblen, The Theory of the Leisure Class					

sleeping and engaging in leisure or cultural activities, such as storytelling, dance, painting and ritual (Sahlins, 1974). The idea of producing material goods over and above immediate needs and accumulating material wealth began for the most part with the advent of agriculture which created settled communities and the more elaborate political and social structures that came with them. In such circumstances the powerful could force the less powerful to produce a surplus and usurp that surplus in the form of taxes, rents or tithes, thus facilitating the existence of a 'leisure class'. The very notion of a surplus over and above subsistence is a contested one, since the requirements for subsistence must be assessed by someone and, down the ages, those in power have generally made this assessment in regard to others, but in their own interest. Thus peasants, slaves and workers have at times been forced into starvation to deliver a 'surplus' to serve the material and leisure demands of elites – the 'leisure class'. When pushed too far, empires and dynasties have come to grief in such circumstances. Critical analyses of contemporary Western society see capital as continuing this practice, although identifying the capitalist class with a significant *leisure* class in Veblen's sense is now difficult to achieve (Rojek, 2000: 51ff). Such ideas reflect the Marxian notion of 'surplus value'. The idea of 'leisure' being linked to 'surplus' is clearly relevant in current political and social discourse but is absent from contemporary economics.

Such considerations can be seen as being in the tradition of 'political economy' but during the twentieth century the discipline of economics moved away from this parent discipline and became a more technical and limited field of study and this has been reflected in the economics of leisure.

How have economists addressed the issue of leisure? At the core of any economic analysis for any product are the 'micro-economic' phenomena of demand, supply and price, how they are determined and how they interact. These relationships are, for most standard products, unremarkable: it is the 'non-standard' characteristics of many leisure products which has attracted much of the attention of leisure economists. In addition to the micro-economics of individual markets, economics is also concerned with the macro-economics of whole economies: the economic significance of leisure and particular leisure sectors and the economic impact of leisure projects on local and national economies has also therefore been a feature of the economics of leisure. Three broad areas can be identified: the work–leisure tradeoff; market sector peculiarities; and public sector issues. These are discussed in turn below. The bulk of the economics of leisure is shaped by what has become known as 'neoclassical' theory: the final section of the chapter considers critiques of this approach and examples of alternative approaches.

Work–leisure tradeoff

The question of how workers balance work-time and leisure-time is one of the most long-standing preoccupations of leisure economists. It is arguably the core of Veblen's work, particularly in regard to the historical, and prehistorical, evolution of a leisure class. The level of interest in the topic has fluctuated among the wider leisure studies community, but it has become arguably the key issue, not only of leisure economics but of leisure studies in general, since the 1990s, when it was observed that a supposed long-term trend in reduced working hours and increased leisure time in Western economies had apparently come to an end.

In the 1960s Clawson and Knetsch (1966: 13) set out some of the relevant issues regarding the work–leisure tradeoff: that leisure and work are clearly competitors for a fixed amount of time; that the number of hours individual workers may spend in paid work is not completely flexible but is partly constrained by social and commercial norms; that increasing wages resulting from productivity gains could result in workers wishing to work either *more* hours or *less* hours; and that in practice, up to the middle of the twentieth century, American workers had opted for a mixture of both, but with the majority (60 per cent) of the share of the fruits of productivity gains secured by workers being taken in the form of increased wages and just 40 per cent in the form of increased leisure. But these observations were just background to Clawson and Knetsch's primary concern with the economics of outdoor recreation, they were not the focus of their interest.

John D. Owen examined the topic in more detail than anyone else before or since in his book, *The Price of Leisure*, published in 1969. Working hours were posited to be affected by a change in the wage rate in two opposing ways, termed the *substitution* effect and the *income* effect. The substitution effect referred to the situation in which workers work *more* hours in response to an increase in the wage rate: since the employer is offering a higher price for labour the worker is prepared to offer more of it. This effect is clearly at work when workers respond to the offer of premium overtime rates by working longer hours. The *income* effect, however, works in the opposite direction since, with a higher wage rate, the worker can secure the same level of income by working *fewer* hours. Which of these effects will dominate in any one situation is therefore an empirical question, depending on the preferences of the individual worker for income as opposed to leisure. In aggregate, the result will reflect the combined preferences of all workers. The extent to which these preferences are able to be exercised in particular labour market conditions, and particularly the extent to which they are reflected in collective bargaining outcomes, is also an empirical question. Owen conducted empirical work using US data for the period 1929–61 and concluded that the *income* effect had been dominant in America in that period – that is, as wages had risen, the supply of labour per worker had declined, resulting in significant reductions in working hours; in economists' jargon: there was a 'backward sloping supply curve for labour'. However, as Clawson and Knetsch had observed, the income effect was not totally dominant, since the reductions in working hours were not sufficient to offset increases in wage rates altogether – incomes rose at the same time as working hours were falling.

Unlike commentators who implied that rising productivity and wages would *inevitably* lead to reduced working hours and a 'society of leisure', Owen indicated that neither economic theory nor empirical evidence suggested that reduced working hours would apply in all conditions of increasing wages. He presented data to suggest that the income effect had been reinforced in the United States during the study period by particular 'leisure supply' features, including the rapid development of the leisure industries and the decline in the price of leisure goods and services relative to other goods and services. Thus the offer of more leisure goods and services in the marketplace led workers to seek more 'consumption time' to enjoy them – a recognition often attributed to Henry Ford (*Time Magazine*, 1998). Further, during the Depression, there had been political and trade union pressure to reduce working hours in order to create jobs (Hunnicutt, 1988: 147ff). So increased wages, increased leisure time, reduced prices of leisure goods and services and political influences resulted in a trend towards growth in leisure consumption. Further, Owen suggested that there was evidence that the 60-hour working week and lack of paid holidays which were common at the beginning of the period, had resulted in levels of fatigue which did not produce optimum levels of productivity. So, when reduced working hours and paid holidays were shown to enhance productivity, and hence could be conceded at little or no cost to employers, resistance to change was reduced. The fatigue–productivity relationship, Owen observed, seemed to level out at a working week of about 40 hours. Indeed, Owen's own data indicates that the decline in the working week in the US stalled in about 1948 at around 41.7 hours.

Gratton and Taylor addressed the topic in 1985 in their book *Sport and Recreation: An Economic Analysis*. They examine the 'demand for time' as a preliminary stage to analysing demand for sport. While they make one reference to Owen's earlier work (p. 36), it is not in regard to his central theory and analysis. They partially replicated his work using British data for the period 1950–80, and obtained similar results, concluding that, since working hours fell during this period while real wages increased, the income effect was dominant, although they note that the existence of continued high levels of overtime working and increasing average hours of paid work by women suggest that the substitution effect was also at work. By 2000, however, the situation had changed: in their volume *The Economics of Sport and Recreation* Gratton and Taylor examine the period 1975–95 in Britain. They note a continuing decline in working hours for both men and women up to 1984 but an increase thereafter, so that, for men, the number of hours worked per week in 1995 actually exceeded the number worked in 1975. Thus there had been a dominant *income* effect up to the mid-1980s but a dominant *substitution* effect thereafter. This trend is confirmed in a later paper (Gratton and Taylor, 2004) in which the analysis is extended to the year 2000: British workers are rejecting increased leisure in favour of increased working hours and increased incomes and consumption. However, the reason for this change in direction in the mid-1980s is not discussed.

The most celebrated analysis of the issue was presented in Juliet Schor's 1992 volume *The Overworked American: The Unexpected Decline of Leisure*. Schor gives scant regard to Owen's earlier work or to the subtleties of the economic theory which underpinned it. She notes that the decline in the working week in the US halted in the 1940s but that 'increasing leisure time' had nevertheless been a mantra of commentators in the intervening years. Owen had shown working hours to be static at around 41 hours per week from 1949 to 1961, but Schor shows that working hours per worker *increased* between 1969 and 1987. She also notes that the US was out of step with other Western countries, particularly Europe, where working hours continued to decline into the 1980s, as the above British example illustrates.

Schor seeks not only to chart this change in trends but to explain it. Owen had used standard neoclassical economic theory to explain the observed income effect in the period 1929–61 and associated increase in leisure time, based on trends in prices and development of the leisure industries, but Schor concludes that, because the *substitution* effect has become dominant, neoclassical economic theory is deficient. Economists had typically argued that whether the income effect or the substitution effect was dominant was an empirical question. By implication, economists are suggesting that the remit of economics stops at that point: people's preferences are a 'given' or 'exogenous' factor in economics. But Schor does not accept such limitations: on the basis of survey evidence she concludes that workers do have a preference for shorter working hours but that the system does not allow them to exercise that choice: employers have the upper hand and, in conditions of high unemployment (which obtained in the 1980s when Schor was doing her research), impose a 'take-it-or-leave-it' regime. Thus she finds neoclassical economics deficient in explaining the late twentieth-century decline of leisure in the United States:

> The crux of the neoclassical story is that workers determine hours [of work]. But do they? Not according to the evidence. Every study I have seen on this topic has found that workers lack free choice of hours ... The failure of the neoclassical approach is rooted in its assumption that there is always full employment and that workers' choices are sovereign ... this characterization is mistaken. ... It is clear that we can no longer rely on the simple assumption that labor and product markets provide optimal outcomes in response to what people want and need. (Schor, 1992: 128–32)

So, even though workers would like to reduce working hours, they are prevented from doing so by employer inflexibility. Schor is not convincing in explaining why American workers were frustrated in achieving their desires in the 1970s and 1980s but had been able to achieve them in earlier decades – although Owen's observations concerning the fatigue–productivity issues, referred to above, may have been relevant. Schor's explanation for increasing working hours is that American workers are caught in an 'insidious cycle of work and spend'. But being caught in some sort of cycle of 'work and spend', insidious or otherwise, is what capitalism, and neoclassical economics, is all about: *Homo economicus* is, in theory, insatiable as regards market goods and services. This is noted by Schor (pp. 132–8) and criticized on the grounds of environmental sustainability and 'Zen'. Thus, while she rejects neoclassical economics, her arguments for doing so are debatable and in its place she offers a sort of anti-materialist/'green' moral crusade.

In a very brief treatment of the subject, Vogel (2000: 11) provides a plausible explanation of the conflicting views on 'income effect' versus 'substitution effect' – the idea that different processes might dominate at different income levels. Economists tend to use simplified, unidirectional curves when demonstrating their theoretical arguments with graphical representations, but such formats are not intrinsic to the theory or the argument. Thus Vogel suggests, as shown in Figure 9.1, that the labour-supply curve may be 'forward sloping' (hours worked increase with wages) at some points (A–B and C–D) and 'backward sloping' (hours worked fall with increasing wages) at other points (B–C). A change in direction may occur when a certain number of working hours is reached, as suggested by Owen, or when a certain level of income is reached. As the economists keep saying, this is an empirical question.

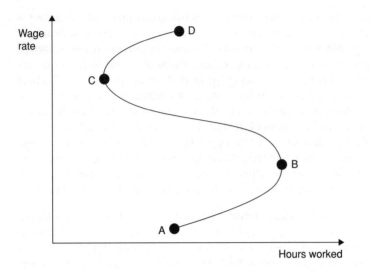

Figure 9.1   Backward- and forward-sloping labour-supply curve

Source: Adapted from Vogel (2000: 11).

The issue of work–leisure tradeoff is arguably the most important in leisure studies in the current era. It is clearly a quintessentially economic issue. There is some dispute over the data used in the above analyses, particularly the use of labour survey data as opposed to time-use budget surveys (see Schor, 1992: 168–9), and there is always difficulty in trying to draw conclusions from aggregated time-series data over substantial time-spans, since many social and economic changes are taking place in addition to those which are the focus of the research. Further, while standard economics is capable of explaining stable relationships between working hours and wage rates, it seems to be incapable of explaining changes in the relationship.

Market sector peculiarities

In predominantly market economies the key challenge in the development of an economics of leisure, or any other area where the public sector is involved, is that the core theory and analytical methods of mainstream economics are concerned with the workings of *market* processes. This phenomenon is predominantly analysed using a model which makes a number assumptions, in particular that any good or service is provided by a large number of competitive, profit-maximizing firms and that consumers are well-informed about the prices and qualities of goods and services on offer and that they behave rationally in making their choices. This model has been widely criticized for being unrealistic, but economists defend it on the grounds that, despite the lack of apparent realism, it is generally supported by aggregate data and is useful for prediction. The substantial proportion of the economics of leisure seems to be concerned with adapting the standard model to take account of 'odd' situations which do not conform to the standard market format or with 'non-market' situations which involve the intervention of governments in the marketplace. In some cases, it is the market peculiarities which form the basis for arguments for government involvement. The 'market peculiarities' are discussed here, while the non-market, public sector issues are discussed in the next section.

The market peculiarities discussed here relate to: competition in sport; composite products; natural monopoly; and inflation in the arts.

Competition and the economics of sport

Sport appears to violate some of the major assumptions of mainstream economics: that firms compete freely with each other, there is open access to the market and typical firms seek to maximize their share of the market, even to the point of market domination (even though this is viewed by economists and governments as undesirable and to be resisted by mechanisms such as anti-trust laws and monopolies commissions). Clearly this does not apply to sport, particularly team sports organized into leagues. At the extreme, for one team or club, or 'firm', to become a monopoly, would not make sense: there would be no one to play. Even the common phenomenon of oligopoly, where a market is dominated by a handful of firms, would not make for a satisfactory sporting competition. Sporting clubs therefore collaborate through leagues and federations to ensure the survival of a number of teams/clubs/firms to make up viable leagues. Practices which would be seen as 'anti-competitive' in other situations – including player salary caps, 'draft' systems for recruitment of players and redistribution of gambling levies and broadcasting revenues – are used to achieve this. In fact, it has been suggested that 'the firm' is not the individual club but the league, since the 'product' being produced is the overall competition, not single matches (Dobson and Goddard, 2001: 5). The 'anti-competitive' measures seek not just to ensure the survival of a number of clubs but also to ensure that all clubs are 'competitive' in a sporting sense, since it is believed that, for a league competition to be attractive to spectators, all clubs must have, from time to time, a reasonable chance of success; and even dominant clubs can experience falling attendances at matches if there is no chance of a close match.

Composite products

A composite product is a product or service made up of a number of elements offered by a number of suppliers. Examples in non-leisure sectors include retailing: shoppers are drawn to Oxford Street in London because of the range of competing products on offer. While the traditional shopping 'high street' has generally evolved historically, partly by accident, in the case of the traditional market and the modern shopping mall this coming together of suppliers is deliberately organized by a public or commercial entity. Of course most products and services result from the input of numerous suppliers, but there is typically only one end-point supplier of the product to the customer. In the leisure sector the composite product is common. The sporting league phenomenon discussed above is an example of the composite product, with a number of clubs and the league – and often broadcasting organizations and sponsors – co-operating to produce the sporting 'product'. In the case of sports consumption, as Gratton and Taylor note (2000: 49–50), even participation in a single activity can involve a composite product because of the need for appropriate clothing, equipment, transport and possibly tuition, as well as actual participation. Tourism is a quintessential composite product. While some tourism operations – such as island resorts with single owners – are relatively self-contained, more commonly the tourism 'product' involves a large number of commercial, public and not-for-profit organizations. Thus a holiday to a major city will involve the numerous owners and managers of attractions and hospitality, accommodation and transport providers. Often a 'tourism commission' seeks to provide some sort of co-ordination, but in many cases such bodies do little more than provide collective promotion and information services – the tourism 'industry' runs itself.

The economics of such industries or products is therefore complex, typically involving analysis of a 'parent' market and of subsidiary markets.

Natural monopoly

The idea of natural monopoly is not unique to leisure, but is common in the sector. Natural monopoly occurs when there can only be one supplier of a particular product. This occurs frequently because of the 'iconic' nature of many leisure attractions, particularly in the tourism sector. Thus there can only be one Parthenon and one Niagara Falls. Some phenomena come close to this status because of historical advantage – thus there could conceivably be a rival to Disneyland one day, but it would take many years for another theme park to achieve the status of Disney in the popular culture. Typically, leisure organizers can take advantage of the natural monopoly – thus only a limited number of hotels can have a view of the Niagara Falls or be within walking distance of the Acropolis and only a limited number of pubs can be on the waterfront. There are two consequences of natural monopolies which we should note: excessive profit and limitation of supply.

Economic theory indicates that monopolies make excessive profits, to the disadvantage of the consumer. In normal markets it is often possible to impose competition, for example, as has been done in the delivery of telephonic services in recent decades, but this is rarely possible with a natural monopoly. In some cases full advantage of achieving excessive profits is not taken because of government ownership of the attraction. In other cases some of the profit is garnered by the state on behalf of the community by licensing and/or taxation of private operators.

The limitation of supply results in the above excessive profit possibility, but can also create additional problems. While the tourism industry in Athens can increase the provision of hotels and restaurants and even provide additional contemporary attractions and possibly open up additional historic sites, everyone visiting Athens will wish to visit the Acropolis – and in conditions of increasing world population and increasing affluence, more and more people will wish to visit, resulting in problems of congestion and even damage to the attraction itself. The 'economic' solution would be to control demand through pricing – that is to raise the price of admission to deter some demand and bring the total in line with capacity. But going all the way with such a strategy would not be acceptable for iconic sites, the visiting of which may be seen as everyone's 'birthright'.

Inflation in the arts

In their 1966 book, *Performing Arts – The Economic Dilemma*, Baumol and Bowen demonstrated that, in conditions of increasing economic prosperity based on technology-based increases in labour productivity, the performing arts are inevitably at a chronic disadvantage since opportunities for increases in labour productivity in the arts are extremely limited – the classic illustration of this being that it takes just as many people just as long to play a Beethoven concerto today as it did when Beethoven composed it. This observation became part of the basis for the claim for ongoing, and increasing, public assistance for the arts, as discussed below. While the argument has been widely accepted, it can also be seen as a typical example of 'privatizing the profits' and 'nationalizing the losses', since there have in fact been significant technological advances in the area of the arts, including various forms of recording, distribution and broadcasting. But the profitable industries which have developed as a result of these technological developments have invariably been separated from the 'parent' arts institutions which historically spawned their talent. Thus the profitable film and television industry is separate from the theatre, the music recording industry is separate from orchestras and opera companies and design is separate from 'fine art'.

Government

The branch of economics known as 'welfare economics' has long developed criteria for government intervention in markets in situations where market processes are considered ineffective at delivering certain goods or services in an efficient or equitable manner. The economist Milton Friedman, who was a 'guru' of economic rationalists in the 1970s and a staunch advocate of the market system, nevertheless quotes approvingly the eighteenth-century 'grandfather' of modern economics, Adam Smith, who outlined three essential duties of government:

> first, the duty of protecting the society from the violence and invasion of other independent societies; secondly, the duty of protecting, as far as possible, every member of the society from the injustice or oppression of every other member of it, or the duty of establishing an exact administration of justice; and, thirdly, the duty of erecting and maintaining certain public works and certain public institutions, which it can never be for the interest of any individual, or small number of individuals, to erect and maintain; because the profit could never repay the expense to any individual or small number of individuals, though it may frequently do much more than repay it to a great society. (quoted in Friedman and Friedman, 1979: 49)

These criteria for government intervention have been extended and elaborated by others and are summarized in Table 9.2. Space precludes a full exposition of these criteria here, but full discussion is presented elsewhere (Veal, 2002: 53ff; Gratton and Taylor, 1991; O'Hagan, 1998; Throsby and Whithers, 1979). The most common arguments deployed in the leisure area are the 'market failure' arguments, which point out circumstances where the market is not efficient in allocating services – that

Table 9.2 Welfare economics: the role of the state in a market economy of leisure

Type of service	Characteristics	Leisure examples
1. National defence	Protecting the nation/maintaining peace – a public good (see below, 3(a))	- Some sporting activities promoted to maintain physical fitness for military preparedness (e.g. ancient Greek games, archery in medieval England) - In 1930s Australia: a National Fitness campaign launched because of concerns about the fitness of men for military service (Hamilton-Smith and Robertson, 1977: 178)
2. Law and order	Providing a legal framework for society, protection of life and property	- Gambling regulation - Licensing of sale and consumption of alcohol - Licensing/regulation of radio and television broadcasting - Copyright laws - Fire and safety regulations in places of entertainment
3. Market failure (a) *Public goods and services*	*Non-excludable* – not practically possible to exclude anyone from enjoying the good or service – so difficult to charge the user *Non-rival* – one person's enjoyment or consumption does not preclude consumption or enjoyment by others – so extra users do not cost more	- Parks – amenity enjoyed by passers-by - Community pride from national sporting success - Firework displays - Public broadcasting - Public sculpture - Heritage conservation (e.g. National Parks, monuments) - Contribution to cultural development by the arts
(b) *Externalities, neighbourhood or third party effects*	Third parties are affected, positively or negatively, by transactions between providers and consumers – market is distorted since third parties do not pay for service received	- Negative example: airport noise pollution or pub/club noise disturbance – need for government regulation/rules and/or levy on polluters - Positive example: community health benefits of sport participation – government may therefore subsidize sport facilities/ services to encourage participation and produce social benefits

(c) Mixed goods	Both public good/service and private dimensions (Baumol & Bowen, 1976)	- Attendance at an arts event (patrons enjoy personal private benefit; general cultural development of society is a public benefit) – government subsidizes production in recognition of public benefit. - Urban parks (visitors enjoy personal private benefit; but passers-by and neighbours enjoy 'neighbourhood' benefit)
(d) Merit goods	Goods and services considered beneficial, but with high learning threshold	- Subsidy and education for some art forms - Cultural heritage - Environmental/heritage appreciation education
(e) Option demand	Goods and services which people want to maintain *in case* they or their successors want to use them in future	- Significant environmental, cultural and heritage items
(f) Infant industries	Industries where it is difficult for new entrants to get started because of power of existing companies	- Local film industry - Local publishing industry - Airlines
(g) Size of project	Projects too large for private sector to invest	- Few examples today – possibly major resort development, Olympic Games
(h) Natural monopoly	Services where only one supplier is technically required	- Unique heritage attractions or environmental resources

4. Socio-political arguments

(a) Equity or humanitarian measures	Facilities or services considered essential for a minimum standard of living or quality of life so must be provided for all (Cushman & Hamilton-Smith, 1980)	- Access to play facilities for all children - Access to open space and physical recreation facilities for all – government provision or subsidy
(b) Economic management & development	Development of facilities or programmes that provide jobs and incomes	- Tourism developments – e.g. resorts – government may provide land, tax 'holidays', infrastructure - Major sports facilities – e.g. Olympic facilities – government may provide land, funds, infrastructure or direct provision
(c) Incidental enterprise	Trading activities which are incidental to a public facility or service	- Restaurants/cafes in museums, leisure centres - Gift shops in visitor information centres
(d) Tradition	Facilities/services which are valued because they have been provided for many years	- Swimming pools in areas where population has declined or use patterns have changed

Source: Veal (2002: 64-5).

151

is, left to its own devices, the production and allocation of resources would not reflect consumer preferences. In these cases, it is argued, the state should intervene. But this presents two problems: determination of the quantum of state intervention and problems of the efficiency and scale of the state itself.

The quantum issue concerns assessment of the *value* to the user and/or the community at large of the services provided against the *cost* of providing them. Within government, expenditure for one purpose must be weighed against alternative competing purposes. More broadly, an assessment must be made of the value of services funded by government from taxation as against the value of services which taxpayers could secure if they spent the money directly in the marketplace. Even where government regulation, rather than expenditure, is involved, there are inevitably costs borne by private individuals or organizations against which the benefits of the government intervention must be assessed; for example, 'local content' rules in broadcasting have an impact on television companies' costs, and heritage orders have financial implications for property owners. Thus the level and distribution of the benefits produced and the costs imposed should all ideally be assessed if government expenditure is to be justified. The techniques of cost-benefit analysis and economic impact analysis have been developed to achieve this and these are discussed below.

Such an 'economic rationalist' stance is often criticized as being mechanistic and unsympathetic to the sector concerned (for example, Garnham, 1987); it is argued that sport, the arts or the heritage should be supported 'for their own sake' and that no amount of money is too much to be spent on important aspects of national culture. Arts economist David Throsby (2001) has recently argued that 'cultural value' cannot be in any way aligned with 'economic value', which would imply that there is no way of ever assessing what an appropriate level of government expenditure should be in the cultural field. But in fact, the approach can be seen as very humanistic: government resources are derived from the community, and in a democratic society the community is entitled to know that its resources are being allocated in a way that will provide optimum benefits for the community, and not just on the say so of a self-selected elite. As it happens, virtually all cost-benefit and economic impact studies in the area of leisure provide overwhelming support for government expenditure in the sector. Examples from the literature are listed in Table 9.3.

This 'cost-benefit' process can be complex, involving estimation of what users of subsidized or free services might, in theory, be willing to pay if it were feasible or desirable to ask them to do so, and estimates of the size of broader costs and benefits to third parties and the community at large. A particular challenge is devising, where possible, economic indicators of social, individual, cultural and environmental costs and benefits which are not routinely the subject of economic exchange. In some fields, such as transport planning, projects are routinely assessed in formal cost-benefit terms before being undertaken, but this is rarely the case in the leisure area: many of the cost-benefit analyses conducted have been *post hoc* case studies designed to establish the value of generic arts, sport, environmental government expenditure, rather than justifying particular projects.

Table 9.3 Cost-benefit and economic impact of leisure – selected studies

Year	Author(s)	Study aims	Method
The Arts			
1988	Myerscough	Economic significance of the arts in the UK	Arts multiplier
1989	Dept. of Finance	Economic benefit of museums in Australia	Efficiency analysis – costs per visit
1990	DASETT	Economic benefit of museums (response to Dept. of Finance, 1989)	Review of Dept. of Finance (1989)
1996	Casey, Dunlop & Selwood	Economic significance of the arts in the UK	Expenditure and audience analysis
1999	Evans	Economic and social impact of performing arts in the UK	Willingness to pay + audience analysis
Outdoor recreation			
1966	Clawson & Knetsch	Value of user benefits of natural areas	Clawson/travel cost method
1993	Garrod, Pickering & Willis	Economic value of botanic gardens	Willingness to pay
Participation in sport/exercise			
1986	Henley Centre for Forecasting	Economic impact of sport in the UK	Compilation of data on benefits
1988	DASETT	Economic value of sport/exercise participation in Australia	Compilation of data on benefits
1990	Hefner	Economic impact of sport	Multipliers and input-output analysis
Sporting events			
1986	Burns, Hatch & Mules	Economic impact of the Adelaide Grand Prix	Cost-benefit, multiplier
1993	KPMG Peat Marwick	Economic impact of Sydney 2000 Olympic Games	Multiplier analysis
2000	Gratton, Dobson and Shibli	Significance of six UK sporting events	Visitor expenditure analysis
2004	Preuss	Economic impact of the Olympic Games 1972–2008	Review of methods and compilation of statistics

153

Of particular note in cost-benefit studies in leisure have been two techniques: the 'Clawson' or travel cost method and 'willingness to pay'. Clawson and Knetsch (1966), as mentioned above, developed a technique for deriving a demand curve, relating costs to demand levels, for a recreation site even when no admission price is charged, based on the way the level of site visitation varies with distance from the site, and hence travel costs. While it measures only the individual benefits accruing to users, and not any wider social benefits, and while it has been subject to some criticism over the years, it has been widely used and remains an important contribution to the field. The 'willingness to pay' or 'contingent valuation' method is not peculiar to leisure; as its name implies, it simply involves discovering, usually be means of a survey, what actual and potential beneficiaries of a service might hypothetically be willing to pay for the benefits received. The technique is conceptually simple and again has been subject to considerable criticism, but has been widely used (Mitchell and Carson, 1989).

Economic impact is a related but different technique: it is concerned primarily with economic outcomes of projects in terms of jobs and incomes and less with costs, or indeed other types of impact. Typically, the aim is to estimate the increase in personal and business income and the corresponding increase in job creation from a development – the technique has been most commonly used in relation to tourism, which is generally developed for economic reasons. Of particular note in such studies is the phenomenon of the 'multiplier', which refers to the fact that expenditure by governments or tourists circulates through a local economy creating additional economic activity as it goes – thus a restaurant employs staff, but also buys in supplies from other businesses who employ staff; the staff themselves spend their money with local businesses, and so on (Archer, 1977). Eventually the effect fades out as a result of 'leakages' – that is, money which is lost to the local economy by external expenditure on such things as imports and taxes. Estimates of the size of the 'multiplier effect' in different environments has been a key feature of many economic impact studies, particularly in the context of tourism.

Broader issues than estimation of costs, benefits and impact of individual projects arise in considering the role of government; namely aggregate government expenditure and 'government failure'. As regards aggregate government expenditure, there has traditionally been controversy in economic policy over the appropriate size of government in a predominantly market economy. Even when individual projects or ongoing services can be fully justified, there are some who believe that a government sector above a certain size inhibits private sector growth, through effects on the capital market and through the disincentive of high taxation rates. At what point this negative effect takes place, if at all, is a matter for debate and political disagreement. An allied issue is the question of 'government failure', that is the belief that government is intrinsically inefficient, so the more of an economy which is in the public sector the greater the drag on overall efficiency. In some cases, the source of the inefficiency is public accountability and this is unavoidable; in other cases, inefficiencies arise from practices which can, in theory, be corrected. In some cases private sector efficiency is sought in the provision of government funded services through 'outsourcing' to the private sector.

Alternatives to neoclassical theory

It is notable that in some of the disciplines which have contributed to leisure studies, there has been considerable development in theory and even sharp paradigmatic change and conflict over the last 40 years. Most notable in this regard is sociology, which has seen Marxist, feminist, postmodern and post-structuralist challenges. By contrast, basic economic theory has remained relatively unchanged. Thus, in discussing the differences between their 2000 book and its predecessor 1985 volume, Gratton and Taylor (2000: viii) referred to the 'wealth of information' which had emerged on the sports industry in the intervening 15 years – but no reference was made to any developments in theory. By and large, economic contributions to the study of leisure adhere to neoclassical economic theory, as developed in the early twentieth century, as their guiding framework. There are some exceptions, but they make only a marginal impact on the central orthodoxy.

Some economists have noted the existence of 'alternative' economic theory and have sought to relate it to leisure phenomena. This is not a widespread practice since economists in general have not given widespread recognition to non-mainstream theory. The practitioners of mainstream economics have shown themselves adept at largely ignoring their critics and alternative paradigms, and leisure economists are no exception. The obvious 'alternative' economics is Marxian economics. This, of course, has been roundly rejected by Western mainstream economists for more than a century. But during the 1970s and 1980s, when neo-Marxism was enjoying its heyday in the sociology of leisure, largely based on Marxist political economy, leisure economists were largely silent. They promulgated the neoclassical economic theory, but did not themselves juxtapose it with Marxian perspectives. While mainstream economists continued to 'do their own thing', sociologists pushed a Marxian or neo-Marxian 'economics of leisure', using terms such as 'surplus value' and denying the existence of consumer sovereignty. Examples include Clarke and Critcher (1985), Aronowitz (1973) and Gorz (1980). Marxist expositions of the economics of leisure by Marxist economists, at least in English, are non-existent.

Recently, in the third edition of *The Economics of Recreation, Leisure and Tourism*, John Tribe (2005) has added a chapter entitled 'Critique, Alternative Perspectives and Change', which considers not only Marxism but also other critical economic perspectives from environmental and anti-free trade groups. Arguably, Sinclair and Stabler (1997: 95ff), in addressing *The Economics of Tourism*, make the most substantial effort to consider alternatives, or modifications of, the supply side of the neoclassical model. A number of these are summarized below.

- *The structure, conduct and performance (SCP)* paradigm in industrial economics accepts much of neoclassical theory but, rather than focusing on the costs and pricing of individual firms and assuming a fully competitive environment, as in the neoclassical model, concentrates on the structure of markets, in terms of the numbers of buyers and sellers, as a key variable in analysing the supply side of a market. If uncompetitive, monopolistic structures emerge they must be countered by government intervention. Such monopolistic tendencies can be seen in a number of commercial sectors with leisure connections, including publishing, brewing and gambling.

- *The Chicago School/contestable markets* model is an alternative to the SCP model, but holds that anti-competitive behaviour of existing firms is kept in check by the potential threat of new entrants into the market – the phenomenon of 'budget airlines' challenging established airlines is an example.
- *The Austrian School* offers an alternative view of the workings of markets which does not require the market to tend towards a static 'equilibrium' state as the neoclassical model does. It views markets as more fluid, with firms learning to adapt to change and uncertainty. The 'neo-Austrian' school focuses particularly on the process of evolution in industrial practices which this implies.
- *Transactions theory* argues that firms cannot behave fully rationally on the basis of complete knowledge of the market, as neoclassical theory assumes, because of the costs of gathering and transmitting information and acting on it – for example in a situation when a firm must source many sorts of supplies from numerous, possibly thousands, of potential suppliers, or where a firm must convey information on its products in numerous markets. 'Short cut' solutions which may or may not produce optimum results are therefore adopted, such as the exclusive use of an agent to sell product or source supplies. Relationships between tour operators and travel agents are an example in the leisure context.
- *Behavioural models of the firm*, based on psychology, which explore how managers make decisions in conditions of uncertainty and incomplete information have challenged the neoclassical theory of the firm which assumes complete knowledge and rational decision-making, and have provided empirical depth to an element of the demand/supply process which has hitherto been predominantly theoretical.
- *Game theory* is suited to analysing situations of oligopoly – that is, where there are very few firms operating in a market and consequently a less than fully competitive market. Game theory seeks to analyse the consequences for each of the firms involved in attempting to 'second guess' each other – for example, with regard to pricing or decisions to enter a given market.

While Sinclair and Stabler illustrate how these theoretical perspectives are particularly suited to analysing aspects of the tourism market, it is clear that there is no established body of tourism-related research which uses these approaches.

Each of the alternative perspectives discussed by Sinclair and Stabler is concerned primarily with the supply side of markets – the behaviour of firms. In general, with the possible exception of the Austrian School, which is a 'root and branch' alternative to neoclassical economics, the approaches explored tend to incorporate aspects of management or organization theory, thus they move into inter-disciplinary territory.

Similar moves can be seen in some economists' consideration of the limitations of, alternatives to and developments of the neoclassical approach to the demand side – the behaviour of individuals as consumers.

While we have seen that there is a literature on the economics of leisure and work time in aggregate, Staffan Linder (1970), among others, pointed out that economic theory had generally neglected the dimension of *time* in its consideration of consumption of goods and services, and the constraints this was likely to place on consumption. While this was to some extent remedied, notably by Becker (1965), it has remained as a somewhat isolated piece of analysis and has not been incorporated into mainstream demand theory.

We have seen how Juliet Schor rejected neoclassical theory as inadequate to explain the changing relationship between work, leisure and income. Her critique is partly aimed at inflexibility of employers, which might be deemed anti-competitive and therefore at odds with how competitive markets are assumed, by neoclassical economics, to behave, but this is not entirely clear from Schor's discussion. The main thrust of her critique is, however, aimed at American consumers and/or the materialist culture in which they live. But traditionally such matters are beyond the scope of neoclassical economics – in the model, consumers' tastes are 'given'. In straying beyond the normal confines of economic analysis Schor is also exploring, although not explicitly saying so, interdisciplinary areas such as environmental analysis and philosophy.

Gratton and Taylor (2000: 48) express 'serious reservations as to whether the neo-classical approach ... can ever completely explain the consumer's decision to take part in sport'. In response to this they offer a short exploration of the work of two authors, Scitovsky and Csikszentmihalyi, on consumer psychology, which suggests the need for a more sophisticated approach to consumer behaviour than the neoclassical model offers.

Critiques of the limitations of neoclassical demand theory are not confined to leisure economists. Douglas and Isherwood (1980: 1–24) note that criticism of the neoclassical limitations are widespread among economists; their own contribution is to use anthropological approaches to understand consumers in their social setting, including their leisure setting (ibid.: 90).

'Public choice' theory links economic theory with political science in drawing a parallel between market processes and political processes in analysing the public sector (Self, 1993). In the political process, it is argued, voters support, in a self-interested way, political parties which offer them more of what they want and this is similar to consumers expressing preferences through their expenditure patterns. As political parties bid against each other to offer voters more of what they want this leads to an expansion of the role of the state – including its role in various sectors of leisure – as parties seek to meet as many needs of as many groups as possible. Since much of government provision is therefore a quasi-market process, public choice theory has been used to support 'rollback of the state' which took place under New Right governments in the 1980s, but it can equally be used to understand the 'non-rational' economics of the public sector.

Finally, we should note Hirsch's (1977) *Social Limits to Growth* thesis, which posits that certain types of consumption are status-related and are limited by restrictions on supply (whereas the neoclassical model assumes that supply will increased in response to rising demand and rising prices). The classic example is the harbourside or riverfront mansion: generally, the supply of such dwellings is very limited and cannot be increased, so their desirability pushes up their prices to exceptional levels. Other, less obvious examples in the leisure domain bring us full circle to Veblen, in that much leisure consumption can be seen as status-driven, an aspect of 'conspicuous consumption'. Examples include the desire to belong to exclusive clubs or have access to other 'exclusives' such as corporate boxes, the attraction of 'designer' labels, travel to 'unspoiled' holiday destinations before mass tourism arrives and pursuit of collectables, such as artworks and antiques. In one sense, neoclassical theory can cope with this phenomenon in isolation, with a very steeply sloping, even vertical, supply curve, but the explanation for the phenomenon, its pervasiveness and its effects on overall consumption demand lies beyond the scope of traditional economics.

This brief review of the limitations and boundaries of neoclassical economics suggests that much of what might be interesting and useful in the economics of leisure lies in these 'fringe' areas. This poses a challenge for economists and those working in the overlapping disciplines to develop an interdisciplinary approach to understanding leisure demand, supply and distribution.

Bibliography

Archer, B. (1977) *Tourism Multipliers*, Bangor, University of Wales Press.

Aronowitz, S. (1973) *False Promises*, New York, McGraw-Hill.

Basso, P. (2003) *Modern Times, Ancient Hours: Working Lives in the Twenty-first Century*, ed. and trans. G. Donis, London, Verso.

Baumol, W. J. and Bowen, W. G. (1966) *Performing Arts – The Economic Dilemma*, Cambridge, MA, MIT Press.

Baumol, W. J. and Bowen, W. G. (1976) 'Arguments for Public Support of the Performing Arts', in M. Blaug (ed.) *The Economics of the Arts*, London, Martin Robertson, pp. 42–57.

Becker, G. S. (1965) 'A Theory of the Allocation of Time', *Economic Journal* 75(3): 493–517.

Blaug, M. (ed.) (1976) *The Economics of the Arts*, London, Martin Robertson.

Bull, A. (1991) *The Economics of Travel and Tourism*, Melbourne, Pitman.

Burns, J. P. A., Hatch, J. H. and Mules, T. J. (eds) (1986) *The Adelaide Grand Prix – The Impact of a Special Event*, Adelaide, Centre for South Australian Economics Studies.

Casey, B., Dunlop, R. and Selwood, S. (1996) *Culture as Commodity? The Economics of the Arts and Built Heritage in the UK*, London, Policy Studies Institute.

Clarke, J. and Critcher, C. (1985) *The Devil Makes Work: Leisure in Capitalist Britain*, London, Macmillan.

Clawson, M. and Knetsch, J. L. (1966) *Economics of Outdoor Recreation*, Baltimore, Johns Hopkins Press.

Cooke, A. (1994) *The Economics of Leisure and Sport*, London, Routledge.

Cushman, G. and Hamilton-Smith, E. (1980) 'Equity Issues in Urban Recreation Services', in D. Mercer and E. Hamilton-Smith (eds) *Recreation Planning and Social Change in Urban Australia*, Malvern, Victoria, pp. 167–79.

DASETT – Department of the Arts, Sport, the Environment, Tourism and Territories (1988) *The Economic Impact of Sport and Recreation – Regular Physical Activity*. Technical Paper No. 2, Canberra, AGPS.

DASETT – Department of the Arts, Sport, the Environment, Tourism and Territories (1990) *What Value Heritage? Issues for Discussion*, Canberra, AGPS.

Department of Finance (1989) *What Price Heritage? The Museums Review and the Measurement of Museum Performance*, Canberra, Department of Finance.

Dobson, S. and Goddard, J. (2001) *The Economics of Football*, Cambridge, Cambridge University Press.

Douglas, M. and Isherwood, B. (1980) *The World of Goods: Towards an Anthropology of Consumption*, Harmondsworth, Penguin.

Evans, G. (1999) 'The Economics of the National Performing Arts – Exploiting Consumer Surplus and Willingness-to-Pay: A Case of Cultural Policy Failure?' *Leisure Studies* 18(2): 97–118.

Feldstein, M. (1991) *Economics of Art Museums*, Chicago, University of Chicago Press.

Fort, R. and Fizel, J. (eds) (2004) *International Sports Economics Comparisons*, Westport, CT, Praeger.

Frey, B. S. (2000) *Arts and Economics: Analysis and Cultural Policy*, Berlin, Springer-Verlag.

Frey, B. S. and Pommerehne, W. (1989) *Muses and Markets: Explorations in the Economics of the Arts*, Oxford, Blackwell.

Friedman, M. and Friedman, R. (1979) 'The Role of Government', in *Free to Choose*, Harmondsworth, Penguin, pp. 47–58.

Garnham, N. (1987) 'Concepts of Culture: Public Policy and the Cultural Industries', *Cultural Studies* 1(1): 24–37.

Garrod, G., Pickering, A. and Willis, K. (1993) 'The Economic Value of Botanic Gardens: A Recreational Perspective', *Geoform* 24(2): 215–24.

Gorz, A. (1980) *Farewell to the Working Class*, London, Pluto.

Gratton, C., Dobson, N. and Shibli, S. (2000) 'The Economic Importance of Major Sport Events: A Case-Study of Six Events', *Managing Leisure* 5(1): 17–28.

Gratton, C. and Taylor, P. (1985) *Sport and Recreation: An Economic Analysis*, London, Spon.

Gratton, C. and Taylor, P. (1988) *Economics of Leisure Service Management*, Harlow, Longman.

Gratton, C. and Taylor, P. (1991) *Government and the Economics of Sport*, Harlow, Longman.

Gratton, C. and Taylor, P. (2000) *Economics of Sport and Recreation*, London, E. & F. N. Spon.

Gratton, C. and Taylor, P. (2004) 'The Economics of Work and Leisure', in J. T. Haworth and A. J. Veal (eds) *Work and Leisure*, London, Routledge, pp. 85–106.

Hamilton-Smith, E. and Robertson, R. W. (1977) 'Recreation and Government in Australia', in D. Mercer (ed.) *Leisure and Recreation in Australia*, Malvern, Victoria, Sorrett, pp. 75–189.

Hanley, N., Shaw, W. D. and Wright, R. E. (eds) (2003) *The New Economics of Outdoor Recreation*, Cheltenham, Edward Elgar, UK.

Harmon, D. and Putney, A. D. (2003) *The Full Value of Parks*, Lanham, MD, Rowman & Littlefield.

Hefner, F. L. (1990) 'Using Economic Models to Measure the Impact of Sports on Local Economies', *Journal of Sport and Social Issues* 14(1): 1–13.

Heilbrun, J. and Gray, C. M. (1993) *The Economics of Art and Culture – An American Perspective*, Cambridge, Cambridge University Press (2nd edn 2001).

Hendon, W. S., Shanahan, J. L. and MacDonald, A. J. (eds) (1980) *Economic Policy for the Arts*, Cambridge, MA, Abt.

Hendon, W. S. and Shanahan, J. L. (eds) (1983) *Economics of Cultural Decisions*, Cambridge, MA, Abt.

Henley Centre for Forecasting (1986) *The Economic Impact and Importance of Sport in the UK*. Study 30, London, Sports Council.

Hirsch, F. (1977) *Social Limits to Growth*, London, Routledge & Kegan Paul.

Hunnicutt, B. K. (1988) *Work Without End: Abandoning Shorter Hours for the Right to Work*, Philadelphia, Temple University Press.

Kelly, J. R. (1985) *Recreation Business*, New York, John Wiley & Sons.

Klamer, A. (ed.) (1996) *The Value of Culture: On the Relationships between Economics and the Arts*, Amsterdam, Amsterdam University Press.

KPMG Peat Marwick (1993) *Sydney Olympic 2000: Economic Impact Study*, 2 Vols, Sydney, Report to Sydney Olympics 2000 Bid Ltd..

Linder, S. B. (1970) *The Harried Leisure Class*, New York, Columbia University Press.

Lundberg, D. E., Krishnamoorthy, M. and Stavenga, M. H. (1995) *Tourism Economics*, New York, John Wiley & Sons.

Mitchell, R. C. and Carson, R. T. (1989) *Using Surveys to Value Public Goods: The Contingent Valuation Method*, Washington, DC, Resources for the Future.

Myerscough, J. (1988) *The Economic Importance of the Arts in Britain*, London, Policy Studies Institute.

Netzer, D. (1978) *The Subsidized Muse: Public Support for the Arts in the United States*, Cambridge, Cambridge University Press.

Noll, R. G. and Zimbalist, A. (eds) (1997) *Sports, Jobs and Taxes: The Economic Impact of Sports Teams and Stadiums*, Washington, DC, Brookings Institute Press.

O'Hagan, J. W. (1998) *The State and the Arts: An Analysis of Key Economic Policy Issues in Europe and the United States*, Cheltenham, Edward Elgar.

Owen, J. D. (1969) *The Price of Leisure: An Economic Analysis of the Demand for Leisure Time*, Rotterdam, Rotterdam University Press.

Peacock, A. T. and Rizzo, I. (eds) (1994) *Cultural Economics and Cultural Policy*, Dordrecht, Kluwer.

Peacock, A. T. and Weir, R. (1975) *The Composer in the Market Place*, London, Faber.

Pearce, S. (ed.) (1991) *Museum Economics and the Community*, London, Athlone Press.

Preuss, H. (2004) *The Economics of Staging the Olympics: A Comparison of the Games, 1972–2008*, Cheltenham, Edward Elgar.

Rojek, C. (2000) *Leisure and Culture*, Basingstoke, Macmillan.

Sahlins, M. (1974) *Stone Age Economics*, London, Tavistock Publications.

Schor, J. B. (1992) *The Overworked American: The Unexpected Decline of Leisure*, New York, Basic Books.

Searle, G. A. C. (ed.) (1975) *Recreational Economics and Analysis*, Harlow, Longman.

Self, P. (1993) *Government by the Market? The Politics of Public Choice*, Basingstoke, Macmillan.

Sinclair, T. and Stabler, M. (1997) *Economics of Tourism*, London, Routledge.

Sloane, P. J. (1980) *Sport in the Market Place? The Economic Causes and Consequences of the 'Packer Revolution'*, Hobart Paper 85, London, Institute for Economic Affairs.

Syme, G. J., Shaw, B. J., Fenton, D. M. and Mueller, W. S. (1989) *The Planning and Evaluation of Hallmark Events*, Aldershot, Avebury, UK.

Throsby, C. D. (2001) *Economics and Culture*, Cambridge, Cambridge University Press.

Throsby, C. D. and O'Shea, M. (1980) *The Regional Economic Impact of the Mildura Arts Centre*, Sydney, Macquarie University, School of Economic and Social Studies.

Throsby, C. D. and Withers, G. A. (1979) *Economics of the Performing Arts*, Melbourne, Edward Arnold.

Time Magazine (1998) 'Builders and Titans: Henry Ford' (7 December), available at <http://www.time.com/time/time100/builder/profile/ford.html> (accessed February 2006).

Tisdell, C. (ed.) (2000) *Economics of Tourism*, Cheltenham, Edward Elgar.

Tisdell, C. (2001) *Tourism Economics: The Environment and Development*, Cheltenham, Edward Elgar.

Towse, R. (ed.) (1997a) *Cultural Economics: The Arts, the Heritage and the Media Industries*, Cheltenham, Edward Elgar.

Towse, R. (1997b) *Baumol's Cost Disease: The Arts and other Victims*, Cheltenham, Edward Elgar.

Towse, R. (ed.) (2003) *Handbook of Cultural Economics*, Cheltenham, Edward Elgar.

Tribe, J. (1995) *The Economics of Leisure and Tourism: Environments, Markets and Impacts*, Oxford, Butterworth-Heinemann.

Tribe, J. (2005) *The Economics of Recreation, Leisure and Tourism*, Oxford, Elsevier.

Veal, A. J. (1987) *Leisure and the Future*, Allen & Unwin, London.

Veal, A. J. (2002) *Leisure and Tourism Policy and Planning*, Wallingford, CABI Publishing.

Veblen, T. (1899) *The Theory of the Leisure Class*, London, Allen & Unwin, 1970.

Vickerman, R. W. (1975) *The Economics of Leisure and Recreation*, London, Macmillan.

Vickerman, R. (1983) 'The Contribution of Economics to the Study of Leisure', *Leisure Studies* 2(3): 345–64.

Vickerman, R. (1989) 'Economic Models of Leisure and its Impact', in E. L. Jackson and T. L. Burton (eds) *Understanding Leisure and Recreation*, State College, PA, Venture Publishing, pp. 331–57.

Vogel, H. L. (2000) *Travel Industry Economics*, Cambridge, Cambridge University Press.

Walsh, R. G. (1986) *Recreation Economic Decisions: Comparing Benefits and Costs*, State College, PA, Venture Publishing.

Wolf, M. J. (1999) *The Entertainment Economy*, Times Books/Random House, New York.

Zimbalist, A. (ed.) (2001) *The Economics of Sport*, Cheltenham, Edward Elgar.

10
The Duality of Leisure Policy

Fred Coalter

The history of public leisure policy in the United Kingdom (but also elsewhere) has been characterized by an essential duality. Government involvement and investment has the dual purposes of extending social rights of individual citizenship while recognizing the potential wider social benefits associated with leisure provision.

Of course, such duality is a common characteristic of most social policies, where the extension of social rights has been accompanied by social obligations and duties (Roche, 1992). Writing about cultural policy, Bianchini (1992) suggests that 'citizenship' represents an attempt not simply to extend social rights, but also to bridge the potentially socially disruptive gap between the individual and the community and between the exercise of individual rights and the common good. Harrison (1973), writing about the growing government interest in leisure policy in the nineteenth century, argues that there is an inherent tension between social and moral reform. Although social reform requires the lessening of constraints on individual liberty, moral reform requires the building up of constraints. Citizenship implies responsibilities and duties as well as rights. The complex relationships between leisure and citizenship, between rights and responsibilities can be seen in discussions surrounding the emergence of modern leisure policy in the nineteenth century.

Bailey (1978: 49–50), in discussing the agitation for reduced working hours, states that: 'only by demonstrating their commitment to the serious duties of recreation could the working class prove their fitness for the shortening of the working day'. When the Ten Hours Bill was passed, Lord Shaftesbury warned the working class 'of the great responsibility they faced now that the bill had passed into law ... to turn to good account the extra free time they had acquired'.

Consequently, much of the nineteenth century government positive interest in various aspects of leisure (sport, libraries, museums, parks) combines genuine concerns to improve the quality of life of the new urban working class with attempts to create a new civic culture and, by implication, 'citizens' (Bailey, 1978). In this context leisure was viewed vaguely as a social and physical space (public buildings, public parks) in which economic inequalities would be unimportant – leisure was ideologically constructed as the realm of social equality, the realm of citizens. Consequently, participation was not simply about individual welfare and rights – the act and process of participation was central to the idea of the citizen. Participation was both an expression and an affirmation of citizenship, of a deeper social consensus. From this perspective the responsible citizen was a participating citizen, non-participation was, and as we will see, continues to be, viewed as a potential threat to social stability.

Further, the politics of leisure policy have been characterized by another duality – a frequently strong political and ideological rhetoric about the importance of various aspects of leisure provision has been combined with government reluctance to be involved directly. For example, despite its presumed role in addressing issues of urban health (parks, washhouses), education (libraries, museums) and broader moral and social cohesion (rational recreation), much leisure provision was a non-statutory responsibility of local government and the voluntary sector.

Leisure as a right of social citizenship

However, systematic central government interest in leisure policy dates largely from the 1960s. As in the nineteenth century, government's interest in leisure policy reflected a concern with the effects of rapid economic, social and cultural change. The understanding of the new context is illustrated by the first annual report of the advisory Sports Council in 1966, which stated that:

> We have entered a new era of dramatic evolution in our material progress ... more and more people are acquiring leisure and the means to enjoy it ... consequently we are faced with the need for better, more abundant and sophisticated facilities for our leisure activities. (Advisory Sports Council, 1966: 5)

This was reflected in a more general concern to promote public planning, provision and management to cater for the demands of the new 'leisure age' (Sillitoe, 1969; Blackie et al., 1979; Veal, 1987: 1–3). The organizational infrastructure for leisure policy was both reorganized and extended. The Arts Council (which was established in 1949) was reformed and, reflecting a more inclusive age, its remit shifted from an elitist concentration on 'fine arts' to a more general definition and a desire to create new audiences (Coalter et al., 1988). An executive Sports Council was established in 1971 to support the voluntary sector and to encourage local authorities to provide for increasing demand 'in the interests of social welfare and the enjoyment of leisure among the public at large' (Sports Council Royal Charter, 1971: 1). The Countryside Commission replaced the National Parks Commission in 1968 to meet rising demands for outdoor recreation and reconcile these with the interests of agriculture and conservation.

Underlying these developments was a vague notion of 'citizenship rights' and a social-democratic consensus about the extension of welfare services (for an analysis of similar developments in the Netherlands see van der Poel, 1993; in Germany, see Nahrstedt 1993; and in France, see Hantrais, 1989). The post-war welfare state had established a variety of social rights of citizenship through an expanding range of publicly organized goods and services – educational reform, health care, personal social services, an expanded public house building programme, and so on. Within this climate of opinion, a broad notion of 'social service' combined with a local government commitment to 'service development' to include increased investment in public leisure provision (although this was never subject to widespread political, public or even theoretical debate) (Roche, 1992). Similar processes were occurring in France, where the public had come to expect state intervention and to see leisure provision as an important social service (Hantrais, 1989).

Within this context continuing inequalities in participation led to the designation of certain groups as 'recreationally disadvantaged'. If all aspects of citizenship were to become a reality, public provision must provide equal opportunities for all. This led to the formulation of policies of 'recreational welfare' (Coalter et al., 1988). Rather than simply respond to expressed demand, policy became concerned to democratize areas of public leisure. The language of leisure policy shifted from a concern with demand to an attempt to address the issues of 'need'. Attempts were made to define the nature of 'leisure need' implied by public provision (Rapoport and Rapoport, 1975; Mennel, 1979) in order to improve the fit between provision and such need (Dower et al., 1981) and lay the basis for the development of a leisure profession.

In Germany, government confirmed that 'leisure policy is part of a social policy, which is directed to the achievement of an adequate standard of human, social and democratic life, and of working conditions for all citizens' (Nahrstedt, 1993). In Britain the 1975 White Paper, *Sport and Recreation*, defined recreational facilities as 'part of the general fabric of the social services'. Policies of positive discrimination were developed with the definition of 'target groups' and associated special concessionary and promotional strategies (Sport for All, democratization of culture, community recreation, animation) aimed at reducing constraints and encouraging participation (for accounts of similar developments in France, see Hantrais, 1984).

However, the ambiguity and duality of leisure policy was also present. The 1975 White Paper promoted the idea of recreation *as* welfare, stating that:

> by reducing boredom and urban frustration participation in active recreation contributes to the reduction of hooliganism and delinquency among young people ... The need to provide for people to make the best of their leisure time must be seen in this context. (Department of the Environment, 1975: 3)

Nevertheless, although the rhetoric of recreation *as* welfare was ideologically potent, it remained politically weak and marginal to core public policy developments – few attempts were made to examine systematically the effectiveness of recreation *as* welfare policies.

Leisure policy under attack

However, the 'golden age' of social-democratic leisure policy (sport for all; democratization of culture) was relatively short-lived, as leisure services came under attack from the political left and right. The left criticized what it viewed as the essentially passive, non-participatory and non-liberatory nature of public leisure services. The emergence of a so-called 'leisure profession' to define, measure and cater for needs meant that the citizen in such policies was essentially passive. Social democracy did things *to* and *for* people, within a paradigm of caring givers and grateful receivers (Corrigan, 1988). Such a system was essentially one way – a top-down democratization of culture rather than a bottom-up 'cultural democracy'. The supposedly liberative, participatory, potential of leisure services was being undermined by bureaucratic structures, managerialist ideologies and the dominance of a form of professional paternalism in the definition of need (Dower et al., 1981; Clarke and Critcher, 1985; Whitson, 1985).

However, this critique was paralleled by much more fundamental moral, economic and political attacks on welfarism *per se* from the political right. Following the election of Margaret Thatcher's neoliberal Conservative government in 1979 we entered a period of what Henry (2001: 78) refers to as 'state flexibilisation and disinvestment' – in which all aspects of welfare were subject to radical critique and attempted reform.

The right's moral critique of social citizenship was also one of passivity – that, in practice, it consisted solely of rights, with few associated *responsibilities* and duties (Roche, 1992). This 'nanny state' had led to passivity and a decline in the willingness, or ability, of recipients to take responsibility for their own consumption and welfare. The *economic* critique was that local governments were financially profligate and, in order to reduce public sector borrowing deficits, there was a need to control local government spending. The *political* critique was of local government *per se* – because of what was seen as bureaucratic inefficiency and lack of accountability and responsiveness to consumer needs, local government's role as a direct provider should be abolished or reduced greatly (Coalter, 1998). Although reflecting different historical trajectories and national circumstances, broadly similar shifts in leisure policies can be identified in the Netherlands (van der Poel, 1993; Lengkeek, 1993) and France (Poujol, 1993).

Although the right critique was aimed at all forms of public provision, there were specific attacks on leisure services at both national and local levels. For example, in an attempt to reduce what was perceived to be a 'welfare mentality' in the arts, greater emphasis was placed on commercial sponsorship and incentive funding (this was eventually extended to sport) (Henry, 2001). Under such pressures the rationale for the arts gradually shifted from community arts and aesthetic issues to an increasing emphasis on the economic importance of the arts (ibid.). Evans (2001: 139) refers to this as the growth of the 'new cultural economy' (also driven partly by the need to find strategies for the economic redevelopment of deindustrializing cities). Evans (ibid.) illustrates that this shift in arts policy was widespread – in addition to the UK (Myerscough, 1988), economic impact studies of the arts were undertaken in Germany, the Netherlands (Kloosterman and Elfring, 1991) and the US (Heilbrun and Gray, 1993).

In terms of local leisure provision it was claimed that universal subsidies were both inefficient and ineffective (Audit Commission, 1989). They were perceived to generate artificially high levels of demand among groups who could afford to take responsibility for their own consumption and they had demonstrably failed to attract the disadvantaged groups for whom they were intended. Such analyses led to the more general policy of Compulsory Competitive Tendering (CCT) being applied to local authority sport and recreation services. This required them to compete to retain the management of their facilities (on the presumption that this would lead to increased efficiency and a greater cutomer focus), while retaining control of strategic policy and methods of implementation (pricing, programming).

Interestingly, despite the left critique of paternalistic and non-responsive leisure services, reaction to the extension of CCT to sport and recreation services was almost uniformly negative. Bramham et al. (1993) argued that welfare rights were being replaced by consumer rights (see also Aitchison, 1992; Clarke, 1992; Ravenscroft and Tolley, 1993). Ravenscroft (1993: 42) argued that public leisure provision had ceased to be a constituent part of a liberal democratic model of freedom and had become 'a *central feature* of a deeply divisive process of constructing a new citizenship, one in which the politics of choice has been replaced by the politics of means' (emphasis added).

One critic of this more general 'defence of welfare' position suggested that the left was viewing the public sector through rose-tinted glasses, confusing symbol with substance, using 'the rhetoric of citizenship … not to understand market society, but simply to express moral distaste for the vulgarity of market values' (Ignatieff, 1991: 30). In relation to leisure policy, Coalter (1998) argued that the 'defence of welfare' position rested on a number of misrepresentations and unexamined assumptions. For example, leisure services' failure to establish a status as part of the core welfare services (Hill and Bramley, 1986) meant that the assertion that such changes were a 'central feature' in the reconstruction of social citizenship was more symbolic than real (Coalter, 1998). Further, such analyses ignored the relative failure of previously highly subsidized 'welfare-oriented' leisure services to cater for disadvantaged groups (Audit Commission, 1989).

Leisure policy: a lottery?

Although the replacement of Margaret Thatcher by John Major in 1990 did not lead to a substantial change in the broader neoliberal policies (for example, CCT proceeded), it led to a more proactive approach to certain aspects of leisure policy – especially in sport, an area of deep personal interest to Major. Major's administration sought to bring some degree of coherence via the establishment of the Department of National Heritage (responsible for broadcasting, arts, sports, heritage and tourism and providing a Cabinet post) and published the first strategy for sport since 1975 – *Sport: Raising the Game* (Department of National Heritage, 1996). However, perhaps most significantly, the National Lottery was established in 1994, to fund the 'good causes' of sports, arts and heritage. Henry (2001: 92) refers to the introduction of the National Lottery as 'a masterstroke in terms of leisure policy, since it allowed the Conservative government to both decrease tax-driven subsidy and to increase financial support for sport, the arts and heritage'.

Although this ensured large sums of money becoming available (by 1999 over £2 billion had been allocated to sport and the arts), Henry (2001) argues that because access to Lottery funding was based on a bidding process and some degree of matched funding it cannot be regarded as a replacement for needs-driven welfare spending. In a similar vein, Evans (1995: 234) argues that an absence of a planning framework for the arts and the adoption of centralized administration of grants (via the Arts and Sports Councils and a Heritage Commission), led to the reinforcement of 'a hegemonic system of leisure intervention' in which welfare-oriented issues of cultural democracy were ignored. Further, as with others, he regards the Lottery as a form of regressive taxation, with the beneficiaries being concentrated in capital and regional cities, in major flagship projects and in the arts, sports and heritage organizations whose participants are predominantly drawn from higher socioeconomic groups (those least likely to play the Lottery) (see also Evans, 1995). This was exacerbated in sport, where a 35 per cent contribution from applicants was required. However, the Sports Council responded to this by adopting a deprived area-based policy, where up to 90 per cent funding was made available (although this was also criticized for leaving out various disadvantaged groups) (Henry, 2001).

Much of John Major's interest in aspects of leisure policy was developed within a traditional Conservative discourse of heritage, nationhood and national pride (Henry, 2001). In the introduction to the strategy for sport, *Sport: Raising the Game*, Major stated that:

> Sport is a central part of Britain's National Heritage ... a binding force between generations and across borders ... one of the defining characteristics of nationhood and local pride. (Department of National Heritage, 1996: 2)

However, the strategy effectively ignored equity issues of 'sport for all' and the central role of local government in mass participation, concentrating on school sport and the promotion of 'traditional sports'. The other major initiative in the strategy related to elite sport – in his introduction, Major argued: 'sport at the highest level engages the wider community'. To combat what was perceived as a relative decline in Britain's international sporting performance it was proposed to establish a Lottery-funded British Academy of Sport on the Australian model (Green, 2004). Because of Major's electoral defeat in 1997, much of this agenda was not implemented, although it was adopted almost wholesale by the 'New' Labour government of Tony Blair.

New Labour and leisure as 'active citizenship'

The election of a New Labour government in the UK in 1997 placed aspects of leisure more centrally on the broader social policy agenda, largely because of the presumed externalities, or benefits, associated with participation. For example, the Scottish Office stated that:

> Arts, sport and leisure activities ... have a role to play in countering social exclusion. They can help to increase the self-esteem of individuals; build community spirit; increase social interaction; improve health and fitness; create employment and give young people a purposeful activity, reducing the temptation to anti-social behaviour. (Scottish Office, 1999: 22)

In England, Policy Action Group 10's action plan for sport and the arts stated that:

> Participation in the arts and sport has a beneficial social impact. Arts and sport are inclusive and can contribute to neighbourhood renewal. They can build confidence and encourage strong community groups. However, these benefits are frequently overlooked both by some providers of arts and sports facilities and programmes and by those involved in area regeneration programmes. (DCMS, 1999: 5)

Although this may look like a simple restatement of the recreation *as* welfare policies of the 1970s and 1980s, the underpinning sociopolitical philosophy of New Labour ensured that such policies have moved beyond their previous often rhetorical status – the link between leisure policies and a new emphasis on 'active citizenship' was made more explicit.

First, the increased emphasis on the potential of leisure services is explained by certain aspects of New Labour's agenda, especially their desire to create a 'Third Way' between the perceived failures of 'Old' Labour policies of state control, state provision and anti-individualism and the Thatcherite neoliberal, free market policies, with their extreme individualism. The Third Way – between the market and the state – is a relatively amorphous term associated with the writings of Giddens (1998) and represents an attempt to modernize and reform all aspects of government and civil society. Drawing loosely on the communitarian ideas of Etzioni (1997), Putnam's (1993, 2000) concepts of social capital, and Hutton's (1995) notions of a 'stakeholder' society, the Third Way seeks to strengthen civil society and empower communities. It seeks to combine responsibilities with rights via the promotion of 'active citizenship' – although Giddens's (1998) Third Way values include equality, protection of the vulnerable and freedom as autonomy, they also include 'no rights without responsibilities'. Much of this was to be achieved by reducing social exclusion.

Giddens (1998: 104) states that social exclusion is 'not about gradations of inequality, but about mechanisms that act to detach groups of people from the social mainstream'. Room (1995) proposes that, whereas policies for addressing poverty were distributional, the concerns of policies to combat social exclusion are relational – it refers to inadequate social participation, lack of social integration and lack of power. Forrest and Kearns suggest that 'social exclusion arises from a combination of unemployment, low income, marital breakdown and a generally resource-poor social network ... trapped within or channelled into specific neighbourhoods' (Forrest and Kearns, 1999: 1). The Social Exclusion Unit (n.d.) define it as a shorthand label for a combination of linked problems – unemployment, poor skills, low income, poor housing, high crime environment, bad health and family breakdown.

Central to this agenda is the rather diffuse concept of social capital, which refers to various social and moral relations that bind communities together. This partly reflects a broad shift from viewing urban regeneration solely in terms of economic and infrastructural development, to a greater emphasis on people and the development of social capital. This has resulted in an increased emphasis on social processes and relationships and the organizational capacities of communities (Forrest and Kearns, 1999). Communities with high levels of social capital are characterized by three main components – strong social networks and civic infrastructure; strong social norms (that is, informal and formal rules about personal and social behaviour and associated sanctions); and mutual trust and reciprocity among members of a community. Although the concept is not new (see Field, 2003, for a review), the recent work of Putnam (2000) on the decline of community in the USA has led to increased policy interest. Evidence suggests that communities high in social capital tend to have a number of positive aspects – lower crime rates, better health and lower rates of child abuse (see Performance and Innovation Unit, 2002, and Office for National Statistics, 2001, for policy-oriented reviews of evidence).

This approach revises the policy rhetoric about the relationship between leisure participation and citizenship being both a right and an affirmation. For example, the Scottish Office wants to promote increased participation because 'people who participate in sports and arts activities are more likely to play an active role in the community in other ways' (Scottish Office, 1999: 22).

Reflecting this new emphasis on active citizenship, Sport England and the Local Government Association, seeking to promote the positive aspects of sports volunteering, argued that:

Voluntary and community activity is fundamental to the development of a democratic, socially inclusive society. Voluntary and community groups ... enable individuals to contribute to public life and the development of their communities ... In so doing they engage the skills, interests, beliefs and values of individuals and groups. (Local Government Association, 1999: 16)

There are striking similarities between this rhetoric and Parker's (1993) analysis, which, borrowing from Stebbins's (1997) concept of 'serious leisure', suggests that leisure time participation in non-commercial community and voluntary organizations offers the potential to develop active citizenship.

This new emphasis has been described as marking a shift from the traditional approach of developing sport *in* the community, to developing communities *through* sport (Coalter et al., 2000; Houlihan and White, 2003) – although this is most marked in sport, these shifts have also occurred in other aspects of leisure services. In New Labour's social inclusion agenda the tests of effectiveness have shifted from the equity-oriented 'Sport for All' to what Richard Caborn, Minister of Sport, has referred to as 'sport for good' – as sport (and leisure provision in general) is called upon more systematically to provide an 'economy of remedies' (Donnison et al., 1965) to a variety of social problems.

Prove it!

However, the emergence of the new centrality of leisure in social policy has been accompanied by a new emphasis on measurement and evaluation. Although the issue of externalities has always been a major rationale underpinning leisure policies (Coalter, 2000), it has been a vague and unexamined rationale. The apparent theoretical strength and coherence of the description of leisure's potentially positive contributions led to widespread failures to undertake systematic monitoring and evaluation of presumed outcomes.

The shift from management by objectives ('catering for the leisure needs of the community') to objective-led management (defining measurable targets) that had begun with CCT, was now reinforced. With CCT being replaced by Best Value, the emphasis has shifted from output-led to outcome-based evaluation (Cabinet Office, 2002). Emphasis was placed on 'welfare effectiveness' and, most importantly, the contribution that all services made to so-called 'cross-cutting agendas' – health, crime, regeneration and education.

Much of this approach is summed up in the phrase 'evidence-based policy-making'. Within New Labour's pragmatic non-ideological stance, 'what matters is what works' became the watchword (Solesbury, 2001). Although much of this evidence-based policy-making is based on monitoring and *ex post* evaluation of current initiatives, a number of organizations have been established to accumulate evidence about the efficacy of practice – in health there is the National Institute for Clinical Excellence and the NHS Centre for Reviews and Dissemination; in education, the Centre for Evidence-informed Education Policy and Practice (EPPI Centre), and the Association of Directors of Social Services has established a 'Research in Practice' (RIP) initiative (Solesbury, 2001).

In the area of leisure there has been a range of research-based initiatives reflecting this new evidence-based, outcome-led approach. In sport, a series of state-of-the art reviews have been commissioned by government and public organizations: *Policy Action Team 10: Report to the Social Exclusion Unit – Arts and Sport* (Department of Culture, Media and Sport (DCMS), 1999); *The Role of Sport in Regenerating Deprived Urban Areas* (Coalter et al., 2001 for the Scottish Executive); *Game Plan* (DCMS/ Strategy Unit, 2002); *The Benefits of Sport* (Coalter, 2005 for Sport Scotland) and the establishment of an online research-based Value of Sport Monitor by Sport England and UK Sport.

In the arts, outcome-oriented reviews have included Jermyn (2001) and Jackson (2003) for voluntary arts. Wavell et al. (2002) reviewed evidence relating to the broader social impacts of libraries, with Slee et al. (2001) reviewing evidence relating to social exclusion and countryside recreation. More generally, the Local Government Association commissioned a range of evidence-based reviews including play, tourism, arts, libraries, parks and museums (Allison and Coalter, 2001; Coalter, 2001a, 2001b, 2001c, 2001d; Coalter and Taylor, 2001).

This literature places varying interpretations on the nature and meaning of 'social exclusion', with some interpreting it narrowly within a traditional paradigm of 'low or non-participation' and seeking to illustrate examples of best practice in increasing access. However, although increased participation in leisure services is a goal of the social inclusion agenda, this is simply a necessary condition for the achievement of the presumed outcomes associated with leisure participation. That this shift towards a much more systematic and evidence-based approach proved difficult for some is indicated by the comment by the Arts Council that, 'expanding access has always been an important part of the work of the funding system ... Advocating the role the arts can play in addressing social exclusion is however a new departure' (quoted in Jermyn, 2001: 2).

Consequently, all the outcome-oriented reviews attempt to illustrate that participation in their part of leisure services is also associated with the achievement of broader personal and social outcomes. For example, Slee et al.'s (2001) review of countryside recreation and social exclusion identifies projects aimed at increasing participation among traditionally under-represented groups (ethnic minorities; people with disabilities), but also examines projects targeting more 'vulnerable groups' (at-risk youth; the homeless). Jermyn's (2001) work on the arts and social exclusion identifies a range of contexts in which the arts may contribute to other processes – educational achievement; rehabilitation of offenders; health and well-being; the construction of social capital and the more traditional concerns of community development and urban regeneration.

The broad assumptions of such approaches are outlined in Figure 10.1. For the more traditional, welfare-oriented concerns with social rights of citizenship the success of a programme could be assessed at the level of 'leisure outcomes' – survey data to illustrate the extent to which issues of equity had been addressed by attracting under-participating groups. However, within the new outcome-oriented social inclusion agendas, evaluation centres on the outcomes associated with such participation. As Figure 10.1 illustrates, the assumption is that participation will lead to *intermediate (individual) impacts* (for example, fitness, sense of well being, self-esteem, social skills and social involvement). Such impacts are then likely to lead to *intermediate outcomes* (changes in behaviour – decreased drug use, decreased anti-social behaviour, increased healthy lifestyle, improved educational performance, increased employability). In fact some commentators suggest that increased employability is the key desired outcome (Levitas, 1996). Collins and Kay (2003: 22) quote a Department of Social Security (1998) document, stating that the government's aim is to rebuild the welfare state around work and conclude that underpinning such policies is 'the belief that work will provide the income, status and self-esteem and thereby make recipients into active citizens, exercising their political and consumer rights'.

The accumulation of such behaviours, plus the more general impact of an improved local leisure infrastructure, will produce *strategic social outcomes* such as increased social capital, community cohesion and social regeneration (for a detailed

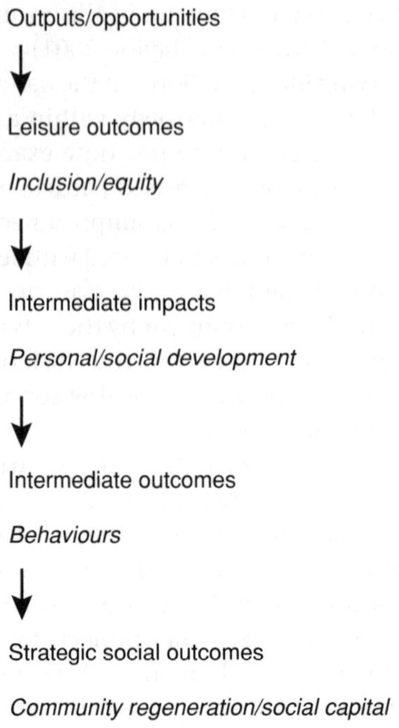

Outputs/opportunities

↓

Leisure outcomes

Inclusion/equity

↓

Intermediate impacts

Personal/social development

↓

Intermediate outcomes

Behaviours

↓

Strategic social outcomes

Community regeneration/social capital

Figure 10.1   The impacts of leisure

discussion of these issues in relation to sport, see Coalter, 2002). Although these issues and approaches appear to be more developed in the UK than elsewhere, others are also seeking to address this new agenda. Crompton, writing from a North American perspective, writes about the need to 'reposition' leisure services. He argues that:

> Providing resources to a leisure department so a minority of residents can have enjoyable experiences is likely to be a low priority when measured against the critical economic, health, safety and welfare issues with which most legislative bodies are confronted. (Crompton, 2000: 65–6)

In order to justify the allocation of additional resources, elected officials have to be convinced that leisure agencies deliver collective or public benefits, and Crompton (2000) argues that the task of leisure service agency managers is to identify the public benefits most desired and demonstrate the agency's potential contribution. However, most of the evidence-based reviews of leisure services conclude that, while there are strong theoretical arguments underpinning the presumption of a range of potential positive outcomes, the empirical evidence is weak (Coalter et al., 2000; Jermyn, 2001). This is not surprising as many of the presumed impacts and outcomes have mostly been vaguely implied and largely taken for granted – part of the vague policy rhetoric – with research being related predominantly to planning and marketing concerns with the nature and volume of participation. In some areas there has even been a reluctance to undertake such evaluation. For example, Jermyn quotes Moriarty's summing up of the wariness of arts workers about 'the anxiety that something very precious may be lost, that the complexity of an experience which included relationship, enjoyment, learning, exploration, expression will be destroyed, diluted or reduced' (Jermyn, 2001: 9).

Of course, in this and other areas, the lack of evidence also relates to more mundane issues such as pressures to deliver services and the lack of resources and expertise to undertake what are often very complex evaluations (Coalter et al., 2000; Jermyn, 2001). Although this is not the place to develop the argument, it is worth noting that there is an important debate about the precise nature of evidence required for such wide-ranging and complex claims. For example, Matarasso, writing about the social impact of libraries, suggests that 'the decision-making processes of public administration ... depend on the balance of probabilities rather than the elimination of reasonable doubt' (Matarasso, 1998: 5).

Pawson (2004) refers to these and similar social policies as 'ill-defined interventions with hard-to-follow outcomes' and suggests that, rather than the traditional quantitative approach to outcome measurement, we need to adopt theory-driven, logic-model approaches to assessing the success of such interventions (Pawson and Tilley, 2000; see also Coalter et al., 2000; Coalter, 2002, for illustrations regarding sport). From a policy perspective, the significance of such an approach is that it requires leisure policy-makers, providers and managers to articulate much more clearly and precisely the nature of their assumptions about each leisure service and how participation in such provision is presumed to lead to specific personal and social outcomes. Consequently it is essential to understand the processes of participation and to provide and manage in order to maximize the possibility of the achievement of the assumed outcomes. In other words there is a need to distinguish between basic necessary conditions (that is, participation in various leisure services) and sufficient conditions (the nature of processes) in achieving desired outcomes (Coalter et al., 2000).

However, it is also worth noting that, for some, the increased emphasis on instrumental, outcome-driven policies is not wholly unproblematic. In 2004, Tessa Jowell (Minister of Culture, Media and Sport) illustrated her perceived dilemmas in a 'personal manifesto'.

As a Culture Department we ... have to deliver the utilitarian agenda, and the measure of instrumentality that this implies, but we must acknowledge that we are doing more than that ... too often politicians have been forced to debate culture in terms only of its instrumental benefits to other agendas ... In political and public discourse in this country we have avoided the more difficult approach of investigating, questioning and celebrating what culture actually does in and of itself. (Jowell, 2004a: 8–9)

From this position she develops arguments for more traditional policies based on the inherent value of culture and policies of democratization of culture – 'giving everyone the possibility of benefiting from what complex culture has to offer' (Jowell, 2004a: 14) and quotes the DCMS funding for free access to museums and art galleries as an example of such a policy. Interestingly, soon after this publication Jowell gave a speech entitled *Realising the Opportunities from Equality in Sport* (Jowell, 2004b), which listed a series of sports-related outcomes related to health, self-esteem, teamwork, and volunteering and social skills and referred to sport's role in addressing the obesity-related problems associated with inactivity. It would seem that although the debate about culture for culture's sake may still have some defenders, sports for sports sake has been abandoned to more pragmatic, outcome-oriented approaches.

Leisure and regeneration

At a macro level, there has been a reinforcing of the role of various aspects of leisure in broader processes of social and economic regeneration and development. Henry (2001) analyses this long-term shift as reflecting cities becoming part of new 'regimes of accumulation' as they move from being Fordist units of industrial production to post-Fordist units of consumption (Henry, 2001). In the former, leisure provision was largely part of welfare provision, part of the social wage. In the latter it occupies a more strategic position as post-industrial cities seek to become tourist-driven centres of consumption, with arts and sport in particular being used in strategies of re-imaging and city marketing (Henry and Gratton, 2001) in an attempt to attract both inward investment and tourists.

The global reach and importance of such developments are illustrated by Evans, who states that:

> cities that have used culture ... are celebrated and looked to as successful proponents not only of culture-led regeneration, but also of urban regeneration generally. Regional capitals such as Barcelona and ... Bilbao in Spain, Glasgow in Scotland, Frankfurt in Germany and several English and French secondary cities have used aspects of the urban cultural planning formula. (Evans, 2001: 213)

However, the extent to which these developments can be regarded as part of a more integrated leisure policy is questionable. For example, while suggesting that the regeneration claims of such projects are often overstated, Evans (2001) also points to significant ambiguities in the relationship between such developments and wider cultural and leisure policies. He suggests that such development-driven investments often take place in the absence of a strategic cultural policy, with minimal involvement of the local cultural sector and in parallel to neighbourhood community arts and cultural activities – leading to 'the narrowing in the range of cultural activities and experience on offer ie homogenisation' (ibid.: 255).

Gratton et al. make a broadly similar point, suggesting that sports-led regeneration efforts have little to do with an overall leisure/sports policy:

investment in sporting infrastructure in cities over the past 20 years was not primarily aimed at getting the local community involved in sport, but was instead aimed at attracting tourists, encouraging inward investment and changing the image of the city. (Gratton et al., 2005: 1)

In an analysis of the Sydney Olympics, Searle (2002) argues that the subsequent financial troubles of Stadium Australia and the SuperDome are explained partly because they were built in response to a passing opportunity rather than rooted in a strategic approach to recreation and leisure planning for the greater Sydney area. Much of the sports-led attempts at regeneration have been based on events and for Gratton et al. (2005) the results are mixed – the relative success of the nationally funded Commonwealth Games in Manchester, the relative failure of the locally funded World Student Games in Sheffield, the growing scepticism in North America about the real value of public investments in stadia for professional team sports (Austrian and Rosentraub, 2002; Coates and Humphreys, 2003) and only a limited number of mega events where direct economic benefit is most likely (for example, the Olympics, the World Cup). However, because of a lack of robust data (see Crompton, 1995, for a detailed critique of the limitations of economic impact studies), Gratton et al. (2005) conclude that the longer-term urban regeneration benefits of sport remain unknown (see also Gratton and Henry, 2001).

In the light of Gratton et al.'s (2005) comment that such investments are rarely aimed at getting the local community involved in sport, it is worth noting Taylor's (2001) analysis that one result of the World Student Games in Sheffield was the closure of a local swimming pool and a city-wide decline in swimming attendances. Further, Coalter (2004) has illustrated that there is little evidence that economically driven large-scale sporting events have any positive longer-term impacts on mass participation (despite this being a regularly expressed rationale). This separation of the macro role of sport from the more traditional equity concerns is illustrated by the increasingly instrumental and success-driven investments in elite sport. Although this approach was outlined in John Major's *Sport: Raising the Game* (Department of National Heritage, 1996) it has been reinforced by New Labour's emphasis on focused investment, outcomes and performance-based approaches (Green, 2004). The emphasis on winning and meeting the government's broader foreign policy and diplomatic objectives has meant that the former, admittedly rather aspirational, model of a sports development continuum, with a relationship between mass and elite participation, is severely eroded. For example, Sue Campbell, the Chair of UK Sport, has stated that:

The reality is that there are some sports in which we can genuinely anticipate success on a world stage, but have to face the fact that they will never be mass participation sports ... you can have a performance strategy based on good quality identification and structure that doesn't necessarily have to link into mass participation. (Campbell, 2004: 18)

In an era of outcome-oriented policy and funding within the context of 'welfare effectiveness', it would seem that the aspiration to an integrated leisure policy is as unattainable as ever – even within specific subsidiary policy areas. For example, *Game Plan* (DCMS/Strategy Unit, 2002) identifies four distinct worlds of sport – the production of excellence, the staging of events, 'mass' participation and social inclusion – each of which has different desired objectives, dynamics and funders and increasingly is the responsibility of different agencies. In the arts there seems to be a stronger belief in the relationship between participation and excellence, although the emphasis on bringing 'the transforming power of the arts to bear on issues of health, crime, education and inclusion' remains (Arts Council, 2003: 4). Further, we have seen the argument that the economic imperatives of the 'cultural economy' bear little relationship to the needs of community arts, or to issues of equity and social citizenship.

Conclusions

Because notions of participation, choice, individual freedom and the 'quality of life' are central to the concept of social rights, many have viewed increased public provision for leisure as being part of an evolutionary process of the development of citizenship. From this perspective, already established civil, political and social rights are augmented by the development of positive public policies for leisure. While not seeking to deny certain aspects of such an analysis, the core argument in this chapter has been that the history of public leisure policy is characterized by an essential duality – a tension between freedom and constraint, between the extension of such social rights of citizenship and a desire to restrain the exercise of potentially socially disruptive individual rights, between the balance of rights and responsibilities. Although the precise emphasis has varied historically, it is difficult to view public leisure policy simply as being the unproblematic extension of social rights of citizenship (Clarke, 1992; Henry, 1995; Ravenscroft, 1993). Although discussions of leisure policy have often been constructed in terms of freedoms and opportunities, the frequent references to participation and public cultures (Bramham et al., 1993) could be viewed as having the implication of duties and obligations of citizenship as well as simple rights.

Despite apparent historical changes in leisure policies, reflecting different governments' ideological priorities, it could be argued that the merit good argument has been the most consistent and strongest rationale underpinning leisure policies (Coalter, 1998) – perhaps paradoxically, leisure has not always been a social right of citizenship, but as one means of achieving certain aspects of citizenship! Not only should citizens be *able* to participate, but also it seems that they *should* participate as this contributes to the greater public good.

This emphasis clearly underpins recent public leisure policy in the UK. Informed by concerns with social inclusion, social capital, active citizenship, community renewal and stakeholding societies, traditionally rather diffuse assumptions about the positive outcomes of participation are now made explicit. Leisure policy is now formulated within a wider discourse of evidence-based policy-making and welfare effectiveness, raising major problems of accountability and lack of robust evidence for what have traditionally been 'ill-defined interventions with hard-to-follow outcomes' (Pawson, 2004). The associated pressure to chase outcome-focused funding which underpins short-term initiatives does little to develop more coherent policies. There is evidence that leisure policies developed within the social inclusion agenda, driven by particular outcome concerns, also have a rather tenuous relationship with broader 'recreational welfare' policies. Such pressures seem to be leading to greater fragmentation in leisure policy, with leisure-based approaches to economic regeneration (for example, large-scale events, iconic buildings), or outcome-driven interventions, having little systematic relationship with broader welfare-oriented policies for increased participation (Evans, 2001; Gratton et al., 2005). Despite being placed closer to the centre of core social policy concerns than ever before, it would seem that such a position represents as much of a threat as an opportunity for the development of a coherent set of policies for leisure.

Bibliography

Advisory Sports Council (1966) *Annual Report*, London, HMSO.

Aitchison, C. (1992) 'Women and the Implications of Compulsory Competitive Tendering in the UK Local Authority Leisure Services', in D. Leslie (ed.) *Perspectives on Provision*. LSA Publication No. 52, Eastbourne, Leisure Studies Association, pp. 37–47.

Allison, M. and Coalter, F. (2001) *Realising the Potential of Cultural Services: The Case for Museums*, London, Local Government Association.

Arts Council of England (1999) *Addressing Social Inclusion: A Framework for Action*, London, Arts Council of England.

Arts Council England (2003) *Ambition for the Arts 2003–2006*, London, Arts Council England.

Audit Commission (1989) *Sport for Whom? Clarifying the Local Authority Role in Sport and Recreation*, London, HMSO.

Austrian, Z. and Rosentraub, M. S. (2002) 'Cities, Sports and Economic Changes: A Retrospective Assessment', *Journal of Urban Affairs* 24(5): 549–63.

Bailey, P. (1978) *Leisure and Class in Victorian England*, London, Routledge & Kegan Paul.

Bianchini, F. (1992) 'Cultural Policy and the Development of Citizenship'. Paper presented at the European Leisure and Recreation Association Conference, 'Leisure and the New Citizenship', Bilbao, June.

Blackie, J., Coppock, T. and Duffield, B. (1979) *The Leisure Planning Process*, London, Social Science Research Council/Sports Council.

Bramham, P., Henry, I., Mommaas, H. and van der Poel, H. (eds) (1993) *Leisure Policies in Europe*, Wallingford, CAB International.

Campbell, S. (2004) Sue Campbell Interview by D. Jenner, *Sports Management* 1: 16–19.

Clarke, A. (1992) 'Citizens and Consumers', in J. Sugden and C. Knox (eds) *Leisure in the 1990s: Rolling Back the Welfare State*. Publication No. 46, Eastbourne, Leisure Studies Association, pp. 109–20.

Clarke, J. and Critcher, C. (1985) *The Devil Makes Work: Leisure in Capitalist Britain*, Basingstoke, Macmillan.

Coalter, F. (1988) *Sport and Anti-Social Behaviour: A Literature Review*. Research Report No. 2, Edinburgh, Scottish Sports Council.

Coalter, F. (1995) 'Compulsory Competitive Tendering for Sport and Leisure Management: A Lost Opportunity', *Managing Leisure* 1(1): 3–15.

Coalter, F. (1998) 'Leisure Studies, Leisure Policy and Social Citizenship: The Failure of Welfare or the Limits of Welfare?' *Leisure Studies* 17(1): 21–36.

Coalter, F. (2000) 'Public and Commercial Leisure Provision: Active Citizens and Passive Consumers?' *Leisure Studies* 19(2): 163–81.

Coalter, F. (2001a) *Realising the Potential of Cultural Services: The Case for the Arts*, London, Local Government Association.

Coalter, F. (2001b) *Realising the Potential of Cultural Services: The Case for Libraries*, London, Local Government Association.

Coalter, F. (2001c) *Realising the Potential of Cultural Services: The Case for Sport*, London, Local Government Association.

Coalter, F. (2001d) *Realising the Potential of Cultural Services: The Case for Tourism*, London, Local Government Association.

Coalter, F. (2002) *Sport and Community Development: A Manual*. Research Report No. 86, Edinburgh, Sport Scotland.

Coalter, F. (2004) 'Stuck in the Blocks? A Sustainable Sporting Legacy', in A. Vigor, M. Mean and C. Tims (eds) *After the Gold Rush: A Sustainable Olympics for London*, London, IPPR and Demos.

Coalter, F. (2005) *The Social Benefits of Sport: An Overview to Inform the Community Planning Process*, Edinburgh, Sport Scotland.

Coalter, F., Allison, M. and Taylor, J. (2000) *The Role of Sport in Regenerating Deprived Urban Areas*, Edinburgh, Scottish Executive.

Coalter, F., Long, J. and Duffield, B. (1988) *Recreational Welfare: The Rationale for Public Sector Investment in Leisure*, Aldershot, Gower/Avebury.

Coalter, F. and Taylor, J. (2001) *Realising the Potential of Cultural Services: The Case for Children's Play*, London, Local Government Association.

Coates, D. and Humphreys, B. R. (2003) 'The Effect of Professional Sports on Earnings and Employment in the Services and Retail Sectors in US Cities', *Regional Science and Urban Economics* 33(1): 175–98.

Collins, M. and Kay, T. (2003) *Sport and Social Inclusion*, London, Routledge.

Corrigan, P. (1988) 'Citizen Gains', *Marxism Today* (August).

Crompton, J. L. (1995) 'Economic Impact Analysis of Sports Facilities and Events: Eleven Sources of Misapplication', *Journal of Sport Management* 9(1): 14–35.

Crompton, J. L. (2000) 'Repositioning Leisure Services', *Managing Leisure* 5(2): 65–75.

Department of Culture, Media and Sport (DCMS) (1999) *Policy Action Team 10: Report to the Social Exclusion Unit – Arts and Sport*, London, HMSO.

Department of Culture, Media and Sport (DCMS)/Strategy Unit (2002) *Game Plan: A Strategy for Delivering Government's Sport and Physical Activity Objectives*, London, Strategy Unit/ Cabinet Office.

Department of Environment (1975) *Sport and Recreation*. Cmd 6200. London, HMSO.

Department of National Heritage (1996) *Sport: Raising the Game*, London, Department of National Heritage.

Department of Social Security (1998) *A New Contract for Welfare: New Ambitions for Our Country*. Cmd 3805. London, Stationery Office.

Donnison, D. V. et al. (1965) *Social Policy and Administration*, London, Allen & Unwin.

Dower, M., Rapoport, R., Strelitz, Z. and Kew, S. (1981) *Leisure Provision and People's Needs*, London, HMSO.

Etzioni, A. (1997) *The New Golden Rule: Community and Morality in a Democratic Society*, New York, Basic Books.

Evans, G. L. (1995) 'The National Lottery: Planning for Leisure or Pay Up and Play the Game?' *Leisure Studies* 14(2): 225–44.

Evans, G. L. (1999) 'The Economics of the National Performing Arts – Exploiting Consumer Surplus and Willingness-to-Pay: A Case of Cultural Policy Failure?' *Leisure Studies* 18(2): 97–118.

Evans, G. L. (2001) *Cultural Planning: An Urban Renaissance?*, London, Routledge.

Field, J. (2003) *Social Capital*, London, Routledge.

Forrest, R. and Kearns, A. (1999) *Joined-Up Places: Social Cohesion and Neighbourhood Regeneration*, York, YPS for the Joseph Rowntree Foundation.

Giddens, A. (1998) *The Third Way: Renewal of Social Democracy*, Cambridge, Polity Press.

Gratton, C. and Henry, I. (eds) (2001) *Sport in the City: The Role of Sport in Economic and Social Regeneration*, London, Routledge.

Gratton, C., Shibli, S. and Coleman, R. (2005) 'Sport and Economic Regeneration in Cities', *Urban Studies* 42(5/6): 1–15.

Green, M. (2004) 'Changing Policy Priorities for Sport in England: The Emergence of Elite Sport Development as a Key Policy Concern', *Leisure Studies* 23(4): 365–85.

Hantrais, L. (1984) 'Leisure Policy in France', *Leisure Studies* 3(2): 129–46.

Hantrais, L. (1989) 'Central Government Policy in France under the Socialist Administration 1981–86', in P. Bramham, I. Henry, H. Mommas and H. van der Poel (eds) *Leisure and Urban Processes*, London, Routledge, pp. 69–89.

Harrison, B. (1973) 'State Intervention and Moral Reform in 19th Century England', in P. Hollis (ed.) *Pressure from Without in Victorian England*, London, Edward Arnold.

Heilbrun, J. and Gray, C. M. (1993) *The Economics of Art and Culture: An American Perspective*, Cambridge, Cambridge University Press.

Henry, I. P. (1995) 'Leisure and Social Stratification: The Response of the State to Social Restructuring in Britain', in K. Roberts (eds) *Leisure and Social Stratification*. Publication No. 53, Eastbourne, Leisure Studies Association, pp. 49–58.

Henry, I. P. (2001) *The Politics of Leisure Policy*, 2nd edn, Basingstoke, Palgrave Macmillan.

Henry, I. P. and Gratton, C. (eds) (2001) *Sport in the City: The Role of Sport in Economic and Social Regeneration*, London, Routledge.

Hill, M. and Bramley, G. (1986) *Analysing Social Policy*, Oxford, Blackwell.

Houlihan, B. and White, A. (2003) *The Politics of Sports Development: Development of Sport or Development through Sport?* London, Routledge.

Hutton, W. (1995) *The State We're In*, London, Vintage.

Ignatieff, M. (1991) 'Citizenship and Moral Narcissism', in G. Andrews (ed.) *Citizenship*, London, Lawrence & Wishart, pp. 26–36.

Jackson, A. (2003) *Doing it Ourselves: Learning to Challenge Social Exclusion through Voluntary Arts*, Cardiff, Voluntary Arts Network.

Jermyn, H. (2001) *The Arts and Social Exclusion: A Review Prepared for the Arts Council of England*, London, Arts Council of England.

Jowell, T. (2004a) *Government and the Value of Culture*, London, Department for Culture, Media and Sport.

Jowell, T. (2004b) Speech to 'Taking Action – Realising the Opportunities from Equality in Sport' Conference, November, London, Department for Culture, Media and Sport.

Kloosterman, R. C. and Elfring, T. (1991) *Werken in Nederland*, Scoonhoven, Academic Service.

Lengkeek, J. (1993) 'Collective and Private Interest in Recreation and Tourism – the Dutch Case: Concerning Consequences of a Shift from Citizen Role to Consumer Role', *Leisure Studies* 12(1): 7–33.

Levitas, R. (1996) 'The Concept of Social Exclusion and the New Durkheimian Hegemony', *Critical Social Policy* 16(1): 5–20.

Local Government Association (1999) *Value of Sport – Best Value Through Sport*, London, Sport England.

Matarasso, F. (1998) *Poverty and Oysters: The Social Impact of Local Arts Development in Portsmouth*, Stroud, Comedia.

Mennell, S. (1979) 'Theoretical Considerations on Cultural Needs', *Sociology* 13(2): 235–57.

Moriarty, G. (1997) *Taliruni's Travellers: An Arts Worker's View of Evaluation*. The Social Impact of the Arts Working Paper 7. Stroud, Comedia.

Myerscough, J. (1988) *Economic Importance of the Arts in Britain*, London, Policy Studies Institute.

Nahrstedt, W. (1993) 'Leisure Policy in Germany', in P. Bramham, I. Henry, H. Mommas and H. van der Poel (eds) *Leisure Policies in Europe*, Wallingford, CAB International, pp. 129–48.

Office for National Statistics (2001) *Social Capital: A Review of the Literature*, London, ONS, Social Analysis and Reporting Division.

Parker, S. (1993) 'Serious Leisure, Citizenship and the Body Politic', in C. Brackenridge (ed.) *Body Matters: Leisure Limit and Lifestyle*. Publication No. 47, Eastbourne, Leisure Studies Association, pp. 179–82.

Pawson, R. (2004) 'Evaluating Ill-defined Interventions with Hard-to-follow Outcomes'. Paper to the ESRC Seminar Series 'The Impact of Sport and the Arts', Metropolitan University, Leeds, January.

Pawson, R. and Tilley, N. (2000) *Realistic Evaluation*, London, Sage.

Performance and Innovation Unit (2002) *Social Capital: A Discussion Paper*, London, Cabinet Office, available at: <http://www.cabinet-office.gov.uk/innovation>, accessed February 2006.

Poujol, G. (1993) 'Leisure Politics and Policies in France', in P. Bramham, I. Henry, H. Mommas and H. van der Poel (eds) *Leisure Policies in Europe*, Wallingford, CAB International, pp. 13–40.

Putnam, R. D. (1993) 'The Prosperous Community: Social Capital and Public Life', *American Prospect* 13(1): 35–42.

Putnam, R. D. (2000) *Bowling Alone: The Collapse and Revival of American Community*, New York, Simon & Schuster.

Rapoport, R. and Rapoport, R. N. (1975) *Leisure and the Family Life-Cycle*, London, Routledge.

Ravenscroft, N. (1993) 'Public Sector Provision and the Good Citizen', *Leisure Studies* 12(1): 33–44.

Ravenscroft, N. and Tolley, J. (1993) 'Ideological Dominance in Recreation Provision: The Response of Local Authorities in Britain to CCT'. Paper presented at the Third International Conference of the Leisure Studies Association, 'Leisure in Different Worlds', Loughborough University, July.

Roche, M. (1992) *Rethinking Citizenship: Welfare, Ideology and Change in Modern Society*, Cambridge, Polity Press.

Room, G. (1995) 'Poverty and Social Exclusion: The New European Agenda for Policy and Research', in G. Room (ed.) *Beyond the Threshold: The Measurement and Analysis of Social Exclusion*, Bristol, Policy Press.

Scottish Office (1999) *Social Inclusion – Opening the Door to a Better Scotland*, Edinburgh, Scottish Office.

Searle, G. (2002) 'Uncertain Legacy: Sydney's Olympic Stadiums', *European Planning Studies* 10(7): 845–60.

Sillitoe, K. K. (1969) *Planning Leisure*, London, HMSO.

Slee, B., Joseph, D. and Curry, N. (2001) *Social Exclusion in Countryside Leisure in the United Kingdom*, Cardiff, Countryside Recreation Network.

Social Exclusion Unit (n.d.) *What is Social Exclusion?* London, Office of the Deputy Prime Minister, Social Exclusion Unit, available at <http://www.socialexclusionunit.gov.uk/page.asp?id=213>, accessed February 2006.

Solesbury, W. (2001) *Evidence Based Policy: Whence it Came and Where it's Going*. Working Paper No. 1, London, ESRC UK Centre for Evidence Based Policy and Practice, University of London.

Sports Council (1971) Royal Charter, London, Sports Council.

Stebbins, R. (1997) 'Casual Leisure: A Conceptual Framework', *Leisure Studies* 16(1): 17–25.

Taylor, J. and Coalter, F. (2001) *Realising the Potential of Cultural Services: The Case for Urban Parks, Open Spaces and the Countryside*, London, Local Government Association.

Taylor, P. (2001) 'Sports Facility Development and the Role of Forecasting: A Retrospective on Swimming in Sheffield', in C. Gratton and I. P. Henry (eds) *Sport in the City: The Role of Sport in Economic and Social Regeneration*, London, Routledge, pp. 214–26.

van der Poel, H. (1993) 'Leisure Policy and the Netherlands', in P. Bramham, I. Henry, H. Mommas and H. van der Poel (eds) *Leisure Policies in Europe*, Wallingford, CAB International, pp. 41–70.

Veal, A. J. (2002) *Leisure and Tourism Policy and Planning*, Wallingford, CAB International.

Wavell, C., Baxter, G., Johnson, I. and Williams, D. (2002) *Impact Evaluation of Museums, Archives and Libraries: Available Evidence Project*, London, Council for Museums, Archives and Libraries.

Whitson, D. (1985) 'Leisure and the State: Theorising Struggles Over Everyday Life', in F. Coalter (ed.) *The Politics of Leisure*, Eastbourne, Leisure Studies Association, pp. 45–62.

Part 3
Axial Principles

11
Leisure and Time
Jiri Zuzanek[1]

Both notions examined in this chapter – time and leisure – pose considerable definitional difficulties. St Augustine, struggling in the fourth century with the concept of time, wrote: 'What then is time? If no one asks of me, I know; if I wish to explain to him who asks, I know not' (St Augustine, *Confessions*, XI, 14). Ennis, in an article published 16 centuries later, expressed a similar puzzlement with the notion of leisure: 'Of all the great categories of life, leisure is surely one of the most untidy' (Ennis, 1968: 525). Yet, paradoxically, time is often used to define leisure. So, what then, is the relationship between leisure and time? Can an equation containing two 'unknowns' be solved with any certainty?

Many doubts have been cast about the relevance of time in defining or measuring leisure. Leisure, we have been told repeatedly, is more than discretionary time. Defining leisure as time would empty it of its content. According to Berger, 'To contrast work and leisure – and we must contrast them, since they have sociological meaning *vis-a-vis* each other – we must conceive of leisure as a kind of *action*' (Berger, 1963: 28). To de Grazia, 'Anybody can have free time. Not everybody can have leisure. Free time refers to a special way of calculating a special kind of time. Leisure refers to a *state of being, a condition of man*' (de Grazia, 1962: 5, emphasis added). But the conundrum of the leisure–time relationship is difficult to escape. For most people leisure remains time free of obligations. In a questionnaire distributed in one of my classes students were asked to choose words that in their opinion best described different activities. The only activity that in the opinion of *all of them* was best described by the word 'leisure' was – guess what – *sunbathing*!

Csikszentmihalyi (1980), recognizing the difficulty of defining leisure unidimensionally, defined it as a crossover of free time, activity and attitude (see Figure 11.1). A similar approach was adopted later by Kelly (1982). It seems though, that in most instances time was accepted as a compromise in a search of a more substantive or germane quality of leisure. Time was viewed as a yardstick or a framework rather than a resource or value in its own right. As we will try to demonstrate, this was caused, in part, by viewing time primarily as duration or 'clock' time (so many hours or so many minutes) and overlooking the fact that time has also an experiential dimension of subjectively perceived *pace* and a social elasticity or *rhythm*.

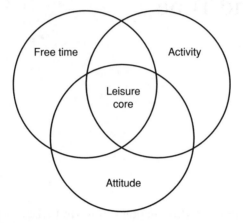

Figure 11.1   Leisure as a cross-section of discretionary time, activity and attitude

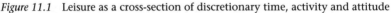

Notes:
Free time: time left after fulfilling personal needs, paid work and school requirements, as well as family and household obligations and other commitments
Activity: recreational, sporting and entertaining activities traditionally defined as leisure, e.g. going to theatre or sporting event, watching TV, visiting friends, playing golf
Attitude/state of mind: psychological dispositions and expectations, e.g freedom to choose the activity, doing things for their own sake, intrinsic motivation, enjoyment, relaxation
Examples of 'fringes':
Professional tennis meets the criterion of activity, but it is not part of free time, nor is it done for its own sake. 'Labour of love' (research, writing a book) may share some attitudinal dispositions with leisure but is not performed in free time nor is it traditionally defined as leisure. Teen's attendance at an opera performance at parents' behest meets criteria of free time and activity but lacks the desired attitude.

Source: adapted from Csikszentmihalyi (1980).

What follows is an attempt to disentangle the relationship between leisure and time from a historical and pragmatic rather than philosophical perspective. To do so, we will focus first on historical changes in the valuation of time and leisure and after that discuss measurements of leisure and time. We will then examine the role of time in seizing the experiential dimension of leisure, and finally address the issue of the subjective and social elasticity of time.

The value of time and leisure from a historical perspective

Time is money. (Benjamin Franklin)

Time is more than money. (S. G. Strumilin)

The valuation of time and leisure are in many ways sign-posts of major social changes in human history. Access to time and leisure served as a defining criterion of humanity and divinity in Ancient Greece, Buddhism and medieval Christianity. As de Grazia (1962) pointed out, in Ancient Greece and Rome it was not leisure that was defined as non-work, but rather work was defined as *negotium* or *'un-leisure'*.

This valuation changed with the advent of Industrial Revolution and modern capitalism. Benjamin Franklin's (1748) famous quotation equating time with money and Max Weber's *The Protestant Ethic and the Spirit of Capitalism* (1904) document a radical shift in the valuation of time. 'The leisureliness was suddenly destroyed ...The idyllic state collapsed under the pressure of a bitter competitive struggle. Respectable fortunes were made ... always reinvested into business' (Weber, 1904: 68).

Time continued to be valued not for its own sake as a source of wisdom, serenity or redemption, but rather as an opportunity to produce, save, invest, and succeed financially. Frederick Taylor's 'time and motion' studies of work efficiency (1911) and Chaplin's parody of it in *Modern Times* (1936) epitomize this trend. The sublime time of the past crumbled under the rigour of business transactions and assembly-line productivity that culminated in today's world of quick buck, fast food, quick sex, fleeting attention span, 'day trading' (of stocks),[2] and an incessant shortage of time.

Not surprisingly, these trends generated opposition and sharp criticism. In the nineteenth century, efforts to rekindle the value of leisure as opposed to work can often be found in the writings of the socialist left. According to Marx, 'The realm of freedom only begins, in fact, where labour that is determined by need and external purposes ceases; it is therefore, by its very nature, *outside the sphere of material production'* (Marx, 1867: 255, emphasis added). Marx's son-in-law, French socialist Paul Lafargue, brought this argument to its logical conclusion in a provocative pamphlet, *The Right to Be Lazy* (1883). For Lafargue, similar to Marx, development of human potentiality for its own sake begins beyond the realm of work and necessity.

Unfortunately when the left came to power, first in Russia, and later in other countries, many good intentions of the past were forgotten. The real socialist state found itself in need of a work ethic, work discipline and work sacrifice. The logic of becoming a ruling rather than an opposition party resulted in the perplexing fact that among the works published in the Soviet Union one finds writings of Frederick Taylor (1911; published in Russian in 1924) – the very epitome of the capitalist exploitation of the workers – rather than Lafargue's *The Right to Be Lazy*. Theories of 'the scientific management of work' rather than the Marxian concept of self-actualization became the major inspiration of Soviet labour policies in the 1920s, and led to considerable tension with the workers.

A leading Soviet economist and statistician, S. Strumilin, tried to bring the value of discretionary time to the forefront of public discussion but political winds blew in a different direction. Gulag and forced labour rather than an enlightened balance of work and free time were looming on the horizon.

Between the two world wars and after the Second World War, discretionary time and leisure found their advocates among liberal educators, philosophers and social scientists.

Authors approaching leisure from an educational perspective emphasized free time's contribution to the person's 'wholesome' development and positive social integration. For Jacks, leisure provides an opportunity to exercise 'creative and imaginative faculties which the general standardization of labour tends to suppress' (Jacks, 1931: 64). Overstreet, in *A Guide to Civilized Leisure*, argues that in a world of scarcity we have had to give our 'hostages to toil'. 'Now, in an age of plenty, we can look forward to an increasing amount of time that is our own. We have, to an extent, grown work-wise. In the future, we shall grow leisure-wise' (Overstreet, 1934: 9). In most publications written by authors of this ilk, free time was heralded as a potential answer to the problems of modern civilization, capable of helping where work failed.

Unlike the educators, Dutch historian Huizinga (1938) and German philosopher Joseph Pieper (1948), focused on leisure as a cultural disposition or attitude rather than time or activity. For Huizinga, play and leisure represent a breeding ground for new ideas, new discoveries, and new political institutions. Only in play and leisure are human beings in full command of their spiritual, physical, and intellectual capacities. Huizinga's book *Homo Ludens* (1938 [1955]) was written in difficult times. Nazi stormtroopers were marching in the streets of Germany and menacing neighbouring countries. Huizinga was craving for a world that was less serious, less deadly, and more open for play, particularly fair play. Historically and personally this turned out to be a dream. Huizinga was arrested by the Nazis after the occupation of the Netherlands, and released from concentration camp shortly before his death. Intellectually, however, his book remains a living manifesto of hope and humanist vision that deeply influenced the subsequent study of leisure.

Joseph Pieper's book *Leisure: The Basis of Culture*, first published in German in 1948, grows out of essentially the same intellectual climate as Huizinga's *Homo Ludens*. It was born out of the tragic experience of the Second World War and expresses a longing for peace of affairs as well as the peace of mind. Pieper views leisure as the basis of human culture and a much-needed counter-balance against the materialistic, instrumental, assertive and overly busy mould of modern Western civilization. 'Leisure', Pieper wrote, 'is not the inevitable result of spare time, holiday, a week-end or vacation. It is, in the first part, an attitude of mind, a condition of the soul' (Pieper, 1948: 40).

Social scientists joined the debate about the role of free time and leisure in modern societies and its relationship with work as early as the 1930s. It was increasingly recognized that time is more than a tool for making money. In *Leisure – A Suburban Study*, Lundberg et al. wrote:

> The main satisfactions of life are to be found in the time and the activities which remain when work, sleep, and the activities necessarily incidental thereto are done. On the basis of this axiom, implicit in the behaviour of people themselves, questions of the well-being of groups must ultimately be measured largely in terms of the amount of leisure which they have and the uses they make of it. (Lundberg et al., 1934: 94)

Lundberg was quick to point out that:

> Clearly, *something more* than a short and easy working day, even with economic security, is needed before we have any assurance that the lives of men [*sic*] will be happier and lighter. It all depends on what we do with the additional leisure and our *attitude toward these activities*. (ibid.: 2)

Free time was seen by most social scientists as a prerequisite of leisure but not necessarily as its equivalent. According to Meyersohn (1972), all leisure occurred during free time, but not all free time was leisure. To qualify as leisure, free time had to fulfil a number of functions. Meyersohn listed four of them: (a) rest or respite; (b) entertainment; (c) self-realization and (d) spiritual renewal. Dumazedier (1967) singled out similar functions: (a) relaxation – an antidote to fatigue; (b) entertainment – an antidote to boredom; and (c) personal development – a cultivation of physical and mental self.

There was a good deal of enlightened optimism in this juxtaposition of leisure and free time. As we know too well, entertainment may be an antidote to boredom as well as its source and respite can reinvigorate as well as breed passivity.

From a policy perspective, there is an agreement that a certain amount of discretionary time is a prerequisite of human development and emotional well-being. Analyses of survey data, however, show that not only a *shortage* of free time but its *excessive amounts* are associated with lower levels of life satisfaction (Robinson, 1977) and may result in a waste of time. 'If the great gift of unbeholden time and discretionary income creates leisure whose dominant motifs are boredom, violence, and escape, the monster turns on its creator and challenges the viability of the democratic ideal' (Berger, 1963: 37).

It seems that the developmental potential of free time materializes only when juxtaposed with the world of necessity. So, how much discretionary time is good for us, and how much of it is too much? It is extremely difficult to answer this question without the help of a time measurement 'rod'. In the following section, therefore, we will examine the use of time duration (clock time) in defining and measuring leisure.

Leisure as time

According to Robinson and Converse (1972), a 24-hour day can be visualized as the available input of lifestyle resources, with the output represented by the choice of activities and the time allocated to them. In the words of these authors, time-use data offer 'a unique view of the intersection between the imperatives of the human condition and the range of individual behavioural choice' (Robinson and Converse, 1972: 19). As such, time-use data provide a valuable instrument for the study of leisure in the context of daily life.

One of the main issues facing time-use researchers is how to develop a comprehensive classification of daily and leisure activities. How functional are the activity categories that we use in time-use studies, and what rationale except for tradition and convenience is there for classifying these activities the way we do?

In discussing activity patterns of urban Americans, Chapin (1974) suggested that an activity has a number of properties. It has duration, a position in time, a place in a sequence of events, and fixed location or a path in space. The activity may involve only the person whose actions are being reported, or the activity may be shared with others. An activity may be defined simply as shopping. However, it can be subdivided into driving from home to shopping centre, buying groceries, and driving back home. Further on, the same activity may be classified in even greater detail, as (a) driving from one's home to the shopping centre; (b) hunting for a parking space; (c) picking up a shopping trolley, and so on.

The problem of grouping daily and leisure behaviour is how to create an 'activity universe' that is both comprehensive and manageable. How many activities should be monitored? How detailed should the activity codes be? Should watching television be combined with watching video or DVD movies? Should we care about the difference between reading books and magazines? Should attendance at popular and symphony concerts be one activity or two? How long can the list of activities be before it loses practical relevancy and methodological consistency?

Chapin states correctly that the classification of activities depends largely on the purpose of the investigation. Existing time-use classifications of daily activities implicitly recognize functional distinctions between economically motivated behaviour (work for pay), biologically or physiologically determined behaviour (sleep, eating, personal hygiene), family-oriented and household activities (child care, household chores), and discretionary or free-time activities. There is no strong consensus with regard to political, voluntary and religious activities. It seems, though, that while the initial entry into voluntary activities is *free*, continuing participation in them is perceived by most participants as a *commitment*. From the time-use perspective, leisure is then defined as discretionary time remaining to the individual after fulfilling all personal needs, contractual obligations and commitments.

A universally acceptable grouping of leisure activities poses a particularly difficult problem. It is not easy to single out *one* specific function or need underlying all leisure activities. As already indicated, leisure activities serve a number of overlapping functions. In classifying leisure activities researchers usually take into account their different functions, physical and psychological requirements, experiential connotations, social-demographic correlations and, last but not least, established cultural traditions.

In most countries leisure activities are divided into several major categories, such as: watching TV and video, socializing with friends and family, sports and outdoor activities, hobbies, attending sporting and cultural events, reading, listening to music, and resting. Among activities that have been added lately to this list one finds computer and video games and the use of the internet. Of course, all of these activities can be further subdivided. Experience sampling data (see following section) indicate that watching video movies has a different experiential 'texture' than watching television, and reading books is different from reading newspapers.

Yet, historically and culturally visual media 'hang together' and represent a critical breach with the 'Gutenberg culture' of reading (McLuhan, 1962).

In the past 40 years, following the seminal multinational time-use study conducted in 12 countries under the direction of Alexander Szalai (Szalai et al., 1972), time-use researchers have made considerable progress in standardizing daily and leisure activities and refining time diary collection methods.

From a measurement perspective, examining daily and leisure behaviour as time carries a number of advantages:

- According to Robinson and Converse (1972), time-use data represent true 'ratio scales'. The amount of time spent in one activity affects and is affected by the amount of time spent in other activities and could be reported as hours and minutes per day or as a percentage of total daily time.
- Compared to 'recall' questionnaires asking respondents to report frequency of participation in selected leisure activities in the past year, month, or week, time diaries focus on short time intervals during the survey day (usually ten minutes long) and cover the entire spectrum of daily activities rather than a single group of activities (for example, leisure). The very design of time-use diaries with a focus on a tedious reconstruction of the sequence of daily events takes normative pressures off the respondent's shoulders and makes the reporting of leisure activities less susceptible to a social desirability bias.
- Because physical or 'clock' time is standardized in a similar fashion around the world, it represents, unlike money or attitudinal measures, a relatively universal and bias-free measurement of human behaviour.

In sum, time-use data are well suited for the analyses of *social differences*, *social changes* and *cross-national similarities and differences* in human behaviour and leisure participation.

Like any method of data gathering, time diaries have some limitations:

- Time-use studies provide effective information about the distribution of time to most common daily and leisure activities, but are of limited use for monitoring participation in less frequently engaged in leisure pursuits. Daily and leisure activities that are performed infrequently or for very short intervals are often under-reported or fall 'between the cracks'. Time-use surveys can be relied upon with regard to information on such activities as watching television, physically active and social leisure (visiting friends and entertaining at home), but offer only a spotty glimpse of telephone conversations, arts attendance or participation in individual sports.
- A question can be asked about whether or to what extent a single diary day is typical of the respondent's overall time use and lifestyle? Is the amount of domestic work and free time reported by a respondent on a particular day, when he or she may have been sick or overburdened with other obligations, representative of his or her routine daily patterns? Or to put this question

differently, how accurately does a sum of random daily observations reflect the dynamics of respondents' lives over prolonged periods of time?

This concern is, of course, valid but it has been addressed in a number of time-use surveys by sampling more than one day of a respondent's life. In the aforementioned multinational time-use study (Szalai et al., 1972), time diary information for each respondent was collected for two weekdays and one day off. In the Netherlands, time diary data have been collected every five years from 1975 to 2000 for the *entire* week. Such data collection strategies ensure a more comprehensive capturing of peoples' lifestyles.

• Time-use studies have also been criticized for containing little or no information about attitudes and meanings accompanying human behaviour and leisure participation. Time-use data, we are told, tell us *what* people do, but not *why* they do it or *what meaning* they attach to what they are doing. As a result, most time-use analyses are descriptive rather than interpretive. This criticism may have been valid with regard to the less sophisticated time-use studies of the past, but does not apply to current large-scale surveys that often elicit supplementary information about respondents' attitudinal dispositions, enjoyment of performed activities, emotional well-being, subjective perception of time pressure, and health.

The 1998 Canadian General Social Survey (GSS) contained, for example, questions about respondents' subjective perception of time pressure and stress, sleeping problems, self-assessed health, life satisfaction, satisfactions with one's job, work–family interface, satisfaction with time use, financial situation, and questions about the most enjoyed activities and activities in which the respondent would like to spend more time. Inclusion of these questions, obviously, provides a unique opportunity to examine relationships between daily behaviour, emotional well-being and health.

International comparisons of time-use data pose considerable methodological challenges that have been extensively discussed in the literature (Szalai et al., 1972; Gershuny, 1991; Lingsom, 1991; Harvey, 1991; Zuzanek, 1991; Niemi, 1993; Robinson and Godbey, 1997; Alsaker et al., 1999). Most of the problems are associated with different data collection procedures (personal versus telephone interviews), different sampling specifications (one or more respondent per household, different age boundaries), and differences in coding. In spite of these difficulties, the collaborative effort of researchers and statisticians from different countries has resulted in the development of a reliable instrument for studying cross-national differences in time use and the direction of time use changes in the past 15–20 years.

To illustrate this point we would like to report selected findings from a comparative study of Adolescent Time Use in ten developed industrial countries (Australia, Belgium, Canada, Finland, France, Germany, the Netherlands, Norway, the UK, and the US) and the 2003 Ontario Study of Adolescent Time Use and Well-Being (OATUS) conducted by the Research Group on Leisure and Cultural Development (University of Waterloo).[3]

Analyses of adolescent time-use data from the ten surveyed countries show that the amount of time spent by adolescents in personal needs (sleep, meals at home) has declined over the past two decades in most countries. In Ontario, 67 per cent of 15–19-year-old students reported sleeping fewer than eight hours on school days; 27 per cent slept fewer than seven hours. On Saturdays, close to 20 per cent of teens went to bed after midnight, and of these almost 8 per cent were not in bed after 1.00 a.m. Not surprisingly, on Sundays, 35 per cent of Ontario teens stayed in bed until after 10.00 a.m., and 6 per cent past midday. Initially, late bedtime hours were associated with watching television, but lately they are related mostly to surfing the internet.

The length of sleep – particularly on school days – affects adolescents' emotional well-being and health. Students who slept fewer than seven hours on school days reported higher levels of perceived time pressure and stress, and a lower level of self-assessed health than students who slept longer hours. Going late to bed and short sleep on school days was also associated with skipping breakfast – a strong contributing factor to teens' obesity. As well, late bedtime was associated with a greater likelihood of smoking and a heightened sense of depression and loneliness. Going to bed early, on the other hand, was associated with less time pressure, less fatigue on the way to school, greater satisfaction with school performance and fewer emotional problems.

Among other trends that have serious lifestyle and health implications and were common to most of the ten surveyed countries, were the declining levels of reading and participation in physically active leisure. In several surveyed countries, the amount of reading reported in the late 1990s and at the beginning of the 2000s had fallen to half or less of the reading time reported in the 1980s. Adolescent participation in physically active leisure fell in Norway, Australia and Germany, and remained at approximately the same levels as in the 1980s in France, Finland and the Netherlands.

The analyses of the Ontario data show that greater amounts of reading, unlike watching television, are associated with positive academic outcomes. Adolescents' participation and interest in sporting activities was positively associated with teens' greater time-use satisfaction, fewer emotional problems, happier outlook on life and better health, while sedentary lifestyles contributed to teens' obesity. These and other similar findings testify to the fact that combined use of time use and 'qualitative' data is much more than simplistic time-budget accounting and can help identify important social and policy issues in the domains of time use, lifestyle and health.

Leisure as experience

As indicated earlier, time-use surveys often include questions about the meaning and valuation of reported activities. However, questions about the qualitative dimensions of life and leisure are usually asked not during the day when the activities are engaged in, but *post factum*, as an afterthought. In the 1998 Canadian General Social Survey, for example, respondents were asked to single out activities that they had enjoyed the most at the very end of the day. Satisfaction with time use was measured in this survey as a global assessment of respondents' feelings about their use of time rather than as a response to particular daily occurrences. It has fallen to the Experience Sampling Method (ESM) developed in the mid-1970s by Mihaly Csikszentmihalyi and associates at the University of Chicago to provide an instrument to study the experiential or qualitative dimensions of human behaviour within the *immediate context* of daily life.

ESM surveys monitor respondents' daily and leisure behaviour and its accompanying moods with the help of electronic tools such as pagers, pocket vibrators, programmable wristwatches, or handheld computers. These electronic devices are pre-programmed or randomly activated by a radio transmitter to produce a 'beep' or 'vibration' (if carried in the pocket) several times a day, usually within two-hour intervals.

At the time of the beep, respondents fill out short self-report forms (usually bound in a booklet) and answer questions about various behavioural and experiential aspects of their daily life. Filling out each self-report form takes approximately one and a half to two minutes. The length of the observed period is usually a week, but may be as short as part of the day or as long as three months (Filstead et al., 1985). While the number of beeps per day and the length of the observed period are determined by researchers' specific interests, they are, obviously, subject to conventional limitations of privacy, interference with daily life, and respondents' attention capacity. Normally, the number of beeps per day varies between seven and ten (Hurlburt et al., 1984).

Although questions included in ESM self-reports depend, to a certain extent, on researchers' interests, during the past two decades a set of 'core' questions monitoring respondents' behaviour and experiential states has been commonly used by researchers engaging in ESM studies. A number of Likert-type and semantic differential questions allow the respondent to be placed on emotional and experiential continua of *affect* (happy–sad; irritable–cheerful; good–bad); *activation* (alert–drowsy; energetic–tired; active–passive); *anxiety* (upset–calm; tense–relaxed; worried–carefree); *control* of the situation, and *flow* (match of the respondent's feelings of challenge with the competence or skill required by the activity).

In a number of ESM surveys respondents have been asked to report their sense of time pressure and stress at the time of the beep, their interest in the performed activity, the sense of how fast or slow the time was passing, and other questions capturing their emotional and physical well-being.

Unlike experimental and laboratory studies, ESM research offers an *in situ* rather than an *in vitro* perspective on daily life and leisure. At the risk of over-generalization, the advantages of ESM can be summarized in several major points:

1. ESM improves our understanding of daily and leisure behaviour at the level at which it is manifested – within its 'immediate time frame' (Alliger and Williams, 1993: 528). The immediacy of ESM observations, perhaps even more than in time diaries, greatly reduces the potential for a failure of recall or 'social desirability' bias.

2. ESM contributes to the understanding of *situational variations* in leisure behaviour and experiences as these relate to the physical location (where?), the social context (with whom?), and the temporal location of the activity within weekly and daily cycles of behaviour (at what time of the day or on which day of the week?). These variations are outside of the reach of traditional recall questionnaires which often obscure important situational and 'within-person differences' (ibid: 529).

3. By monitoring motivational, cognitive, and emotional aspects of daily life and leisure, ESM studies allow us to examine human behaviour as a *meaningful experience*, a *purposeful activity* within a *natural context*, and a part of the *dynamics of daily life*, something that neither laboratory research nor traditional time diary or activity questionnaires can do.

4. To a degree, ESM studies combine characteristics of cross-sectional and panel research designs. The fact that human behaviour and emotional states are observed through repeated observations for a period of one week (or more) provides the opportunity to study *causal* links between antecedent and subsequent emotional states.

5. In an interesting discussion of leisure indicators, Ennis (1968) listed as an important criterion of the effectiveness of such indicators their 'meaningfulness', an ability to tell something *unambiguous* about the activity under study. This is one area where ESM can both complement and enhance information obtained through time diaries.

   Much academic and public policy discussion has lately focused on the trends in the length of working hours in industrialized countries (Schor, 1991; Robinson and Godbey, 1997; Zuzanek et al., 1998). The issue that seems to have been overlooked in this discussion, however, is the *composition* and *content* of working hours. According to Kubey et al., 'one simple but intriguing ESM finding from the world of work shows that workers actually report working only about 65% of the time they are at their jobs' (Kubey et al., 1996: 114). This finding is corroborated by Zuzanek and Mannell's 1985 and 1987 ESM surveys. The ESM data may help us to assess how much 'slack' there is in the present workplace and how much of such slack is indispensable for an effective functioning of the workplace and employees' job satisfaction.

6. ESM surveys by providing rich information about the emotional, cognitive and motivational connotations of daily and leisure behaviour can help researchers to refine the classification of a number of daily and leisure activities that pose measurement problems. The ESM data suggest, for example, that combining travel with activities to which such travel is related (a conventional practice in time diary analyses), is justified. Travel to work appears experientially closer to work than to travel for shopping or travel associated with leisure. The ESM data call into question, however, the frequent practice in time diary studies of classifying adult and special interest education as free time. The experiential connotations of time spent studying put it closer, for the adult population, to paid work than to leisure, and justify its inclusion into total workload rather than leisure (see Zuzanek, 2000).

Housework obligations and child care contain activities with different experiential profiles as well. Gardening is experienced differently than cooking, home upkeep, or bookkeeping. Playing with children elicits a different emotional and experiential reaction than does physical child care. These observations lend considerable support to the notion of 'semi-leisure' advocated by Dumazedier (1967) for activities that do not fit traditional notions of leisure, family obligations, or housework.

In short, ESM surveys provide more refined information for a functional grouping of daily and leisure activities than traditional time use or activity recall surveys. By rendering researchers an opportunity to assess immediate and circumstantial meanings and motivations of human activity, ESM has greatly contributed to our understanding of behavioural and experiential patterns of daily life and leisure. One has to agree with Stone and Shiffman's statement that, when conducted well, ESM studies can provide 'an unparalleled wealth of data' (Stone and Shiffman, 1992: 127) for a better understanding of the behavioural and emotional challenges of modern life.

Subjective and social elasticity of time

Subjective and social elasticity of time has long attracted attention of anthropologists, psychologists, geographers, sociologists and economists (Evans-Prichard, 1940; Fraisse, 1963; Linder, 1970; Zerubavel, 1985; Levine, 1998). The interest in the subjective perception of time was given a boost by a widely shared sense that the rhythms of modern life have sped up, run out of control, and need to be curbed. Robinson and Godbey (1997) have drawn attention to the paradox that people in modern societies may have gained additional free time, yet subjectively feel more 'time-crunched' than they were a decade or two ago. Concerns with countering the speeding up of modern life found an expression in an advocacy of individual efforts to 'downshift' the pace of life (Lefkowitz, 1979; Schor, 1991), and broadly conceived policy initiatives such as 'slow cities', 'slow food', *'tempo giusto'* (right speed), and so on (see Honoré, 2004).

Pieper (1946 [1948]) was among the first to point out that to be at ease with oneself and the world around we need to immerse in time. In the world of frequent time interruptions, fragmented time, and multitasking, we may be losing the joy of time.

The conflict between the sped up rhythms of modern life and the *joie de vivre* was well captured in an episode that occurred during my visit to the World Wine Fair in Bordeaux. While tasting wines, I was approached by a salesman who looked for an opportunity to enter North American markets with a new product, called a Vinotron. Here is a brief description of this product from a promotional pamphlet:

The 'Vinotron' is a device which accelerates the maturing process in wines, improving their quality at the same time. After four or five weeks of use, the maturing process is accelerated by two to three years. The design of the 'Vinotron' is revolutionary. It speeds up maturing in the bottle by using a physical process which generates non-ionizing radiation, presenting no danger to health.

I told the fellow that as a heritage buff I was not the right contact for him. 'Just give it a thought,' he said, 'you buy a 1990 Mouton Rothschild today and instead of waiting 15 or 20 years, you radiate it to maturity in no time.' There was no room in this 'cash for time' proposal for the pleasure of waiting, drinking or talking about Bordeaux's fabulous first growths. I felt rather relieved that the new invention did not catch on with the Bordeaux crowd.

The subjective dimensions of time passage are difficult to capture empirically. We do not have good measures for serenity or peace of mind, but ESM provides some interesting insights into the *subjective pace* and *social elasticity* of time.

ESM data collected as part of the Ontario Survey of Adolescent Time Use and Well-Being offer an opportunity, among other things, to examine the complex relationship between feelings of *time pressure* and perceived *pace of time* in the context of daily life. Data reported in Table 11.1 suggest that the feelings of time pressure and perceived pace of time are correlated, but surprisingly have opposite effects on respondents' moods.

Table 11.1 Relationships between affect, time pressure and pace of time (Pearson '*r*')

	Affect	Time pressure	Time passing	Choice
Affect (1–7)	1.00	–.18	.14	.15
Time pressure (1–9)	–.19	1.00	.15	–.16
Time was passing (0–9)	.14	.36	1.00	.26
How much choice doing activity (0–9)	.25	–.36	.36	1.00

Notes: Data in Tables 11.1, 11.2 and 11.3 were collected as part of the 2003 Ontario Survey of Adolescent Time Use and Well-Being (*n* = 219 adolescents aged 12–19 plus one parent from each family). Affect was computed as a composite of three semantic differential scales: feeling bad to good, sad to happy, irritable to cheerful (alpha = .83). Time pressure was measured by asking respondents how pressed for time they felt at the time of the beep (1 = not at all; 9 = very much). Pace of time ranged from 0 (very slow) to 9 (very fast). To establish the amount of choice in doing an activity, respondents were asked how free they were in choosing what they were doing (0 = not at all; 9 = very much).

The inter-correlation between the subjective feelings of time pressure and perceived pace of time at the time of the beep is .15 for adolescents and .36 for their parents. However, the correlation between the feeling of *time pressure* and *affect* is *negative* (*r* = –.18), while the relationship between *affect* and perceived *time pace* is *positive* (*r* = .14). In other words, we dislike to be pressed for time but enjoy it – up to a point – when time passes quickly.

A positive relationship between the pace of time and 'affect' is true for most but not all activities or situations. Time flies quickly when teens are immersed in sporting activities and passes slowly when they are in class or waiting (Table 11.2). However, for some activities or situations higher levels of affect are associated with a slower rather than faster pace of time. Gardening, reading, praying, being in church are examples of activities that are enjoyed when the time flows slowly.

In short, a sense of joy may be derived from a fast as well as a slow passage of time depending on cultural and intellectual expectations associated with particular activities or situations. Nothing new, perhaps, 'to every thing there is a season ... a time to laugh and a time to mourn ... a time to keep silence, and a time to speak' (Ecclesiastes, 3:1).

Table 11.2   Relationships between daily activities, affect and perceived pace of time (mean scores)

	Affect 1–7	Time passing 0–9
Adolescents		
Class work	5.23	3.34
Doing homework	4.96	4.53
Paid work	4.94	3.67
Free time	5.40	4.60
Socializing with friends	5.54	4.68
Watching TV	5.29	4.20
Watching video/DVD movies	5.66	5.02
Playing computer/video games	5.41	5.20
Participating in sports	5.89	6.10
Reading books	5.37	4.03
Reading newspapers/magazines	5.15	4.26
Religious activities	5.75	3.15
Waiting	4.91	2.62
All daily activities: adolescents	5.26	4.30
Parents		
Paid work	5.11	5.73
Housework	5.18	5.26
Cooking	5.24	5.62
Housecleaning/maintenance	5.12	4.93
Book keeping/finances	4.94	5.04
Gardening	5.71	5.75
Child care	5.29	5.50
Physical child care	5.21	5.50
Play/socialize with children	5.63	5.49
Free time	5.32	4.77
All daily activities: parents	5.21	5.27

Notes: see Table 11.1.

The *social elasticity* of time is a by-product of the collective rhythms of life. The same amount of 'clock' time can be perceived as longer or shorter, slower or faster depending on social, cultural, personal, and situational circumstances. Linder (1970) contrasted the concept of time in industrial societies with the *mañana* attitudes of Latin Americans where there is 'no great need of precision in reckoning and measuring time' (Linder, 1970: 17). Evans-Pritchard (1940) observed and wrote about the 'fortunate' people of Nuer totally oblivious to the Western notion of time. The different pace of time in different cultural contexts has been extensively documented by Levine in *A Geography of Time* (1998).

The ESM studies support observations about the social elasticity of time. Time is perceived as running faster or slower depending on the type of activity engaged in, its location, respondents' demographic characteristics, or calendar days.

The subjective perception of the passage of time seems to be driven not by clock time but by the amount of change happening during a given period of time. This may be the reason why older teens experience time as running faster than their younger counterparts (Table 11.3). This may also explain why, for teens, time runs faster on Sundays than on weekdays – a window of new opportunities – while the opposite is true of their parents whose time runs slower on Sundays than on weekdays – a respite from a hurried work week.

Table 11.3 Relationships between location of daily activities, adolescents' age, the day of the week, affect and perceived pace of time (mean scores)

	Affect *1–7*	*Time passing* *0–9*
Location (adolescents)		
Class room	5.23	3.38
School gym, sports field	5.63	5.52
Home	5.16	4.55
Workplace	4.77	3.38
Shopping mall/store	5.33	4.53
Movie theatre	5.48	5.09
Theatre/concert hall	5.69	5.92
Church	5.73	3.38
Age (adolescents)		
12–14 years	5.46	4.12
15–17 years	4.92	4.50
18–19 years	5.20	4.77
Day of the week (adolescents)		
Weekdays	5.23	4.24
Weekends	5.32	4.44
Day of the week (parents)		
Weekdays	5.17	5.39
Weekends	5.32	4.98

Notes: see Table 11.1.

One of the most interesting questions raised in the research literature concerns relationships between weekly calendar rhythms, moods and activities. According to Sorokin (1943),

> We apprehend time in 'week' units; we localize the events and activities in 'week' units; we co-ordinate our behaviour according to the 'week', we live and feel and plan and wish in 'week' terms. It is one of the most important points of our 'orientation' in time and social reality. (Sorokin, 1943: 420)

Analyses of ESM data show that experiential moods and perceptions of time pace vary systematically across the week. The moods resonate not only with the behaviour which they accompany, but also with the *calendar expectations* of a particular day. In a way, different days 'colour' the experiencing of activities differently.

Free time activities are perceived more positively on weekends than on other days of the week, while the reverse is true of housework activities. The surge of positive feelings, accompanying free time activities on Sundays, may be a result of an 'experiential consonance', a resonating match of positive calendar and activity mood expectations. The 'downgrading' of housework-related moods on Sundays could be attributed, in turn, to a mismatch between calendar and activity mood expectations. This, it seems, would explain why women feel least positive while shopping and doing errands on Sundays (see Zuzanek and Mannell, 1993).

Analyses of ESM data suggest that time is not duration only. It has subjective and social dimensions as well. Clock time may be a useful instrument in examining the distribution of leisure as a developmental resource, while analyses of the subjective and social dimensions of 'live' time provide us with important insights into the temporal *structure* and *quality* of our lives.

Conclusion

There seems to be an agreement that leisure is more than time, and is best described as a crossover of activity, time and experience (attitude). It is difficult, however, to operationalize this definition for practical research needs, particularly in cross-cultural research. From a research and measurement perspective it is easier to operationalize leisure as either discretionary time, or a socially defined activity, or an experience, *one at a time*, rather than opt for the conceptually appealing but methodologically elusive combination thereof. From this perspective, time use, leisure participation and experience sampling surveys provide complementary rather then competing strategies for studying daily life and leisure behaviour. Combining time diary, recall and ESM approaches in studying leisure will bring more forcefully into the forefront of social science research questions about the structure, the changes, and the meanings of everyday life in the complex and hurried world in which we live.

Notes

1. I would like to thank Roger Mannell and Margo Hilbrecht for their comments and assistance in preparing this chapter.
2. Day trading involves computerized purchase of stocks when they begin to move up and an almost instantaneous sell-off, resulting in a gain of a few pennies. When this is done repeatedly by low-paid employees working on commission (no thought or knowledge required) this apparently can be profitable.
3. The comparative study of adolescent time use in ten developed industrial countries was supported by the Canadian Institute for Health Information. The 2003 Ontario Survey of Adolescent Time Use and Emotional Well-Being (OATUS/ESM) was supported by a SSHRC strategic grant. It was administered in 11 Ontario schools selected from different SES neighbourhoods (total sample 2,113). Both surveys were conducted by the Research Group on Leisure and Cultural Development of the University of Waterloo (Jiri Zuzanek, principal investigator).

Bibliography

Alliger, G. M. and Williams, K. J. (1993) 'Using Signal-Contingent Experience Sampling Methodology to Study Work in the Field: A Discussion and Illustration Examining Task Perceptions and Mood', *Personnel Psychology* 46: 525–49.

Alsaker, F. D., Flanagan, C. and Csapo, B. (1999) 'Methodological Challenges in Cross-national Research: Countries, Participants, and General Procedures', in F. Alsaker and A. Flammer (eds) *The Adolescent Experience: European and American Adolescents in the 1990s*, Hillsdale, NJ, Lawrence Erlbaum Associates.

Augustine, *Confessions*, XI, 14.

Berger, B. M. (1963) 'The Sociology of Leisure: Some Suggestions', in E. O. Smigel (ed.) *Work and Leisure. A Contemporary Social Problem*, New Haven, College and University Press, pp. 21–40.

Chapin, F. S. (1974) *Human Activity Patterns in the City: Things People Do in Time and Space*, New York, Wiley.

Czikszentmihalyi, M. (1980) 'Subject Delineation of the Proposed Leisure Information Network', in L. Bollaert et al. (eds) *The First International Leisure Information Network Conference*, Brussels, V. U. B.

de Grazia, S. (1962) *Of Time, Work, and Leisure*, Garden City, NY Doubleday and Company.

Dumazedier, J. (1967) *Toward a Society of Leisure*, New York, The Free Press.

Ennis, P. (1968) 'The Definition and Measurement of Leisure', in E. Sheldon and W. Moore (eds) *Indicators of Social Change*, New York, Russell Sage.

Evans-Pritchard, E. E. (1940) *The Nuer: A Description of the Modes of Livelihood and Political Institutions of Nilotic People*, Oxford, Clarendon Press.

Filstead, W., Reich, W., Parrella, D. and Rossi, J. (1985) 'Using Electronic Pagers to Monitor the Process of Recovery in Alcoholics and Drug Abusers'. Paper presented at the 34th International Congress on Alcohol, Drug Abuse and Tobacco, Calgary, Alberta, Canada.

Fraisse, P. (1963) *The Psychology of Time*, New York, Harper & Row.

Franklin, B. (1748) *Advice to a Young Tradesman Written by an Old One*, Philadelphia, New Printing Office.

Gershuny, J. (1991) 'International Comparison of Time Budget Surveys: Methods and Opportunities', in *The Changing Use of Time: Report from an International Workshop*, Luxembourg, Official Publications of the European Communities, pp. 13–43.

Harvey, A. S. (1991) 'The Use of Time of the Non-employed. Historical, Cross-national Comparisons', in *The Changing Use of Time: Report from an International Workshop*, Luxembourg, Office for the Official Publications of the European Communities, pp. 95–122.

Honoré, C. (2004) *In Praise of Slow*, Toronto, Alfred A. Knopf Canada.

Huizinga, J. (1938) *Homo Ludens*, Boston, Beacon Press, 1955 (written in 1938, first published in Switzerland in 1944).

Hurlburt, R. T., Lech, B. C. and Saltman, S. (1984) 'Random Sampling of Thought and Mood', *Cognitive Therapy and Research* 8: 263–75.

Jacks, L. P. (1931) *The Education of the Whole Man*, New York, Harper & Brothers.

Kelly J. R. (1982) *Leisure*, Englewood Cliffs, NJ, Prentice-Hall.

Kubey, R., Larson, R. and Csikszentmihalyi, M. (1996) 'Experience Sampling Method Applications to Communication Research Questions', *Journal of Communication* 46(2): 99–120.

Lafargue, P. (1883) 'The Right to be Lazy', in E. Larrabee and R. Meyersohn (eds) *Mass Leisure*, Glencoe, IL, The Free Press.

Lefkowitz, B. (1979) *Breaktime: Living Without Work in a Nine to Five World*, New York, Hawthorn Books.

Levine, R. (1998) *A Geography of Time*, New York, Basic Books.

Linder, S. B. (1970) *The Harried Leisure Class*, New York, Columbia University Press.

Lingsom, S. (1991) 'Age and Behaviour. A Cross-national Comparison of Contemporary Changes', in *The Changing Use of Time: Report from and International Workshop*, Luxembourg, Office for the Official Publications of the European Communities, pp. 49–91.

Lundberg, G. A., Komarovsky, M. and McInerny, M. A. (1934) *Leisure – A Suburban Study*, New York, Columbia University Press.

Marx, K. (1867) *Selected Writings in Sociology and Social Philosophy, Capital*, Vol. 3/2, New York, McGraw-Hill Book Company, 1964.

McLuhan, M. (1962) *The Gutenberg Galaxy: The Making of Typographic Man*, Toronto, University of Toronto Press.

Meyersohn, R. (1972), 'Leisure', in A. Campbell and P. E. Converse (eds) *The Human Meaning of Social Change*, New York, Russell Sage Foundation.

Niemi, I. (1993) 'Sensitivity of Comparative Time Use Measurement to Survey Design', in *Time Use Methodology: Toward Consensus*, Rome, Istituto Nazionale di Statistica, pp. 229–31.

Overstreet, A. B. (1934) *A Guide to Civilized Leisure*, New York, W. W. Norton & Co.

Pieper, J. (1948) *Leisure: The Basis of Culture*, New York, New American Library, 1963 (first published in German in 1948).

Robinson, J. (1977) *How Americans Use Their Time. A Social-Psychological Analysis of Everyday Behavior*, New York, Praeger Publishers.

Robinson, J. P. and Converse, P. E. (1972) 'Social Change as Reflected in the Uses of Time', in A. Campbell and P. E. Converse (eds) *The Human Meaning of Social Change*, New York, Russell Sage Foundation.

Robinson, J. P. and Godbey, G. (1997) *Time for Life: The Surprising Ways Americans Use their Time*, University Park, PA, Pennsylvania State University Press.

Schor, J. B. (1991) *The Overworked American: The Unexpected Decline of Leisure*, New York, Basic Books.

Sorokin, P. (1943) *Sociocultural Causality, Space and Time*, Durham, NC, Duke University Press.

Stone, A. A. and Shiffman, S. (1992) 'Reflecting on the Intensive Measurement of Stress, Coping, and Mood, with an Emphasis on Daily Measures', *Psychology and Health* 7: 115–29.

Strumilin, S. G. (1982) *Problemy ekonomiki truda (Problems of the Economics of Work)*, Moskva, Nauka (first published in 1923).

Szalai, A. et al. (eds) (1972) *The Use of Time*, The Hague, Mouton.

Taylor, F. W. (1911) *The Principles of Scientific Management*, New York, Harper Bros.

Weber, M. (1904) *The Protestant Ethic and the Spirit of Capitalism*, New York, Charles Scribner's Sons, 1958 (first published in German in 1904).

Zerubavel, E. (1985) *The Seven Day Circle*, New York, The Free Press.

Zuzanek, J. (1991) 'Time-Budget Research: Methodological Problems and Perspectives', in E. J. McCullough and R. L. Calder (eds) *Time as a Human Resource*, Calgary, University of Calgary Press, pp. 243–51.

Zuzanek, J. (2000) *The Effects of Time Use and Time Pressure on Child–Parent Relationship: Research Report*, Waterloo, Ontario, Otium Publications.

Zuzanek, J., Beckers, T. and Peters, P. (1998) 'The "Harried Leisure Class" Revisited: Dutch and Canadian Trends in the Use of Time from the 1970s to the 1990s', *Leisure Studies* 17: 1–19.

Zuzanek, J. and Mannell, R. C. (1993) 'Leisure Behaviour and Experiences as Part of the Everyday Life: The Weekly Rhythm', *Loisir & Société/Society & Leisure* 16(1): 31–55.

12
Overturning the Modernist Predictions: Recent Trends in Work and Leisure in the OECD

Juliet B. Schor

The optimistic predictions of social scientists about the coming of a leisured future are increasingly being discredited (Gershuny, 2000; Robinson, 1986; Robinson and Godbey, 1999; Juster and Stafford, 1985, 1991). As early as the 1960s, the optimists expected that by the twenty-first century, citizens of the advanced industrialized nations would be living lives of leisure, perhaps suffering from a 'crisis of leisure time', brought on by boredom and a failure to know how to spend time. But instead of boredom, time poverty and high levels of daily life stress appear to be widespread. (On the 'crisis of leisure time', see Schor, 1992; on time pressure, see Robinson and Godbey, 1999, and Galinsky et al. 2001.) The trends in the subjective measures are readily explainable by developments in actual hours of work, and in particular a break from earlier patterns of rapid decline in work time. For example, in the OECD, over the last 20 years average hours per working age person fell a meagre 2 per cent, not per year, but for the entire two decades. Hours per employee have fallen by 7 per cent. This is a far cry from the 18 per cent decline over the period 1950–80, the experience that presumably led to such optimistic longterm predictions about declining hours of work and rising leisure time. The experience of the United States, where both predictions and explanations of the 'growth of leisure time' were pervasive, is an even more cautionary tale for the teleological, modernist perspective. According to internationally comparative sources, working hours per employee rose 3 per cent in the period 1980–2000, and a whopping 16 per cent per working-age person. Estimates from household survey data show even more substantial increases. The US experience is important because throughout the twentieth century, it has led the way in trends in working hours and leisure. A number of other OECD countries have also seen increases in worktime in the last two decades by this latter metric. These include the Netherlands, Australia and Canada.

Seen in historical perspective, recent trends are striking. The combination of rising US hours, plus rising hours in a subset of Western European countries, means that for the last decade, the majority of the working population in the most affluent parts of the world have been *increasing* rather than *decreasing* their annual hours of work. Furthermore, these increases in hours (and output) are occurring just as evidence of ecological overshoot has become far more pervasive, and the need to moderate the environmental impact of consumption far more compelling. As an oft-cited solution to excessive consumption, worktime reduction has implications beyond the quality of life perspective with which it is frequently associated. (On ecological overshoot, see Wackernagel et al., 2002.)

The recent data suggest the need for radical revision in our thinking about work and leisure. Over the last decade, as evidence of rising hours of work in the US has surfaced, its experience has not been taken seriously by observers of trends in hours. On the one hand, there has been debate about whether or not hours have actually risen in the US (see Robinson and Godbey 1999 and the rebuttal by Schor 2000. See also Gershuny 2000). On the other hand, the relevance of the US case to European and other OECD nations has not been universally appreciated. In this chapter, I argue that thinking about current and future trends in work and leisure may need to be radically revised. My argument begins with a rethinking of the long trends in work time over the last three centuries, and a re-evaluation of the modernist, conventional wisdom concerning the impact of capitalist development on worktime. I then consider recent trends in hours in the OECD, and consider the question of whether the US is continuing in its historic role as leader in trends in work time. If so, then the future path of hours throughout the OECD will be far different than the leisure optimists expect.

A short introduction to conventional thinking about trends in work and leisure

The history of the social scientific perspective on leisure time that prevailed from the 1960s through at least the 1980s is by now well known, especially within leisure studies. Indeed, the field owes its existence in part to sociological treatments of time use from the beginning of this era. The hegemonic view was that technical change, bureaucratic rationalization, increased educational attainment and the general march of progress would result in steady declines in working hours. Leisure time was thought to be increasing, and there was every expectation that those increases would continue indefinitely (for example, Gershuny (2000: 32) defines modern industrial or 'post-industrial' societies as being characterized by 'declining work time'). Indeed, simple projections of current trends suggested that working time would eventually reach negligible levels. If working hours were declining in excess of 1 per cent per year, as was the case in a substantial number of Western European countries between 1950 and 1980, the reality of a four-day week or even a four-hour day was not far off. The United States, which had a slightly lower pace of change, began the post-1950 period already having achieved the five-day work week, and with lower annual hours than many other OECD members. There too expectations of a leisured future were widespread, inside and out of academia.

Social scientists such as Jonathan Gershuny, social psychologist John Robinson, economists Thomas Juster and Frank Stafford, and others put forward the thesis of declining work and rising leisure time. The standard explanations for why leisure time would rise included both technological and economic factors. On the one hand, labour-saving technological change, which was proceeding rapidly throughout the advanced capitalist countries, was expected to continue indefinitely. Technical change led to productivity growth, which made possible the production of additional output for any given level of labour hours. Technology can thus be thought of as a facilitating condition, making possible higher wealth or more leisure. Economic analyses suggested that workers would prefer to take at least some significant portion of that potential wealth in the form of shorter hours of work, that is, more leisure. In the standard terminology of economics, the idea is that leisure is a normal good, and as individuals (and by extension, societies) become richer, they will demand more of it. This so-called 'income' effect operates in the opposite direction from the 'substitution' effect, according to which higher productivity makes leisure more expensive, thereby leading people to want less of it. In general, where accounts were explicit, productivity growth and worker choice of hours were the mechanisms which were deployed to explain both what was thought to be a trend toward more leisure time, as well as predictions of future increases.

Underneath the economic and technological analyses lurked the larger frameworks of post-industrial society, modernization theory and a virtually unquestioned belief in progress. Expectations of a leisured society were very much a part of that teleological view. Technological and economic 'progress' would bring freedom from toil, a social good. For example, in a recent book on time-use Gershuny goes so far as to argue that there 'seems to be a certain natural trajectory of development shared in all countries' (2000: 20–1). He talks about 'developmental sequences', on the one hand trying to distinguish his views from widely discredited notions like Rostow's 'stages', but ending up reproducing a fairly standard stages theory nonetheless, with concepts such as 'the logic of progress or modernization' (ibid.: 28). However, my claim must be qualified. There was also concern about a possible 'crisis of leisure time', an expectation which spurred the establishment of leisure studies departments and leisure 'experts' who could facilitate this transition and educate people about how to use leisure time well. But this was a problem that was believed to be readily manageable, a small concern that did not shake the larger edifice of belief in progress and modernization.

As is common with hegemonic ideologies, the historical and social assumptions and evidence underlying this modernist, progressive worldview went unquestioned. (They would only be seriously critiqued later by postmodernists, among others.) If we consider the scholarship on leisure time, it seems likely that the unreflective belief in a continuous path of increasing leisure was partly due to myopic historical vision, brought on by an ideological attachment to capitalism as a progressive system. The myopia involves the fact that contemporary accounts of leisure time typically start in the mid-nineteenth century, and chronicle the substantial reductions in hours which occurred in Western Europe and the United States from roughly the last quarter of the nineteenth century through the post-Second World War period. Gershuny's 2000 book compares working hours in 1780 to 1984, conveniently beginning at a historically high point in working time and ending not far in advance of the reversal of the trends to more leisure (Gershuny, 2000: 23–35).

The focus on this period can also be seen in the widespread attention paid to the calculations of Angus Maddison, who has put together internationally comparative data for OECD countries. Maddison's estimates begin in 1870, arguably the peak of working hours in all of human history. Maddison finds that annual hours worked per person declined dramatically from 1870 to 1950. Annual hours were just under 3,000 in all six of his countries at the beginning of the period. By 1950 they had all fallen to within a range of 1,800 to 2,300. In France, the decline was 956, or roughly a third; in Germany, 625; in Japan, 656; in the Netherlands, 756; in the UK, 1,056; and in the United States, annual hours fell from 2,964 to 1,867, a decline of 1,097 (Maddison, 1987: 686, table A-9). The practical import of choosing this historical period, rather than a longer one beginning for example in 1800 or even 1750, is that capitalism came to be widely believed as an economic system in which 'progress', be it technological, through market expansion, or education, would more or less automatically yield increasing amounts of leisure.

But capitalism did (and does) not automatically yield hours reductions. Quite the reverse. An investigation of the course of capitalist development in Britain, the United States and other Western European countries finds that industrialization and the growth of the market led to substantial increases in daily hours of work, and an even greater growth in the number of days worked per year. There were technological aspects to the increase in hours, such as the possibility of nighttime work brought on by electricity. There were practical aspects such as the protection from weather afforded by indoor work. And of course there were economic factors. The latter are probably most important. The growth of markets made possible the accumulation of enormous profits. This in turn created powerful incentives for capitalists to find and retain labourers who could work at maximum effort for maximum hours. For example, upward pressures on hours were clearly in evidence in the early period of capitalist growth, 1600–1800, before technological change was occurring to any significant effect (Rule, 1981; see also the discussion in Schor, 1992). In Britain, for example, during the eighteenth century there were significant and steady increases in home-based piece-work in apparel and related industries (for example, lace-making). Hours were long and the seasonality of work associated with an agrarian economy also declined, as more year-round production became the norm. Similar conditions have been found in home-based work in the United States, as for example, among the piece-workers studied by Stansell (1982).

An upward movement of hours also developed once home-based and workshop production gave way to factory labour. In these workplaces the majority of labourers were women and children, two groups relatively unable to resist the coercive environment of the factory, and the considerable upward pressure on hours that emanated from owners. Long factory hours, especially in textiles, were the subject of Marx's famous chapter ten of *Capital*, in which he described the expansion of the working day associated with industrialization and the factory system. Marx also chronicled the ongoing conflicts between owners and labourers about hours of work, exacerbated in part by a compensation regime in which pay was set by the day, week or the month, rather than the hour. Upward pressure on work time was also present in agriculture, where the shift to capitalist farming was associated with fewer holidays and longer daily hours. Expansive days and few holidays were also characteristic of domestic service, a large nineteenth-century occupation. And it can be seen most dramatically in the mobilization of a huge slave labour force bound for North and Latin American plantations, where hours were long and holidays relatively rare. Taken together, the developments in workshops, factories, farms, households and plantations paint a picture of societies experiencing widespread expansion in working time. Indeed, from this vantage point, capitalism as an economic system is shown to have been associated with a historically unprecedented rise in the quantity of human labour deployed in economic activity. It is peculiar, then, that the post-war discourse totally ignored this history, focusing instead on a shorter, possibly anomalous period of time (1875–1980). With this background in mind, I turn now to discuss the post-war trends in working hours.

Post-war trends in working hours in the OECD

Trends in hours across the OECD are presented in Table 12.1. This data was compiled by Burgoon and Baxandall (2004), using a cross-national database from University of Groningen which provides more internationally comparative estimates than earlier data sets. (Burgoon and Baxandall are interested in emerging differences in work time between political regimes, hence the grouping by political type, an interesting categorization I have retained.) The data show annual hours per employee in 18 OECD countries over the period 1950–2000. As one would predict from the aforementioned discourse, reductions in hours of work in the early post-Second World War decades were substantial. Reductions were most rapid between 1950 and 1980. For example, among all countries, the average decline in hours per employee was by 18 per cent. This translates to an annual average decline of 0.57 per cent per year between 1950 and 1973, and 0.7 per cent from 1973–80. There was some variation among countries, although in all cases, hours fell by at least 10 per cent. For example, reductions reached or exceeded 25 per cent in Sweden, Norway, Belgium, Germany and the Netherlands. The more 'liberal' market-oriented countries (Australia, Canada, Ireland, the UK and the US) had the least reduction during those decades. Both the Social Democratic and Christian Democratic groupings witnessed significant declines – 22 per cent and 20 per cent, respectively.

After 1980, hours fell much less, by an average of only 0.3 per cent per year, for a total reduction of 7 per cent over the period 1980–2000. In the United States and Sweden, hours reductions ended altogether, and working time increased. In a number of other cases, such as Australia and Canada, reductions were negligible (less than 0.1 per cent per year). By contrast, continental Europe, or the Christian Democratic countries, did continue to experience a significant decline in hours. For example,

Table 12.1 Annual work hours per employee (1950–2000) and per working-age person (1973–2000)

	Annual work hours per employee								Annual work hours per working-age person				
	1950	1960	1973	1980	1990	2000	Change 1950–80	Change 1980–2000	1973	1980	1990	2000	Change 1980–2000
Social Democratic													
Denmark	2071	1929	1580	1582	1492	1541	−24%	−3%	1188	1178	1137	1166	−1%
Finland	2035	2041	1707	1756	1677	1637	−14%	−7%	1195	1258	1228	1098	−13%
Sweden	2038	1905	1641	1503	1546	1623	−26%	8%	1207	1192	1269	1197	0%
Norway	2040	1939	1671	1512	1432	1376	−26%	−9%	1130	1100	1039	1062	−4%
Average	*2046*	*1953*	*1650*	*1588*	*1537*	*1544*	*−22%*	*−3%*	*1180*	*1182*	*1168*	*1131*	*−4%*
Christian Democratic													
Austria	2100	2073	1889	1755	1683	1519	−16%	−13%	1277	1112	1103	1035	−7%
Belgium	2404	2289	1971	1805	1699	1554	−25%	−14%	1197	1022	949	919	−10%
France	2045	2025	1849	1696	1558	1540	−17%	−9%	1186	1060	923	939	−11%
Germany	2372	2152	1848	1723	1616	1532	−27%	−11%	1271	1143	1029	1010	−12%
Italy	1957	2018	1815	1724	1674	1634	−12%	−5%	1155	1103	1069	1034	−6%
Netherlands	2156	2002	1709	1569	1414	1347	−27%	−14%	926	833	860	981	18%
Switzerland	2092	2015	1883	1821	1641	1589	−13%	−13%	1463	1352	1365	1284	−5%
Average	*2161*	*2082*	*1852*	*1728*	*1612*	*1531*	*−20%*	*−11%*	*1211*	*1089*	*1042*	*1029*	*−6%*
Liberal													
Australia	2023	1945	1880	1815	1806	1797	−10%	−1%	1283	1192	1241	1262	6%
Canada	2090	1994	1899	1806	1799	1789	−14%	−1%	1186	1179	1237	1261	7%
Ireland	2437	2320	2177	2025	1922	1700	−17%	−16%	1305	1154	1030	1114	−3%
New Zealand					1759	1756	n.a.	n.a.			1179	1248	n.a.
United Kingdom	2112	2134	1919	1758	1698	1653	−17%	−6%	1345	1202	1208	1170	−3%
United States	2166	1967	1882	1831	1819	1879	−15%	3%	1217	1207	1313	1396	16%
Average	*2166*	*2072*	*1951*	*1847*	*1801*	*1762*	*−15%*	*−5%*	*1267*	*1187*	*1201*	*1242*	*5%*
Japan	1958	2095	2042	2000	1956	1799	2%	−10%	1427	1403	1419	1346	−4%
All OECD average	*2123*	*2050*	*1845*	*1746*	*1677*	*1626*	*−18%*	*−7%*	*1233*	*1165*	*1144*	*1140*	*−2%*

Sources: Burgoon and Baxandall (2004); Groningen University (2002); OECD, *Labour Force Statistics*, various years.

in Austria, Belgium, the Netherlands and Switzerland, reductions were between 13 per cent and 14 percent overall, or nearly 0.7 per cent annually. Reductions were also significant in France (9 per cent) and Germany (11 per cent). Ireland had the largest overall decline among all the OECD nations, for a total decline of 16 per cent, or 0.8 per cent per year. However, the rate of decline slowed considerably between 1980 and 1990 and 1990 and 2000. Among the Social Democratic or Nordic countries, where the change was most dramatic, the total reduction fell from 3.2 per cent in the first period to 0.45 per cent in the second. In the continental group the decline was from 6.7 per cent to 5.0 per cent. In the third group, the fall was from 2.5 per cent in the first period to 2.2 per cent in the second. From 1980 to 1990 these data show hours increasing in only one country: Sweden. From 1990 to 2000, hours increased in Denmark, Sweden and the United States, and stayed constant in New Zealand.

Annual hours per working-age person reveal an even greater shift toward higher levels of work effort in the OECD. A comparison of the average among all countries finds that whereas hours per employee declined by a total of 7 per cent between 1980 and 2000, hours per working-age person declined only 2 per cent. Between 1990 and 2000, the change in hours per working-age person was only a four-hour total decline, or 0.3 per cent. In the Nordic countries, the differences between the two measures are small (only 1 per cent), but in the continental group, they are substantial (11 per cent versus 6 per cent). Among the third group, the differences are even sharper. While hours per employee fell on average 5 per cent, hours per working-age person rose by an equivalent amount (5 per cent).

It may also be interesting to consider trends in hours in relationship to trends in productivity growth. Productivity data are provided by Maddison (1987), and the calculations are mine (also contained in Schor, 2005). The data show a marked shift from the first half of the post-war period to the second. In 1950–73, the excess of productivity growth over hours reductions was substantial – on average nearly a 4 per cent gap existed. That gap fell to 1.7 per cent in the 1973–90 period, as productivity growth slowed and hours reductions continued at nearly the rate of the earlier period. In the 1990s, there has been more variation, with some countries taking nearly all productivity growth in the form of shorter hours (for example, Austria, at 0.318). For the 12 countries as a whole, the gap has narrowed to just 1.505 per cent.

Curiously, when Gershuny considers the reversal of earlier trends, he concludes that the 1980s and the 1990s are an 'exception to the general pattern', and that the longer one's time period, the more exceptional the 1980s appears. This conclusion is curious for a number of reasons, including the fact that he only has data for one country in the 1990s, despite the 2000 publication date for his book. It is also pure speculation, which has not been borne out by non-diary sources of data on hours. An even more curious discussion is what he calls an *ad feminam* (Gershuny, 2000: 74) attack on the 'running out of time' thesis to the fact that he suspects its proponents are middle-aged mothers with busy, hectic careers (if he was alluding to me, it's pure fantasy).

The US case: the end of leisure?

The virtue of the foregoing data is that they are comparative. However, on the basis of the case I know relatively well, the United States, questions about these data arise, because the magnitude and timing of hours increase is not matched by a widely used national data set. To get a more detailed, and I believe accurate, picture I rely instead on estimates of annual hours from a household survey called the Current Population Survey (CPS) that is jointly produced by the Bureau of the Census and the Department of Labor. One virtue of the household survey is that it captures the growing 'casualization' of the labour market, that is, the decline of stable full-time employment in favour of higher rates of part-time work, a growing tendency to combine multiple part-time jobs, more self-employment, more casual and part-year work, more independent consultancy and the like. Because the household survey asks people about total hours of work, without tying those hours to particular jobs, it avoids the biases associated with measurements of hours which are job-based rather than person-based (the CPS data has been criticized by proponents of time-diary measures on the grounds that the quality of recall data is poor. For this argument, see Robinson and Godbey, 1999, and the discussion in Schor 2000).

Annual hours estimates from the CPS have been produced by Economic Policy Institute. These data cover the period from 1973 to 2000, and are reproduced in Table 12.2. They show that although hours fell slightly from 1967 to 1973, since then they have increased in every sub-period. (Correcting for the growth of involuntary unemployment and under-employment reverses the 1967–73 decline, and also makes the increase since then considerably larger. For calculations with this correction, over the period 1969–1989, see Leete and Schor, 1994.) The total increase in hours between 1973 and 2002 is 199 hours per year – or nearly an additional five weeks of work per year (assuming a 40-hour work week). Hours have risen steadily since the 1980s, by about half a per cent per year. The rise can be attributed both to the fact that weekly hours have gone up (about a tenth of a percentage point a year), and because people are working more days and weeks each year. Furthermore, productivity growth has been positive throughout this period. The excess rate of productivity growth over hours change increased to a nearly four-decade high of 3.1 per cent in the period 1995–2000 (see Table 12.3). The National Survey of the Changing Workforce of employees found that average hours at all jobs reached 47.1 per week, an substantial increase from the 43.6 hours registered in 1977, the year the survey was first conducted (Bond et al., 1997: 72–3).

The US story would be incomplete without a discussion of rising labour force participation rates, which has combined with growing hours to produce substantial increases in hours. This trend can be seen in the data from Table 12.1, where the rise in hours per working-age person exceeds the rise for employees by 13 per cent from 1980 to 2000. Data measured by household show even greater increases. According to the Council of Economic Advisers, between 1969 and 1999 annual hours of work for married-couple households rose 18 per cent (497 hours) and 28 per cent in single-parent households (297 hours) (Council of Economic Advisers, 1999). Estimates from the Economic Policy Institute also highlight the growth of hours, when measured on a household, rather than individual basis. For example, among all married-couple households, with heads of households in the 25–54 age range, total hours of paid work by both husbands and wives rose between 1979 and 2000 by a very substantial 388 per year, a gain of nearly 12 per cent. The increase has been even larger for some subgroups. Among those in the mid-point of the income distribution (the famously 'squeezed middle class') the average increase in hours was 660 per year, a rise of just over 20 per cent (Mishel et al., 2002: 100, table 1.27).

Table 12.2 Annual work hours in the US, 1967–2000

Year	Annual work hours
1967	1,716
1973	1,679
1979	1,703
1989	1,783
1995	1,827
2000	1,878

Source: Mishel et al. (2002: 115, table 2.1).

Table 12.3 Growth in annual work hours and productivity in the US, 1967–2000 (average annual change)

Period	Change in hours (1)	Change in productivity (2)	Productivity minus hours (2) – (1)
1967–73	–0.04	2.5	2.46
1973–79	0.2	1.2	1.4
1979–89	0.5	1.4	1.9
1989–95	0.4	1.5	1.9
1995–2000	0.6	2.5	3.1

Source: author's calculations from Mishel et al. (2002: 115, table 2.1).

Not surprisingly, surveys of US workers have begun to show that significant numbers feel 'overworked', and are experiencing excessive levels of job-related time pressure and stress. These sentiments have grown over time. A 2001 survey from the Families and Work Institute found that 28 per cent of workers had felt overworked often or very often in the last three months, 28 per cent reported being 'overwhelmed by how much work they had to do' (often or very often in the last three months), and 29 per cent 'didn't have the time to step back and process or reflect on the work they're doing' (often or very often in the last three months). Only 24 per cent of the sample responded that they rarely or never experience any of these feelings of overwork. More than half the sample reported these feelings 'at least sometimes in the last three months'. A majority of the workers in the sample, as in the Institute's 1997 study of similar issues, now report that they are working more hours than they would like to (data from Galinsky et al., 2001: 73–4).

The US: anomaly or leading indicator?

How relevant is this experience for other countries? Will the United States continue to be the leading country in the determination of working hours, as it has been for more than a century, or are we witnessing a significant divergence in which the path of hours reductions embarked on in many European and non-European OECD countries will continue? While it is impossible to answer this question definitively, it is worth considering the historical context and the causal background to the US change. Historically, the United States led the way internationally with early reductions in the length of the working day, Saturday and Sunday work, and the institution of a full-time standard. These developments began in the late nineteenth century, and gathered momentum in the first half of the twentieth century. European countries followed a broadly similar pattern although on a lagged timetable. Similarly, the slowdown in hours reductions began in the United States in the 1950s and 1960s and only later spread to other parts of the OECD. And finally, the reversal of the downward trend and the rise of hours began early in the 1970s by my calculations, and gathered steam in the 1980s. As noted above, some other countries have now begun to follow suit, with a trend to increased hours in some countries during the 1990–2000 decade.

The causal factors behind rising hours in the US also suggest that it may be a leading indicator. One factor is the rise of married women's labour force participation, and the movement of educated women into professional, managerial and other demanding jobs. The US has been temporally ahead of the remainder of the OECD with respect to this trend, but other countries appear to be following, at least in broad outline. This is likely to increase average hours, especially if gender composition effects are taken into account. A second factor is that recent analyses suggest one culprit for the rise of hours is worsening income inequality. This argument was first made by Linda Bell and Richard Freeman, who argued that as workers' relative position worsens, they respond by increasing desired and actual hours of work. They applied this line of reasoning to explain differences in hours of work between the US and Germany (Bell and Freeman, 1998). This argument has also been explored in a cross-national data set. Bowles and Park (2001) have found that in countries with higher levels of income inequality (as measured by Gini coefficients), hours of work in the manufacturing sector are higher, and that the inequality effect is quite substantial – a one standard deviation change in the Gini coefficient is associated with a 3–7 per cent change in annual hours. Once again, the US has been a leading country in terms of the rise of income inequality, where the so-called 'Great U-turn' (Bluestone and Harrison, 1990) began in the mid-1970s. Now, many countries are experiencing deterioration in their distributions of income, a fact which suggests that rising desired (and actual) hours may result over time.

A third trend for which the US has been a leading country is in the use of new information and other so-called 'high-tech' technologies. While the conventional wisdom holds that these labour-saving innovations will in fact save labour, the historical evidence is far from supportive of that position. Indeed, the experience of the first Industrial Revolution that I discussed above, suggests the reverse. Massive technical change led to tremendous increases in hours of work. The reason was that these technologies hold the possibility for reaping large increases in profitability, which employers took advantage of. Only when workers were able to organize to resist employers' demands did productivity growth begin to be translated into shorter hours. I believe that we are in a period now which is analogous to the pre-1875 period. That is, employers' desire to reap profitability from technology is outstripping employees' ability to withstand upward pressure on hours. The work-inducing nature of technology is hinted at by a question from the 2001 Families and Work Institute survey. A total of 41 per cent of the sample said that they use technology (cell phones, beepers, pagers, computers, email and fax) 'often or very often' during non-work hours, and this use of technology is correlated with the likelihood of feeling overworked. The argument that technology is driving hours higher, rather than reducing them, is also supported by the pattern of hours increase in the US, where the rise in the 1990s was even greater than that in the 1980s. Unless employees are able to amass more collective power in the labour market, either through a revitalization of unions or new collective forms, it seems unlikely that they will be able to do much to stem the tide of rising hours. More likely, the individual exit option, colloquially known as 'downshifting', which has become popular in recent years, will remain the major avenue of resistance. (For a discussion of downshifting, see Schor, 1998, chapter 5.)

The post-war experience suggests that conventional accounts of the path of working hours that rely on either technological determinism or employee sovereignty are misguided. The first point I have already addressed with respect to the historical experience – the introduction of labour saving technologies was associated with rising work effort in the nineteenth century, and in the US again in the late twentieth century. At the very least, the impacts of technological change can go either way. On the question of employee sovereignty, the post-war experience is also revealing. A growing body of survey evidence and analytic models suggest that the claim that employees *qua* individuals can choose hours is not supported. The US is probably the case where this perspective has been most vigorously advanced, by mainstream economics. It is even less plausible in the case of other OECD countries with high rates of unionization, where hours are determined through a collective bargaining process. However, in surveys very high fractions of US workers report not being able to choose their hours, and the evidence is far more supportive of what has been termed a 'tied wage-hours' offer (for evidence on this point, see the citations in Schor, 1992). At the very least, the 'market' in hours is a very incomplete one. A view closer to the truth, I suggest, is that the typical worker is now out of equilibrium with respect to hours choice. The majority of employees report that they are working considerably more hours than they would like. In the 1997 National Survey of the Changing Workforce (NSCW) roughly 64 per cent were working more than they preferred, with 11 hours as the median level of excess hours. This was a substantial increase from the 47 per cent who reported overworking in the 1992 survey (Bond et al., 1997: 74). (A significant minority is working fewer hours than they would like. In the NSCW the figure was 13 per cent.) Precisely because firms, rather than workers, have choice in hours, the hours determination process is neither socially rational nor economically efficient.

Conclusion: the future of working time in the OECD

What can we conclude from the recent history of both the US and the OECD as a whole as it pertains to future trends in work and leisure? One obvious conclusion is that deterministic, teleological and modernist accounts of the future of work time should be avoided in favour of analyses that stress market and political power. This is hardly a revolutionary point, although it is one that economists, who have become more engaged with the study of hours in the last decade, would do well to take seriously. And perhaps the point is relevant to more than economics. Despite the growing influence of institutionalist and social constructionist analyses in the social sciences, thinking about work time continues to be embedded in determinist frameworks. The policy discourse on working hours remains heavily influenced by old-fashioned economic models and overly deterministic views of global competition. That having been said, future trends in work time in the OECD are hard to predict. In the absence of deliberate intervention to reduce hours, it seems likely that the trend toward a US-style increase will grow, rather than subside. However, the link between ecological degradation and long hours noted in the introduction could provide an added impetus for reducing hours, at least outside the US, where sustainability concerns are beginning to be taken seriously.

Bibliography

Bell, L. and Freeman, R. (1998) 'Working Easy: Hours Worked and Earnings Dispersion in Germany', Haverford College and Harvard University, unpublished paper.

Bluestone, B. and Harrison, B. (1990) *The Great U-Turn: Corporate Restructuring and the Polarizing of America*, New York, Basic Books.

Bond, J. T., Galinsky, E., and Swanberg, J. E. (1997) *The 1997 National Study of the Changing Workforce*, New York, Families and Work Institute.

Bowles, S. and Park, Y. (2001) 'Emulation, Inequality, and Work Hours: Was Thorstein Veblen Right?' Santa Fe Institute, unpublished paper.

Burgoon, B. and Baxandall, P. (2004) 'Three Worlds of Working Time: The Partisan and Welfare Politics of Work Time Hours in Industrialized Countries', *Politics and Society* 32: 439–73.

Council of Economic Advisers (1999) 'Families and the Labor Market, 1969–1999: Analyzing the "Time Crunch"', Washington, DC, Council of Economic Advisers, unpublished mimeo.

Galinsky, E., Kim, S. and Bond, J. T. (2001) 'Feeling Overworked: When Work Becomes Too Much', New York, Families and Work Institute, unpublished mimeo.

Gershuny, J. (2000) *Changing Times: Work and Leisure in Post-Industrial Society*, Oxford, Oxford University Press.

Groningen University (2002) 'University of Groningen and The Conference Board', GGDC Total Economy Database. <http://www.ggdc.net> accessed April 2006.

Juster, T. and Stafford, F. P. (1985) *Time, Goods and Well-Being*, Ann Arbor, MI, Survey Research Center, Institute for Social Research, University of Michigan.

Juster, T. and Stafford, F. P. (1991) 'The Allocation of Time: Empirical Findings, Behavioral Models, and Problems of Measurement', *Journal of Economic Literature* 29(2): 471–522.

Leete, L. and Schor, J. B. (1994) 'Assessing the Time Squeeze Hypothesis: Estimates of Market and Non-market Hours in the United States, 1969–1989', *Industrial Relations* 33(1): 25–43.

Maddison, A. (1987) 'Growth and Slowdown in Advanced Capitalist Economies: Techniques of Quantitative Assessment', *Journal of Economic Literature* 25(2): 649–98.

Mishel, L., Berstein, J. and Allegretto, S. (2002) *The State of Working America 1998–99*, Ithaca, NY, Cornell University Press.

OECD (various years) *Labour Force Statistics*, OECD Department of Economics and Statistics, Paris, OECD.

Robinson, J. P. (1986) 'Trends in Americans' Use of Time: Some Preliminary 1965–1975–1985 Comparisons', Final Report to Office of Technology Assessment, Washington, DC, US Congress, mimeo, September.

Robinson, J. P. and Godbey, G. (1996) 'The Great American Slowdown', *American Demographics* (June): 42–8.

Robinson, J. P. and Godbey, G. (1999) *Time for Life: The Surprising Ways Americans Use Their Time*, 2nd edn, State College, Pennsylvania, PA, Pennsylvania State Press.

Rule, J. (1981) *The Experience of Labour in Eighteenth-Century English Industry*, London, Palgrave Macmillan.

Schor, J. B. (1992) *The Overworked American: The Unexpected Decline of Leisure*, New York, Basic Books.

Schor, J. B. (1998) *The Overspent American: Upscaling, Downshifting and the New Consumer*, New York, Basic Books.

Schor, J. B. (2000) 'Working Hours and Time Pressure: The Controversy about Trends in Time Use', in L. Golden and D. M. Figart (eds) *Working Time; International Trends, Theory and Policy Perspectives*, London, Routledge, pp. 73–86.

Schor, J. B. (2005) 'Sustainable Consumption and Worktime Reduction', *Journal of Industrial Ecology* 9 (1, 2): 37–50.

Stansell, C. (1982) *City of Women: Sex and Class in New York 1789–1860*, New York, Knopf.

Wackernagel, M. et al. (2002) 'Tracking the Ecological Overshoot of the Human Economy', *Proceedings of the National Academy of Sciences* 99(14) (9 July): 9266–71.

13

Leisure and Gender: Challenges and Opportunities for Feminist Research

Karla A. Henderson and Susan M. Shaw

The centrality of gender as an organizing principle of leisure practice has been the focus of a considerable body or research conducted over the past couple of decades (for example, Deem, 1986; Wimbush and Talbot, 1988; Henderson et al., 1996; Wearing, 1998). Researchers revealed how gender relates not only to leisure activities and behaviours, but also to the experiences and meanings of leisure in everyday life. The gender stereotyping of activities, evident in many realms of leisure practice, was shown to be associated with gendered opportunities, constraints, and patterns of time use. Men's time was seen as segmented with often a clear differentiation between work and non-work, and men seemed to have a greater availability of leisure activities and relaxation. The more holistic nature of women's lives, despite dramatic increases in labour market participation of some groups of women in the later years of the twentieth century, was seen to reflect women's caregiving roles, family responsibilities, and the lack of access to leisure that was free of socially prescribed obligations.

The early research on leisure and gender tended to use an 'add women and stir' approach (Henderson, 1994; Wimbush and Talbot, 1988), with a tendency to focus on issues such as gender differences in participation, constraints and time use. The early research sometimes lacked a solid theoretical underpinning. Over the years, though, the theoretical grounding for this body of research has developed rapidly, and has reflected some of the variation between North American and British/Australian research.

Research emphases in the United States and Canada have typically been placed on women's meanings and perceptions (for example, Allen and Chin-Sang, 1990; Henderson, 1990; Shaw, 1985) and on societal expectations about women's family and caring roles and responsibilities (for example, Bedini and Guinan, 1996; Shaw, 1997; Tirone and Shaw, 1997) as well as femininity, sexuality and appearance (for example, Frederick and Shaw, 1995; Shaw, 1992). Women's leisure is seen to be socially constructed in a variety of ways, due to ideological imperatives and societal expectations associated with femininity, motherhood and familism, and so on (for example, Henderson et al., 2002; Shaw, 2001).

In contrast, research in Britain and Australia has tended to incorporate a more overt focus on social structures and gendered power relations (for example, Green et al., 1990; Yule, 1997). The macro-sociological perspective of these scholars directed attention toward structural dimensions of power, and moved the debate toward issues of class and economic inequalities as well as gender. This body of research also incorporated notions of social reproduction, and the role of leisure in the reproduction of (and sometimes resistance of) dominant ideologies (for example, Green et al., 1990; Wearing, 1998).

The North American and British/Australian approaches tended to reflect micro and macro perspectives, respectively. The complementary nature of the gender relations and social constructionist approaches with the shared focus on power, ideologies and inequities and the need for social change helped to develop theoretical linkages and provided a common basis for understanding in many ways. Thus the development of the two somewhat separate bodies of research led to some mutual reinforcement and a cross-fertilization of ideas. Furthermore, as the general area of gender and leisure research progressed, the complexity of the issues being addressed gained greater recognition along with recognition of the need to critique essentialist notions of sex and gender and simplistic notions of gender difference (for example, Aitchison, 2000; Henderson, 1994).

Nevertheless, as the twentieth century came to an end, the rapid expansion of gender-related research on leisure seemed to slow down. A number of challenges emerged, both from within and from outside the leisure field, which appeared in some ways to challenge the fundamental assumptions and liberatory purposes of the gender agenda. In this chapter we will discuss some of these challenges, the impact they have had on research on leisure and gender, and the potential for new approaches which might enhance rather than weaken this body of research.

Ghettoization

One of the challenges faced by the emerging area of gender scholarship has been its isolation or 'ghettoization' from other areas of leisure research. Deem (1999) argued forcefully that research on women's leisure has typically been ignored, and has rarely been acknowledged or integrated outside the narrow confines of researchers who study it. Despite claims by Henderson and Bialeschki (1999), Coalter (1999) and Kelly (1999) that feminist research can contribute to a broader understanding of epistemological and theoretical aspects of leisure research, feminist studies seem to be cited only infrequently in the 'mainstream' leisure literature. Where the concept of gender is incorporated in other areas of leisure research, it is often treated as an independent variable (presumably in recognition of the fact that it is a predictor of leisure behaviour). Theoretical constructions developed through research on gender are rarely used to inform social analysis in other areas of the leisure literature.

In North America the ghettoization of gender research on leisure may be less evident. For example, some gender researchers have been at the forefront of the move towards greater acceptance of qualitative and interpretative methodologies in leisure research (for example, Henderson, 1991; Samdahl, 1999). In addition, feminist research has contributed to understanding leisure through a focus on meaning and lived experience, and has been noted for developing ties and linkages with British leisure research (Coalter, 1997). Nevertheless, feminist publications in general may not be widely read or incorporated into required readings for undergraduate and graduate students, and conference sessions dedicated to gender often receive little attention (Deem, 1999).

One explanation for the ghettoization of gender research in leisure studies may be that it is simply symptomatic of the isolation of leisure research in general. Samdahl and Kelly (1999) suggested that research on leisure is rarely read or cited by research in other fields of study. Similarly, Pedlar (1995) and Shaw (2000) discussed the isolation and perceived lack of relevance of research on leisure. The isolation of the gender and leisure research seems to be particularly evident within rather than outside the leisure field. Therefore, different causes may underlie this phenomenon.

Another explanation for the isolation of gender research is that it is inferiorized (Aitchison, 2000; Deem, 1999). This isolation may be consistent with the oft-noted inferiorization of women and women's work in general (Andersen, 1993), as well as with the fact that most of the researchers studying gender are women and most of the research has directed attention towards understanding women's leisure and women's lives. Thus the topic area of gender and leisure may seem to be narrow or exclusionary, and appears to have little applicability to 'male-stream' research. One evident challenge to gender research, therefore, is the challenge of whether and what ways this body of knowledge should be applied to enhance understanding of men and masculinities. On the one hand, it would be unfortunate if men were added simply to make gender research more acceptable as 'legitimate research'. On the other hand, notions of gender clearly do apply to men and men's lives as well (Brod and Kaufman, 1994; Messner and Sabo, 1990), so the lack of research on the gendered nature of men's leisure would seem to be an obvious gap in understanding.

Another possible explanation for the apparent 'ghettoization' of gender and leisure research is its focus on white middle-class Western women (Aitchison, 2000; Wearing, 1998). This assessment is consistent with other the criticisms of Second Wave feminism for its focus on women who were relatively advantaged, and for ignoring the glaring inequities between women from different social classes and from different cultural and racial backgrounds (for example, hooks, 1989). The challenge to gender research here relates to the question of recognizing and incorporating ideas of diversity as an important aspect of the gender analysis.

Cross cutting these issues, and adding a theoretical dimension, is the challenge of postmodernism and post-structuralism as means for expanding leisure and gender meanings. Feminist researchers within the leisure field, and in other fields, have at times been criticized for 'holding onto' an outdated conceptualization of social structure (for example, Rojek, 1997). Thus, for example, understanding gender through reference to structured power relations and dominant ideologies is thought, by some theorists, to ignore recent social change and the advent of the postmodern world. Holding on to 'old' explanations may isolate leisure researchers from asking 'new' questions (Kelly, 1997; Roberts, 1997; Rojek, 1995).

Perhaps the challenges of including men, diversity, and emerging theories must become a part of the feminist agenda if gender research is to be given more attention and recognition within the field of leisure studies. These challenges raise the question of whether gender research remains relevant today, and whether these specific criticisms represent a fundamental challenge to feminist researchers or not. We turn in the remainder of this chapter to discussion of these challenges.

Men and masculinities

Given the growth, range, and depth of research about women, femininity and leisure, it is interesting to speculate about why so little research has been done about men, masculinity and leisure. In one sense, a considerable volume of research about men's leisure does exist. The rationale is that the research about men is as old as scholarship itself, and that the historical study of social life has been the study of men and their undertakings. This mainstream study of men, however, has paid scant attention to the meanings of masculinity and has not focused on men as gendered beings (Coltrane, 1994). Rather, the historical study of men's activities including their participation in leisure as well as their participation in all other realms of social life has been based on the idea that men's lives (at least white middle- and upper-class Western men's lives) are the 'norm'. Women have been designated the 'other' because of their biological sex and/or because of their gender. No assumption has been made about the necessity to understand the gendered nature of men's lives. Therefore, this research on men and masculinity sits outside the field of gender studies.

The focus on women within gender studies could be seen to be based on a taken-for-granted assumption that women's lives are gendered (and, by inference, that men's lives are not). The incorporation of a gender relations framework for understanding women's lives makes apparent that gender is relational, and that the relations of power influence men's lives as well as women's lives, albeit in different and divergent ways. The relatively new area of 'men's studies' (for example, Kimmel and Messner, 1998) takes this assumption as a starting point for understanding men's lives. In general, however, research on men and masculinity from a gendered perspective remains rare, and is almost non-existent within the field of leisure studies.

The focus on women's lives within the gender and leisure field is not because gender is thought to lack relevance to men's lives. Rather, the focus on women's leisure probably reflects the fact that most gender scholars are women who want to see their research contribute not only to enhanced understanding but also to social action and social change. The feminist perspective adopted by these researchers represents a desire to make women's lives visible and to reduce gender inequities within the realm of leisure as well as other areas of social life (Henderson and Bialeschki, 1999), and to reduce oppression and improve the quality of women's lives. Nevertheless, since gender is relational and socially constructed, and since men also face problems (as well as advantages) associated with the gendered nature of their lives, a case could be made about expanding gender research to include more focus on men and masculinity.

This challenge of expanding gender and leisure scholarship is one that we believe needs to be addressed for various reasons: (1) to promote a broader understanding of gender, (2) to incorporate the neglected area of men's studies, (3) to gather information about both the positive and negative aspects of men's lives, and (4) to understand the implications of men's gendered lives for women and vice versa. The developing academic area of men, masculinity and sport (for example, McKay et al., 2000) is a starting point. This research has pointed to some problems that men face because of their gender (for example, Kimmel and Messner, 1998; Messner and Sabo, 1990). For example, men who do not fit the ideal image of masculinity or who are not competitive, tough, successful, or heterosexual may face a variety of problems (for example, discrimination, harassment) in their lives including their sporting lives. This research needs to be expanded to look at other areas of men's leisure lives as well. Another starting point could be the expansion of the women and leisure research to include a focus on men as well as women. For example, researchers could examine the work–leisure–family nexus for men who are fathers or have other caregiving responsibilities.

Whatever the starting point for future research on men and leisure, previous gender scholarship underscores the necessity of incorporating the relational aspects of gender, and examining how the construction of masculinities is interwoven with constructions of femininities. Sports sociologists within the men's studies tradition (for example, Messner and Sabo, 1990), have incorporated feminist theories and frameworks to enhance their understanding of men's lives, and we suggest that this approach needs to be taken in future research on men and leisure. Such an approach could focus on ways that gender relations may negatively influence men's lives. For example, narrow constructions of masculinity may disadvantage or constrain men and their options and choices. Alternatively the role of gender as a facilitator or enabler of leisure for men (and for advantaged women as well) may provide additional insight. This analysis also requires a focus on power and the uneven distribution of power among men, among women, and between men and women. This type of research on uncovering the lives of people with power, as opposed to those without power, may be controversial but would clearly facilitate knowledge of relational dynamics. In addition, research on the reproduction and resistance to hegemonic masculinity and femininity (Shaw, 2001) could provide additional insights into societal aspects of gender relations and gender ideologies.

One of the difficulties of expanding gender research to focus on men as well as women is the issue of standpoint theory (Harding, 1991). The emphasis among standpoint theorists on how subordinate social positioning determines consciousness and makes specific sorts of knowledge available would seem to make the gender perspective more relevant to research on women's than men's lives. Nevertheless, an expansion of gender research to men and masculinities suggests that benefits and insights can be gained if researchers are able to bring their own experiences and consciousness to bear on research studies. Thus, although both men and women can do research on gender in our opinion, by incorporating the experiences of being male or female, advantages would exist to the study of men if some male researchers were involved in the research process. Unfortunately, relatively few male scholars seem to be interested in research on gender (Henderson and Shaw, 2003). Male scholars may feel reluctant to enter a field that has come to be seen as a 'women's realm', or they may fear uncovering information that is uncomfortable or personally challenging. Nevertheless, we hope that this perception will become less of an issue in the future as more young male scholars become involved in gender research.

Another potential difficulty in broadening the base of gender studies is that male scholarship or research on men and masculinities could start to dominate the field. In this case, once again women's lives and the need for social change could be inferiorized or made invisible. This debate has been widely discussed with regard to 'women's studies' versus 'gender studies' (Evans, 1990). Evans argued that the shift from women's studies to gender studies may allow the difference between the sexes to replace the study of sexual inequality and the social subordination of women. We are personally optimistic, however, that progress can be made with vigilance, attention to gender/feminist theoretical understanding, and with a relational approach that promotes an understanding of the complex interrelationships between masculinity and femininity. We are suggesting that the challenge to incorporate the study of men should be accepted and encouraged, and that collaborative work between female and male researchers and between researchers focusing on men's as well as women's lives will contribute to a more inclusive understanding of gender and leisure.

Diversity and globalization

Diversity is a challenge that requires attention to issues of difference not only between women and men, but also among women and among men. These multiple identities seem to be related to the construction of opportunity and constraint in leisure. Yet, the examination of the intersection of identity markers such as gender, race, (dis)ability, ethnicity, age and maturity, sexual identity and class does not seem prevalent in the feminist leisure literature (Henderson et al., 2002), and is certainly not common in the general leisure literature either. Parallel to past research on leisure and gender, characteristics such as race and ethnicity most typically have been studied as separate and distinct aspects of social life. This research on race and ethnicity has been of value (for example, Floyd, 1998; Gramann and Allison, 1999). The idea of diversity, however, suggests the need for greater attention to and integration of a wide range of cultural indicators including customary beliefs, social forms and material conditions as well as physical traits and characteristics. From the perspective of gender scholarship, a critical analysis of issues such as institutionalized sexism, racism, ageism and homophobia is needed to move beyond the discussion of people who are identified as female, non-white, gay/lesbian or 'other' (Aitchison, 2000).

Queer theory is an example of an emerging area of social thought that has direct ties to issues regarding diversity. Queer theory, like current feminist theory, rejects the idea that gender or sexuality is essential and immutable. This challenge led to the concept of selfhood as a constructed idea with gender seen as a system of shifting signifiers rather than an innate or essential category (Butler, 1990). In previous generations and even today, definitions of sexuality through biology, religion, politics and economics have produced categories of right and wrong, which are usually linked to ideas about reproduction and family life. These traditional definitions result in notions of 'normal' and 'deviant', while queer theory examines and politically critiques anything that falls into normative and deviant categories, particularly sexual activities and identities. Thus queer theory moves thought away from the binary ideas of heterosexuality as 'normal' and anything else as 'other' to an examination of how encompassing sexual identity might be. For example, Butler argued that the assumption that sex (that is, male, female) causes gender (that is, feminine, masculine), which causes desire towards the other gender should be challenged because gender and desire are flexible rather than biologically determined. A feminist-queer perspective could be useful to leisure studies because it would shift thinking from a narrow social psychological perspective to a more critical sociological analysis (Kivel and Pearce, 1999). Further, this perspective can address the rigid and mutually exclusive categories of identity (for example, male/female, heterosexual/homosexual) that typically organize social science and leisure research. Queer theory opens the door to a broader understanding of diversity that moves beyond dualistic ways of thinking such as normal/deviant, heterosexual/homosexual, male/female or able-bodied/disabled.

Queer theory, though, while addressing the issue of essentialism, is less able to address structural and political economy issues such as questions of globalization and global economic justice. Cross-cultural and cross-national diversity, and the movement towards globalization, represent another set of challenges to gender scholarship. Globalization has significant implications with regard to economic, political, cultural and geographic processes, and suggests an increasingly transnational world (Moghadam, 1999). However, this transnational world has different implications and different outcomes for people in different cultural, material and geographic circumstances.

In terms of women's lives, globalization makes apparent the need for both economic and gender justice because of the diverse ways that women live around the world (DAWN, 2001). Many critics fear that globalization exacerbates gender inequality. The global economy has generated jobs for some women in developing countries, and this has enabled them to earn and control income and sometimes to break away from patriarchal structures including traditional household and familial obligations (Moghadam, 1999). Nevertheless, at the same time, much of the work that has become available to women is badly paid, demeaning, or insecure. In some countries, women are exploited in low-wage sweatshop settings or impoverished through the loss of traditional sources of income (Fernandez-Kelly and Wolf, 2001).

In addition, sex tourism and sexual slavery have flourished in some areas as a direct result of global economic and political systems, adding to the spread of disease and the disempowerment of women and children (Victims of Trafficking and Violence Protection Act, 2000).

The benefits of globalization have also been unevenly distributed among men, with many of those already living in poverty becoming further marginalized. World political economic systems have resulted in policy shifts in a number of countries towards greater privatization and lowered public spending, particularly in social services. Thus the need for justice includes justice for both women and men and the need to address economic as well as gender inequities.

Globalization challenges leisure researchers as well as political economists. The 1995 Beijing Declaration and Platform for Action listed a number of issues that related to women's lives such as poverty, education, health, violence, human rights, the media, the environment and discrimination against female children. All of these issues have direct implications for leisure and the quality of life for girls and women (Bialeschki and Henderson, 1996). Further, economic discrimination and other forms of injustice also affect the leisure of boys and men, in both similar and dissimilar ways.

The significance of diversity and globalization are evident, but finding ways to address these issues is not easy. Post-colonial feminist theory provides a critique of Western feminism that has focused on equal rights for educated women while ignoring the experiences of women who are economically or educationally disadvantaged (Wearing, 1998). Adopting a post-colonial feminist theoretical perspective allows the silenced voices of marginalized women to be heard as well as the voices of colonized men and boys. Despite globalization's negative impact on the lives of many people worldwide, it may offer a way to link gender justice with economic justice at global, national and local levels.

The challenge of diversity related to gender research includes taking global inequities and forces of globalization into account and is not just a question of understanding multiple identities and experiences, or structural systems of inequality within Western nations. Clearly greater articulation of these issues and their relationships to gender and leisure are required. Moreover, while sensitivity to these diversity issues is an important and necessary step, enhanced understanding will also require collaboration among male and female researchers from varied cultural backgrounds and from different parts of the world. Although feminist researchers have worked to make the lives of (Western) women visible, more work is needed to develop understanding of women and men from diverse backgrounds, different material conditions and with varying degrees of access to power and resources.

'Postisms' and gender

The emergence of postmodernism and post-structuralism has also presented a major challenge to gender research and feminist theory. The challenge appears to be twofold and relates to both the characterization and articulation of society and societal change, and also to the critique of scholarship and empirical research.

Postmodernist descriptions of the fragmentation of today's society focus on the loss of meaning and enduring cultural markers, and the raised consciousness of life as contingent and uncertain as opposed to fixed and stable (Rosenau, 1992; Rojek, 1995). These characterizations, along with post-structuralists' emphases on the breakdown of structured relations of power, present a new and radically altered articulation of social life (Rogers, 2001). Moreover, the concept of the subversion of the subject problematizes the notion of personal and social identity and suggests multiple, varied and contradictory identities (Rosenau, 1992; Wearing, 1998). Accordingly, the concept of 'woman' (or of 'man') is questioned (Green, 1998) along with notions of dominant ideologies, hegemonic masculinity/femininity, and structured relations of power. Thus postmodernism and post-structuralism can be seen to contradict current gender scholarship in many ways with their emphasis on unequal access to power, unequal opportunities for leisure and the reproduction of dominant ideologies of gender.

The postmodern/post-structural critique of empirical scholarship also represents a challenge to the epistemological basis of most social science research including gender research. The anti-realist stance of post-structuralism is not a major issue for many feminists because of the widespread acceptance of constructionism and the social construction of meaning. However, the more extreme position of some postmodernists in which all traditional methodological approaches are rejected including the rejection of interpretivism as well as positivism, is much more problematic. This position seems to provide little opportunity for the continuation of gender (or any other) scholarship. In addition, the denial of any privileged voice is also an issue of concern. Although feminist researchers have long rejected the idea of a central voice of authority, or 'expert opinion', they have sought to give voice to women and to members of other marginalized groups. They have also made use of ethnographic, phenomenological and other approaches to provide insight, interpretation and understanding of gender issues. These approaches would seem to be discredited by post-structural critiques of epistemology.

The reaction of gender researchers to these challenges from postmodern/post-structural thinking has been mixed with perhaps the strongest negative reactions to the idea that structured inequities are melting away (Aitchison, 2000; Scraton, 1994). Researchers who have focused on understanding and improving women's lives are aware of the continuing lack of access to power and material resources for many women. That is, considerable evidence suggests that women are more likely than men to live in poverty, to be marginalized, and to be subjected to abuse and sexual exploitation. Gender, like race and ethnicity and other social markers, continues to predict material conditions and life opportunities. All women are not marginalized, but the postmodern era seems to have brought few benefits to those women and others who lack power. The danger of postmodernist thinking for many feminists is that it may usher in a new post-feminist era and an end to the politics of emancipation (Scraton, 1994) because of the failure to recognize continued power inequities. Moreover, a lack of focus on inequalities could lead to a return to the 'blaming the victim' approach (Henderson et al., 1996; Wearing, 1998) if the postmodern era is seen to present individuals with multiple options and opportunities.

It is not surprising that few gender researchers have accepted uncritically the postmodern/post-structuralist paradigm. Nevertheless, many of the same researchers have found some of the ideas from within this paradigm to be useful in raising important issues for consideration. The ideas of multiple identities, the reflexive self, the breakdown of clear divisions between work and leisure and the ambiguous and contradictory aspects of postmodern existence resonate with many feminist scholars (for example, Green, 1998; Wearing, 1998). These ideas suggest that gender (and other) researchers need to recognize the varied experiences of different women and men and the existence of many femininities and masculinities. They also reinforce the need to be wary of totalizing or unidimensional depictions or explanations of gendered society (Aitchison, 2000). Thus, the emphasis needs to be placed on understanding diversity and difference in its many forms within particular societies as well as globally.

A tension remains, however, between recognition of diversity and multiple identities and the idea of commonality of experience among women. This concern could be seen as a major dilemma for feminist researchers who have documented shared experiences of women. For other researchers, perhaps the concept of tension itself is just an additional aspect of the contradictory notion of social life that includes gender and family experiences (Shaw, 1997). In other words, it may be important for researchers to take into account unique situations and subjectivities of individuals as well as the possibility of shared experiences among some women, which result from commonalities linked to race, ethnicity, sexuality, age, poverty, motherhood or caregiving responsibilities.

The idea of diversity and the acceptance of tensions and contradictions within postmodernism may also provide a way forward in terms of competing methodologies. Feminist researchers, as mentioned earlier, support the need to provide a voice for women (and men) in different life circumstances. Thus, although feminist researchers (like other social science researchers) may be reluctant to abandon traditional epistemological approaches that have provided understanding and have facilitated social action in the past, they may be willing to accept other avenues of insight. New approaches from auto-ethnography to deconstructionism, could provide a contribution to scholarship as could new methods of dissemination such as poetry, plays, and other forms of artistic representation (Richardson, 1997). These strategies may not be seen as a satisfactory answer to some postmodernists, but they would be consistent with feminist ideals of praxis and inclusion.

The 'postisms' overall have presented a challenge to feminist researchers, but this challenge could lead to a new and expanded feminism rather than an abandonment of gender research. Specifically, postmodernist and post-structuralist ideas have encouraged feminist researchers to become more open to new ideas, more flexible, and more focused on issues of individual and cultural diversity as well as globalization. At the same time, however, feminist researchers have not rejected the critical issues of power and justice. This commitment is evident from the focus, even among postmodernist feminists (for example, Wearing, 1998), of continued attention to the role of dominant ideologies associated with femininity, motherhood or familism, and the role of resistance in seeking to combat these oppressive ideologies (Shaw, 2001). Thus feminist research in the postmodern era can continue to focus not only on enhanced understanding of the gendered nature of social life, but also continues its agenda of emancipation.

Looking towards the future

The challenges that gender scholars have faced in recent years has encouraged researchers to examine the basic tenets and principles of this area of research and to give serious consideration to emerging ideas and perspectives. The fact that this body of research has focused primarily on understanding the lives of women and girls has its roots in the historical exclusion of women from traditional social science research, and the need to make women's lives visible (Henderson and Bialeschki, 1999; Shaw, 1999). As a result, the research about leisure and gender has largely ignored questions related to men's lives and the social construction of masculinity. We believe that it is now important to rectify this gap in gender research, and to give more attention to understanding the gendered lives of men. This research needs to build on existing gender scholarship and to add to, rather than replace, existing research on women. Moreover, this new direction has the potential to greatly enhance understandings of leisure and gender and will be facilitated if male as well as female scholars become engaged with this project.

The related issues of diversity and globalization also need greater attention by gender scholars. Researchers have expounded on the need to broaden the basis of understanding gender, and yet a focus on diversity is not evident in most of the research to date (Henderson et al., 2002). Although the intersection of gender with other characteristics such as race and class is acknowledged (for example, Bialeschki and Walbert, 1998; Phillipp, 1998; Scraton and Watson, 1998), clearly more analyses need to be done. A greater focus on diversity and globalization would be enhanced with greater diversity among leisure scholars. The relative lack of scholars of colour from different parts of the world with diverse cultural backgrounds studying leisure is a reflection of global and cultural inequities, and is another area of concern that deserves attention. Greater collaboration among scholars worldwide would be an important step forward.

Post-colonial theory may represent a useful approach for critiquing Western perspectives and for incorporating new voices into the field of leisure and gender research (Wearing, 1998). In this way, globalization may offer a way to link leisure and gender justice with economic justice at global, national and local levels. Issues related to the gendered nature of paid and unpaid labour as well as health, education, working conditions and militarism cannot be separated from questions of leisure and the quality of life for women, men, children and families worldwide.

As indicated earlier, postmodernism and post-structuralism also offer some insights that can be helpful for leisure researchers studying gender. These perspectives are consistent with the emphasis on diversity and individual identities and subjectivities. They also serve to illuminate the many tensions and contradictions of modern life including the tension between the commonalities and uniqueness of experiences and situations as well as the ambiguity and lack of certainty related to postmodernism and rapid social change.

For gender scholarship to remain relevant and meaningful, researchers need to take account of the current challenges. Part of the relevancy and meaning may be wrapped up in how feminism is used as a philosophical foundation for research on gender theory. Henderson and Bialeschki (1999: 171) noted that feminism in the past has enhanced interpretations of leisure and should 'have implications for broader, not narrower, theory'. In other words, gender scholars do not have to conform to one narrow perspective, but can continue to grow through exposure to and incorporation of varied approaches and paradigms (Walker, 1995). New feminist approaches, also referred to as Third Wave feminism with the emphasis on individual and sexual freedom and its toleration of difference may also have something to offer to leisure researchers. Like postmodernists, Third Wave feminists argue that absolute rules of behaviour no longer exist either for men or women (Hogeland, 2001). Followers of new feminism also claim to be building upon, rather than negating, earlier feminist work. They accept many of the basic tenets of earlier feminism such as the need for women's empowerment and emancipation, but they place greater emphasis on diversity and bring new applications especially related to women's sexual freedom (Howry and Wood, 2001).

Many gender scholars see some potential for new ideologies of feminism to add fresh dimensions of understanding human behaviour. Nevertheless, they are also concerned that care be taken to ensure that the emancipatory project of feminist research does not get lost or forgotten in the process. For example, questions need to be asked about whether emphasis on female sexuality with its potential for enhanced freedom and choice might also, under some circumstances, lead to conformity to a sexualized ideal for girls and women and the danger of increased sexual exploitation. In addition, similar to concerns about post-structuralism (Aitchison, 2000), gender scholars need to ensure that ongoing structural inequalities (such as those between between women and men, young and old, gay/lesbian/bisexual/ transgendered and others, community and global inequalities) are not ignored by new feminist approaches.

These concerns reflect ongoing tensions between the competing ideas of structure and agency that have been evident in all areas of social research for many decades (Wearing, 1998), and which have perhaps come to the fore with the challenge of the 'postisms' and new feminisms. We would argue, though, that this tension itself is of particular relevance to scholarship on leisure and gender. Feminist leisure researchers have argued for two decades that freedom and choice are the basis for leisure in the lives of individual women and men (for example, Henderson et al., 1996; Wimbush and Talbot, 1988). As Steinam (1995: xxvi) reiterated: 'The greatest gift we give one another is the power to make a choice. The power to choose is even more important than the choices we make … We have to learn to cherish one another's choices.' At the same time, continuing evidence of unequal access to material goods and resources based on gender and other attributes requires continuing vigilance with regard to structured power relations. Therefore, enhancing freedom requires overcoming disadvantage as well as resistance to dominant relations of power, while at the same time recognizing that these power relations are constantly changing and subject to renegotiations and reconstructions.

From the perspective of choice and the creation of self, leisure is relevant for both women and men who use the freedom of leisure to express and reinvent themselves through culture, music, media, clothing and relationships with others. Therefore, leisure can lead to empowerment and resistance to oppressive ideologies and behavioural strictures (Shaw, 2001; Wearing, 1998). Consistent with this broad view of leisure, the study of leisure and gender needs to focus on becoming more diverse and more inclusive if it is to continue to be relevant and meaningful, and to resist processes of ghettoization and marginalization. This research requires recognition of individual choice and agency as well the multiple systems of inequality and constraint. It also means incorporating new ideas, focusing on a wide range of issues, and making use of different methodological and theoretical approaches to enhance understandings. An emerging focus on men and masculinities and on diversity and globalization need to become part of the agenda. Leisure and gender together and separately have numerous implications to how people live their lives and the quality of those lives. Much remains to be uncovered.

Bibliography

Aitchison, C. (2000) 'Poststructural Feminist Theories of Representing Others: A Response to the "Crisis" in Leisure Studies Discourse', *Leisure Studies* 19: 127–44.

Aitchison, C. (2001) 'Gender and Leisure: The Codification of Knowledge', *Leisure Sciences* 23: 1–19.

Allen, K. R. and Chin-Sang, V. (1990) 'A Lifetime of Work: The Context and Meanings of Leisure for Aging Black Women', *The Gerontologist* 30: 734–40.

Andersen, M. L. (1993) *Thinking about Women: Sociological Perspectives on Sex and Gender*, New York, Macmillan Publishing Co.

Anderson, K. L. (1999) 'Snowboarding: The Construction of Gender in an Emerging Sport', *Journal of Sport and Social Issues* 23: 55–79.

Bedini, L. A. and Guinan, D. M. (1996) '"If I Could Just Be Selfish…": Caregivers' Perceptions of Their Entitlement to Leisure', *Leisure Sciences* 18: 227–39.

Bialeschki, M. D. and Henderson, K. A. (1996) 'Women, Leisure, and Global Issues', *World Leisure and Recreation Association* 38(4): 41–4.

Bialeschki, M. D. and Walbert, K. L. (1998) '"You Have to Have Some Fun To Go Along With Your Work": The Interplay of Race, Class, Gender, and Leisure in the Industrial New South', *Journal of Leisure Research* 30(1): 79–100.

Brod, H. and Kaufman, M. (1994) 'Introduction', in H. Brod and M. Kaufman (eds) *Theorizing Masculinities*, Thousand Oaks, CA, Sage Publications, pp. 1–10.

Butler, J. (1990) *Gender Trouble*, New York, Routledge.

Coalter, F. (1997) 'Leisure Sciences and Leisure Studies: Different Concept, Same Crisis?' *Leisure Sciences* 19(4): 255–68.

Coalter, F. (1999) 'Leisure Sciences and Leisure Studies: The Challenge of Meaning', in E. L. Jackson and T. L. Burton (eds) *Leisure Studies: Prospects for the Twenty-first Century*, State College, PA, Venture Publishing, pp. 507–19.

Coltrane, S. (1994) 'Theorizing Masculinities in Contemporary Social Science', in H. Brod and M. Kaufman (eds) *Theorizing Masculinities*, Thousand Oaks, CA, Sage Publications, pp. 39–60.

DAWN (Development Alternatives with Women for a New Era) (2001) 'Gender Justice and Economic Justice: Reflections on the Five Year Reviews of the UN Conferences of the 1990s', <http://www.dawn.org.fj/global/health/gender_justice.html>.

Deem, R. (1986) *All Work and No Play? The Sociology of Women and Leisure*, Milton Keynes, Open University Press.

Deem, R. (1999) 'How Do We Get Out of the Ghetto? Strategies for Research on Gender and Leisure for the Twenty-first Century', *Leisure Studies* 18(3), 161–77.

Evans, M. (1990) 'The Problem of Gender for Women's Studies', *Women's Studies International Forum* 13(5): 457–62.

Fernandez-Kelly, P. and Wolf, D. (2001) 'A Dialogue on Globalization (Women's Employment)', *Signs* 26(4): 1243.

Floyd, M. F. (1998) 'Getting Beyond Marginality and Ethnicity: The Challenge for Race and Ethnic Studies in Leisure Research', *Journal of Leisure Research* 30(1): 3–22.

Frederick, C. J. and Shaw, S. M. (1995) 'Body Image as a Leisure Constraint: Examining the Experience of Aerobic Exercise Classes for Young Women', *Leisure Sciences* 17: 57–73.

Gramann, J. H. and Allison, M. T. (1999) 'Ethnicity, Race, and Leisure', in E. L. Jackson and T. L. Burton (eds) *Leisure Studies: Prospects for the Twenty-first Century*, State College, PA, Venture Publishing, pp. 283–97.

Green, E. (1998) '"Women Doing Friendship": An Analysis of Women's Leisure as a Site of Identity Construction, Empowerment and Resistance', *Leisure Studies* 17(3): 171–85.

Green, E., Hebron, S. and Woodward, D. (1990) *Women's Leisure, What Leisure?* London, Macmillan Education Ltd.

Harding, S. (1991) *Whose Science? Whose Knowledge? Thinking from Women's Lives*, Ithaca, NY, Cornell University Press.

Henderson, K. A. (1990) 'The Meaning of Leisure for Women: An Integrative Review of the Research', *Journal of Leisure Research* 22(3): 228–43.

Henderson, K. A. (1991) *Dimensions of Choice: A Qualitative Approach to Recreation, Parks, and Leisure Research*, State College, PA, Venture Publishing.

Henderson, K. A. (1994) 'Broadening an Understanding of Women, Gender and Leisure', *Journal of Leisure Research* 26(1): 1–7.

Henderson, K. A. and Bialeschki, M. D. (1999) 'Makers of Meanings: Feminist Perspectives on Leisure Research', in E. L. Jackson and T. L. Burton (eds) *Leisure Studies: Prospects for the Twenty-first Century*, State College, PA, Venture Publishing, pp. 167–76.

Henderson, K. A., Bialeschki, M. D., Shaw, S. M. and Freysinger, V. J. (1996) *Both Gains and Gaps: Feminist Perspectives on Women's Leisure*, State College, PA, Venture Publishing.

Henderson, K. A., Hodges, S. and Kivel, B. (2002) 'Context and Dialogue in Research on Women and Leisure', *Journal of Leisure Research* 34(3): 253–71.

Henderson, K. A. and Shaw, S. M. (2003) 'Leisure Research about Gender and Men: The Weaker Link?' Paper presented to the Leisure Research Symposium of NRPA in St Louis, Missouri, October.

Hogeland, L. M. (2001) 'Against Generational Thinking, or, Some Things that "Third Wave" Feminism Isn't', *Women's Studies in Communication* 24: 107.

hooks, b. (1989) *Talking Back: Thinking Feminist, Thinking Black*, Boston, MA, South End Press.

Howry, A. L. and Wood, J. T. (2001) 'Something Old, Something New, Something Borrowed: Themes in the Voices of a New Generation of Feminists', *The Southern Communication Journal* 66: 323.

Kelly, J. (1997) 'Leisure as Life: Outline of a Poststructuralist Reconstruction', *Loisir & Société* (Society and Leisure) 20(2): 401–18.

Kelly, J. R. (1999) 'Leisure Behaviors and Styles: Social, Economic, and Cultural Factors', in E. L. Jackson and T. L. Burton (eds) *Leisure Studies: Prospects for the Twenty-first Century*, State College, PA, Venture Publishing, pp. 135–50.

Kimmel, M. S. and Messner, M. A. (eds) (1998) *Men's Lives* (4th edn), Boston, MA, Allyn and Bacon.

Kivel, B. and Pearce, K. (1999) 'Shifting Identities, Shifting Paradigms: Leisure and Feminist-Queer Theory'. Paper presented to the Leisure Research Symposium of NRPA in Nashville, Tennessee, October.

McKay, J., Messner, M. and Sabo, D. (2000) *Masculinities, Gender Relations and Sport*, Thousand Oaks, CA, Sage Publications.

Messner, M. A. and Sabo, D. (eds) (1990) *Sport, Men, and the Gender Order: Critical Feminist Perspectives*, Champaign, IL, Human Kinetics.

Moghadam, V. M. (1999) 'Gender and Globalization: Female Labor and Women's Mobilization', *Journal of World Systems Research* 2: 367–88.

Pedlar, A. (1995) 'Relevance and Action Research in Leisure', *Leisure Sciences* 17(2): 133–40.

Phillipp, S. F. (1998) 'Race and Gender Differences in Adolescent Peer Group Approval of Leisure Activities', *Journal of Leisure Research* 30(2): 214–32.

Richardson, L. (1997) *Fields of Play: Constructing an Academic Life*, New Brunswick, NJ, Rutgers University Press.

Roberts, K. (1997) 'Why Old Questions are the Right Response to New Challenges: The Sociology of Leisure in the 1990s', *Loisir & Société* (Society and Leisure) 20(2): 369–81.

Rogers, M. F. (2001) 'Contemporary Feminist Theory', in G. Ritzer and B. Smart (eds) *Handbook of Social Theory*, London, Sage Publications, pp. 285–96.

Rojek, C. (1995) *Decentring Leisure*, London, Sage Publications.

Rojek, C. (1997) 'Leisure Theory: Retrospect and Prospect', *Loisir et Société* (Society and Leisure) 20(2): 383–400.

Rosenau, P. M. (1992) *Postmodernism and the Social Sciences: Insights, Inroads, and Intrusions*, Princeton, NJ, Princeton University Press.

Samdahl, D. M. (1999) 'Epistemological and Methodological Issues in Leisure Research', in E. L. Jackson and T. L. Burton (eds) *Leisure Studies: Prospects for the Twenty-first Century*, State College, PA, Venture Publishing, pp. 119–33.

Samdahl, D. and Kelly, J. (1999) 'Speaking Only to Ourselves? Citation Analysis of Journal of Leisure Research and Leisure Sciences', *Journal of Leisure Research* 31(2): 171–80.

Scraton, S. (1994) 'The Changing World of Women and Leisure: Feminism, "Postfeminism," and Leisure', *Leisure Studies* 13: 249–61.

Scraton, S. and Watson, B. (1998) 'Gendered Cities: Women and the Public Leisure Space in the "Postmodern City"', *Leisure Studies* 17: 123–37.

Shaw, S. M. (1985) 'The Meaning of Leisure in Everyday Life', *Leisure Sciences* 7: 1–24.

Shaw, S. M (1992) 'Body Image among Adolescent Women: The Role of Sports and Physically Active Leisure', *Journal of Applied Recreation Research* 16: 349–57.

Shaw, S. M. (1997) 'Controversies and Contradictions in Family Leisure: An Analysis of Conflicting Paradigms', *Journal of Leisure Research* 29(1): 98–112.

Shaw, S. M. (1999) 'Gender and Leisure', in E. L. Jackson and T. L. Burton (eds) *Leisure Studies: Prospects for the Twenty-first Century*, State College, PA, Venture Publishing, pp. 271–81.

Shaw, S. M. (2000) 'If Our Research is Relevant, Why is Nobody Listening?', *Journal of Leisure Research* 33(1): 147–55.

Shaw, S. M. (2001) 'Conceptualizing Resistance: Women's Leisure as Political Practice', *Journal of Leisure Research* 33(2): 186–201.

Steinam, G. (1995) 'Foreword', in R. Walker (ed.) *To Be Real*, New York, Anchor Books, pp. xiii–xxviii.

Tirone, S. C. and Shaw, S. M. (1997) 'At the Center of Their Lives: Indo Canadian Women, Their Families, and Leisure', *Journal of Leisure Research* 29(2): 225–44.

Victims of Trafficking and Violence Protection Act of 2000 (LS 106–386) (2000) Retrieved on 28 June 2004 from <http://www.state.gov/documents/organization/10492.pdf>.

Walker, R. (1995) 'Being Real: An Introduction', in R. Walker (ed.) *To Be Real*, New York, Anchor Books, pp. xxix–xl.

Wearing, B. (1998) *Leisure and Feminist Theory*, London, Sage Publications.

Wimbush, E. and Talbot, M. (eds) (1988) *Relative Freedoms*, Milton Keynes, Open University Press.

Yule, J. (1997) 'Engendered Ideologies and Leisure Policy in the UK. Part 1: Gender Ideologies', *Leisure Studies* 16: 61–84.

14
Leisure and Ageing

Yvonne Harahousou

In the field of ageing, three basic areas of enquiry have been pursued by gerontologists over the past half-century: 'the aged' as members of increasingly aged populations in human societies; basic 'processes and mechanisms of ageing' in cells, organisms and individuals within ageing populations, and 'age as a dimension' of social organization and public policy in industrialized societies (Bengtson et al., 1999). In social gerontology, especially, there has been an increase in theoretical and empirical analyses concerning the consequences of population ageing, the changing status of ageing individuals in society, the social processes of ageing in complex and changing societies, and the interdependency of age groups in the generational compact (Johnson, 1996). From a comparative perspective studies on ageing seek to understand processes of ageing and the status of the elderly in different cultural and historical contexts.

Research and theoretical interest in some of these topics within gerontology has spread to the field of recreation and leisure. Fuelled by the growing commitment of public resources to the study and support of an ageing population in most developed countries, and the subsequent awareness of the beneficial role of leisure in later life, many leisure scholars have re-focused their research from children and youth to the study of middle-aged and ageing adults. More specifically, the pressing demographic trends worldwide, with a projected worldwide population of over 1 billion persons (aged 60 and over) by the year 2025, of whom 860 million are estimated to be in the developing world, the different challenges that will be present in the developed versus the developing regions, and most importantly the economic problems imposed by these trends in terms of social security and health-care costs (MacNeil et al., 2003), have created an even greater necessity to increase the quality and quantity of research about later life leisure.

To date, leisure studies about older adults have primarily focused on their participation patterns, leisure needs, preferences, and the constraints preventing or inhibiting leisure involvement. Much of this research has focused on, the role of active leisure or physical activity in preventing disease, in promoting health through lifestyle development (MacNeil, 1995; Mobily, 1987), and on enhancing the quality of life of older adults. Today, however, under the pressing demographic shifts noted above, leisure researchers need to understand the magnitude of the shifts in each community, region or nation. Therefore, more studies with large representative samples of older adults across two or three generations are needed, with well-validated cross-cultural and cross-national standardized measures. Yet, to arrive at a more complete understanding of leisure in later life, researchers should not segregate leisure research from a much larger and more comprehensive body of literature about the elderly. Leisure scholars must integrate the basic gerontology and geriatrics literature – theories, concepts and research findings – into their own research. Ideally, the research agenda should involve multidisciplinary teams of researchers studying the same group of older adults using an interdisciplinary approach to understanding leisure in older adults.

It is widely recognized that the world population is increasingly ageing, due to increased longevity, low fertility and improved health that has been witnessed during the last century in both developed and developing nations. Ageing is becoming less associated with dependency and more with activity and independence. 'Active ageing' is a new definition of 'ageing' which has emerged and reflects the desire and ability of many seniors to remain engaged in all life's activities, such as work, retirement, education and leisure (US Department of Health and Human Services, 1997). Consequently, the course of life no longer follows its traditional age-segregated stages: education during childhood and adolescence; work during early and middle adulthood; and leisure following retirement during later life. This current pattern appears to have an *age-integrated* structure wherein education, work and leisure are possible, and desirable, at all stages across the life course (McPherson, 2004).

Positive images about ageing have also started to replace negative ones that are traditionally associated with ageing (Johnson, 1995). The attribution of passivity to the elderly is no longer valid as a cultural image. Rather, more active images of being old are being defined and promoted by older adults who are expected to be more physically active in their later life than were their parents or grandparents. Additionally, since older adults currently live healthier and longer lives, and are generally better off financially than the previous generation, they are no longer looked upon as necessarily poor, needy or victimized people. In fact, they are no more likely to be poor than any other age group, and some of them are even one of the wealthiest societal groups (Godbey, 1994). Thus it is not surprising that some segments of the elderly population are increasingly viewed as 'a shot of economic adrenalin' (Hoffman, 1990).

Consequently, leisure has grown in qualitative importance and has come to be more central in the lifestyles of older individuals. Leisure is no longer viewed as a way to 'kill time' or an alternative to work, but an important element of older people's lives, which provides them with meaning and a sense of personal identity. Leisure according to the new definition of active ageing means an active way to experience successful ageing, life satisfaction, and higher quality of life in later life. Thus older adults, due to their economic advantages and increased health, spend more on all forms of leisure and have become a very large segment of the travel and tourism industry. Additionally, more older adults engage in various forms of active leisure, including sports and active recreation (Wankel and Berger, 1990), since the importance of exercising to health and well-being is well known (Blair, 1993).

In summary, the current status of the elderly population, as it appears in most developed countries, encompasses more activity and independence, more positive and active images, an age-integrated structure within education, work and leisure, with an emphasis in leisure involvement that includes active recreation and sports. This current status, however, does not appear in less developed countries where life expectancy is much lower (around 45 years for both sexes in some countries) due to poor health and lifestyle factors, as well as to such societal events as wars, famines and natural disasters. To achieve a more universal knowledge, regarding the current pattern of the ageing population, as well as a valid picture of elderly leisure involvement worldwide, more studies are needed on older adults living in developing or emerging nations, and on those living in rural, small or remote communities in developed countries. Additionally, more comparative studies would provide valuable information regarding the leisure needs, demands and constraints of older adults in different cultural or economic settings.

Theoretical perspectives on ageing and leisure involvement

Several theories in social gerontology have attempted to explain the process of leisure involvement and successful ageing. Amongst them, activity theory, disengagement theory and continuity theory have been used most in leisure studies (Howe, 1988). *Activity theory* (Burgess, 1960) holds that maintaining a high level of physical, social and intellectual activity upon retirement increases satisfaction with life. Feelings of social isolation among the older age group are reduced when seniors learn to substitute their 'lost roles' with new interests and activities. *Disengagement theory* (Cumming and Henry, 1961), on the other hand, views ageing as a process of withdrawal of the individual from society in a pattern of voluntary reduction, as well as that of society from the individual. *Continuity theory* (Atchley, 1971), holds that the smooth passage into the realities of old age comes from the uninterrupted pursuit of one's favourite pre-retirement activities after retirement. Another approach, analysed in the context of leisure continuity by Baltes and Baltes (1990), is a pattern of *selective optimization with compensation*. By focusing energy and resources on selected activities, even to the exclusion of others, the older adult can still achieve a satisfying lifestyle. Compensation involves adaptation to altered conditions and abilities to maintain as much continuity as possible.

While the above theoretical perspectives have provided some valuable insights, they have frequently also provided unidimensional explanations, concentrating on social roles, psychological variables, or physical processes of ageing. Conversely, other perspectives have adopted a multidimensional approach, such as the *life course developmental perspective* (Levinson, 1978), and a more critical approach such as the *feminist perspective* (Henderson and Bialeschki, 1991) and the *postmodern perspective* (Laws, 1995). Levinson proposed three components that should be examined collectively: the sociocultural world, the self, and the individual's participation in the external world in order to understand life structure. Individuals in their later years are faced with choices concerning the central constituents of their lives. These include retirement, family structure and leisure. In the domain of leisure the life course, which is broken into theoretically meaningful stages, provides a context for understanding differences in leisure behaviour. Age cannot explain the differences in leisure behaviour across the lifecycle without the consideration of changes such as alterations in the family structure or employment status, which may occur simultaneously (Lawton, 1985). Leisure behaviour across the lifecycle can better be understood when focused on the effects of all these changes as an individual moves from one stage to another.

The *feminist perspective* highlights the structural disadvantage that the majority of elderly women experience in leisure, reflecting broad social and economic structures that determine gender inequalities and material constraints (Watson et al., 1996). Recently feminists have discussed ways in which women and men can resist oppressive societal forces. Indeed, leisure may provide a context in which individuals can experience freedom of choice and feel more in control of their lives (Shaw, 1996).

The *postmodern perspective* uses a constructionist approach on ageing that views the differences across ages as parallel to socially constructed gender differences and argues that specific differences in behaviour between young and old people cannot simply be reduced to a universal cause (Laws, 1995). Furthermore, social relations are manifest in particular historical and geographical contexts. Thus understanding ageing variations is subject to cohort variations, different historical periods, or geographical regions. Another approach of this perspective suggests that social relations are constantly contested and recreated in struggles over identity politics (Young, 1990). Leisure participation of the elderly in general, and active leisure participation in particular, challenges the hegemony of a youth-oriented culture by reconstructing public images of the elderly. Thus, instead of being depicted as frail and dependent, they are viewed as active and independent. Leisure practices are part of an array of cultural practices that imbue old age with meaning.

To date, there has been little application of theoretical knowledge from leisure gerontological research. This often raises a scepticism about the importance of theory in leisure, and in gerontology research in general, which has led some researchers to substitute empirical models for theory and others to abandon any attempt at building a theory. According to Bengtson et al. (1999), the concern for theory development in gerontology has become devalued due to the following four trends: a) the failed quest for 'grand theory', b) the drive for applications and solutions, c) postmodernist epistemological critiques, and d) the resistance to cross-disciplinary and interdisciplinary investigations in gerontology. As the above authors explain, 'without theory, the contributions of individual studies in aging are likely to have little impact. Empirical generalizations are but discrete building blocks in the development of knowledge. As researchers we have a responsibility to act also as theorists, to interpret and explain our findings within a broader context of inquiry' (Bengtson et al., 1999: 16).

Leisure patterns in later life

Leisure participation levels of older adults have increased in most developed countries, as there is more available time, better provision of medical care, nutrition, fitness activities and a healthful environment in many retirement communities and centres. Information technology and new forms of communication have also contributed to this increase by rapidly shaping and exchanging leisure types and experiences around the globe. Therefore, older adults welcome the opportunity for relaxation and enrichment and, although most of them continue to participate in the same leisure activities they enjoyed in earlier years, others are more selective and/or compensatory due to health decrements, limited income and/or loss of leisure companions, while many are eager to try new endeavours, including tourism, sport and cultural activities (Kelly, 1996a).

The degree and type of leisure participation varies along dimensions such as gender, race, ethnicity and social stratification, as well as religion, geographic region and education. Other dimensions include economic resources, marital status, language and cultural traditions. In addition, some research findings suggest that involvement in leisure (Tarrant et al., 2001), as well as in sports (Lalive d'Epinay et al., 1996) may be more a function of cohort/generation effects than of simply getting older.

With regard to active leisure participation, cross-cultural and cross-sectional studies report a decline in participation in physical activity and sporting activities with increasing age (Fisher et al., 2002). Although it has been established that significant health benefits can be gained from moderate levels of regular physical activity for all ages, a significant proportion of the elderly population remain sedentary. There are exceptions, notably China and Japan, however, where most elderly persons engage in active pastimes, including physical exercises (Sivan, 2002). In Europe, Lalive d'Epinay et al. (1996) have found a general increase of individuals, particularly older adults, participating in sports in recent decades. Most of the above findings, however, are available from studies involving older adults who live in urban areas, and are members of the mainstream population (i.e., home-dwelling, healthy, mobile elderly persons), and many involve subjects found in handy/intact groups at a particular leisure centre or sports site. As Kelly (1996b) states, 'it is a mistake to concentrate only on age-designated programs and organizations when trying to understand the community leisure involvement of older adults. Rather, the entire spectrum of organized activity is relevant, including those, which continued from earlier life periods. Senior programs are on the margins of the entire pattern.'

The pattern of activity appears as diverse as the elderly population itself. Activities range from television viewing to participating in Elderhostel programmes, and playing cards at the community centre to providing child care for grandchildren. There are also an increasing number of seniors who engage in competitive sports, such as track and field, swimming, cycling and various team sports. Activities also serve a variety of purposes. While some activities are purely enjoyable in and of themselves, others fulfil higher cognitive or psychosocial needs (King, 1996). There is also a need for information about intergenerational leisure activities or interests, both within the extended family *per se*, and across society in general. For example, it is important to know to what extent, how, and why the elderly are segregated from, or integrated with, other age cohorts in their pursuits; yet, to what extent their social and leisure involvement should be age-segregated or age-integrated.

Specific activities, leisure preferences and values over time may change as individuals make the transition from the middle-aged to the later life stage. Their underlying motivations and complex needs, however, remain a source of continuity. For many elderly persons this continuity of activity patterns is not only a preference for the familiar but also a way of compensating for the effects of ageing, that is, minimizing the negative effects of physical and mental ageing, facilitating decision-making regarding activities, and meeting the expectations of others (Atchley, 1993). But even where there is consistency and continuity in leisure interests, there is also room for experimentation and new experiences. This reflects the tendency to seek new leisure experiences in later life (Iso-Ahola et al., 1994).

Constraints in later life

Engagement in leisure is rarely free from constraints. This is more pronounced in the elderly, who have lost control in many areas of their life, due to forced retirement, declining health, loss of leadership roles in organizations, loss of driver's licence, reduced income, and so on (McGuire, 1985). These leisure constraints can inhibit people's desire to initiate, maintain and/or replace leisure activities, limit their full involvement, reduce their enjoyment, and even cause them to cease participation (Alexandris and Carrol, 1997; Tsai and Coleman, 1999).

Constraints that affect older people's leisure involvement are usually classified in two broad categories. These categories typically include *societal* (structural) and *individual* (personal) constraints that are further divided into intrapersonal and interpersonal (Crawford and Godbey, 1987). At the *societal level*, leisure constraints are imposed due to various reasons, including lack of information and availability of leisure opportunities within the community, lack of programmes and facilities for older adults within the public and private sector, high cost of leisure activity, poor communication and transportation system, and so on. At the *individual level*, interpersonal constraints (the result of interpersonal interaction) may include: fear of victimization in an unsafe neighbourhood, existence of ageist stereotypes and sociocultural norms that discourage participation in certain leisure activities (sport, education, computer usage, and so on), and marginality specifically of less acculturated immigrants (Tsai, 2000). Additionally, other interpersonal constraints are social isolation, lack of a partner due to widowhood or divorce, loss of freedom due to caregiving responsibilities, and lack of independence and spontaneity in leisure (Bedini and Guinan, 1996). *Intrapersonal* constraints involve psychological states and attributes, such as declining energy and health, perceived lack of skills, increasing stress, depression and anxiety. Other intrapersonal constraints include loss of interest or fluctuating interests, decreased economic resources, less discretionary income, declining health of a spouse and inability to drive a car or use public transportation (McPherson, 1998).

The presence of constraints varies among elderly people and is characterized not only by degree and type, but also by a unique combination of constraints, as well as by a hierarchy of constraints (Crawford et al., 1991). Thus, while constraints such as lack of facilities, opportunities and costs for some seniors, and time commitments, largely due to caregiving responsibilities (Brattain-Rogers, 1997) for others, may affect their leisure, these constraints may not affect those who have skill deficiencies and are geographically isolated. Likewise, some individuals experience intrapersonal constraints first and perceive them as more powerful than the societal ones. Clearly, constraints to pursuing leisure in later life are not only shaped by age, but also by its intersection with gender, ethnicity/race, able-bodied-ness and social class, and particular historical and sociocultural contexts which reframe possibilities and constraints (Stodolska, 1998; Freysinger, 2002). To understand these variations we require more research of an explanatory and comparative nature to find out why the degree and type of leisure constraints vary so widely, or why some of these constraints are more pronounced in specific communities or countries. Similarly, we need to know why many older adults are not involved, or are less involved than their peers, in specific leisure activities.

Although the aforementioned constraints may seriously affect older people's leisure involvement and/or its enjoyment, for many individuals these constraints may no longer be viewed as insurmountable obstacles. Rather, they are conceived as 'negotiable' (Jackson et al., 1993). This means that many people adopt innovative strategies to alleviate these obstacles either by modifying their leisure activities or altering other aspects of their lives (Henderson et al., 1995). Although relatively little is empirically known about how older individuals negotiate their constraints, it appears that as they become increasingly resource-rich through adult education and technological advantages, they become more successful in the negotiation of constraints by employing selection, compensation and optimization strategies in everyday functioning (Lang et al., 2002). This in turn helps them to obtain optimal results from their leisure.

With regard to physical activity and sports participation, the constraints (real or perceived) may represent significant potential obstructions to the initiation, maintenance, or resumption of participation by older persons. Available findings although limited report as essential constraints lack of motivation, presence of illness/disability and fear of injury, as well as lack of leisure time and/or money (Chinn et al., 1999). Other constraints cited by older women were lack of interest in sports, resistance due to upbringing, missing sport opportunities earlier in life (Harahousou, 1995), as well as fear of ridicule in a gym when women might expose their body by doing an activity, and fear due to harassment (Dowling et al., 1997). Lastly, the form of an ageing body itself and its limited modification and reconstruction pose an additional constraint (Shilling, 1994).

Constraints in old age may also be imposed by the sport itself. That is, although sport is a legitimate source of pleasure for older adults, the inherent characteristics of competition, and athleticism, may constrain older adults from pursuing them as a form of leisure (Freysinger, 2002). In this way sport for older adults may be in danger of becoming part of a set of cosmetic and preventive efforts to hide one's ageing from oneself and others (Lolb, 2000). Furthermore, it may create a new hegemony, which disallows change and diversity within and among older advantaged or disadvantaged individuals (Featherstone, 1993), and denies individuals or values them only as sport consumers. This fails to consider their right to be old or to maintain control over their own lives (O'Beirne, 1999).

Leisure benefits in later life

Leisure activities and especially physical activities have been linked to physiological, psychological, and social benefits in elderly people (Alfermann and Stoll, 2000; McAuley and Rudolph, 1995). With regard to physiological benefits, physical activity and exercise are closely connected with the improvement and maintenance of physical health and functioning, as well as with enhanced longevity (Lee et al., 1997; Wannamethee et al., 1998). More specifically, research shows that regular physical activity can reduce the risk of obesity, high blood pressure, heart disease and stroke (Cordes and Ibrahim, 1996). In addition, regular physical activity also helps preserve and improve muscular strength, balance and aerobic capacity. This allows individuals the ability to undertake activities of daily living and thus to maintain independence (Shephard, 1995), and it helps to reduce the likelihood of falls. Physical activity positively affects other aspects of health including diabetes, osteoporosis, cholesterol and general functioning (Elward and Larson, 1992).

In terms of cognitive benefits, leisure activities offer many opportunities that positively affect various lifestyle factors, which as recent research shows are associated with cognitive ageing. Most of these factors are potentially modifiable or manageable, and some are protective. For example, lifelong learning, mental and physical exercise, continuing social engagement, stress reduction and proper nutrition may be important factors in promoting cognitive vitality in ageing (Fillit, 2002). The cognitive benefits from physical activity are related to mental skills and abilities, such as thinking, learning and reasoning, that are frequently assumed to deteriorate greatly with ageing. In older women, specifically, exercise is associated with decreased reaction time and anxiety, and increased memory span and well-being. These findings are found in cross-sectional studies but not in longitudinal or experimental studies (Fox, 1999), where findings tend to show stability in most cognitive areas throughout life. Other intervening variables, however, such as physical health, economic status, education and sociocultural context, are often suspected to influence the performance of older individuals (MacNeil and Teague, 1992). For example, Blanchard-Fields and Chen (1996), who focused on sociocultural influences on cognitive functioning among older persons, used the term 'adaptive cognition' to describe the practical aspects of mental function on problem solving, decision making and coping, as well as moral reasoning, affection and social motivation.

Other equally important benefits related to psychological and emotional health are connected with feelings, values, emotions, attitudes and personal-social skills.

Terms such as 'personality', 'motivation', 'life satisfaction' and 'adaptation' are commonly used in the domain of mental health. Thus recent studies show that physical activity is associated with improved mental health (Hassmen et al., 2000; Hilleras et al., 1999). There is also an association between lack of exercise and depression among elderly persons (Ruuskanen and Ruoppila, 1995). Other important benefits that contribute to successful ageing are competence and efficacy (Baltes and Baltes, 1990), in other words, the facility for achievement, success and mastery in older adults. The need for achievement, success and mastery does not change with age, as does the availability of opportunities due to various social losses. As evident from the above studies, the benefits reported from older adults are mostly associated with their physical activity involvement and less with leisure involvement *per se*. Clearly, more research is needed on the relationship between leisure in every form and degree of involvement and health, especially mental health, and, on how to enhance cognitive involvement through a variety of leisure activities.

Attitudes and values are also influenced by leisure participation and physical activity and make people like or dislike many forms of leisure. For example, by participating in leisure activities, people may become more aware, and appreciative of or sensitive and protective in terms of environment issues. Satisfaction can be derived from leisure activities when these fulfil specific needs of older adults or become sources of enjoyment. Research suggests that there is a strong correlation between life satisfaction and participation rates in recreation, but a weak correlation between life satisfaction and the use of free time by older individuals (Zuzanek and Box, 1988). It is likely that the impact of recreation activities is related to a number of interactive factors, two of which are type (formal–informal) and meaning of the activity (McPherson, 1998). Furthermore, the enjoyment derived from the recreational experience often enhances personal motivation, which in turn keeps older people active.

In terms of social benefits, leisure experiences offer opportunities to interact productively and socialize with others (Harahousou, 1999). This social interaction, facilitated by recreational activity, may be competitive, co-operative or simply informal socializing. Group activities also help participants satisfy their need for belonging and provide opportunities to develop long-lasting friendships and romantic relationships. In some cases, participating in prestigious types of activities, such as golf, tennis and sailing, may help to enhance social status and to make important professional connections (Harahousou, 2000).

Successful ageing is defined as an optimal state of overall functioning and well-being, but only a small proportion of older adults meets these criteria. Most older persons, however, view successful ageing as a process of adaptation. In this way, many more persons could be considered successfully aged (Faber et al., 2001). During the adaptation process, some seniors see their decrease in societal roles as an opportunity to feel free and to be themselves; others may feel satisfied by withdrawing from the wider world; while others may seek to maintain a former lifestyle over which they feel they have personal control and strength to meet life's demands (MacNeil and Teague, 1992).

Social support and leisure in later life

Social support evolves from interaction within a social network. The structure of social networks typically involves the number of associates, how these associates may know one another and relate with one another, particularly in terms of hierarchy, and the degree of solidarity in this network (Adams and Blieszner, 1995). Having a strong formal and/or an informal network, such as friends, age-peers, family and/or professional staff, respectively, is frequently mentioned by scholars as providing an individual with a group wherein social interaction serves as a buffer against stress, or as a mechanism to enhance well-being (Gottlieb, 1994; O'Brien Cousins, 1994; Rowe and Kahn, 1998). In contrast, social isolation or the lack of a strong social network places older people at risk of poor health. Leisure involvement in a group creates and strengthens friendship networks, which in turn can elicit positive cognitive, affective and behavioural responses. Other studies suggest that self-empowerment, with the assistance of a peer group, is an effective health promotion strategy to change activity behaviour for weight reduction or for general physical and mental health (Haper, 1994). An age-related peer support group, especially, can provide role models, mentors and activity partners; information and knowledge; emotional release as a confidant; encouragement and counselling; and, can establish new cognitive and behavioural norms in later years.

Finally, the effectiveness of social support depends on the situation, the person, and his or her needs (Rowe and Kahn, 1998). More specifically, knowledge about the characteristics of the target leisure group is needed, such as, past leisure experience; current cognitive and physical capacities; current perceived leisure needs; the size, composition and availability of the existing social network; level of self-efficacy concerning leisure activity potential or competence; and, sources of perceived negative support and perceived barriers (McPherson, 1996). Therefore, before resources are dedicated to developing networks and providing support to older adults, the above issues should be considered. To give an example, if the demonstration of independence for some older adults is important, they may reject attempts to provide support in various forms. For some others, imposing social support may be inappropriate and perhaps counterproductive, and as Rowe and Kahn (1998) noted, 'goodness of fit is essential'.

Older women's leisure

In order to understand the impact of gender on all aspects of older people's lives, and on leisure behaviour in particular, one should address the complexities of expectations, roles and behaviour for women and men. In addition, other important factors, such as cultural situations and income that often facilitate or restrict leisure experiences in later life, should be addressed. With regard to women's leisure, feminist analyses over the past 15 years have consistently found that any investigation of women's leisure must take into account multidimensional and cumulative antecedent constraints, such as women's socioeconomic and employment status, level of education, ethnicity and domestic commitments, such as caregiving responsibilities (Henderson et al., 1996).

In their early years, the current generation of older women were socialized almost exclusively around the importance of the family role (that is, childrearing, caregiving, housekeeping), a primary role they should fulfil above all others. As Gottlieb (1989) explains, these women were primarily relegated to the personal and domestic sphere, and their two corollary imperatives were the centrality of relationships and affiliate activities, as well as the obligation to nurture others and be responsible for their emotional and social well-being. These women experienced a lack of power in both the public and private sphere. On a personal level, many older women were aware of their economic dependence on their husbands, and this made it difficult to question his decisions and his greater power in the home. On a public level, these women were less affected by the women's movement than their younger counterparts because few women addressed their concerns or could alter their sense of powerlessness. Moreover, they were even less likely to attend or graduate from school, especially professional schools, and to enter the workforce. The few who were able to do so were mainly employed in secondary status jobs, referred to as poorly paid 'women's jobs'.

These socialization messages have had profound consequences for the development, behaviour, and leisure activities of older women. As a result, for these women, it has always been difficult to conceptualize leisure in the traditional way, since it has never been related to their everyday experiences (Juniu and Henderson, 2001). Women's perception of leisure time and work is very much intertwined and work and leisure often coexist. This happens because women often perform multiple activities at the same time, combining work and leisure activities. For example, older women combine work and leisure when they perform domestic duties or caregiving responsibilities, while at the same time watching television. Thus the duality between paid work and leisure, as a dimension of leisure for women is not evident, since much of women's work occurs within the home. Even the freedom of individual choice, a basic element of leisure, is manifested as 'a relative freedom' in women (Wimbush and Talbot, 1988). For example, as Juniu (2002) explains, outdoor cooking (barbecues), which is recreational for men, could be considered an obligation for women.

Other consequences of socialization, when combined with the existing ageist ideology, have also had an impact on the value and pattern of leisure activities for older women. Thus these women attribute little value to leisure behaviour and many do not believe they deserve nor have the time to engage in it (Wearing and Wearing, 1988). Many older women have missed the opportunity that school offers to learn and engage in a variety of leisure and physical activities. In addition, they are mainly dependent on other members of the family – especially husbands – for financial, social and emotional support, and for companionship in any leisure involvement. However, the leisure behaviour of these women varies greatly in how these experiences occur. For example, Bialeschki and Michener (1994) suggest that as women grow older and relinquish some of the roles of motherhood, they are more likely to return to personal leisure activities. Therefore, when older women are released from parenting they become more dominant compared to their male counterparts who become less dominant in the renegotiation of gender differentiation that takes place in later life (Fry, 1996).

The most popular leisure activities of older women documented in cross-cultural studies have been home-based and family-oriented activities such as TV viewing, reading and resting, gardening, talking on the phone, home-based hobbies and crafts, socializing with family and friends, walking and folk dancing (Harahousou, 1995; Green et al., 1990). Retirement from paid work might also make a difference for older women's leisure repertoire, as Gibson and her associates (2000) showed in their study. Their findings revealed that apart from participating in popular activities, retired women participated in exercise classes, as well as in outdoor sports such as golf and tennis. Church-related activities and folk dancing in religious festivities – socially approved public activities which allow older women to temporarily escape from the confinement of their domestic roles – are also very popular among older women in many cultures (Harahousou, 1999).

Another important issue that older women face today is the lack of preparation for the extended and increasingly healthy period of their life past their childrearing years. Overall women live longer than men, and therefore more so by themselves, as reflected by an increasing number of divorced, single and widowed older women. Older women also are more likely to live in poverty than their male counterparts, since on average they earn less, are more likely to work part-time and spend more time out of the workforce, all of which negatively impact their social security and pension earnings. Therefore, although older women may have the physical capacity for activities, including physical activity, they are little prepared for roles other than family roles (Gottlieb, 1989) that will replace the lost ones during their extended remaining years. In addition, because level of involvement in some leisure activities decreases across the life span, many women may not be as likely to begin new activities as they age. On the other hand, as Henderson (2000) explains, women's ability to form social networks and maintain social integration appears to be an advantage to them in old age. This advantage may occur because women are able to view themselves as more independent than dependent, and the maintenance of their social connectedness is seen as very helpful for the initiation and maintenance of leisure activities.

Other intervening constraints, such as fear of violence (both physical and psychological), especially being alone on the streets at night, as well as 'no access to private transport', and relying on 'public transport' to travel to and from the leisure facility, have been reported as major constraints on many women's participation in public leisure (Scraton, 1993). Dowling and his associates (1997) indicate that the fear women experience can manifest itself in many ways, ranging from the elimination of physical activity to the considerable planning that must be undertaken to overcome the fear. Income has also been an important factor that may broaden or restrict the range of leisure choices available. Coalter (1993) found that women tend to spend less on their leisure than do their male counterparts, and this stems from them not asserting their right to engage in leisure activities. In addition, activity involvement of women is often mediated by their socioeconomic status and level of education. According to Kelly and Freysinger (2000), middle-class individuals tend to participate in a greater variety of leisure pursuits than working-class individuals. Culture is considered also as likely to differentially impact on older women's experiences. Across cultures women generally receive less deference than men (Fry, 1988), and this may determine their degree and quality of involvement in leisure pursuits.

Leisure policies and programmes

Ageing involves biological, psychological and social processes, during which older individuals are influenced not only by genetic and personality factors but also by sociocultural ones. These factors influence older people's behaviour, opportunities, experiences and interests, specifically those related to leisure behaviour. Leisure policy-makers and professionals should recognize these factors and take into consideration the following trends when developing and implementing effective leisure policies and programmes for older adults.

- The elderly cohort is comprised of a heterogeneous mix of individuals who are different in terms of gender, ethnicity, religious beliefs, geographic region, education, marital status, language and cultural traditions. This means that the voices of older persons, who can best portray the realities of their everyday lives, should be heard in order to design appropriate leisure policies and recreation prescriptions.
- In multicultural societies, where ethnic minorities experience a disproportionately greater number of problems such as vulnerability or lack of dignity and respect (Hawkins and McLean, 1993), the provision of ethno-specific leisure services and/or cross-culturally trained leisure leaders will better serve the specific interests and needs of these individuals (Tsai, 2000). In addition, policy-makers and practitioners should communicate, share, and adapt good practice in leisure provision from different cultures so they will be more able to meet the needs and interests of a culturally diverse population.
- The family as a potential leisure and recreation centre for older adults is declining and meaningful leisure recreation activities for older adults have become less available. Thus alternate social network structures and services are needed to provide meaningful leisure experiences for them. Leisure and recreation providers should cater for the efficacy of specific activities on the functional status and life satisfaction of ill, frail or disabled elders in long-term care facilities, as well as in community-based service delivery (Hawkins, 1999).
- Women experience more health and financial problems, for more years, than men in later life, and face gender, age and racial discrimination. These problems have contributed to a low level of leisure and recreation involvement throughout their lifecycle. Thus, leisure policies should give priority to all forms of provision to this increasing female cohort and create sensitive and

varied programmes that account for content and ability. Special consideration should be given to access and location, as well as personal security outside the home. In addition, leisure policies must eliminate the constraints associated with the female gender, and encourage women by creating leisure programmes more gender sensitive in nature.

- An increasing number of older people have shown an interest in becoming involved in organized senior sports and games, such as Master Games and Senior Olympics. The rapid growth of competitive senior games and sports in recent years has created concern over the quality of events and the safety of participants. Professionals in physical recreation must know and communicate their scientific knowledge to ensure that competition among older persons is promoted, conducted and judged by appropriate standards.

- In developing nations, more elderly persons are beginning to show an interest in the better use of their free time, due to increasing information and globalization. This interest applies to leisure services and products as well as tourism, which is also growing in these regions. More effective leisure services and programmes will grow, though, if the providers avoid imposing values, experiences or practice from developed nations, and instead take into account the aspirations and needs of the population makeup of the developing nations. Any new form of leisure and recreation activity should interact with tradition to foster positive attitudes, produce positive lifestyle changes and maintain continuity (Harahousou, 2000).

- Environmental conditions (housing, traffic, crime, safety), especially in urban places, severely restrict older individuals' leisure pursuits, and in many cases force them to be 'prisoners' in their own homes. Similarly, in rural areas, older persons are often limited in the quality of housing, availability of health, social and leisure services, in terms of both diversity and quality. Thus provision of leisure services in the community, neighbourhood, and home should be available to promote independence and well-being. For the homeless, the frail elderly, the bedridden and the geographically isolated, outreach strategies should provide meals on wheels, health care and leisure possibilities.

- A healthier, knowledgeable and demanding 'grey' market is emerging in most countries, due to the increase in active life expectancy. This means more adults are capable of engaging in active leisure, sports and tourism opportunities for a longer period in their later life. Among them many belong to the oldest age cohort, who are the healthiest of the elderly – that is, they are the survivors of their birth cohort (McPherson, 2001). This sociodemographic 'grey' power needs to be seriously considered in every leisure programme site or facility, by incorporating older people's specific needs, interests and leisure patterns.

- Finally, the ageing population of tomorrow – the current baby boomers – will present a challenge to leisure professionals, since it is expected to show the following characteristics: higher levels of education, higher health conscientiousness and higher commitment to the importance of leisure. In terms of preferred leisure activities, it is predicted that they will shift towards individualized activities rather than group events, since baby boomers today prefer to socialize in smaller groups and typically stay within their extended family circles (Ziegler, 2002). In terms of group events, older adults are likely to be more interested in programmes that promote stress reduction, meaningful social interaction, nutritional benefits and intergenerational exchange (Adkins, 1994). Volunteerism will change dramatically to a new form that involves concentrated bursts of time to a specific task (Ziegler, 2002). According to Ziegler (ibid.), the emerging senior programmes of tomorrow should facilitate transition away from games and activities, such as bingo, bridge and shuffleboard, currently associated with senior citizens, and accommodate the boomers' busy schedule that will remain so in their retirement. Thus workshops of six- or eight-week classes, as well as weekend and night classes, will better fit the busy schedule of tomorrow's older adults, many of whom will work after retirement.

Concluding, the challenge today for the research, policy and practitioner communities in the field of leisure is how to design and deliver policies for an ever-expanding and increasingly diverse older population so that leisure life potential can be realized. This challenge is even more difficult because this growing older population is ageing in a rapidly changing social and economic world. To meet this challenge, it is equally important to consider the micro-issues of older people's leisure preferences and needs, as well as the macro-issues concerning policies most likely to be effective in encouraging more active, health enhancing lifestyles, such as publicity and promotion, provision of subsidized facilities/programmes and/or tax incentives, and so on.

Bibliography

Adams, R. G. and Blieszner, R. (1995) 'Aging Well with Friends and Family', *American Behavioral Scientist* 39(2): 209–24.

Adkins, K. D. (1994) 'The Leisure of the Aging: We've Only Just Begun', *Illinois Parks & Recreation* (November/December): 30.

Alexandris, K. and Carrol, B. (1997) 'An Analysis of Leisure Constraints based on Different Recreational Sport Participation Levels: Results from a Study in Greece', *Leisure Sciences* 19: 1–15.

Alfermann, D. and Stoll, O. (2000) 'Effects of Physical Exercise on Self-Concept and Well-being', *International Journal of Sport Psychology* 30: 47–65.

Atchley, R. C. (1971) *The Social Forces in Later Life*, Belmont, CA, Wadsworth Publishing Co.

Atchley, R. C. (1993) 'Continuity Theory and the Evolution of Activity in Later Adulthood', in J. R. Kelly (ed.) *Activity and Aging: Staying Involved in Later Life*, Newbury Park, CA, Sage, pp. 5–16.

Baltes, P. B. and Baltes, M. M. (1990) 'Successful Aging: Perspectives from the Behavioral Sciences', New York, Cambridge University Press.

Bedini, L. A. and Guinan, D. M. (1996) 'The Leisure of Caregivers of Older Adults: Implications for CTRS's in Non-Traditional Settings', *Therapeutic Recreation Journal* 30: 274–88.

Bengtson, V. L., Rice, C. J. and Johnson, M. L. (1999) 'Are Theories of Aging Important? Models and Explanations in Gerontology at the Turn of the Century', in V. L. Bengtson and K. Warner Schaie (eds) *Handbook of Theories of Aging*, New York, Springer, pp. 3–20.

Bialeschki, M. D. and Michener, S. (1994) 'Re-entering Leisure: Transition within the Role of Motherhood', *Journal of Leisure Research* 26(1): 57–74.

Blair, S. N. (1993) 'Physical Activity, Physical Fitness and Health', *Research Quarterly of Exercise and Sport* 64: 365–76.

Blanchard-Fields, F. and Chen, Y. (1996) 'Adaptive Cognition and Aging', *American Behavioral Scientist* 39(3): 231–48.

Brattain-Rogers, N. (1997) 'Centrality of the Caregiving Role and Integration of Leisure in Everyday Life: A Naturalistic Study of Older Wife Caregivers', *Therapeutic Recreation Journal* 31: 230–43.

Burgess, W. (1960) *Aging in Western Societies*, Chicago, University of Chicago Press.

Chinn, D., White, M., Harland, J., Drinkwater, C. and Raybould, S. (1999) 'Barriers to Physical Activity and Socio-Economic Position: Implications for Health Promotion', *Journal of Epidemiology Community Health* 53: 191–2.

Coalter, F. (1993) 'Sports Participation: Price or Priorities?' *Leisure Studies* 12: 171–82.

Cordes, K. and Ibrahim, H. (1996) *Application in Recreation and Leisure*, Mosby Year Book, Inc.

Crawford, D. W. and Godbey, G. (1987) 'Reconceptualizing Barriers to Family Leisure', *Leisure Sciences* 9: 119–27.

Crawford, D. W., Jackson, E. L. and Godbey, G. (1991) 'A Hierarchical Model of Leisure Constraints', *Leisure Sciences* 13: 309–20.

Cumming, E. and Henry, W. (1961) *Growing Old: The Process of Disengagement*, New York, Basic Books.

Dowling, R., Potrac, P. and Jones, R. (1997) 'Women and Leisure: A Qualitative Analysis of Constraints and Opportunities'. Working Papers in Sport & Leisure Commerce, No. 2, University of Memphis.

Elward, K. and Larson, E. B. (1992) 'Benefits of Exercise for Older Adults. A Review of Existing Evidence and Current Recommendations for the General Population', *Clinics in Geriatric Medicine* 8(1): 35–50.

Faber, M., Bootsma-van der Wiel, A., van Exel, E., Gussekloo, J., Lagaay, A. M., van Dongen, E., Knook, D., van der Geest, S. and Westendorp, R. (2001) 'Successful Aging in the Oldest Old: Who Can Be Characterized as Successfully Aged?', *Archives of Internal Medicine* 161(22): 2694–700.

Featherstone, M. (1993) 'The Mask of Aging and the Postmodern Life Course', in M. Featherstone, M. Hepworth and B. Turner (eds) *The Body: Social Process and Cultural Theory*, (4th edn), London, Sage.

Fillit, H. (2002) 'The Role of Hormone Replacement Therapy in the Prevention of Alzheimer Disease', *Archives of Internal Medicine* 162(17): 1934–42.

Fisher, J. K., Pickering, A. M. and Li, F. (2002) 'Healthy Aging Through Active Leisure: Design and Methods of SHAPE – A Randomized Controlled Trial of a Neighborhood-based Walking Project', *World Leisure* 1: 19–28.

Fox, K. R. (1999) 'The Influence of Physical Activity on Mental Well-Being', *Public Health and Nutrition* 2: 411–18.

Freysinger, V. J. (2002) 'Sport as Leisure in Later Life: Possibilities and Constraints', *ADOZ, Boletin del Centro de Documentaci n en Ocio* 24: 36–44.

Fry, C. (1996) 'Age, Aging and Culture', in R. Binstock and L. George (eds) *Handbook of Aging and the Social Sciences* (4th edn) San Diego, CA, Academic Press, pp. 117–36.

Fry, C. L. (1988) 'Theories of Age and Culture', in J. Birren and V. L. Bengston (eds) *Emergent Theories of Aging*, New York, Springer, pp. 447–81.

Gibson, H. J., Ashton-Shaeffer, C. and Sanders, G. (2000) 'Leisure in the Lives of Retirement Aged Women: The Florida Experience'. Paper presented in the 6th World Conference 'Leisure and Human Development', Bilbao, 3–7 July.

Godbey, G. (1994) *Leisure in Your Life. An Exploration* (4th edn), State College, PA, Venture Publishing.

Gottlieb, B. (1994) 'The Meaning and Importance of Social Support', in H. A. Quinney et al. (eds) *Toward Active Living*, Champaign, IL, Human Kinetics Publishers.

Gottlieb, N. (1989) 'Families, Work, and the Lives of Older Women', in J. D. Garner and S. Mercer (eds) *Women As they Age. Challenge, Opportunity, and Triumph*, New York and London, The Haworth Press.

Green, E., Hebron, S. and Woodward, D. (1990) *Women's Leisure: What Leisure?* Basingstoke, Macmillan.

Haper, D. (1994) *Health Promotion and Aging*, New York, Springer.

Harahousou, Y. (1995) 'Older Greek Women and Their Physical Recreation Involvement in Greece', in S. Harris, E. Heikkinen and W. Harris (eds) *Towards Healthy Aging – International Perspectives, Part 2. Psychology, Motivation and Programs. Vol. IV: Physical Activity, Aging and Sports*, Albany, NY, Center for the Study of Aging, pp. 327–37.

Harahousou, Y. (1999). 'Elderly People, Leisure and Physical Recreation in Greece', *World Leisure and Recreation* 3: 20–4.

Harahousou, Y. (2000) 'Leisure Potential for Personal and Social Development of Aging People', in M. Cuenca Cabeza (ed.) *Leisure and Human Development*, Spain, University of Deusto, pp. 145–52.

Hassmen, P., Koivula, N. and Uutela, A. (2000) 'Physical Exercise and Psychological Wellbeing: A Population Study in Finland', *Preventive Medicine* 30: 17–25.

Hawkins, B. (1999) 'Population Ageing: Perspectives from the United States', *World Leisure and Recreation* 41(3): 11–14.

Hawkins, B. and McLean, D. (1993) 'Delivering Services to a Diverse Aging Population: Challenges for the Future', *Journal of Physical Education, Recreation and Dance* (April) 31–4.

Henderson, K. (2000) 'Leisure, Gender, and Later Life', *ADOZ, Boletin del Centro de Documentación en Ocio* 24: 21–6.

Henderson, K. A. and Bialeschki, M. D. (1991) 'A Sense of Entitlement to Leisure as Constraint and Empowerment for Women', *Leisure Sciences* 13: 51–65.

Henderson, K. A., Bialeschki, M. D., Shaw, S. and Freysinger, V. J. (1996) *Both Gains and Gaps: Feminist Perspectives on Women's Leisure*, State College, PA, Venture Publishing.

Henderson, R. A., Bedini, L. A., Hecht, L. and Schuler, R. (1995) 'Women with Physical Disabilities and the Negotiation of Leisure Constraints', *Leisure Studies* 14: 17–31.

Hilleras, P. K., Jorm, A. F., Herlitz, A. and Winblad, B. (1999) 'Activity Patterns in Very Old People: A Survey of Cognitively Intact Subjects Aged 90 Years or Older', *Age and Ageing* 28: 147–52.

Hoffman, C. (1990) 'Retirees Just Love Hendersonville and the Feeling is Mutual', *Appalachia* 23(3): 18–25.

Howe, C. Z. (1988) 'Selected Social Gerontology Theories and Older Adult Leisure Involvement: A Review of the Literature', *Journal of Applied Gerontology* 6: 448–63.

Iso-Ahola, S. E., Jackson, E. and Dunn, E. (1994) 'Starting, Ceasing and Replacing Leisure Activities over the Life-Span', *Journal of Leisure Research* 26(3): 227–49.

Jackson, E. L., Crawford, D. W. and Godbey, G. (1993) 'Negotiation of Leisure Constraints', *Leisure Sciences* 15: 1–11.

Johnson, M. L. (1996) 'Interdependency and the Generational Compact', *Ageing and Society* 15(2): 243–65.

Johnson, T. (1995) 'Aging Well in Contemporary Society: Introduction', *American Behavioral Scientist* 39(2): 120–30.

Juniu, S. (2002) 'Perception of Leisure in Latino Women Immigrants', *World Leisure* 1: 48–55.

Juniu, S. and Henderson, K. (2001) 'Problems in Researching Leisure and Women: Global Considerations', *World Leisure* 4: 3–10.

Kelly, J. R. (1996a) 'Activities', in J. E. Birren (ed.) *Encyclopedia of Gerontology*, Vol. 2, San Diego, CA, Academic Press, Inc., pp. 37–49.

Kelly, J. R. (1996b) 'Leisure', in J. E. Birren (ed.) *Encyclopedia of Gerontology*, Vol. 2, San Diego, CA, Academic Press, Inc., pp. 19–30.

Kelly, J. R. and Freysinger, V. J. (2000) *21st Century: Current Issues*, Boston, Allyn & Bacon.

King, R. (1996) 'Volunteerism by the Elderly as an Intervention for Promoting Successful Aging', in R. G. Stone (ed.) *Volunteerism and Successful Aging*, Gerontology Manual, School of Occupational Therapy & Physical Therapy, University of Puget Sound, WA.

Lalive d'Epinay, C. J., Manidi, M. J. and Stuckelberger, A. (1996) 'Aging and Physical Activity: A European Perspective'. Paper presented at the 4th International Congress 'Physical Activity, Aging and Sports', Heidelberg, Germany, 27–31 August.

Lang, F. R., Rieckmann, N. and Baltes, M. M. (2002) 'Adapting to Aging Losses: Do Resources Facilitate Strategies of Selection, Compensation, and Optimization in Everyday Functioning?', *Journals of Gerontology: Series B: Psychological Sciences and Social Sciences* 57B(6) (November): 501–9.

Laws, G. (1995) 'Understanding Ageism: Lessons from Feminism, and Postmodernism', *The Gerontologist* 35(1): 112–18.

Lawton, M. P. (1985) 'Activities and Leisure', in M. P. Lawton and G. L. Maddox (eds) *Annual Review of Gerontology and Geriatrics 5*, New York, Springer, pp. 127–64.

Lee, I. M., Paffenbarger, R. S. Jr and Hennekens, C. H. (1997) 'Physical Activity, Physical Fitness and Longevity', *Aging* (Milan) 9: 2–11.

Levinson, D. (1978) *The Seasons of Man's Life*, New York, Alfred A. Knopf.

Lolb, M. (2000) 'Motivated Ageing: The Perspective of Sports Educational Gerontology', in S. Bailey (ed.) *Physical Activity and Ageing, Perspectives*, ICSSPE, Vol. 2, pp. 85–103.

MacNeil, R. D. and Teague, M. L. (1992) *Leisure Aging: Vitality in Later Life* (2nd edn), Dubnque, IA, Brown and Benchmark.

McAuley, E. and Rudolph, D. (1995) 'Physical Activity, Aging and Psychological Well-being', *Journal of Aging and Physical Activity* 3: 67–96.

McGuire, F. A. (1985) 'Constraints in Later Life', in M. G. Wade (ed.) *Constraints on Leisure*, Springfield, Charles C. Thomas, pp. 335–53.

MacNeil, R. D. (1995) 'Leisure Programs and Services for Older Adults: Past, Present, and Future Research', in L. A. Barnett (ed.) *Research about Leisure: Past, Present, and Future*, Champaign, IL, Sagamore, pp. 149–76.

MacNeil, R. D., Winkelhake, K. and Yoshioka, N. (2003) 'Gerontology Instruction in Recreation and Leisure Studies Curricula: A Two Decade Status Report', *Educational Gerontology* 29(2): 279–94.

McPherson, D. B. (1996) 'Aging, Social Support and Involvement in Physical Activity'. Paper presented at the 4th International Congress on Physical Activity, Aging and Sport, Heidelberg, Germany, August 27–31.

McPherson, D. B. (1998) 'Population Aging and Leisure in a Global Context: Factors Influencing Inclusion and Exclusion Within and Across Cultures', *World Leisure and Recreation* 41(3): 5–10.

McPherson, B. (2001) 'Population Aging, Social Development and Older Adults: Global and Local Realities for the Promotion of Leisure in Later Life'. Invited Keynote Presentation, World Leisure Asia Conference on Social Development, Leisure and Older Persons, Shanghai, 24–28 April.

McPherson, D. B. (2004) 'Leisure in Later Life', in G. Gross et al. (eds) *Encyclopedia of Recreation and Leisure in America*, New York, Charles Scribner's Sons.

Mobily, K. E. (1987) 'Leisure, Lifestyle, and Lifespan', in M. L. Teague and R. D. MacNeil (eds) *Aging and Leisure: Vitality in Later Life*, (2nd edn), Englewood Cliffs, NJ, Prentice-Hall, pp. 179–206.

O'Beirne, J. (1999) 'Growing Older, Getting Better: Than What?', in J. Onyx, R. Leonard and R. Reed (eds) *Revisioning Aging*, New York, Peter Lang Publishing, pp. 7–37.

O'Brien Cousins, S. (1994) 'The Role of Social Support in Later Life Physical Activity', in H. A. Quinney et al. (eds) *Toward Active Living*, Campaign, IL, Human Kinetics, pp. 247–53.

Rowe, J. W. and Kahn, R. L. (1998) *Successful Aging*, New York, Pantheon Books.

Ruuskanen, J. M. and Ruoppila, I. (1995) 'Physical Activity and Psychological Well-being among People Aged 65 to 84 Years', *Age and Ageing* 24: 292–6.

Scraton, S. (1993) 'The Changing World of Women and Leisure: Feminism, Post-feminism, and Leisure', *Leisure Studies* 12: 294–61.

Shaw, S. (1996). 'The Gendered Nature of Leisure: Individual and Societal Outcomes of Leisure Practice', *World Leisure & Recreation* 38(4): 4–6.

Shephard, R. J. (1995) 'Physical Activity, Health, and Well-Being at Different Life Stages', *Research Quarterly for Exercise and Sport* 66: 298–302.

Shilling, C. (1994) *The Body and Social Theory*, London, Sage Publications.

Sivan, A. (2002) 'Leisure Participation of Hong Kong Elderly: Policy and Practice', *World Leisure* 1: 11–18.

Stodolska, M. (1998) 'Assimilation and Leisure Constraints: Dynamics of Constraints on Leisure in Immigrant Population', *Journal of Leisure Research* 30(4): 521–51.

Tarrant, A. M., Cordell, H. K. and Green, T. G. (2001) 'Cohort Versus Age Effects On Leisure Involvement'. Paper submitted to the World Leisure Asia Pacific Conference on Social Development, Leisure and the Older Persons, Shanghai, 24–28 April.

Tsai, E. H. (2000) 'The Influence of Acculturation on Perception of Leisure Constraints of Chinese Immigrants', *World leisure* 4: 33–42.

Tsai, E. H. and Coleman, D. J. (1999) 'Leisure Constraints of Chinese Immigrants: An Exploratory Study', *Society and Leisure* 22(1): 241–62.

US Department of Health and Human Services (1997) 'Active Aging: A Shift in the Paradigm'. Paper presented at the Denver Summit by experts on ageing, May.

Wankel, L. M. and Berger, B. G. (1990). 'The Psychological and Social Benefits of Sport and Physical Activity', *Journal of Leisure Research* 22: 167–82.

Wannamethee, S. G., Shaper, A. G. and Walker, M. (1998) 'Changes in Physical Activity, Mortality, and Incidence of Coronary Heart Disease in Older Men', *Lancet* 351: 1603–8.

Watson, B., Scraton, S. and Bramham, P. (1996) 'Leisure Lifestyles, Elderly Women and the Inner City', *World Leisure & Recreation* 38(4): 11–14.

Wearing, B. M. and Wearing, S. L. (1988) 'All in a Day's Leisure: Gender and the Concept of Leisure', *Leisure Studies* 7: 111–23.

Wimbush, E. and Talbot, M. (1988) *Relative Freedoms*, Milton Keynes, Open University Press.

Young, I. M. (1990) *Justice and the Politics of Difference*, Princeton, NJ, Princeton University Press.

Ziegler, J. (2002) 'Recreating Retirement', *Parks & Recreation* 37(10): 56.

Zuzanek, J. and Box, S. (1988) 'Life Course and the Daily Lives of Older Adults in Canada', in K. Altergott (ed.) *Daily Life in Later Life*, London, Sage Publications, pp. 147–85.

15

Race and Leisure

Valeria J. Freysinger and Othello Harris

In this chapter race and leisure are examined. Interest in race, and how and why it shapes leisure practices and experiences – and leisure (re)constructs perceptions and notions of race – is relatively recent in the field of leisure studies. The discussion in this chapter is informed by the scholarship on race and ethnicity in the field of recreation and leisure as well as well as that in sport sociology, cultural studies, race and ethnic studies, and feminist studies. That is, leisure is broadly constructed in this chapter and the thinking in fields outside of recreation and leisure is considered as relates to the subject of race and leisure. The literature reviewed is primarily North American, British and Australian. In other words, this chapter presents particular ways of thinking and talking about leisure and race that are rooted in the cultures and scholarly traditions of particular societies, most notably, white-dominated cultures where aboriginal and (select) immigrant peoples are marginalized.

The chapter begins with an examination of notions of race and ethnicity and how these notions have framed the questions asked (or not) about leisure and race. Then the extant research on leisure and race is reviewed and summarized in four subsections: the invisibility of race in leisure, race differences in leisure/race as leisure constraint, leisure as opportunity, and perceptions of 'racial' difference/ distinctiveness as a form of leisure. These sub-topics roughly reflect a chronology or history of how race and ethnicity have been considered and realized in the study and practice of recreation and leisure. Still, the boundaries between them are not absolute and there was/is overlap. That is, while having an historical genesis, remnants of each way of thinking, or construction of race and leisure, carried over into subsequent thinking and all are still present today. This literature also suggests questions that we might ask about race and leisure in the future and that discussion concludes the chapter.[1]

Notions of race and ethnicity

An examination of the meanings of race and ethnicity historically and today shows that notions of race and ethnicity have been constructed, challenged and reconstructed across time. For example, in its earliest usage, race was used to denote kinship linkages (McLemore and Romo, 1998) and to differentiate people by religion (for example, the Jewish race), colour (such as the Caucasian, Mongoloid and Negroid races), and nationality (for example, the Italian and Irish races) (Hraba, 1994).

Today many people take for granted that there are a number of different races that are biologically determined. A fairly typical rendition of this notion of race in the United States was put forth by Richard Kraus (1994) in his book *Leisure in a Changing America: Multicultural Perspectives*:

> a race is a statistical aggregate of people who share a composite of genetically transmissible *physical* traits, such as 'skin pigmentation, head form, facial features, stature, and the color, distribution and texture of body hair. Since gross similarities are to be noted among human populations, many attempts have been made to classify the people of the world racially. Estimates of racial types range from three – Caucasoid, Mongoloid, and Negroid – to thirty or more.' (Rose, cited in Kraus, 1994: 86)

While advocating a biological definition of race, the meaninglessness of such a categorization is contained within the definition itself. Which biological traits would allow us to classify people into (how many) races? What traits would result in clear boundaries – clearly demarcating those who belong in and outside of the racial group of interest? How could skin colour – one of the most pervasive markers of race, particularly in post-slavery United States – indicate one's race when there is great variation within every group that is considered a race? Just as 'Asians' vary in skin colour, so do 'blacks', 'whites', and others who are widely thought of as races. One would do no better (and perhaps, no worse) to classify people by eye shape (for example, epicanthic eye fold which characterizes groups as different as Japanese and !Kung San Bushmen), eye colour or blood type (see Begley, 1995, for a brief but clear discussion of problems inherent in devising biological race).

While race as a biological construct is probably meaningless, race is nonetheless important; that is, race matters (West, 1993). Race matters because it defines social relations (and vice versa). In many societies, race is correlated with income and wealth, access to health care, the quality of education one receives, one's relative status and access to various forms of leisure and recreation. That is, race stratifies power and privilege. Even though race has no biological bases, if people learn to perceive differences between groups of people designated as races, they will act on those perceived differences. 'Individuals cannot separate where they stand in the web of reality from what they perceive' (Kincheloe and Steinberg, 2000: 3). As such, it is more accurate to say that race is socially constructed.[2] That is, each society takes what it deems to be important physical differences and creates racial categories from them. As van den Berghe (1967) suggests, it is not the presence of physical differences that makes a society multiracial. Rather, it is the social significance that is attributed to whatever physical differences are deemed to exist that results in societies of many races. In a similar vein, McClaren states that 'People do not discriminate against groups because they are different; rather, the act of discrimination itself constructs categories of difference that hierarchically locate people as "superior" and "inferior" and then universalizes and naturalizes such differences' (McClaren, 2000: 64).

This process can be seen in the United States where, for many years, 'biological' notions of race resulted in one white and several non-white categories (Spencer, 1999). White meant, and probably continues to mean, the absence of anything other than white heritage, while black has not historically meant the absence of anything other than black heritage. By way of example, in the late nineteenth century, Homer Plessy was prohibited from riding in the 'white' section of a train in Louisiana because he was determined to be 'coloured'. Plessy was one-eighth black (meaning only one of his eight great-grandparents was black). More than 50 years later, in 1948, Davis Knight was sentenced to five years in jail for violating the state of Mississippi's miscegenation law. Although Knight claimed no knowledge of having black lineage, the state proved that one of his great-grandmothers had been a slave. He was one-sixteenth black, but in the state of Mississippi he was, indeed, black. In 1983 Susie Phipps sued the state of Louisiana to have her racial designation on her birth certificate changed from 'coloured' to 'white'. She lost her case, which went as high as the Supreme Court, when the state determined she was one-thirty-second black. The one black ancestor rule meant that she, too, could not be white in America. Ironically, if any of the above claimed they had only one white ancestor, they would not be considered white. As these examples demonstrate, whiteness in America has historically meant the absence of black blood.

The social construction of 'race' and ethnicity is evidenced not only historically but also contemporaneously. Stodolska and Yi (2003) provide an example of this from their study of the impact of immigration on the ethnic identities and leisure behaviour of Korean, Mexican and Polish adolescents. They found that prior to immigrating to the US, the adolescents did not think of themselves as having common cultural traits (or as Korean, Mexican and Polish). As they became established in the US, however, they began to think of themselves as members of ethnic minority groups distinct from 'mainstream Americans' and other ethnic groups in this country. They also used comparisons with other individuals in their own ethnic group in constructing their ethnic identities. For example:

> Korean adolescents positioned themselves along a continuum ranging from a 'Korean–Korean' ('FOB' in young people's slang) – a person who has stayed in the United States for a relatively short time, shows adherence to traditional Confucian values ... and speaks primarily Korean language to a 'Korean-American' (or a 'Twinky') – a person who speaks fluent English and is usually of higher socio-economic status. (ibid.: 63)

Further, 'outside labelling' was also significant in the teens' development of an ethnic identity. Being seen as 'ethnic' by, and experiencing discrimination from, their 'mainstream peers' led them to see themselves as culturally distinct and to search for their cultural roots.

Kevin Hylton's (2005) recent review and discussion of 'race' critical theory and critical race theory (CRT) provide further insight into the social construction of race. Based on post-structuralist notions of 'race' and his own and others' research on race (blackness and whiteness) in sport (for example, Birrell, 1989; Carrington and McDonald, 2001; Long and Hylton, 2002; Scraton, 2001), Hylton notes that while race has little meaning biologically, it is a powerful social category. Yet people do not experience race and racism in the same way. Racial identity is not fixed but relational and sociohistorically situated (see also Li, 1990). These tensions or seeming contradictions surrounding 'race', however, must be accepted:

> at the same time we must accept a theoretical frame from which to move if inequality, 'race' and racism in society are to be the ultimate foci of our energies ... [Further], to acknowledge the social and physical differences that make up these 'races' ... is not the same as *agreeing* that they essentially determine intellectual, social or physical attributes. (Lewis, cited in Hylton, 2005: 90–1)

Citing Chong-Soon Lee's criticism of Appiah's contention that race has no basis 'to give it meaning apart from where there is racist intent', Hylton notes that 'Appiah's argument that ethnicity or culture should substitute for "race" is a belief that does not fully recognize the institutionalized discourse of "race" and therefore the historical cultural markers that go with it' (Hylton, 2005: 91). That is, the import of 'race' cannot be reduced to ethnicity at the same time individual differences cannot be denied. Similarly, to argue as Spencer (1999) does against the notion of the social construction of 'race' because the myth of biological race is the foundation for the social construction of race, is to argue that 'race', racial inequality and racism do not exist in social relations and leisure. Hence Hylton calls 'for a critical navigation of the definitions of "race" and a focus on its related social processes rather than becoming stymied by unceasing debates (about notions of race) and their limiting outcomes' (Hylton, 2005: 91).

One direction for such critical work has been the investigation of 'Whiteness'. Such study is important in order to deconstruct 'race' (that is, decentre whiteness) and understand the process of white privileging that occurs in racializing others. That is, '(r)ace as a category is usually applied to "non-white" peoples. White people usually are not seen and named. Whites center themselves as the human norm. "Others" are raced; "we" are just people' (Apple, 2000: x). Whiteness is neutrality, the 'raceless norm', the 'human ordinary' against which those who are 'Other' exist. Grounded in critical and post-structuralist theory, Whiteness is seen as relational and historically conferred.[3] Context matters. In fact, racism is reproduced when context is ignored, when the artificiality of race is denied (Banton, 1980; Guinier and Torres, 2002). Racial identities – including Whiteness – are not natural, given or fixed, rather they are ever-changing, produced in an ongoing process and hence subject to redefinition, resistance and change (Apple, 2000; Kincheloe and Steinberg, 2000). According to Haney-Lopez (1996), individuals are not born White, rather they become White through their social context as well as the choices they make. Whites become white through producing, naming and marginalizing others (Frankenberg,

1993). Of course there are many ways to be White – or any 'race' – as whiteness intersects with age, class, sexual orientation, gender and other material and cultural factors. The examples noted previously indicate the fluidity of 'race' and its social construction. According to Kincheloe and Steinberg:

> the Irish, Italians, and Jews have all been viewed as nonwhite in particular places at specific moments in history. Indeed, prior to the late 1600s, Europeans did not use the label Black to refer to any race of people, Africans included. Only after the racialization of slavery by around 1680 did whiteness and blackness come to represent racial categories. (Kincheloe and Steinberg, 2000: 8–9)[4]

For these reasons, Ella Shohat contends that 'it might be worthwhile to focus less on identity as something one "has," than on identification as something one "does"' (Shohat, 1995: 177).

While ethnicity may be seen as a more neutral or less politically charged concept than race,[5] *ethnic group* is a relatively new term; many groups that are now considered ethnic groups were once considered races. McLemore and Romo define an ethnic group as 'a group or category of people whose inclusion in the group or category is based primarily on similarities of nationality, religion, language or other aspects of a person's social and cultural heritage' (McLemore and Romo, 1998: 16). James also conceives of ethnicity as defined by people with a common heritage, but adds that their 'sense of identity and belonging stems from not only their perception of "being different," but also from their realization that they are seen as different by others' (cited in Tirone and Pedlar, 2000: 148). That is, ethnic groups often share a cultural tradition (an objective dimension) and share some degree of consciousness (a subjective dimension). Much like racial groups, ethnic groups are often unequal in status, wealth and power. There is often intergroup competition and conflict but also cooperation and accommodation between ethnic groups (Farley, 1982). In a multicultural society, ethnicity is a critical determinant of who gets what. It often shapes peoples' interactions with each other and often affects participatory patterns in leisure and recreation. Ethnicity, like race, is a social construction (Barth, 1969; Long and Hylton, 2002; Solomos and Back, 1996). It is an identity that is constructed and reconstructed across time and place in relation to others. Also like race, not all people are seen as possessing 'ethnicity'. In fact, the absence of a sense of ethnicity – or lack of a 'validated' ethnicity – among many whites in the United States is seen as one reason for their racism and ethnocentrism (Kincheloe and Steinberg, 2000).

These various notions of and tensions surrounding 'race' and ethnicity have shaped the research on leisure and race. In the following sections, the questions this research has asked – and thus how 'race' has been (re)produced – are discussed.

Race, ethnicity and leisure

Just as constructions and understandings of race and ethnicity have changed across time, leisure has been and continues to be conceptualized in a variety of ways as well as discussed in other chapters in this book. These conceptualizations have influenced how race and ethnicity are understood or thought about within the field of recreation and leisure studies. For example, when the dominant notion of leisure is one of particular forms or types of activity – going to parks, reading, television viewing, or visiting museums – then racial groups may be compared in terms of differences in their participation and various explanations for those differences proffered. In contrast, when psychological/social psychological thinking prevails and leisure is constructed as a quality/experience of time/activity/being or a state of mind then issues of race and ethnicity are rarely addressed as leisure may be seen as possible for anyone and everyone, regardless of social and structural inequalities. These and other viewpoints are presented in the subsequent sections.

The invisibility of race in leisure research

Early research in the field of recreation and leisure paid little attention to the subject of race. In fact, in reading the nascent work in the field one might come to the conclusion that race was not a social category that stratified life conditions and chances, including opportunities for and practices of leisure. In North America and elsewhere, this perspective was strongly influenced by notions of racial superiority or dominance, normal and marginal, and the predominance of psychological/social psychological thinking about leisure noted above. The hegemony of thinking of leisure as an experience of a 'race-less' individual is perhaps not surprising given the history of the professional practice of recreation and leisure. Recreation and leisure were activities of individuals, communities, organizations and society long before they were a field of study. The organization and provision of leisure activities during the industrial period in Western cultures can be read as obliviousness to, and perhaps even an attempt to 'erase', race and racial difference. For example, in the United States the 'playground movement' and other work of philanthropists and social reformers of the time had, as one of their purposes, the socialization of immigrant groups into 'mainstream' (that is, white/Anglo and middle class) society. However, as noted by Murphy (1974) it was white immigrant and lower-class youth in particular who were the focus of these early efforts (see also Taylor, 1999, for a discussion of urban parks, social class and social control). The lack of recorded history of similar attempts made with more 'obviously' different racial groups from this mainstream in the US (that is, American Indians, Japanese, Mexican, Chinese and African) may indicate nothing more than neglect of particular histories;[6] or, it may suggest that fewer attempts were made to use recreation as a stepping stone to becoming an 'American' with some racial groups (Bialeschki and Walbert, 1998).

In the United States, it was not until the 1960s that the recreation profession turned its attention to the leisure needs of people of colour (Kraus, 1971) and then only because of public protest and social unrest (that is, the Civil Rights Movement). According to Murphy (1974), in the 1960s and early 1970s questions were raised about recreation and leisure services as a site of social (in)equality (Jenkins, 1963; Kraus, 1968; Murphy, 1972; Staley, 1968). In this same book, Murphy predicted 'a lessening of distinct leisure class differences' in the United States due to increased affluence across the population, the growth of mass leisure, and increasing free time (Murphy, 1974: 99). Similarly, in the UK, Roberts (1970) wrote that the end of the twentieth century would bring a 'leisure democracy' and expected that differences in leisure activities would be an outcome of various small 'taste publics'. Scholarship a decade later, however, offered little support for these predictions (Clarke and Critcher, 1985; Featherstone, 1987; Rojek, 1985).

In the early to mid-twentieth century when a scholarship on leisure and recreation emerged, social and political institutions and practices that continued to deny opportunity to racial minorities in the United States was quite consistent with notions of leisure as an experience of the individual. After all, if leisure resided in the mind of the individual and was a *perception* of freedom or choice (Neulinger, 1981), then access to leisure was an individual problem and structural inequalities predicated on race could be ignored. Further, as argued by Rojek (1985), beginning in the 1960s a sociology of leisure was produced that constructed a leisure without society (see also Coalter, 1997). However, by the end of the 1960s and start of the next decade, in both North America and Britain, conflicts arose between 'racial' groups over access to the economy, education, social and political life, and leisure. This is not to say that these were the first 'racial' conflicts. They were not and were preceded by numerous others, often involving recent immigrant white ethnic groups (for example, in the United States, Jews and Italians) as well as people of colour (see Rowe, 1998, for a discussion of 'race' and social conflict in Britain). In fact, Clarke and Critcher (1985) contend that it was such struggles and conflicts, as well as the alliances of marginalized social groups, and not industrialization, that produced both the right to leisure and the ability to pursue certain forms of leisure in Britain.

Race differences in leisure/race as leisure constraint

Perhaps at least in part because of the racial conflicts of the 1960s and 1970s, researchers within and outside the field of recreation and leisure began examining race differences in leisure. In fact, in terms of research on recreation and leisure, no other topic to date has attracted as much attention. Initially race and ethnicity were constructed as categorical/biologically determined variables that could be distinguished. Racial differences were essentialized and both race and ethnicity were seen as homogeneous and universal. Because of these renderings of race and ethnicity their impact on leisure and recreation was seen as measurable and a valid basis of comparison. Two explanations of different leisure participation rates among races came to dominate: marginality and ethnicity.

Edwin Gomez (2002), in discussing the development of marginality and ethnicity explanations of racial differences in leisure, identifies the work of Lindsay and Ogle as setting the groundwork for marginality theory. While discussing the influence of poverty and segregation on opportunity for recreation, Gomez notes that Lindsay and Ogle did not mention race. For them, if cost or economic barriers were removed, there would be no differences in participation between high and low income groups; that is, race and racial discrimination did not exist outside of class differences.

Gomez (2002) credits the research of Craig for introducing the ethnicity perspective into leisure research in North America. Craig conducted a study of the leisure patterns of urban and suburban Southern Blacks and concluded: 'the extent to which people identify with their ethnic/racial group is an important variable to consider' (cited in Gomez, 2002: 125). However, while Craig saw black identity as externally produced (that is, defined in terms of White attitudes) he did not recognize institutionalized racism.

Washburne (1978), according to Gomez, 'provided recreation researchers with the conceptual definitions for ethnicity and marginality as explanations of underutilization of recreation resources by ethnic/racial group members (specifically Blacks)' (Gomez, 2002: 125). In Washburne's conceptualization of these perspectives, he maintained that Blacks do not participate in the same recreation and leisure as Whites 'because of poverty and various consequences of socioeconomic [note: not racial] discrimination' (Washburne, 1978: 176) – the marginality perspective – *or* that the leisure patterns of Blacks are a reflection of their subcultural style – the ethnicity perspective. Gomez asserts that while researchers subsequently 'treated ethnicity as synonymous with race or ethnic group designation' (Gomez, 2002: 125), this actually deviates from Washburne's notion of ethnicity as subcultural style. That is, according to Washburne, research should not focus on the 'race' or ethnicity of individuals but on the identification people have towards a subculture. While Washburne's thinking about ethnicity allowed for the possibility that 'race' and ethnicity are not biologically based, it also suggested that individuals can choose to be racial or ethnic – or not – and that socioeconomic status inequality underlay racial inequality.

Clearly both in their origins and their interpretations, the marginality and ethnicity 'theories' of racial differences in recreation and leisure were apolitical, devoid of notions of power and race and (in)equality. Yet this should not be surprising given that 'race' as a biological category is neutral. Perhaps it should also not be surprising then that these theories have proved inconsistent in their explanatory power and of little value for understanding 'race' and leisure (see Floyd, 1998; Gramann and Allison, 1999; Johnson et al., 1998; Phillip, 1994, 1999; Rehman, 2002; Shinew et al., 2004a, for further discussion of the limits of these perspectives).

Research on race and leisure in the 1990s attempted to get beyond the reduction of racial differences in leisure activity participation to economic circumstances/ opportunity or ethnic identification/subcultural style. For example, some scholars examined the meanings of leisure to different racial groups and how 'race'/ ethnicity shape individuals' lives and their notions of leisure. This research, most of it interpretive, indicates that 'race' frames individuals' lives and leisure but does so in intersection with gender and age (Allison and Geiger, 1993; Khan, 1997; Taylor, 2001; Tirone and Pedlar, 2000; Tirone and Shaw, 1997; Watson and Scraton, 2001). Others shifted the research lens from social class and ethnic identification as explanations for leisure activity participation and focused instead on differences in *how* various racial groups participated or the meanings they attached to their participation in leisure and recreation. Rather than finding differences in activity participation, this body of research suggests various racial groups' involvement in the same activities or experiences may be pursued differently and/or for different reasons (Carr and Chavez, 1993; Gramann and Allison, 1999; Irwin et al., 1990; Schneider et al., 2002). Still, the results of this research were often interpreted in light of the ethnicity and/or marginality perspectives.

Some researchers, rather than examining factors of social class and race separately, explored the interaction of the two as well as their intersection with other social status factors such as gender and age.[7] For example, Floyd et al. (1994) studied leisure preferences and the interaction of race and class. They found that the effects of race on leisure preferences were mediated by class membership. Shinew and colleagues (1995) studied gender, race, class and leisure preferences and again found that leisure preferences were influenced by the intersection of these three status factors. Phillip, in a study of race, gender and adolescent leisure, concluded that race was a more powerful predictor than gender of adolescent peer group approval of leisure for both Black and White teens but that 'race and gender are *defining* features of African American adolescent leisure experience' (Phillip, 1998b: 214, emphasis added). An examination of the influence of age, 'race' and residential location on park preferences and behaviours found that both age and race were important to these dimensions of recreation (Payne et al., 2002). Two interpretive studies on the impact of immigration on individuals' leisure (Juniu, 2000; Stodolska and Yi, 2003) provide insight into the ways social class differentially shapes the experience of immigration and being an ethnic minority.

In was not until the 1990s that a critical mass of scholars both within and outside the field of recreation and leisure studies began documenting and directly investigating the historical and contemporary centrality of discrimination to racial and ethnic minority individuals' experiences of common everyday pastimes and leisure and their engagement in more organized and planned recreation, as well as the programming and policy implications of such (Allison and Schneider, 2000; Blahna and Black, 1992; Chavez, 2000; Gramann and Allison, 1999; Jarvie and Reid, 1997). This research has consistently found that experiences and perceptions of racism, discrimination, or 'unwelcomeness' (Phillip, 1999) is a leisure constraint that shapes not only opportunities for participation (Aron, 1999; Bialeschki and Walbert, 1998; Holland, 2002; Long et al., 1997; Phillip, 1994) but also comfort in and enjoyment of participation (Bairner and Shirlow, 2003; Hibbler and Shinew, 2002; Holland, 1997; Phillip, 1999; Ross, 1997; Tirone, 1999–2000; Watson and Scraton, 2001), attitudes toward leisure (Floyd and Gramann, 1995; Phillip, 1998b), 'style' of participation (West, 1989) and outcomes of participation (Phillip, 1997, 1998a, 2000; Ross, 1997).

Relatively recent research, much of it examining immigrants' experiences of recreation and leisure, also challenges the universality and homogeneity of 'race', racism and discrimination in leisure and recreation (Carrington et al., 1987; Junui, 2000; Rublee and Shaw, 1991; Stodolska and Yi, 2003; Tsai and Coleman, 1999; Yu and Berryman, 1996). For example, in studying a white ethnic minority (Polish immigrants to Canada), the work of Stodolska et al. (Stodolska, 1998, 2000a; Stodolska and Jackson, 1998) found among other things that kinds of discriminatory treatment and contexts where such took place were different for the 'less visible' Polish-

Canadian ethnic minorities than has been reported for more visible racial minorities. In other words, the experience of racism in leisure is shaped by perceived degree of 'Otherness' (for example, skin colour, distinctiveness of dress and traditions, language skills). Research has also found that gender distinguishes the experience of some recent immigrants. In research on South Asian immigrant youth in the UK, females were often more constrained in their leisure participation than males but males experienced more discrimination because of their greater involvement in public spaces (Carrington et al., 1987; Glyptis, 1985; Taylor and Hegarty, cited in Stodolska, 2002). In a study of a diverse group of migrants to Australia, Taylor (2001) reported that age, years of residence, and degree of assimilation differentiated the meanings attached to and the constraints these women experienced in leisure (see also Stodolska, 1998). At the same time, a study of Chinese immigrants to Australia found that gender, age, length of residence, and income did not differentiate the perception of leisure constraints (Tsai and Coleman, 1999). Finally, a study of leisure preferences and constraints among African American and Caucasian adults found that while having distinct leisure preferences, in contrast to previous research, African Americans may not be as constrained as Caucasians (Shinew et al., 2004a). Despite methodological issues that limit the study's results (for example, participants were confined to Chicago park-users), Shinew et al. propose a new framework for understanding African Americans' and Caucasians' experiences of leisure using Shaw's (1994) discussion of leisure as resistance, that moves beyond reductionistic notions of economic marginality and ethnicity.

The study of racial differences in leisure practices has certainly become more 'critical' in perspective in the past ten years in that the complexity of 'race' has begun to be acknowledged and explored. In these explorations the lack of homogeneity and universality of 'race' is evidenced. Still, concerns exist over the usefulness and interpretation of this research (Gramann and Allison, 1999; Floyd, 1998; Henderson, 1998; Hylton, 2005; Kivel, 2000; Stodolska, 2000b). These concerns and some proposed solutions that provide directions for future research are discussed further in the last section of this chapter.

Leisure as opportunity

Leisure has also been studied as a context of racial and ethnic opportunity for at least four reasons: (1) the ideology of recreation as beneficial and desire for the field/profession to justify its importance and right to public funds, (2) evidence that leisure and recreation can hold benefits for individuals and communities, (3) an increased understanding of agency and structure and the dynamics of power relationships and (4) research that started giving voice to previously silenced 'Others'. The scholarship on leisure as opportunity ranges from the politically conservative to radical, from leisure as a site of cultural reproduction and the maintenance of social order to leisure as a context for resistance and social and cultural transformation.

As noted previously, the efforts of early recreation practitioners was predominantly about assimilating (white) immigrants and/or the underclass into capitalist and patriarchal society. Such efforts continue today in programmes such as 'Midnight

Basketball' and 'Work to Ride' in the US which are aimed at keeping young or unemployed, primarily Black males off the streets and hence out of trouble – as well as prepare them to fit into social institutions of education and work. Underlying the ethnic festivals and celebrations that comprise much of the public recreation enterprise as well is the notion that interracial/ethnic contact reduces prejudice and hence enhances social cohesion and a sense of community. Research on this 'contact hypothesis' (Allport, 1954; Farley, 1982; Prentice and Miller, 1999; Sherif, 1961), some of it conducted within the context of sport (Coakley, 1998; Eitzen, 2003; Freysinger et al., 2002; Grey, 1992; McClendon and Eitzen, 1975), indicates that the relationship between interracial/ethnic contact and perceptions of racial/ethnic differences and racial tensions is mediated by a number of factors including the interdependency of the group, one's group status (majority or minority), common goals, as well as societal and cultural ideologies of race and ethnicity (see also Shinew et al., 2004b for an examination of the contact hypothesis in the context of community gardens). In contexts of interracial/ethnic contact it is typically the minority group member who is expected to conform to the White norm (Gramann and Allison, 1999).

In general the research shows that ideologies of race are not easily disrupted nor are racial divides easily bridged (for example, see Evans-Pritchard, 1989, and the response of Laxon, 1991; also, Long and Hylton, 2002; Rublee and Shaw, 1991). The belief that interracial/ethnic contact has the potential to reduce racial conflicts and tensions ignores inequalities in power that go along with 'race'. For example, it ignores the fact that Whites who 'transgress' or cross racial borders through their participation in and identification with other racial/ethnic cultural practices (such as music, dress, language, recreation) – something increasingly seen among youth today – are still White and do not lose the power being White bestows. That is, it is a privilege of Whites as the 'raceless' and the arbiters of power, to be 'nomadic' in identity (Kincheloe and Steinberg, 2000; McClaren, 2000).[8] For persons of colour, crossing the boundaries of 'race' is not so easy both because their entry into white culture is limited and always contested, and because such crossings often carry a heavy cost – that of 'giving up' one's own 'race' – something that ultimately, in a society where 'Whiteness reigns' (Kincheloe et al., 2000), is not allowed. Racial identity is central to a sense of self and community, especially for those daily confronted by the devaluation and marginalization of racism. Some adapt to the 'burden of racism' (Holland, 1997) through the strategy of 'selective acculturation', a process whereby some traits or characteristics of 'White identity' are adopted (for example, language, styles of dress) in order to be able to improve economic opportunity while much of one's 'traditional' culture is maintained (Gramann and Allison, 1999). Even where such a strategy is employed, adoption may be temporary or fluid as social context changes.

As noted by Gramann and Allison (1999), in North America many members of established (as opposed to recent immigrant) racial and ethnic minority groups (for example, French Canadians, American Indians, African Americans) are not assimilating culturally but rather just the opposite, and emphasizing their ethnic or 'racial' distinctiveness. While some see leisure as a context both for 'selective acculturation' and 'ethnic boundary maintenance' (Barth, 1969; Gramann and Allison, 1999; Shaull and Gramann, 1998) research also suggests that attempts to express or enact non-white racial identities in leisure rarely occurs without notice by Whites and is often contested (Long et al., 1997; Long and Hylton, 2002; McAvoy, 2002; Tirone and Pedlar, 2000). Still others believe that, consistent with the ethnicity perspective, there is evidence that leisure is a site for the expression of culture (Allison, 1982, 1988; Carr and Chavez, 1993; Hutchinson, 1987; Irwin et al., 1990; Tirone and Shaw, 1997).

More recently, scholars have 'reframed' the notion of leisure as cultural expressiveness by recognizing the power that defines 'race' and 'race' relations. From this perspective, leisure is seen as (potentially) a site of resistance – a space where oppressive structures and processes are challenged and sometimes transformed. This perspective has also received some research attention and mixed support (Carrington, 1998; Taylor, 2001). In her research on racial/ethnic minority female adolescents in Australia, Betsy Wearing (1998) found that because of their marginalization these young women constructed cultural practices of resistance. Shinew et al. (2004) suggest that their findings that African American adults reported fewer leisure constraints and preferred different leisure activities than Caucasian adults may be read as resistance in some of the ways that Shaw (2001) conceptualizes resistance. That is, African Americans in their study may have perceived fewer leisure constraints because they 'have become more accustomed to negotiating constraints, and thus have developed strategies of resistance to empower themselves in life and leisure' (Shinew et al., 2004a: 194). Further, that the African American adults in their study preferred different leisure activities than their Caucasian counterparts could be interpreted as 'African Americans "freely choosing" not to participate in stereotypical Caucasian leisure pursuits, suggesting an individual form of resistance and "self-determination"' (ibid.: 195). Or it could be that those African Americans in the study who reported a preference for activities identified as 'white', may be 'pioneers' as suggested by Washburne (1978); individuals who 'resist conformity and sanctions associated with their particular group and break through barriers that tend to exclude their participation' (Shinew et al., 2004: 195).

Clearly, as noted by Susan Shaw (2001), the concept of resistance is complex and its application as a framework to interpret human practices challenging. Researchers must think critically about ideologies of 'race' and ethnicity when studying 'race'/ethnicity in leisure and interpreting 'race'/ethnic differences in leisure and recreation practices so as not to over-interpret individual action or create new victims.

Perceptions of 'racial' difference/distinctiveness as a form of leisure

Race may also be interpreted as a form of leisure in that beliefs about 'race' and racial difference are constructed or manifested in cultural practices that become sources of pleasure and/or entertainment. In constructing 'Otherness' a number of things happen. On the one hand, such difference is made strange, foreign and potentially threatening or dangerous. On the other hand, such difference is also constructed as interesting, fascinating and exotic. As cultural theorist Eric Lott states:

in rationalized societies, becoming 'white' and male seems to depend on the remanding of enjoyment, the body, an aptitude for pleasure. It is the other who is always 'excessive' in this respect, whether through exotic food, strange and noisy music, outlandish bodily exhibitions, or unremitting sexual appetite. Whites in fact organize their own enjoyment through the other, Slavoj Zizek has written, and access pleasure precisely by fantasizing about the other's 'special' pleasure. Hatred of the other arises from the necessary hatred of one's own excess; ascribing this excess to the 'degraded' other *and indulging* in it – by imagining, incorporating, or impersonating the other – one conveniently and surreptitiously takes and disavows pleasure at one and the same time. This is the mixed erotic economy, what Homi Bhabha terms the 'ambivalence' of American whiteness. (Lott, cited in McClaren, 2000: 66–7)

Either way, the different-ness (or non-Whiteness) of 'Others' and their subordinate status because of that different-ness are reproduced. Hence, the same leisure pursuit may be experienced in very different ways for different racial/ethnic individuals and be not only a source of pleasure but also pain and oppression. Ross (1997) concluded this from a study of British television where she found that the representation of blacks on television was both irritating and worrisome for black audiences. The limited and stereotypical construction of 'ethnic' identities was seen by black audiences as evidence of the ignorance and racist assumptions on the part of white writers. Such productions' disregard of cultural authenticity was also taken as disregard for black viewers. Not only did television's stereotypical constructions of 'black' identity worry these adults because of their impact on themselves and black children, but also because of their impact on white audiences who, 'without first-hand knowledge of black communities, assume that their vicarious experience of televisions' portraits of "blackness" is the real thing' (Ross, 1997: 233).

Similar concerns have been voiced by those who study both tourism and sport. Tourism, according to Hollinshead (1998: 125), is 'the quintessential industry of "difference" or "otherness"'. In tourism, cultures and ethnicities are constructed in ways that (re)produce inequalities.[9] Sport has also been examined in this way. For example, sporting audiences are predominantly white, while in some sports, blacks are increasingly visible as athletes or players. Such predominance of black (male) athletes is read by many whites as evidence of innate or physiological differences between races and all the attendant mental and emotional distinctions that have been constructed around the mind–body duality. Hence sport is a leisure practice through which people are 'racialized' and racism is (re)produced (Birrell, 1989; Carrington, 2004; Davis and Harris, 1998; Hylton, 2005; Jarvie and Reid, 1997; Long and Hylton, 2002; Scraton, 2001).

What of the future?

The previous discussion has identified a number of challenges and directions for future research on race and leisure. Based on this discussion several concluding thoughts are offered here.

- We must be cautious that in focusing on or emphasizing 'racial' difference, we do not '(mask) the conditions that give some forms of difference value and power over others' (Hylton, 2005). Further, to ignore 'race' renders it invisible but to focus on it may render it essential. Similar to feminist scholarship, leisure and 'race' scholars must grapple with their focus on difference and the extent to which it reproduces 'race' as a category of difference – and further oppresses and disadvantages individuals of colour by focusing on their difference from (often having less or a lack of in comparison to) Whites, the 'raceless norm' (Dyer, 1997).
- Studying Whiteness is one attempt to decentre Whiteness, reveal the social construction of 'race' and create an awareness of the processes of empowerment and privileging (Fine et al., 1997). Questions that might be asked in the study of whiteness include: how does whiteness function in the lives of white people?; how is whiteness 'received very differently by individuals standing at different intersections of various race, class, gender, religious, and geographical axes of identity'?; how does whiteness as the norm shape 'the lives of those who are both included and excluded by the categorization' (Kincheloe and Steinberg, 2000: 17)? Specific to leisure, how are leisure and recreation part of the 'white power bloc – the loose alignment of various social, political, education, and economic agents as well as agencies that work in concert around particular issues to maintain white power' – and how might leisure and recreation be contexts for a 'pedagogy of whiteness', attempts to reinvent whiteness in non-racist ways (ibid.: 18)? Some of the recent research on race and leisure, particularly that on the leisure of white ethnic minority immigrants conducted by Stodolska et al., begins to untangle the culture of whiteness. Stodolska also calls for integrating research on minorities into the broader field of leisure in order to '(build) a coherent theoretical framework that could be consistently applied to study the leisure experience of both minorities and the mainstream' and laments the 'focus on narrowly defined problems whose applicability is limited to specific groups and specific situations' (Stodolska, 2000b: 158). It is suggested here that this research would be strengthened by post-structural theorizing about race and culture because only by seeing individuals as embedded in culture/race/ethnicity can we understand leisure (see Aitchinson, 2000; Hollinshead, 1998; Hylton, 2005; Scraton, 2001; Shaw, 2001 for applications of post-structural thinking to leisure research).[10]
- At the same time, we must be careful that in shifting attention to whiteness we do not, in the words of Michael Apple, '[lapse] into the possessive individualism that is so powerful in this society. That is, such a process can serve the chilling function of simply saying "but enough about you, let me tell you about me"' (Apple, 2000: xi). That is, we must be careful that in focusing on whiteness we do not recentre dominant voices – or generate white guilt, hostility and feelings of powerlessness. There is often a discomfort that whites feel when put under racial scrutiny and in realizing that Others represent and imagine them (hooks, 1992).

- A number of leisure researchers have called for change in leisure research (for example, Aitchison, 2000; Allison, 2000; Coalter, 2000; Floyd, 1998; Hemingway, 1999; Henderson, 1998; Hylton, 2005; McDonald and McAvoy, 1997; Stodolska, 2000b). Included in that call is the need to (re)centre social justice as an aim of the practice and study of recreation and leisure. In order to do this, a critical examination of 'race' must be undertaken. According to Hylton, 'writers need to centralize "race" and racism in their analyses and research agendas. Where "race" has been ignored, include it, where it has been marginalized, centre it, and where it has been problematized, theorize it' (Hylton, 2005: 89). Further, the critical study of 'race' must go beyond armchair theorizing and work for positive social change (Hylton, 2005; Kincheloe and Steinberg, 2000).

Lani Guinier and Gerald Torres (2002) argue that we ignore 'race' at our own peril. Like the miner's canary whose distress alerted coalminers to poison in the air, we also need to heed the distress of the 'race' – whether it be among Whites or Blacks – and enlist race to resist power. Guinier and Torres call this *political race* whose aim is to empower people of all races to struggle together to improve life chances of all who have been 'raced' black regardless of skin colour. A critical understanding of race may finally allow an opportunity for the building of non-racist communities through leisure.

Notes

1. The thinking presented in this chapter should not be read as definitive but rather as exploratory and suggestive. While an attempt was made to present and integrate a diverse literature on leisure and race, there clearly is much missing from this discussion. Readers of this chapter are urged to consult the references cited for further and more in-depth discussion of the many issues raised only briefly here.
2. Ranier Spencer (1999) argues against the use of a social construction of race, declaring that the myth of biological race is the foundation for the social construction of race. That is, even as we deny the validity of biological race, we use the same categories devised by those who believe in race as science to discuss and declare race as socially constructed. While cognizant of the US government's need to collect data to monitor discrimination, Spencer believes federal race categories have not only served to reveal patterns of racism, which is of great importance, but they have also helped to substantiate the flawed belief in race. Spencer's goal in writing *Spurious Issues* is to expose the myth of race in an attempt to eliminate the false idea of race.
3. See Kincheloe and Steinberg (2000) for a discussion of the history of whiteness.
4. Indeed, according to Long and Hylton (2002: 101), 'whiteness [continues to make] "others" of Jews, the Irish, travelers and refugees from Eastern Europe today'.
5. In the US, it has become common practice, at least among Whites, to avoid the usage of the term 'race' and to use the term 'ethnic group' or 'ethnicity' instead, particularly when referencing situations of inequality. This avoidance seems to increase in relation to increases in evidence of the subordination and oppression of people of colour.
6. See work by Bialeschki and Walbert (1998) on the intersection of race, class and gender in the leisure of working-class women in the industrial New South and the work of Holland (2002) on the history of Black recreation in the US.
7. Hylton (2005) cites Ladson-Billings (1998) and Parker (1998) as discussing the necessity of recognizing the connection between race and racism and other forms of oppression.

See Scraton (2001) for cautions against adding race to other contexts or discourses of oppression in an additive fashion.
8. See the work of Yasser Mattar (2003) for insight into how the internet facilitates individuals' crossing of 'racial' boundaries, the hybridity of identity and the reproduction of racism.
9. Hollinshead calls for tourism researchers within the field of leisure studies to think more deeply about their subject and advocates using the cultural-theoretical thinking of Homi Bhabha (1990, 1994) as a framework for such study. Hollinshead's presentation of Bhabba's writing on culture and ethnicity provides insights for leisure and recreation research generally.
10. This is not meant to be an uncritical endorsement of post-structural thinking. See hooks (1990), Maynard (2002) and Hylton (2005) for a critique of such theory.

Bibliography

Aitchison, C. (2000) 'Poststructural Feminist Theories of Representing Others: A Response to the "Crisis" in Leisure Studies' Discourse', *Leisure Studies* 19: 127–44.
Allison, M. T. (1982) 'Sport, Culture and Socialization', *International Review for the Sociology of Sport* 17: 11–37.
Allison, M. T. (1988) 'Breaking Boundaries and Barriers: Future Directions in Cross-cultural Research', *Leisure Sciences* 10: 247–59.
Allison, M. T. (2000) 'Leisure, Diversity, and Social Justice', *Journal of Leisure Research* 31(1): 2–6.
Allison, M. T. and Geiger, C. (1993) 'The Nature of Leisure Activities among the Chinese American Elderly', *Leisure Sciences* 15(4): 309–19.
Allison, M. T. and Schneider, I. E. (eds) (2000) *Diversity and the Recreation Profession: Organizational Perspectives*, State College, PA, Venture Publishing.
Allport, G. W. (1954) *The Nature of Prejudice*, Cambridge, MA, Addison-Wesley.
Apple, M. W. (2000) 'Foreword', in J. L. Kincheloe, S. R. Steinberg, N. M. Rodriguez and R. E. Chennault (eds) *White Reign: Deploying Whiteness in America*, New York: St Martin's Griffin, pp. ix–xiii.
Aron, C. S. (1999) *Working at Play: A History of Vacations in the United States*, Oxford: Oxford University Press.
Bairner, A. and Shirlow, P. (2003) 'When Leisure Turns to Fear: Fear, Mobility, and Ethno-sectarianism in Belfast', *Leisure Studies* 22(3): 203–22.
Banton, M. (1980) 'The Idiom of Race: A Critique of Presentation', in C. B. Marret and C. Leggon (eds) *Research in Race and Ethnic Relations*, Greenwich, CT, JAI Press.
Barth, F. (1969) *Ethnic Groups and Boundaries: The Social Organization of Cultural Difference*, London, George Allen & Unwin.
Begley, S. (1995) 'Three is Not Enough', *Newsweek* (13 February): 67–9.
Bhabha, H. (1990) *Nation and Narration*, London, Routledge.
Bhabha, H. (1994) *The Location of Culture*, London, Routledge.
Bialeschki, M. D. and Walbert, K. L. (1998) '"You Have To Have Some Fun To Go Along With Your Work": The Interplay of Race, Class, Gender, and Leisure in the Industrial New South', *Journal of Leisure Research* 30(1): 79–100.
Bierstedt, R. (1948) 'The Sociology of Majorities', *American Sociological Review* 13: 700–10.
Birrell, S. (1989) 'Racial Relations Theories and Sport: Suggestions for a More Critical Analysis', *Sociology of Sport* 6: 212–27.
Blahna, D. and Black, K. (1992) 'Racism a Concern for Recreation Managers', in P. H. Gobster (ed.) *Managing Urban and High-use Recreation Settings* (General Technical Report NC-163, pp. 111–18). St. Paul, MN, USDA Forest Service Northcentral Forest Experiment Station.
Carr, D. S. and Chavez, D. J. (1993) 'A Qualitative Approach to Understanding Recreation Experiences: Central American Recreation on the National Forests of Southern California',

in A. W. Ewert, K. J. Chavez and A. W Magill (eds) *Culture, Conflict, and Communication in the Wildland–Urban Interface*, Boulder, CO, Westview Press, pp. 181–94.

Carrington, B. (1998) 'Sport Masculinity and Black Cultural Resistance', *Journal of Sport and Social Issues* 22(3): 275–98.

Carrington, B. (2004) *Leisure Studies: Special Issue on Race/Nation/Sport* 23(1).

Carrington, B., Chievers, T. and Williams, T. (1987) 'Gender, Leisure and Sport: A Case Study of Young People of South Asian Descent', *Leisure Studies* 6: 265–79.

Carrington, B. and McDonald, I. (2001) *Race Sport and British Society*, London, Routledge.

Chavez, D. J. (2000) 'Invite, Include, Involve! Racial Groups, Ethnic Groups, and Leisure', in M. T. Allison and I. E. Schneider (eds) *Diversity and the Recreation Profession: Organizational Perspectives*, State College, PA, Venture Publishing, pp. 179–94.

Clarke, J. and Critcher, C. (1985) *The Devil Makes Work: Leisure in Capitalist Britain*, Chicago, University of Illinois Press.

Coakley, J. (1998) *Sport in Society* (6th edn), St. Louis, MO, McGraw-Hill.

Coalter, F. (1997) 'Leisure Sciences and Leisure Studies: Different Concept, Same Crisis?' *Leisure Sciences* 19(4): 21–36.

Coalter, F. (2000) 'Leisure Studies, Leisure Policy and Social Citizenship: A Response to Rosemary Deem', *Leisure Studies* 19(1): 21–36.

Davis, L. and Harris, O. (1998) 'Race and Ethnicity in U.S. Sports Media', in L. A. Wenner (ed.) *MediaSport: Cultural Sensibilities and Sport in the Media Age*, New York, Routledge, pp. 154–69.

Dyer, R. (1997) *White*, New York, Routledge.

Eitzen, S. D. (2003) *Fair and Foul: Beyond the Myths and Paradoxes of Sport*, Lanham, MD, Rowman & Littlefield.

Evans-Pritchard, D. (1989) 'How "They" See Us: Native Americans' Images of Tourists', *Annals of Tourism Research* 16: 89–105.

Farley, J. E. (1982) *Majority–Minority Relations*, Englewood Cliffs, NJ, Prentice-Hall, Inc.

Featherstone, M. (1987) 'Lifestyle and Consumer Culture', *Theory, Culture, and Society* 4(1): 55–70.

Fine, M., Weis, L., Powell, L. and Wong, L. (eds) (1997) *Off White: Readings on Race, Power and Society*, New York, Routledge.

Floyd, M. F. (1998) 'Getting Beyond Marginality and Ethnicity: The Challenge for Race and Ethnic Studies in Leisure', *Journal of Leisure Research* 30(1): 3–22.

Floyd, M. F. and Gramann, J. H. (1995) 'Perceptions of Discrimination in a Recreation Context', *Journal of Leisure Research* 27: 192–9.

Floyd, M. F. and Shinew, K. J. (1999) 'Convergence and Divergence in Leisure Style among Whites and African Americans: Toward an Interracial Contact Hypothesis', *Journal of Leisure Research* 31(4): 359–84.

Floyd, M. F., Shinew, K. J., McGuire, F. A. and Noe, F. P. (1994) 'Race, Class, and Leisure Activity Preferences: Marginality and Ethnicity Revisited', *Journal of Leisure Research* 26: 158–73.

Frankenberg, R. (1993) *The Social Construction of Whiteness: White Women, Race Matters*, Minneapolis, University of Minnesota Press.

Freysinger, V. J., Harris, O., Kimball, A. C. and Spencer, M. (2002) 'Leisure and Majority–Minority Relations: Bridging the Gap or Widening the Divide?' Paper presented at the 10th Canadian Congress on Leisure Research, University of Alberta, Edmonton, Alberta, Canada, 22–25 May.

Glyptis, S. (1985) 'Women as a Target Group: The Views of the Staff of Action Sport – West Midlands, *Leisure Studies* 4: 347–62.

Gomez, E. (2002) 'The Ethnicity and Public Recreation Participation Model', *Leisure Sciences* 24: 123–42.

Gramann, J. H. and Allison, M. T. (1999) 'Ethnicity, Race, and Leisure', in E. Jackson and T. Burton (eds) *Leisure Studies at the Millennium*, State College, PA, Venture Publishing, pp. 283–97.

Grey, M. (1992) 'Sports and Immigrant and Anglo Relations in Garden City (Kansas) High School', *Sociology of Sport Journal* 9: 255–70.

Guinier, L. and Torres, G. (2002) *The Miner's Canary: Enlisting Race, Resisting Power, Transforming Democracy*, Cambridge, MA, Harvard University Press.

Haney-Lopez, I. (2000) 'The Social Construction of "Race"', in R. Delgado and J. Stefancic (eds) *Critical Race Theory: The Cutting Edge*, Philadelphia, Temple University Press, pp. 163–75.

Hemingway, J. L. (1999) 'Critique and Emancipation: Toward a Critical Theory of Leisure', in E. L. Jackson and T. L. Burton (eds) *Leisure Studies: Prospects for the Twenty-first Century*, State College, PA, Venture Publishing, pp. 487–506.

Henderson, K. A. (1998) 'Researching Diverse Populations', *Journal of Leisure Research* 30(1): 157–70.

Henderson, K. A. (2001) 'Researching Leisure and Physical Activity with Women of Color: Issues and Emerging Questions', *Leisure Sciences* 23(1): 21–34.

Hibbler, D. K. and Shinew, K. J. (2002) 'Interracial Couples' Experience of Leisure: A Social Network Approach', *Journal of Leisure Research* 34(2): 135–56.

Holland, B. L. (1997) 'Surviving Leisure Time Racism: The Burden of Racial Harassment on Britain's Black Footballers', *Leisure Studies* 16: 261–77.

Holland, J. W. (2002) *Black Recreation: A Historical Perspective*, Chicago, Burnham, Inc.

Hollinshead, K. (1998) 'Tourism, Hybridity, and Ambiguity: The Relevance of Bhabha's "Third Space" Cultures', *Journal of Leisure Research* 30(1): 121–56.

hooks, b. (1990) *Yearning: Race, Gender and Cultural Politics*, Boston, MA, South End Press.

hooks, b. (1992) 'Representing Whiteness in the Black Imagination', in L. Grossberg, C. Nelson and P. Treichler (eds), *Cultural Studies*, New York, Routledge.

Hraba, J. (1994) *American Ethnicity* (2nd edn), Itasca, IL, F. E. Peacock Publishers, Inc.

Hutchinson, R. (1987) 'Ethnicity and Urban Recreation: Whites, Blacks, and Hispanics in Chicago's Public Parks', *Journal of Leisure Research* 19(3): 205–22.

Hutchinson, R. (1988) 'A Critique of Race, Ethnicity, and Social Class in Recent Leisure-Recreation Research', *Journal of Leisure Research* 20(1): 10–30.

Hylton, K. (2005) '"Race," Sport and Leisure: Lessons from Critical Race Theory', *Leisure Studies* 24(1): 81–98.

Irwin, P. N., Gartner, W. G. and Phelps, C. C. (1990) 'Mexican American/Anglo Cultural Differences as Recreation Style Determinants', *Leisure Sciences* 3: 129–55.

James, C. (1995) *Seeing Ourselves: Exploring Race, Ethnicity, and Culture*, Toronto, Thompson Educational Publishing, Inc.

Jarvie, G. and Reid, I. (1997) 'Race Relations, Sociology of Sport and the New Politics of Race and Racism', *Leisure Studies* 16: 211–19.

Jenkins, S. (1963) *Comparative Recreation Needs and Services in New York City Neighborhoods*, New York, Community Council of Greater New York.

Johnson, C. Y., Bowker, J. M., English, D. B. K. and Worthen, D. (1998) 'Wildland Recreation in the Rural South: An Examination of Marginality and Ethnicity Theory', *Journal of Leisure Research* 30(1): 101–20.

Juniu, S. (2000) 'The Impact of Immigration: Leisure Experiences in the Lives of South American Immigrants', *Journal of Leisure Research* 32(3): 358–82.

Kew, S. (1981) *Ethnic Groups and Leisure*, London, The Sports Council and Social Science Research Centre.

Khan, N. A. (1997) 'Leisure and Recreation among Women of Selected Hill-farming Families in Bangladesh', *Journal of Leisure Research* 29(1): 5–20.

Kimball, A. and Freysinger, V. J. (2003) 'Leisure, Stress and Coping: The Sport Participation of Collegiate Student-athletes', *Leisure Sciences* 25(2/3): 115–37.

Kincheloe, J. L., Steinberg, S. R., Rodriguez, N. M. and Chennault, R. E. (eds) *White Reign: Deploying Whiteness in America*, New York, St Martin's Griffin.

Kincheloe, J. L. and Steinberg, S. R. (2000) 'Addressing the Crisis of Whiteness', in J. L. Kincheloe, S. R. Steinberg, N. M. Rodriguez and R. E. Chennault (eds) *White Reign: Deploying Whiteness in America*, New York, St Martin's Griffin, pp. 3–29.

Kivel, B. D. (2000) 'Leisure Experience and Identity: What Difference does Difference Make?' *Journal of Leisure Research* 32(1): 79–81.

Kraus, R. (1968) *Public Recreation and the Negro: A Study of Participation and Administrative Practices*, New York, Center for Urban Education.

Kraus, R. (1971) *Recreation and Leisure in Modern Society*, New York, Appleton-Century-Crofts.

Kraus, R. (1994) *Leisure in a Changing America: Multicultural Perspectives*, New York, Macmillan.

Ladson-Billings, G. (1998) 'Just What is Critical Race Theory and What's it Doing in a Nice Field Like Education?' *Qualitative Studies in Education* 11(1): 7–24.

Laxon, J. (1991) 'How "We" See Them: Tourism and Native Americans', *Annals of Tourism Research* 18: 365–91.

Li, P. S. (1990) 'Race and Ethnicity', in P. S. Li (ed.) *Race and Ethnic Relations in Canada*, Toronto, Oxford University Press, pp. 3–17.

Long, J., Carrington, B. and Spracklen, K. (1997), '"Asians Cannot Wear Turbans in the Scrum": Explorations of Racist Discourse within Professional Rugby League', *Leisure Studies* 16: 249–50.

Long, J. and Hylton, K. (2002) 'Shades of White: An Examination of Whiteness in Sport', *Leisure Studies* 21(2): 87–104.

Mattar, Y. (2003) 'Virtual Communities and Hip-hop Music Consumers in Singapore: Interplaying Global, Local and Subcultural Identities', *Leisure Studies* 22(4): 283–300.

Maynard, M. (2002) '"Race", Gender and the Concept of "Difference" in Feminist Thought', in S. Scraton and A. Flintoff (eds) *Gender and Sport: A Reader*, London, Routledge, pp. 111–26.

McAvoy, L. (2002) 'American Indians, Place Meanings, and the Old/New West', *Journal of Leisure Research* 34(4): 383–97.

McClaren, P. (2000) 'Whiteness is … The Struggle for Postcolonial Hybridity', in J. L. Kincheloe, S. R. Steinberg, N. M. Rodriguez and R. E. Chennault (eds) *White Reign: Deploying Whiteness in America*, New York, St Martin's Griffin, pp. 63–75.

McClendon, M. J. and Eitzen, D. S. (1975) 'Interracial Contact on Collegiate Basketball Teams: A Test of Sherif's Theory of Superordinate Goals', *Sociology of Sport Quarterly* 55: 926–38.

McDonald, D. and McAvoy, L. (1997) 'Native Americans and Leisure: State of the Research and Future Directions', *Journal of Leisure Research* 29(2): 145–66.

McLemore, S. D. and Romo, H. D. (1998) *Racial and Ethnic Relations in America* (5th edn), Boston, MA, Allyn & Bacon.

Murphy, J. F. (1972) 'Egalitarianism and Separatism: A History of Approaches in the Provision of Public Recreation Service for Blacks, 1906–1972'. Unpublished Dissertation, Oregon State University.

Murphy, J. F. (1974) *Concepts of Leisure: Philosophical Implications*, London, Prentice-Hall.

Neulinger, J. (1981) *The Psychology of Leisure*, Springfield, IL, Charles C. Thomas.

Parker, L. (1998) '"Race Is Race Ain't": An Exploration of the Utility of Critical Race Theory in Qualitative Research in Education', *Qualitative Studies in Education* 11(1): 25–41.

Payne, L. L., Mowen, A. J. and Orsega-Smith, E. (2002) 'An Examination of Park Preferences and Behaviors Among Urban Residents: The Role of Residential Location, Race, and Age', *Leisure Sciences* 24: 181–98.

Phillip, S. F. (1994) 'Race and Tourism Choice: A Legacy of Discrimination', *Annals of Tourism Research* 21: 479–88.

Phillip, S. F. (1997) 'Race, Gender, and Leisure Benefits', *Leisure Sciences* 19: 191–207.

Phillip, S. F. (1998a) 'African-American Perceptions of Leisure, Racial Discrimination, and Life Satisfaction', *Perceptual and Motor Skills* 87: 1418.

Phillip, S. F. (1998b) 'Race and Gender Differences in Adolescent Peer Group Approval of Leisure Activities', *Journal of Leisure Research* 30(2): 214–32.

Phillip, S. F. (1999) 'Are We Welcome? African American Racial Acceptance in Leisure Activities and the Importance Given to Children's Leisure', *Journal of Leisure Research* 31(4): 385–403.

Phillip, S. F. (2000) 'Race and the Pursuit of Happiness', *Journal of Leisure Research* 32(1): 121–4.

Prentice, D. and Miller, D. (eds) (1999) *Cultural Divides: Understanding and Overcoming Group Conflict*, New York, Russell Sage Foundation.

Rehman, L. A. (2002) 'Recognizing the Significance of Culture and Ethnicity: Exploring Hidden Assumptions of Homogeneity', *Leisure Sciences* 24(1): 43–57.

Roberts, K. (1970) *Leisure*, London, Longman.

Rojek, C. (1985) *Capitalism and Leisure Theory*, London, Tavistock.

Ross, K. (1997) 'Viewing (P)leasure, Viewer Pain: Black Audiences and British Television', *Leisure Studies* 16: 233–48.

Rowe, M. (1998) *The Racialisation of Disorder in Twentieth Century Britain*, Aldershot, Ashgate.

Rublee, C. and Shaw, S. M. (1991) 'Constraints on the Leisure and Community Participation of Immigrant Women: Implications for Social Integration', *Loisir et Société (Society and Leisure)* 14(1): 133–50.

Schneider, I. E., McAvoy, L. H. and Frakt, A. N. (2002) 'Cross-cultural Claims on Devils Tower National Monument: A Case Study', *Leisure Sciences* 24(1): 79–89.

Scraton, S. (2001) 'Reconceptualising Race, Gender and Sport: The Contribution of Black Feminism', in B. Carrington and I. McDonald (eds) *Race, Sport and British Society*, London, Routledge, pp. 170–87.

Shaull, S. L. and Gramann, J. H. (1998) 'The Effect of Cultural Assimilation on the Importance of Family-related and Nature-related Recreation among Hispanic Americans', *Journal of Leisure Research* 30(1): 47–63.

Shaw, S. M. (1994) 'Gender, Leisure and Constraint: Towards a Framework for the Analysis of Women's Leisure', *Journal of Leisure Research* 26: 8–22.

Shaw, S. M. (2001) 'Conceptualizing Resistance: Women's Leisure as Political Practice', *Journal of Leisure Research* 33: 186–201.

Sherif, M. (1961) *Intergroup Conflict and Cooperation: The Robbers Cave Experiment*, Norman, University of Oklahoma Book Exchange.

Shinew, K., Floyd, M., McGuire, F. and Noe, F. (1995) 'Gender, Race, and Subjective Social Class and their Association with Leisure Preferences', *Journal of Leisure Research* 27: 75–89.

Shinew, K., Floyd, M., McGuire, F. and Noe, F. (1996) 'Class Polarization and Leisure Activity Preferences of African Americans: Intragroup Comparisons', *Journal of Leisure Research* 28(4): 219–32.

Shinew, K. J., Floyd, M. F. and Parry, D. (2004a) 'Understanding the Relationship between Race and Leisure Activities and Constraints: Exploring an Alternative Framework', *Leisure Sciences* 26(2): 181–200.

Shinew, K. J., Glover, T. D. and Parry, D. C. (2004b) 'Leisure Spaces as Potential Sites for Interracial Interaction: Community Gardens in Urban Areas', *Journal of Leisure Research* 36(3): 336–55.

Shohat, E. (1995) 'The Struggle Over Representation: Casting, Coalitions, and the Politics of Identification', in R. de la Campa, E. A. Kaplan and M. Sprinker (eds), *Late Imperialism Culture*, New York, Verso.

Sigelman, L. and Welch, S. (1993) 'The Contact Hypothesis Revisited: Black–White Interaction and Positive Racial Attitudes', *Social Forces* 71: 781–95.

Solomos, J. and Back, L. (1996) *Racism and Society*, Basingstoke, Macmillan.

Spencer, R. (1999) *Spurious Issues: Race and Multiracial Identity Politics in the United States*, Boulder, CO, Westview Press.

Staley, E. J. (1968) *An Instrument for Determining Comparative Priority of Need for Neighborhood Recreation Services in the City of Los Angeles*, Los Angeles, Recreation and Youth Services Planning Council.

Stodolska, M. (1998) 'Assimilation and Leisure Constraints: Dynamics of Constraints on Leisure in Immigrant Populations', *Journal of Leisure Research* 30: 521–51.

Stodolska, M. (2000a) 'Changes in Leisure Participation Patterns after Immigration', *Leisure Sciences* 22: 39–63.

Stodolska, M. (2000b) 'Looking Beyond the Invisible: Can Research on Leisure of Ethnic and Racial Minorities Contribute to Leisure Theory?', *Journal of Leisure Research* 32(1): 156–60.

Stodolska, M. (2002) 'Ceasing Participation in Leisure Activities After Immigration: Eastern Europeans and Their Leisure Behavior', *Loisir et Société* (*Society and Leisure*) 25(1): 79–117.

Stodolska, M. and Jackson, E. L. (1998) 'Discrimination in Leisure and Work Experienced by a White Ethnic Minority Group', *Journal of Leisure Research* 30(1): 23–46.

Stodolska, M. and Yi, J. (2003) 'Impact of Immigration on Ethnic Identity and Leisure Behavior on Adolescent Immigrants from Korea, Mexico, and Poland', *Journal of Leisure Research* 35(1): 49–80.

Taylor, D. (1999) 'Central Park as a Model for Social Control: Urban Parks, Social Class, and Leisure Behavior in 19th Century America', *Journal of Leisure Research* 31(4): 420–77.

Taylor, T. (2001) 'Cultural Diversity and Leisure: Experiences of Women in Australia', *Loisir et Société* (*Society and Leisure*) 2: 535–55.

Tirone, S. (1999–2000) 'Racism, Indifference, and the Leisure Experiences of South Asian Canadian Teens', *Leisure/Loisir* 24(1–2): 89–114.

Tirone, S. and Pedlar, A. (2000) 'Understanding the Leisure Experiences of a Minority Ethnic Group: South Asian Teens and Young Adults in Canada', *Loisir et Société* (*Society and Leisure*) 23: 145–69.

Tirone, S. and Shaw, S. M. (1997) 'At the Center of their Lives: Indo Canadian Women, Their Families, and Leisure', *Journal of Leisure Research* 29(2): 225–44.

Tsai, E. H. and Coleman, D. J. (1999), 'Leisure Constraints of Chinese Immigrants: An Exploratory Study', *Loisir et Société* (*Society and Leisure*) 22: 243–64.

van den Berghe, P. (1967) *Race and Racism: A Comparative Perspective*, New York, John Wiley and Sons, Inc.

van Wel, F. and Linssen, H. (1996) 'Ethnicity and Youth Cultural Participation in the Netherlands', *Journal of Leisure Research* 28(2): 85–96.

Walker, G. J., Deng, J. and Dieser, R. B. (2001) 'Ethnicity, Acculturation, Self-construal, and Motivations for Outdoor Recreation', *Leisure Sciences* 23: 263–83.

Washburne, R. F. (1978) 'Black Under-Participation in Wildland Recreation: Alternative Explanations', *Leisure Sciences* 1(2): 175–88.

Watson, B. and Scraton, S. (2001) 'Confronting Whiteness? Researching the Leisure Lives of South Asian Mothers', *Journal of Gender Studies* 10(3): 265–77.

Wearing, B. (1998) *Leisure and Feminist Theory*, London, Sage.

West, C. (1993) *Race Matters*, Boston, MA, Beacon Press.

West, P. C. (1989) 'Urban Regional Parks and Black Minorities: Subculture, Marginality, and Inter-racial Relations in Park Use in the Detroit Metropolitan Area', *Leisure Sciences* 11: 11–28.

Woodward, M. D. (1988) 'Class, Regionality, and Leisure among Urban Black Americans: The Post-civil Rights Era', *Journal of Leisure Research* 20: 87–105.

Wray, S. (2002) 'Connecting Ethnicity, Gender and Physicality: Muslim Pakistani Women, Physical Activity and Health', in S. Scraton and A. Flintoff (eds) *Gender and Sport: A Reader*, London, Routledge, pp. 127–40.

Yu, P. and Berryman, D. L. (1996) 'The Relationship Among Self-Esteem, Acculturation, and Recreation Participation of Recently Arrived Chinese Immigrant Adolescents', *Journal of Leisure Research* 28: 251–73.

16
A Touch of Class[1]

Chas Critcher

Class as category

This chapter is about the relevance of the concept of class for understanding leisure. Unless prompted, we do not habitually describe our social experience, at work or in leisure, in class terms. There is in any case a world of difference in how a word like 'class' is used in everyday language compared with the specialized terminology – some would say jargon – of the social sciences.

Class is one form of social division. Others include gender, age and ethnicity. All of these

- are perceived as being substantially different materially or culturally;
- are long-lasting and sustained by dominant cultural beliefs, the organization of social institutions and individual interaction;
- confer unequal access to resources – and thus different life chances and lifestyles;
- engender shared identities in terms of perceived difference from those in an alternative category of the same division. (Braham and Janes, 2002: xiii)

Here we adopt a working definition of social classes as groups of people, more strictly speaking families or households, who can be ranked in terms of their access to income and wealth.

Classifying classes

Various ways of measuring social class follow similar procedures. The working population is divided into occupational groupings, defined by their level of skill and authority. These are reclassified into a smaller number of socioeconomic groups, usually between six and eight. These may then be divided into a few social classes. The key problem here is where to draw the boundaries, especially between the

271

working and middle classes. Some put all non-manual occupations in the middle class; others put routine non-manual (office) workers into the working class. This is the crucial decision, since of the working population in the 1991 UK Census this group contained 11 per cent of men, 39 per cent of women and 24 per cent overall (Reid, 1998: 21). A further distinction may be made at the upper end, where some professionals and managers are taken to have higher status and authority than others.

Until very recently most government statistics used a scale of six socioeconomic groups:

- professional
- employers and managers
- intermediate and junior non-manual
- skilled manual
- semi-skilled manual and professional services
- unskilled manual.

Using such categories, we can estimate the size of each class in contemporary Britain. Savage (2001) estimated them as

- the middle class: 40.1 per cent overall, comprised of 29.4 per cent professional and managerial and 10.7 per cent self-employed
- the working class: 59.9 per cent overall, comprised of 27.2 per cent routine white-collar and 32.7 per cent manual.

If we define the higher echelons of professional and managers as upper class and leave the routine non-manual workers as a genuinely ambiguous group, we could come up with figures like these for the UK (derived from Reid, 1998: table 2.1):

- upper class 4 per cent
- unequivocally middle class 27 per cent
- borderline middle and working-class 24 per cent
- unequivocally working class 45 per cent.

The size of the respective classes depends on how we construct the categories and aggregate them together. 'Formidable technical problems are associated with the questions of how many classes there are and where their boundaries lie' (Abercrombie and Warde, 2000: 129). A recent decision to change the Census definitions of socioeconomic groups has proved controversial because they are claimed not to be 'hierarchical'.

Two dimensions of class are crucial to our, or any, discussion of leisure: class as inequality and class as culture. For each we shall explain what class in general is taken to mean, indicate how it applies to modern Britain and pose some questions about its relevance to leisure. The second half of the chapter answers the questions about class and leisure; considers arguments about the impact of recent economic and cultural change; and ends by indicating the status of class in leisure sociology.

Class as material inequality

Class is a way of explaining the patterns of inequality in society: how and why some groups have more material resources than others. Not only income matters. Wealth is important, whether it can be cashed in or not (known as marketable or non-marketable wealth). Into the class equation come ownership of houses, cars or consumer goods, as well as savings, stocks and shares or pension rights. Two questions arise about material class inequality. First, where does it come from? Second, what effects does it have?

Class is an attribute of households rather than individuals. Household income is the total sum of what all the members of the family bring in. The largest component is usually the earnings of adults, especially men. What they are paid depends upon their position in the labour market. Position in the labour market is closely related to level of education. We can forecast reasonably accurately where in the labour market, and thus the class structure, somebody will end up who has no formal academic qualifications. Their level of education points them towards particular kinds of jobs: whether they drive a bus, follow a trade, have a routine office job or manage the activity of others.

Class inequalities are rooted in the labour market but their effects extend way beyond employment prospects to encompass what sociologists call 'life chances'. One of these is, quite literally, a matter of life and death. The higher anyone's social class, the longer they will live and the better their physical and psychological health will be. It does not end there.

> There is virtually no aspect of a person's life chances that is not shaped by class: people's income, their job prospects, their housing conditions, leisure interests and social life continue to be associated with their class. (Savage, 2001: 82)

The annual government publication *Social Trends* (ONS, 2003) yields some simple facts about class inequality (all percentage figures have been rounded to the nearest multiple of five).

- *Wealth* (excluding home ownership). The top 1 per cent of the population own 25 per cent of all wealth; the top 5 per cent own 50 per cent. The top half own 95 per cent so that the remaining half own just 5 per cent of wealth.
- *Housing tenure and type*. A total of 30 per cent of all households own their houses outright; 40 per cent have a mortgage. Of the remainder, 20 per cent rent their homes from councils or other social housing agencies and 10 per cent from private landlords. Over 40 per cent of professional and employers/ managers live in detached houses, compared with fewer than 20 per cent of the skilled, semi-skilled or unskilled manual.

- *Car ownership.* Just under 30 per cent of households have access to more than one car; just over 40 per cent have one car; 30 per cent have no car at all.
- *Holidays* (defined as four or more nights away). A total of 35 per cent of households have two or more holidays; 40 per cent have one holiday; 25 per cent have no holiday at all.

British society has become more unequal in the last 25 years, a deliberate consequence of taxation policies pursued by both political parties. Everybody is better off than before but the rich are getting richer much faster than the rest of us and the relative position of the poor has changed little. Trends in the labour market affect the class structure. We are becoming more middle class because there are more middle-class and fewer working-class jobs than there used to be. Popular culture, especially pop music, show business and sport, provide many examples of individuals who have gone from humble origins to join the super rich but social mobility between classes is much less dramatic. The middle class seems to be the most fluid, with individuals moving in and out of it. Fewer individuals join or leave the upper or working classes, generally to or from the nearest social class.

Now we can ask: how does class inequality in all its forms affect leisure behaviour? An answer would examine the effect on leisure behaviour of such factors as income levels, educational qualifications, housing standards, access to private transport. These may affect leisure behaviour as whole and specific leisure activities. Of course, individuals will vary. People with the same level of disposable income will choose to spend it in their own way. But if class inequality does affect leisure, we should be able to identify some patterns to people's behaviour, regardless of personal preferences. Such patterns may be produced by material inequality and reinforced by cultural habit.

Class as cultural difference

One indicator of class inequality is housing. Those similarly placed in the class structure will live in similar kinds of houses in similar kinds of areas. The consequence is class segregation by residence. This aspect of class is clearly visible. A journey through any urban or rural environment will quickly encounter different kinds of housing (detached, semi-detached, terraces, high- or low-rise flats and so on). Sometimes different types press upon each other; at others, whole areas are of one type such as suburbs, public housing estates, inner-city neighbourhoods.

Most people find that their neighbours are pretty much like themselves. They will have similar income levels, send their children to the same type of school, use the same shops, visit the same pubs or bars, have access to the same parks, libraries, sports or community centres. Sharing the same physical environment does not make people mix very much or have the same outlook on life. But it does increase the potential for the emergence of common patterns of experience or values. Since they are based upon and reflect class position, they are called class cultures.

If we can identify distinctive boundaries between upper-class, middle-class and working-class lifestyles, this may suggest that those who share the same class position are also likely to share and express a common outlook on life. Lifestyles can be explored by quantitative indicators. We can ask members of the same or different classes a whole range of questions in a survey about aspects of their daily lives which we can measure. This might include:

- their attitudes – to work experiences, political parties, neighbourhood life
- their perceptions of themselves and others as members (or not) of classes or other kinds of grouping
- their networks of families, friends and work colleagues
- their membership of trade unions, political groups, voluntary associations.

If members of objectively defined class groupings do tend to have similar kinds of attitudes, perceptions, networks and memberships, these shared characteristics may together endorse a particular way of seeing the world, which is distinct from those of other classes. This would provide systematic empirical evidence for the existence of class cultures.

But class cultures do not only consist of attitudes or behaviour which can be measured. They may also be embedded in everyday life, so taken for granted as to be almost unconscious. In everyday social life we mobilize what might be called signs of class. A simple example is how we speak. We may habitually register from their accent where in Britain somebody comes from, apparently regardless of class. But in practice, working-class people have much more pronounced accents, shading off into dialect where the meaning may be instantly recognizable only to others in the same language community. Working-class Sheffielders, for example, habitually use what is called the glottal stop – 'I've been t'shops'; use archaic words – 'I've been waiting to see thee', or employ local expressions – 'He's a bit nesh'. 'Love', pronounced 'luv', is used as a familiar form of address, even by men to men, whereas a few miles south in Derbyshire the equivalent term is 'duck' pronounced 'dook'. All this is regarded as quite normal; it is how ordinary people speak. But, often though not always, it is not how middle-class people speak, even in Sheffield. They aspire to a 'proper' way of talking which, though not always eradicating the local accent entirely, certainly dispenses with those forms of speech which appear to be 'common'. And a sign of the upper class, wherever they live, is precisely that they speak 'posh', eliminating traces of local accent and dialect. Additionally, class differences may be found in the range and extent of vocabulary and, more controversially, in what the language is designed to do, express abstract concepts or express emotion. Linguists have not resolved the issue of class differences in language (Argyle, 1994) but how we speak may be a routine marker or sign of class, of who belongs in which group.

Another everyday 'sign' of class may be food, which Warde (2001) examined in detail. The professional and managerial class contained a distinctive grouping of independent professionals characterized by 'eating out in stylish restaurants, experimenting with domestic cuisine and eating more healthily' (ibid.: 213). They were a minority, even within their own class. More striking were differences between the classes. Compared with the middle class, the working class spent more on bread, sausages, cooked meats, beer, fish and chips, sugar, tea and canned vegetables, and less on fresh vegetables, processed fruit, wine, meals out and fresh fruit (ibid.). Warde concluded that the working class 'retains distinctive dietary practices, suggesting the persistence of class taste, class culture and a firm class boundary with higher classes' (ibid.: 214). Even amongst the very varied middle class it was 'possible to identify the occupational class category of two middle-class individuals out of three by reading their weekly grocery bills' (ibid.: 217).

Now we can begin to identify some questions about the potential relationship between such class cultures and leisure. How far can leisure be situated as part of the way of life which defines class cultures? Does leisure not merely reflect but express class culture? Are particular kinds of leisure activities 'signs' of class membership? Even where members of different classes apparently pursue the same leisure activities, are there significant class differences in the form they take, as we saw with food?

Class patterns in leisure: quantitative

Leisure involvement can be measured in different ways: by money and time spent or by rates of participation in nominated activities. Unsurprisingly, we find that the more disposable income a household has, the more proportionally it will spend on leisure and related expenditure, such as transport. The less well-off have to spend proportionally more of their income on the basic necessities of life, as Table 16.1 shows.

Table 16.1 Household expenditure by income grouping 1998-99: largest three categories (%)

Category	Top fifth	Next top fifth	Middle fifth	Next bottom fifth	Bottom fifth	Average of all
Motoring and fares	19	18	17	13	13	17
Leisure goods and services	19	17	17	14	13	17
Food and non-alcoholic drinks	13	16	18	21	22	17
Total %	51	51	52	48	48	51

Source: Adapted from *Social Trends*, (ONS, 2003, table 6.8).

The total percentages for each group are very similar but how they are apportioned is different. Those with higher incomes spend not only more money but a higher proportion of their incomes on leisure related goods and services. Such economic inequalities affect leisure, for example in the home.

The influence of class on home-based activities is obvious. (Table 16.2.) The rate of participation declines as we go down the class structure. There are hardly any activities where lower social groups participate more than higher ones. Middle groups consistently participate more than lower ones and less than higher ones. As *Social Trends* notes dryly:

In general, smaller proportions of those in the manual socio-economic groups, such as the unskilled, participated in certain home-based leisure activities than those in the non-manual groups, such as professionals and managers. (ONS, 2001: 226)

This pattern repays some careful examination. Three activities show few class differences: watching TV, needlework, etc., and visiting/entertaining friends or relations. The really significant class differences in home-based leisure are found in five activities: listening to the radio, listening to music, reading books, DIY and gardening.

Table 16.2 Participation in home-based leisure activities: by gender and socioeconomic group, 1996–97 (% of population aged 16 and over participating in the activity in previous four weeks)

	Professional	Employers and managers	Intermediate and junior non-manual	Skilled manual	Semi-skilled manual	Un-skilled	All
Males							
Watching TV	99	99	99	99	98	99	99
Visiting/ entertaining friends or relatives	95	96	96	95	94	88	95
Listening to radio	93	92	93	87	85	83	89
Listening to records, CDs, tapes	83	80	85	74	73	67	78
Reading books	81	69	68	48	49	39	58
DIY	66	65	50	52	46	42	52
Gardening	62	63	50	52	46	42	52
Needlework, etc.	4	4	3	3	3	2	3
Females							
Watching TV	98	99	99	100	99	98	99
Visiting/ entertaining friends or relatives	100	98	97	95	97	96	97
Listening to radio	96	89	90	85	82	78	87
Listening to records, CDs, tapes	93	83	80	72	70	64	76
Reading books	91	80	77	63	61	54	71
DIY	41	36	32	30	27	22	29
Gardening	49	55	51	42	41	39	45
Needlework, etc.	30	36	39	40	36	36	36

Source: Social Trends (ONS, 2001, table 13.4) (online).

The biggest class difference of all is for reading books, more evident amongst men than women. This also applies to listening to the radio and playing music, though the 'intermediate and junior non-manual' group has an exceptionally high rate for both. There is a pattern here; these activities are all interests cultivated early in life and part of the lifestyle of the group. An interest in reading and music, regardless of personal tastes, is more likely to occur amongst higher than lower classes.

The other two large class differences are in DIY and gardening. Men do more of both but still participation rates increase up the class scale. The bigger a family's house or garden, the more likely its members are to spend time on their care. Maintaining and improving the house and garden are more likely to become a 'project', a financial and psychological investment, on which leisure time and money are spent. A range of television programmes now seek to satisfy this fascination with changing rooms or houses.

Consistent patterns of class differentiation are evident within and between activities. This is not to deny the existence of avid readers or keen gardeners amongst the working class. Individuals can and do depart from the leisure norms of their class. But the home as a leisure project and a site for a variety of leisure activities is correlated with class: the higher the social class, the more central to leisure these versions of the home are likely to be.

Class appears to influence out-of-home activities as well. (Table 16.3.)

Table 16.3   Participation in selected leisure activities away from home, by social grade, 1996 (% of population aged 16 and over participating in last three months)

Activity	AB	C1	C2	D	E	All
Visit a public house	74	69	64	66	48	65
Meal in a restaurant (not fast food)	87	73	58	45	36	62
Drive for pleasure	54	47	48	46	38	47
Meal in fast-food restaurant	48	44	42	43	29	42
Library	59	43	31	30	21	39
Cinema	47	42	35	30	21	36
Short-break holiday	41	33	28	22	18	29
Disco or nightclub	26	29	27	31	20	27
Historic building	41	31	17	15	10	24
Spectator sports event	30	25	23	18	7	22
Theatre	35	26	17	11	7	20
Museum or art gallery	36	24	14	11	12	20
Fun fair	14	13	19	16	10	15
Exhibition (other than museum/gallery)	24	18	13	7	4	14
Theme park	14	11	14	12	10	12
Visit a betting shop	5	6	11	12	12	9
Camping or caravanning	8	9	11	9	5	9
Bingo	2	5	8	10	14	7

Note: A: higher managerial, professional or administrative; B: intermediate managerial, professional or administrative; C1: supervisory or clerical and junior managerial, professional or administrative; C2: skilled manual workers; D: semi- and unskilled manual; E: pensioners, widows, casual workers or unemployed.

Source: *Social Trends* (ONS, 1998, table 13.12).

On only a few measures – disco/nightclub, fun fairs, betting shops and bingo – is there any variation from the consistent pattern of decreasing attendance as we go down the class scale.

Beneath the surface of leisure behaviour, we find more rather than less evidence of class differences (Reid, 1998). Higher social classes watch considerably less television than either the middle or working classes. Working-class viewers are more likely to watch commercial television, middle-class radio listeners to tune into BBC Radio 4. Newspaper preference is clearly divided along class lines. Higher social classes are less likely to have no car and more likely to have two than other classes. They also consistently play more sport and take other forms of physical exercise, such as walking or jogging. And so the list of greater participation amongst the higher social classes continues, including some which are obvious (visits to the countryside, museums and stately homes, attending plays and concerts) and some which are not (going to the cinema, drinking alcohol inside and outside the home).

The conclusion has to be that class is a highly salient factor in basic quantitative measures of leisure participation.

> All leisure activities demand time, many require money and some need skill and/or opportunity for their pursuit. While such factors are not necessarily the determinants of leisure behaviour, they obviously affect it and their distribution is related to the social strata. (Reid, 1998: 214)

Quantitative evidence of the effects of class on leisure behaviour is substantial but this does not necessarily imply that class differences are also qualitative. A different kind of argument is required.

Class patterns in leisure: qualitative

Qualitative differences in class leisure can easily be illustrated by the case of sport. In the British context sports can be readily identified with different classes, especially at the extremes. Upper-class sports include yachting, rowing, show jumping; working-class sports include snooker, darts, rugby league. Some sports extend across the upper and middle classes but generally exclude the working class: tennis, golf, rugby union. A few sports bring together the upper and working classes, excluding the middle class, such as horse racing or boxing. Some sporting activities can be seen to have changed class position. Watching professional football is now so expensive that it has lost some of its working-class adherents whilst increasing its middle-class audience. An apparently individual choice, whether or not to play or watch a sport, is shaped by class, in terms of both material resources and cultural patterns.

Sport is the most transparent but not the only example of class differences being reproduced or rearticulated within particular kinds of leisure activity. As argued 20 years ago (Clarke and Critcher, 1985), there are at least three ways of understanding class differences within apparently similar kinds of leisure activity: differences in kind, differences in meaning and differences in context.

A simple example of differences in kind is the consumption of food and drink. As well as class differences in the frequency of such activities, there are also likely to be class differences in their nature. Exactly what is eaten or drunk, the willingness to experiment, knowledge about foreign food, wines and beers, and so on; all will differ. The whole world doesn't love a sushi bar. Another example would be gambling, with bingo and football at a different end of the continuum from casinos, the fastest-growing area of the sector. As Adonis and Pollard (1997: 270) have pointed out, the

National Lottery is predominantly a working-class activity, though the proceeds appear to be distributed much further up the class scale. In all these instances, the same category of activity will hide differences in kind.

Differences in meaning may be found even where the nominated activity is more closely defined. A fishing, rugby or gentlemen's club may incorporate very different ideas about what and who the club is for, what is entailed in being or becoming a member, and so on. Joining the local playgroup rota is different in purpose and ethos from membership of the Women's Institute or Mothers' Union, though both may be classified as 'voluntary associations'.

Differences in context refer to how discrete leisure activities are patterned along class lines. A golf club may provide access to networks which prove no handicap to business while deals of a rather different kind may transpire in a working men's club.

Individuals may cross class boundaries but, precisely because we tend to do the kinds of things that people like us do, leisure bears the imprint of class. 'Patterns of sociability continue to be class bound, which contributes to the separation of one class from another' (Abercrombie and Warde, 2000: 155).

Very little has been done to pursue this line of enquiry. A significant exception is Bourdieu (1984), who proposed a new way of conceptualizing culture in class terms. Findings from a large-scale survey in France confirmed that 'all cultural practices (museum visits, concert-going, reading etc.) and preferences in literature, painting and music, are closely linked to educational level (measured by qualifications or length of schooling) and secondarily to social origin' (Bourdieu, 1984: 1). Such differences are attributable to the unequal distribution of three kinds of capital: economic (derived from position in the labour force); cultural (transmitted by families) and academic (acquired through prolonged education). Since these often, though not invariably, reinforce each other, whole classes or groups within them have their own *habitus*. This framework designates the cultural/leisure activities of the group as superior to those of other groups. The consequence is that 'the manner of using symbolic goods ... constitutes one of the key markers of "class"' (ibid.: 66). Class distinction becomes a matter of 'taste'. The same goods in different contexts (the *habitus*) take on different meanings: 'the very meaning and value of a cultural object varies according to the system of objects in which it is placed' (ibid.: 88). Such objects include music, sports, furniture, films, food, clothing, even cosmetics.

This argument is not easy to understand and even harder to summarize. Some of the ideas are frankly obscure. The logic seems at times contradictory. It is not clear whether, even if true for France in the mid-1960s, these ideas have any relevance to Britain or any other nation 40 years later. However, Bourdieu has provided a new vocabulary with which to tackle the kinds of class differences suggested earlier: differences in kind, meaning and context.

Class, consumption and change

Class, as material inequality or cultural form, is never fixed; it is constantly changing. Over the last 40 years change appears to have accelerated markedly, so that the whole existence of classes is now being questioned. In the past 'there were strong class-based cultures, visible from clothing, audible from accent and embodied in mannerisms' (Abercrombie and Warde, 2000: 147), yet surely this is now much less accurate. Distinctive class cultures have dissolved with changes in occupations, housing and consumerist patterns of living. The rise of a new middle class has collapsed previous class distinctions. Ethnic divisions have arisen within the working class which is no longer economically or culturally homogeneous. The changes within this class especially seem momentous.

> Mass consumption, the seductiveness of the products of commercial producers, and the time and organization required to pursue material comforts have probably diluted the distinctiveness of working-class culture. Sources of solidarity that arose from the daily patterns of interaction within working-class communities, particularly those based on mining, heavy engineering, shipbuilding and the like, have contracted. (Abercrombie and Warde, 2000: 167)

As the working class has shrunk and its culture fragmented, the middle class has risen to prominence. It includes both professionals and managers, materially and culturally closer to the upper class, as well as routine white-collar workers, materially and culturally closer to the working class. It also includes the self-employed. Sharp divisions exist between employers, employed and self-employed and between private and public sectors. Though very mixed and interested in individual rather than group identity, the middle class are highly class conscious. 'This is not a homogeneous class. But it is aware of class and class matters' (Abercrombie and Warde, 2000: 182).

Within leisure, two trends seem to have diminished the importance of class. One is the increased 'privatization', better termed 'privatism', of leisure. The home is increasingly the premier leisure site. The privatism of leisure, found especially amongst the burgeoning middle class, is punctuated by occasional excursions into the countryside or holiday resort. Yet the home remains the essential base of, and final refuge for, leisure as a totality.

The second trend is the massive expansion of commercialized leisure. Leisure has become above all something to be consumed in the marketplace. According to Lury (1996), the consumer society has a multitude of characteristics amongst which can be found: the mass availability of consumer goods; the penetration of the market into almost all spheres of life; the use of advertising and promotion to attract consumers; the popularity of shopping in all its forms; the importance of selling and buying style, perhaps even lifestyle. These are typical of the economy as a whole but in the consumer society sport and leisure are central to the commercial enterprise, being sold in their own right and as a vehicle for the marketing of other goods and services, noticeable in every single televised sports event.

The result is a leisure market in which any class preferences are likely to be overridden by individual choices, patterned if at all by the consumption of pre-packaged lifestyles:

with the rise in standards of living, it is argued that issues related to consumption, rather than production, are becoming more relevant; and that 'lifestyles', rather than 'classes' are playing an increasingly important part in shaping a whole range of attitudes and behaviours. (Crompton, 1998: 140)

And yet it is more complex. Not only does access to all this depend upon disposable income; a visit to a theme park or shopping mall does not imply commitment to a whole lifestyle. When examined, lifestyles turn out to adhere stubbornly to class patterns.

> Lifestyles are not the idiosyncratic properties of individuals, however much everybody believes that he or she has freely chosen his or her lifestyle. Rather, elements of a lifestyle hold together in some way and are held in common by a number of individuals. Social groups, in other words, are often constituted by the possession of the same lifestyle. (Abercrombie and Warde, 2000: 344)

Each class still demonstrates, in highly complex ways, a set of lifestyles which differentiates it from those above and below.

Devine (1992) revisited the Affluent Worker studies from the 1960s. These had identified car workers in Luton as prototypes of the then 'new' and affluent working class. While the affluent workers had not adopted the lifestyles and outlooks of the middle class, there were signs of significant change. Evident were: an 'instrumentalist' attitude to work (motivated solely by money); a privatism of lifestyles, including leisure; and an individualistic attitude towards politics. Devine was sceptical. Her intensive interviews with 32 Luton couples in the mid-1980s produced very different findings. Attitudes to work included both intrinsic and extrinsic rewards and, in any case, financial incentives were not peculiar to the working class. Support for the Labour Party remained, in the expectation that it represented the interests of 'ordinary people' as a group. Devine could find little evidence of the alleged privatism of lifestyle. Extended family networks were strong, with some, if limited, sociability with neighbours and workmates. Men still undertook leisure outside the home, especially sport and drinking. Women were more home-centred, but this was expected and accepted. The home-centredness of those with young children was less an active choice than a necessary adjustment to a tight budget and the constraints of child care. Devine found a negotiated balance between public and private lifestyles. Changes in working-class life had been more gradual and were less easily labelled than earlier studies had assumed.

Wynne (1998) used the ideas of Bourdieu to investigate the lifestyles of the new middle class. He surveyed, interviewed and observed the residents of a new exclusive residential development with its own integral social and sporting facilities. Crudely summarized, Wynne found the crucial distinctions were between two groups. One group had worked their way up from the working class without the benefit of formal education. They tended to retain some forms of working-class sociability and used the social facilities mainly for drinking. The other group, often from similar backgrounds, owed their occupational advancement to educational professional qualifications. They preferred the sports facilities. Tensions were evident between the two groups.

Wynne argues that he had found clear evidence of 'cultural capital' producing different forms of *habitus*, but these were differences within the middle class rather than between it and other classes. The crucial lifestyle distinctions were situated and expressed within leisure. Within a fragmented middle class, leisure was increasingly important to the expression and maintenance of subtle distinctions of lifestyle.

The upper class demonstrate most starkly how a class position creates and is defended by a class culture. A small elite, no more than 0.1 per cent of the population, dominates the upper echelons of British business and the state. They own or control the commanding heights of the economy and the wealth (land, property and shares) which goes with it. If part of the political elite, they determine the conditions under which this wealth is created and distributed. The very few studies of the upper class scarcely mention leisure, even Scott (1982). Those near enough to this class to observe it, like journalists, agree that the upper class sustains itself primarily through networks. Such networks are not only economic but social.

The upper class meet each other all the time. Upper-class children move together through preparatory and public schools to the top universities, especially Oxford and Cambridge. Young adults mix with other members of the upper class, whom they will generally marry. They move in the same restricted social circles, go to and are seen at the same social events, habitually mixing business with pleasure. However hard-headed their business or political decisions may be and however much they may appear to compete with each other, members of the upper class know that their continuing economic and political supremacy depends upon their daily interaction with other members of the same class, at work and in leisure. The continuing influence of class culture on the fabric of British social life is here very obvious.

The empirical evidence, quantitative and qualitative, suggests that class has continued to exert a fundamental influence upon leisure choice and behaviour. This is all too frequently glossed over by exaggerating the scale and nature of social change. In particular two mistaken assumptions are very common: first, that what or how people consume has become more important than what or how people produce; and second, that individual choice has become paramount. 'It would be wrong to mistake contemporary society's increased individual capacities to manipulate the cultural trappings of identity as meaning that class no longer matters' (Scott, 2000: 53). This, it might be feared, is the trap into which the sociology of leisure has fallen.

Class and leisure theory

Twenty years ago, the argument was made about the importance of class to leisure analysis:

> Inequality of leisure opportunity has both a material and a cultural aspect. The material aspect includes access to key resources, especially those of time

and money. The cultural aspect includes the perception of what is appropriate leisure behaviour for a member of a particular social group. (Clarke and Critcher, 1985: 146)

The thesis may now seem dated, yet, as the preceding discussion has shown, the essentials of the argument can be sustained. Society and its class formations have, as they constantly do, undergone change. The details alter but the significance of class appears to have endured. However, while debates about class and other forms of social division took place in the 1980s, contemporary leisure theory, at least in Britain, seems to have given up on class. Indicative is its treatment in the work of two leading leisure scholars, Kenneth Roberts and Chris Rojek.

Roberts (1999) does not argue that class is irrelevant to understanding leisure. That would be to deny basic statistical evidence. But, he suggests, its influence is now restricted to income. Higher social classes do more of nearly everything because they can purchase it but qualitatively different cultures have declined. Leisure preferences converge, as the elite take to popular culture and the mass gains access to activities once reserved for the privileged elite. Hence his conclusion:

> It is more accurate to speak of present-day leisure as class related than class based. By far the strongest class relationship nowadays is that the higher social strata do more of virtually everything that has a cash price. It has become more difficult than in the past to identify qualitatively distinct leisure patterns that are typical of entire social classes or even specific occupations. The main differences are now quantitative and are maintained primarily through financial inequalities. (Roberts, 1999: 85)

Here Roberts concedes some influence on leisure of class as material inequality, but denies the influence of class as cultural difference. Yet later he states:

> The main differences in leisure behaviour are still by social class, age and sex ... Sex, age and socio-economic status continue to be related to leisure differences; clearer than the differences between the intra-class lifestyles that have been identified in existing research. (ibid.: 212)

Here differences between classes are presented as more significant than differences within classes, and these seem to be qualitative as well as quantitative. The argument, perhaps like the influence of class itself, seems inconsistent.

Rojek (2000) has also demoted class, even though he concedes its fundamental importance to leisure behaviour.

> The evidence supports the view that class inequality continues to be fundamental in modern (and postmodern!) societies ... Leisure continues to be a badge of membership to the richest class. Holiday homes, private yachts, jets and luxury cars are prestige leisure accessories. Social gatherings like Ascot, Henley, private fashion shows and operas are all common leisure events for the rich. Membership

of gentlemen's clubs, luxury ski and health resorts, yacht clubs, hunting clubs all serve to further identify the richest in society. By contrast the conditions of the leisure poor are marked by lack of money, a lack of personal space, low geographical mobility and a homologous range of activities. (Rojek, 2000: 68)

The status of such observations is, for Rojek, banal. We already know this; it will lead us back to some old questions and their habitual dead ends. Reducing leisure to a simple reflection of class ignores the really interesting questions about leisure as cultural play, where identities are secured and realized by transgressing the borders of conformity. The massive transformation of leisure symbols by the mass media in a consumerist society will simply be missed if we keep on relating everything back to what social surveys or community studies tell us about socioeconomic groups. Class is, as it were, the setting for the drama of leisure; if we concentrate on the scenery, we will miss the action.

Different positions emerge about the significance of class for leisure. In contrast to the emphasis on the material inequalities and cultural differences of class as fundamental to understanding leisure, we can reduce its influence to the factor of income, take some of it for granted and move on to other more interesting questions, or simply wish class out of existence altogether. Alternatively, it can be held that other social divisions may be as, if not more important than class, notably gender and ethnicity. Class is the only or even the primary way in which contemporary leisure should be understood. A range of factors influence, we might say sociologically 'structure', leisure choices and practices. Moreover, any full understanding of leisure has to understand it at some point in its own terms as the effort to realise human qualities of sociability and pleasure. However, it would be a grave error to deny or ignore how patterns of leisure are intimately related to class inequalities and cultures.

Conclusion

We are finally left with a mystery. The influence of class on leisure has been and is changing in complex ways, yet, as we have seen, the quantitative evidence for class inequality in leisure continues to be compelling and the qualitative evidence at least provides a case to answer. None of this seems central to the sociology of leisure which denies, ignores or takes for granted the influence of class. This is part of a wider trend in public and intellectual debate about class.

> The *facts* about class – in Britain and a number of other western countries – show that inequality has widened quite dramatically since about 1980. But, over just this same period, fashionable *theories* and influential *ideologies* have appeared to say almost the opposite. While rich and poor have in fact grown further apart, predominant ideology has set out to dismiss this; and both predominant ideology and leading social theory have come to argue that it does not much matter anyway. (Westergaard, 2001: 69)

This chapter has taken issue with the view that 'it does not much matter anyway'. The challenge to leisure scholars is that, whatever other questions and topics they may wish to pursue, they may have to begin by confronting the claims about the influence of class on leisure. It may be blindingly obvious, but that does not make it insignificant or uninteresting.

Note

1. The evidence and examples in this chapter are taken from Britain, the context the author knows best. Britain may be unusual. It is often thought by those outside it to be an exceptionally class-ridden and class-conscious society. The relationship between class and leisure in other nations may deviate from the British case. How far this is so can be evaluated by following the logic suggested by this chapter:

   - defining class
   - establishing its measurement in official statistics
   - summarizing evidence about class inequalities in life chances
   - ascertaining cultural differences between classes, such as speech or food
   - examining survey evidence about class participation rates in leisure
   - reviewing studies of class cultures in leisure
   - critiquing how leisure scholars currently assess class factors.

   Such an enterprise for any society might reveal differences from the British case. Whether they are differences of detail or substance would require careful consideration.

   I am grateful to Peter Bramham for comments on an early draft of this chapter. It would have been a better piece, had I taken any notice.

Bibliography

Abercrombie, N. and Warde, A. (2000) *Contemporary British Society*, (3rd edn), Cambridge, Polity Press.

Adonis, A. and Pollard, S. (1997) *A Class Act: the Myth of Britain's Classless Society*, London, Hamish Hamilton.

Argyle, M. (1994) *The Psychology of Class*, London, Routledge.

Bourdieu, P. (1984) *Distinction: A Social Critique of the Judgement of Taste*, London, Routledge & Kegan Paul.

Braham, P. and Janes, L. (2002) 'Social Differences and Divisions: Introduction', in P. Braham and L. Janes (eds) *Social Differences and Divisions*, Cambridge, Blackwell.

Clarke, J. and Critcher, C. (1985) *The Devil Makes Work*, Basingstoke, Macmillan.

Crompton, R. (1998) *Class and Stratification*, (2nd edn), Cambridge, Polity Press.

Devine, F. (1992) *Affluent Workers Revisited: Privatism and the Working Class*, Edinburgh, Edinburgh University Press.

Lury, C. (1996) *Consumer Culture*, New Brunswick, NJ, Rutgers University Press.

Office for National Statistics (ONS) (1998) *Social Trends*, London, HMSO.

Office for National Statistics (2001) *Social Trends*, online.

Office for National Statistics (2003) *Social Trends*, London, Office for National Statistics, available online at: <www.statistics.gov.uk> (accessed April 2006).

Reid, I. (1998) *Class in Britain*, Cambridge, Polity Press.

Roberts, K. (1999) *Leisure in Contemporary Society*, Wallingford, CAB Publishing.

Rojek, C. (2000) *Leisure and Culture*, Basingstoke, Macmillan.

Savage, M. (2001) 'The Condition of the Contemporary Middle Classes', in N. Abercrombie and A. Warde (eds) *The Contemporary British Society Reader*, Cambridge, Polity Press.

Scott, J. (1982) *The Upper Classes: Property and Privilege in Britain*, Basingstoke, Macmillan.

Scott, J. (2000) 'Class and Social Stratification', in G. Payne (ed.) *Social Divisions*, Basingstoke, Macmillan.

Warde, A. (2001) 'Food and Class', in N. Abercrombie and A. Warde (eds) *The Contemporary British Society Reader*, Cambridge, Polity Press.

Westergaard, J. (2001) 'The Persistence of Class Inequalities', in N. Abercrombie and A. Warde (eds) *The Contemporary British Society Reader*, Cambridge, Polity Press.

Wynne, D. (1998) *Leisure, Lifestyle and the New Middle Class: A Case Study*, London, Routledge.

17
Leisure and Subculture
Chris Jenks

We have come a long way since Veblen (1899) first described the conditions of leisure and provided a forward-looking analysis that would nevertheless lock the concept in relation to a whole series of other structural conditions now rendered more fluid. Despite these inevitable penalties of historicism Veblen achieved far more than the election of ideas, still current, such as 'conspicuous consumption'. In analytic terms his lasting insight was the detailed revelation of the ideology of those with power in society. At a different level he demonstrated that this ruling ideology, through imitation, envy and sad comparison became the ideology of a particular historical period.

In many senses leisure was a relatively simple and straightforward idea held in a network of binary oppositions such as work/leisure, public/private and labour/ pleasure (Slater, 1998). As such, the disposition of leisure began to claim an identity as an absence, something other than that which was clear, specific and intended (or should we say purposive). Modernity was concerned with the development of industrial capitalism, with the harnessing of human plasticity to the machine as a recipe for surplus and excess, and the combination of these tactics within the strategy of reason. Modernity marked out work and productivity as essential, desirable, ethical (see Weber's Protestant ethic) and species specific (see Marx's *Homo laborens*). Indeed, leisure took on the conceptual status of the temporary open spaces within modernity's project; it signified something apart from the 'real' purpose of being human and, in fact, social.

Of course, the idea of leisure as a more or less sophisticated version of 'not-work' could not sustain within a rapidly developing society where notions of rest and recuperation were becoming not just subtle masks for economic investment and necessity but also, and primarily, elements of a new pastoral philosophy of self-realization. Indeed, in a late-modern world people may expend more time, physical and mental energy in pursuit of their leisure activities than they do in relation to their paid labour. All of these issues are complicated by the significance of gender in relation to unpaid labour (Green et al., 1990; Deem, 1986) and also by simple socioeconomic status of the individual but nevertheless 'leisure' has become an active rather than a passive signifier in contemporary society. Further complications arise from the emergent structural conditions of what we might call a postmodern society where new versions of the life course derive from both voluntary and also enforced changes in the patterns of employment including: working from home; job-sharing; early retirement and work as leisure, accompanied by the boom in fictional and fantasy worlds provided through the rise and success of leisure industries (Rojek, 1994, 1995). The grand work narratives of modernity are slowly being eroded but their lingering ethic still attaches to notions of identity and self-worth. Unemployment has not yet morphed conceptually into 'work-freedom' and still carries a residual stigma in relation to self-esteem and societal evaluation.

It is the essentially moral evaluation of normative conduct revealed above which is to become the topic of this paper specifically in relation to the idea of leisure. Among the vast range of social problems that confront the modern world there are two, namely crime and delinquency, which have been enquired into with considerable thoroughness and diligence; and the subsequent research conducted in these areas has revealed quite dramatically both the shortcomings and the possibilities of sociology as an applied science. Crime and delinquency would appear to have claimed more public attention and academic concern than any other social problem over the last 50 years. This is in part because of the exponential increase in their incidence, despite repeated waves of governmental policy across the political spectrum, and partly because other problems closely associated with the growth of modernity, such as poverty, have diminished in both significance and occurrence, relatively speaking. Perversely, and perhaps in origin due to the Durkheimian view of crime as a functional necessity in the perpetuation of rule systems, crime has come to be viewed as 'normal' (in the sense of anticipated, expected, not a transitory event). Criminality has assumed a certain normative alterity contained in 'alternative economies', 'underworlds', 'criminal mentalities' such that it is both mainstreamed and totalized. Ironically then, and this is largely due to positivist criminologies which expound the manifestation of an inverted or pathologically skewed rationality, crime can be viewed as an alternative form of work, as in 'ducking and diving', 'making a living', 'getting-by', 'career criminals', 'professional criminals' – indeed, the dark side of modernity's elan towards surplus and excess. What I want to assert here is that we might profitably view crime as a sustaining mode of leisure. Subsequently I shall argue that such alternative realities are maintained through the fragile consensus and value systems upheld in subcultural forms (Jenks, 2004).

Crime is a juridical definition of an act, crime is not in the least the same thing as transgression, yet within any particular sociohistorical-political order a transgressive act may become identified as such and thus processed in the form of criminality. The populace does not engage in such interpretive niceties. We, as members of a society, do not seek to understand the assault, the loss, the disarray and the violence that surrounds us through the subtleties of theory. Non-normative deeds are 'bad' deeds and the collective consciousness attempts to reconcile these irregularities through the methods of positivist criminology, or a commonplace version thereof.

What are the causes of crime? Well, as a liberal society we have come to address this question, regularly, through an equation of nature and nurture. People's intrinsic nature or their upbringing have made them as they are and statistical and correlative analysis can lead to a high degree of predictability, or at least a high degree of *post hoc* explainability, in relation to their current actions.

We have learned, however grudgingly, that bad acts perpetrated today are brought about through the past. Previous dispositions and events precipitate criminality. To this extent criminals are victims of the past and our understanding of the etiology of their acts provides a mitigation for the 'abnormal' urge that could have possibly motivated such acts. However, this positivist criminological mode is not without difficulties, the first being its singular failure, as a driver of policy, to diminish let alone contain the levels of criminality within modern society but the second is more epistemological. It can be routinely demonstrated that, however compelling the data and whatever the veracity of the biogenetic, psychological, sociohistorical, political or even ecological variables concerning crime, it is clearly the case that many people who similarly occupy these causal categories appear wholly unmoved by them. That is, individuals who share similar or identical causal backgrounds to known criminals do not themselves commit crime. Beyond this many individuals who commit criminal acts do not occupy all or any of the significant causal categories. And further still, individuals who do and individuals who do not fit the causal categories may either commit or not commit the anticipated crimes for extended periods – the science cannot predict a single way of life. Such recognitions begin to divert our understandings of the criminal act away from determinism along the continuum towards free will, or at least the issue of choice.

Katz, a leading and in many senses an isolated figure in existential criminology, begins his stimulating thesis in the following provocative manner:

> The study of crime has been preoccupied with a search for background forces, usually defects in the offenders' psychological backgrounds or social environments, to the neglect of the positive, often wonderful attractions within the lived experience of criminality. The novelty of this book lies in its focus on the seductive qualities of crimes: those aspects in the foreground of criminality that make its various forms sensible, even sensuously compelling, ways of being. (Katz, 1988: 3)

So people may, and indeed do, commit criminal acts because they choose to, because they want to or, perhaps most difficult to grasp, because they like it! They like it, they take pleasure in it, they pass their time through it, they may acquire mastery in it, they may exercise choice through it, find fulfilment through it, it may be exciting and distracting – it might constitute a leisure pursuit not the exercise of labour power. If the transgressive act and the criminal act are often compounded, which in an increasingly governed society they inevitably are, then it is essential that the element of choice is elected as a sovereign principle (Jenks, 2003). We cannot conceive of a truly existential transgressive act where the individual was driven to it by the past, by forces out of his or her control. This would be a life of marginalization not a life on the edge. If boundaries, prohibitions and taboos are to be tested in a transgressive manner then the relationship between the perpetrator and the act must be wilful and intended, not accidental or unconscious.

> Whatever the relevance of antecedent events and contemporaneous social conditions, something causally essential happens in the very moments in which the crime is committed. The assailant must sense, then and there, a distinctive constraint or seductive appeal that he did not sense a little while before in a substantially similar place. Although his economic status, peer group relations, Oedipal conflicts, genetic makeup, internalized machismo, history of child abuse, and the like remains the same, he must suddenly become propelled to commit the crime. Thus, the central problem is to understand the emergence of distinctive sensual dynamics. (Katz, 1988: 4)

Katz, quite precisely, illuminates the wilful and the intended, he recommends the study of the foreground rather than the background of crime, and he invites us to attend to the qualities that the transgressive act may hold for its perpetrator rather than attending to legal sanction or social outrage. This is no right-wing backlash theory attempting to diminish the impact of decades of liberal tolerance, this is an action theory attempting to demonstrate how assumed categories of being become transformed into actual and particular courses of action, how choice disposes time spent. We conventionally explain and attempt to understand crime in a fixed relation with rationality. A classical and highly influential example of this is provided by Merton (1968) who argues, in short, that some forms of criminality may be a manifestation of people attempting to achieve an appropriate end through an inappropriate means, that is, we all need money, not all of us have money, not all of us can earn money, so some of us have to steal to acquire money. With this kind of thinking the normative structure is retained at the highest level of generality – shared value-orientations. In Merton's model crime displaces work as a form of acquisition, production and accumulation (albeit misplaced and disapproved of). On the streets real people rob and even kill for no significant or even discernable material gain. Surely what we are dealing with is not a rational issue but a moral and emotional issue. An issue that might well be considered as a form of leisure.

> The closer one looks at crime ... the more vividly relevant become the moral emotions. Follow vandals and amateur shoplifters as they duck into alleys and dressing rooms and you will be moved by their delights in deviance ... Watch their strutting street display and you will be struck by the awesome fascination that symbols of evil hold for the young men who are linked in the groups we often call gangs ... The careers of persistent robbers show us, not the increasingly precise calculations and hedged risks of 'professionals,' but men for whom gambling and other vices are a way of life, who are 'wise' in the cynical sense of the term, and who take pride in a defiant reputation as 'bad.' And if we examine the lived sensuality behind events of cold-blooded 'senseless' murder, we are compelled to acknowledge the power that may still be created in the modern world through the

sensualities of defilement, spiritual chaos, and the apprehension of vengeance. (Katz, 1988: 312)

What Katz is also telling us, and this is an issue critical to our thesis on leisure, is that such acts, be that defined as deviant, transgressive, criminal, wicked, non-normative, naughty or bad, are not just the province of particular groups. The desire, their sensual attraction, belongs to us all.

> Perhaps in the end, what we find so repulsive about studying the reality of crime – the reason we so insistently refuse to look closely at how street criminals destroy others and bungle their way into confinement to save their sense of purposive control over their lives – is the piercing reflection we catch when we steady our glance at those evil men. (ibid.: 324)

This chilling reflexive turn in Katz's conclusion, the 'know thyself' clause which steadies the hand of the social theorist but weakens the foundations of his moral highground can be instructive in ways other than the spuriously democratic. Here let us sustain the theme of the transgressor 'saving their sense of purposive control over their lives' (Katz quoted above) which may well be an accelerative feature of the late-modern condition. Lyng (1990) develops the concept of 'edgework'. We can produce 'edgework' as on a spectrum with all excessive conduct previously considered but as micro, interactional and, most crucially, intended. Its function to transgress I nevertheless ascribe to a condition of contemporary social life. Edgework might take the form of rock and ice climbing, bungee jumping, parachuting, hang-gliding, flying microlights, motor racing, white-water rafting, downhill skiing – activities that announce sport and leisure but also carry significant and recognized threats to personal safety. That an activity should be potentially life-threatening is essential to the notion of 'edgework'. The 'edge', Lyng suggests, can be defined variously through dichotomies opposing life/death, consciousness/unconsciousness, and the ordered self/disordered self. There is a tendency to transfer of training in edgework, so rock climbers, for example, may also be excessive drinkers or obsessive trainers. What is central to the activity is a sense of self-realization or determination. It is critical that the ego becomes realized in an almost histrionic context. It is not the case, either, that edgeworkers are fearless. Precisely part of the frisson of the activity is the experience of fear, its control and the perverse pleasure that this combination can provide. The capacity that such sensation has for pressing the individual beyond the experience of the normal and the everyday, on a dramatic scale, enables us to suggest that edgework has an elitist orientation; it always elevates the individual above the mundane. Apart from the obvious chemical reactions that sudden infusions of adrenalin can produce, the approach to the edge, the excessive step across the boundary, ensures that the individual's perceptions become extremely acute and concentrated. This, in turn, has an effect on the experience of time. Such temporal mastery is not without appeal, no longer do we wait but instead time stands still or is held at the convenience of completion. Another experience at the edge is that of cognitive mastery of a situation, but also a symbiosis with the environment

– people become 'at one with their machines', 'part of the wave' or 'continuous with the rock'. All these symptoms and sensations, inventoried by Lyng, resonate strongly with the postmodern preoccupation with the 'hyperreal'. Quite often the experience of edgework is too overwhelming to be expressed in language (in the same way that the actions of the Kray Twins, Ian Brady and Myra Hindley, Fred and Rose West and child killers just walked off the edge of language). Rock climbers fall back on mundanities like 'because it was there ...'.

Unlike chance activities such as gambling, but just like violent crime against the person, edgework demands a level of control and never simple abandonment. Random chance or caprice do not signify. Edgework becomes coherent when understood in relation to the contemporary 'risk society' that Beck (1992) and Douglas (1992) have introduced us to. If our governance, technology and social strategies seek to minimize and militate against risk, then edgework provides the individual antidote; it is the 'spontaneous, anarchic, impulsive character of experience' (Lyng, 1990: 864). Lyng also tells us that for Turner (1976) identity construction takes place between the polarities of 'institution' and 'impulse' and that we are not all evenly distributed between the expression of 'constraint' and 'spontaneity'. This is leisure juxtaposed not to work but to moral constraint.

Modern social theory is not wholly pessimistic concerning our inevitable compliance with late-modernities over-socialization and potential alienation, and many suggest that a central dynamic of today is the incessant search for self. This can become corrupted, however, into the narcissism that Lasch (1980) describes through infatuated and obsessional consumption, or what Giddens (1991) sees as the nostalgic management of ontological anxiety through psychoanalysis. People often seek spontaneity and freedom from constraint through 'edgework' which imitates the characteristics of such action. 'Edgework' focuses on the general ability to maintain control of a situation that verges on total chaos. It does so however, through the luxury of desired choice and through the exercise of highly specific skills, both hyperbolic instances of leisure defining practices.

The mediating concept selected to organize these sets of concerns is that of subculture. What is being argued is that crime, a major sociological phenomenon conventionally categorized as a problem, though sometimes reasoned into a misplaced form of work, income and productivity, might as easily and usefully be understood as a form of leisure. As demonstrated it shares a number of the definable characteristics of leisure activities. Why it has not been previously understood as a form of leisure, a pastime, an enjoyment and a mode of self-realization is that such a move might appear to justify and approve what is commonsensically 'known' to be immoral conduct. However, this move is neither unthinkable nor libertarian if one conceives of the value system that supports such pursuits being held outside of the mainstream consciousness and perpetuated through subcultural codes and symbolism. This is, of course, a perhaps over exaggerated bifurcation and insulation of the 'good' and the 'bad' given the spectrum of criminality that occurs across the spectrum of the populace, but it demonstrates that there are symbolic places for individuals to occupy if they need to justify their conduct as something other than absurdly pathological. Let us look at what subcultures supposedly do, what they are for.

Hebdige's (1979) excellent exposition of subculture, though in many ways historically specific, has evolved, ironically, into an orthodoxy on the topic. His ethnographic case studies of punks, mods, teds and rastas are clearly reminiscent of an earlier era and his conceptualization of the central analytic issues in terms of Gramsci via Althusser (with interventions from Situationism) have also been outstripped by more contemporary developments in social, cultural and political theory. Hebdige, of course, emerged from a tradition that followed in the wake of Hoggart's (1985) neo-Leavisite representation of working-class England's folkways and mores. Hebdige and the scholars focused around the Birmingham Centre for Contemporary Cultural Studies (CCCS) group mobilized the idea of subculture to articulate the unspoken, or perhaps unheard, voices of a populist proletariat within a critical vision and still with an eye to radical social change. Stuart Hall provided the drive and the impetus of that group and his particular version of Marxism provided the theoretical framework. The whole Birmingham CCCS tradition, however, seemed largely content to restrict the idea of subculture to the pastime and possession of youth and, for some of its indigenous critics (McRobbie, 1981; Gilroy, 1987), mostly male youth and perhaps even white male youth:

> There have been studies of the relation of male youth to class and class culture, to the machinery of the State, and to the school, community and workplace. Football has been analyzed as a male sport, drinking as a male form of leisure, and the law and the police as patriarchal structures concerned with young male (potential) offenders. I don't know of a study that considers, never mind prioritises, youth and the family; women and the whole question of sexual division have been marginalised. (McRobbie, 1981: 111)

In such a context the previously powerful device presented in the form of the concept 'subculture' begins to degrade. As such it becomes interpretable as little more than the noise of white, male adolescence, irksome at times but reparable through maturation.

However, the concept subculture did not begin either with Hebdige or the Birmingham group. Subculture is a concept with a long, but largely forgotten, history. An archaeology of the concept 'subculture' reveals trace elements of the idea even to within the classic sociological tradition. The founding fathers employed such devices to reconcile the desired stability of the post-revolutionary European society with the inevitable recognition of accelerative and compound social change wrought through modernity's relentless progress. For example, Durkheim's vision of the multiple mechanicisms of workgroups and guilds functioning as a microcosms for the overall interdependence of organic solidarity.

At a different stage in the development of our discipline the Chicago School in the US had made strenuous efforts to elevate the lifeworld of the 'underdog' into an intelligible, and manageable, form through urban studies, biographical methods, social reaction theory, labelling theory, typification vignettes and essentially through the assembling device of the subculture. At its most modest the Chicago School can be seen to employ the concept of subculture to highlight the symbolic normative structure of groups smaller than the society as a whole. This is a micro-sociology, or perhaps a microcosmic sociology, that gives voice to and directs our attention to the ways in which such groups differ in such elements as their language, belief systems, values, mannerisms, patterns of behaviour and lifestyle from the mainstream, larger society of which they are also a part.

From a wholly different political position Talcott Parsons claimed the concept of subculture and incorporated it in a masterly fashion within the cybernetics and autopoesis of the *Social System* such that all deviant and non-normatively oriented conduct could be absorbed within the scheme of central values. This was no simple diversion, it was this arresting appropriation of the concept subculture that informed much of the positivist criminology and social pathology emanating from the US and setting the ground rules for this subdiscipline up to the late 1950s. What we have here is a much more conflictual model. The subculture is not a part within a part within a whole. In the Parsonian universe, central values stay central and the concept of a subculture designates a group, an enclave, a cult or a distraction of antithetical values that are expressions of either frustrations with or interventions into the dominant structure of legitimation and control within society. These are usually realized in terms of the pathological relationship between social structure and personality and are largely viewed in a remedial manner.

Definitions and versions proliferate and origins are obscure. It has been argued by Wolfgang and Ferracuti (1967) that the term 'subculture' was not widely employed in the social science literature until after the Second World War. Lee (1945) is cited as making the first use of the term, closely followed by Gordon (1947), who is quoted defining subculture as:

> a subdivision of a national culture, composed of a combination of factorable social situations such as class status, ethnic background, regional and rural or urban residence, and religious affiliation, but forming in their combination a functional unity which has an integrated impact on the participating individual. (Gordon, 1947: 40)

Another definition from around the same time states that:

> The term 'subculture' refers ... to 'cultural variants displayed by certain segments of the population.' Subcultures are distinguished not by one or two isolated traits – they constitute relatively cohesive social systems. They are worlds within the larger world of our national culture. (Komarovsky and Sargent, 1949: 143)

And so we evolve through:

> A society contains numerous subgroups, each with its own characteristic ways of thinking and acting. These cultures within cultures are called subcultures. (Mercer, 1958: 34)

to:

> Such shared learned behaviors which are common to a specific group or category
> are called subcultures. (Young and Mack, 1959: 49)

These preceding examples are not isolated, the history of the concept comprises a
vivid mosaic but each segment demonstrates a political move, and each exemplar
reveals a step outside of the kernel sense of the social, for supportive or critical reasons.
In this context, the concepts of identity, difference and selfhood are addressed and
from within a post-structuralist paradigm the politics of knowledge are now reviewed
in terms of identity politics, affinity politics, standpoint epistemologies and the
narratives of post-colonialism. Each of these moments is itself held in a tension
with tenuous clusterings of the social, or rather the subcultural and we look to the
heroic potentialities for liberation within the groupings of, for example, women,
'queer' folk, black consciousness, childhood or even cyborgs. These moments, in
turn, highlight the necessity of a theory or mode of concept formation that enables
what has come to be known as the middle range. That is, an order of construct,
like subculture, which retains the causal necessity of the social but overcomes
the mysterious leap between, for example, Durkheim's structural constraints (the
outside) and an individual act of self-destruction (the inside). Such argument both
retains the necessity of the social and relocates the subcultural.

As early as 1960, Yinger wrote in the US:

> In recent years there has been widespread and fruitful employment of the concept
> of subculture in sociological and anthropological research. The term has been used
> to focus attention not only on the wide diversity of norms to be found in many
> societies but on the normative aspects of deviant behaviour. The ease with which
> the term has been adopted, with little study of its exact meanings or its values
> and its difficulties, is indicative of its utility in emphasizing a sociological point
> of view in research that has been strongly influenced both by individualistic and
> moralistic interpretations. To describe the normative qualities of an occupation,
> to contrast the value systems of social classes, or to emphasize the controlling
> power of the code of a delinquent gang is to underline a sociological aspect of
> those phenomena that is often disregarded. (Yinger, 1960: 625)

This is in large part supportive of the endeavour of a number of subcultural theorists
to honour the norms, life ways and values of members of some groups which at
a systems level might be disregarded as dysfunctional, irrational, sick or deviant.
However, addressing more metatheoretical considerations, he continues:

> It is unfortunate that 'subculture,' a central concept in this process, has seldom
> been adequately defined. It has been used as an *ad hoc* concept whenever a writer
> wished to emphasize the normative aspects of behavior that differed from some
> general standard. The result has been a blurring of the meaning of the term,

confusion with other terms, and a failure frequently to distinguish between two levels of social causation. (ibid.: 625–6)

And I would concur with this point. We cannot simply elect to define a group of people whose proximity or range of activities has fallen under our analytic gaze as a subculture unless we express a clear epistemological purpose. Now if that purpose is to indicate the very difference of that group of people or the conscious antagonism of that group of people to what the body of people in their wider society think or believe then, as Yinger (1960) points out, we might properly employ the concept of a 'contraculture'. Perhaps the purpose of subcultural work is to demonstrate inconsistencies between a particular group's practices and that of the mainstream and to reveal further the systematic strategies that they employ to guarantee a reproduction of those inconsistencies then we may be implying that subcultures exercise agency, their difference is self-consciously meaningful action. As such they might sustain as leisure what the majority excise as pathological. However far we push the definitional necessity of subcultures bearing a relationship to some sense of a wider normative structure (be that a soft or hard conceptualization) then we are still left with the problem of boundaries. Downes (1966) interrogating the concept in relation to an explanation of delinquent activity expresses this well:

> no culture can be regarded as a completely integrated system. Most cultures, like personalities, can be regarded as permeated by apparent contradictions.
> The concept of the 'subculture' embodies one such contradiction. What constitutes the 'culture' of a complex society: all its subcultures, their uniformities only, or the dominant subculture? Where, to put it crudely, does culture end and subculture begin? Does subculture merely refract or totally displace culture? Any vagueness over the boundaries of the overall culture will automatically extend to subcultures. (Downes, 1966: 4–5)

Downes continues to address the elusive nature of this boundary yet is drawn to proceed in his criminological analysis on the basis of his own typology which, though clear, continues to evade the question that he himself has raised. He says that subcultures may be classified into two main kinds, one of which contains two subcategories:

(a) those which precede, or are formed *outside* the context of the 'dominant culture': for example, the 'culture' of immigrant groups which become 'subcultures' in the context of the host culture; also, regional subcultures which precede, but come to co-exist, merge with or differentially respond to the enveloping 'dominant culture'.
(b) those which originate *within* the context of the dominant culture: these fall into two sub-categories:
  (i) those which emerge in *positive* response to the demands of the social and cultural structures; for example, occupational subcultures, age-group subcultures, and

298 A Handbook of Leisure Studies

      (ii) those emerging in *negative* response to the social and cultural structures' demands; e.g. delinquent subcultures; religious-messianic-revivalist subcultures; political-extremist subcultures. (Downes, 1966: 9)

One of the evasions here is concerning the internal coherence and ontological status of such subcultures, that is, are we to assume that the members of such groups know that they are members of such groups and that such groups actually exist as reality structures. The other evasion concerns the epistemological status of such subcultures, that is, are they all, in a significant sense, actually theoretical devices used to formulate collective action for specific rhetorical, political or moral purposes. For example, the maintenance of a coherent sense of criminal activities as leisure activities.

Although the motivation to describe and explain slices of life in the mould of subcultures may, in most non-Parsonian instances, be to insulate, to ideal-type, to retain a difference and an essence, to politicize and to render equivalent, it is also a dereliction of the sociologist's commitment to explain the social in terms of the social (or at least engage with the problems that such an imperative entails). Now the situation is clearly not an either/or but without the buttress of intervening theorizing about levels, constraint and social control, and to opt unreflexively for the use of subculture as a source of explanation begins a reduction. Yet we must concede alternative, self-sustaining definitions of the situation, however fragile or implausible at first glance. Subcultures can, and do, support leisure activities even though their binding value-systems may appear strange, alien or abhorrent. Strange as it may seem, this author can understand, but not appreciate, watching football as a valid form of leisure.

Perhaps the story begins rather further back. Totalizing concepts like 'society' and 'social systems' have never had a practical currency within the explanatory frameworks of lay members of any particular social group. Perhaps we might argue that since the 1960s in the West 'society' has become part of a quasi-political rhetoric of mitigation for the unwanted or unintended consequences of human action. It designates a dull, deep-seated, impersonal causality for which no one person has to claim unique responsibility. Even at times of severe external threat, like war, when Durkheim convincingly disserted that social solidarity would reach an unprecedented intensity, it is empirically unlikely that previously experienced forms of difference, stratification, inclusion and exclusion would become resolved through more than the expressive mode of a new and transitory sense of nationhood. Society then is essentially an analytical device both contrived and espoused by sociology in its earliest incarnations, to establish the specific and distinct ontology that all scientific paradigms require to announce their difference from all previous types of understanding. Society is a structuralist trope routinely employed to designate and summarize all of the universal, ideal, essential and peculiarly human dispositions that ensure their tendency to opt for clustering rather than isolation. More than this, society is an inevitable growth out of moral philosophy that saves humankind from the sad and shallow reductions that are required through its explanation with reference to psychology's 'behaviour', 'market forces' in economics, and 'the state' in politics. The actual empirical referent of 'society' is people's perpetual, though variable, sense of the 'social' and 'sociality'. The laudation and illumination of this fine and irrepressible human sentiment was sociology's rightful purpose at its inception, not some cynical attempt at intellectual entrepreneurship or epistemological imperialism. And this is worthy of retention.

Real, material people know about love, attraction, affection, care, altruism, obligation, contracting, expectation, togetherness, solidarity, loyalty, belonging, and so on, without being able to, or indeed needing to, point at an object form called society. Sociologists speak of society while lay members know about and act in relation to family, friendship, community, organization, institution and group membership. Clearly what is at work here is not a confusion or a competition between different reality structures, nor even the existence of parallel world. In reality what we are witnessing is the practice of construction or transformation from one order, the 'lived', into another order, the 'conceptual'. This transformation implies no hierarchy of validity, but certainly the latter seeks to understand more fully the former and to do so by extraction, clarification, and releasing the everyday world from the grip of commonsense (or what ethnomethodology would refer to as the taken-for-granted). In a strong sense then, the sociologist's invocation of 'society' makes reference to the lay member's cognitive and affective architecture which enables his or her bonding with others.

It has been argued that the signifier 'society' implies a description of a nation-state or a population, but this is relatively worthless in attempting to discern meaning. Nation-states are historical, arbitrary, sometimes geographical and almost always internally divisive units symbolically united by language – sometimes. Population, on the other hand, is a strictly statistical category. Demographic trends are *post hoc* descriptions of stability or instability, they are not explanations of meaningful human action and motive.

Society must remain an ideal conceptualization of a collective consciousness which exerts constraint upon individual action with the function of sustaining groups, formations and networks of interaction. This is the level that sociologists have continued to refer to as the 'macro' as opposed to the 'micro'. Any shift towards the micro, as is instanced by the espousal of the term 'subculture' must take care not to liberate its object of study from the constraints of the totality. Subcultures cannot in any sense be meaningfully insulated from the society of which they are an inevitable part. Subcultural theories are obliged to express their coherence with social theories from which they emerged.

Gelder and Thornton (1997), addressing a similar range of concerns, state the following:

What is a 'subculture'? What distinguishes it from a 'community'? And what differentiates these two social formations from the 'masses', the 'public', 'society', 'culture'? These are obstinate questions to which there is no agreed answer, but rather a debate – the problem at the root of which is about how scholars imagine and make sense of people, not as individuals, but as members of discrete populations or social groups. Studies of subcultures are attempts to map the social world and, as such, they are exercises in representation. In attempting to depict the social world or translate it into sociology (or cultural studies or any of the other disciplines that are active in the field), we are unavoidably involved in a process of construction. (Gelder and Thornton, 1997: 1)

But they go on to say:

'Community' is perhaps the label whose referent is closest to subculture, to the degree that several contributors use the term interchangeably. Nevertheless, there are subtle disparities between the two concepts, which affect when and why one or the other is applied in any case. (ibid.: 2)

They then remind us that communities conventionally suggest a greater permanence than subcultures, that they tend to be geographically aligned to a specific locale, and that in general they comprise of families and kinship groups. All of this is coherent with what we came to know as British community studies through, for example, the work of Young and Willmott (1957), Willmott (1963), Townsend (1957) and Jackson and Marsden (1962). However, there is a more analytic point to be made which is illuminated by Harris (2001) when he says:

Community is an old and venerable sociological concept that developed in sociology's 'classic period' and has only recently begun to be problematised. It is, moreover, one area of debate within which sociology can plausibly claim to be part of the 'reflexivity of modernity'. Community is a concept with powerful resonances among non-sociologists, and lay and sociological uses inform each other. To call something a community is to link it into an intense signifying chain with positive connotations such as locality, solidarity, closeness and mutual support. (Harris, 2001: 37)

What this opens up is a further, important, distinction in the classifications that sociologists might employ which is often confused or conflated in the application of the concept subculture. We can attempt to classify different forms of social group and we can attempt to classify different forms of social relationship. The former is about scale and proximity the latter is about texture and integration.

When we speak about classifying social groups we might make reference to Simmel's (1902) highly sophisticated micro-sociology, his analyses of the dynamics within dyads and triads and his exposition of the interwoven links between the physical size of a group, the organization or structure of a group and character of the relationships that exist within such groups. All this Simmel refers to as 'the quantitative determination of certain divisions and of certain groups'. Much later Homans (1948) attempted a not wholly satisfactory taxonomy of human groups based not so much on how they diverge as on the ways in which they overlap. This was a micro-sociological attempt to elicit high-level generalizations concerning the nature of social interaction. Subsequently Gurvich (1957) set out an extremely abstract and complex matrix through which different types of social group may be determined.

> It is clear that every organised group is also structured. However, a group may not only be structurable, but also structured, without also being organised, nor even capable of being organised, not even capable of being expressed in a single organisation (such as social classes, which are a patent example of this). Further, when organisation enters into the equilibrium of a structure, it is no more than one element, and not even an indispensable one at that. (Gurvich, 1957: 60)

He exercises 15 criteria which include size, proximity, duration, function, and so on. The scheme claims to be exhaustive.

When we speak about classifying different forms of social relationship we enter into a far less cold, technical and empirical realm (though this would not be a fair way to describe Simmel's work which is equally instructive about the texture of relationships). In this context we are aggregating and disaggregating different manners of relationship, social bond or solidarity. It is this context that classical sociological theory has made some of its most telling and lasting pronouncements. Perhaps most noticeably Durkheim, in his thesis on the division of labour in society, provided us with two formative modes of collection and integration that he referred to as 'mechanical' and 'organic' solidarity. These were intangible entities yet experienced as the social sentiments of societal members; sociologically these are powerful devices for establishing a link between the social bond and the symbolic order in terms of both chronology and complexity. Mechanical solidarity is a highly condensed symbolic experience and organic is much more diffuse, one may well evolve from the former, both absolutely fit the going order and both appropriately demonstrate the intense interrelation between action, affect and social structure. Even before Durkheim, Tönnies (1887) had developed his thesis which distinguished between '*Gemeinschaft*' and '*Gesellschaft*', concepts which have come to be transposed as ideal-typical representations of 'community' and 'association' (or 'society'). This twofold scheme can and has been applied to the distinction between groups as well as the distinction between societies but, as in the case of Durkheim, the idea was clearly inspired by the advent and march of modernity along an evolutionary yet unpredictable path. And earlier still, in 1876, the anthropologist Maine drew an enlightening separation between those societies whose relationships are ordered by 'status' and those that are ordered by 'contract'. In Maine's writing, this primary distinction parallels a second, namely the distinction between 'static' and 'progressive' societies. The gradient from stasis to progress often being specified by the development of civil laws which shift the focus of control from the individual to the family. There are striking homologies between these various lines of theorizing.

The idea of subculture takes us to a range of places and opens up a spectrum of debate. It challenges us to question our firmly held views of 'proper' or 'appropriate' conduct. Subculture takes us to a series of locations not populated solely by the 'mad, bad and dangerous to know' but by groups, collectivities, shared values, perhaps another collective unconscious which inverts our 'looking glass selves'. In a subcultural world leisure may not be restricted to sport, trainspotting, hiking, surfing the net, watching TV and all of those decent and respectable activities that we variously honour and applaud. Rather we might confront a vocabulary of leisure that includes theft, vandalism, violence against the person, exotic sexual practices and perhaps even murder.

This is no postmodern dystopia but a conscious acknowledgement of what we have always known. Any discussion of postmodernism has to begin with a discussion of what modernity is and has been. Subculture, a fragmentary device, may be employed in the context of this debate to see these wider issues in relation to ourselves as temporal, that is as operating through a time consciousness, but also to our positioning in space. Modernity, with its implicit clarity concerning issues like work and leisure, may well be an incomplete project but we are therefore left with a series of contemporary politics that drop into all of the traps that postmodernity sets up for them. Not least that pitfall concerning morality which is difficult to reconstitute on a subcultural basis. Where to take politics now? How to make judgements concerning the 'good' on grounds which are other than short term or merely pragmatic?

Bibliography

Beck, U. (1992) *Risk Society: Towards a New Modernity*, London, Sage.

Deem, R. (1986) *All Work and No Play: The Sociology of Women and Leisure*, Milton Keynes, Open University Press.

Douglas, M. (1970) *Purity and Danger*, Harmondsworth, Penguin.

Douglas, M. (1992) *Risk and Blame: Essays in Cultural Theory*, London, Routledge.

Downes, D. (1966) *The Delinquent Solution: A Study in Subcultural Theory*, London, Routledge.

Gelder, K. and Thornton, S. (eds) (1997) 'General Introduction' to *The Subcultures Reader*, London, Routledge.

Giddens, A. (1991) *Modernity and Self-Identity: Self and Society in the Late Modern Age*, Oxford, Polity Press.

Gilroy, P. (1987) *There Ain't No Black in the Union Jack*, London, Unwin Hyman.

Gordon, M. (1947) 'The Concept of the Sub-culture and its Application', *Social Forces* 26 (October): 27–42.

Green, E., Hebron, S. and Woodward, D. (1990) *Women's Leisure, What Leisure: A Feminist Analysis*, London, Macmillan.

Gurvich, G. (1957) *The Social Framework of Knowledge*, (English translation), Oxford, Blackwell, 1971.

Harris, K. (2001) 'Transgression and Mundanity: The Global Extreme Metal Music Scene'. Unpublished PhD thesis, University of London.

Hebdige, D. (1979) *Subculture: The Meaning of Style*, London, Routledge.

Hoggart, R. (1985) *The Uses of Literacy*, Harmondsworth, Penguin.

Homans, G. (1948) *The Human Group*, London, Routledge.

Jackson, P. and Marsden, D. (1962) *Education and the Working Class*, London, Routledge.

Jenks, C. (2003) *Transgression*, London, Routledge.

Jenks, C. (2004) *Subculture: The Fragmentation of the Social*, London, Sage.

Katz, J. (1988) *Seductions of Crime: Moral and Sensual Attractions of Doing Evil*, New York, Basic Books.

Komarovsky, M. and Sargent, S. (1949) 'Research into Subcultural Influences upon Personality', in S. Sargent and M. Smith (eds) *Culture and Personality*, New York, The Viking Fund.

Lasch, C. (1980) *The Culture of Narcissism*, London, Abacus.

Lee, A. (1945) 'Levels of Culture as Levels of Social Generalization', *American Sociological Review* 10 (August): 125–43.

Lyng, S. (1990) 'Edgework: A Social Psychological Analysis of Voluntary Risk Taking', *American Journal of Sociology* 95(4): 851–86.

McRobbie, A. (1981) 'Settling Accounts with Subcultures: A Feminist Critique', in T. Bennett (ed.) *Culture, Ideology and Social Process*, London, Batsford.

Maine, S. (1876) *Village Communities in the East and West*, London, John Murray.

Mercer, B. (1958) *The Study of Society*, New York, Harcourt-Brace.

Merton, R. (1968) *Social Theory and Social Structure*, New York, Free Press.

Parson, T. (1951) *The Social System*, New York, Free Press.

Rojek, C. (1994) 'Leisure and the Dreamworld of Modernity', in I. Henry (ed.) *Leisure: Modernity, Postmodernity and Lifestyles*, London, Leisure Studies Association.

Rojek, C. (1995) *Decentring Leisure: Rethinking Leisure*, London, Sage.

Simmel, G. (1902) 'The Number of Members as Determining the Sociological Form of the Group', *American Journal of Sociology* 8: 200–18.

Slater, D. (1998) 'Work/Leisure', in C. Jenks (ed.) *Core Sociological Dichotomies*, London, Sage.

Tönnies, F. (1887) *Community and Association* (English translation), London, Routledge, 1955.

Townsend, P. (1957) *The Family Life of Old People*, London, Routledge.

Turner, R. (1976) 'The Real Self: From Institution to Impulse', *American Journal of Sociology* 81(3): 983–1016.

Veblen, T. (1899) *The Theory of the Leisure Class: An Economic Study of Institutions*, New York, Mentor, 1953.

Willmott, P. (1963) *The Evolution of Community*, London, Routledge.

Wolfgang, M. and Ferracuti, F. (1967) *The Subculture of Violence: Towards an Integrated Theory in Criminology*, London, Tavistock.

Yinger, M. (1960) 'Contraculture and Subculture', *American Sociological Review* 25(5) (October): 625–35 (October).

Young, K. and Mack, R. (1959) *Sociology and Social Life*, New York, American Books.

Young, M. (1963) *Family and Class in a London Suburb*, London, Routledge.

Young, M. and Willmott, P. (1957) *Family and Kinship in East London*, London, Routledge.

18
Leisure and Consumption
Daniel Thomas Cook

Forms and practices of leisure exist in dynamic and uneasy tension with the interests and demands of commerce. Conceptually, leisure and consumption appear to be at odds with one another; practically, in everyday life, they are difficult to disentangle. The steady rise to prominence of a culture of consumption over the course of the twentieth century has been accompanied by the presence of markets and the dominance of a market logic in virtually every corner of social life in the twenty-first (Cross, 2000; Slater, 1997). Leisure, often conceptualized by theorists and practitioners as an escape from the vicissitudes of productive life, can itself hardly escape the pull of capital. New forms of leisure, in fact, are dependent upon media and market forces to garner audiences and procure adherents.

The relationship between leisure and consumption is decidedly one-sided. A perennial concern expressed by scholars and commentators centres on the idea that commercialization presents an incipient challenge to the authenticity and freedom thought to be definitive of leisure (see Dumazedier, 1967; Hemingway, 1999). This is a perspective derived from an essentialist view of leisure, stemming in part from classical Hellenic thought, which holds that the realm of leisure represents an unqualified good, something above and beyond the mundane, perhaps something pure (Sylvester, 1999). For some contemporary thinkers, leisure can be the basis of liberation (Hemingway, 1999), the conduit of community (Arai and Pedlar, 2003) and the vehicle for the movement and expansion of social capital and civic engagement (Putnam 2001; Hemingway, 1999; but see Glover, 2004).

The pursuit of leisure, interestingly, never quite rises to the level of posing a threat to consumption, but rather is often seen as having been taken over by money and the money economy. Kelly and Freysinger lay out the problem – and the structure of the problem – succinctly in a series of questions they pose to the audience for their textbook:

> Has leisure become more consumption and less a dimension of life? ... Have many come to identify leisure with spending money rather than building deeply

satisfying experiences? ... Has the market for mass leisure become so central to our perceived quality of life that we identify satisfaction with spending, and freedom with discretionary income?

What are the contemporary images of leisure? Are they the real: the forest path, the deep conversation, and the moment of shared lightness? Or are they the fake: Las Vegas and the easy excitement of gambling, Disney and the pretend trip around the world, 'ethnic' theme restaurants that actually microwave their menu...? (Kelly and Freysinger, 2000: 60)

The queries, posed with didactic intent, nevertheless reinforce and reveal an underlying contrast. Echoing the critiques of Frankfurt School theorists Adorno and Horkheimer (1944), Kelly and Freysinger superimpose the real/fake dichotomy onto the life/consumption distinction: leisure is real, or can lead to a real existence, while spending and consumption, particularly when focused on entertainment, are facades posing as true experience. Note how consumption is positioned as counter-indicative of a 'dimension of life'.

These distinctions draw upon fundamental and largely unarticulated assumptions and beliefs about the nature of commercial enterprise and the exigencies of money. When examined closely, they map out uneven moral landscapes of value which inform everyday, taken for granted understandings not only about the relationship between leisure and consumption, but also about the uneasy place of economic value in social life. In this chapter, I address the implications of the proposition that leisure has virtually become consumption by examining key theoretical, conceptual and historical underpinnings of leisure consumption. In the process, I situate the moral discourses about leisure and consumption within a larger frame of the tensions and ambivalences surrounding contemporary life under consumer capitalism. The upshot of this endeavour is to offer an analysis which rejects the received dichotomies in favour of a view that neither celebrates or vilifies leisure or consumption outright, but which sees them as culturally viable vehicles for the expression and enactment of various levels and kinds of social meaning. In so doing, I hope to clear a path for a less essentialized, more critical approach.

Veblen and the leisure class

Thorstein Veblen's *The Theory of the Leisure Class* (1899) remains a necessary point of departure for any examination of leisure and consumption. In this oft-celebrated, widely-cited, century-old tract, the American-born Norwegian scholar not only laid out a theory of the named social class under scrutiny but, as well, outlined a conception of human motivation that is generative of social arrangements. Veblen situates his key concepts – pecuniary emulation, conspicuous leisure, conspicuous consumption and invidious distinction – in a social evolutionary framework which plots a linear movement of society in a familiar, modernist trajectory from savagery to barbarism to civilization.

Humans, particularly men, according to Veblen are driven by two basic motivations: a 'distaste' for anything futile or, we might say, non-utilitarian, and a desire to be thought well of by our fellows (ibid.: 15–16). In the early barbarian, predatory state of society, the necessities of hunting (or 'exploits') gave expression to both. Success in hunting by an individual, although readily visible to immediate others at the time of the kill, was not so apparent at other times. The taking and display of trophies (that is, 'booty') – such as the animal pelt, the lion's head and, in the case of warfare, the capture of slaves – gave visual and material evidence of one's overall prowess or success beyond a single act. 'Esteem is gained and dispraise avoided by putting one's efficiency in evidence' (ibid.: 16) and thus 'booty serves as *prima facie* evidence of successful aggression' (ibid.: 17).

In this societal stage, Veblen contended, physical labour like hunting is an honourable undertaking and the best hunters and warriors were held in places of high esteem. But later, labour and physical exertion became 'irksome' and thus devalued (ibid.: 18). This is a change in social value for which he gives no explanation.

Ownership, rather than exploits, became the preferred form of status display. A number of implications flow from this assertion. For one, according to Veblen, the institution of private property, wherever it is found, forms the basis of competition or 'struggle' (ibid.: 23). Possessing wealth is thus a sign of a successful outcome of a struggle. It is economic booty symbolic of a certain kind of skill and prowess. Consumption, rather than being an unworthy end in itself (mere accumulation), serves a different function and a different master. Ownership, as displayed by consumption, is based on the motive of emulation – the desire to be like worthy others (ibid.: 25). Since wealth can be more easily quantified and compared than, say, the exploits of hunting, it is at the ready to be used for social comparison and distinction: 'The possession of wealth confers honour; it is an invidious distinction' (ibid.: 26).

One's wealth, and thus one's social position – like one's hunting prowess – is not readily available for all to see at any one time and must therefore be symbolized and put on display. Leisure and consumption, when made conspicuous, signify social position within the leisure class and between the leisure and non-leisure classes. It is a way of signalling social status. The best way to symbolize one's wealth – a sign of one's success – is to engage in conspicuous waste (ibid.: 85), for example, to use one's time in 'non-productive' ways thereby distancing oneself from productive work (ibid.: 43) and to own, use and display things which are clearly beyond utility (ibid.: 69–71).

Standards of dress (ibid.: 167–87), the elaboration of specified eating utensils for each course of a meal, the vast landscaped gardens of the idle rich, the mansions with rooms and wings rarely occupied and the conspicuous presence of servants are all iconic of the social strata Veblen located as the leisure class. Within the class he described, the keeping of servants as well as the dress, taste and activities of women, particularly of wives, function as a vicarious means of consumption and leisure, giving indication through canons of taste that the male head of the household does *not* engage in productive work. In a similar way, table manners, heraldic devices, forms of speech, ceremonial deference, among other practices, often speak to the social standing of persons present in the encounter as well as refer to their social lineage (ibid.: 68–81). In the descriptions of the symbolic activities of the leisure class, Veblen offers some early intimations of Bourdieu's (1984) notions of cultural capital and habitus.

The expressive, performative dimensions of leisure and consumption

The contemporary relevance of Veblen may, at first, be unclear. No viable leisure class exists today in the so-called developed societies of the global North that would be recognizable to Veblen. The extremely rich who dominate turn-of-the-millennium capitalism, as Rojek (2000: 59–63) points out, are known more for their work ethic and not so much for the conspicuousness of their leisure and consumption. Mary Douglas and Baron Isherwood (1979), furthermore, pose a strong challenge to the notion that emulation and distinction constitute primary or driving motives in social relations, suggesting in their stead the human need to make sense and meaning out of the world.

It is not, I contend, either in the historical reality of a leisure class or in the details of this class that provide scholars insight into contemporary leisure. It is rather in the linking together of leisure and consumption from the outset as expressive activities, as practices which encode social meaning, which keep Veblen's concepts on the tips of the tongues of many consumption-leisure theorists. Veblen offers, in sum, what amounts to an algorithm for social semantics whereby displaying one's position vis-à-vis others is inseparable from enacting status competition, performing social distinction and emulating the behaviour of desired others.

Veblen's work stands side by side important works of his contemporaries, most notably Sigmund Freud's *The Interpretation of Dreams* (originally published in 1900) and William James's *The Principles of Psychology* (originally published in 1890), in that all three thinkers posit a view of humans as expressive, signifying social creatures. Freud's psychic realm of dreams and James's unfolding phenomenological reality both require interpretation, a deciphering of codes. Veblen's arena is that of the interpersonal, rather than the intrapsychic, where meaning is encountered in and as social display and social action. Leisure and consumption serve foremost as vehicles, as symbols, for the creation and expression of social relationships. Like all symbols, they condense various kinds and levels of meaning into summary form (that is, encoding), requiring interpretation by others to assess their particular import (that is, decoding).

Pecuniary emulation, conspicuous leisure, conspicuous consumption and invidious distinction, however, do not require an identifiable leisure class to be active in social affairs.

A vibrant, working-class street life of entertainment and amusement animated industrial American cities at the time of Veblen's writing. As Kathy Peiss (1986) describes, nickelodeon theatres, trips to amusement parks like Coney Island in New York, socializing in taverns and frequenting dance halls offered both male and female workers their own proprietary spaces and times distinct from the spaces and times owned and controlled by the capitalists in the factories. The workers did not constitute a class of leisure by any means. Yet their leisure and consumption practices were no 'less' symbolic of their social standings, of their social skills and of the social distinctions pertaining between various groups, ethnicities and neighbourhoods than those of the class targeted by Veblen for criticism and satire (see Ewen, 1985; Nasaw, 1993; Chauncey, 1994).

The conception of leisure as liberation seems to describe well the realities of the working classes at the height of the industrial city at the opening of the twentieth century. Another kind of 'liberation' accompanied the concomitant rise to prominence of a consumer-oriented economy and culture in the early twentieth century. Increased productive capacity coupled with a general increase in real income for many in the US context expanded the availability of, and access to, an ever widening array of goods. The urban department store put these goods on display and putatively offered a space where people, particularly women, of different classes could mix and mingle in a variety of ways (Benson, 1986; Leach, 1993).

Consumer culture effectively reorganized many of the social and symbolic arrangements that had pertained between the classes. A kind of 'democratization' of fashion (Kidwell and Christman, 1974), made possible by the ready availability of inexpensive, factory-made goods, disrupted standing modes of class display and class location in that those without much wealth could appear in styles and fabrics once reserved for the wealthy. Those seeking social distinction through exclusive dress and furnishings were thus put into the position of continually distancing themselves from the encroachment of mass fashions, ushering the 'chase-and-flight' dynamic of fashion change theorized by Simmel (1971), elaborated by Bell (1949) and found in modified form in Bourdieu (1984). Progressive, stylistic obsolescence in everything from clothing to home furnishings to automobiles and telephones became a conscious marketing strategy in the 1920s and was made tangible to the buying public with the co-operation and encouragement of the advertising industry (Marchand, 1985; Leach, 1993).

If one strips away the historical particularities of Veblen's leisure class and gives up on the question of whether there is or was such a class exactly in the way he described, then one is left with a view of leisure and consumption as intertwined, socially expressive activities which form the basis, in Rojek's (2000) terms, of contemporary performative culture. The shuffling and reshuffling of social codes and identities brought about by the onslaught of consumer culture did not extinguish the expressive dimensions of leisure and consumption, but exploded them in many directions. Accompanying an increasingly consumption-oriented mode of life have been material and cultural arrangements whereby the co-ordinates of social identity are loose and variable, not fixed upon any single set of attributes or practices, traditions or histories. Leisure and consumption today remain expressive, not of a cleanly identified position in an identifiable hierarchy of a known social class, but of a variety of social locations and cultural positions within a dynamic realm of signs, signifiers and symbols. Absent solid co-ordinates, identity and meaning – because they are not intrinsic stagnant states, but social constructions – are in almost constant need of affirmation and reiteration in order to be kept socially useable, that is, they must be exercised and performed (Goffman, 1967).

Performative culture requires performative selves (Featherstone, 1991) as well as audiences and stages on which to perform. Leisure continues to grow in prominence as a key cultural arena where self and other are at the ready for mutual monitoring, and perhaps for emulation, as the social value of work continues to dissipate (Rojek, 2000, 2001). It is in and through leisure and its display – for example, in the decor of one's home (Miller, 2001), in the staging of romantic encounters (Illouz, 1997), in the entertainments preferred, in the pictures and artefacts on view from the places visited, in the admiration of celebrity (Rojek, 2003) – where selves and identities can be practised, tested out, acquired or discarded. Every performer, as George Herbert Mead (1934) pointed out many decades ago (albeit in different terms), is also simultaneously an actor and an audience member, a necessary partner in the dance between self and not-self. Leisure allows for the play of the self to be engaged even as it embodies and makes material larger arrangements of power, particularly economic power.

The inescapably of the economic

Leisure pursuits can never be divorced completely from economic pursuits. The social meanings of leisure, recreation and entertainment in no way exist apart from the economic system and social arrangements from which they have arisen, but must be understood as derived in some way from them.

For Veblen's class, leisure was not a 'time out of time' or a way to escape the world – it was a way to engage with and in a particular, circumscribed world. Conspicuous leisure was not a retreat but an interaction. It was a form of display of a particular kind to a particular audience. Money, wealth and pecuniary considerations were part and parcel of the social order so described. One look at the classical Greek conception of *schole* shows that it fits easily within Veblen's general approach – only citizens, not slaves or commoners, could be involved in it and it was completely a male undertaking. *Schole* was, in this way, invidious, conspicuous and thus expressive of social position. There were no pretensions about its exclusivity based on gender, class and wealth.

Similarly, if one examines the myriad of leisure forms and practices outlined in Gary Cross's *A Social History of Leisure* (1990), it becomes evident that virtually every such practice – from wagering on bull-baiting to spending time at the ale house, from the playground to modernized, rationalized sports – involved either actual expenditures of money or were implicated in class relations. Peiss's (1986) working-class women, as well, forged their identities through, not despite, commercial leisure. These were not necessarily 'coopted' by capital as much as they were experienced through consumption.

Examples of contemporary, non-commodified leisure are hard to come by because virtually any conceivable activity, regardless of how 'simple' or 'local' it may appear at first, can be found to have been informed by market considerations. Physical exercise requires some sort of gear which often have visible corporate logos and attendant status implications. Having conversations with family or friends often occurs over meals, in coffee shops and on shopping trips. Engaging in hobbyist pursuits – a key site for Putnam's (2001) conception of voluntary, civic engagement – does not free one from the grip of economic capital, as Richard Butsch (1984) pointed out several decades ago. Acts and forms of resistance, like those of Dick Hebdige's (1987) punks or the everyday practices of the women Susan Shaw (1994, 2001) discusses, nevertheless enact and *express* their resistance through forms of consumption – be it in the display of a girls' hockey uniform and gear or in the private spaces of their bedrooms (McRobbie, 1991).

The issue in this regard facing twenty-first-century scholars is not so much the question of whether leisure has been commodified – that much is evident. It is recognizing that many leisure forms, contexts, practices and cultural arenas have arisen *in and as* commercial activity from their inception. Amusement/theme parks, various kinds of urban entertainment as well as the entire spectrum of electronic media from radio to television to the digital play of computer games (Kline et al., 2003) might be some obvious examples. A less obvious, but equally pertinent, illustration would be common behaviour when attending an American baseball game. Having peanuts, ice cream, a hot dog and a drink, wearing insignia of a team and purchasing a scorecard or a souvenir are not separate from the experience of the 'game' but are part and parcel of the experience and have been for the better part of a century. Consumption is not so much brought in to baseball as extracted out of it.

Those concerned about the merging of leisure and consumption fear that consuming leisure – as opposed to, say, engaging in it or 'pursuing' it – destroys the very experience sought. For many people, however, it is evident that 'consuming' leisure is integral to the experience of enjoyment which could not be had otherwise. To return to baseball, Ritzer and Stillman (2001) demonstrate how the postmodern ball park (for example, Pac-Bell park in San Francisco, Comerica Park in Detroit) becomes a hybrid site for entertainment by combining extravaganza with shopping mall features in such a way that attending to the game on the field appears to be secondary to the experience. Leisure, in a similar vein, directly enfolds into consumption when shopping becomes spectacle, as in the great shopping malls in Edmonton and Minnesota (Sorkin, 1992). In addition, the sports store/restaurant/ museum, ESPNZone (Sherry et al., 2001), the NikeTown stores (Sherry, 1998) and American Girl Place in Chicago (Diamond et al., 2004) seamlessly blend 'fun' and spending in a new kind of themed environment (Gottdiener, 1997). Questions of authenticity or purity do not dominate the assessment of visitors' experience here, just as one would not ask about the 'reality' of an amusement park. The staging itself is primary – the staging *is* the event and experience – while elements of 'authenticity' (for example, the NikeTown Chicago display of shoes that Michael Jordan wore) can be sprinkled throughout.

From this perspective, leisure has not virtually *become* consumption. Economic considerations have not merely invaded some pre-existent, untouched realm of leisure in contemporary times, but have been part of the construction of its social meaning perhaps from time immemorial. The sanctified, essentialized view of 'pure' leisure as somehow residing above or beyond economic consideration and as existing in categorical opposition to consumption and pecuniary considerations is itself a relatively new social invention. The idea of authentic or uncontaminated leisure is a reaction similar to those made against the ravages of industrialization in the nineteenth century. That era gave us the familiar notions of pure nature (Lears, 1981), innocent childhood (Zelizer, 1985; Higgonet, 1998) and the celebration of the noble native (Sheller, 2003), all of which have become prime fodder for colonization and commodification.

Purity is a place of moral refuge incompatible with critical analysis. The search for economically untainted leisure is the scholar's version of the touristic quest for authentic experience – an unattainable flight of fancy. It is, as well, an intellectual and analytic cul-de-sac with no way out except by a reverse in direction. Ignoring the necessary interconnections between consumption and avocational practices condemns scholarship and social thought to a kind of futility.

Freedom circumscribed

To make these points, however, in no way endorses or celebrates the ongoing and rampant commodification of leisure evident in contemporary media-saturated societies. Recognizing the inescapability of the economic dimension of all leisure does not then exonerate those interests that continually seek to monopolize the access, meanings, content and boundaries of cultural life.

Over a century ago, Georg Simmel (1900) pointed out that a money economy encourages the exercise and expression of personal freedom which was, for the most part, unencumbered by kin and traditional ties. He couldn't foresee the coming prominence and eventual dominance of media, particularly electronic media, over cultural production and reception. Consequently, he wouldn't have anticipated that the kind of personal freedom which arises out of a monetary system could only be realized, paradoxically, by remaining fastened to the images, structures and relations assembled by, and ultimately for, that system. The 'freedom' of making and finding identities through leisure consumption, to put it another way, has been met by the power of corporate structures and interests to set the parameters from which choices are seen to be choices.

The commodification of leisure and of virtually every important aspect of life (Strasser, 2003), including childhood and the life course itself (Cook, 2004), continues apace because consumption offers an ideologically and practically viable means of asserting and expressing self in a globalizing economy constituted by fractured, quasi-transient social relations and identities. In recent decades in the global North, there has been an ongoing reconciliation or, better, a conflation of market value with social value whereby concerns about the polluting effects of the money economy on everyday life now appear – if they are noted at all – as benign by-products of an essentially free, liberal, capitalist democracy of goods and relations. Goods and consumption have come to be understood by many as being the *means* by which the self can be found, experienced and expressed, not obstacles to it (Miller et al., 1995; Fiske, 1989; Twitchell, 1999). The democratization of goods and the democratization of leisure have enfolded upon one and other to promise a larger realization of the democratization of desire whereby the pursuit of, or the longing for, things and experiences need not be restricted by one's income, social station or ascriptive identity. We can, ideally, all want the same things, pursue the same leisure. In the ideology of corporate democracy now dominant in the early twenty-first century, we are equalized not just by our access to the world of goods and leisure experiences, but by the trajectory of our aspirations.

Distended social aspirations form the crux of Juliet Schor's (1992, 1998) neo-Veblenesque analysis of American work, consumption and leisure. Schor contends that Americans, on average, spend more time working and are in deeper financial debt than in the 1970s (Schor, 1992). They have traded personal, non-work time to acquire the money needed to pay for their increasingly costly consumer lifestyles – lifestyles which have put many into serious, recurring financial debt. The 'upscaling of the American dream' (Schor, 1998) has come about because consumers no longer, as in the past, compare themselves and compete with the neighbours next door who might have slight material and status symbolic advantages. Americans increasingly compete and compare themselves with lifestyles often unattainable for most consumers. These lifestyles exist mainly on television in sitcoms, dramas and shows that laud extravagant homes, vacations and exquisite daily living. The result, according to Schor, is an insidious cycle of see-want-borrow-and-buy that keeps families overworking in pursuit of an unattainable life.

These cycles take place not only along a single dimension of aspiration leading toward the single goal of the large, suburban home and professional lifestyle, but also along multiple dimensions spreading out in many directions. The difference between Veblen's analysis and contemporary experience is not simply one of the degree or range of status display, it is in the ownership of the means of transmission of status display. Television – and electronic media more generally – remain the most prominent forms of leisure activity for Americans and Europeans. The primary purpose for its owners is to deliver segmented audiences to advertisers; entertainment and information are means to that end. It is a commercial medium which, like money, simultaneously individualizes viewers and segments them into lifestyle/consumption groupings the ownership of which is monopolized by an alarmingly few corporate entities (McChesney, 1999).

Pecuniary interests take hold in social cleavages and power relations, particularly those inflected in gender-, sexual-, ethnic-, class- and age-related identities and practices, which themselves serve as the basis for more nuanced marketing categories and advertising appeals. In the multiply referential fields of everyday social display, leisure and consumption continuously interpenetrate and become manifest through performance in specific contexts oriented toward specific audiences. In rave and clubbing culture (Redhead, 1997; Glover, 2003), in African-American street life (Anderson, 1990), on the streets of Rio de Janeiro (Diversi, 2006), on boulevards of upscale shopping districts (Zukin, 2004), on the football field, basketball court or in the stands where the fans reside, identity is enacted in a conversation between reference group exigencies and the corporate owned means of consumption.

Conclusion

We don't live near or beside consumer society, but within it. Consequently, we don't seek, experience, make or find leisure and recreation anywhere else. But, having or making leisure in consumer society does not require that those activities and experiences necessarily take on the same priorities, agendas and postures toward markets as their profit-maximizing creators intend. Having a child's birthday party at a commercial venue does not make that party any less real or important to the child or the parent, especially if the child requested it (McKendrick et al., 2000). In a similar vein, attending a film, playing a video game, trading Pokemon cards (Cook, 2001), engaging in instant messaging on the internet, taking ecstasy at a rave party or listening to music loudly while loitering on a street corner are no less 'real' than hiking the Grand Canyon or practising one's Tai Chi.

The moments of 'real' leisure – the 'deep conversation', the 'forest path' – alluded to by Kelly and Freysinger above gain a good measure of their social value not because they are free in and of themselves, but because of what they are not. They are not immediately and apparently commercialized. They are not motivated exclusively by self interest or profit. Yet as forms of avocational activity in contemporary consumer capitalism, they are also, in Stuart Hall's (1997) term, signifying practices.

One may share a casual evening with friends over a bottle of wine – a bottle that is branded and logoed. The brand of wine may not matter in the enjoyment of the evening, but it nonetheless sits, as a third party, on the table between the friends and, with regard to social analysis, its status as a commodity cannot be ignored. Leisure, 'real' or not, exists *in relation* to the world of commerce. It is not something free in and of itself, but tethered always in some way to the socio-economic world.

The crucial questions posed about leisure and consumption should no longer be framed in terms of real or not real, authentic or inauthentic, pure or polluted, but in terms of whether citizen-consumers will abdicate all thought of questioning and contesting the means through which leisure contexts and experiences become available. The trick here is to avoid leisure fetishism – similar to Marx's kindred notion – and realize that leisure and its meanings can never be exclusively located 'in' objects and venues, but are produced in social relations, including economic, power relations. Arguing over whether this or that moment of recreation is or is not commodified takes away from examining how the recreation is produced and distributed, owned and sold, shared and experienced. The danger of commercialized leisure lies not so much in its commercial origins but in its socio-political trajectories – whether it will be merely reproductive, or decidedly transformative, of our social relations and our lives.

Bibliography

Adorno, T. and Horkheimer, M. (1944) *The Dialectic of Enlightenment*, London, Verso.
Anderson, E. (1990) *Streetwise: Race, Class, and Change in an Urban Community*, Chicago, University of Chicago Press.

Arai, S. and Pedlar, A. (2003). 'Moving Beyond Individualism in Leisure Theory: A Critical Analysis of Concepts of Community and Social Engagement', *Leisure Studies* 22(July): 185–202.

Bell, Q. (1949) *On Human Finery*, New York, A. A. Wyn.

Benson, S. P. (1986) *Counter Cultures: Saleswomen, Managers, and Customers in American Department Stores, 1890–1940*, Champaign, University of Illinois Press.

Bourdieu, P. (1984) *Distinction*, Cambridge, MA, Harvard University Press.

Boyer, C. (1992) 'Cities for Sale: Merchandising History at South Street Seaport', in Michael Sorkin (ed.) *Variations on a Theme Park: the NEW AMERICAN CITY and the End of Public Space*, New York, Hill and Wang.

Butsch, R. (1984) 'The Commodification of Leisure: The Case of the Model Airplane Hobby', *Qualitative Sociology* 7(3): 217–35.

Butsch, R. (ed.) (1990) *For Fun and Profit*, Philadelphia, Temple University Press.

Chauncey, G. (1994) *Gay New York*, Chicago, University of Chicago Press.

Cook, D. T. (2001) 'Exchange Value as Pedagogy in Children's Leisure: Moral Panics in Children's Culture at Century's End', *Leisure Sciences* 23: 81–98.

Cook, D. T. (2004) *The Commodification of Childhood*, Durham, Duke University Press.

Cross, G. (1990) *A Social History of Leisure*, State College, PA, Venture Publishing.

Cross, G. (2000) *An All-Consuming Century: Why Commercialism Won in Modern America*, New York, Columbia University Press.

Diamond, N., Kozinets, R., Sherry, J. F. et al. (2004) 'Making Intergenerational Memories at American Girl Place'. Paper presented at the 2004 Society for Applied Anthropology Annual Conference, Dallas, Texas.

Diversi, M. (2006) 'Street Kids in Nikes: In Search of Humanization Through the Culture of Consumption', *Cultural Studies, Critical Methodologies* (forthcoming).

Douglas, M. and Isherwood, B. (1979) *The World of Goods*, New York, W. W. Norton.

Dumazedier, J. (1967) *Toward a Society of Leisure*, New York, Free Press.

Ewen, E. (1985) *Immigrant Women in the Land of Dollars: Life and Culture on the Lower East Side, 1890–1925*, New York, Monthly Review Press.

Featherstone, M. (1991) *Consumer Culture and Postmodernism*, London and Newbury Park, CA, Sage Publications.

Fiske, J. (1989) *Understanding Popular Culture*, Boston, Unwin Hyman.

Freud, S. (1900) *The Interpretation of Dreams*, Cutchogue, NY, Buccaneer Books, 1985.

Glover, T. D. (2003) 'Regulating the Rave Scene: Exploring the Policy Alternatives of Government', *Leisure Sciences* 25: 307–25.

Glover, T. D. (2004) 'Social Capital in the Lived Experiences of Community Gardeners', *Leisure Sciences* 26: 143–62.

Goffman, E. (1967) *Interaction Ritual: Essays in Face-to-Face Behavior*, Chicago, Aldine.

Gottdiener, M. (1997) *The Theming of America*, Boulder, CO, Westview Press.

Hall, S. (ed.) (1997) *Representation: Cultural Representations and Signifying Practices*, London and Thousand Oaks, CA, Sage.

Hannigan, J. (1998) *Fantasy City*, London, Routledge.

Hebdige, D. (1987) *Subculture: The Meaning of Style*, London and New York, Routledge.

Hemingway, J. L. (1999) 'Critique and Emancipation: Toward a Critical Theory of Leisure', in E. L. Jackson and T. L. Burton (eds) *Leisure Studies: Prospects for the 21st Century*, State College, PA, Venture Publishing, pp. 497–506.

Higgonet, A. (1998) *Pictures of Innocence: The History and Crisis of Ideal Childhood*, New York, Thames & Hudson.

Illouz, E. (1997) *Consuming the Romantic Utopia: Love and the Cultural Contradictions of Capitalism*, Berkeley, University of California Press.

James, W. (1890) *The Principles of Psychology*, New York, H. Holt and Company.

Kelly, J. R. and Freysinger, V. (2000) *Leisure in the 21st Century: Current Issues*, Boston, Allyn & Bacon.

Kidwell, C. B. and Christman, M. C. (1974) *Suiting Everyone: The Democratization of Clothing in America*, Washington, DC, Smithsonian Institution Press.

Kline, S., Dyer-Witherford, N. and de Peuter, G. (2003) *Digital Play: The Interaction of Technology, Culture, and Marketing*, London, McGill-Queen's University Press.

Leach, W. (1993) *Land of Desire: Merchants, Power and the Rise of a New American Culture*, New York, Pantheon Books.

Lears, J. (1981) *No Place of Grace: Antimodernism and the Transformation of American Culture*, New York, Pantheon Books.

Lury, C. (1996) *Consumer Culture*, London, Routledge.

MacCannell, D. (1976) *The Tourist*, New York, Schocken Books.

Malbon, B. (1998) 'Clubbing: Consumption, Identity and the Spatial Practices of Every-night Life', in T. Skelton and G. Valentine (eds) *Cool Places: Geographies of Youth Cultures*, London and New York, Routledge, pp. 266–86.

Marchand, R. (1985) *Advertising the American Dream*, Berkeley, University of California Press.

McChesney, R. W. (1999) *Rich Media, Poor Democracy: Communication Politics in Dubious Times*, Urbana, University of Illinois Press.

McKendrick, J. H. et al. (2000) 'Time for a Party! Making Sense of the Commercialization of Leisure Space for Children', in Sarah L. Holloway and Gill Valentine (eds) *Children's Geographies*, London, Routledge.

McRobbie, A. (1991) *Feminism and Youth Culture: From Jackie to Just Seventeen*, Boston, Unwin Hyman.

Mead, G. H. (1934) *Mind, Self & Society from the Standpoint of a Social Behaviorist*, Chicago, University of Chicago Press.

Miller, D. (ed.) (2001) *Home Possessions*, Oxford, Berg.

Miller, D., Jackson, P., Thrift, N., Holbrook, B. and Rowlands, M. (eds) (1995) *Shopping, Place and Identity*, London, Routledge.

Nasaw, D. (1993) *Going Out: The Rise and Fall of Public Amusements*, New York, Basic Books.

Peiss, K. (1986) *Cheap Amusements*, Philadelphia, Temple University Press.

Putnam, R. D. (2001) *Bowling Alone: The Collapse and Revival of American Community*, New York, Touchstone.

Redhead, S. (ed.) (1997) *The Clubcultures Reader*, Oxford, Blackwell.

Ritzer, G. and Stillman, T. (2001) 'The Postmodern Ballpark as a Leisure Setting: Enchantment and Simulated De-McDonaldization', *Leisure Sciences* 23(2): 99–113.

Rojek, C. (2000) *Leisure and Culture*, New York, St. Martin's Press.

Rojek, C. (2001) 'Leisure and Life Politics', *Leisure Sciences* 23(2): 115–25.

Rojek, C. (2003) *Celebrity*, London, Reaktion Books.

Schor, J. (1992) *The Overworked American: The Unexpected Decline of Leisure*, New York, Basic Books.

Schor, J. (1998) *The Overspent American*, New York, Basic Books.

Shaw, S. M. (1994) 'Gender, Leisure and Constraints: Towards a Framework for the Analysis of Women's Leisure', *Journal of Leisure Research* 26(1): 8–23.

Shaw, S. M. (2001) 'Conceptualizing Resistance', *Journal of Leisure Research* 33(2): 186–201.

Sheller, M. (2003) *Consuming the Caribbean*, London, Routledge.

Sherry, J. (1998) 'The Soul of the Company Store: Nike Town Chicago and the Emplaced Brandscape', in J. Sherry (ed.) *Servicescapes: the Concept of Place in Contemporary Markets*, Lincolnwood, NTC Business Books, pp. 109–46.

Sherry, J. F. Jr, Kozinets, R. V., Storm, D., Duhachek, A., Nuttavvthisit, K. and DeBerry-Spence, B. (2001) 'Being in the Zone: Staging Retail Theatre at ESPN Zone Chicago', *Journal of Contemporary Ethnography* 30(4): 465–510.

Shoval, N. (2000) 'Commodification and Theming of the Sacred', in M. Gottdiener (ed.) *New Forms of Consumption*, Boulder, Rowman & Littlefield.

Simmel, G. (1971) 'Fashion', in D. N. Levine (ed.) *On Individuality and Social Forms*, Chicago, University of Chicago Press, pp. 294–323.

Simmel, G. (1900) *Philosophy of Money*, London and Boston, Routledge & Kegan Paul, 1978.

Slater, D. (1997) *Consumer Culture and Modernity*, London, Polity Press, 324–39.

Sorkin, M. (1992) 'See You in Disneyland', in M. Sorkin (ed.) *Variations on a Theme Park: The New American City and the End of Public Space*, New York, Hill & Wang, pp. 205–32.

Strasser, S. (2003) *Commodifying Everything: Relationships of the Market*, New York, Routledge.

Sylvester, C. (1999) 'The Western Idea of Work and Leisure: Traditions, Transformations, and the Future...', in E. L. Jackson and T. L. Burton (eds) *Leisure Studies: Prospects for the 21st Century*, State College, PA, Venture Publishing, pp. 17–31.

Twitchell, J. (1999) *Lead Us Into Temptation: The Triumph of American Materialism*, New York, Columbia University Press.

Veblen, T. (1899) *The Theory of the Leisure Class*, New York, Viking Press, 1967.

Zelizer, V. (1985) *Pricing the Priceless Child: The Changing Social Value of Children*, New York, Basic Books.

Zukin, S. (2004) *Point of Purchase: How Shopping Changed America*, New York, Routledge.

19

Leisure, Mass Communications and Media

David Rowe

The leisure–mass communications nexus

Leisure and mass communications have an established and increasingly intimate relationship. The two institutions have developed in parallel and in consort, with communication across time and space essential to the popularization and extension of leisure structures and practices, and the media constituting important sites of leisure in their own right. This chapter will, therefore, focus on two key aspects of the leisure–mass communications nexus. First, it will examine the uses of media as forms of leisure activity such as watching television and film; reading newspapers, magazines and books; listening to recorded music and radio; and 'surfing' the internet. Here it can be seen that mass communications and leisure are virtually inseparable in the contemporary world – to the consternation of those who see in this trend a threat to 'serious' and 'healthy' forms and values of leisure. But the apparatus of mass communications also sometimes takes leisure as its object – the leisure of looking at leisure. Second, therefore, the representation of leisure in the media will be considered and analysed as it appears in such forms as tourist brochures and leisure advertisements, and leisure-oriented television programmes and internet sites. Leisure is also represented and scrutinized, more critically, by the media as a social object in relation to such phenomena as health, the body, sexuality, deviancy, violence, labour, idleness and so on. Here media representations of leisure are the means to the exploration of social issues and, frequently, constructed as opportunities for what Cohen (1980: xx) describes as 'moral entrepreneurship', whereby a social problem is identified and solutions proposed under conditions of a self-sustaining 'moral panic'.

Before pursuing these lines of enquiry, though, it is necessary to examine the evolving relationship between mass communications and leisure. As noted above, the media make many forms of leisure possible, and leisure is a key object of media attention. Leisure Studies, as a field of scholarship, has much in common with Media, Communication and Cultural Studies in its commitment to interdisciplinarity and concern with the range of interpenetrating structures and processes shaping contemporary social life (Rowe, 2002). It can be difficult to differentiate these approaches, but the consistent thread within Leisure Studies is its orientation around the leisure–work dialectic. The concept of leisure emerged in response to the rationalization of industrial work-time in the nineteenth century (Clarke and Critcher, 1985) and, despite the constant redrawing of the boundaries between, and the content of, work and leisure since then, the utility of the analytical distinction between paid work and leisure as 'relatively freely undertaken non-work activity' (Roberts, 1978: 3) remains. The process of mass communication and the services provided by the media have been central to the development of contemporary leisure. Indeed, it can be argued that a progressive 'mediatization' of the world has occurred under modernity, as mass communication has become increasingly central to all major (macro and micro) social institutions – political, economic, military, educational, familial, and so on (Curran and Gurevitch, 2000). Whereas the development of mass transport enabled many more people than previously to travel within and between villages, regions and countries, the combination of mass transport and mass communications enabled the media (first in print form, then electronic) to bring the world to increasingly large audiences without ever having to leave home. However, the media's highly efficient delivery of leisure products – standardized items delivered from a single source to widely dispersed populations (Watson, 1998) – involves more than the availability of new forms of leisure provision. The commercial media are also the 'display windows' of the goods and services created in great profusion by the capitalist mode of production.

As leisure became increasingly commodified and industrialized, the old methods of soliciting customers, such as advertising on sandwich boards carried around the streets or through the shouts of traders in marketplaces, could no longer be relied upon. The leisure industries have come to rely on the mass media to connect them to their customer base. The 'discretionary' nature of leisure expenditure means that the requirement to prime demand through the media is especially central to the operation of the leisure industries. This task can be achieved through explicit media advertising and promotion, but also as a by-product of media coverage of leisure practices and organizations. By such means the relationship between mass communications and leisure can be shown to be both extensive and intense, overt and hidden, especially when the popular use of media constitutes leisure practice itself.

Mass communications *as* leisure

The last few centuries, in what we can loosely call the era of modernity – and, now perhaps, the age of postmodernity (Harvey, 1989) – have been characterized by a vast expansion in the institution of the mass media, with knowledge and experience increasingly stored for posterity and communicated to dispersed and disparate human populations. One of the most important existential consequences of this development has been the increased access of larger numbers of people to a widening variety of experiences and to glimpses of 'other worlds'. This access was first provided by the print media, but technological development has enabled many of the world's citizens both to experience distant events vividly and instantaneously, and also to enjoy sights and sounds, such as films and pop songs, that have been specially manufactured for their information and entertainment. The influence of mass communications on leisure activity has been so thoroughgoing that it is difficult to find an appropriate analytical entry point, but initial attention can be given to the leisure activity at which most people (in the Western world at least) spend most of their leisure time – watching television.

Television time use

While there are many different forms of media, and they can be used in various combinations (such as reading a newspaper review of a CD while listening to it), over the last five decades television has been the most important medium for leisure. As Veal and Lynch (2001: 414) have argued, 'Broadcasting dominates modern leisure', a statement that is consistently supported by leisure time-use studies. Golding and Murdock (2000: 86), for example, note that the 'television set [is] an increasingly dominant hub of leisure time and expenditure', with '[o]n average British adults in the 1990s [spending] 26 hours a week watching television broadcasts, and an as yet uncalibrated amount of time using television for related activities, such as viewing videos or playing computer games'. Empirical studies have shown that TV watching is the paramount leisure activity in both gross and relative terms, followed by other media-related leisure activity.

For example, an Australian Bureau of Statistics survey of adult participation in leisure activities in the early 1990s found that 94 per cent of people watched television, followed by listening to radio (76 per cent) and reading (70 per cent), with listening to music (65 per cent) the fifth most popular leisure activity (Brown and Rowe, 1998: 95). In other words, four out of the five leisure activities with the highest levels of participation in this nation-wide study involved media and mass communications. The 'odd' activity out, visiting friends and relatives, no doubt often involved the media in some way, such as watching television together or talking about the latest film or television programme as part of the process of mediatization discussed earlier. The increasing flexibility and availability of mass communications technology mean that it can be integrated into many leisure activities, such as jogging while listening to a Sony Walkman, or being induced to shop for new leisurewear by persuasive product advertisements. The media, therefore, are seamlessly woven into all aspects of everyday leisure and working lives.

Of course, the raw popularity of individual leisure pursuits cannot disguise patterned variations in them. For example, the French sociologist Pierre Bourdieu (1984), in his famous late 1960s empirical study *Distinction*, discerned a strong relationship between social class and cultural taste. An empirical study of 'Australian everyday cultures' in the late 1990s sought to replicate Bourdieu's study, while also adjusting its theoretical framework to take account of the contribution of the work of Michel Foucault (1977). Foucault had challenged the Marxist emphasis (reflected in the analyses of Bourdieu and others) on the determination of economic power through the workings of the class structure by stressing that power is dispersed from a range of different sites, and takes many different forms. The Australian study, conducted in another country, three decades later, and operating with a modification of Bourdieu's social class model and, following Foucault, a greater range of variables, discovered both resemblances and differences in the leisure and media taste patterns discovered by Bourdieu. For example, it found considerable age variations in preferred television genre type, class differences in musical genre preferences, and gender influences on tastes in film (Bennett et al., 1999). Thus, unsurprisingly perhaps, 75.1 per cent of people over 60 years of age preferred news programmes, compared with only 14.4 per cent of 18–25-year-olds; 18.5 per cent of professionals ranked classical music as their favourite type of music, compared with only 2.9 per cent of manual workers; and men were proportionately more than twice as likely as women to prefer adventure films (25.3 per cent and 11 per cent, respectively).

Leisure taste preferences in mass communications are, however, rather more complex and less predictable than these starker variations suggest – according to the same study, similar proportions of older and younger people have preferences for quality TV drama (2.5 per cent and 3.3 per cent respectively); professionals and manual workers are less differentiated in their liking for Top 40 pop music than might be expected (10.7 per cent and 15.6 per cent); and men and women are virtually indistinguishable in preferences for film comedy (23.7 per cent and 24.9 per cent). When such social categories are related and cross-tabulated, age, class and gender provide additional complexities for the analysis of leisure and mass communications – younger women of higher socioeconomic class, for example, were shown in the 'Australian Everyday Cultures' study to vary in their tastes in film from older women, younger men, and from either sex if occupying different social class positions. Irrespective of such permutations, however, mass communications in general are demonstrably integral to contemporary leisure. This phenomenon has provoked considerable anxiety about its potential distortion of the development of leisure values, discouraging physically healthy pursuits in favour of sedentary leisure, and stimulating unhealthy sensations, especially among the young (Miller, 2002).

Because of its conspicuous success as a leisure resource, and also on account of its 'democratizing' capability of making the same cultural fare available in almost every home, television has provoked strong concerns. From its inception, television viewing has been criticized as a leisure pursuit with a socially destructive impact. The 'box in the corner', having entered the living rooms of most Western dwellings by the 1970s, and proliferating in many other rooms since, has often been denounced for abusing its domestic power. The prime measures of success for television programmers – aggregate viewers and viewing hours – are, according to television's critics, indices of the failure of more productive and wholesome forms of leisure. The content of television is often condemned on the grounds that it is trivial at best and dangerous at worst (Mander, 1980). Regular exposure of viewers (especially the young) to violence, promiscuity, banality, avarice, sexism, homophobia, racism, ethnocentrism, ageism, and so on, are seen to lead to imitative, anti-social behaviour and to create a 'toxic' public culture. Society's most popular leisure activity based on mass communications, therefore, is also regarded by various critics as eroding its moral foundations. This is not only a question of television's damaging content, but also of its capacity to displace other, worthier activities. Watching sport on television, for example, is often condemned for encouraging the population to forgo physically and mentally active, outward-looking forms of leisure in favour of passive, homebound reception (Cashmore, 2000).

Televised sport

Following its emergence as codified physical activity in nineteenth-century Britain, modern sport has developed into a globally favoured leisure activity. Physical education in the form of sport (especially for males) was made compulsory in schools for a variety of reasons, including its assumed capacity to discharge 'unhealthy', especially youthful energies, to enhance the fitness of the population for the purposes of socially efficient longevity and combat readiness in case of war, and to instil appropriate moral values such as group co-operation, positively sanctioned competition, and observance of norms of hierarchy and the division of labour (Hargreaves, 1986). The values being promulgated here fell under the rubric of amateur sport (playing for the love of the game), but sport has been subject to the same pressures of commercialization and professionalization as other leisure pursuits. Sport has forged an enormously successful alliance with mass communications in forms including novels, films, newspapers and magazines, and, above all, television (Rowe, 2004). If watching television has been the most important and popular leisure pursuit of the last 50 years, sport on television has been one of its most successful genres. Sport supplies large, regular audiences for television and, on the occasions of major national and global sports events, spectacular collective viewing occasions. For example, the cumulative audience for the 2002 Korea–Japan soccer World Cup has been estimated at 28.8 billion viewers (FIFA, 2002), while the International Olympic Committee (IOC) estimated that nine out of ten of people in the world with access to television watched at least some of the Sydney 2000 Olympic Games (2002).

While television figures of this size are likely to excite peak sports bodies, individual sports, sponsors, advertisers and television networks, they are also signs for moral entrepreneurs of a 'couch potato' world of lazy, increasingly obese viewers in the light of statistics such as those that the population is over three times more likely to watch sport on television than ever to engage in organized sport or even in casual sports activities (McKay, 1990: 131). Seen in this way, television is positioned as a malign influence on leisure, creating a population of *voyeurs* instead of one actively engaged in a range of approved leisure pursuits. The origins of modern Leisure Studies in the healthy leisure movements of the twentieth century have tended to predispose its practitioners to be critical of television viewing as leisure. This perspective can itself be criticized on the grounds that it is prejudiced by an elitist disdain for the common people, who are seen as being at the mercy of media manipulators whom they are unable to resist, and so have to be 'saved' from their own frailties by an enlightened minority of Leisure Studies professionals. This 'mass society' tradition in both Leisure Studies and Media Studies has both left- and right-wing variants, and can be traced to the Frankfurt School and Leavisite critiques of 'mass culture' (Swingewood, 1977). The subsequent development of Cultural Studies and postmodern theory has been characterized by a less categorically damning critique of media and popular culture (Real, 1996), and a greater emphasis on the struggle for power over and within leisure between dominant and subordinate groups in which the former's 'hegemony' is neither total nor uncontested.

Contesting communications leisure

The history of the relationship between mass communications and leisure, then, is a highly politicized one, with the potentially educative and improving aspects of the media constantly pitted in debate against media uses that are seen to 'dumb down' an atrophying populace. Television has not been the only target of such critiques. For example, when recorded music first became available via the radio and the gramophone, some proponents of 'high culture' tended to view the technology as a new means of bringing Mozart and Beethoven to the 'common people', only for it to be used more commonly to listen to 'cheap' popular music (Rowe, 1995). Similarly, the video cassette recorder freed the viewer from the tyranny of broadcast television schedules, and offered the possibility of both selective viewing and 'time shifting' (watching what the viewer wanted to watch when they wanted to watch it). However, with the introduction of video came debates about 'video nasties', gratuitously violent and sexually explicit media material to which children could now be exposed in the domestic environment (Barker, 1984). Each new technological and/or cultural innovation, including daily newspapers, comics, film, DVD, computer games and the internet, has, therefore, prompted new anxieties about the effects of its adoption and use as a leisure resource.

Some of these technological innovations have, to some degree, problematized the conception of 'mass communication'. In television, for example, the availability of subscription-based multichannelling via cable, satellite and microwave has meant that broadcasting is increasingly giving way to 'narrowcasting', so enabling the customization of media for relatively small taste and language groups. At the same time, audiences are being reconceptualized as active and discerning rather than the victims of predatory media marketing plans. Earlier critiques of the media tended to highlight the aspects of media texts that were found to be ideologically objectionable, but contemporary audience and reception studies have placed more emphasis on how people in different leisure contexts interact with the media, and the ways in which uses of the media occur in varying social settings and are combined with other activities (Balnaves et al., 2002). Empirical studies of television viewing, for example, have shown that levels of attention vary widely, and that interpretations of what has been seen are similarly variable, both between different research subjects and between researchers and those that they are observing (Watson, 1998). Viewers are also, some conclude, more empowered in their engagement with media than is often believed (Fiske, 1987). Indeed, studies of media use often reveal as much about the researcher as the researched. Popular forms of television such as soap operas and sport tend to be highlighted in such critiques – there are rarely complaints that television audiences might watch Sunday night classical music performances on the small screen rather than travel to 'live' venues, or that 'quality' television drama deters audiences from attending live theatre. There is a class cultural dimension to such debates, therefore, that echoes those of long-standing between forms of leisure regarded by social elites as edifying, and those stigmatized as either cause or symptom of societal decline (Clarke and Critcher, 1985). But, as was noted above, leisure and media taste preferences do not always neatly observe class boundaries – which, in any case, are rather more fluid than a binary dominant-subordinate model will allow (Dandaneau, 2001). Media audiences are not disempowered simply by being the targets of mass communications, and developments in media technology, such as the emergence of the internet, may challenge the idea of a unidirectional flow between sender and receiver (Holmes, 1997).

The internet and the network society

The most recent media technology innovation, popularly available in the West for only a little over a decade, is an intriguing test case for the analysis of leisure's relationship with mass communications. Because it is, simultaneously, a medium of one-way mass communications and computer-mediated communication (CMC) that can be 'narrowcast' and interactive, the internet is capable of many leisure and other uses. The internet is a vast treasure house of leisure opportunities, with some of these virtually indistinguishable from traditional publishing and broadcasting. Most major broadcast and newspaper groups, for example, provide online content, while major publishers and record companies make written and audio texts available to online audiences either for promotional purposes (such as excerpts from novels and songs) or on a commercial exchange basis (downloading whole novels and musical albums). But there are also relationships between media and audiences that are much more interactive and/or small scale. These include discussion groups and research databases offering access to opinion and information not provided by the major commercial and public media organizations that dominate contemporary mass communications. In more strictly leisure-oriented terms, internet 'chat rooms' and computer games create communicative opportunities that blur the lines between media producer and consumer, and between 'active' and 'passive' leisure forms (Mayer, 1999). The internet also creates space for small independent producers of music, film and other such cultural forms without the advertising and promotional resources of large, transnational media corporations. Of course, this availability of low-budget web pages and links cannot destroy the advantage of corporate media capital – search engines, for example, can be manipulated to favour large internet clients. Similarly, highly capitalized companies are better placed than minor ones to take advantage of new, converging combinations of media experience that, as in the case of many 'reality shows' such as *Big Brother*, involve broadcast television, the internet and telephony. Nonetheless, some significant change can be detected, especially among younger people, in leisure media use patterns, with a gradual fragmentation of audiences within and between media. The vast growth of audiovisual channels and the many options provided by computer-mediated communication are inevitably having an impact on mass communications, including a reduction in gross hours of television viewing, and within that activity a reduction in the audiences for the established television networks (Castells, 1996: 367). But these shifting patterns signify the expansion and diversification of media leisure use, rather than a retreat towards a pre-technological leisure practice.

The intensification of communications convergence has been described as heralding the coming of the 'network society', conceived as a 'set of interconnected nodes' in which the 'inclusion/exclusion in networks, and the architecture of relationships between networks, enacted by light-speed information technologies, configurate [*sic*] dominant processes and functions in our societies' (Castells, 1996: 470). Networking can reshape the leisure dimensions of mass communications, which can become even more 'massified' through instantaneous global broadcasting (Dayan and Katz, 1992), and, simultaneously, more customized or even individualized by appropriating the small-scale interactive capabilities of new communications technologies in response to the demands of their users. The enhanced connectivity facilitated by, for example, mobile phones with capacity for emails, short messages, still images and video; 'peer-to-peer' programs that bypass music copyright legislation; lightweight, digital camcorders and satellite phones capable of instantly recording, encoding and transmitting information and images from both proximate and remote locations; and dispersed networked computers that make traditional forms of censorship and control difficult and expensive, are helping to redraw a leisure landscape once characterized by the physical transport of people and cultural objects, or the dissemination of cultural imagery from single, identifiable sources (Castells, 1996). Communications on both macro- and micro-scales can be seen, therefore, to facilitate and, indeed, to constitute leisure in a wide variety of forms. The widely-used terms 'infotainment' and 'tabloid' describe the merging of the informational and entertainment functions of the media to a degree that imposes an almost universal leisure imperative, thereby turned the work-like activity of consulting the 'serious' media into a more leisurely encounter with a media culture in which celebrity gossip and scandal fuses with important news (Sparks and Tulloch, 2000; Turner, 2004).

In April 2004, for example, a British Sunday tabloid newspaper carried a lead front-page story, supported by many inside pages inside, alleging infidelity by the leading English football player, David Beckham. At the time Beckham was one of the world's most prominent celebrities (Cashmore, 2002), not least because of his high-profile marriage to Victoria Beckham, formerly known as 'Posh Spice' of the successful but disbanded female pop group, the Spice Girls. There followed an orgy of media attention about Beckham's conduct, the state of his marriage, new allegations of infidelity with other women, the implications for football, and so on. The 'Posh 'n' Becks' story dominated the British print media for several weeks, often overshadowing major 'hard news' stories like the insurgencies against the Allied Forces in Iraq, threats of terrorism, the Palestinian-Israeli conflict, and the proposed ratification of a European Union Constitution. While there was a good deal of straightforward voyeurism and celebrity gossip in the story, it also provided some opportunities to discuss issues of some import, such as the conflict between spouses over career and family priorities, the gender politics of work and sexual conduct, media ethics, and the rights of privacy. Simultaneously, therefore, this media celebrity scandal of little objective importance provided opportunities for voyeuristic leisure and – of lesser weight, it must be acknowledged – for popular political debate about social issues that resonate with everyday life (Lull and Hinerman, 1997). Thus media discourse and leisure practice cannot simply be reduced to a 'zero sum' game in which the use of the news media for leisure purposes automatically excludes all possibility of a more serious sociopolitical engagement. The popular media, however, do more than create and enhance such leisure opportunities. By representing various areas of social and cultural experience in which leisure concepts and practices are implicated, leisure is also turned into a subject of mass communications.

Leisure *in* mass communications

Leisure is represented by various means in the media, and these representations feed back into leisure values and practices. Public broadcasters such as the British Broadcasting Corporation (BBC), for example, have taken as part of their role the representation of selected leisure events (especially those of a sporting nature, such as the Grand National and FA Cup Final) and their projection, promotion and thus reproduction as national cultural pastimes (Whannel, 1992). More routine representations by broadcasters, newspapers and magazines of leisure activities ranging from gardening to arts and crafts may be defended on the grounds that they simply reflect the popularity of particular types of leisure in particular contexts. But no media representation is value-neutral (Curran and Gurevitch, 2000), and any assertion of the 'typicality' of leisure pursuits involves a judgement that is simultaneously inclusive and exclusive. For example, television feature programmes showing pastoral English life in which country gardens are lovingly tended are, at one level, valid reflections of the lives and leisure practices of some (albeit a privileged minority) members of the UK population. Yet, by their nature, such representations of 'typically English' leisure do not correspond to the lived experiences of urban, working-class apartment dwellers, especially those whose origins may be in the Caribbean or the Indian sub-continent, or who may identify as Scots or Welsh. The concentration on leisure, in any case, is unlikely to reveal the connections between leisure and various forms of structured social inequality – the garden products made by exploited workers in developing countries, the supporting services provided by unemployed and underemployed local people, the housing market forces that govern the size or even availability of gardens, and so on. In other words, the demand for most electronic and print media to be more entertaining means that leisure's representation is encouraged to be in soft focus and to bypass awkward differences in leisure opportunity and preference in favour of a spurious national typicality.

The commercial media, as noted above, explicitly represent leisure in its various forms as part of an overall advertising, promotion and marketing function – the exposure of leisure products to potential consumers. The mass media are, therefore, key actors in shaping – or, more critically, manipulating – leisure patterns. In television, for example, there has been a veritable explosion of 'infotainment' or 'lifestyle' programmes, especially those involving the 'makeover' of houses and gardens, supported by established and new glossy home living magazines. Broadly, such programmes encourage homes to be seen as a (or, indeed, the) leisure site as well as an economic asset to be improved for capital exchange. Viewers are instructed in the design of domestic leisure sites (such as games rooms and external spas) and introduced to the range of products and services by which they are created. The commodities can be both displayed during the programme through the technique of product placement and around it through paid spot advertising. The equivalents in the case of magazines are written texts about and photographs of the goods, often with suppliers and prices in a byline, and contiguous advertising. The most overt commercial media display of leisure products occurs in paid 'infomercials' and 'advertorials'. The media's promotion of home renovation as leisure may seem a relatively harmless practice, especially if, as is the case with television cooking programmes, many viewers only gaze on but do not engage in the prescribed activities. But there are social implications in encouraging more inward looking, homebound forms of leisure and, whether explicitly or implicitly, stimulating competition between neighbours for the creation of domestic leisure sites distinguished by conspicuous consumption. Despite this current emphasis on the domestic sphere, mass communication is also central to the advertising and promotion of leisure beyond the home, such as in the representation of a key leisure industry – tourism.

Mass communication of tourism

The media carry information about tourism by a variety of means, including consumer-oriented 'Holiday' TV programmes and mass-circulated tourist brochures and catalogues. Here it can be seen that domestic and external leisure can be interdependent, with the media-induced planning and anticipation of tourism experiences a significant aspect of leisure in the home. For example, browsing through holiday brochures bringing sunny summer images into homes during the northern hemisphere winter is for many a pleasurable activity, while the television programmes that 'consumer test' holidays and tourist destinations can be enjoyed as forms of vicarious travel mediated by various forms of language (Dann, 1996). Media and tourism can, therefore, be regarded as mutually interdependent in a similar way to the media and sport linkage described earlier. Tourism is a specific form of industrialized leisure that requires participants to be attracted to stay away from home. Potential customers have first to be made aware that a tourism opportunity exists, and then be persuaded to choose it from among the myriad competing tourism products. The mass media are particularly efficient means of connecting tourism operators and customers given that tourism is an image-based industry. Access to mass communication, as in all other spheres, provides a clear advantage to some tourism operators and destinations over others. It enables those in a position to purchase more media advertising space to gain greater consumer visibility, and by this means to generate the visitor volumes, especially for 'packaged' holidays, that result in the economies of scale conferring a cost advantage. The success of such media-linked tourism promotion can also be self-reinforcing, with some holiday types and destinations becoming almost 'normative' in some countries. For example, in Britain during the 1960s and 1970s the heavy, integrated media promotion of packaged holidays in Mediterranean Spain stimulated a major shift in summer vacation patterns, becoming an almost ritualized practice for many members of the British (especially northern English) and some other northern European working classes (especially the German). Here, mass communication can be seen to do rather more than advertise leisure – it is capable, under propitious circumstances (including the arrival of inexpensive charter air travel and a rise in disposable income) to influence leisure patterns.

This mass communications influence on leisure in the form of tourism, however, does not entirely determine it. As Urry (2002) has argued, there is a long-established tension between mass (working-class) and less high-volume contemplative (middle-class) forms of tourism, and the very success of packaged tourism has prompted a reaction in which many tourists search for new, more authentic cultural experiences through tourism. The media also supply such information through guidebooks like the *Lonely Planet* series that claim to seek out tourism locations that are relatively 'unspoilt' by tourists, although in which are to be found an uncommon number of visitors carrying *Lonely Planet* guides. Niche forms of tourism (such as culture- and nature-based) that distinguish themselves from standardized 'mass' tours in favour of a smaller scale, deeper, educational immersion in the tourist destination, are no less dependent on the media. The internet is especially well suited to the task of linking tourism 'producers' and consumers of this kind, and the more targeted, interactive nature of some communication through the internet departs considerably from traditional conceptions of mass communications. But all forms of tourist image-making work largely by projecting brand identities that are relatively easy to recognize and assimilate. Thus, the media are crucially implicated in the tendency of tourist destinations to be classified stereotypically, often in simple binary terms as wild, untamed and unspoilt, or as civilized, sophisticated and advanced (Rowe, 1998). Tourism, one the most economically important forms of leisure (Urry, 2002), requires the media to stimulate public attention, but as a consequence the complexity and diversity of whole nations and peoples aspiring to be prime tourism destinations tend to be narrowed to small, readily digestible lists of 'typical' qualities – colourful, traditional, exotic, simple, exciting, cultured, and so on. In some cases, countries heavily reliant on tourism are required to live up to the media-projected tourism image by 'performing' it for the cameras of visitors, thereby ossifying a culture that is discouraged from changing or displaying its many different facets for fear of tourism marketing confusion (MacCannell, 1992). It is for this reason that, for example, Indigenous peoples in Australasia, North America and elsewhere have sought to exercise control over the image of their life and culture as it is projected to tourists in media advertising campaigns (Butler and Hinch, 1996). The manner in which people and places are represented touristically by the media, and the principal signifiers that are used in the process of mass communication in seeking to capture their 'essence', are of necessity, then, subjected to considerable scrutiny and debate.

Leisure, tourism and mass communications are linked in many other ways. Mass mediated sports spectacles, such as the Olympic Games, the Ashes series in cricket, and the soccer and rugby World Cups, are effortlessly fused in the case of sport tourism, where spectators travel to the site of the event and become, often through vivid, noisy displays of national partisanship (like that of England's 'Barmy Army' of cricket fans) part of the media spectacle itself, visible to television viewers around the world (Hinch and Higham, 2004; Weed and Bull, 2004). Here, mass communications enhance the leisure forms of sport and tourism, with visiting broadcasters often projecting touristic 'postcard' features as well as the sports action. Ethnographic and nature television documentaries have long had a touristic element that is now supplemented by 'reality' TV shows like *Survivor* and *I'm a Celebrity, Get Me Out of Here!*, which are staged in 'jungle' and similarly exotic locations, as well as 'fly on the wall' TV shows like *Ibiza* that represent people at work and play in leisure spaces. Even reality television shows set in conventional domestic environments and showing people doing relatively ordinary things, such as *Big Brother*, may produce tourist sites like the *Big Brother House* on the Gold Coast in Australia. Thus the media–tourism linkage is multidimensional, highly creative but also controversial, not least where the media have, intentionally or otherwise, been responsible through saturation coverage for the establishment of 'dark tourism' sites (Rojek, 2000) such as the tunnel in Paris where Diana, Princess of Wales was fatally injured. This leisure phenomenon raises another important question concerning the leisure–mass communications nexus – what do the media classify as leisure, and of which forms and agents of (in)activity do the media (dis)approve?

Mass communications, leisure prescriptions and moral panics

The commercial market for leisure, as noted above, is substantially shaped by mass communication, but the marketplace of social and leisure values is similarly influenced by news and current affairs media. Just as there are debates about the role of mass communications in leisure (such as watching television), the media also put leisure under the microscope. Both public and commercial media sometimes carry information about leisure services and commend positively sanctioned forms of leisure as part of healthy lifestyle campaigns. Here the mass communication of leisure takes on a public service complexion, with the media adopting a role that is 'disciplinary' in its application of what Foucault (1991) calls 'governmentality' to the citizenry. According to Foucault, modern societies have increasingly sought to manage their populations by replacing the strategic imposition of external, coercive force with an internalized self-control. It is often in the name of social efficiency, therefore, that the media encourage people to take daily exercise, participate in 'fun runs', consume less alcohol and no cigarettes or illicit drugs, recognize and counter excessive gambling and gaming, and strike a better 'work–life' balance by modifying their leisure practices. Media campaigns that intervene in the field of leisure seek to harness the persuasive power of mass communications – ironically, by encouraging media users to spend less time exposing themselves to the media (in the case of television viewing) or by trying to counter the effect on some members of the population of excessive adoption of leisure practices that the commercial media themselves energetically promote (such as drinking and gambling). While the media may, again with some irony, receive advertising revenue from both the promoters of 'unhealthy' leisure and from those who seek to counter it, the state has intervened in many countries to limit or ban the media exposure of unhealthy leisure products such as tobacco. Thus leisure is caught up in the continuing and ever-changing contestation between the state and media organizations over which leisure products and activities can be promoted, and in what ways.

The media's positive sanctioning of certain forms of leisure can be matched by negative sanctioning of leisure activities that are seen to be dangerous, anti-social or destructive. This practice is defensible when both symptoms and causes are represented within a tenable explanatory framework. For example, the problem of petrol sniffing or binge drinking among Australian Aboriginal children can be legitimately discussed in the context of the continuing legacy of Indigenous dispossession. But it is also common, especially among the more populist forms of TV, radio and the press, to 'blame the victim' and/or to stigmatize some leisure practices and practitioners in a moralizing manner that neither accepts sociocultural diversity nor entertains structural explanations for leisure behaviour. As Rojek (1995: 101) notes, affixing and evading labels of 'deviant' leisure is a highly ideological process in such areas as drug taking and trespassing on enclosed land. There is a considerable literature in Sociology, Media and Cultural Studies that interrogates the media coverage of 'unconventional' leisure (for example, Hall and Jefferson, 1993; Redhead, 1990), often finding an hegemonic reinforcement of power structures in seeking to contain and marginalize overt and covert challenges through leisure to the status quo. Youth-oriented subcultures, including teddy boys, hippies, punks, New Age travellers, ravers and rappers, have all been recipients of media condemnations of 'deviant' leisure, just as the unemployed have been subjected to recurrent media claims of idleness and aversion to work (Aitchison, 2000; Clarke and Critcher, 1985; Critcher, 2003). The representation of leisure in the media, therefore, often paints a politicized picture of currently approved and denigrated leisure forms, and of the posited relationships between leisure practices and the characteristics of those who indulge in them.

Conclusion: communicating leisure

In this chapter I have sought to demonstrate that, while the tools and timing of leisure may be in constant flux, mass communications remain an integral, institutional aspect of the structure and experience of leisure. The term itself has an old-fashioned ring in what is often heralded as a 'digital age' in which interactive, personalized communication in cyberspace has replaced the previously dominant one-to-many transmission of leisure texts. The communicative landscape of the twenty-first century is, however, marked by the co-existence of mass and minor communications, and by the constant interplay of highly formalized, capitalized media and the 'cottage' media production and consumption that is especially well facilitated by digital technology. It is increasingly easy, therefore, to capture mass communicated images, modify them, and disseminate them in pursuit of leisure – 'serious' or otherwise. Leisure time, for the foreseeable future, will be devoted largely to, or deeply implicated in, the reception and relay of communicative texts. At the same time, leisure remains a consistent object of mass communications – for the purposes of consumer advice, commodity marketing, vicarious pleasure, anthropological education, moral instruction and ideological contestation. Contemporary leisure and mass communications, therefore, display an unprecedented degree of mutual, institutional interdependence.

Bibliography

Aitchison, C. (2000) 'Poststructural Feminist Theories of Representing Others: A Response to the "Crisis" in Leisure Studies' Discourse', *Leisure Studies* 19 (3): 127–44.

Balnaves, M., O'Regan, T. and Sternberg, J. (eds) (2002) *Mobilising the Audience*, St Lucia, University of Queensland Press.

Barker, M. (ed.) (1984) *The Video Nasties: Freedom and Censorship in the Media*, London, Pluto Press.

Bennett, T., Emmison, M. and Frow, J. (1999) *Accounting for Tastes: Australian Everyday Culture*, Melbourne, Cambridge University Press.

Bourdieu, P. (1984) *Distinction: A Social Critique of the Judgement of Taste*, Cambridge, MA, Harvard University Press.

Brown, P. and Rowe, D. (1998) 'The Coming of the Leisure Society? Leisure Time Use in Contemporary Australia', in D. Rowe and G. Lawrence (eds) *Tourism, Leisure, Sport: Critical Perspectives*, Melbourne, Cambridge University Press, pp. 89–99.

Butler, R. and Hinch, T. (eds) (1996) *Tourism and Indigenous Peoples*, London, Thomson.

Cashmore, E. (2000) 'Television', in E. Cashmore (ed.) *Sports Culture: An A-Z Guide*, London, Routledge, pp. 405–9.

Cashmore, E. (2002) *Beckham*, Cambridge, Polity.

Castells, M. (1996) *The Information Age: Economy, Society and Culture: Volume I: The Rise of the Network Society*, Cambridge, MA, Blackwell.

Clarke, J. and Critcher, C. (1985) *The Devil Makes Work: Leisure in Capitalist Britain*, London, Macmillan Education.

Cohen, S. (1980) *Folk Devils and Moral Panics: The Creation of the Mods and Rockers* (new edn), London, Martin Robertson.

Critcher, C. (2003) *Moral Panics and the Media*, Maidenhead, Open University Press.

Curran, J. and Gurevitch, M. (eds) (2000) *Mass Media and Society* (3rd edn), London, Arnold.

Dandaneau, S. P. (2001) *Taking it Big: Developing Sociological Consciousness in Postmodern Times*, Thousand Oaks, CA, Pine Forge Press.

Dann, G. (1996) *The Language of Tourism: A Sociolinguistic Perspective*, Wallingford, CAB International.

Dayan, D. and Katz, E. (1992) *Media Events: The Live Broadcasting of History*, Cambridge, MA, Harvard University Press.

FIFA (2002) '41,100 hours of 2002 FIFA World Cup TV coverage in 213 countries'. Press Release, 21 November, Zurich, Federation Internationale de Football Association.

Fiske, J. (1987) *Television Culture*, London, Methuen.

Foucault, M. (1977) *Discipline and Punish: The Birth of the Prison*, Harmondsworth, Penguin.

Foucault, M. (1991) 'Governmentality', in G. Burchell, C. Gordon and P. Miller (eds) *The Foucault Effect: Studies in Governmentality*, London, Harvester Wheatsheaf, pp. 87–104.

Golding, P. and Murdock, G. (2000) 'Culture, Communications and Political Economy', in J. Curran and M. Gurevitch (eds) *Mass Media and Society* (3rd edn), London, Arnold, pp. 70–92.

Hall, S. and Jefferson, T. (1993) *Resistance Through Rituals: Youth Subcultures in Post-War Britain* (new edn), London, Routledge.

Hargreaves, J. (1986) *Sport, Power and Culture*, Cambridge, Polity Press.

Harvey, D. (1989) *The Condition of Postmodernity: An Inquiry into the Origins of Cultural Change*, Oxford, Blackwell.

Hinch, T. and Higham, J. (2004) *Sport Tourism Development*, Clevedon, Somerset, Channel View.

Holmes, D. (ed.) (1997) *Virtual Politics: Identity and Community in Cyberspace*, London, Sage.

International Olympic Committee (2002) *Marketing Fact File*, Lausanne, Switzerland, IOC, available at: <www.multimedia.olympic.org/pdf/en_report.344.pdf> (accessed January 2006).

Lull, J. and Hinerman, S. (eds) (1997) *Media Scandals: Morality and Desire in the Popular Culture Marketplace*, New York, Columbia University Press.

MacCannell, D. (1992) *Empty Meeting Grounds: The Tourist Papers*, New York, Routledge.

Mander, J. (1980) *Four Arguments for the Elimination of Television*, Brighton, Harvester.

Mayer, P. (ed.) (1999) *Computer Media and Communication: A Reader*, New York, Oxford University Press.

McKay, J. (1990) 'Sport, Leisure and Social Inequality in Australia', in D. Rowe and G. Lawrence (eds) *Sport and Leisure: Trends in Australian Popular Culture*, Sydney, Harcourt Brace Jovanovich, pp. 125–60.

Miller, T. (ed.) (2002) *Television Studies*, London, British Film Institute.

Real, M. (1996) *Exploring Media Culture: A Guide*, Thousand Oaks, CA, Sage.

Redhead, S. (1990) *The End-of-the-Century Party: Youth and Pop towards 2000*, Manchester, Manchester University Press.

Roberts, K. (1978) *Contemporary Society and the Growth of Leisure*, London, Longman.

Rojek, C. (1995) *Decentring Leisure: Rethinking Leisure Theory*, London, Sage.

Rojek, C. (2000) *Leisure and Culture*, Basingstoke and London, Macmillan.

Rowe, D. (1995) *Popular Cultures: Rock Music, Sport and the Politics of Pleasure*, London, Sage.

Rowe, D. (1998) 'Tourism, "Australianness" and Sydney 2000', in D. Rowe and G. Lawrence (eds) *Tourism, Leisure, Sport: Critical Perspectives*, Melbourne, Cambridge University Press, pp. 74–85.

Rowe, D. (2002) 'Producing the Crisis: The State of Leisure Studies', *Annals of Leisure Research* 5(1): 1–13.

Rowe, D. (2004) *Sport, Culture and the Media: The Unruly Trinity* (2nd edn), Maidenhead, Open University Press.

Sparks, C. and Tulloch, J. (eds) (2000) *Tabloid Tales: Global Perspectives on the Popular Media*, Boulder, CO, Rowman & Littlefield.

Swingewood, A. (1977) *The Myth of Mass Culture*, London, Macmillan.

Tomlinson, A. (1999) *The Game's Up: Essays in the Cultural Analysis of Sport, Leisure and Popular Culture*, Aldershot, Ashgate.

Turner, G. (2004) *Understanding Celebrity*, London, Sage.

Urry, J. (2002) *The Tourist Gaze* (2nd edn), London, Sage.

Veal, A. J. and Lynch, R. (2001) *Australian Leisure* (2nd edn), Melbourne, Longman.

Watson, J. (1998) *Media Communication: An Introduction to Theory and Process*, London, Macmillan.

Weed, M. and Bull, C. (2004) *Sports Tourism: Participants, Policy and Providers*, Oxford, Elsevier.

Whannel, G. (1992) *Fields in Vision: Television Sport and Cultural Transformation*, London, Routledge.

Part 4
Leisure Forms and Settings

20
Sport and Sport Studies

Susan Birrell[1]

Sport is such a pervasive feature of contemporary life that, while not everyone participates in it actively or can be considered a fan, no one is unaffected by its presence. In all its forms and levels, sport exerts enormous significance in our cultural life. The billions of dollars pumped into the economy every year by sport and fitness consumers, the huge salaries of professional athletes, the extent to which the Olympic Games rivet the world's attention every two years, the impact of intercollegiate and interscholastic sport in the US, and the symbiotic relationship between sport and television which has resulted in 24-hour-a-day all-sports networks – all point to the ways that sport has insinuated itself into the fabric of society.

Yet despite its undeniable presence as a cultural force, sport, like leisure, was virtually ignored by serious scholars for many years. While excellent scholarship could be found scattered within other academic disciplines, it was not until 1964 and Franklin Henry's famous paradigm shifting article 'Physical Education: An Academic Discipline' that a critical mass of scholars emerged from within physical education to found the disciplinary fields that would comprise exercise science (now called kinesiology) and sport studies. A year later Gerald Kenyon and John Loy (1965) elaborated on Henry's argument, urging the development of the social science and humanities side of the field. Drawing on previous work from scholars both within physical education and outside the field, they outlined the steps necessary to formalize sociology of sport as a new academic discipline focused on the significance of sport in culture. Although Kenyon and Loy's specific call was for a sociology of sport, their vision encompassed a multidisciplinary field that would study sport from sociological, historical, psychological, philosophical, geographical, anthropological and literary perspectives. Today the fields that comprise sport studies are represented by at least 22 specialized organizations, and research is published in at least 20 specialized journals.[2]

Sport, in all its forms, continues to provide fascinating grounds for study. In the past four decades, sport at all levels – recreational, youth, interscholastic, intercollegiate, amateur, professional – has exploded in popularity and assumed a level of prominence that surely justifies the attention of these serious scholars.

In this chapter I review the growth of our understanding of cultural meanings of sport as that understanding has been fostered by the academic enterprise of sport studies. I trace the history of sport studies, touching on its early connections to leisure studies; discuss current theoretical and methodological practices; and review selected topics to demonstrate the range of critical work in the field of sport studies, particularly within the sociology of sport.

Developing sport studies

The serious study of sport developed in both North America and Europe in the mid-1960s. In Britain sport studies was part of the new multidisciplinary field of leisure studies; in North America, sport studies and leisure studies developed separately (more on this below). These early differences have had a significant impact on the course of history for the two fields. This review traces that process in the North American context.

In North America, sport studies has developed in two broad stages: an early stage characterized by differentiation, specialization and multidisciplinarity, as sport studies emerged as a discipline-based response to the dominant focus on professional training within the field of physical education; and a current stage of increasing interdisciplinarity as sport studies blurs disciplinary boundaries and genres to forge intellectual connections with humanities based disciplines and with critical cultural studies. Running through this short but eventful history are several interrelated themes: the evolution from a multidisciplinary to an interdisciplinary field; an increasingly explicit attention to theory; an increasingly sophisticated critical approach to the subject matter; and the move toward a cultural studies of sport.

Creating a multidisciplinary field

The early years in the development of sport studies as a field of academic interest were characterized by moves to establish the focus of the field by a series of differentiating moves that distinguished sport studies from other academic enterprises. The process of differentiation of the field took place in at least four rather rapid stages of development: a departure from traditional physical education practices, a divergence of interests between sport studies and leisure studies, the establishment of clearly defined subdisciplines, and an ongoing effort to distinguish between the disciplinary interests of sport studies and the applied fields that grew from it. Throughout this period, the hallmark of sport studies was its development as a multidisciplinary field.

In Australia, interest in sport studies grew out of sociology, and in Britain, sport and leisure studies grew out a variety of academic fields including sociology, geography, psychology, economics, architecture, and media studies as well as physical education and recreation management. In North America, interest in the scholarly study of sport was also found within these disciplines but the impetus for the formal study of sport grew out of physical education thus necessitating the first of the discipline-defining moves. The crucial event in that process was Franklin Henry's (1964) influential essay that differentiated a new academic or discipline based approach from the traditional professional orientation of physical education. Very quickly after Henry reimagined the possibilities of the field, physical education programmes underwent major restructuring, and a variety of discipline-defined subspecialty areas was the result. One cluster of subdisciplines developed into programmes of exercise science, or kinesiology. These subdisciplines included anatomy, biomechanics, exercise physiology, kinesiology, motor development and motor control. Following the lead of Kenyon and Loy (1965), a second cluster of subdisciplines, whose focus was primarily social science and humanities oriented, developed as programmes of sport studies. These included the sociology of sport, the psychology of sport, the history of sport, the philosophy of sport, the anthropology of play and, occasionally, a focus on the literature of sport.

Though owing its formal origins to physical education, sport studies did not develop wholly out of that field but through interactions between scholars within physical education and those in the cognate disciplines who had laid the early groundwork for the scholarly study of sport. In differentiating themselves from the predominantly professional training model of physical education, sport studies scholars cultivated these connections with their colleagues in other academic fields. Students in the first sport studies graduate programmes took a significant proportion of their academic training in cognate fields. Founding members in the scholarly organizations devoted to the study of sport were drawn from physical education and from the parent disciplines, and the editorial boards of sport studies journals included those trained specifically in the newly formed sport studies programmes and those outside the field.

The second differentiating move in the development of sport studies in North America came in terms of subject matter, and this move resulted in the separate development of sport studies and leisure studies. In the US, although sport studies and leisure studies are parts of the larger enterprise signalled, acronymically at least, by AAHPERD (the American Alliance for Health, Physical Education, Recreation, and Dance), the two fields have developed separately as the components that make up that large professional organization have redefined themselves and their relationship to the whole. Sport studies descended from its origins in physical education, while leisure studies grew out of recreation education, with heavy influence in the US from the National Recreation and Parks Association (NRPA). For a while in the mid-1960s, in the excitement of forging new disciplinary identities, the connections between sport and leisure were explored, and a potential convergence between sport studies and leisure studies seemed logical. The contents of the founding anthology (Loy and Kenyon, 1969) and the curriculum for the first classes in sociology of sport in North America reflect attention to play, games, and leisure as well as sport. In addition, we claimed a common scholarly ancestry, recognizing Huizinga (1950) and Veblen (1899), for example, as foundational texts.

But despite this common ancestry, the interests and approaches of sport studies and leisure studies rather quickly diverged. Every new field must seriously address the unique subject matter that defines its focus of enquiry, and sport studies and leisure studies differentiated themselves along these lines. Where leisure studies scholars claimed leisure as their conceptual focus, sport studies scholars carved out the territory of sport. Early essays on the development of both fields reflected this fundamental issue. In John Loy's (1968) classic essay 'The Nature of Sport: A Definitional Effort', for example, Loy clearly attends to leisure as an important partner to sport, but he does not trace the descent of the concept of sport through leisure, moving instead from Huizinga to Caillois (1961) as he traces the relationship from play to games to sport. Those in leisure studies also ponder these connections, with a general conclusion, in the UK as well as North America, that sport and leisure are very closely related.

As a result, leisure studies directs considerable research energy toward sport, specifically recreational sport. The interests of sport studies are quite naturally broader, given that sport comprises the entire substantive focus of the field. A range of activities and experiences vie for our attention under the rubric of sport. These include physical activities organized through the fields of personal fitness activities; recreational sport opportunities organized through community youth leagues or college intramural programmes; sport programmes sponsored through educational institutions from the elementary school level through interscholastic high school programmes at intercollegiate sport; amateur sport participation that ascends to the elite level all the way to the Olympic Games; and the wide realm of professional sport. While sport studies casts our net broadly in terms of subject matter, our major focus has been on collegiate, professional and elite levels of sport participation and on the cultural contexts these sport forms illuminate and reproduce.

In North America, sport studies and leisure studies work on sport also is differentiated in terms of the unit of analytical interest. Leisure studies generally works from a social psychological model as they study recreational sport involvement; sport studies has developed a multidisciplinary approach, drawn from sociology, history, psychology and anthropology, and focuses attention on the cultural contexts in which sport is embedded. Increasingly, interrogations into the meanings of the sport experience and how that experience is influenced by cultural forces have focused attention on the continued inequities in sport and on the increasing commercialization, globalization and mediation of sport.

A third stage of differentiation resulted in the development of distinctive subdisciplinary groups which together provided the multidisciplinary approach that marked sport studies in its earliest years. Each member of this multidisciplinary project followed different epistemological routes as it developed as a separate subdiscipline through interaction with its cognate discipline. Discipline specific organizations sprang up on both the national and international stages.[3]

These acts of disciplinary independence were necessary in order for each group to distinguish itself with its own substantive focuses and its own theoretical and methodological approaches. The boundary between the sociology of sport and the psychology of sport was a particularly important negotiation that was not accomplished until the 1980s. By then the different epistemological assumptions of the two fields became more difficult to reconcile, and a shared focus on the social psychology of sport was ceded to sport psychology as sport sociology increasingly defined itself in terms of its critical focus on the cultural aspects of sport. Sport psychology continued to focus on the individual, alone or in groups, as the unit of analysis while sport sociology was more likely to use broader units of analysis such as social organizations and institutions.

Finally, sport studies continues to struggle to differentiate the more scholarly aspects of the field from the more applied.[4] One example is the struggle to determine the proper relationship between sport studies and the fields variously known as sport management, sport administration, or athletic administration. In recent years, these focuses have developed into subspecialization areas with their own organizations and their own journals. The best of these programmes use the critical base of sport studies to ground their professional training.

A more heated debate exists within sport psychology between those who advocate that maintaining the field's academic focus must remain paramount and those urging the field in a more applied direction. Unlike their colleagues in other subdisciplines, sport psychologists sometimes are caught in a jurisdictional debate with their colleagues in psychology. The creation in 1986 of an Exercise and Sport Division within the American Psychological Association, for example, is seen by some as an attempt to take control of this increasingly popular – and lucrative – field. One solution was the development of the Association of Applied Sport Psychology (AASP), an offshoot of the North American Society for Psychology of Sport and Physical Activity (NASPSPA) which was created to focus on applied matters. Another is the creation of formal processes for designating Certified Consultants within sport psychology.

Moving toward an interdisciplinary and critical sport studies

As we have seen, the early years in the development of sport studies as a field of academic interest were characterized by moves to establish the focus of the field by differentiating sport studies from other academic enterprises and by its conceptualization as a multidisciplinary field.

Sport studies today is more appropriately characterized as interdisciplinary. Having established disciplinary legitimacy, sport studies became part of the broader trend toward interdisciplinary work taking place throughout academia and began to build methodological and theoretical bridges between the sport disciplines. At the same time, important connections were established with scholarly traditions outside the original conceptualization of the field, most notably media studies and the humanities. Exciting theoretical and methodological changes have resulted.

Within the sociology of sport these moves began with a turn away from the dominant sociological paradigm of the time which was marked by quantitative methods and a usually unarticulated reliance on the principles of structural functionalism. Increased attention to symbolic interactionism and other interpretative theoretical traditions and a greater use of ethnographic methods was one outcome. The emergence of critical anthropology offered a model, and some sport scholars followed closely the anthropological debates over epistemology and method, the exploration of 'blurred genres' and the related academic 'turns':

the turn to the humanities, the interpretative turn and the critical turn. All were adopted to some extent in the evolving field of sport studies.

Another move was a more enthusiastic embracing of critical theories from Marxist and feminist traditions. Classical Marxism and the critical traditions that descended from it, particularly the influences of Gramsci and Stuart Hall, significantly strengthened analyses of the power of ideology working in and through sport. Feminist theories moved beyond liberal and radical approaches toward more synthetic and critical theories, including socialist feminism and critical theories focused on the 'matrix of domination' that included gender, race and class. These complex critical traditions became part of the interdisciplinary project of critical cultural studies which has had a major influence on sport studies.

The turn to the humanities brought sport studies within the sphere of radical theoretical interventions, most significantly post-structuralism and theories of the postmodern. The turn to poststructuralist interpretations is a turn away from modernist, realist epistemological positions and a move from identity politics to a politics of representation. The analysis of mediated images and representations, once limited to more descriptive quantitative content analysis, now offers more nuanced interpretative analyses, through the critical intervention of discourse analysis, narrative analysis, and the metaphor of 'reading' culture adapted from literary fields. All have had profound effects on the quality of cultural analysis in sport studies.

Understanding contemporary sport

No one who seriously studies sport these days can fail to see that sport has departed greatly from the idealized notion of sport as a site where our most treasured cultural values are nurtured and celebrated. The demythologizing of sport was an early focus of sport studies, and as commercial imperatives appear to shape or exploit sport even further, the critical tradition in sport scholarship counters with increasingly sophisticated theoretical frameworks.

To illustrate this process, I review four themes selected to represent some of the current work of critical scholars who explore the cultural meanings of contemporary sport. I begin with discussions of the dominant focus of critical sport scholarship – the continuing inequities structured into sport – and the increasing importance of critical media studies in our understanding of contemporary sport, then provide shorter discussions of everyday sport and the resistant work of sporting subcultures and spatial dimensions of the sport experience.

Patterns of continuing inequality in sport

Sport scholars never subscribed to the common misperception that sport is some sort of equal opportunity activity – a level playing field where athletic excellence is welcomed and rewarded regardless of who displays it. From the beginning, sport studies scholars realized that inequality, structured along lines of gender, race and class, is a dominant characteristic of the world of sport. Our earliest efforts to understand the nature and extent of sport involvement by charting patterns of sport participation immediately revealed patterns of unequal access and opportunities. The realization that sport does not merely mirror societal inequities but is a site where such inequality is reproduced, indeed celebrated, has become a central theme of critical work in the field.

Active involvement in sport has increased steadily over the past decades, with significant exceptions.[5] But more important than surveying the numbers of participants and charting the rise in popularity of particular sport and fitness activities, sport scholars work to plumb the depths of meaning for these participation trends. What does it mean that although fitness club memberships continue to rise, the number of adults categorized as unfit also increases (American Sports Data, Inc., 2000)? Perhaps these patterns provide evidence that commercial interests disguised as public health policies and not personal commitments are driving the 'fitness boom'. Gender and race have always been complicating factors in sport involvement. What does it mean that although dramatically more girls and women are finding organized opportunities to participate in sport, from grade school all the way to the pros, fewer opportunities now exist for them to fill leadership positions as coaches, officials or administrators of the sports they love? What does it mean that although more athletes from minority groups are involved in sport, they are still limited in the positions they may play and the leadership positions they may aspire to, and they are more likely to see themselves represented as team mascots than enfranchised as team owners? For that matter, what does it mean that professional sport continues to restrict opportunities for leadership to wealthy white men? What does it mean that the long established inverse relationship between age and physical activity appears to be reversing so that in the US, grandparents might be more active than their grandchildren (American Sports Data, Inc., 2001)?

While these patterns clearly illuminate patterns of unequal access manifested in sport, they are just the starting point for more fundamental enquiries into the nature of sport as a productive force in the construction of relations of power structured along lines of gender, race and ethnicity and class, as well as sexuality, nationality, age and ability/disability. Early work by sport sociologists explored these patterns, particularly those reflecting unequal treatment of female athletes and black athletes, and a focus on social class and the anti-democratizing of sport have been staples of sport historians from the very beginning. Critiques informed by feminist and Marxist theories, and more recently critical race theory, have reformed our approaches to these issues. The most provocative scholarship now focuses on the dynamic intersection of power lines of race, class and gender and the complex relations of power that result. Critical analysis of the inequities structured into sport is now the dominant theme in sport studies.

Exploring gender and sexuality

The trajectory of feminist scholarship on sport has been documented elsewhere in essays that explore the evolution from modernist theories such as liberal and radical feminism to the more synthetic or intersectional theories that characterize the critical project. Current critical feminist work in sport is grounded in materialist critiques such as socialist feminism or feminist cultural studies and in post-structuralist theories that trace their heritage from Barthes to Lacan to Foucault to Butler.

Critical scholars, particularly those interested in gender and sexual differences, centre their analyses in a politics of the body. The growing recognition of lesbian and gay male presence in sport, and the availability of postmodern and post-structuralist theories, particularly queer theory, enable scholars to explore the ways subjectivities are formed by discourses written on and through the sporting body. Huge potential exists for expanding this work to include race and ethnicity, social class, age, and physical ability/disability, all also written on the body. Because bodies bear the markers of all their social subjectivities simultaneously, synthetic analyses capable of handling these complexities are imperative.

Following from the feminist insight that women are controlled through the control of their bodies, sport scholars recognize the athletic body as a site for this struggle, or as Messner (1988) phrased it, as 'contested terrain'. Feminists generally see women's involvement in sport as a form of empowerment centred in the body, but focus as well on the extent to which these sport experiences are co-opted by dominant cultural forces and turned into a disciplining of the body for male consumption. Often this issue is addressed by focusing on fitness and exercise activities such as aerobics and weight training and the struggle to define the meaning of these experiences. Analyses try to assess who ultimately controls the desire for women to be fit, and to what extent women's fitness is merely another aspect of a cultural demand for heterosexual attractiveness.

Perhaps the most provocative research questions the simple binaries of male/female by exploring competing masculinities and the differences among women. These themes promise to provide the basis for more complicated intersectional analyses.

Exploring social class

Marxist critiques of sport have been an important part of sport studies from the beginning. Scholars who follow this tradition explore the ways that sporting experiences are structured by and limited by the 'social locations' of class and the ways that the process of capitalism invades every aspect of sport, from professional through recreational. The most incisive critiques of the commercialization and commodification of sport – a major theme in critical analyses – originate from Marxist insights.

As an important cornerstone in the development of cultural studies, Marxist scholarship is a site for spirited debates over the relative merits of materialist and idealist conceptualizations of cultural reproduction. In sport studies these debates play themselves out between those who favour the more economically grounded materialist approaches of classical Marxism and those who endorse post-Marxist approaches, following Gramsci and Hall, and focus on the role of ideology in the reproduction of privilege and power. Both approaches provide crucial insights into the ways that capitalist practices and ecnonomic interests manipulate sport.

Marxist analyses are the foundation of the study of globalization and the increasing capitalization of the world sport market and the extension of capitalist power through post-colonialism. Focusing on globalization interrogates the ways that apparently national sporting concerns are actually manifestations of a global marketplace controlled by multinational conglomerates such as Nike. Such relations of dominance are often abetted by the globalization of attractive and iconic figures such as Michael Jordan and David Beckham. Here again the complications of intersectional models will provide more profound understandings of the ways in which the processes and outcomes of globalization and post-colonialism are raced and gendered.

Exploring race and ethnicity

Our earliest scholarship on race and ethnicity, like our early focus on women, was well intentioned but descriptive. Documenting patterns of exclusion and recovering and celebrating the achievements of women and athletes of colour too long ignored by mainstream sport memory is the necessary first step in uncovering more dynamic and insidious patterns of power.[6] More recently we have moved from the study of structural aspects of discrimination such as stacking, which remains a strikingly robust residual tradition, to more nuanced studies of the meanings of minority involvement in sport. Indeed, the whole meaning of the term 'minority' is provocative when the statistical minority in some of our most dominant sport forms is actually white athletes.

The impact of our work has been compromised by our restrictive view of the nature of racial and ethnic presence in sport. Our focus is primarily fixed on black male athletes though recent exposés on the painful practice of Native American mascots have received deserved attention. We are only beginning to explore race as a category of experience for 'majority' white athletes through the application of insights from 'whiteness' studies. Recent applications of critical race theories to sport are deepening our understanding of the meanings of these patterns and phenomena.

Although Native peoples have been involved in sporting activities for centuries, even critical scholars neglect their presence. Those with some anthropological training are most likely to focus their research attention here, a situation that runs the risk of making them appear to be a sort of cultural artefact rather than the real athletes they are. Ethnographies of First Nation sporting traditions in Canada, Aboriginal sporting traditions in Australia, and Native American sporting traditions in the US tell us a great deal about boundaries between mainstream and resilient and resistant cultures. Finally, considerable attention has recently been directed to the insulting tradition of reducing Native American identities to serve as sport team mascots.

Representations of sport

While critics of sport often complain that watching sport has replaced active participation in sport, it is more accurate to argue that although active involvement continues to rise, involvement in sport through the media has risen even faster. ESPN's reach is global, with over 20 networks in 20 countries and on every continent (Freeman, 2000: 6). In the US, most homes can graze four or more ESPN channels

24 hours a day. *ESPN: The Magazine* is challenging *Sports Illustrated* for dominance in the North American print market. Sport scholars work to understand and explain the increasing power of the media, particularly television, as the primary supplier of sport experiences and the major delivery system of images and cultural understandings about sport.

In this, scholars have benefitted greatly from critical work in communication studies, the theoretical insights of Gramscian theories of ideology, and postmodern and post-structuralist approaches that replace modernist and realist epistemologies with epistemologies that take the representational as the crucial site of cultural struggle. Traditional quantitative content analysis has been displaced by narrative analyses and discursive analyses in which an individual is understood not as an independent agent fully authorized in the construction of his or her messages but as a subject of cultural representation.

Sport scholars blend together the insights of these traditions as they explore all three sites for the making of meaning: the producer, the message, and the audience. In fact most work focuses on the message since that artefact lends itself most readily to analysis. Attention is paid to the processes of encoding and decoding that mediate between the producer and consumer through the message, conceptualized as a site for struggle over meanings: the preferred meaning proffered by the producer, the dominant reading urged by cultural interests, and resistant readings produced by the reader or consumer. Relatively few have studied the media production process, but these studies have yielded invaluable insight into the ways representations are produced, chosen, and circulated. On the other end, only a few have undertaken the audience studies that would help us understand how these messages are read and understood by the consumer. Marxist and feminist analyses are appropriate at both ends of the process, questioning who produces the images that surround us and how these processes then work to interpellate us as readers, calling us out to consume representations, commodities and ideologies all nicely packaged as sport. In the end, scholars must recognize that producers and audiences are, like the messages they circulate and consume, themselves subjects of the cultural discourses that surround them and themselves historically produced.

Representations are of particular interest to scholars because they produce particular understandings that work to reaffirm dominant relations of power structured along the lines of race, gender, sexuality, and so on. Women, who have won some opportunities to participate in sport, now find that the battleground has shifted to the ways their involvement and their athletic bodies are represented in mainstream media. Against a long history of the sexualization, objectification and commodification of women's bodies and a shorter history of the celebration of women's athleticism, critical sport scholars ponder new equations of strength and sexiness and the current confusion over the proper representations of active women.

Exploring the cultural meanings that circulate around athletes of colour through media representations is also a productive venue for critical analysis. A primary theme here is the ways that the athletic achievements of racial and ethnic minorities are undermined or dismissed. One example is the contention that African

American athletes owe their successes to their 'natural' athletic abilities rather than their dedication and hard work. Another variation on this theme interrogates the cultural categorizations, constructed through the media, that dominate our public perceptions of black athletes. The simplistic separation of black athletes into categories of good citizen (Michael Jordan, of course, and Tiger Woods, despite his mitigating multicultural identity) and 'bad boys misbehaving' (Dennis Rodman and Mike Tyson, for example) forms the basis for penetrating questions about the cultural imperatives apparently operating to produce these categories and categorizations. Even more revealing are studies of the narratives constructed in the popular press to make cultural sense of the good man gone bad: O. J. Simpson and Kobe Bryant offer the best examples here. In these cases the event is framed not as the tragic tale of a great hero falling from grace but as the tawdry tale of fundamental badness finally revealed. Comparable work on the cultural meanings of women athletes of colour has focused on the Williams sisters and Nancy Lopez, for example, and on the ways that the women of the WNBA are constructed as good girls in contrast to the bad boys of their brother organization, the NBA.

Sporting subcultures and resistant action

The rampant commercialism that invades virtually all levels of sport today alienates some people so much that they abandon sport altogether, but others seek out alternative experiences, often on the margins of the mainstream, and intentionally construct resistant sporting subcultures where they themselves organize and define the activity. Using ethnographic methods and interpretive theories such as symbolic interactionism, researchers explore the social conditions under which these subcultures form, how the group forges and maintains its identity, and how it responds to pressures from mainstream culture to conform or disband.

Sport scholars have investigated a wide range of such subcultures or groups which use sport as the site for resistant or subversive action. Some sporting subcultures are unabashedly confrontational, like English soccer hooligans, who actively challenge the strictures of mainstream culture. The rebellion of others, such as skateboarders and rock climbers, utilizes a strategy of evasion. Others challenge selective aspects of culture, such as women who band together to invade the male preserve of sports in order to participate in 'inappropriate' sports: rugby and bodybuilding are the most common examples.

However resistance does not have to take place within the social support system of a subcultural community. Whenever an individual chooses an activity that goes against the cultural grain, he or she is using sport as a site for resistance, perhaps even subversive action.

Resistant groups have a history of using sport as a means for expressing and preserving their own cultural identity, such as in the black baseball leagues, or of tailoring sport to fit their own needs, such as feminists' efforts to replace a traditional form of sport (softball, for example) with their own variations. Sport can also be a site for cultural transference, when new, sometimes subordinated cultures take up dominant cultural forms and, substituting appropriation for assimilation, produce their own forms and meanings: Pueblo baseball and Trobriand cricket are two classic examples. Such intentional manipulations imbue signifiers of mainstream sport with new meanings (gay male appropriations of David Beckham, for example) disrupting their power to carry uncontested meanings. Other interventions force mainstream sports into new configurations, creating hybrid forms of sport and validating alternative subjectivities such as female masculinity (within bodybuilding, for example) which disrupt commonsense notions of the body and modernist assumptions about the relationship between sex and gender. Conceptualizing such subversive actions as part of the power struggles in which sport is embedded is central to the cultural studies project.

Spatial dimensions of sport

Sport is a dynamic activity that takes place in time and space, but while we have well developed theories on the temporal patterns of sport provided by sport historians, the spatial dimension of sport has been less thoroughly explored. Now, guided by new insights from Marxist scholarship, cultural geography, critical geography, and postmodern geography, the spatial dimension of sport opens up as exciting new territory.

Space has many dimensions, from the concrete to the metaphorical to the ideological, and all can offer insights into the cultural meanings of sport. Realist epistemologies which privilege more concrete conceptualizations of space characterize the early work in the geography of sport. This work documented the geographic distribution of athletes and mobility patterns in a relatively descriptive manner. More recent work conceptualizes this issue as athletic migration and locates the patterns within Marxist and materialist frameworks, extending the scope of analysis to the global stage. Other scholars explore issues of urban sport by examining the politics of stadium placement and the migration of sport franchises in terms of economic costs and impact on the production of community.

Sport is infused with metaphors of space. Many sports are both literally and metaphorically described in spatial term: football with its territorial imperatives is the most obvious example; the division of the schedule into home and away games unleashes a barrage of spatial metaphors about the protection of home turf; and the vast expanses of green that constitute the cricket pitch and the baseball diamond conjure up peaceful visions that signify home and nation. We use metaphors of space as well to illustrate other power dynamics in sport: 'sport as a male preserve', for example, or 'women's bodies as contested terrain'.

But many of these situations are not metaphorical at all, as when particular sporting venues are restricted, officially or surreptitiously, to particular members: the protest at the Masters Tournament at Augusta National in 2002 is a reminder of the long history of keeping Jews, blacks, women and other undesirables out of country clubs, athletic clubs and swimming pools. But resistant action emerges here as well as athletes produce their own resistant spaces such as public spaces appropriated by skateboarders or gay male runners.

Space is a dynamic force, not the static backdrop to social life. Explorations of the process of spatialization, urged by critical and postmodern geographers, reveal dialectical tendencies within space: space produces meanings just as meanings produce space; space is both socially constructed and constitutive of social experience. Interrogations into the productive capacity of space might be particularly promising within sport as we explore the ways sporting spaces acquire social signification and how these meanings circulate within the immediate and extended environment. Sport lends itself well to ethnographies of cultural space and scholars have begun to focus attention on the ways that subjectivities are produced and circulated in relation to particular spaces. Clearly postmodern theories of space and place promise to take critical geography of sport in provocative new directions.

Conclusion

The serious study of sport has developed rapidly in the past 40 years, and the shift toward more critical and more interdisciplinary work has strengthened our abilities to provide cogent social commentary about the world around us. These insights are not limited to the specific subject matter of sport: the best work in sport studies is not really about sport *per se* but about power as power is manifested and reproduced in and through sport, and how sport might serve as a site for resistance, transformation and the redistribution of power. More exciting prospects lie ahead. To continue our critical trajectory, we must remain alert to the sea changes of academia and maintain our intellectual connections with other disciplines so that we do not become isolated within our own departments.

Our interdisciplinary project can be enriched even further through increased interactions with those within sport studies as well as our colleagues in other disciplines. Connections might be strengthened, for example, if critical sport studies scholars whose work is located within particular disciplines, such as sport history and sport sociology, sponsored joint conferences occasionally rather than relying on the interdisciplinary commitments of individual scholars to make those connections. Potentially even more intriguing is the possibility of North American sport studies scholars and leisure studies scholars beginning dialogues across the disciplines. As it is, North American sport studies has a stronger epistemological affinity to leisure studies in the UK than within the US. Crossing those borders might open new possibilities for both fields.

Many new themes, new theories, and new topics await our scholarly attention. Critical work is grounded in a commitment to pursue issues of inequality but our analyses are limited by the incompleteness of our understandings of the impact of the social categories of experience around which privilege is structured. Strong traditions of critical scholarship on the relationships of gender, sexuality, race, ethnicity and class to sport have been developed, but there are limits to our conceptualizations of these social experiences. Our work on race and ethnicity, for example, does not extend far enough to include groups such as Asian Americans, Latinos and Native Americans in any meaningful way. A glaring omission on our research agenda is the almost total absence of critical theoretical work that engages the ways that age and physical ability/disability are implicated in the ideological work of sport. Extending our scholarship in these directions brings the possibility for connection to leisure studies, with its focus on therapeutic recreation and leisure through the lifespan. Even more important, we need to move beyond analyses of inequality that explore only one of these lines of power at a time. Models of intersectional analysis that explore the complicated ways in which these power lines cross and intersect promise much more complex and complete pictures of the ways that power is exercised in and around sport.

Notes

1. I thank my Iowa colleagues Tina Parratt and Dawn Stephens for sharing with me their insights into the fields of sport history and sport psychology, and Pennington Winberg and Kirsten Wolfe for their excellent and timely research assistance. Mary McDonald offered keen insights into the trends of the field, suggested new sources, and read several drafts of this chapter. It is a pleasure to acknowledge her invaluable assistance.
2. Among these journals, the sociology of sport accounts for seven, sport psychology supports six, and sport history four.
3. Sport sociology and sport psychology began with international organizations. The sociology of sport grew out of the International Council of Sport Science and Physical Education (ICSSPE) and in 1964 moved to join the cognate group, the International Sociology Association as the International Committee on Sociology of Sport, then became an autonomous group, the International Sociology of Sport Association. The North American Society for the Study of Sport (NASSS) began in 1980. National organizations were also formed in France, Japan and Korea, but not in Britain, where only recently has a Sport Study Group formed within the British Sociological Association. Sport psychology began with the International Society for Sport Psychology, also in 1964. The North American Society for Psychology of Sport and Physical Activity was founded three years later. In 1986 part of that group formed the Association for Applied Sport Psychology to support the more applied part of that field. Also that year, an Exercise and Sport division was added to the American Psychological Association. Sport history began in 1973 with the formation of The North American Society for Sport History (NASSH). The International Society of History of Physical Education and Sport was founded in 1989 as a merger of smaller international groups, and national sport history organizations exist around the world – in Britain, Australia, Brazil, Holland, Finland, Japan, Norway and France, to name a few. The Anthropological Association for the Study of Play (TAASP) began in 1974, changing its name to The Association for the Study of Play (TASP) in 1987 to reflect a more interdisciplinary approach. The Sport Literature Association began its association with the Modern Language Association in the 1980s. Sport philosophy formed the Philosophic Society for the Study of Sport in 1972, then became the International Association for the Philosophy of Sport in 1999. All these organizations sponsor research conferences, most annually, and most sponsor journals in their area of expertise. Many of these associations are listed in the Scholarly Sport Sites maintained by the University of Calgary at <http://www.ucalgary.ca/librar/ssportsite/assoc.html> (accessed 11 January 2005). The US has no separate scholarly organization focused on leisure studies; the Canadian Association for Leisure Studies has existed since 1983.
4. In contrast, professional affiliations and identities remain a more central part of North American leisure studies, a part of its long-standing connections to the parks and recreation field.
5. Sport participation continues to increase at all levels: recreational, scholastic, collegiate, professional and elite amateur. Increases in recreational sport and fitness activities can be attributed to interacting individual and cultural (often commercial) forces: increased awareness by individuals of the relationship between physical activity and health on the one hand and the increased profits generated by the fitness industry on the other. At the competitive levels of interscholastic and intercollegiate athletics, much of the growth is

attributable to increased opportunities for women (attributed in the US to the impact of Title IX) but men's opportunities to participate in organized sports has increased steadily as well. Opportunities to participate at the professional and elite levels have also increased, though of course not on the same scale. Increased participation here can be directly attributed to commercial interests. Professional sports leagues add franchises as soon as new markets become viable investments. Even more important, the demand for content matter to satisfy the voracious television audience it has created drives networks such as ESPN to seek out, even invent, more televisable sport. The one glaring exception to this trend of increased sport involvement is found, sadly and ironically, among children and youth. For those not involved in the official teams that represent their schools or for those whose parents do not facilitate their participation in sponsored youth sport leagues, the trend is discouraging: physical activity levels of children and youth have decreased dramatically in recent years as more and more US schools drop compulsory physical education classes.

6. Richard Lapchick's annual Racial Report Card (available from <http://www.sportinsociety. org/>) and Acosta and Carpenter's annual report on Title IX (<http://webpages.charter. net/womeninsport/>) provide important databases for documenting inequities and raising critical questions about opportunities in sport.

Bibliography

American Sports Data, Inc. (2000) 'Booming Health Clubs, Slipping Fitness Participation and Healthier Diets all Coexist in the Overweight Society' <http://www.americansportsdata. com/pr-fitnessrevolution.asp>. Posted August 28, 2000. Accessed November 26, 2004.

American Sports Data, Inc. (2001) 'Grandparents Fitter than Grandchildren?' <http://www. americansportsdata.com/pr-generations.asp>. Posted July 23, 2001. Accessed November 26, 2004.

Caillois, R. (1961) *Man, Play and Games*. Trans. by M. Barash. Glencoe, IL, Free Press.

Freeman, M. (2000) *ESPN: The Uncensored History*, Dallas, Taylor Publishing Company.

Henry, F. (1964) 'Physical Education: An Academic Discipline', *Journal of Health, Physical Education, and Recreation* 35: 32–3, 69.

Huizinga, J. (1950) *Homo ludens*, Boston, Beacon Press.

Kenyon, G. S. and Loy, J. W. (1965) 'Toward a Sociology of Sport', *Journal of Health, Physical Education, and Recreation* 36: 24–5, 68–9.

Loy, J. W. (1968) 'The Nature of Sport: A Definitional Effort', *Quest*, Monograph X, pp. 1–15.

Loy, J. W. and Kenyon, G. S. (eds) (1969) *Sport, Culture and Society: A Reader on the Sociology of Sport*, New York, Macmillan.

Messner, M. (1988) 'Sport and Male Domination: The Female Athlete as Contested Ideological Terrain', *Sociology of Sport Journal* 5: 197–211.

Veblen, T. (1899) *The Theory of the Leisure Class: An Economic Study of Institutions*, New York, The Macmillan Company.

Further reading

This list is suggestive rather than comprehensive. Excellent essays providing overviews of most topics in this review can be found in Coakley and Dunning (2000) and Guilianotti (2004); specific chapters are not separately cited below. Other sources cited are representative of particular trends within the field.

Developing sport studies

Adelman, M. (1983) 'Academicians and Athletics: A Decade of Progress', *Journal of Sport History* 10: 80–106.

Burdge, R. (1989) 'The Evolution of Leisure and Recreation Research from Multidisciplinary to Interdisciplinary', in E. Jackson and T. Burton (eds) *Understanding Leisure: Mapping the Past, Charting the Future*, State College, PA, Venture Publishing.

Coalter, F. (1999) 'Leisure Sciences and Leisure Studies: The Challenge of Meaning', in E. Jackson and T. Burton (eds) *Leisure Studies: Prospects for the Twenty-first Century*, State College, PA, Venture Publishing.

Gill, D. (2000) 'The History of Sport and Exercise Psychology', *Psychological Dynamics of Sport and Exercise*, Champaign, IL, Human Kinetics Press.

Jackson, E. and Burton, T. (eds) (1989) *Understanding Leisure and Recreation: Mapping the Past, Charting the Future*, State College, PA, Venture Publishing.

Jackson, E. and Burton, T. (eds) (1999) *Leisure Studies: Prospects for the Twenty-first Century*, State College, PA, Venture Publishing.

Leisure Studies Association. Organizational website. <http://www.leisure-studies-association.info/LSAWEB/History.html> (accessed 16 January 2005).

Loy, J., McPherson, B. and Kenyon, G. (1978) *Sociology of Sport as an Academic Specialty*, Ottawa, Ontario, CAHPER monograph.

Loy, J. and Sage, G. (eds) (1997) 'Sociology of Sport: Traditions, Transitions, Transformations', Special issue of *Sociology of Sport Journal* 14.

Moving toward an interdisciplinary and critical sport studies

Andrews, D. L. (2002) 'Coming to Terms with Cultural Studies', *Journal of Sport and Social Issues* 26(1): 110–17.

Coakley, J. and Dunning, E. (eds) (2000) *Handbook of Sports Studies*, London, Sage.

Guilianotti, R. (ed.) (2004) *Sport and Modern Social Theorists*, London, Palgrave Macmillan.

Hargreaves, J. A. (ed.) (1982) *Sport, Culture and Ideology*, London, Routledge & Kegan Paul.

Howell, J., Andrews, D. and Jackson, S. (2002) 'Cultural Studies and Sport Studies: An Interventionist Practice', in J. McGuire and K. Young (eds) *Theory, Sport & Society*, Boston, JAI.

McDonald, M. G. and Birrell, S. (1999) 'Reading Sport Critically: A Methodology for Interrogating Power', *Sociology of Sport Journal* 13: 344–65.

Rail, G. (ed.) (1998) *Sport and Postmodern Times*, Albany, SUNY Press.

Sage, G. (1998) *Power and Ideology in American Sport*, (2nd edn), Champaign, IL, Human Kinetics.

Sugden, J. and Tomlinson, A. (eds) (2002) *Power Games: A Critical Sociology of Sport*, London, Routledge.

Exploring gender and sexuality

Birrell, S. (1988) 'Discourses on the Gender/Sport Relationship: From Women in Sport to Gender Relations in Sport', *Exercise and Sport Science Reviews* 16: 459–502.

Birrell, S. and Cole, C. L. (eds) (1994) *Women, Sport and Culture*, Champaign, IL, Human Kinetics.

Cahn, S. K. (1994) *Coming on Strong: Gender and Sexuality in Twentieth-century Women's Sport*, New York, Free Press.

Cole, C. L. (1994) 'Resisting The Canon: Feminist Cultural Studies, Sport and Technologies of the Body', in S. Birrell and C. L. Cole (eds) *Women, Sport and Culture*, Champaign, IL, Human Kinetics.

Cole, C. L. (ed.) (2001) 'Bodies', Special issue of *Journal of Sport and Social Issues* 25.

Costa, D. M. and Guthrie, S. (eds) (1994) *Woman and Sport: Interdisciplinary Perspectives*, Champaign, IL, Human Kinetics.

Duncan, M. C. (1994) 'The Politics of Women's Body Images and Practices: Foucault, the Panopticon, and Shape Magazine', *Journal of Sport and Social Issues* 18(1): 48–65.

Dworkin, S. L. and Wachs, F. L. (1998) 'Disciplining the Body: HIV-positive Male Athletes, Media Surveillance and the Policing of Sexuality', *Sociology of Sport Journal* 15(1): 1–29.

Eskes, T., Duncan, M. C. and Miller, E. M. (1998) 'The Discourse of Empowerment: Foucault, Marcuse, and Women's Fitness Texts', *Journal of Sport and Social Issues* 22(3): 317–44.

Hall, M. A. (1996) *Feminism and Sporting Bodies: Essays on Theory and Practice*, Champaign, IL, Human Kinetics.

Hargreaves, J. (1994) *Sporting Females: Critical Issues in the History and Sociology of Women's Sport*, London, Routledge.

Hargreaves, J. A. (2000) *Heroines of Sport: The Politics of Difference and Identity*, London, Routledge.

Mangan, J. A. and Park, R. (eds) (1987) *From 'Fair Sex' to Feminism*, London, Frank Cass.

Messner, M. (1992) *Power at Play: Sports and the Problem of Masculinity*, Boston, Beacon Press.

Messner, M. (2002) *Taking the Field: Women, Men, and Sports*, Minneapolis, University of Minnesota Press.

Pronger, B. (1990) *The Arena of Masculinity: Sports, Homosexuality, and the Meaning of Sex*, New York, St. Martin's Press.

Pronger, B. (2002) *Body Fascism: Salvation in the Technology of Physical Fitness*, Toronto, University of Toronto.

Scraton, S. and Flintoff, A. (2002) 'Sport Feminism: The Contribution of Feminist Thought to our Understandings of Gender and Sport', in S. Scraton and A. Flintoff (eds) *Gender and Sport: A Reader*, New York and London, Routledge.

Vertinsky, P. (1994) *The Eternally Wounded Woman: Women, Doctors, and Exercise in the Late Nineteenth Century*, Urbana, IL, University of Illinois Press.

Exploring social class

Brohm, J. M. (1978) *Sport: A Prison of Measured Time*, trans. Ian Fraser, London, Ink Links.

Cantelon, H. and Gruneau, R. (eds) (1982) *Sport, Culture, and the Modern State*, Toronto, University of Toronto Press.

Gruneau, R. (1983) *Class, Sports, and Social Development*, Amherst, University of Massachusetts Press.

Gruneau, R. (1988) 'Modernization or Hegemony: Two Views on Sport and Social Development', in J. Harvey and H. Cantelon (eds) *Not Just a Game: Essays in Canadian Sport Sociology*, Ottawa, University of Ottawa Press.

Hargreaves, J. A. (ed.) (1982) *Sport, Culture and Ideology*, London, Routledge & Kegan Paul.

Exploring race and ethnicity

Andrews, D. L. (1995) 'The Facts of Michael Jordan's Blackness', *Sociology of Sport Journal* 16: 125–58.

Banet-Weiser, S. (1999) 'Hoop Dreams: Professional Basketball and the Politics of Race and Gender', *Journal of Sport and Social Issues* 23(4): 403–20.

Birrell, S. (1989) 'Racial Relations Theories and Sport', *Sociology of Sport Journal* 6: 212–27.

Birrell, S. (1990) 'Women of Color, Critical Autobiography and Sport', in M. Messner and D. Sabo (eds) *Sport, Men, and the Gender Order: Critical Feminist Perspectives*, Champaign, IL, Human Kinetics.

Carrington, B. (1998) 'Sport, Masculinity, and Black Cultural Resistance', *Journal of Sport and Social Issues* 22(3): 275–98.

King, C. R. (ed.) (2004) 'Re/claiming Indianness', Special issue of *Journal of Sport and Social Issues* 28.

Jackson, S. (1998) 'A Twist of Race: Ben Johnson and the Canadian Crises of Racial and National Identity', *Sociology of Sport Journal* 15(1): 21–40.

Jamieson, K. (2003) 'Occupying a Middle Space: Toward a Mestiza Sport Studies', *Sociology of Sport Journal* 20(1): 1–16.

McDonald, M. G. (1996) 'Michael Jordan's Family Values: Marketing, Meaning and Post-Reagan America', *Sociology of Sport Journal* 13(4): 344–65.

McDonald, M. G. (2002) 'Queering Whiteness: The Peculiar Case of the WNBA', *Sociological Perspectives* 45(4): 379–96.

McDonald, M. G. (ed.) (2005) 'Whiteness and Sport', Special issue of *Sociology of Sport Journal* 22(3).

Spencer, N. (2004) 'Sister Act VI: Venus and Serena Williams at Indian Wells: "Sincere Fictions" and White Racism', *Journal of Sport and Social Issues* 28: 223–44.

Representations of sport

Andrews, D. L. (ed.) (2001) *Michael Jordan, Inc.: Corporate Sport, Media Culture and Late Modern America*, Albany, SUNY Press.

Andrews, D. and Jackson, S. J. (2001) *Sport Stars: The Cultural Politics of Sporting Celebrity*, London, Routledge.

Birrell, S. and McDonald, M. (eds) (2000) *Reading Sport: Critical Essays on Power and Representation*, Boston, Northeastern University Press.

Gruneau, R. and Whitson, D. (1994) *Hockey Night in Canada: Sports, Identities, and Cultural Politics*, Aurora, Ontario, Garamond Press.

Jamison, K. (1998) 'Reading Nancy Lopez: Decoding Representations of Race, Class, and Sexuality', *Sociology of Sport Journal* 15: 343–58.

MacNeill, M. (1996) 'Networks: Producing Olympic Ice Hockey for a National Television Audience', *Sociology of Sport Journal* 13(2): 103–24.

Whannel, G. (2002) *Media Sport Stars: Masculinities and Moralities*, London, Routledge.

Sporting subcultures and resistant action

Birrell, S. and Richter, D. (1987) 'Is a Diamond Forever? Feminist Transformations of Sport', *Women's Studies International Forum* 10: 395–409.

Birrell, S. and Theberge, N. (1994) 'Feminist Resistance and Transformation of Sport', in D. M. Costa and S. Gutherie (eds) *Women and Sport: Interdisciplinary Perspectives*, Champaign, IL, Human Kinetics, pp. 361–76.

Caudwell, J. C. (1999) 'Women's Football in the United Kingdom: Theorizing Gender and Unpacking the Butch Lesbian Image', *Journal of Sport and Social Issues* 22(4): 390–402.

Cole, C. L. (ed.) (1998) 'Power/Resistance/Sport', Special issue of *Journal of Sport and Social Issues* 22.

Theberge, N. (2000) *Higher Goals: Women's Ice Hockey and the Politics of Gender*, Albany, SUNY Press.

Spatial dimensions of sport

Andrews, D. L. (2003) 'Sport and the Transnationalizing Media Corporation', *Journal of Media Economics* 16(4): 235–51.

Bairner, A. (2001) *Sport, Nationalism, and Globalization: European and North American Perspectives*, Albany, SUNY Press.

Bale, J. (2003) *Sports Geography*, (2nd edn), New York, Routledge.

Bale, J. and Cronin, M. (eds) (2003) *Sport and Postcolonialism*, New York, New York University Press.

Bale, J. and Maguire, J. (eds) (1994) *The Global Sports Arena: Athletic Talent Migration in an Interdependent World*, London, Frank Cass.

Curry, T., Schwirian, K. and Woldoff, R. (2004) *High Stakes: Big Time Sports and Downtown Redevelopment*, Columbus, Ohio State University Press.

Cole, C. L. (2002) 'Sports Facilities', Special issue of *Journal of Sport and Social Issues* 26.

Cole, C. L. (2003) 'Space', Special issue of *Journal of Sport and Social Issues* 27.

LaFeber, W. (1999) *Michael Jordan and the New Global Capitalism*, New York, Norton.

Reiss, S. (1989) *City Games: The Evolution of American Urban Society and the Rise of Sports*, Urbana, IL, University of Illinois Press.

Rooney, J. (1974) *A Geography of American Sport*, Reading, MA, Addison-Wesley.

Silk, M. (2004) 'A Tale of Two Cities: The Social Production of Sterile Sporting Space', *Journal of Sport and Social Issues* 28: 349–78.

Smith, J. and Ingham, A. (2003) 'On the Waterfront: Retrospectives on the Relationship between Sport and Communities', *Sociology of Sport Journal* 20: 252–74.

VanIngen, C. (2004) 'Therapeutic Landscapes and the Regulated Body in the Toronto Front Runners', *Sociology of Sport Journal* 21: 253–69.

Vertinsky, P. and Bale, J. (2004) *Sites of Sport: Space, Place and Experience*, London, Routledge.

21

The Arts and Entertainment: Situating Leisure in the Creative Economy

Deborah Stevenson

Among the many products and practices categorized as art and entertainment are some of the most popular forms of leisure in contemporary society. Of particular significance are such commodities and activities as the expressive arts, popular music, motion pictures, television and multimedia. Indeed, the leisure experiences and priorities of people living in the West, increasingly, are being satisfied by, and understood in terms of, the cultural industries sector rather than the leisure and recreation industries as they traditionally have been defined. Even tourism is now often included under the remit of culture rather than leisure. The creative industries are also at the centre of a range of city reimaging and city branding exercises which seek to turn former places of work and production into spaces of leisure and consumption (Stevenson, 2003). Such places have become key sites for economic development and the expression and maintenance of local and regional identities.

The creative industries are acknowledged as being one of the fastest growing sectors of the economy – central pivots of what Sharon Zukin (1997) describes as the 'symbolic economy'. Moreover, the majority of what is classified as art or entertainment is provided by the private rather than by the public sector. And even those 'elite' cultural forms, such as major art galleries or theatre companies, that are funded or heavily subsidized by governments are under considerable pressure to succeed as 'industries' by either finding complementary sources of funding or tailoring their programmes to meet the (popular) preferences of audiences/markets rather than the creative priorities of artists and producers (Stevenson, 2000).

The study of contemporary culture and the cultural industries has developed as a truly interdisciplinary endeavour straddling the social science and humanities fields of cultural studies, media studies and sociology, in particular. It is noteworthy, however, that despite the merging of leisure and culture at the level of lived experience, leisure studies scholars have contributed surprisingly little to this research *oeuvre*. This is worrying because leisure studies has the potential to add considerably to our understanding of the arts and entertainment as social phenomena and our ability to explore the intersections between the activities that now define the sector. In addition, discussions occurring within other disciplinary fields can complement existing knowledge about leisure both as a set of practices and as an industry sector. Of particular relevance to leisure studies are debates concerning the cultural industries and the creative city which have problematized the relationship between leisure, government, entertainment and the arts at the local level. Beginning with a discussion of the way in which the arts and entertainment sector is being understood, a task of this chapter is to explore key aspects of the debate about cities and their cultures and to reflect on the place of leisure within it. Also considered is the role of government in shaping the sector, particularly local government, where the trend towards cultural planning occurring as part of a cultural industries development agenda, is now one of the major influences shaping contemporary (urban) leisure and one of the most significant sites of cultural policy.

Cultural industries, creative leisure

Delineating what is meant by the categories 'art' and 'entertainment' is no easy task. Indeed, it is almost impossible to determine unequivocally what should be included within each category and to identify where one begins and the other ends (Avery, 2000; Hughes, 2000: 14; Lynch and Veal, 1997: 220–2). Conventionally, the arts have been understood fairly narrowly as traditional forms of creative expression, such as classical music and theatre, while entertainment has been taken to refer to more contemporary popular forms, including festivals and events. But these divisions, ultimately, are unsustainable especially when one considers that no matter how each is configured the arts and entertainment are central elements of the culture of any society. Following Raymond Williams (1989), culture in this context is usually understood very broadly as encompassing not only the artefacts of creative expression, but also the activities, meaning systems, rituals and rhythms of everyday life that define a group or society (Bennett, 1998; Hawkins, 1993). The task for scholars is as much to examine the intersections, interactions and disarticulations between these different elements of culture as it is to interrogate the nature and boundaries of its component aspects and forms.

Partly because the notion of culture is amorphous, especially as the object of government policy, there has been a trend in recent years for some scholars and policy-makers to speak of the 'creative' rather than the 'cultural' sector (O'Regan, 2002). This shift has been prompted by recognition also that the arts and entertainment (including the media and broadcasting) are important aspects of the 'new economies' of cities and nations (see, for instance, Florida, 2002). There is a lively debate within academic circles concerning the differences between the cultural and the creative industries and the relative usefulness of each as an explanatory frame and the focus of government policy (Cunningham, 2002; Miller, 2002). As Jo Caust explains, at its broadest the cultural industries sector embraces:

> ...all activities connected with the arts, as well as sectors far removed. [while] The creative model can include a broad range of activities including broadcasting, fashion, multi-media, journalism, publishing, the popular music industry and both commercial and not-for-profit activity. (Caust, 2003: 54)

In its highly influential *Creative Industries Mapping* document Britain's Department of Culture, Media and Sport (1998, 2001) suggests that the creative industries are:

> those industries which have their origin in individual creativity, skill and talent and which have a potential for wealth and job creation through the generation and exploitation of intellectual property.

While the creative is intended to provide the definitional space to be more focused than the cultural it, nevertheless, remains a very elastic concept. As Andrew McNamara explains in relation to *Creative Industries Mapping*:

> The idea behind the 'creative industries' retains the cultural focus upon individual creativity, skill and talent, but it transforms both the creative arts and cultural industries because it hooks on to this new capacity for wealth and job creation 'through the generation and exploitation if intellectual property'. (McNamara, 2002: 67)

O'Regan and Ryan (2004) suggest that the relationship between the cultural and creative sectors is actually quite symbiotic and the cultural industries (comprised of 'cultural institutions, libraries and museums') are a producer or 'holder' of content that is regarded as an 'asset' of the creative industries. However, at the local government level (in Australia, at least) understandings of the two sectors are extremely blurred with there being a tendency to use the terms interchangeably, as synonyms (Stevenson, 2005). As a result, many of the definitional and operational problems associated with the idea of culture are being overlaid onto the idea of the creative. As argued below, the reason for this blurring, in part, is because local lifestyles, rituals and everyday leisure activities – the 'way of life' dimensions of culture – are actually at the centre of how cultural policy has come to be imagined at the local level. Indeed, these expansive dimensions and their potential were pivotal to the marketing, by the Australia Council, of cultural planning to local governments in Australia in the late 1980s and 1990s (see, for instance, contributions to the Cultural Planning Conference – EIT Pty Limited, 1991).

Cultural planning thus has never been conceptualized narrowly as focusing solely on creative products and artefacts but has from the outset sought to intervene in, and connect with, other policy areas, such as those concerned with the built environment, social life and economic development and to work at the intersections between the creative and the lived (Mercer, 2002). In addition, cultural tourism, which is also an important aspect of many local government cultural planning strategies, pivots on local cultures and civic identities as well as on positioning the arts as an industry (ibid.: 174).

The issue of how the creative and/or cultural industries should be understood is much more than an academic debate. Because of their status as the objects of government policy, and because governments at all levels are deeply involved in fostering the sector(s) in some way, it is extremely important to work through definitional assumptions and their consequences. What soon becomes apparent when one does this is that many of the issues being debated relate to the nature of the interface between the public and the private sectors and to the ways in which this relationship is being negotiated with respect to the arts and entertainment (and leisure) within an industry development framework. Of particular concern is to determine what the 'appropriate' role of government should be in relation to the creative/cultural sector and what this role might mean for what were once core concerns of cultural policy – achieving active participation in, and equitable access to, creativity by and for all citizens.

Private interest and public good

No matter where the definitional lines are drawn it is undeniable that the arts and entertainment are big business and that a considerable industrial complex has developed to broker the production and consumption of a bewildering array of activities and practices, as well as (directly and indirectly) to intervene in the rhythms and experiences of everyday life. Not only are the cultural/creative industries increasingly provided by the commercial sector, but they frequently are highly individualized experiences which, more often than not, occur within the private rather than the public sphere – in lounge rooms and private homes, not on the streets or in community halls. And even when activities are undertaken as part of a collective experience, participation is often as an individual consumer attending a privately owned and operated facility, such as a cinema, a nightclub or a sports stadium, rather than as a member of a community or citizenry. Given these trends, it is hard to dispute Jim McGuigan's (1996: 74) assessment that the idea of the cultural industries is an 'assert[ion] of the prevalence of mainly commercial culture over publicly subsidised culture'.

It is undeniable too that the ethos of economic growth that underpins the idea of the creative/cultural industries challenges (some would say compromises) the goal of the public good that has been a central element of the cultural agenda of governments at all levels (Stevenson, 2004). In addition, the discursive spaces within which to consider aesthetic priorities have also been reduced considerably (Caust, 2003). Indeed, the ideology of the free market and the objective of profit maximization have fused with the idea and goal of creativity, and a view has emerged that the proper role of government is to be a facilitator that fosters the provision of cultural resources and services by the private sector rather than being a direct provider of art – the marketplace thus has become the key arbiter of cultural provision, creative priorities and aesthetic value. Within this context, facilitation by government can occur in a range of ways, including through legislation, regulation and, increasingly, by entering into formal 'partnerships' with industry. For instance, it is not uncommon for governments to bear the initial infrastructure costs associated with a cultural/creative initiative in order to encourage private sector investment and to minimize that sector's commercial risk. Such public–private funding partnerships are usually referred to as 'pump priming'.

As a result of these types of associations, both the public and private sectors in various combinations and alliances play central roles in fostering creative expression. Hence the cultural/creative industrial complex comprises shifting alliances of governmental, quasi-governmental and commercial interests. The primary challenge for governments entering into such alliances is to find ways of fostering productive and sustainable partnerships with the private sphere without subordinating the interests of the public (Gibson, 2001). The evidence suggests, however, that this balance is difficult to achieve. As Lisanne Gibson (2002: 26) explains, the 'logics' of the cultural/creative industries and those of the public good are (on the surface at least) 'competing'. The fulcrum of this competition lies in 'the complexities involved in marrying together enterprise processes for cultural support while retaining the centrality of public-interest rationales for cultural policy' (ibid.: 27). Gibson further argues (2002) that there is compelling evidence that the 'creative industries' paradigm is being attached predominantly to those cultural/creative forms that are, or will be, most profitable, rather than to those which will ensure access to, and equity in, cultural production and participation *and* be economically sustainable. Government's role in the arts/cultural provision has never been straightforward (Rowse, 1985; Stevenson, 2000), but where the concern in the past was to balance aesthetic priorities with the goals of access and equity, the task for contemporary governments is to try and achieve these objectives as outcomes of the imperatives of economic development and profit accumulation.

One area of cultural industry development where government involvement routinely takes the form of a partnership with the private sector, and where commercial interests may well overshadow aesthetic priorities and those of the public good, is the use of the cultural/creative industries in the redevelopment of urban precincts into places of leisure and consumption. At one extreme of this creative industries redevelopment spectrum are high profile entertainment zones, such as Darling Harbour in Sydney, the South Street Seaport in New York, and Harbor Place in Baltimore, where such attractions as festival marketplace shopping spaces, cinema complexes, restaurants, aquaria, convention centres and maritime museums are featured (Harvey, 2000). At the other end are those initiatives that seek to focus on local creative production and industry development rather than on themed entertainment and spectacle. Emblematic of this more low-key approach is the trend to establish designated cultural precincts or quarters where a range of synergistic creative endeavours are co-located. Precincts may provide spaces for activities, such as multimedia, computing, recording and broadcasting, or for the traditional creative arts, theatres, rehearsal, performance and exhibition spaces, artist's studios and craft workshops. There will often also be retail outlets in these precincts for the sale of locally produced items.

The policy framework through which many creative industries precincts are being developed and the arts, entertainment and cultural development responsibilities of local government pursued is cultural planning. Thus it is with relation to cultural planning and cultural precinct development that many of the tensions between the commercialization of culture and the public good occur. But, because of its focus on the local, it is also in relation to this policy framework that leisure merges most closely with the cultural and creative.

Leisure and the creative city

In Western nations, including Australia, Canada and the UK, one of the most significant local cultural development initiatives of recent years has been cultural planning. While it is not a cohesive body of thought or policy framework (indeed, the term 'cultural planning' is not even used universally), it is, nevertheless, the case that around the world similar blueprints are being developed and claims being made regarding locally focused and co-ordinated approaches to the governance of the arts and culture. These blueprints pivot on positioning the arts and entertainment as 'industries' and often include the development of entertainment zones or creative industries precincts (Landry, 2002; Mercer, 2002). Significantly, a broadly focused cultural planning paradigm is seen as having the potential to contribute to a range of economic, urban and social goals (McNulty, 1988, 1991; McNulty et al., 1986). In short, it is asserted that local governments should foster local culture in its widest sense because it is believed that a comprehensive cultural plan that incorporates leisure, recreation, artistic and entertainment pursuits can achieve wide-ranging objectives and considerably improve the 'quality' of everyday life (Evans, 2001; Landry et al., 1996). As Mercer explains:

> a broad and enabling [cultural] policy framework ... can simultaneously address the (soft) 'intangibles' of affirmation, identity, quality of life, celebration and social justice and the (hard) 'tangibles' of economic development, leverage, industry strategies, infrastructure development, training programs, domestic and inbound tourism revenue, urban design, town planning and transport. (Mercer, 1991: 3)

The scope of cultural planning is vast and leisure and recreation as well as the arts and entertainment are at its core. Moreover, cultural planning is frequently replacing community arts as the local cultural policy framework through which a range of social welfare objectives are being pursued – including being a strategy for achieving social inclusion (Stevenson, 2004). Many of these initiatives are focused on controlling activities that occur in public space. Indeed, public space in all its guises – parks, streetscapes, roads, neighbourhoods and urban precincts – are central to the social and creative agenda of cultural planning. It is public space that cultural planners seek to 'animate' (and tame) by nurturing the creative industries and fostering local cultural expression. The aim is to make these places attractive, safe and economically productive – environments where entertainment, the arts and leisure merge and supposedly thrive.

In what has become an influential reference work for cultural planners, Charles Landry (2002) highlights the importance of public space to a cultural planning/ creative city approach:

> At their best they function as showcases for creative ideas and activities generated in all parts of the city and places where the majority of public facilities agglomerate – ranging from museums to cafés, public squares, cinemas, pubs, restaurants, theatres and libraries. They are key locations for the public realm. (Landry, 2002: 120)

The cultural planning literature is filled with examples of once-derelict or dangerous urban precincts that have been turned into vibrant quarters or precincts (many of which were developed through public–private partnerships) that pivot on the creative industries.

Driving the trend to redevelop and reimage public space is the aim to foster the lifestyle and consumption choices of, what is being called, the 'creative class'. Indeed, it is the cultures and creative preferences of this group that are seen as pivotal to the revitalization of cities and regions. Richard Florida (2002) claims that the 'transformation' of leisure is a fundamental aspect of the 'rise of the (urban) creative class'. In transforming leisure, public space is also being transformed. The result is that some forms of leisure and the cultural production/consumption priorities of some groups are being nurtured at the expense of others. The direct and indirect control or marginalization of the leisure choices and cultural expression of groups outside the 'creative' (middle) class, whose presence in public space is viewed with suspicion, is necessary because of the challenge they pose to the cultural, leisure and creative industries agenda that is being set. For instance, Zukin (1997) describes how the parks of New York City have, in recent years, become the spaces of middle-class leisure and the homeless who once occupied them effectively have been displaced. She explains that '[b]ecause of the police and security guards, the design, and the food, the park has become a visual and spatial representation of a middle-class public culture' (Zukin, 1997: 31–2). This is a trend that is being repeated in cities around the world. As an aspect of this same process, activities such as graffiti, skateboarding and 'car culture', once deemed to be anti-social or criminal, are increasingly being reconceptualized as forms of cultural expression in the hope of rendering them manageable through cultural policy rather than overt policing initiatives or targeted strategic social policy. At the heart of these related processes are fundamental tensions between creative expression, public good and economic accumulation which are embedded in a cultural/creative industries agenda and lie at the core of cultural planning. They are central also to contemporary understandings of leisure, particularly as it occurs within urban environments.

Conclusion

It is becoming increasingly difficult to examine the arts and entertainment and their place in society without either directly or indirectly slipping onto the terrain of leisure and leisure studies. The concern of this chapter has been that nowhere within debates about the cultural and/or creative industries which are central to contemporary scholarship about the arts and entertainment, is this slippage and its consequences being examined. Nor is it a concern of leisure studies. However, there can be no doubt that deliberations regarding the cultural or the creative industries are relevant to leisure studies if for no other reason than it highlights an important way in which leisure is being framed/appropriated within contemporary cultural policy. However, leisure is positioned differently depending on which term is used. For instance, in relation to the creative industries, leisure emerges as an important consideration largely (albeit not solely) with respect to the contexts within which creative goods and services are produced and/or consumed. In addition, leisure can often be 'content' for the creative industries. However, when the sector is conceptualized as the cultural industries, it is no longer a matter of whether a particular artefact or activity is produced or consumed as part of a leisure experience. Rather, the relationship is far more absolute. The cultural necessarily embraces all forms of leisure within its sphere – leisure is part of culture – and there is no language within this paradigm for separating the two. Leisure is thus by definition the object of all cultural policy frameworks that are underpinned by an understanding of culture as way of life.

The level of government where this merging is most evident is local government where cultural planning strategies are being developed which seek to manage leisure and recreation as part of a cultural industries development agenda, particularly through the provision and control of urban public space, parks and cultural precincts. These debates do not just talk to the framing of leisure through a cultural/creative industries paradigm but point to the way in which cultural policy frameworks operate to control and regulate leisure particularly in urban environments. The aim of this chapter, therefore, was to consider some of these intersections and trends both in an effort to highlight current concerns within the study of the arts and entertainment and to underline their consequences and significance to leisure studies. It is imperative that this dialogue continues.

Bibliography

Avery, P. (2000) 'City Culture as the Object of Cultural Tourism 2000', in M. Robinson, R. Sharpely, N. Evans, P. Long and J. Swarbrooke (eds) *Reflections on International Tourism: Developments in Urban and Rural Tourism*, Sunderland, Business Education Publishers.

Bennett, T. (1998) *Culture: A Reformer's Science*, St Leonards, Allen & Unwin.

Caust, J. (2003) 'Putting the "Art" Back into Arts Policy Making: How Arts Policy has been "Captured" by the Economists and the Marketers', *International Journal of Cultural Policy* 9(1): 51–63.

Cunningham, S. (2002) 'From Cultural to Creative Industries: Theory, Industry and Policy Implications', *Media International Australia* 102 (February): 54–65.

Department of Culture, Media and Sport (1998, 2001) *Creative Industries Mapping*, London, DCMS.

EIT Pty Limited (1991) *The Cultural Planning Conference*, Mornington, Engineering Publications.

Evans, G. (2001) *Cultural Planning: An Urban Renaissance?* London, Routledge.

Florida, R. (2002) *The Rise of the Creative Class: And How it's Transforming Work, Leisure, Community and Everyday Life*, London, Basic Books.

Gibson, L. (2001) 'Cultural Development Meets Rock and Roll (or What Government can Learn from Pop Music Festivals)', *International Journal of Cultural Policy* 7(3): 479–92.

Gibson, L. (2002) 'Creative Industries and Cultural Development – Still a Janus Face?' *Media International Australia* 102 (February): 25–34.

Hannigan, J, (1998) *Fantasy City: Pleasure and Profit in the Postmodern Metropolis*, London, Routledge.

Harvey, D. (2000) *Spaces of Hope*, Edinburgh, Edinburgh University Press.

Hawkins, G. (1993) *From Nimbin to Mardi Gras: Constructing Community Arts*, St Leonards, Allen & Unwin.

Hughes, H. (2000) *Arts, Entertainment and Tourism*, Oxford, Butterworth Heinemann.

Landry, C. (2002) *The Creative City: A Toolkit for Urban Innovators*, London, Earthscan.

Landry, C., Greene, L., Matarasso, F. and Bianchini, F. (1996) *The Art of Regeneration: Urban Renewal Through Cultural Activity*, Stroud, Comedia.

Lynch, R. and Veal, A. J. (1997) *Australian Leisure*, South Melbourne, Longman.

McGuigan, J. (1996) *Culture and the Public Sphere*, London and New York, Routledge.

McNamara, A. (2002) 'How "Creative Industries" Evokes the Legacy of Modernist Visual Art', *Media International Australia* 101: 66–77.

McNulty, R. (1988) 'What are the Arts Worth?', *Town and County Planning* 57: 266–8.

McNulty, R. (1991) 'Cultural Planning: A Movement for Civic Progress'. EIT Ltd, *The Cultural Planning Conference*, Mornington, Engineering Pulbications.

McNulty, R., Penne, R., Jacobson, D. and Partners for Livable Places (1986) *The Return of the Livable City*, Washington, DC, Acropolis Books.

Mercer, C. (1991) '"Little Supplements of Life": Cultural Policy and the Management of Urban Populations'. Unpublished paper presented at the Institute for Cultural Policy Studies, March.

Mercer, C. (2002) *Towards Cultural Citizenship: Tools for Cultural Policy and Development*, Stockholm, Bank of Sweden Tercentenary Foundation.

Miller, T. (2002) 'A View from a Fossil: The New Economy, Creativity, and Consumption'. Paper to the Symposium on the 'New Economy, Creativity and Consumption', Queensland University of Technology, Brisbane, December.

O'Regan, T. (2002) 'Too Much Culture, Too Little Culture: Trends and Issues for Cultural Policy Making', *Media International Australia* (incorporating *Culture and Policy*) 102: 9–25.

O'Regan, T. and Ryan, M. (2004) 'Centering the ICT Infrastructure for the Knowledge Economy'. Unpublished paper.

Rowse, T. (1985) *Arguing the Arts: The Funding of the Arts in Australia*, Ringwood, Penguin.

Stevenson, D. (2000) *Art and Organisation: Making Australian Cultural Policy*, Brisbane, University of Queensland Press.

Stevenson, D. (2003) *Cities and Urban Cultures*, Maidenhead and Philadelphia, Open University Press.

Stevenson, D. (2004) '"Civic Gold" Rush: Cultural Planning and the Politics of the Third Way', *International Journal of Cultural Policy Studies* 10(1): 119–30.

Stevenson, D. (2005) 'Cultural Planning in Australia: Texts and Contexts', *Journal of Arts Management, Law and Society* 35(1): 36–49.

Williams, R. (1989) *Keywords: A Vocabulary of Culture and Society*, London, Fontana.

Worpole, K. (1992) *Towns for People: Transforming Urban Life*, Buckingham, Open University Press.

Zukin, S. (1997) *The Culture of Cities*, Cambridge, MA, Blackwell.

22
Outdoor Recreation

John M. Jenkins and John J. Pigram

The significance of outdoor recreation is rarely found in prominent legislation or public policy, and it is not a stated priority or strategic initiative of many academic or other institutions. However, outdoor recreation is an important and active field of scholarly activity and is as important as work is to everyday life. Leisure and outdoor recreation are important to personal development, and viewed holistically, they bring 'a degree of balance to spirit, mind, and body' (Walmsley and Jenkins, 2003: 279). Outdoor recreation provides opportunities for psychological and spiritual renewal, for testing one's skills and knowledge, for building family relationships and friendships. Through outdoor recreation, people can explore, and become more familiar with, natural and cultural environments. The relaxation, peace and solitude people experience during outdoor recreation activities in wilderness areas, for example, helps people escape the mundane and reduces stress in daily living. Simultaneously, they gain a greater appreciation of landscapes and ecosystems.

This chapter defines outdoor recreation and explains its significance. The nature and orientation of outdoor recreation studies are discussed. A selection of important associations, interest groups and government agencies are briefly reviewed. Key issues in outdoor recreation research are identified and described, though the focus is mainly on outdoor recreation in natural settings. Selected innovative management models and frameworks, developed mainly but not exclusively for application in protected areas and other natural environments, are noted and their origins are briefly explored.

Outdoor recreation: definitions and scope

According to the *Macquarie Dictionary*, the word recreate comes from the Latin *recreare* ('to restore'; *creare* being 'to create') and recreation from the Latin *recreatio*. Generally, recreation implies physical and psychological revitalization of the individual, although purists would argue that *re-creation* is, or should be, the culmination of recreational activity – 'the activity is the medium: it is not the message' (Gray and Pellegrino, 1973: 6). Recreation should not be defined in terms of end-results, because potentially re-creative activities which, for whatever reason, fail to revitalize the participant, would be excluded. The term 'outdoor recreation' is more familiar in certain cultural contexts than others, yet outdoor recreation is just what the category 'outdoor recreation' portrays – recreation that occurs outdoors in, for example, urban and rural environments or terrestrial and marine environments. It includes recreational activities such as hiking/rambling, fishing, hunting, swimming in the outdoors, surfing, scuba-diving and snorkelling, climbing and abseiling, hang-gliding, orienteering, golf and tennis, but it does not include amusement and theme parks or riding the lift of a large tower. Some authors stress the central feature of interactions in outdoor recreation between recreationists and 'an element of nature' (Ibrahim and Cordes, 1993: 4), a theme which we pursue in this chapter.

The concept of recreation, like that of leisure or work, is personal and subjective. This conceptual ambiguity seems to have led Mercer (2003: 414) to suggest that perhaps the term 'recreation' ought to be defined every time it is used. Mercer's suggestion, especially given the diverse orientations of outdoor recreation research and curricula, has considerable merit, but it does raise a concern. Definitional debate can create problems in clarifying the position and contributions of a field of study. It may contribute to confusion in how to develop and orientate educational and research programmes and can foster uncertainty in public policy-making.

The significance of outdoor recreation

The 'leisure explosion' in the developed world has been paralleled by a striking upsurge in all levels and forms of recreation activity and associated economic, physical and social impacts (for example, Clawson, 1963; Coppock and Duffield, 1975; Pigram, 1983; Liddle, 1997). Institutional, technological and socioeconomic factors have been influential in this upsurge (for example, see Cushman et al., 2005a; Pigram and Jenkins, 2006). Much leisure activity is, of course, home-centred, and increasingly home-technology-centred (for example, television, computers, videos), a feature which is being reinforced and cultivated in Western society. Nevertheless, participation in outdoor recreation in Australia, Canada, New Zealand, the UK, the US and other industrialized nations has grown rapidly since the Second World War, and particularly since the 1960s.

Expenditure on recreation is increasing as a proportion of household expenditures in countries such as Canada and Australia. In Australia, in the 12 months to June 1999, average household expenditure on recreation was A$89 per week. Local government 'spending on recreation and culture has grown to around 20% of local government outlays' (Montgomery, 2004).

The UK's countryside attracts not only a large number of people, but also a high frequency of participation. In 1990, as much as 19 per cent of the UK population aged 16 and over had visited the countryside within the week before they were surveyed, and nearly half had done so within the previous month. At the other extreme, only 2 per cent had never been to the countryside (Glyptis, 1993: 5–6). Most recent surveys (for example, Countryside Agency, 2004) indicate that total leisure day visits in England fell from 5.9 billion trips in 1998 to 5.2 billion in 2002/03 (a 14 per cent reduction). Of these visits, 24 per cent were to the countryside, 5 per cent to the seaside or coast and 71 per cent to a town or city (with the English and Welsh more likely to visit the countryside than the Scottish). Total expenditure decreased from approximately £69.9 billion in 1998 to £61.9 billion in 2002/03. The most popular leisure activities were going out for a meal or drink (18 per cent), walking, hill walking, rambling (16 per cent), visiting friends and relatives (14 per cent) and shopping (12 per cent). In the 2002/03 survey, 62 per cent of adults in Britain had visited the countryside at least once in the year prior to survey; 21 per cent of respondents had visited in the two weeks prior to the survey.

The Australian Bureau of Statistics (ABS) conducts the Environmental Attitudes and Practices Survey, a household survey which seeks to collect data on environmental topics, such as visits to national and state parks and World Heritage Areas. In the 2001 survey it was found that approximately 54 per cent of all adults visited such areas at least once in the 12 months prior to survey, but interestingly, visitation to these areas had declined between 1992 and 2001 (ABS, 2005). The ABS (2005) also published data on participation in recreation and sports activities. These data highlight the importance of outdoor recreational activities, but more detailed analysis shows that there are some marked differences (and some similarities) occurring in recreation participation among people of different ages and among men and women. In fact, at the leisure/recreational/sport activity level, for example, in Australia and many other countries, substantial differences in men's and women's participation rates can be seen (for example, see Cushman et al., 2005a).

In the United States, a 1994/95 survey of outdoor recreation participation revealed that 94.5 per cent of respondents aged 16 years or older participated in at least one outdoor recreation activity. In the recent National Survey on Recreation and the Environment for 2000/01, about 97 per cent of the US population aged 16 or older participated in some kind of outdoor recreational activity. Walking, viewing natural scenery, family gatherings and visiting nature centres were among the most popular terrestrial activities. Motor-boating, fresh- and warm-water fishing, swimming in a lake, river or ocean, and visiting a beach were the most popular water-based activities (see Cordell et al., 2005).

In Western societies, many specific land- and water-based or related activities have experienced varying rates of growth; for example, golf; bicycle riding; walking/day-hiking and backpacking; photography; nature study; horseback-riding; orienteering, mountaineering, rock-climbing and caving; off-road (four-wheel) driving; rafting, windsurfing, waterskiing, tubing and jet-skiing; snow-skiing/snowboarding, and cross-country skiing. Participation in, and demand for, nature-based recreation and tourism activities appear to be growing, and viewing or observing nature and wildlife is an increasingly popular attraction. This also appears to be the case in less developed countries. National and global figures are revealing, but there are regional and local variations where participation in nature-based recreation may actually be declining or at least stagnating.

Outdoor recreation research and study: foci, approaches and influences

Participation in outdoor recreation activities is influenced by, among other things, socioeconomic factors. Income and education, which are often reflected in occupation and correlate highly with car ownership and accessibility to a range of recreational opportunities, have substantial impacts on recreation. Demographic variables such as age, sex, family structure, immigration and concomitant cultural assimilation and diversity, are also important in explaining recreation patterns. Participation in many recreational pursuits tends to decline progressively with age, although television-watching, golf and bowls have higher participation rates among the older age groups than the young (see Cushman et al., 2005b: 289). In short, among many other factors, people's recreational motivations, the types of leisure pursuits and recreational activities they undertake and the intensity with which they are pursued, in most cases change throughout a person's lifecycle.

Other factors researchers have been investigating as means of explaining outdoor recreation in contemporary society include: population growth; populations ageing; migration and immigration; gender and lifecycle-based issues; economic impacts and valuation of recreational resources; increasing attention to health and fitness programmes and improved health care and diets; changing family structures and the increasing number of non-traditional family units; the length of the working week and the nature of employment (increasing casualization of the workforce; growth of service industries; holiday entitlements and other workplace arrangements for men and women); urbanization and suburbanization; the influence of commercial interests (public relations and marketing); environmental impacts and recreational ecology; motivations, behaviours and experiences; the roles and impacts of the media; public policy; technological developments in recreational equipment and infrastructure; the promotion of high-risk recreational activities; growth in environmental and cultural awareness and interests; shifts in the age of retirement; and tourism development.

The field of outdoor recreation studies is now very broad and gaining greater academic attention and respectability (for example, Mercer, 1980; Chubb and Chubb, 1981; Patmore, 1983; Van Lier and Taylor, 1993; Lynch and Veal, 1996, 2001; Jenkins and Pigram, 2003). The latter has come about after much questioning of the integrity and academic rigour associated with the field and a lengthy gestation period characterized by a lack of co-ordinated effort in many countries. Exceptions include the large volumes of work of prominent agencies such as the UK's Countryside Agency (formerly the Countryside Commission), the US Department of Agriculture's Forest Service and Parks Canada.

Early studies in outdoor recreation have closely parallelled those of leisure studies, but across the world there have been some remarkably different orientations and lags. Indeed, it appears that outdoor recreation research has been far more prominent in North America, especially in the US, where outdoor recreation is a highly visible field in government agencies, research programmes and university curricula (see below). In countries such as Australia, New Zealand, the UK and Canada, it tends to be embodied in leisure and/or tourism programmes or in outdoor education studies.

In a review of Clayne Jensen's (1970) *Outdoor Recreation in America: Trends, Problems, and Opportunities*, Sal Prezioso (former President of the National Recreation and Park Association) wrote: 'America today is in a state of transition and so is the park and recreation movement. It is timely, then, to examine and study the changing times and trends and problems that confront us in the park and recreation field.' In the above book and a collection of papers published as *Issues in Outdoor Recreation* (1977), Jensen and Thorstenson saw that there was scholarly attention given to the history of outdoor recreation in America (going back 300 years!), recreational need, social and economic forces, public policy and government, private lands, public lands, economics, preservation, resource management.

Nevertheless, an interesting point of debate about outdoor recreation studies emerged in the 1980s. Writing in the early 1980s, David Mercer (then a geographer at Monash University, Australia), a highly influential and pioneering Australian academic in leisure and recreation, attempted to draw distinctions between 'those active and interested in the relatively narrow field of "recreation" research and those who consider that their major area of endeavour is either "leisure" or, more broadly, "collective consumption"'. Mercer argued that recreation researchers:

- were 'fairly pragmatic in their stated aims and objectives';
- saw little or no problem in dividing up the social world into categories or segments labelled 'work', 'play' and so forth;
- concentrated on apparently straightforward measurements of activities and facilities;
- embarked on usually census-like quantitative research focusing on participation and activities with little grounding 'in any kind of social or economic theory'. (Roberts, quoted in Mercer, 1981: 3–4).

Some might consider these harsh criticisms, but reviews like this are salutary to the development of any discipline or field of study. Mercer went further and recounted that '"Leisure" research, on the other hand, attempts to look at the wood rather than the trees. It takes a "broad brush" approach to contemporary society, sees work, leisure and consumption as inextricably related, and argues that the very definition of leisure is problematic and open to considerable debate and conflicting interpretation' (ibid.: 4). Mercer placed English sociologist Kenneth Roberts, who had previously raised two important objections to the recreation approach, in this second group. Roberts argued that the recreation approach was far too narrow and that

recreation is only part of leisure. Suggesting that the quality of life depends upon sports complexes and fun centres smacks of 'bread and circuses'. The second objection is that the recreation approach is asociological, meaning that it takes too little account of how both the supply and demand for recreation facilities are likely to be influenced by the wider social system. (ibid.)

Mercer noted that an individual's academic training and organizational affiliations strongly affected their research foci. Many young Australians, for example, attended overseas universities to gain planning and recreation qualifications, and most to American institutions. They brought home American ideas. American and Canadian recreation planning thought infiltrated Australia universities and recreation planning generally. In fact, as early as the 1960s, staff of the New South Wales National Parks and Wildlife Service had studied ranger training in the US and adopted many of their practices – from clothing to fieldwork and organization.

Other prominent writers in the field of outdoor recreation around this time were reflecting on related issues in outdoor recreation research, but were also addressing the broader concerns of Mercer, as Mercer himself and Hamilton-Smith had been (for example, Mercer and Hamilton-Smith, 1980). Amidst some fine work, which has stood the test of time, we must necessarily be pragmatic.

In a widely cited and influential book (*Outdoor Recreation and Resource Management*, 1983), John Pigram traversed an extensive array of outdoor recreation concepts, theory and practice. Reflecting Pigram's position as a geographer with a substantial background in resource management (for example, water management), the book had a coherent theme: 'Outdoor recreation is recognised as an important form of resource use and particular attention is given to the adequacy of the resource base to provide a quality environment for sustained use' (ibid.: Preface). The extensive coverage of the book can be illustrated by reference to the second chapter. It was here that Pigram pointed to 'confusion concerning the nature of recreation demand' (ibid.: 16) and the very limited application of much demand and participation focused research. He described various types of demand, the socioeconomic and other characteristics of people which serve to influence participation as well as many other variables such as people's perceptions of recreation opportunity, access and accessibility, disability, travel behaviour and mobility, social need, gravity models of travel behaviour, recreational experiences, recreational management and visitor impacts. He also described the key elements and practical relevance of Clark and Stankey's (1979) now highly influential Recreation Opportunity Spectrum.

Also published in 1983 was J. Allan Patmore's *Recreation and Resources: Leisure Patterns and Leisure Places*. The conceptual and structural overlaps in the books by Pigram and Patmore and a later text on *Rural Resource Management* by (Paul Cloke and Chris Park, 1985) are interesting – all three books were written by geographers. The latter focused their attention on rural areas. Patmore, on the other hand, took a very similar approach to Pigram and addressed such matters as the relationships between work and leisure, use of leisure and recreation demand, recreation in the city, recreation in rural/countryside areas, coastal development, linear and water resources, resource evaluation, and dimensions of carrying capacity. Patmore states:

> The explosion of leisure activities during the 1960s, and in particular the rapid growth of the use of the countryside for recreation, sparked an academic interest that closely paralleled the practical concern of planners with the phenomenon. Much of this interest came from geographers and led to several papers and texts

of note in the late 1960s and early 1970s. (Patmore, 1983: 1; see also Hall and Page, 2002)

In fact, the historical interest was lengthier than Patmore implied in his references to various sources, involved many contributors across the disciplines, and was simultaneously working its way around the globe.

Historical dimensions

Pinpointing with any degree of accuracy the crucial periods and influences in a field of study is never an easy task. The purpose here is not to give a history of leisure or outdoor recreation itself, but to trace some important contemporary aspects. For detailed histories readers should consult the references cited below as well as those of ORRRC (1962); Jensen (1970), Cunningham (1980), Mercer (1981), Rosenzweig (1983), Cross (1990), Mommaas (1997) and Hall and Page (2002). In these studies, there is strong evidence of leisure's prominence, rising with social and cultural change in industrial society, and becoming an aspect of public policy with which national and local governments continue to contend. Indeed, in the early 1800s we can observe that outdoor recreation research, planning and management were at least a concern in early legislation and planning and that research in these areas has a lengthy history.

In the US, the Outdoor Recreation Resources Review Commission (ORRRC) (1962) provided a 'Chronology of Significant Events in the History of Outdoor Recreation', beginning with the establishment of the Municipal Forest in Newington in 1710!

In Australia, references to recreation and the need for outdoor recreation space can be found in orders issued from the Colonial Offices in London to Governors in the colony. Governor Darling, for example, was directed

> to constitute Commissioners for Lands, and they were to report what lands it might be proper to reserve for various public purposes including places fit to be set apart for the recreation and amusement ... and for the promoting of the health of such inhabitants ... or which it may be desirable to reserve for any other public convenience, utility, health or enjoyment. (*HRA* I, XII: 117)

Shortly thereafter, in 1830, J. T. Maslen's book, *The Friend of Australia – A Plan for Exploring the Interior and for Carrying out a Survey of the White Continent of Australia*, offered advice on a range of issues to Australian planners, including the provision of open space:

> all the entrances to every town should be through a park that is to say, a belt of park about a mile or two in diameter should entirely surround every town, save and excepting such sides as are washed by a river or lake. This would greatly contribute to the health of the inhabitants in more ways than one, as well as pleasure... it would render the surrounding prospects beautiful, and give a

magnificent appearance to the town from whatever quarter viewed. (Maslen, 1830: 263)

Charles La Trobe, Victoria's first Lieutenant Governor, reflected the reform movement's ideal of fresh air for all in his call for parks to be set aside in Melbourne as '"lungs for the city", and in the provision of public parklands ... in the town centre by 1840' (Pescott, 1982, cited in Stewart, 1991: 7).

In 1833, a Report by a Select Committee of the House of Commons on Public Walks in England considered the benefits of open space and recreation to industrialization and industry, and recognized the existence of a class-based society:

> open spaces reserved for the amusement [under due regulations to preserve order] of the humbler classes, would assist to wean them from low and debasing pleasures. Great complaint is made of drinking houses, dog fights, and boxing matches, yet, unless some opportunities for other recreation is afforded to working men, they are driven to such pursuits. The spring to industry which occasional recreation gives, seems quite necessary to the poor as to the rich. (p. 8, cited in Daly, 1987: 15)

More than a century later, steps taken to protect the countryside in the UK's Town and Country Planning Act 1947, were reinforced in legislation establishing the National Parks and Access to the Countryside Act 1949. The 1949 Act was intended to preserve, by designation, those rural landscapes considered to be of national importance from the prospect of development and led to the establishment of national parks, of which there are now twelve. The Act was also a vehicle for recreational access to the countryside. However, the post-war period saw a dramatic increase in recreational use of the countryside, and in 1966, the White Paper *Leisure and the Countryside* recommended the establishment of country parks which would

> make it easier for the town dwellers to enjoy their leisure in the open, without travelling too far and adding to the congestion on the roads; they would ease the pressure on the more remote and solitary places; and they would reduce the risk of damage to the countryside – aesthetic as well as physical. (Minister of Land and Natural Resources, 1966)

Elsewhere, leisure had become a great cause for concern in the Great Depression of the 1930s, and, with the spread and dominance of Western ideology and values became a problem for the developed and developing worlds.

Between the 1930s and 1960s there was important scholarly activity, but it was rather sporadic and disjointed, awaiting academic and practical consolidation. Max Kaplan's (1960) *Leisure in America: A Social Inquiry*, is one publication which bears testimony to an expanding range of work in the leisure and recreation fields from the 1930s. Early publications, several cited by Kaplan, included Veblen's classic *The Theory of the Leisure Class* (1899), Bowen and Mitchell's *Theory of Organized Play:*

Its Nature and Significance (1923), Castle et al.'s *The Coming of Leisure: The Problem in England* (1935), Mander's *6pm Till Midnight* (1945), Lundberg et al.'s. *Leisure: A Suburban Study* (1934), Huizinga's *'Homo Ludens': A Study of the Play Element in Culture* (1955), Meyer and Brightbill's *Community Recreation* (1948), Brockman's *Recreational Use of Wildlands* (1959), Brightbill's *Man and Leisure: A Philosophy of Recreation* (1961), Neumeyer's *Leisure and Recreation* (1958), Florence Robbins's *The Sociology of Play, Recreation and Leisure* (1955), and articles by many including those cited by Hall and Page (2002), whose focus was on geography.

The United States Outdoor Recreation Resources Review Commission was established by an Act of June 1958 (Public Law 85–470, 72 Stat. 238) to answer the following questions:

- What are the recreation wants and needs of the American people now and what will they be in the years 1976 and 2000?
- What are the recreation resources of the Nation available to fill those needs?
- What policies and programs should be recommended to insure that the needs of the present and future are adequately and efficiently met?' (ORRRC, 1962: iii)

While the ORRRC began investigating recreation in 1958 and produced its volume of work beginning in 1962, it was also around that time that universities such as Clemson and North Carolina were establishing courses in outdoor recreation. In 1963, the School of Natural Resources, the University of Michigan and the Bureau of Outdoor Recreation of the US Department of the Interior co-sponsored the National Conference on Outdoor Recreation. The ORRRC provided great impetus to the outdoor recreation research and education 'movement'. From this impetus, and that elsewhere in the form of researchers, government agencies, interest groups, and individual recreationists and activitists (for example, Myles Dunphy and others among the bushwalking and environmental movement in Australia; Ramblers in the UK; John Muir) and associations, conferences and publications in the United States and abroad saw some key themes developing:

- quantitative regional to national surveys of recreation demand in particular, and supply to a lesser extent
- profiles of visitors – demographic and geographic
- recreation ecology – focusing on impacts, capacities and management options generally targeted at limiting visitor numbers
- recreational access to public and private lands
- conservation of natural and cultural resources in tandem with recreational use
- multiple use
- resource management concepts, models, frameworks and principles
- economics of outdoor recreation and assessments of resource values and opportunity costs.

In the 1960s there was a heavy concentration of research in the natural sciences and particularly ecology. Liddle's (1997) earliest evidence of recreation ecology was Stillingfleet's (1759) *Observations on grasses in Miscellaneous Tracts Relating to Natural History, Husbandry and Physics*. However, Liddle states that it was from the 1960s that recreation ecology research expanded exponentially. Influential scholars included N. G. Bayfield, M. Liddle and D. Cole, and many reports on recreation impacts are to be found in journals such as *Biological Conservation, Environmental Management* and the *Journal of Wildlife Management* (Liddle, 1997), as well as the more specific leisure, recreation and tourism journals. There were also monographs such as Wall and Wright's (1977) and Hammett and Cole's (1987 and later editions) works which proved to be influential.

Growth in interest in social impacts (for example, conflict, crowding, vandalism) (e.g., see Jacob and Schreyer, 1980; Driver and Bassett, 1975; Clark, 1976) economics (Clawson and Knetsch, 1966), geography (Duffield and Owen, 1970; Coppock and Duffield, 1975), social psychology (Driver, 1970; Hendee et al., 1971) and forestry (for example, Brockman, 1959) were evident. These and other publications signified the emergence of and need for broad-based scholarly research engaging with a range of disciplines. However, even by the 1980s there were still some strong signals that the theoretical basis of many leisure and outdoor recreation studies was lacking (e.g., Riddick et al., 1984), though these criticisms were sometimes poorly conceived and based on narrow reviews. Challenges to such views were soon published, and by 1994, the conceptual and theoretical strength and development of outdoor recreation research had been highlighted by Henderson (1994) and others, but had been increasingly evident for some time. Henderson's observations were also evident in the application of recreation research to recreation management. Specifically, the development and application of outdoor recreation concepts, models and frameworks initially applied in the UK and North America in the 1970s and even earlier.

In 1971, Vedenin and Miroschnichenko undertook a resource-based classification of recreation potential for the Soviet Union. They classified the country into broad zones according to suitability for summer and winter recreation and for tourism on the basis of selected climatic and physiographic factors which favour or inhibit outdoor recreation (Vedenin and Miroschnichenko, 1971). The classification and associated maps indicated large areas of the former USSR suitable for extended periods of recreation across both seasons.

Perhaps one of the most ambitious and exhaustive schemes for classification of recreation potential was carried out in Canada as part of the Canada Land Inventory, a comprehensive project to assess land capability for five major purposes – agriculture, forestry, ungulates, waterfowl and recreation. The inventory was applied to settled parts of rural Canada (urbanized areas were excluded) and was designed for computerized data storage and retrieval as a basis for resource and land-use planning at local, provincial and national levels.

Academic interest in leisure and outdoor recreation has grown, with the late 1960s to early 1970s critical turning points in the legitimizing of leisure and outdoor recreation studies as acceptable fields of academic enquiry. The early publications of scholars and government agencies in the UK, North America and Australia began to shape the leisure and outdoor recreation research agendas of Western societies. Courses in leisure and outdoor recreation slowly emerged and expanded their scope and content. As Mercer points out, leisure studies programmes were being offered at Advanced Colleges of Education in South Australia and Victoria in the early 1970s. Other institutions began to develop courses in 'recreation administration, landscape design and wildlife and national parks management' (Mercer, 1981: 2). Nevertheless, few programmes of study (that is, degrees, degree majors) or courses outside the US dealt with outdoor recreation (or recreation for that matter) as a core element or in a substantial way.

There was a solid progression of publications through the 1960s and 1970s, and major tangents or affiliated work also emerged in the areas of sport, tourism, and culture and cultural industries. Evidence of the extent to which leisure and outdoor recreation studies have grown can be seen in publications of books and journals, the staging of academic and professional conferences and the establishment and evolution of professional associations. That said, by and large, outdoor recreation researchers remain a diverse group spread among many disciplines across a variety of institutions.

Examples of influential agencies and associations

For more than 50 years the Countryside Commission in Britain has been active in promoting the conservation of the natural beauty and amenity of the English countryside, within the framework of efficient agricultural land use. A particular concern has been the provision and upkeep of recreational footpaths and rights of way and encouragement of the establishment of farm trails in co-operation with landholders.

In 1999, the Countryside Agency was formed from a merger of the Countryside Commission and the Rural Development Commission. The Countryside Agency is a statutory body aimed at conserving and enhancing the countryside, promoting social equity and opportunity for the people who live there, and helping everyone to enjoy this national asset. Among the priorities of the Countryside Agency are homes, services and opportunities for rural people, access to rural areas for outdoor recreation, reducing the impact of traffic growth on the rural environment, and maintaining farming at the heart of a strong rural economy with attention both to conservation and the production of food and fibre (<http://www.countryside. gov.uk>).

Several industry associations closely linked to outdoor recreation have been influential in the development of the recreation education and industry, organizing conferences and other means of sharing information, developing training programmes and certification and accreditation criteria for professionals and academic programmes, codes of ethics, providing scholarships, and acting as voices for professionals and educators.

The National Recreation and Parks Association (NRPA) was established in the US in 1965. NRPA has a lengthy history with its origins closely linked to the Playground Association of America of the early 1900s and subsequently the National Recreation

Association (1926). NRPA is an independent and nonprofit organization, whose mission is to 'advance parks, recreation and environmental conservation efforts that enhance the quality of life for all people' (<http://www.nrpa.org/>). 'Specific goals of the association are to promote public awareness and support, to support and advance public policies and programs, to enhance professional development, and to promote, disseminate, and expand knowledge' (Tynon, 2003: 325).

NRPA publishes three journals: *Parks & Recreation*, which gives monthly reviews of industry related trends and standards, the refereed *Journal of Leisure Research* and *SCHOLE: A Journal of Leisure Studies and Recreation Education*.

Parks and Leisure Australia (PLA) is the peak Australian industry association that 'services parks and leisure professionals, who plan, develop and manage or provide for community parks and leisure opportunities, which enhance and improve the quality of life for all Australians' (<http://www.parks-leisure.com.au>). PLA has several specialty interest groups which it actively supports, including the natural resource management group and the recreation specialists in disabilities/specialist populations, local government recreation services, aquatics and amenity horticulture. PLA's history, which reflects a long held interest in horticulture, is an interesting one traced by Stewart (1991). The Victorian Tree Planters' Association was formed in 1926, comprising about 50 nurserymen and park curators. The VTA evolved to become the Institute of Park Administration of Victoria in 1955, reflecting members' expanded interests in parks administration and professional education. IPAV became the Australian Institute of Parks and Recreation (later the Royal Australian Institute of Parks and Recreation) after IPAV had held annual conferences which repeatedly attracted national interest and attendance.

Other influential associations include those specifically oriented towards leisure and recreation studies, e.g., the Leisure Studies Association, established in the UK in 1975; the Australian and New Zealand Association of Leisure Studies (established in 1991). Other associations, sometimes related to specific disciplines, recognized the significance of recreation (for example, Association of American Geographers).

The United States Department of Agriculture (USDA) Forest Service is a federal government agency established in 1905. The Forest Service manages 193 million acres of public lands (155 national forests and 20 grasslands and more than 200 research and experimental forests). 'The mission of the USDA Forest Service is to sustain the health, diversity, and productivity of the Nation's forests and grasslands to meet the needs of present and future generations' (<http://www.fs.fed.us/aboutus/mission.shtml>). The outdoor recreational resources include wilderness areas, scenic rivers and byways, trails and national monuments. Recreational opportunities available on Forest Service lands range from hiking and camping to skiing; from wildlife viewing to fishing and hunting. The Service is very strongly committed to the principle of land stewardship and multiple use. It is world renowned as the home of an extraordinary wealth of research on recreation demand and behaviour, diversity in use, access, impacts, ecology and management. Indeed, some of the most influential recreation management models and frameworks have emerged from the Forest Service, as well as agencies such as Parks Canada.

Outdoor recreation management

Many outdoor recreation management models and frameworks have been applied since the 1970s. These models and frameworks have been discussed at length and critically reviewed in various publications (for an overview see Pigram and Jenkins, 2006; Newsome et al., 2002).

Carrying capacity

Like many concepts in outdoor recreation management, the term 'carrying capacity' is bedevilled by varying and sometimes conflicting interpretations. The concept of 'recreation carrying capacity' derives from the practice, in livestock and wildlife management, of referring to the estimated number of animals an area of rangeland or a given habitat can support. In its initial application in outdoor recreation, the concept was seen as a technique to limit use to the maximum number of visitors a recreation resource or site could tolerate, without damage to the biophysical or social conditions.

Most definitions of recreation carrying capacity attempt to combine the notion of protection of the resource base from overuse with, simultaneously, the assurance of enjoyment and satisfaction for participants. Thus, in broad terms, recreation carrying capacity involves both the biophysical attributes of the environment as well as the attitudes and behaviour of users. An early definition of recreation carrying capacity by the Countryside Commission (1970: 2) reflected this duality: 'The level of recreation use an area can sustain without an unacceptable degree of deterioration of the character and quality of the resource or of the recreation experience.'

Widespread application of the concept of recreation carrying capacity led to growing scrutiny of its effectiveness as a management technique. The relationship between use and impact, typically, is not direct, and is affected by the type of recreation activity; its timing and distribution on the one hand, and the attributes of the environment where use occurs, on the other. Consequently, recent years have seen the adoption of a number of alternative approaches to monitor and manage the impacts of outdoor recreation on the environment. McCool's view was:

> The change in the character of the question driving concern about impacts from recreational use reflects a different paradigm defining recreational impact issues. It focuses not on one of the principal input variables – use level – but rather on the output or results of management. This conceptualization of use-impact relationships renders the theory of carrying capacity, as applied to recreation, out-of-date and of little practical utility to managers or theoretical value to scientists … In summary, the carrying capacity theory has probably outlived its usefulness. (McCool, 2003: 44)

McCool's statement is perhaps rather harsh and runs the risk of dismissing a historically useful concept both for thinking about environmental capacity and relationships. Brown et al.'s response to a comment on their work applying the concept of ecological carrying capacity in the Maldives and Nepal by Lindberg and McCool (1998) offers a more cautious view:

> we are circumspect on the use and application of the carrying capacity concept, and we argue that whilst ecological and tourism capacity may be of use, that use is limited, and indeed social and cultural factors may be more important in determining the extent and impacts of tourism development. (Brown et al., 1998: 293)

If applied in a dynamic way, carrying capacity invites us to think about how different physical and human conditions can affect the ability of an environment to sustain different uses. Indeed, the concept of carrying capacity has more than one dimension (for example, ecological, social, cultural), and these dimensions are now more recognizably interrelated, particularly in the application of the concept in recent research. Brown et al.'s research comment acknowledges this situation.

The Recreation Opportunity Spectrum

In many ways, the Recreation Opportunity Spectrum (ROS) is an application of behaviour setting analysis from environmental psychology (Barker, 1968; Ittelson et al., 1976; Levy, 1977). This approach suggests that all human behaviour should be interpreted with reference to the environment or behaviour setting in which it occurs. It is further suggested that, given knowledge of the behaviour setting for a specific recreation experience, such as a park visit, it should be possible to identify the human values and expectations associated with that experience. Examination of the human and non-human features of the behaviour setting should then indicate those contributing to or detracting from satisfaction.

Within this conceptual approach, a recreation opportunity allows the individual to participate in a preferred activity, in a preferred setting to realize a desired experience (Driver and Brown, 1978). The focus is on the setting in which recreation occurs. The ROS describes the range of recreational experiences which could be demanded by a potential user clientele if a full array of recreation opportunity settings was available through time. Clark and Stankey define a recreation opportunity setting as:

> the combination of physical, biological, social and managerial conditions that give value to a place (for recreation purposes). Thus, a recreation opportunity setting includes those qualities provided by nature (vegetation, landscape, topography, scenery), qualities associated with recreational use (levels and types of use) and conditions provided by management (roads, developments, regulations). By combining variations of these qualities and conditions, management can provide a variety of opportunities for recreationists. (Clark and Stankey, 1979: 1)

The basic premise underlying the concept of the ROS is that a range of such settings is required to provide for the many tastes and preferences that motivate people to participate in outdoor recreation. Quality recreation experiences can be best assured by providing a diverse set of recreation opportunities. Failure to provide diversity and flexibility ignores considerations of equity and social welfare, and invites charges of discrimination and elitism (Clark and Stankey, 1979). A sufficiently broad ROS should be capable of handling disturbances in the recreation system. These might stem from such factors as social change (for example, in demographic characteristics) or technological innovations (for example, all-terrain recreation vehicles) (Stankey, 1982).

The ROS offers a framework within which to examine the effect of manipulating environmental and situational attributes or factors to produce different recreation opportunity settings. Clark and Stankey (1979) suggest that the most important of these 'opportunity factors' are:

- access
- non-recreational resource uses
- on-site management
- social interaction
- acceptability of visitor impacts, and
- acceptable regimentation.

By packaging a recreation opportunity setting in some combination of the six factors described, a variety of recreation opportunities or options can be generated and the ROS materially enlarged.

Limits of Acceptable Change

Out of the questioning of the application of the concept of carrying capacity to recreation management evolved a more comprehensive and systematic framework for recreation decision-making, known as the 'Limits of Acceptable Change' (LAC). The planning framework based on LAC is essentially a reformulation of the recreation carrying capacity concept. The emphasis is on the ecological and social attributes sought in an area, rather than on how much use the area can tolerate. Elements of LAC found their way into planning in wilderness areas in the early 1980s (Eagles and McCool, 2002). First tested in the Bob Marshall Wilderness Complex in Montana around 1985 (Stankey et al., 1984; USDA Forest Service, 1985), the system has received widespread endorsement as a rational planning approach to recreation and parks management. Establishing and implementing the Limits of Acceptable change management framework involves a multistage process, involving nine interrelated steps.

Essentially, the Limits of Acceptable Change approach turns the recreation–environment relationship on its head, transferring the focus from the supposed cause (numbers of visitors) to the desired conditions – the biophysical state of the site and resource base, and the nature of the recreation experience. Moreover, change in nature is seen as the norm, and a certain level of natural variation in the environment is to be expected. The central question for recreation planners then becomes – how much, and what type of change can be accepted? Whereas the response must necessarily be subjective, it needs also to be guided by reference to more than ecological criteria. Socioeconomic and political considerations can also be important elements of the consultative process in setting the Limits of Acceptable Change.

The Visitor Activity Management Process

Tensions between resources and visitors led to the development of the Visitor Activity Management Process (VAMP) by the Canadian Parks Service (now Environment Canada). VAMP offers a fundamental change in orientation in parks management, from a product or supply basis to an outward-looking market-sensitive approach (Graham et al., 1988). Resource managers are encouraged to develop and market visitor experiences which will appeal to specific market segments.

> VAMP is a pro-active, flexible, conceptual framework that contributes to decision-building related to the planning, development and operation of park-related services and facilities. It includes an assessment of regional integration of a park or heritage site, systematic identification of visitors, evaluation of visitor market potential, and identification of interpretive and educational opportunities for the public to understand, safely enjoy and appreciate heritage. The framework was developed to contribute to all five park management contexts: park establishment; new park management planning; established park planning and plan review; facility development and operation. (Graham, 1990: 279)

The VAMP, like earlier frameworks (for example, ROS and LAC), uses information from both social and natural sciences to facilitate decision-making with respect to access to and use of protected areas (although it has the potential to be applied to a wider range of environments), and incorporates an evaluation requirement to measure effectiveness in outcomes and impacts (Graham, 1990). VAMP has not been applied widely, save for a limited number of sites in Canada (for example, Glacier National Park, British Columbia; Cross-country (Nordic) skiing, Ottawa; Mingan Archipelago; Point Pelee National Park; Kejimkujik National Park).

The Visitor Impact Management framework

The development of Visitor Impact Management (VIM) in 1990 demonstrates the increasingly widespread view that recreational management requires scientific and judgemental consideration (for example, Vaske et al., 1995: 36), and that effective management of the recreation resource is much more than setting visitor use levels and specific carrying capacities (for example, Graefe et al., 1984; Vaske et al., 1995: 36).

The VIM framework resulted from a study by the US National Parks and Conservation Association (NPCA). The study had two objectives: (1) to review and synthesize the existing literature dealing with recreational carrying capacity and visitor impacts, and (2) to apply the resulting understanding to the development of a methodology or framework for visitor impact management, that would be applicable across the variety of units within the US National Park system.

The review of the scientific literature relating to carrying capacity and visitor impacts identified five major considerations underpinning the nature of recreation impacts, which should all be incorporated into visitor impact programmes:

1. *Impact relationships*: impact indicators are interrelated so that there is no single, predictable response of natural environments or individual behaviour to recreational use.
2. *Use–impact relationships*: use–impact relationships vary for different measures of visitor use, and are influenced by a variety of situational factors. The use–impact relationship is non-linear (that is, it is not simple or uniform).
3. *Varying tolerance to impacts*: not all areas respond in the same way to encounters with visitors. There is inherent variation in tolerance among environments and user groups; for instance, different types of wildlife and user groups have different tolerance levels in their interactions with people.
4. *Activity-specific influences*: the extent and nature of impacts vary among, and even within, recreational activities.
5. *Site-specific influences*: seasonal and site-specific variables influence recreational impacts. (Graefe, 1990: 214; Vaske et al., 1995: 35)

These five issues represent important considerations for the management of ecological, physical and social impacts (Graefe, 1990). In brief, the VIM framework is designed to deal with the basic issues inherent in impact management; namely, the identification of problem conditions (or unacceptable visitor impacts), the determination of potential causal factors affecting the occurrence and severity of the unacceptable impacts, and the selection of potential management strategies for ameliorating the unacceptable impacts (Graefe, 1990: 216). Graefe (1990) and Vaske et al. (1995) note that the task of managing visitor impacts is not over when management strategies are implemented, and that continuous monitoring and evaluation are necessary.

VIM has been applied in Australia (for example, Jenolan Caves), Canada (for example, Prince Edward Island), and in the US (for example, Icewater Spring Shelter, Great Smoky Mountains National Parks; Logan Pass/Hidden Lake Trail, Glacier National Park; Florida Keys National Marine Sanctuary, Florida; Buck Island Reef National Monument, Virgin Islands; and the Youghiogheny River, Western Maryland) as well as Argentina, Mexico and the Netherlands (for example, see Graefe, 1990; McArthur, 2000; Newsome et al., 2002).

Visitor Experience and Resource Protection

The US National Parks Service is finding it more difficult to fulfil 'its dual mission to provide for the enjoyment of national parks while conserving resources for future generations' (US Department of the Interior, National Park Service, 1997: 4). The Visitor Experience and Resource Protection (VERP) framework was developed in the early 1990s and first applied in about 1993 by the United States National Parks Service as a response to increasing visitor pressures and impacts in US National Parks and growing concerns about carrying capacities. The 1978 *National Parks and*

Recreation Act (P.L. 95–625) actually requires the National Park Service 'to address the issue of carrying capacity in general management plans' (US Department of the Interior, National Park Service, 1997: 8). VERP evolved from the earlier LAC model in a fashion to suit the National Parks Service's mission, structures, functions and operations. It also has close links to VIM, and an emphasis on managing visitor use and resources simultaneously and continuously. Hence, VERP is: 'a planning and management framework that focuses on visitor use impacts on the visitor experience and the park resources. These impacts are primarily attributable to visitor behavior, use levels, types of use, timing of use, and location of use' (ibid.).

The management of recreation resources is inherently difficult because of the extensive range of variables involved in the recreation–environment relationship. Geographic Information Systems (GIS) are also now being used, among other things, to identify ecologically sensitive areas and to plan tourist development. GIS can be integrated into various models and frameworks in order to identify, develop, implement, monitor and evaluate strategies for outdoor recreation and visitor management.

Conclusion

> Constructive use of leisure time is of vital importance to the well-being of the individual, the community and the nation, since the growth of an individual is determined as much by how he occupies his leisure hours as by the time spent upon his daily tasks. Technological progress has developed an essentially urban pattern of life, raised our standard of living, increased our leisure time and expanded our transportation facilities. These factors, together with the growth and changing composition of our population, indicate that the future will witness increasing pressure on all existing recreational facilities ... recreational needs will be subject to an increasing amount of regimentation. We may not like it, but in the future individual preferences will necessarily have to be tempered by consideration for the many. (Brockman, 1959: 21)

> Outdoor recreation is big business. (Brockman, 1959: 179)

One could be forgiven for thinking Brockman, writing as a Professor of Forestry in specific reference to *Recreational Use of Wildlands*, had written these words in the twenty-first century. Outdoor recreation still brings joy and pleasure to many people, with the provision of appropriate recreational opportunities 'critical to the satisfaction of an individual's need for cognitive and aesthetic stimulation, one of six needs identified by Maslow (1954) as basic to human well-being' (Faulkner, 1978, in Walmsley and Jenkins, 1994: 89). People will continue to treasure the outdoors, as they have throughout human history – tracts of land will continue to be set aside for recreation; the beauty of nature will continue to be expressed in art and the development of formal gardens, as it was during the Renaissance; and consumptive activities such as hunting and fishing (whether or not people support such activities), and more passive activities in wilderness areas, such as bushwalking, will afford some the opportunities to experience 'a closer affinity between primitive and modern concepts of outdoor recreation' (Jensen and Thorstenson, 1977: 15).

This chapter has presented a rather selective overview of aspects of outdoor recreation studies in Western developed countries. It is clear there are monumental challenges ahead for outdoor recreation planners, researchers and policy-makers.

Outdoor recreation may have lost some of the prominence it began to gain in the 1970s and 1980s, but it is now well entrenched in research in many disciplines and fields of study. What we find is that outdoor recreation research now appears widely in publications stemming from those working in the traditional disciplinary areas, as well as a broad range of related fields such as sport, tourism and cultural studies, and of course, leisure.

Bibliography

Australian Bureau of Statistics (ABS) (2002) *Participation in Sport and Physical Activities*, Australian Bureau of Statistics, Canberra (Cat. No. 4177.0).

Australian Bureau of Statistics (ABS) (2005) *Year Book Australia*, Australian Bureau of Statistics, Canberra (Cat. No. 1301.0).

Barker, E. (c.1947) *Reflections on Leisure*, London, National Council on Social Service.

Barker, R. (1968) *Ecological Psychology*, Stanford, Stanford University Press.

Bowen, W. P. and Mitchell, E. D. (1923) *Theory of Organized Play: Its Nature and Significance*, New York, A. S. Barnes & Co.

Brightbill, C. K. (1961) *Man and Leisure: A Philosophy of Recreation*, Englewood Cliffs, NJ, Prentice-Hall.

Brockman, C. F. (1959) *Recreational Use of Wildlands*, New York, McGraw-Hill.

Brown, K., Turner, R. K., Hameed, H. and Bateman, I. (1998) 'Comment: Reply to Lindberg and McCool: A Critique of Environmental Carrying Capacity as a Means of Managing the Effects of Tourism Development', *Environmental Conservation* 25(4): 293–4.

Burns, C. D. (1932) *Leisure in the Modern World*, London, Allen & Unwin.

Castle, E. B., Ottaway, A. K. C. and Rawson, W. T. R. (eds) (1935) *The Coming of Leisure: The Problem in England*, London.

Chubb, M. and Chubb, H. (1981) *One Third of Our Time. An Introduction to Recreation Behavior and Resources*, New York, John Wiley & Sons.

Clark, R. (1976) 'Control of Vandalism in Recreation Areas – Fact, Fiction or Folklore', *USDA Forest Service General Technical Report PSW-17*, Oregon, US Department of Agriculture Forest Service.

Clark, R. and Stankey, G. (1979) *The Recreation Opportunity Spectrum: A Framework for Planning, Management and Research*, General Technical Report, PNW-98, Seattle, US Department of Agriculture Forest Service.

Clawson, M. (1963) *Land and Water for Recreation: Opportunities, Problems and Policies*, Chicago: Rand McNally & Company.

Clawson, M. and Knetsch, J. (1966) *Economics of Outdoor Recreation*, Baltimore, Johns Hopkins Press.

Cloke, P. and Park, C. (1985) *Rural Resource Management*, London, Croom Helm.

Coppock, J. T. and Duffield, B. S. (1975) *Recreation in the Countryside: A Spatial Analysis*, London, Macmillan.

Cordell, H. K., Green, G. T., Leeworthy, V. R., Stephens, R., Fly, M. J. and Betz, C. J. (2005) 'United States of America: Outdoor Recreation', in G. Cushman, A. J. Veal and J. Zuzanek (eds) *World Leisure Participation: Free Time in the Global Village*, Wallingford: CAB International.

Countryside Agency (2004) *Leisure Day Visits: Report of the 2002–3 GB Day Visits Survey*, Cheltenham, UK, Countryside Agency.

Countryside Agency (n.d.) <http://www.countryside.gov.uk/>, accessed 20 June 2005.

Countryside Commission (1970) *Countryside Recreation Glossary*, Cheltenham, Countryside Commission.

Cross, G. (1990) *A Social History of Leisure Since 1600*, State College, PA, Venture Publishing.

Cunningham, H. (1980) *Leisure in the Industrial Revolution*, London: Croom Helm.

Cushman, G., Veal, A. J. and Zuzanek, J. (eds) (2005a) *World Leisure Participation: Free Time in the Global Village*, Wallingford, CAB International.

Cushman, G., Veal, A. J. and Zuzanek, J. (2005b) 'Leisure Participation and Time-use Surveys: An Overview', in G. Cushman, A. J. Veal and J. Zuzanek (eds) *World Leisure Participation: Free Time in the Global Village*, Wallingford, UK: CAB International, pp. 1–16.

Daly, J. (1987) *Decisions and Disasters: Alienation of the Adelaide Parklands*, Adelaide, Bland House.

Driver, B. (ed.) (1970) *Elements of Outdoor Recreation Planning*, Ann Arbor, University of Michigan Press.

Driver, B. L. and Bassett, J. (1975) 'Defining Conflicts Among River Users: A Case Study of Michigan's Au Sable River', *Naturalist* 26: 19–23.

Driver, B. and Brown, P. (1978) 'A Social-physiological Definition of Recreation Demand, with Implications for Recreation Resource Planning', Appendix A of *Assessing Demand for Outdoor Recreation*, Washington, DC, US Bureau of Outdoor Recreation.

Driver, B., Brown, P., Stankey, G. and Gregoire, T. (1987) 'The ROS Planning System: Evolution, Basic Concepts and Research Needed', *Leisure Sciences* 9: 201–12.

Duffield, B. and Owen, M. (1970) *Leisure and Countryside: A Geographical Appraisal of Countryside Recreation in Lanarkshire*, Edinburgh, University of Edinburgh Press.

Eagles, P. F. J. and McCool, S. F. (2002) *Tourism in National Parks and Protected Areas: Planning and Management*, Wallingford, CABI Publishing.

Glyptis, S. (ed.) (1993) *Leisure and the Environment: Essays in Honour of Professor J. A. Patmore*, London, Belhaven.

Graefe, A. R. (1990) 'Visitor Impact Management', in R. Graham and R. Lawrence (eds) *Towards Serving Visitors and Managing Our Resources*, Proceedings of a North American Workshop on Visitor Management in Parks and Protected Areas, Waterloo, Tourism Research and Education Centre, University of Waterloo, pp. 213–34.

Graefe, A. R., Vaske, J. J. and Kuss, F. R. (1984) 'Social Carrying Capacity: an Integration and Synthesis of Twenty Years of Research', *Leisure Sciences* 6(4): 395–431.

Graham, R. (1990) 'Visitor Management in Canada's National Parks', in R. Graham and R. Lawrence (eds) *Towards Serving Visitors and Managing Our Resources*, Proceedings of a North American Workshop on Visitor Management in Parks and Protected Areas, Waterloo, Tourism Research and Education Centre, University of Waterloo, pp. 271–96.

Graham, R., Payne, R. J. and Nilsen, P. (1988) 'Visitor Activity Planning and Management in Canadian National Parks', *Tourism Management* 9(1): 44–62.

Gray, D. and Pellegrino, D. (1973) *Reflections on the Recreation and Park Movement*, Dubuque, IL, Brown.

Hall, C. M. and Page, S. J. (2002) *The Geography of Tourism and Recreation* (2nd edn), London, Routledge.

Hammitt, W. and Cole, D. (1987) *Wildland Recreation Ecology and Management*, New York, Wiley.

Hendee, J. C., Gale, R. P. and Catton, W. P. (1971) 'A Typology of Outdoor Recreation Activity Preferences', *Journal of Environmental Education* 3(1): 28–34.

Henderson, K. (1994) 'Theory Application and Development in Recreation, Parks and Leisure Research', *Journal of Park and Recreation Administration* 12(1): 51–64.

Historical Records of Australia (*HRA*) Volume I (1913) Sydney, Library Committee of the Parliament of the Commonwealth.

Huizinga, J. (1955) '*Homo Ludens': A Study of the Play Element in Culture*, Boston, Beacon Press.

Ibrahim, H. and Cordes, K. (1993) *Outdoor Recreation*, Dubuque, IL, Brown and Benchmark.

Ittelson, W., Franck, K. and O'Hanlon, T. (1976) 'The Nature of Environmental Experience', in S. Wapner, S. Cohen and B. Kaplan (eds) *Experiencing the Environment*, New York, Plenum Press.

Jacob, G. and Schreyer, R. (1980) 'Conflict in Outdoor Recreation: A Theoretical Perspective', *Journal of Leisure Research* 12(4): 368–80.

Jenkins, J. M. and Pigram, J. J. (eds) (2003) *Encyclopedia of Leisure and Outdoor Recreation*, London, Routledge.

Jensen, C. R. (1970) *Outdoor Recreation in America: Trends, Problems, and Opportunities* (3rd edn), Minneapolis, Burgess.

Jensen, C. R. and Thorstenson, C. T. (1977) 'A Brief History of Outdoor Recreation in America', in C. R. Jensen and C. T. Thorstenson (eds) *Issues in Outdoor Recreation* (2nd edn), Minneapolis, Burgess, pp. 3–13.

Kando, T. M. (1975) *Leisure and Popular Culture in Transition*, Saint Louis, MO, The C.V. Mosby Company.

Kaplan, M. (1960) *Leisure in America: A Social Inquiry*, New York, John Wiley & Sons.

Levy, J. (1977) 'A Paradigm for Conceptualising Leisure Behaviour', *Journal of Leisure Research* 11(1): 48–60.

Liddle, M. (1997) *Recreation Ecology*, London, Chapman & Hall.

Lindberg, K. and McCool, S. F. (1998) 'Comment: A Critique of Environmental Carrying Capacity as a Means of Managing the Effects of Tourism Development', *Environmental Conservation* 25(4): 291–2.

Lundberg, G. A., Komarovsky, M. and McInerny, M. A. (1934) *Leisure: A Suburban Study*, Columbia, Columbia University Press.

Lynch, R. and Veal, A. J. (1996) *Australian Leisure*, Melbourne, Longman.

Mander, A. E. (1945) *6pm Till Midnight*, Melbourne, Rawson's.

Maslen, J. T. (1830) *The Friend of Australia – A Plan for Exploring the Interior and for Carrying out a Survey of the White Continent of Australia*, London, Hurst, Chance and Co.

Maslow, A. (1954) *Motivation and Personality*, New York, Harper & Row.

McArthur, S. (2000) 'Visitor Management in Action: An Analysis of the Development and Implementation of Visitor Management Models at Jenolan Caves and Kangaroo Island', PhD thesis, University of Canberra, ACT.

McCool, S.F. (2003) 'Carrying Capacity', in J. M. Jenkins and J. J. Pigram (eds) *Encyclopedia of Leisure and Outdoor Recreation*, London, Routledge, pp. 42–4.

Mercer, D. C. (1970) 'The Geography of Leisure – Contemporary Growth Point', *Geography* 55(3): 261–73.

Mercer, D. C. (1980) *In Pursuit of Leisure*, Melbourne, Sorrett.

Mercer, D. C. (1981) 'Trends in Recreational Participation', in D. Mercer (ed.) *Outdoor Recreation: Australian Perspectives*, Melbourne, Sorrett, pp. 24–44.

Mercer, D. C. (1994) 'Monitoring the Spectator Society: an Overview of Research and Policy Issues', in D. C. Mercer (ed.) *New Viewpoints in Australian Outdoor Recreation Research and Planning*, Melbourne, Hepper Marriott and Associates, pp. 1–28.

Mercer, D. C. (2003) 'Recreation', in J. M. Jenkins and J. J. Pigram (eds) *Encyclopedia of Leisure and Outdoor Recreation*, London, Routledge, pp. 412–15.

Mercer, D. and Hamilton-Smith, E. (eds) (1980) *Recreation Planning and Social Change in Urban Australia*, Melbourne, Sorrett.

Meyer, H. D. and Brightbill, C. K. (1948) *Community Recreation*, Boston, MA, D.C. Heath.

Minister of Land and Natural Resources (1966) *Leisure and the Countryside*, London, HMSO.

Mommaas, H. (1997) 'European Leisure Studies at the Crossroads? History of Leisure Research in Europe', *Leisure Sciences* 19(3): 241–54.

Montgomery, M. (2004) Opening address to the Regional Cooperation and Development forum, National General Assembly of Local Governments, Canberra, 7 November, <http://nga.alga.asn.au/generalAssembly/2004/01.presentations/01.mikeMontgomery.php>, accessed 2 March 2005.

Neumeyer, M. H. and Neumeyer, E. S. (1958) *Leisure and Recreation* (3rd edn), New York, Ronald Press.

Newsome, D., Moore, S. A. and Dowling, R. (2002) *Natural Area Tourism: Ecology, Impacts and Management*, Clevedon, Channel View Publications.

Outdoor Recreation Resources Review Commission (ORRRC) (1962a) *Outdoor Recreation Literature: A Survey: Report to the Outdoor Recreation Resources Review Commission by the Library of Congress*, Study Report 27, Washington, DC, US Government Printing Office.

Outdoor Recreation Resources Review Commission (ORRRC) (1962b) *Outdoor Recreation for America*, Washington, DC: US Government Printing Office.

Parks and Leisure Australia (n.d.) <http://www.parks-leisure.com.au/>, accessed 14 June 2005.

Patmore, A. J. (1983) *Recreation and Resources: Leisure Patterns and Leisure Places*, Oxford, Blackwell.

Pigram, J. J. (1983) *Outdoor Recreation and Resource Management*, London, Croom Helm.

Pigram, J. J. and Jenkins, J. M. (2006) *Outdoor Recreation Management* (2nd edn), London, Routledge.

Riddick, C., DeSchriver, M. and Weissinger, E. (1984) 'A Methodological Review of Research in the Journal of Leisure Leisure Research from 1978 to 1982', *Journal of Leisure Research* 16(3): 311–21.

Robbins, F. (1955) *The Sociology of Play, Recreation and Leisure*, Dubuque, Iowa, Brown.

Rosenzweig, R. (1983) *Eight Hours for What We Will: Workers and Leisure in an Industrial City, 1870–1920*, New York, Cambridge University Press.

Stankey, G. (1977) 'Some Social Concepts for Outdoor Recreation Planning', in *Proceedings of Symposium on Outdoor Advances in the Application of Economics*, Washington, DC, US Department of Agriculture, Forest Service, General Technical Report WO-2.

Stankey, G. (1982) 'Carrying Capacity, Impact Management and the Recreation Opportunity Spectrum', *Australian Parks and Recreation* (May): 24–30.

Stankey, G., Cole, D., Lucas, R., Peterson, M. and Frissell, S. (1985) *The Limits of Acceptable Change (LAC) System for Wilderness Planning*, Ogden, USDA Forest Service.

Stankey, G., McCool, S. and Stokes, G. (1984) 'Limits of Acceptable Change: A New Framework for Managing the Bob Marshall Wilderness Complex', *Western Wildlands* (Fall): 33–7.

Stewart, E. (1991) *Places in the Park: A History of the Royal Australian Institute of Parks and Recreation*, Canberra, Royal Australian Institute of Parks and Recreation.

Stillingfleet, B. (1759) *Observations on grasses in Miscellaneous Tracts Relating to Natural History, Husbandry and Physics*, London.

Tynon, J. (2003) 'National Recreation and Parks Association', in J. M. Jenkins and J. J. Pigram (eds) *Encyclopedia of Leisure and Outdoor Recreation*, London, Routledge.

US Department of Agriculture Forest Service (1985) *Bob Marshall Great Bear Scapegoat Wilderness Action Plan for Managing Recreation (The Limits of Acceptable Change)*, Flathead National Forest, USDA Forest Service.

US Department of Agriculture Forest Service (2000) *National Survey on Recreation and the Environment*, USDA Forest Service and the University of Tennessee, Knoxville, Tennessee.

US Department of the Interior (1978) *National Urban Recreation Study*, Washington, DC, United States Department of the Interior.

US Department of the Interior, National Parks Service (1997) *VERP: The Visitor Experience and Resource Protection Framework: A Handbook for Planners and Managers*, Denver, US Department of the Interior, National Parks Service. Also available online at: <http://planning.nps.gov/document/verphandbook.pdf>, accessed February 2006.

Van Lier, H. N. and Taylor, P. D. (eds) (1993) *New Challenges in Recreation and Tourism Planning*, Amsterdam, Elsevier Science.

Vaske, J. J., Decker, D. J. and Manfredo, M. J. (1995) 'Human Dimensions of Wildlife Management: An Integrated Framework for Coexistence', in R. L. Knight and K. J. Gutzwiller (eds) *Wildlife and Recreationists: Coexistence through Management and Research*, Washington, DC, Island Press, pp. 33–47.

Veal, A. J. and Lynch, R. (2001) *Australian Leisure* (2nd edn), Sydney, Longman.

Veblen, T. (1899) *The Theory of the Leisure Class*, New York, Dover Publications, Inc.

Vedenin, Y. and Miroschnichenko, N. (1971) 'Evaluation of the National Environment for Recreation Purposes', *Ekistics* 184: 223–6.

Wall, G. and Wright, C. (1977) *The Environmental Impact of Outdoor Recreation*, Department of Geography Publications Series No. 11, Waterloo, University of Waterloo Press.

Walmsley, D. J. and Jenkins, J. M. (1994) 'Evaluations of Recreation Opportunities: Tourist Images of the New South Wales Coast', in D. C. Mercer (ed.) *New Viewpoints in Australian Outdoor Recreation Research and Planning*, Melbourne, Hepper Marriott an Associates, pp. 89–98.

Walmsley, D. J. and Jenkins, J. M. (2003) 'Leisure', in J. M. Jenkins and J. J. Pigram (eds) *Encyclopedia of Leisure and Outdoor Recreation*, London, Routledge, pp. 452–5.

23
Tourism

Adrian Franklin

As a form of leisure studies the study of tourism has largely been concerned with why modern tourism emerged when it did, how we can account for it sociologically and culturally (that is, what sort of behaviour is it?) and what sort of social, cultural, political and economic impact/effects it has had. All of those questions have produced lively debates over the 30-odd years during which tourism has been studied academically, and there is still widespread disagreement over some core questions. In part this is because tourism is a moving target; it is itself a changing reflexive part of modern consumer behaviour if not modern life itself, and it is extremely sensitive to a wide range of social and political issues. One has only to think about such issues as nature and environment, indigenous peoples, sexualities, local identity, consumer choice and risk to realize how they have all transformed what we want to see and do, how we approach tourism in relation to them and how tourism itself becomes configured in the issue itself. To take just the first of these, nature and environment, we can appreciate how increasing parts of the natural world have become managed as places of visitation, how visits to nature have become transformed into pilgrimages to spiritually uplifting and sacred sites and how that visitation itself has become a conservation problem, altering the way we approach its management and visitor attitudes to it. And one has only to think of mobility itself under changing historical contexts. Fifty years ago, almost everyone would have very limited personal transport and live most of their lives in their home locality. Tourism then would be crammed into one or two weeks at most. Today, by contrast most of us have access to personal, public and private transport and we use this to travel and tour a great deal more at other times of the year – during weekends and public holidays. We are also more likely to take more than one holiday a year and for these to be more mobile than the sedentary beachside holiday of the 1950s. But even more than this in a globalized society, with companies and organizations stretched over greater spaces and with more spatially scattered interests, our working lives are now more mobile than ever before. Rather than making our travel-rich working lives more like the everyday we have seen these more mobile lives take on a more touristic quality. The hotels that these workers-on-the-move stay in are exactly the same as tourist hotels, they are situated in scenic and attractive touristic locations in major cities and guests mix indistinguishably with those at play or attending conferences. Globalization also brings the world of others and otherness to our own doorsteps in the form of foreign tourists and students, foreign imported goods in malls and supermarkets and dining halls and the entire world at our finger tips in the form of internet pages, sites and connections.

It is frequently noted to be the world's biggest industry and the saviour to marginalized former industrial and rural areas as well as those on the geographical periphery, but it is also globally significant in the way it has transformed our stance to other people and places and ordered the way globalization has occurred. These two claims mean that tourism is a major rather than a minor social and cultural force in contemporary times, worthy of much more attention, research and governmental attention, yet tourism is curiously still seen as a rather shallow, insignificant presence in the world, something that takes place when the serious, important things in life have been attended to. In remaining sections of this chapter I will illustrate the pitfalls and difficulties of defining tourism, describe tourism in terms of its social and cultural content, contextualize contemporary tourism in relation to preceding its defining social history, identify and outline key analysts and perspectives in tourist studies and indicate the new agenda and pathways for research in tourism.

Defining tourism

In trying to understand whether tourism constitutes a singular phenomenon, a single industry, and tourists and tourist companies a singular economic activity, economists, geographers and government analysts and planners have persuaded themselves that there is sufficient coherency and universal meaning for a definition to be useful. Even though it is hard to find any text that does not point up the dangers, pitfalls and contradictions of defining tourism, few allow it to stop them. Even so, despite the fact that the word 'tourist' first appeared in the English language in the early nineteenth century, 'we still cannot agree on a definition' (Cooper et al., 1998: 8).

Hence for example, Mathieson and Wall (1982: 1) define tourism as 'the temporary movement of people to destinations outside their normal places of work and residence, the activities undertaken during their stay in those destinations and the facilities created to care to their need'. Similarly, for Burkart and Medlik (1974: v) '[t]ourism denotes the temporary short-term movement of people to destinations outside the places where they normally live'. This is almost a routine assumption about tourism: O'Reilly (2000: 43), for example, argues that many theorists, including Graburn (1978), Smith (1978) and Voase (1995), define tourism 'more by what it is not than by what it is – it is *not* home and it is *not* work; it is a change of scenery and lifestyle, an inversion of the normal'. Typically, such definitions bring together groups and activities that seem at best unrelated and at worst opposites. They bunch together, perhaps on the same aircraft travelling from a capital city such as Cardiff, Wales to a major tourist city such as London, those going on holiday and those going to work or on business or perhaps to a specialist hospital for treatment. For this reason, formalist procedures typically invoke subdefinitions to cover these extreme variations. Hence we obtain the 'non-business tourist' ('a person who undertakes one or more recreational activities in leisure time, at a location temporarily away from the normal place of residence and at locations at which such recreational activities are normally undertaken') as distinct from the 'business tourist' ('a person who undertakes work related activities at a location temporarily away from their normal place of residence and work') (Carroll et al. 1991). It is not clear how this definition distinguishes tourism from, say, travel. The geographers Shaw and Williams (1994: 5) and urban sociologists Judd and Fainstein (1999) adopt the formal definition preferred by international organizations such as the World Tourism Organization, that 'tourism includes all travel that involves a stay of at least one night, but less than one year, away from home'. This therefore includes travel for such purposes as visiting friends or relatives, or to undertake 'business'. Such a definition places the travel–accommodation connection and its associated industry at the heart of tourism, signalling at the same time that it is the provision and purchase of these commodities rather than tourism behaviour and culture that is central to our interest. Cooper et al. (1998) worry that this definition is dominated by 'demand-side' factors and wish to balance this, following Leiper, with 'supply-side definitions of tourism'. Their supply-side definition emphasizes 'those firms, organisations and facilities which are intended to serve the specific needs and wants of tourists', but quite clearly these organizations are also continuously shaping the wish and desire for tourism that constitutes demand and shape tourism as a cultural form (for a good discussion of this see Zigmunt Bauman as interviewed in *Tourist Studies* (Franklin, 2003b)).

These formal definitions, driven by the desire to quantify tourism and to measure the performance of the tourism economy, not only denude tourism of some its more interesting and important characteristics, they tend to reduce tourism to acts of leisure and recreation at the end of acts of travel. This takes formalist theorists into the quicksands of defining leisure and recreation (notoriously difficult, see Rojek 1985, 1995) and away from the more fruitful and firmer practice of locating tourism as a *mode* of relating to the world in postmodern cultures. It undermines the consumptive, playful, ironic, intellectual, mental, passive, romantic, aesthetic, reflexive, performative, embodied and spiritual content of tourism whilst overemphasizing mobile, physical, active and muscular dimensions. Because tourism cannot properly reduce to the acts of travel and the leisure and recreation activities at the end of discrete bouts of travel, some authors have gone in for the opposite of narrow abstraction in favour of mindless incorporation and extension. Tourism becomes absolutely everything associable with acts of tourism, or put into its proper tautological form, 'tourism is tourism' or 'tourism is what tourists do'. An example of this style of incorporation comes from Weaver and Opperman:

> Tourism is the sum of the phenomena and relationships arising from the interaction among tourists, business suppliers, host governments, host communities,

origin governments, universities, community colleges and non-governmental organisations, in the process of attracting, transporting, hosting and managing these tourists and other visitors. (Weaver and Opperman, 2000: 3)

With some exception, the tendency has been to regard tourism as simply a part of the entertainment industry – a separate and not altogether respectable or admirable industry. Clearly a lot of tourism is structured around entertainment and pleasure, but as with the sociology of sport or food, the sociological importance and meaning of soccer, cricket or eating out is not simply about entertainment and pleasure. Reducing tourism to an industry that delivers a service (pleasure, entertainment) tends to obscure its wider sociological significance. Significantly, such a perspective places all the action and agency in the hands of the tourism industry, its companies, designers and organizations. It is as if they produce the tourist product and deliver it to a passive consumer-tourist. Consumers and their aesthetic taste are constituted in complex ways from a variety of sources and not just by creators of tourist sites and activities. As we know very well, some extremely successful tourist markets can get dumped by consumers who previously saw such activities at the high point of their lives. The dramatic decline of the English seaside is a good example of this, as is the holiday camp and the attraction of post-war industrial infrastructures such as power stations and hydro schemes. Moreover, focusing tourist studies only on those industries, places and exchanges ignores the cumulative effects that tourism has on individuals, cultural groups, nations and global society. All this is to suggest that tourism is always and everywhere historically constituted. It is not a universally 'found' activity nor does it well up from the physiological or psychological nature of our being, always trying to find expression. Certainly we can say that there are many examples of mobility and highly specific forms of non-everyday travel emanating from premodern cultures. We know that ritual for example was typically undertaken in specific spaces away from the everyday, often involving a period of travel, and often involving ludic activities creating great anticipation, excitement and social effervescence. But it would be a mistake to imagine that contemporary tourism was an essentially similar outlet for common needs and drives, even if it is also expressed in ritualistic ways. Equally, there are examples from the anthropological record of travel and pleasurable activities being undertaken out of boredom or to escape oppressive situations such as disagreements and unresolved disputes. But again, we would not want to base our understanding of modern tourism just on our species' tendencies to be bored, or escape problems through mobility. As with all cultural forms, important theoretical links have to be made within the cultures of which they are a part. Although historical and cross-cultural forms of travel and tourism type activities may share some things in common, they do not derive their content from irreducible characteristics of our species and neither can they be arranged in some kind of evolutionary path towards modern tourism, as some histories and sociologies of tourism imply. The best accounts to date tend to derive, at least in the first place, from sociology. We can single out some of the more prominent of these in recent years to show how both tourism *and* accounts of tourism are anchored in specific period of modernity.

Sociological explanations

Although more adequately framed as a social and cultural phenomenon and historically constituted sociological explanations tend, perhaps inadvertently, to reproduce some of the problems noted above. Almost all definitions of tourism identify one or two things that *distinguish* it from other activities: firstly it involves travel away from an individual's home environment; second, it consists of the exposure of individuals to activities and places that are different and unusual (critical here is a necessary contrast between the familiar and the unfamiliar). These vary in interesting ways: some employ the 'escape' metaphor to highlight the essentially problematic conditions of everyday life in modern capitalist societies. For many the realm of work, whether at home or in the labour market, involves a series of pressured, alienating and stressful conditions that require the occasional timeout.

Owing to an in-built bias in the social sciences in favour of production, particularly technology science and manufacturing, tourism and other leisure and consumption activities were not taken very seriously from the 1950s to 1970s; indeed, they were treated rather like superfluous or decorous activities of little consequence. Considering the sheer scale of the expansion of mass tourism in the 1950s and 1960s it produced very little by way of response or comment from sociology, geography or the other business disciplines that now champion tourism. MacCannell's *The Tourist* of 1976 has to be judged in this context. Viewed from the position of American sociological theory at the time it was not surprising that it problematized and tried to explain tourism almost as a *deviant* activity, a somewhat disturbing behaviour resulting from the alienation and cultural disturbance of modernization and modern social relations. Tourism was treated somewhat clinically as a necessary period of recovery from the intolerable conditions of modern life. Some of the classical anxieties of 1960s sociology were wrapped up in this book: alienated workers, dysfunctional family life, a world of synthetic unreality, a highly differentiated and fragmented world ruled by rationalized and bureaucratized procedures and strong states. In comparison with premodern cultures where the individual was locked into a stable and secure social framework, the modern individual was at sea, literally, looking for meaningfulness and finding it the categorical opposites of modernity: the past, the exotic other, pristine nature. In short, MacCannell declared the modern world to be inauthentic and troubling and tourism was the somewhat pathetic and pointless search for the authentic and an antidote of some short-lived kind. While plausible in itself it left tourism very much in the same place it was found: a marginal, somewhat spurious escape attempt from the true reality. Of course, the better studies of tourism refused to see tourists as cultural dupes, preferring to acknowledge a commonplace sense of ironic self-deception among tourists (Cohen and Taylor, 1976; Feifer, 1986; Urry, 2002). But conceptualizing tourism and tourists as intellectually challenged and culturally vacuous is extremely common but also revealing of something important (see Rojek, 1993).

Accounts influenced by the philosopher Friedrich Nietzsche argue that capitalist societies of the West have trapped people inside the disciplines of work and education and buried them inside a bureaucratic and stifling culture of control.

These accounts underlie the manner by which a so-called true human nature has been stifled and constrained and needs to be released for more creative, physically demanding and less inhibited activities. Tourism in particular is identified as a principal escape valve of this sort. This is nowhere better demonstrated than in Cartmill's analysis of the dominant hunting and outdoor leisures in the US, and the development of the national park areas and policy debates that even drew in Presidents (see Cartmill, 1993). After all, does not tourism take place outside normal everyday disciplines and beyond the gaze of everyday surveillance? Other accounts, while not emphasizing this liberational rationale nonetheless take as axiomatic that tourism provides a compelling series of pleasures that derive from the simple relief from the monotony of everyday life. So in Urry's account tourism is explained in terms of the pleasurabilty of the different and the unusual. How else are we to explain the somewhat bizarre objects that tourists will pay money to see? For Urry, the ultimate goal of tourists is to feast their eyes on different and unusual objects, landscapes and townscapes. It is as if these visions are a reward in themselves, visions that can be captured by visual technologies and stored and kept rather like any other commodity. Urry's *The Tourist Gaze* (2002) is the other landmark in theoretical developments in tourism of this period although it is a very different sort of thesis. Urry does not offer a particularly clear link between tourism and the *conditions* of modern life, and certainly tourism is not explained as a *response* to the conditions of modern life. Rather tourism is located very clearly as an emerging cultural activity in modernity and a positive outcome of modernity, clearly linked to the extension of leisure and holidays to workers, the democratization of travel (and security in travel), an extension of the Victorian notion of improvement and approved leisures; and globalization. Writing in the late 1980s Urry linked tourism theoretically to patterns of social change in the last quarter of the twentieth century. Urry does not provide a particularly clear explanation for touristic behaviour *per se*, and this is a weakness. Vague references to the pleasurability of 'the different' and 'the unusual' or the non-everyday only *asserts* some form of pleasurability from these abstract things, it does not account for it. Missing is an account of the aesthetic sensibilities of tourism, especially in the new tourisms of recent decades. At best Urry's account draws on an historical momentum in which the educated middle classes acted as the initial travellers and tourists establishing a pattern of touristic consumption that working class and mass markets simply emulate and copy through critical innovations such as Thomas Cook's package tours. Here though, the emphasis is on notions of personal improvement through education, experience, exposure to different places and people, and the pursuit of health and fitness – all established values of Victorian modernism. However, the implicit aesthetic content of this diffusion model is based upon the older notion of high and low culture: tourism offered those born to low culture the opportunity of glimpsing and being improved by icons and displays of high culture. Urry accounts for more recent forms of tourism consumption in terms of the social and economic restructuring implicit in the notion of post-Fordism.

The fragmentation of mass tourism of the mid-twentieth-century resort holiday into a series of different and niched markets by the 1980s is explained by Urry in terms of the collapse of Fordist or mass forms of production and consumption. Fordist styles of production were based on the extension of mass produced markets through innovations in production line and assembly plants. Fordism describes the extension of former luxuries such as cars to all workers and indeed the growth of capital generally. Fordist styles of consumption were standardized and monotonous. Henry Ford himself was quoted as saying that consumers could have any colour Model T Ford they liked so long as it was black. Post-Fordist forms of production which grew rapidly from the late 1970s favoured smaller, leaner and more flexible forms of production that could respond better to fluctuations in the shaky aftermath of the post-war boom economy and the growing power of consumers in the credit-rich affluent markets of the Western world. Under conditions of greater choice, greater credit and the breakdown of mass popular culture, individuals tended to identify less with older repositories of identity such as social class, political alignment, gender, region and workplace, and more in terms of lifestyle groups with their emphasis on consumption, leisure and style. In a way, teenagers of the 1960s began this style, establishing youth subcultures, ways of life separable from their parents and grandparents. The idea took off and expanded, creating fresh rounds of separation or de-differentiation (where former distinctions become blurred and confused). Tourism industries responded to the emergence and proliferation of lifestyle groups by providing a range of specialist niche markets, greater flexibility, choice and self-direction. The tourism market became segmented into a series of consumer groups catering quite specifically for different tastes and styles. Again, early examples were based on the desire of young people to spend their holidays together. Age, income, class, occupation continued to frame broad patterns of taste, but other dimensions such as generation, sexual orientation, subculture, style, family cycle stage, leisure and enthusiasms provided templates for quite specific forms of consumption (for example, it seems that Goth style can be summed up by the maxim 'buy or wear anything providing it is black'). Even though such a general characterization as this is widely agreed upon, it sits awkwardly with Urry's emphasis on the necessary pleasurability of difference and the unusual at the heart of the tourism experience. To a major extent then, tourism is *increasingly not* offering an essentially different or unusual set of experiences for tourists but tailoring their experiences in line with their chosen forms of *everyday* culture: their style, their preferences, their fellow travellers their fantasies, taste, and so on. This can be seen perhaps through corporate executive trends in tourism and the standardization of the international five-star hotel. If you have been in one you have been in them all.

In all of these accounts the tourist is a passive consumer of services (museums, lookouts, art galleries, historical monuments, nature reserves, and so on) that are crafted and commodified by a knowledgeable industry that knows what it is they seek or need. Even these lifestyle groups are presented as the innovation of a clever marketing and advertising industry. The degree of passivity varies of course. Some people put a lot of effort into researching and planning their tourism. At the other extreme are the fully guided tour-bus consumers who simply pay and watch.

So what is wrong with these accounts? Surely people need to move out of their everyday spaces and to do that they need to travel? Surely they are looking for pleasure and difference? Surely people do lead humdrum lives and need relief from the monotony?

It is not that these accounts are completely wrong so much as confused and incomplete. Because they see the tourist as an essentially passive subject driven by forces external to and greater than them, this emphasis on escape, search and the pleasurability of a world beyond their own is completely compelling. For these accounts, travel away from the everyday and the *rupture* that this is held to produce is central to their theoretical understanding of tourism. I disagree with most of this.

Certainly, these claims are largely asserted with barely any empirical justification or follow-up. This is not a serious objection to theoretical claims *per se*, but I mention it in passing. I would also mention that these accounts echo many of the anxieties of sociology as a discipline. It has never been entirely comfortable with capitalist consumer society (see, for example, Miles's 1998 book, *Consumerism: As a Way of Life)* and has always tended to shroud it in negative, pathological and more recently, in unsustainable terms. Its belief has always been that capitalist relations undermine a true human potential or its development. In this way tourism is portrayed as a kind of displacement activity: a slightly sad perversity, a less than satisfactory or fruitless search for compensation. But sociology is only a subset of intellectual opinion, and the broader intellectual opinion on tourism has been largely negative: tourism is mindless, moronic and futile (see Rojek, 1993: 174–5, for more on this). Crick (1989: 308) specifically mentions the activity of a collective social science representation of tourism and asked 'whether we yet have a respectable scholarly analysis of tourism, or whether the social science literature on the subject substantially blends with the emotionally charged cultural image relating to travel and tourists'. Commenting on the failure of social scientists to take mass tourism and tourists seriously, O'Reilly argues that

> more recent researchers in the fields of geography, social policy and sociology have only been able to approach the topic since it became defined in terms of the elderly, retirement, tourism and the environment, or in terms of migration and poverty; in other words they were able to approach it only as something serious as opposed to the frivolous and trivial. (O'Reilly, 2000: 19)

I mention all this merely to reinforce the point that there is a long tradition of thinking about tourism in this way.

Tourism, modernity and nationalism

Can we find an explanation of tourism that does not assume it to be a vaguely negative reaction to the oppressiveness of capitalist production or the mundaneness and spread of everyday consumer society? We would do well to revisit the early moments of tourism to see if there are any clues there. One such clues lies within Rob Shields's refreshing look at the English seaside in his classic book *Places on the Margin* (1991). Shields's thesis is that tourism relates to modern day transformations of the ritual life of traditional sedentary communities. He compares the modern mass seaside of the early twentieth century with the carnivalesque holy day rituals of premodern Britain, seeing a great deal that has survived albeit it in a weakened form. Just as the carnivalesque rituals often took place away from the village and towns, on the social margins, the seaside can be seen as the social margin to the industrial town. Here, behaviour, such as illicit and free expression of sexuality that would be disapproved of in the home town, was tolerated and facilitated. Places such as Brighton offered an escape from the panoptic order of modernity. This is not an escape from drudgery and monotony of life in industrial capitalism but a Dionysian transgression of its disciplinarity. Brighton was undoubtedly such a place for the adventurous middle classes of London, but whether it was generalizable is doubtful. If Blackpool, as recorded by the Mass Observation exercise of the late 1930s, is in any way representative of the working-class seaside holiday during this period, then there is far more to take stock of than transgressive sexuality, which was found to be largely absent (see Franklin, 2003a; Cross, 1990). Furthermore, it is a mistake to see the seaside as an initial form of mass tourism merely as a development from the original spa resorts and medicinal sea-bathing. While having superficial similarities and influences it was not simply a case of one initiating a market for the other. The spa resorts of the eighteenth and nineteenth centuries owe their origins to a combination of factors specific to the aristocracy and the new industrial middle classes. As a culture spatially scattered on their various estates, large gatherings had always featured during specific parts of the year, 'the season' and at specific places, especially London, in and around courtly activities. The spa towns added not only a new form of therapy, water cures, for common maladies, but new opportunities for specific types of social gathering, particularly the problem of meeting sexual and marital partners. Jane Austen's writings illustrate the extreme delicacy and absence of opportunity for this through much of the year and how places such as Bath Spa maximized the chance to meet, match and court. The spa's great popularity as a social and sexual space overlaid the medicinal rituals and encouraged great innovations which ultimately resulted in a different kind of place, a place dedicated to these sorts of play. This 'resort' space took on an otherworldly appearance consistent with their transformative, liminal and transgressive character and was assisted by music, theatre and games. These resorts were the new playthings of an already mobile bourgeois culture. Modern mass tourism, starting with the seaside, belongs to quite a different set of cultural and historical features. Although they borrow from the idea of a resort, it is not simply an extension of the idea to more people because there are new concepts and practices at work here that relate to major transformations in society, the extension of modernity and nationalism.

Thomas Cook may have begun his company ferrying and guiding wealthy clients around the Romantic hot-spots of Europe of the mid-nineteenth century, creating even more as he proceeded to grow his business, but Thomas Cook was also a revolutionary, one of modernity's great innovators. He was from a relatively humble background and was caught up in the non-conformist religious revivals in the 1830s and 1840s. These religious movements had a strong political character and sought social and economic reform, particularly the improvement of the working classes. So Cook was inspired to transform the status quo, and saw travel and tourism as an important medium of improvement and education, to be added to schooling – for all classes, but especially the otherwise sedentary working classes. He realized that mass mobility was within their grasp, given the new technical innovations with steam trains and ships and given certain organizational/logistical innovations that he could make. But Cook was not only an innovator; he was operationalizing the new spirit of *nationalism* as it reached new heights of development through the second half of the nineteenth century. The truly revolutionary process in nationalism was not merely the reorganization of political geography and new mass social identification with it but the fact that suddenly, the universal themes of national high cultures replace the parochial and particular concerns of village and region. Suddenly and dramatically, all individuals, as national citizens, share much broader horizons, interests and histories. Without nationalism and the new universal culture it produced, particularly the new culture of citizenship, it was unlikely that 'mass' cultures such as seaside and tourism would have occurred. The new nations wrote often for the first time national histories, they searched for the constituent elements of folk history that created a national people and culture; there were national geographies, natural histories that were typically those bounded by national boundaries. For exactly the same reasons nationalism built an infrastructure of national shrines, places of national significance, and encouraged people to gather and visit them. Capital cities were rebuilt to be shrinic centres of national solidity; for rallies, school visits, holiday celebrations, pageant and ceremony. But nationalism was also strengthened by the identification of new sacred sites, dedicated to or celebrating moments of national significance or nation making. Battlefields, birthplaces of important writers and scientists, significant landmarks of national geography, major building such as castles and cathedrals, places celebrated in national poetry and romantic writing, all of these and more began to become desired places to see and visit. To see and visit them was more than just the gaining of experience, it was also performing small ritual acts of national solidarity and citizenship. To be a modern citizen of a modern nation was to eschew the parochial concerns of family and locality and to branch out and to participate in this much larger and exciting world. And, as with the Anglo-Saxon kings such as Athelstan who unified England for the first time through encouraging pilgrimage to princely supported Christian shrines, the first nation-building governments saw travel and tourism in a positive light, building modern sensibilities and social solidarities that bridge former divisions, and rivalry. Many people in the Victorian period understood and believed in the contribution that travel and tourism could make to the overcoming of xenophobia and the achievement of a universal culture. The great American tourist and travel writer Mark Twain wrote that tourism is the great enemy of prejudice.

Thomas Cook and his generation of modernizing nationalists sought to democratize both travel and leisure in these approved forms. The seaside then was a culmination of these processes opened up first by national public holidays and later by the granting of national paid holidays. As I have argued in my book *Tourism* (Franklin, 2003a) the seaside is not a transformation of the former carnivals that characterized most if not all rural communities across Britain and Europe, but an entirely new, modern form that is predicated on nationalism, citizenship and modernism. I argue that the seaside was not looking back and supporting the tested structures of tradition, but forward-looking, offering a glimpse at the new world of future technology and consumerism. This is supported by Tony Bennett's (1983) analysis of Blackpool in which he shows quite clearly how new technologies were often show-cased first at seasides – street lighting being an excellent example. Other research also confirms that the seaside experimented with new forms of consumerism. So, for example Cross (1990) underlines the incredible drawing power of the first ever superstore at Blackpool in the 1930s. As an entirely novel and astonishing form of consumerism in an otherwise austere world, the Mass Observation researchers discovered that this superstore was the first port of call for those alighting from trains at the Central station, and not the beach or the tower. For those travelling to the seaside then, their sense of anticipation and excitement was not merely to stop work and play but to take part in the ritual life of the seaside and as with all rituals the initiates were exposed to and changed by the experience. Above all else, the seaside was experienced as a transformation. The transformative effect on health and vigour was a prominent theme. Blackpool, for example, was represented in its famous lights as an enormous machine, 'the rejuvenator'. Here the initiates enter old and frail and emerge as youthful and robust. But we must not overdo the rituals of health at the expense of the centrality of rituals of modernization that were stamped on most surfaces of the seaside. The seaside was an experience of a new world and a new lifestyle that was promised by modernity. It was a world of leisure and consumerism in which new technologies would liberate the human condition. Emphasis was given to new architectures, new innovations and futurism. Indeed, the seaside attractions that remained the hub of most resorts were modelled directly on the sorts of technological marvel that were displayed at the international exhibitions which began in 1851. And it should come as no surprise that one of Thomas Cook's first tourist ideas was to carry thousands of workers to the Great Exhibition in London in 1851, which expressly showcased new advances in British technology.

Whereas Urry's thesis emphasizes the visual nature of tourism, making tourists somewhat remote if not distant from the objects of their gaze, this new analysis of the seaside places the body at the centre of things. The body at the seaside is clearly the most significant subject and it is clearly engaged in embodied action with tourist objects, the seawater, the sun, the sand, the exciting thrill rides, the sexual encounter or romance, the big bands at the bandstand or dance hall, more alcohol and food.

Unlike the participant in the carnivalesque, which presupposed membership of a local traditional, hierarchical, social order, the holidaymaker in modern times does so as an individual and a citizen. While the carnivalesque was a ritual of renewal and affirmation of the social order, of social reproduction, the modern tourist is engaged in self-making, exploring the modern world, exploring what it is possible to be in this world for unlike the conservative social order of traditional Europe, the modern world offers no limits, no proper social identity, no fixed social role or status. Tourism offers opportunities for this sort of self-making because it opens up spaces of experimentation and difference.

This embodied perspective on tourism is consistent with other perspectives that emphasize the performative and phenomenological dimensions of tourism. Those approaches that stress the performative nature of tourism show how the meaningfulness of tourist sites and objects is only revealed through performing the act of visiting and being there. Edensor (1998) shows in his study of tourists at the Taj Mahal that the tourist experience differs considerably as a result of differences in the way a site is approached walked around and responded to in sensual terms. More generally it makes clear that despite attempts to give sites an interpretation meanings cannot be grafted onto tourist objects in a manner that provides a stable set of signifiers for all tourists. Rather it is what tourists bring to the site, their own background, experiences, history and identity that will contribute to unstable and contested meanings and experiences. Mike Crang (1994) has argued this phenomenological line in relation to debates on the nature of heritage tourism. It is clear that heritage sites offer a range of experiences and meanings that are contingent on differences among the viewing audience. Some sites are clearly used by local cultural groups to achieve visibility. In others, heritage tourism has allowed some peoples and localities to write their past onto an historical record that has hitherto ignored them or their significance. In these ways some tourist sites are not merely items of consumption but makers and markers of cultural identity, institutional responses to maintain community, political expressions in contested histories. As with the role of tourism in nation formation, offering sites of sacredness and significance for display and visiting has important social and political consequences and effects.

In a recent paper, I have argued that the longer-term effects of tourism have been ignored, largely because tourism theory had atrophied around early contributions from Urry and MacCannell. Not only has tourism had profound influences on nationalism and local solidarity but more generally it has played an important role in global affairs. First I have argued that it has had a profound influence on economic globalization by spreading a rather global cosmopolitanism around the world. We consume tourism products at tourist sites but we are also changed by the experience and take something of it away with us. A good example of this is the way tourism has produced a more globally cosmopolitan taste in food. Because we associate the foods we eat while away on holiday with the exotic and the pleasurable, we can invoke these pleasures again, rather like souvenirs, when we are back home. Before the British began taking holidays in Spain, foods such as olive oil, garlic, peppers and chillies were barely obtainable back in Britain and often the subject of loathing. But when the Spanish tourism experience extended to embracing the tastes of Spain things began to change. First, the massive influx of tourists produced a summer demand for far more food, which in turn stimulated market gardening in Spain on a much greater scale. But then with the transformation of British and northern European taste, it then became possible for Spanish farmers and British retailers to organize to make these foods available all year around, almost everywhere. So globalization can be produced in this way, by tourism, and this runs counter to the cultural imperialism thesis of globalization as suggested by the metaphor of Coca-Cola-ization.

Second, I have argued that it has produced beneficial effects on cultural and racial tolerance. Such observations were often made by early tourists but we seem these days to take it for granted or even see tourism as creating only cultural dissonance. Soon after he began an epic tour, the great travel writer Mark Twain said, with some relish: 'We are getting foreignized rapidly and with facility', and at the conclusion he remarked that

> Travel is fatal to prejudice, bigotry and narrow-mindedness, and many of our people need it sorely on these accounts. Broad, wholesome, charitable views of men and things can not be acquired by vegetating in one little corner of the earth all one's lifetime. (Twain, 1993: 38)

Information technology can give us instant access to the world but we have to be careful not to fall into what might be called the fallacy of technological determinism. Crawshaw and Urry's essay on photography (1997), for example, argues that the 1841 technological breakthrough that produced photography was called into being by a prexisting need or desire for it, a desire not unrelated to the development of modern tourism in the same year. A similar argument can be made here that the global aesthetic and the desire for global information preceded its actual technological development and that tourism was a principal ordering of that desire. In the same way that tourism brought people out of essentially local lives, taste worlds, material cultures, and so forth, creating an interest in universal 'national' themes, tastes and values, tourism itself is interesting because as an ordering it was not confined to national boundaries; indeed, it was one of the earliest activities to test the necessity of borders and boundaries. The global aesthetic is a generalized view that we are not shackled to specific local, ethnic, national or regional aesthetics, or at least the view that to limit oneself in any particular way is to exhibit a lack of curiosity, adventure and diversity. It is to be narrow. Unlike information *per se*, tourism is an embodied, sensual experience and one has to physically be there; one has to eat, smell, see and touch in order to develop an appreciation and knowledge of other aesthetic worlds. Tourism is perhaps unique in making travel a new aesthetic experience as an end in itself, a transformation of the self, and an experimentation in self-making. This performative character of tourism is critical for leaving traces and consequences; it is additive and unbounded. In the early days of Japanese overseas travel (1960s), when it was shrouded in suspicion and guilt, they used to travel the world in a tourist bubble with suitcase loads of Japanese food. Some 40 years later, having been more exposed to the routines and character of international tourism, they are now the opposite: recent research has shown that what they are most seeking is '*jibun no hada ni snaka suru*', to 'participate with their own skin' (Moeran, 1983: 96).

Tourism is most frequently referred to as a blight of local cultures, churning away at the foundations of local life, excluding them from their own space, placing property prices beyond their reach, trinketizing their material culture and reducing them to performing clowns, pimps and prostitutes. However much truth there is to such accounts this view, which has been propagated by anthropologists in the main, relates as much to their anxieties about cultural change as it does to a balanced view of host–guest relationships. What is most often missing from their accounts are the longer term traces and consequences of visiting and being visited by others. The anthropologists have generally not been so interested in what the tourists take away with them or what the locals gain from having them stay. Two rather obvious but infrequently mentioned effects are the establishment of cosmopolitanism in place of the fear and suspicion of foreigners, and communitas.

I do not want to say very much about cosmopolitanism except to say it is quite generally the case that tourism and travel is believed to generate the favourable qualities associated with cosmopolitanism. The well-travelled person, the person who has experienced the world, is very widely believed to be an improved version of the less travelled. It is now the case that corporate Japan, for example, now believes that their executive class needs to be well travelled in order to fully partake in its international projects and affairs, and of course travel and tourism is now a routine item of CVs. All over the world young Japanese and others are clocking up air miles in this touristic finishing school. It is not just the guests who take away the wisdom and benefits of travel, it is also local people, and indeed these days we are all both local people and tourists. Thomas Cook invented the guidebook. That may seem like a fairly mundane thing to have done, except that at the time he began writing them there was absolutely no way of knowing what you will find, where to find it, how to comport yourself and how to understand and fit in with the local host culture – *anywhere* in the world. Cook's guides had maps in them, the necessary geography and trails, notes on cuisine and foods, dos and don'ts, histories of the locality, and a suggested itinerary to experience what these places were like *as places*. That innovation of course we take for granted these days, and in the globalization literature such information necessary to globalization is identified merely by the growth in information. However, the guidebook part of the tourism industry is working very hard to update travel guides and the amount of information we now regard as desirable is considerably more than in the mid-nineteenth century and is used by far more people than tourists. In many parts of the world they are as valuable to local nationals as they are to tourists. Indeed, it is probably true to say these days that you can't live in London without a *London A–Z*.

Taken together, what sort of literature do all the guidebooks add up to if not an account of and a technology for a globalized world? And to ask the same question again, could we imagine a globalized world without them? Of course not. These days the guidebooks are now finely tuned from backpacker travel to gourmet wine trail, from literary tourisms in Cook Country to assassination tours in Dallas, Texas, and they make a world available and accessible in a way it has never been before. Again, it is not just the amount of information available, it is also its potential to order experience that matters.

Cosmopolitanism used to be the sole preserve/gain/objective of the elite travelling class, but while we must note Bauman's intervention on vagabondism and the oppressive nature of immobility as the quintessential marker of the failed consumer, it is nonetheless true that these days flows of visitors, travellers and tourists are now a tourist spectacle in their own right for local people. There is now interest in what has been called reverse tourisms, broadly the idea that it is not only Western eyes feasting on the Other, but the other way around too. Similarly, a point I make in *Tourism* (Franklin, 2003a) is that tourist spaces, whether in the UK and the US, or in Bali or Goa, are now not the sole preserve of tourists themselves, and touristic space is increasingly a hybrid, cosmopolitan space. While there are still examples of spatial segregation in luxury tourism, this is on the wane, and there are good economic reasons for making them duel spaces: reducing everyone to the common status of visitor maximizes returns.

Communitas is one of the effects that confirm tourism as a ritual activity. The ready, spontaneous and close bonds established between tourists are well documented (see, for example, Cross, 1990), but international tourism binds together in a variety of ways people from different countries as well as those from guest and host countries. Again, it is the embodied, particular and personal nature of these encounters that drives their particular effects and their performative quality secures more than information and knowledge: it secures brief or extended friendships, romances, exchange visits, correspondence. Even the Lonely Planet backpackers, ostensibly always distinguishing themselves from 'bloody tourists', may go out one day not to return until the money runs out, but when out there they tend to form travelling groups, not unlike the pilgrims of Chaucer's *Canterbury Tales*. And when out there those companions are most unlikely to be exclusively fellow-nationals. Photographic surveys show communitas at work on an epic scale and possibly as rich as those who do identify as tourists, but it is also the case that backpacking reproduces and orders routinized encounters which, like other forms of global information, shrink the planet.

Bauman has recently made the point that tourism is a sort of failed attempt to produce the kinds of understanding, respect and global community that Twain assumed would happen as a result of the growth of tourism (Franklin, 2003b). While a laudable experiment to convert our natural curiosity for the other into a more mundane understanding and familiarity, tourism he feels falls far short of achieving it. Tourists spend too much time in deterritorialized spaces, those places that are created especially for tourists and which are the same the length and breadth of the planet: malls, hotel lobbies, resort beaches, heritage centres, airports and city centres. Tourists are unwittingly perhaps detoured from meeting and mixing with local peoples and see only a selected few in highly selective pleasurable episodes. In Bauman's view it would be better if people spent their time exploring those parts of their own city that they never normally see; using their natural curiosity to create connections and familiarity with the strangers that these days live on our own doorsteps. While overly pessimistic about the longer-term effects of tourism, the point he makes is an interesting one and not dissimilar to another made a long time ago by Xavier de Maistre, a 27-year-old Frenchman who embarked on a tour around his bedroom in 1790 (De Botton, 2002: 243). The point that Maistre wished to make is that the exotic and unfamiliar are all around us but that we need to develop ways of seeing the everyday in a new light. While de Maistre's tourism was not an immediate success, it is true that in the second half of the twentieth century we did begin to explore the everyday cultural and material worlds around us, calling the revealed and interpreted findings 'heritage' and 'cultural studies' and 'centres'. Kirshenblatt-Gimblett (1998) illustrates the same point with Boltanski's exhibition of the contents of his own medicine cabinet, and modern art has exploited the depth and significance of our immediate surroundings – Tracey Emin's bed, for example. But to return to Bauman's argument, it is extraordinary perhaps that we seem to express hardly any interest in those multiple cultures that form so much of our own social composition. While in 2002 the number of international tourist arrivals topped the 700 million mark, it is the case that nearly four-fifths of international tourists travel within their own region and most tourist sites throughout the world are dependent on the trade from the day-trippers from their immediate region. This, alongside the growth in heritage tourism, suggests that we are becoming more used to exploring our own backyards, local cultures and histories. According to the World Tourism Organization, the rise of attacks on airlines and tourists has created a panic with the result that more local trips are made. 'These adverse conditions resulted not so much in a decrease in overall volume but, above all, in the reinforcement of the shifts in demand towards trips to domestic and familiar destinations that were closer to home, and travel by car, coach or train instead of by plane' (World Tourism Organization, 2003). But it is not just the distance travelled that has changed in recent years, there is also a marked change in the extent to which tourists consume tourist packages and deterritorialized spaces of travel. In 2002 they seemed to be cutting loose from this dependency:

> Individual (not organized) travel proliferated, while tour operators faced relatively hard times. 'Do-it-yourself' is becoming more and more common, particularly for the mature and experienced travellers, vigorously stimulated by the possibilities offered by low-cost airlines and the Internet. (ibid.)

So for a number of different reasons the tourism market could shift towards different types of curiosity, and we have to remember that ultimately there is no inevitable type of tourism that will proliferate over others. We can perhaps remember that for a long time the English viewed both France and Scotland as places of great darkness and danger. However, both have become intensely interesting and attractive places for tourists. This aesthetic shift can happen by chance or it can be promoted. Perhaps we should promote tourism more in the name of global peace and understanding, as Bauman suggests, as well as in the name of physical renewal and self-making.

Bibliography

Bennett, T. (1983) 'A Thousand and One Troubles: Blackpool Pleasure Beach', in *Formations of Pleasure*, London, Routledge & Kegan Paul, pp. 138–55.
Boorstin, D. (1964) *The Image: A Guide to Pseudo Events in America*, New York, Harper.
Burkart, A. J. and Medlik, S. (1974) *Tourism: Past, Present and Future*, London, Heinemann.
Campbell, C. (1987) *The Romantic Ethic and the Spirit of Consumerism*, Oxford, Blackwell.

Carroll, P., Donohue, K., McGovern, M. and McMillen, J. (1991) *Tourism in Australia*, Sydney, Harcourt Brace Jovanovich.

Cartmill, M. (1993) *View to a Death in the Morning*, Cambridge, Mass., Harvard University Press.

Cohen, S. and Taylor, L. (1976) *Escape Attempts*, Harmondsworth, Penguin.

Cooper, C., Fletcher, J., Gilbert, D. and Wanhill, S. (1998) *Tourism: Principles and Practice*, Harlow, Pearson Education Ltd.

Crang, M. (1994) 'On the Heritage Trail: Maps and Journeys to Olde Englande', *Environment and Planning D: Society and Space* 12(3): 341–55.

Crang, M. (1999) 'Knowing Tourism and Practices of Vision', in D. Crouch (ed.) *Leisure/Tourism Geographies: Practices and Geographical Knowledge*, London, Routledge, pp. 238–56.

Crawshaw, C. and Urry, J. (1997) 'Tourism and the Photographic Eye', in C. Rojek and J. Urry (eds) *Touring Cultures*, London, Routledge.

Crick, M. (1989) 'Representations of International Tourism in the Social Sciences', *Annual Review of Anthropology* 18: 307–44.

Cross, G. (ed.) (1990) *Worktowners at Blackpool: Mass Observation and Popular Leisure in the 1930s*, London, Routledge.

De Botton, A. (2002) *The Art of Travel*, London, Hamish Hamilton.

Edensor, T. (1998) *Tourists at the Taj: Performance and Meaning at a Symbolic Site*, London, Routledge.

Eriksen, T.H. (2001) *Tyranny of the Moment*, London, Pluto Press.

Feifer, M. (1986) *Tourism in History*, New York, Stein & Day.

Franklin, A. S. (2003a) *Tourism: An Introduction*, London, Sage.

Franklin, A. S. (2003b) 'The Tourist Syndrome: An Interview with Zygmunt Bauman', *Tourist Studies* 3(2): 205–17.

Franklin, A. S. and Crang, M. (2001) 'The Trouble with Tourism and Travel Theory?', *Tourist Studies* 1(1): 5–22.

Gellner, E. (1983) *Nations and Nationalism*, Oxford, Blackwell.

Graburn, N. (1978) 'Tourism: The Sacred Journey', in V. Smith (ed.) *Hosts and Guests*, Philadelphia, University of Pennsylvania Press.

Hannigan, J. (1998) *Fantasy City*, London, Routledge.

Horne, D. (1985) *The Great Museum*, London, Pluto Press.

James, P. (1996) *Nation Formation*, London, Sage.

Judd, D. R. and Fainstein, S. S. (eds) (1999) *The Tourist City*, New Haven, Yale University Press.

Kirshenblatt-Gimblett, B. (1998) *Destination Culture: Tourism, Museums, and Heritage*, Berkeley, University of California Press.

MacCannell, D. (1976) *The Tourist: A New Theory of the Leisure Class*, New York, Schocken.

MacCannell, D. (1992) *Empty Meeting Grounds: The Tourist Papers*, London, Routledge.

MacCannell, D. (2001) 'Tourist Agency', *Tourist Studies* 1(1): 23–38.

Mathieson, A. and Wall, G. (1982) *Tourism: Economic, Physical and Social Impacts*, London, Longman Cheshire.

Miles, S. (1998) *Consumerism as a Way of Life*, London, Sage.

Moeran, B. (1983) 'The Language of Japanese Tourism', *Annals of Tourism Research* 10(1): 93–108.

O'Connell Davidson, J. (1995) 'British Sex Tourists in Thailand', in M. Maynard and J. Purvis (eds) *(Hetero)Sexual Politics*, London, Taylor and Francis.

O'Reilly, K. (2000) *The British on the Costa Del Sol: Transnational Identities and Local Communities*, London, Routledge.

Rojek, C. (1985) *Capitalism and Leisure Theory*, London, Tavistock.

Rojek, C. (1993) *Ways of Escape*, London, Macmillan.

Rojek, C. (1995) *Decentring Leisure: Rethinking Leisure Theory*, London, Sage.

Rojek, C. and Urry, J. (eds) (1997) *Touring Cultures*, London, Routledge.

Ryan, C. and Hall, M. (2001) *Sex Tourism*, London, Routledge.

Seabrook, J. (1996) *Travels in the Skin Trade: Tourism and the Sex Industry*, London, Pluto Press.

Shaw, G. and Williams, A. (1994) *Critical Issues in Tourism: A Geographical Perspective*, Oxford, Blackwell.

Shields, R. (1991) *Places on the Margin*, London, Routledge.

Smith, V. (ed.) (1978) *Hosts and Guests*, Philadelphia, University of Pennsylvania Press.

Twain, M. (1993) *The Innocents Abroad*, London, Random House.

Urry, J. (1999) 'Automobility, Car Culture and Weightless Travel: A Discussion Paper' Department of Sociology, Lancaster University, at: <http://www.comp.lancaster.ac.uk/sociology/soc008ju.html>.

Urry, J. (2002) *The Tourist Gaze*, London, Sage; second edition.

Voase, R. (1995) *Tourism: The Human Perspective*, London, Hodder & Stoughton.

Weaver, D. and Opperman, M. (2000) *Tourism Management*, Brisbane, John Wiley & Sons.

Withey, L. (1997) *Grand Tours and Cook's Tours: A History of Leisure Travel, 1750 to 1915*, New York, William Morrow & Co.

World Tourism Organization (2003) First WTO World Tourism Barometer shows Steadily Improving Conditions for International Tourism, News Release, 24 June, Madrid, WTO, available at: <http://www.world-tourism.org/newsroom/Releases/2003/june/barometer.htm> (accessed April 2006).

24
Eating Out and the Appetite for Leisure

Joanne Finkelstein and Rob Lynch

Dining out is not a new social convention, however, its character has changed dramatically from being a necessity for those who travelled and had no choice of meals, say, at inns and wayfarers' stations, to now being a source of entertainment and a valuable part of the economy of the leisure industries. The modern restaurateur has long known that people do not eat out just for the food. A smart decor, gimmick menu, performing waiters and a price list that promises a bargain, all give a decisive edge over the competition. When César Ritz styled the grand dining room at the Savoy Hotel in 1889 as a promenade for the bourgeoisie, he appeared well aware that the diners' interests extended beyond the menu, and his success rested with meeting those social rather than gustatory needs (Norman, 1972). The recognizability of certain foods also works to make them appealing, not necessarily for their taste but for their familiar associations. For instance, national cuisine is a dubious construction as it is a conglomeration of various regional tastes, yet it works to make foods such as the hamburger, meat pie, croissant and sausage into an immediate source of recognition, identification and comfort (Richter, 2002: 180).

In contemporary urban societies, there is now a wide range of restaurants but not necessarily a diversity of tastes. Many restaurants appear to have developed according to a formula designed to offer the diner an experience that is largely predictable and consistently appealing. The dining out experience is limited, in general terms, to three kinds of restaurant – the chain outlet, *le bistro* or café, and the special-occasion, spectacular restaurant. There are variations within these parameters; for instance, the recent fashion for the massive sized and upmarket, such as Terence Conran's 700-seater Mezzo in London, combines the qualities of the chain restaurant with the spectacular. For analytic purposes, however, the three category classification system works to expound the separate qualities of each type of dining experience.

The classic forms of eating out

All restaurants share the task of providing comestibles to paying customers. The variations on this task arise from the types of food offered, the manner of serving the food, the conduct of the restaurant personnel including the front of house (if there is one) to the kitchen hand and dishwasher (if there is one). Some restaurants are self-serve and there is no host to greet the customers at the door and show them a table and menu. Some restaurants are so automated and serviced that there are no dishes to wash and no cooking utensils to clean, as the foods are pre-prepared and delivered to the kitchen, which is really an assembly area. Across this wide variety, the restaurant has in common the business of serving meals at almost any time of the day and night, to a great variety of paying customers.

The chain restaurant

Fast foods were initially popular as novelties. Pillsbury (1990: 56–7) has described the change in the restaurant in the 1920s to 1930s, in America, where hamburgers, hot dogs and ice cream became the attractions at drive-in restaurants and purpose-built theme outlets such as the Krystal chain and distinctive White Castle. Over time, the enduring success of the chain restaurant has come to rest on its elementary promise: to be always the same, to offer reliable products that are reassuring in a world otherwise buffetted and battered by the challenging and unexpected (Schlosser, 2002).

McDonald's is probably the most well-known of the chain restaurants and it is as famous for its application of the philosophy 'Keep It Simple, Stupid' (KISS), as it is for its products – hamburgers and french fries. The KISS system of food handling and delivery is not unique to the food business, indeed, it is a system that characterizes many social institutions in the modern world. The chain restaurant has proved popular; the promises made to customers have largely been met – the food is always the same, it is delivered quickly, it is cheap to purchase and reliably hygienic. These services revolutionized the restaurant business and suceeded in capturing a massive number of consumers and ensuring their repeat custom. The chain restaurant applied the same principles used in the mass manufacture of other popular commodities such as furniture, cars, televisions, denim jeans and Reebok trainers. In more formal terms, KISS describes Weber's concept of instrumental rationalization. The application of this to the restaurant transformed the business into a factory flow system or mass assembly line that could expand worldwide and still maintain the consistent quality of its services and products (Ritzer, 1996).

Le bistro

Many contemporary restaurants employ various gimmicks to enhance the drama of dining out, such as names that are meaningless but arresting – 'The Quilted Giraffe', 'Liquidity', 'Arc', 'Nood', 'The Seagoing Vegetable'. They also use distinctive styles of cuisine, the apparel of waiters, location of the kitchen, size of the wine glasses, design of the crockery, decor and cost of service to enhance the eating experience. These gimmicks and affectations function as signatures of the place and often have the effect of distracting the diner from the quality of the food. The recent fashion for placing the working kitchen at the centre of the bistro, for example, seems to intensify the focus on the food while at the same time distracting the diner by highlighting the antics of the performing chef. Another feature of *le bistro* is its menu which is often an element of the decor and ambience. It may be written on the walls, scribbled on the paper table cloth, it may be delivered to the table on a small carved slate, or have the appearance of an elegantly printed pamphlet using the full aesthetic potential of newly designed fonts.

Le bistro is all style; its background music is as carefully selected as the personalities of the waiters who attend the tables and engage the patrons in conversations from the formal and servile to the engaging, suggestive and slightly hectoring. The economic viability of the bistro is determined by the restaurateur's reading of the fashions and identification of the bistro's 'demographic'. The importance of style has always been understood by the successful *bistroistas*. The celebrated chef Antonin Carême (1784–1833) popularized the gimmick of food sculptures for precisely these reasons. He was especially well-known for ornamental sculptures made from spun sugar which could stand four- and five-feet in height and were shaped into bucolic scenes that included exotic pagodas, fountains and elaborate temples with cherubs adorning every possible nook and cranny. The purpose of these confectionaries was to make the expense of dining out more akin to the purchase of a nebulous marvel, an experience that singled out the individual from others. It was the necessary ingredient which transformed dining out into a display of conspicuous consumption. Now the style is for foods arranged on the plate in homage to abstract impressionism following Mondrian's bold, squared forms or Jackson Pollocks's drizzled colours. Irrespective of the change of aesthetic, the intention is the same – to distract the diner from the quality of the comestibles.

La spectacular

The third category of restaurant is the well-known tourist attraction which draws its patrons by its reputation. That reputation may be based on its location – 360-degree view overlooking a great metropolitan city, or a 500-year-old vineyard; it might be based on its celebrated chef, unique decor, antique silverware or established wine cellar. This type of restaurant is usually expensive, but not necessarily because of its quality comestibles or standards. Such restaurants provide the backdrop for important occasions. *La spectacular* is listed in the travel guides as an imperative for the well-heeled tourist visiting Florence, Paris or New York; it is where small wedding celebrations are held or milestone birthdays. It is a 'once off' that forms part of the claim for social superiority in terms of the diner's *savoir faire*, fashionability, affluence, and so on.

It is significant that the restaurant has a long history, that it has transcended the ruptures of eighteenth-century political revolution, nineteenth-century industrialization and the reconfiguration of empire, and the twentieth-century global shifts in population arising from migration and economic reform. Its durability is not simply a result of its variety and ubiquity. It has much to do with the practice of eating out itself and how this works to immerse the individual in the aestheticized and commodified dimensions of the social world. The remainder of the chapter addresses the sociological meanings of eating out in terms of the pleasures and tensions it delivers to the modern diner, whether they have chosen to eat in the fast food outlet, the unique tourist spot or the charming local bistro.

The allure of food

The centrality of food as an organizing principle has been a feature of most human societies. Food is about sustenance and appetite, both physical and symbolic, and the distribution of food is about the organization of society. Who eats what, where and with whom are questions which attach to the political, economic and cultural fabric. Following the same logic, the variety of comestibles on offer can be thought of as an extension of the range of human desires. How people live, what they do with their time, how they pursue their pleasures, what they find entertaining and desirable are also practices that attach to the circulation of food. Eating is both a physical necessity and a cultural site where elaborate social rituals take place. As such, in the contemporary world of mass advertising and marketing, food has become a prominent feature of everyday domestic expectations and habits.

In Schlosser's (2002: 3) study of popular fast foods, he remarks that Americans 'spend more money on fast food than on higher education, personal computers ... new cars ... on movies, books, magazines'. Not only does this trend have a direct effect on the US and related national economies, it is also significant for understanding the position of food in the everyday consciousness of individuals going about their business. The manufacture, marketing and consumption of foods in the large cities and urbanized societies of the world constitutes a new industry which has had a profound influence on all aspects of social life, on both a local and global scale. Nestle (2002: 2–28) has shown in her critical and detailed analyses of global food politics that the food industries exert a strong influence on government policies and national economies. The food industries are global, powerful and well capitalized, and they function as politically active lobby groups that protect their colossal interests in much the same way as the alcohol and tobacco industries.

From the beginning of the twentieth century, the message from public health programmes and government and related industries was to eat more food, and eat more varied foods to ensure improved personal health. Those industries involved with large-scale food manufacture and marketing helped promulgate this message, and in so doing established their products (namely, Coca-Cola, Kellogg's cornflakes, Schweppes bottled beverages) as ordinary features of everyday life. Since the latter half of the twentieth century, cosmopolitan societies have generated a deep investment in various food businesses including the restaurant, supermarket, gourmet emporium and the publication of myriad recipe books. In part, this privileging of food has promoted the circumstances in which the current epidemic of overeating and obesity has become visible. In contrast to the beginning of the twentieth century, now the message from government and public health agencies is to eat less food, much less food, as a means of slowing the trend toward obesity and improving widespread health standards.

To arrive at this end point means that the food industries have been highly successful in building the market demand for industrialized food products, and in changing the meaning of food from a basic form of nutrition into a variety of forms of leisure and entertainment that are to be enjoyed both inside and outside the home. The rise of the restaurant industry has simultaneously sustained the strong growth in the mass marketing of standardized foods, and it has produced a consumer who is interested in food as a convenience, a form of entertainment, leisure, pleasure, and as a status symbol. Driving the revolution in the food business is not only the enlarged market of consumers who have developed expectations about food as a continuous source of entertainment and novelty, but it is also the aestheticization of foods as displayed in *haute cuisine* and on the various cooking programmes that repeatedly appear on television and in glossy magazine publications.

The circumstances and influences which shape food into a variety of entertainments and pleasures also distance it from its basic naturalism. It is taken for granted as a form of bodily sustenance and elevated into a cultural and aesthetic form which delivers private and social pleasures in tandem with the physical ones. How and what we choose to eat, and when and with whom we do it, are choices which also carry messages about taste, as defined by Bourdieu (1984: 54). That is, what we do and how we do it creates a variety of social claims which we use to display our sense of social position, and which others interpret in a more or less sympathetic manner. Food, eating, taste, pleasure and leisure form a junction where social position and personal identity are put on display, in much the same way that Bourdieu argued class position is made evident through practices such as food manners and preferences. It is not food or eating *per se* which provides insights into the experiences of pleasure, but rather the role or presence that food can have in the gamut of leisure pursuits available to us.

The private pleasures of eating out

The prominence of food in everyday life indicates how eating has long been an essential ingredient in the formulation of social practices that define the individual's position. Eating in restaurants adds a further dimension to this as the restaurant itself is a complex social site with its own inherent constraints and rules about social intercourse. As a cultural practice, dining out has various beginnings, one being the nineteenth-century Parisian habit of taking *restaurants*, a concentrated consommé made from reduced beef and partridge *jus*. The formalization of the restaurant is often dated to the last quarter of the eighteenth century, in Paris, where those with the skill to make a consommé were granted a legal right to sell it along with 'all sorts of creams, rice and vermicelli soups, fresh eggs, macaroni, stewed capons, confitures, compotes, and other delicate and salutary dishes'. This type of business was expected to be run on the 'principles of cleanliness, decency, and honesty'; it was expected to show a specific and fixed price for its fare, to serve its products at all hours and to admit women. In short, a restaurant was where meals were almost always available, and where the various types of foods were served in set portions and their prices were clearly advertised (Spang, 2000: ix–x). These strictures subtly distinguished the restaurant from other sources of cooked foods such as travellers' inns, chop houses and coffee houses. Thus the public space we now know as a restaurant has had a significant influence on how individuals understand pleasure, how desires are defined and met, and how the strangers encountered in the public sphere become absorbed into the intricacies and drama of our own pleasures. In this way, the restaurant is associated with changes in sensibilities and the democratization of luxury; it is a force in the rise of industrialization and conspicuous consumption, and has functioned as both a symbol of civility and a mechanism for spreading the civilizing process (Elias, 1978).

The Parisian habit of taking a restorative to treat a sickly disposition or restore physical strength was the practice that re-defined a therapeutic regime into an aesthetic sensibility and source of pleasure.[1] The consumption of *restaurants* or restoratives became the fashion which in turn supported a thorough renovation of social relations between individuals. The new bourgeois fashion of taking a restorative was an opportunity to see how others behaved in the public domain. For the aristocracy, the same behaviour was another means of interweaving the sexual appetites with the gustatory. There was a lingering suggestion in this fashionable new habit of eating out that the need to be reinvigorated by a restorative bouillon was the result of a debauched lifestyle which had left the individual too dissipated, too weak, too preoccupied with the carnal, to eat. While the bourgeoisie were learning the new social arts of the public domain and finding in it both entertainment and sociability, the more antique class was indulging the appetites both alimentary and sexual. The elision of the therapeutic *restaurant* with the cultivation of new manners of sociability defined an important moment in the changing structure of the social world. In this way, the fashion of taking bouillon in public was part of the development of the modern public sphere.

Dining out, as a cultural practice and preferred form of sociability, has continually changed since its early modern formulation in the purchase of bouillons which in turn has given its name to the place of consumption – not 'houses of health' as they were then quaintly called, but restaurants, as we now know them. In the continuous evolution of the restaurant, there can be seen a history of the private and public realms and how these different social spheres has each provided specific opportunities for women and men to define their gustatory longings as well as other aesthetic and personal tastes (Spang, 2000).

When the restaurant became a place where women and men could be seen in public, separately and together, it was immediately important as a site where experimental forms of human exchange and play were negotiated and practised. The restaurant contributed to the visibility of the individual and social status by being a place where people could parade themselves and watch others also on display. The restaurant made evident the complex interdependencies between individuals and their socioeconomic circumstances, and in these ways, it became the background against which individuals learned to disport themselves, and even dissemble, for social advantage. This atmosphere constructed the restaurant as a site of spectacle in which the objects on display included both people and comestibles. These attributes of the modern restaurant persist into the contemporary; the restaurant was (and still remains) an eloquent signifier of sociability and of the mechanisms by which status and privilege are put on exhibition.

From its earliest incarnation, the restaurant has also been intricately involved with particular styles of human conduct. Despite its association with health spas and the revitalizing demitasse of bouillon, the restaurant was not simply a commercial enterprise where goods and services were systematically exchanged. It quickly became a crucible in which appetites and desires were cultivated, and where new social experiences were manufactured (Gronow, 1997). Spang has described the restaurant as a site where the individual was able to consider his or her own needs and desires and 'to concentrate on that most fleeting and difficult to universalize sense: taste' (2000: 75). Furthermore, it was an encounter with the novel and aesthetically exquisite. Restaurateurs soon learned that one of the strongest attractions for customers was the decor and ambience of the restaurant (such as in *le bistro*) which, in turn, distracted individuals from their ordinary, everyday concerns. In contrast to cafés and inns, the restaurant provided private spaces for diners in the form of separate tables (in contrast to the long, communal table at the travellers' inn). It provided private rooms or cabinets which could hold two, four, six, and occasionally eight people. It was in the restaurant where the novel pleasure of infusing public life with private intimacies was being tested. The desire for privacy while being in a crowd was the impulse behind the new architecture of the restaurant with its separate cabinets designed for clandestine assignations.

The creation of new pleasures was also inscribed onto the menu. The governing assumption was that variety must be offered in order to respond to all the possible maladies, sensitivities and complaints of the nervous system that the customer might be enduring. In this way, the provision of choice in menu items meant that the diner was forced to reflect on their own tastes and become capable of expressing their needs and desires. The choice provided by the invention of the menu came to have long-term consequences in terms of heightening the level of self-consciousness of the new restaurant diner. Spang describes how the differentiation of the café from the restaurant was crucial in the changing levels of self-consciousness insofar as individuals learned to behave differently in each locale. 'Café patrons read newspapers, and thought about the world around them; restaurant customers read the menu, and thought about their own bodies' (Spang, 2000: 79).

Social opportunities in the restaurant

The pleasures attached to socializing over food and drink did not only arise with the modern restaurant. Forerunners to these establishments had been in existence for hundreds of years. Coffee houses, the commonly cited precedents of the restaurant, were noted to exist in Constantinople as early as 1560, and they proliferated throughout most European cities from the mid-seventeenth century. London, for example, had 82 coffee houses in 1663 and well over 500 six decades later, in 1734. Coffee houses have been noted as important in the historical currents undergirding the emergence of the public and administrative domains. It was in these places that novel tastes and desires especially in social and political matters were being cultivated and refined. In London, the coffee houses were known as 'tattling universities', a description that alluded to the busy exchanges of ideas which took place over a drink of coffee as well the chaotic mix of social classes that mingled there. It was this new social space that encouraged traders, landed gentry, aristocrats and the new urban professionals to speak to one another across the otherwise constraining barriers of class and status, and it was from such social commerce that an outpouring of ideas and ambitions took form.

Spang has described the formulation of the modern restaurant as an evolution from an eighteenth-century 'sensibility' in which various practices surrounding health and vigour were closely cultivated into nineteenth-century expressions of 'taste'. It was in these fashionable practices that new social forms and interpersonal exchanges were being shaped alongside new practices of gastronomy itself (ibid.: 3–5). Food habits and social forms were mutually constitutive. Spang makes the bold claim that restaurants were simultaneously in the business of feeding people and producing the modern concept of identity: she states that 'restaurant service was reserved for, defined by, and perhaps instrumental in creating, individuals' (ibid.: 75).

The restaurant as an imaginary location in human consciousness delineated a new social space in which the semi-private and the semi-public came to sit together in a relatively unproblematic fusion. Brillat-Savarin (1825: 310–13) described the interior of the restaurant as a social arena in which various types of individuals learned both to express desires and control them. He recognized in the restaurant a distinctive space where individuals could, for the first time, cultivate additional layers to their own storehouse of social knowledge and experience. He observed, for instance, the lone male diner who seemed always to request his meal in an overly loud voice, who always seemed to wait impatiently until served and then ate as quickly as possible in order to leave the place. Such conduct, Brillat-Savarin thought, revealed the discomfort of the man who expected dining out to be a communal and pleasurable event, and who revealed a lack of ease and a degree of discomfort at being alone. Brillat-Savarin noted the behaviour of families who seemed to relish the busy atmosphere of the restaurant, and the different foods and drinks that they could savour. The restaurant also attracted married couples who seemed to not have much to say to one another. They looked about them as if in a theatre and, in this way, Brillat-Savarin opined, they escaped from the inherent barrenness of married life. The restaurant attracted lovers as a place they could be together without being compromised by discovery. It also functioned for them as a device which intensified their mutual desire while restraining its unmediated expression. The restaurant provided a romantic setting; it gave a sense of privacy and comfort but, at the same time, it forced lovers to invent new ways of speaking and acting that expressed their sexual desires while remaining obedient to the *moeurs* of public decorum.

For travellers and strangers, Brillat-Savarin noted, the restaurant was a haven in which they could follow their gastronomic fancies and over-indulge without fear of recrimination. Their anonymity allowed them to be self-indulgent without embarrassment. Brillat-Savarin also observed that the restaurant was popular with regular diners who could act with familiarity toward other patrons and restaurant personnel even though they did not have a sustained relationship that went beyond the restaurant door. In this way, the restaurant allowed for the pretence of belonging. The restaurant was also the setting for accidental experiments in human commerce. The styles of human exchange and social relations evidenced over the dining table were closely aligned with emergent bourgeois values; that is, they emphasized the importance of physical appearance and the opportunity to gain the good opinion of others. In this respect the restaurant can be seen to play a crucial role in the convergence of the personal and the social, the private and public. For the new bourgeoisie, it was a crucible in which cultural formations and the individual's new knowledge about the importance of social style was fermenting.

Many of the nineteenth-century observations about human behaviour in the restaurant continue into the present. Brillat-Savarin recognized the potential of the restaurant to be a distinctive social experience for its diverse patrons while, at the same time, it captured the array of activities, moods and desires that spoke eloquently of emergent cultural forms. Thus, from its modern beginning, eating out has been a practice that shapes the very styles of interactional exchange that individuals then learn to desire and cultivate. In the history of manners, Norbert Elias (1978: 68) observed that 'conduct while eating cannot be isolated. It is a segment – a very characteristic one – of the totality of socially instilled forms of conduct.' With this comment he also included how the practices around food were indicative of other social changes taking place such as the shifting thresholds of tolerance towards others and in turn the levels of civility that they implied.

Playing with taste

Much of the social significance of the restaurant lies in its capacity to encourage exhibitionist conduct. During its history it has enticed the social classes to imitate one another, it has been the arena in which class divisions have been safely breached, and where diverse human exchanges such as business deals, seductions, family quarrels, and so on, have taken place. It is where displays of social pretension, guile and the dictates of fashion have all been in evidence. In the restaurant, one is not only consuming food, but one is consuming social positions and experiences. In a restaurant, anyone can pretend to be rich, urbane and powerful. One can play the role of gastronome, bon vivant, good father, benevolent mother, ardent lover, and so on without any fear that someone will challenge the display. In many ways, this makes the restaurant into a forerunner of the contemporary entertainment industry.

The astute observations of Brillat-Savarin in the early nineteenth century foreshadow the fundamental ideas of contemporary play theory articulated by Dutch historian Johan Huizinga and French sociologist Roger Caillois in the mid-twentieth century. The connection between eating out in restaurants and the realm of play and leisure is well illustrated in *Homo Ludens*. Huizinga (1949: 7–13) points out that play is 'free activity standing quite consciously outside "ordinary life". It proceeds within its own proper boundaries of time and space' cut off from the everyday world to which play returns. Play is not 'ordinary' or 'real' but rather 'a stepping out of "real" life into a temporary sphere of activity with a disposition all of its own'. According to Huizinga, there is a secludedness and limitedness to play which allows it to express its own momentum and meaning. Play proceeds within this space according to a set of rules and conventions. 'Play demands order' and the rules 'determine what "holds" in the temporary world circumscribed by play'. Deviations from this order 'spoil the game' and rob the activity of its character. These ideas readily attach to Brillat-Savarin's exposition of the restaurant as a new arena in which the fledgling bourgeois played with the possibilities of the space.

In the separate realm of play, Huizinga well understood how the diner in a restaurant would tend to form a special bond or community with others, and how this spontaneous creation of community and belonging would become self-rewarding and pleasurable in its own right. A play-community tends to form through the feeling of 'being apart together' in an exceptional situation of sharing something important and of mutually withdrawing from the rest of the world. Just as Brillat-Savarin noted that the restaurant encouraged exhibitionist conduct and individual expressiveness, so Huizinga (1949) and Caillois (1961) have both noted the *as if* quality of the ludic. In the separate realm of play, people are free to act *as if* they were someone else, temporarily cut off and released from the normal constraints of the everyday life world. It is this *as if* quality of play which lends itself to the relative absence of recriminations such that Brillat-Savarin noted following the over indulgences and liberties which can be taken in the restaurant. For as long as dining out is regarded as 'not real' activity, then the consequences of transgressions have less weight than they would in the normal, everyday world.

Embedded in the customs of dining out are prevailing ideas of entertainment, health, social prestige, gender differentiation, privilege, and so on. The restaurant has become, in the modern era, a convenient mechanism for circulating a wide variety of ideas and cultural practices. Indeed, all restaurants – whether they are spectacular tourist attractions, theme restaurants or chain outlets – are in the business of creating atmosphere and influencing the conduct of their patrons. As such they impinge directly on the mobilization of certain social practices through which individuals mediate their everyday exchanges with others. This explains, in part, how the restaurant has emerged as a central feature of the changing nature of the public domain, and how it has made styles of eating – whatever the character of the restaurant – into a cultural feature directly linked to the commodification of leisure as a consumer product and a part of the entertainment industries. The entertainment industries are in the business of marketing desires, and constructing appetites; they promote certain practices through which we can interpret our own personal longings. Indeed, the ultimate accomplishment of these industries is the replacement of the consumer's sense of pleasure and reality with that promoted by the purveyor of manufactured goods. This is precisely what dining out can do, especially as it becomes more of a habit deeply located in the everyday regimes of pleasure.

Cultivating the appetites

The popularity of eating out in Westernized societies has become a significant economic phenomenon. At the close of the twentieth century, two out of every three meals were purchased and consumed outside the home (Nestle, 2002). The popularity of contemporary restaurants is often connected to the changing patterns of the family and the increased numbers of working women. Adults away from the home for much of each day readily employ the services of the restaurant to create a sense of family life; indeed, some self-identified 'family restaurants' trade on precisely this circumstance. In addition, the restaurant can function as a site for gathering food knowledge; the diner can collect gastronomic experiences, follow trends in cuisine, become an epicure. This is often exploited by the enterprising restaurateur who elaborately describes the food on the menu or temptingly depicts it on wall paintings in order to amplify the diner's desires. Certainly this was the successful practice of César Ritz at London's Savoy Hotel. He understood his bourgeois patrons to be interested in the theatricality of the restaurant and the opportunities it offered to disport oneself, to play act, to occupy an extravagant and opulent setting as if it were one's own. Seated in the restaurant, one could look about and stare at others as if they were on stage, and such practices would not necessarily look out of place. Ever since, popular restaurants have continued to provide this voyeuristic pleasure; they are a vehicle for being seen in public, seeing who else is out and about, for finding entertainment in the other diners and experimenting with new sensory pleasures.

The appeal of the restaurant can be explained in social, economic and aesthetic terms but it is the entertainment of food and eating, that sustains much of the restaurant's popularity.[2] As the restaurant offers the opportunity for individuals to act in ways largely removed from the actualities of the everyday, it offers a means of realizing private fantasies. In this way, the restaurant is like a theatre in which individuals can appear as they desire without any of the risks that would be encountered were they to try to cross social barriers in other spheres of activity. The restaurant transforms bodily nourishment into a public event subject to prescriptive rules; it brings individuals, figuratively and literally, into the public arena and exposes them to the scrutinizing eye of the other. When, what and how we eat becomes a narrative retelling aspects of biography and cultural knowledge; it is an indication of how deeply we are embedded in the fluctuating social imperatives of our times, such as styles in fashion and popularity. Bourdieu (1984: 196) has described how the act of eating is more than a process of bodily nourishment – it is an elaborate performance of gender, social class and self-identification. And it is an elaborate denial of the 'crude materiality' of eating itself. Bourdieu points out that the complex organization of a meal functions to obscure its actuality – the order in which foods are presented, their arrangement on the plate, the utensils used for bringing food to the mouth, the ways in which food is served, the seating arrangements of individuals at a dining table, the size of the portions served, are all features of eating which deliberately distance the diner from the crude materiality of the food itself.

The ethos of mass consumerism which emerged in the nineteenth century and which has stridently continued into the late twentieth century has effectively stirred up and shaped new and previously unrealized personal appetites. The early twentieth-century social theorist of modernity, Georg Simmel (1903) recognized that people sought out new entertainments as a means for making life easier; the continuous production of new pleasures and pastimes meant that the individual's time and attention were fully absorbed by the material world. Simmel well understood how a vast array of newly manufactured objects could be exciting, but he saw as well that such a fascination with the material diverted the individual from moral thinking about how society should be and what constituted proper social relations. Simmel saw that as the products of the objective culture became available to more people, a putative consensus appeared to exist: people came to act more alike and to enjoy similar interests. It was as if the more people came into contact with the material products of civilization, the narrower became the base of values and qualities upon which social life rested. The consequence of such a narrowing of interests was that the existence of alternative competing values became rare and, in turn, this brought about a dilution of those intellectual pursuits, namely, doubt, critique and invention, which many have argued are the impetus of civility itself (Akerman, 1993).

Various social commentators on modernity have glided over the restaurant and other venues of leisure as slightly too trivial to provide much insight into social life. The works by Elias, Huizinga, Simmel and others, alongside more contemporary studies such as that by Rebecca Spang, have been a corrective to those views. Modes of sociability and leisure forms such as eating out, provide a basis for arguing that the specificities of the social setting are more influential in shaping the public sphere than the idiosyncrasies or psychological characteristics of individuals (Simmel, 1971: 34–5). Styles of sociability are intimately related to the opportunities offered in the public domain. In one sense sociability is a form of interaction devoid of content: it is the 'pure form' of society (ibid.: 129). Simmel meant by this that forms of leisure and play as well as the pursuit of aesthetic pleasures (such as art) can be thought of as interactions devoid of utilitarian purpose thus they create the opportunity for discovering and inventing the play form (ibid.: 130). As sociability has no ulterior end, no content and no result outside of itself, it is a pure form of creativity in which individuals are engaged in the production of their own pleasures and social positions. In this way, what we do in a restaurant, how we eat meals, what leisure practices we associate with food, all impinge on our own capacities to extract pleasure from the social setting and from other human beings – be they strangers or intimates. All this makes the restaurant – in its various guises – a successful social form that has brought individuals together for centuries, and has sustained them in the exploration of pleasure.

Notes

1. Meat broth made from a concentrated liquid essence of many pounds of animal flesh was a triumph of French cuisine. The idea behind such a gastronomic preference was a belief in the virtue of bypassing the mouth, teeth and stomach and directly infusing an essence of nutritive juice directly into the bloodstream. The term 'restaurant' or 'restauration' literally means 'restorative', and from its early modern beginnings, the imbibing of foods purchased from these new establishments had an aura of health and virtue about it.
2. It is ironic that the original restaurants, from which our modern counterparts take their definition, began as establishments offering health and medicinal potions, whereas now,

the type of restaurant most commonly frequented by consumers, namely, the mass-market chain restaurant, has been identified as a leading contributor to the new epidemic of obesity which promises to become, in the next decade, a serious public health problem throughout the industrialized societies.

Bibliography

Akerman, N. (1993) *The Necessity of Friction*, New York, Springer-Verlag.

Bourdieu, P. (1984) *Distinction: A Social Critique of the Judgment of Taste*, Cambridge, MA, Harvard University Press.

Brillat-Savarin, J. A. (1825) *The Physiology of Taste*, New York, Liveright, 1970 edition.

Caillois, R. (1961) *Man, Play and Games*, New York, Free Press.

Elias, N. (1978) *The Civilizing Process*, New York, Urizen.

Elias, N. (1982) *Power and Civility*, New York, Pantheon.

Finkelstein, J. (1989) *Dining Out. A Sociology of Modern Manners*, Oxford, Polity Press.

Goldman, R. and Papson, S. (1996) *Sign Wars*, New York, Guilford.

Gottdiener, M. (2001) *The Theming of America*, Boulder, CO, Westview.

Gronow, J. (1997) *The Sociology of Taste*, London, Routledge.

Huizinga, J. (1949) *'Homo Ludens': A Study of the Play Element in Culture*, London, Routledge & Kegan Paul.

Mintz, S. (1996) *Tasting Food, Tasting Freedom: Excursions into Eating, Culture and the Past*, Boston, Beacon.

Nestle, M. (2002) *Food Politics*, Berkeley, University of California Press.

Norman, B. (1972) *Tales of the Table: A History of Western Cuisine*, New Jersey, Prentice Hall.

Pillsbury, R. (1990) *From Boarding House to Bistro*, Boston, Unwin Hyman.

Richter, S. (2002) 'Food and Drink: Hegelian Encounters with the Culinary Other', in A. Phipps (ed.) *Contemporary German Cultural Studies*, London, Arnold.

Ritzer, G. (1996) *The McDonaldization of Society*, Thousand Oaks, CA, Pine Forge Press.

Schlosser, E. (2002) *Fast Food Nation*, London, Penguin.

Simmel, G. (1971) *The Metropolis and Mental Life and Sociability*, in *On Individuality and Social Forms*, ed. D. Levine, Chicago, University of Chicago Press.

Spang, R. (2000) *The Invention of the Restaurant: Paris and Modern Gastronomic Culture*, Cambridge, MA, Harvard University Press.

Williams, R. (1982) *Dream Worlds: Mass Consumption in Late Nineteenth-Century France*, Berkeley, University of California Press.

25

Family Leisure

Maureen Harrington

Researchers in Leisure Studies know that for most people, most of the time, leisure takes place within and around the home and usually occurs with members of their family and close friends (Bhatti and Church, 2000; Clarke and Critcher, 1985; Horna, 1994; Rojek, 1985; Veal and Lynch, 2001). This has come to be known as *the privatization thesis* and has been stated in various ways, some of which emphasize home-centredness more so than family-centredness, but all capture the idea that in contemporary society, family and friendship-based home-life has taken precedence over leisure in the public sphere (Allan and Crow, 1991). In general proponents of the thesis argue that compared to earlier historical periods, people give priority to home-centred or domestic leisure rather than seeking communal leisure experiences and sociability in public places. Several factors related to the organization of modern capitalist society have been identified as contributing to the privatization of leisure. These factors include innovative and mass produced micro-electronic home entertainment equipment (Rojek, 1985), fear of crime in public spaces and 'higher material standards, greater geographical mobility, more leisure time, and less hierarchical familial ideologies' (Allan and Crow, 1991: 19). Allan and Crow (ibid.) argue that the privatization thesis has been overstated (see also Allan and Crow, 1989), in that not all family members have private space within the home, and most people enjoy a greater diversity in leisure settings and companions than simply the home and immediate family members. Nevertheless, most leisure theorists acknowledge domestic leisure as the arena in which family members establish and maintain their relationships with one another (Godbey, 1999).

However, if we take a longer historical view, technological and social processes of the late twentieth century seem less explanatory of domestic leisure than social and cultural forces that have been set in motion since the end of the Middle Ages. As Ariés (1962) argued in rich historical detail, family life in contemporary society is the legacy of several interconnected social and cultural changes that occurred during the thirteenth to the seventeenth centuries. Private, family and child-centred home life and domestic leisure was a result of the breakdown of communal public life, a changing concept of childhood and the rise of the modern concept of the family within the formation of the class system. A brief discussion of these broad historical changes is instructive to readers interested in understanding the social conditions under which family-based leisure originated.

The origins of family leisure

During the Middle Ages children were an integral part of everyday social life in work, sport and play. Infants wore swaddling-bands and were 'coddled', but under conditions of high fertility and high infant and child mortality, children that survived were treated more or less indifferently, with no special meaning given to their nature. There was no marked transition from child to adult; after all, children were dressed in similar garments to those worn by adults. From the age of three or four years, children participated along with adults in communal games, pastimes and amusements, most of which we would find childish today. These communal activities included all social levels and were one of the main ways society could 'draw its collective bonds closer, to feel united' (Ariés, 1962: 72), particularly during seasonal and traditional festivals such as carnival (see also Rojek, 1985: 26–8; Cross, 1990: 13–16). Games of chance were regarded with 'moral indifference' into the seventeenth century (Ariés, 1962: 82) but during this and the eighteenth century a new attitude arose and some games, such as bowls and skittles that led to brawls, were decried from the pulpit as evil. Police magistrates also banned games from time to time, classifying them 'among quasi-criminal activities such as drunkenness and prostitution, which could be tolerated in a pinch, but which had to be forbidden at the slightest sign of excess' (ibid.: 88). Children were discouraged from playing 'evil' games and encouraged to play 'good' games. Jesuits went so far as to incorporate into school curricula those games and pastimes deemed as wholesome, along with dancing and play-acting. Childhood was beginning to be regarded as a distinct life stage in which the child, by virtue of possessing an immortal soul and a personality, was seen to need both moral guidance and education.

Over the course of the late seventeenth and eighteenth centuries, adults of the upper classes abandoned the games that were once found among all social levels – from nobility to villeins, leaving them to the lower classes and children. Ariés explains:

> it is important to note that the old community of games was destroyed at one and the same time between children and adults, between lower class and middle class. This coincidence enables us to glimpse already a connection between the idea of childhood and the idea of class. (ibid.: 99)

He traces the meaning of childhood from the fourteenth century to the nineteenth century to show how contemporary ideas about parenting and privatized, child-centred family life originated.

Art, iconography and religion had depicted the 'special nature' of children from the fourteenth century, and by the sixteenth and seventeenth centuries children of the upper classes, particularly boys, were dressed in clothing that distinguished them from adults (ibid.: 129). Mothers and nannies, which had always 'coddled' young children, were the first to express a new view of children, as amusing and a source of relaxation to adults, like 'charming toys' (ibid.: 133). However, 'moralists and pedagogues' did not share this view of children but rather took more of a 'psychological interest' in and 'moral solicitude' for children (ibid.: 131), wanting to instil 'disciplined, rational manners' in the 'fragile creatures of God' (ibid.: 133). In the eighteenth century, both the notion of providing amusement and the need for moral safeguarding were found in the concept of childhood, along with a new concern for hygiene and physical health. At this stage, Ariés argues, 'the child has taken a central place in the family' (ibid.: 133).

From his analysis of medieval iconography, Ariés deduces that the concept of the family, as distinct from the bloodline, was not known in the Middle Ages, but rather began in the fifteenth and sixteenth centuries, then flourished in the seventeenth century. There was family life in medieval society, but it was shrouded in silence, not valued nor considered worthy of poetic or artistic expression. The family was not able 'to nourish an existential attitude between parents and children' (ibid.: 368). From the age of seven children were sent away to live in another house, as a servant or an apprentice, to prepare for knighthood or to go to school (ibid.: 366). Children learned 'the art of living' from mingling indiscriminately in the places adults worked and played (ibid.: 368). Beginning in the fifteenth century the family was to undergo 'a slow and profound revolution' (ibid.: 369) with the replacement of apprenticeships by formal schooling of boys, particularly those in the middle levels of the social hierarchy. According to Ariés, this marks a convergence of two distinct concepts, the family and childhood, as the family 'centred itself on the child' (ibid.: 369). Schooling brought parents and children closer emotionally, but it was the gradual dominance of private, domestic life over the older pattern of general sociability that allowed the modern child-centred family with its privatized domestic leisure to emerge in the eighteenth century.

Ariés depicts society in seventeenth-century France as 'graded clienteles' formed through tight relational networks in daily contact 'involving an unimaginable number of calls, conversations, meetings and exchanges' (ibid.: 376) that took place on the street, or in the only other public places, 'big houses', since there were no cafés nor pubs at the time and decent people did not frequent taverns (ibid.: 391). These houses of the well-to-do (compared to the single-room hovels of the poor) housed not only the members of the family but 'a whole population of servants, employees, clerics, clerks, shop-keepers, apprentices, and so on' and 'a constant flow of visitors' (ibid.: 392). The big houses became the cultural milieux for the nascent modern concepts of childhood and the family as they gradually made room for familial privacy. These houses were inevitably crowded by both residents and visitors day and night, no distinction was made between social and professional affairs, and the household slept, ate, danced, talked and worked in general purpose rooms with collapsible beds for sleeping and folding trestle-tables for dining. Even when beds became permanent fixtures in the corners of the room, the room remained a public place, and the family who lived in the house was a focal point of a 'crowded social life' consisting of 'concentric circles of relations, increasingly loose toward the periphery: circles of relatives, friends, clients, protégés, debtors, etc.' (ibid.: 395). The lack of privacy entailed with this more generalized sociability (and associated promiscuity) impeded the development of the concept of the family as a sphere of physical and moral intimacy, but the two existed together in some families in the well-to-do classes. The private sphere of the family as a refuge from the outside world became more realizable in the eighteenth century, with a curtailment of ceremonial etiquette and particularly with changes in architectural design in the layout of rooms. The new arrangement of independent rooms off a common corridor meant that people did not need to pass all rooms to go from one room to another. From this period we find the reduction of the family to the parents and children, with all others, including servants, excluded from the private life of the modern family. The family

> cuts itself off from the world and opposes to society the isolated group of parents and children. All the energy of the group is expended on helping the children to rise in the world, individually and without collective ambition: the children rather than the family. (ibid.: 404)

Here lie the origins of modern concepts of domesticity, privacy and isolation along with the comfort they avail, and for present purposes, the birthplace of family leisure.

It is important to bear in mind that domestic leisure, and its main form, family leisure, both historically and in contemporary times has been most closely associated with the middle classes. The emerging middle class of mid-nineteenth-century Victorian society and across the British Empire embraced the domestic realm with the mother (now a homemaker, albeit one with servants) creating a 'haven in a heartless world' (see Lasch, 1977) for her husband and children. With fewer children, childraising became more permissive and playful (Cross, 1990), and the mother had more time not only for her own leisure but also to organize morally uplifting home-centred leisure for her husband and children, in what has become known as the 'cult of domesticity' imbued with the ideology of 'familism', which will be discussed later. The 'hearth' stood in contrast to the 'saloon'; the 'angel in the parlour' a guardian against drink and public disorder (Cross, 1990: 104; see also Rojek, 1993: 51–96). The principle behind the cult of domesticity was undoubtedly 'private constraint against public excess' (Cross, 1990: 108) but it also spawned an array of family-friendly leisure activities, like board games, fiction, singing and piano-playing, and lawn games like croquet (ibid.), some of which remain popular today – at least among lower-income families (Harrington, 2003). The working and lower classes continued to engage in public leisure, in the pubs, streets and saloons of their neighbourhoods. We can glimpse this form of leisure in Seabrook's reminiscences of the history of his own working-class family:

> Every Saturday night for half a century the women of Green Street gathered in the Snug of 'The Garibaldi'. It was a time of intimacy and relaxation, a time for

mutual commiseration and sympathy, a time for gossip and scandal. But it became something else too. It became a time for self-justification against the outside world:..their conversation evolved into a declaration of faith in themselves and the standards they lived by, an exposition of their profoundest beliefs and thoughts. (Seabrook, 1973: 85)

As the emerging middle class embraced the privatized family centred on the children, it shrank from contact with the lower classes. The middle class 'seceded ... from the vast polymorphous society to organize itself separately, in a homogenous environment, among its families, in homes designed for privacy, in new districts kept free from all lower-class contamination' (Ariés, 1962: 415). Prior to the eighteenth century, most families depended on children working from an early age, but the growing economic power of the middle classes meant they no longer needed their children to labour, and thus argued that 'children *generally* should not work, even though in most families children's labour remained economically essential' (Gittins, 1985: 3). As the middle classes grew politically more powerful, they were able to press for legislation to prohibit child labour, creating 'severe economic problems for working class families ... only partly resolved when working-class men organised unions and pressed for a "family wage"' (ibid.). Underpinned by an ideology of familism, in the nineteenth century the respectable classes felt it their civic and religious duty to lead moral and leisure reform among the disrespectable (or at least disreputable) lower class, under the banner of the Rational Recreation Movement. Recreational programmes offered in such organizations as boys' clubs, girls' clubs, Boys' Brigade, the Boy Scouts and Girl Guides, as well as churches, arose as part of middle-class reform campaigns in Britain, the US, Canada and Australia to impart wholesome, middle-class family values to counter the vice and danger of the use of urban public spaces by children and young people, particularly during night-time. Child labour laws and juvenile curfews were also part of this attempt to keep children and young people out of 'harm's way'. For example, writing about Brisbane newsboys from the 1880s to the First World War, Jamison explains:

The Rational Recreation Movement sought to reform the manners and tastes of what its proponents considered the irrational excesses of a popular culture based putatively on alcohol, gambling, sexual profligacy and myriad other forms of 'unacceptable' street behaviour. Through the provision of 'wholesome' counter-attractions, it was argued plebeian leisure could be transformed from a potential threat to the social order into a vehicle for transmitting the normative, conservative values espoused by the dominant class. (Jamison, 1999: 61)

A similar concern can be seen among middle-class city dwellers in the United States, who wanted to shield working-class children from 'both nightlife and night work' (Baldwin, 2002: 594). Middle-class children were at home in the evening and sent to bed early whereas working-class children were not; rather they 'would loiter in the "bright lights sections" ... waiting for excitement' (ibid.). Middle-class reformers and public officials were united in their 'cultural evangelism' to bring a 'proper childhood' to the working classes and urban poor (ibid.: 596). Their efforts did not supplant popular leisure, but arguably many in the working class 'added elements of the reformers' ideal into their leisure repertory' (Cross, 1990: 101).

The privatization of leisure is also connected to the fact that the Victorian middle class was the class to first experience the 'time–space compression' of modernity (Harvey, 1989, cited in Gillis, 2003) which overturned existing temporal and spatial orders, so that the clock seemed to advance faster and distances between places seemed shorter. As a response to feeling an ebbing connection to the past, and growing uncertainty about a definite future, Victorians innovated new ways to mark cyclical time, to give their lives more continuity and certainty in a seemingly chaotic world. As Gillis explains,

> an entirely new set of highly ritualized daily, weekly, and annual occasions came to serve the purpose not only of synchronizing the presence of family members but, even more important, of providing a common sense of family past and family future. Family time ceased to be merely time spent with kin and became time spent anticipating and remembering family, often in idealized ways that did not necessarily correspond to existing realities. (Gillis, 2003: 154)

The rituals of family time, from daily events like father coming home from work, family dinner and children's bedtime, to weekly attendance at church on Sundays and the eventual diffusion of the modern weekend (ibid.; see also Rybczynski, 1991), and the annual seasons of Christmas, Easter and summer holidays all became family time. These 'repetitive series of occasions … create[d] an experience of cyclical time unavailable in the linear temporal structures of work, school and everyday existence' (Gillis, 2003: 155). Gillis argues that even today family time (defined also as 'quality time') gives us the illusion of regaining a sense of the past, 'bringing to life that which seems irretrievably lost in the time-space compression of the modern world' (ibid.).

The study of family leisure

Leisure Studies has not been very well equipped to study 'family leisure', primarily because leisure has been viewed essentially as an individual phenomenon (Dawson, 2000), and the field is still grappling with an adequate conceptualization of 'family leisure'. Leisure behaviour has mainly been studied through aggregated survey data on individuals, precluding the family, or all the members that constitute it, being the unit of analysis (Kelly, 1997). For psychologists and social psychologists, leisure is a state of being emanating from individual 'freedom of choice, intrinsic motivation and the quality of or enjoyment of the experience' (Mannell and Kleiber, 1997, cited in Shaw and Dawson, 2001: 218). This psychological concept of leisure obviously lends itself to studying individuals, but researchers have also examined socialization processes within the family (see Iso-Ahola, 1980) and the nature of familial relationships (Mannell and Kleiber, 1997). In fact, research on family leisure began with the assumption that family leisure was good for both individual and family development. Many authors, including Orthner (1975), Orthner and Mancini (1980, 1991), Couchman (1982), Holman and Epperson (1984) and Hill (1988) valued family leisure as a means of facilitating family interaction and bonding, particularly for the marital couple. Reviewing the family leisure literature, Orthner and Mancini (1991) found general consensus across the field that shared leisure experiences have positive benefits for the quality of family relationships, in terms of family stability, family interaction and family satisfaction (for example, Orthner, 1975). However, empirical work on leisure and the family almost exclusively focused on the married couple, rather than the family as a whole (but see Couchman, 1982), with the emphasis on the relationship between leisure activity patterns and marital satisfaction.

Leisure Studies has paid little attention to negative aspects of family leisure (Shaw, 1992). The few works that touched on conflict in family leisure lacked empirical grounding (for example, Orthner, 1985) or the research design measured 'leisure' inadequately as a single survey item (for example, Strauss et al., 1980). More recent work acknowledges the inherent contradiction between the ideals or 'fantasy' of family leisure and how it is lived as experience within families, in terms of tensions and conflict arising among family members, and for parents, guilt and disillusionment when the reality falls short of the ideal (Shaw, 1997; Daly, 2001a). Clarke and Critcher argued that the ambiguity and contradictions in both the work and rituals of family life highlight the conceptual limitations of 'leisure' itself; for them, 'family life is a complex mix of work and play, tension and relaxation, constraint and choice' (1995: 59). Most importantly, some researchers realized that family leisure had been reified, gender inequality had not been considered a key factor in understanding it, nor was the concept itself problematized (Shaw, 1992).

Among the overviews of the state of family and leisure research over the past two decades, Kelly's work figures prominently (Holman and Epperson, 1984; Kelly, 1983, 1995, 1997; Orthner and Mancini, 1991; Freysinger, 1997). Kelly recognized the paradoxical nature of the family–leisure relationship, in that family leisure is 'both constrained and preferred, least free and most valued' (Kelly, 1995: 44). He described leisure as one of the 'returns' for the emotional and economic 'investments' in the family and suggested several 'leisure functions' of the nuclear family (ibid.: 47). For Kelly, leisure provides an interactional and communicative focus; 'a social space for parenting'; ways for developing new facets of existing family relationships; and 'an opportunity for autonomy and independence' for both adults and children (ibid.: 48). Family leisure also reduces role rigidity and eases emotional tension between dominant and subordinate family members. Moreover, leisure interaction develops companionship and trust among family members that 'contributes to the overall relationship [including] various kinds of support over the life course' (ibid.: 48).

Kelly did not elaborate on the paradox entailed in the relationship between family and leisure, but he suggested the field might respond to 'structural and stylistic changes in the family' (ibid.: 53) by addressing 'leisure and intimacy' (ibid.: 53) instead, as family is only one of many possible contexts within which intimate communities develop. Intriguingly, Kelly's reformulation of leisure as 'interaction environment' (ibid.) would open up the field to study leisure within other intimate communities, including those most marginalized from mainstream leisure research; for example, gay and lesbian people, migrants and refugees, street children and other homeless people.

Freysinger (1997) offered a broader critique of the field pointing to the descriptive nature of most empirical research, inconsistency in measurement and the shallowness of theoretical formulations in family leisure studies. Aside from recognizing these shortcomings of scholarship, it seems that more consideration has gone into identifying ongoing and emerging substantive issues in the field (for example, Rehman, 2001) with less given to understanding their bases in wider historical, structural and cultural terms.

Feminist contributions to an understanding of gendered family leisure

Prior to the 1980s leisure researchers viewed leisure time and activity as the purview of the individual rational actor of free will who engaged in leisure during non-work time. Leisure was assumed to be a universal concept, applicable to all, at least in Western democracies, with an implicit reference to a male adult. Feminist leisure researchers began to question the appropriateness of this conceptualization to convey women's experience of leisure, particularly within the family context (Bella, 1989; Deem, 1986; Green et al., 1990; Wearing and McArthur, 1988).

The experience of women in the family, particularly their responsibility for housework and child care was taken as the point of departure for a feminist critique of the traditional concept of leisure as time and activity outside of and dichotomous to work (for example, Glyptis and Chambers, 1982; Hantrais, 1983; Deem, 1986; Lenskyj, 1988; Bella, 1989; Henderson, 1990). Some researchers argued that primarily due to the 'ethic of care' (Gilligan, 1982, cited in Henderson et al., 1989, 1996) women's time free from paid work or housework is implicated in caring for other members of the family in ways that men's non-work time usually is not. They pointed out the difficulties women faced to make time for 'self' and engage in personal leisure, and/or pursue leisure activities outside the home. Feminist leisure researchers concluded that the concept of 'leisure time' may be inappropriate for women, and one such researcher was prepared to challenge the assumption that 'leisure is pleasure in the same way for both men and women' (Wearing, 1996: 170).

In theorizing about leisure for women, researchers found the concept of 'familism' particularly useful in explaining why women's leisure is mainly domestic and assumed to be encompassed by family leisure. However, the area of research on women and leisure has not been as fruitful for understanding family leisure as it promised to be. It is as though understanding women's leisure became the destination for feminist researchers, rather than gaining an understanding of the family context of leisure and how that may differ in meaning and experience for women, men and children. For example, in my diary interview research on Australian families and their leisure, a mother talks about her most enjoyable recreational activities:

squash and swimming because it is a social outlet and I have friends I have been doing it with for a number of years. When I go to squash or swimming I don't have the children or my husband and we talk about our sport and we don't cover those subjects, kids or husband, so it is another world. (Mother, Family #9)

An interview with her husband tells a different, more revealing side of the story of how this woman has negotiated, organized and compromised her playing of sport while, not incidentally, her husband has not had to do the same with his sport:

we are both into sport as we can both appreciate the time it takes up. Her swimming was from 6.00 to 7.15 p.m. and to a lot of households that would be a no-no because that is the time to have tea on the table, but [my wife] is organized and has everything set up and I just had to switch on the stove ... If I wasn't a sporting person it wouldn't go down too well. She has played squash for many years and that's where we first met and she is finding it now that the trouble [with squash] is she gets there at 8.00 and gets home at midnight and pays $6 and she either wins easily or loses easily and feels she gets as much enjoyment swimming being away for an hour and a half paying a couple of dollars and she is home at 7.15 compared to midnight. I do the same thing, I have played squash for about 30 years and I like the night outing because you get to see the guys and I play and get home at 12.30 p.m. and don't mind that. (Father, Family #9)

Both of these respondents clearly enjoy the chance to get away from the family and play sport with their same-sex friends. For the mother, she can momentarily enter 'another world' not inhabited by husband and children. For the father, he feels entitled to his late night out with 'the guys' but feels he is being understanding by allowing his wife to organize the evening meal beforehand, so she can spend a little over an hour swimming with her friends. We learn more about the family context of this woman's leisure by seeing how her husband's interests circumscribe it.

The ideology of familism, first associated with the cult of domesticity in the mid-nineteenth-century middle-class family, has been defined as

a belief system which argues that the best way for adults to live is in nuclear families ... as a socially and legally recognized heterosexual couple ... who normally expect to have children [which provides] the most stable, intimate, loving relationship possible. (Luxton, 1988: 238)

This ideology has been criticized on the grounds that it assumes a monolithic nuclear family, with all members having the same positive experience of family life (Bella, 1989; Horna, 1994). Moreover, the notion of a normative family is rendered problematic by the diversity in types of families today, with a heterosexual couple living with their biological offspring no longer the predominant family form.

Bella (1989) argues that familist assumptions underlying the ideal of family leisure obscures the work usually done by women to reproduce family leisure, and that much of what passes for 'family leisure' is women working to facilitate the leisure of other family members. The gendered nature of the work entailed in family leisure is most clearly evident in the reproduction of 'special events' such as birthday parties, picnics, family vacations and, in Bella's most extended example, Christmas (see Bella, 1992; see also Wearing, 1996).

Socialist-feminist research in the UK (Deem, 1986; Wimbush and Talbot, 1988; Green et. al., 1990) argued that material conditions and hegemonic masculinity shapes leisure relations between men and women in the family and beyond. Liberal feminist research in North America adopted a social psychological framework. They interpreted symbolic interactionist theory to throw light on subjective experiences, significant relationships and meanings of leisure in the family (Shaw, 1985; Henderson et al., 1989; Bella, 1989, 1992; Samdahl, 1988; Samdahl and Jekubovich, 1997). Like earlier work on family leisure, the focus was on interaction between the marital couple. Wearing (1998) criticized the symbolic interactionist perspective as overly concerned with individual agency while ignoring the influence of social structure. Along with Shaw (1997), Wearing has begun the work of informing leisure research and by extension family leisure research through a feminist reading of post-structuralist power analysis. She views leisure as 'personal space' (Wearing, 1998: 157) where the subjectivities of men, women, and children are able to resist, challenge and subvert both hegemonic masculinity and inferiorized femininity. Feminist post-structuralist theory has been used to frame a new agenda on family research (Shaw, 1997) calling for an inclusive approach to the study of family leisure drawing on insights from both the dominant social psychological and the 'sociological-feminist' perspectives. It is apparent that in order to be relevant to family life today the concept of 'family leisure' needs to be deconstructed, shorn from its normalized formation and applied across a diversity of family forms and structures.

Shaw and Dawson (2001) attempted to rethink the concept of family leisure by coining the term 'purposive leisure' to describe family leisure as 'purposive' to the achievement of parental goals. Their research on Canadian families shows that parents put considerable effort into organizing and facilitating family leisure activities to two short and long-term ends: to enhance the family's functioning as a cohesive, communicative and bonded unit, and to provide opportunities for children to learn what parents hope will become lifelong values. Family leisure or 'purposive leisure' is highly valued by parents for transmitting values, interests and a sense of family which parents believe originated with previous generations and hopefully will continue to guide their children into their adult and future family lives. However, purposive leisure is a uniform concept that does not account for how family leisure may be mediated by class, ethnicity and other cultural processes. While purposive leisure refers to shared family leisure, it is not clear whether it also may be used to refer to the opportunities for learning values through leisure activities organized or sanctioned by parents for their children and for which shared family leisure may be foregone.

In the remainder of this chapter the state of family leisure research as sketched here will be amplified with some recent sociological work about the family and childrearing, and work in other disciplines that presents family activity, including leisure, from the perspective of the child, rather than the parent, as social actor.

Researchers outside of the field of Leisure Studies may help us reconceptualize family leisure leading to a better understanding of leisure relations in the family.

Family time, quality time and children's leisure: views from beyond leisure studies

A search of the wider social science literature yields other works addressing what members of families do together outside of productive time, both as cultural expectation and experience, although the term 'family leisure' is rarely used. Since the mid-nineteenth-century privatization of family life (Ariés, 1962; see also Zaretsky, 1976), 'family time' has been seen as 'time-out – of time', time set apart from the industrial organization of everyday life (Gillis, 1996: 8, cited in Daly, 2001a: 284), as a means of coping with modernity and its temporal demands. Like 'family leisure' the term 'family time' has been used as a self-evident and positively valued aspect of family life and, as Daly points out, a uniform and coherent concept representing a universally desirable goal (2001a: 283). In his interviews with parents about the meaning and experience of 'family time' Daly found it has certain defining characteristics. Family time bridges the past and present, invoking the past while creating and storing memories of the present to be remembered and cherished in the future. Also, not surprisingly, parents place a high value on togetherness and having a positive, enjoyable experience as a family, in occasions such as shared meals, children's bedtimes, and 'down-time' on weekends. As well, family time is expected to be spontaneous and unscheduled, when families have nothing in particular they have to do (Daly, 2001a).

'Family time' is usually used with reference to the demands and pressures of 'work time' in the 'work-family balance' discourse (ibid.: 283), but the concept itself has much in common with family leisure, to the extent that Daly cites Shaw (1997) on 'family leisure' in support of the concept 'family time' (Daly, 2001a: 284). Like family leisure, there are a number of constraints to family time. For one, paid work and scheduled activities, including the children's organized sport and leisure activities, pervade family time so that it seems there is never enough time to spend 'as a family'. Also, time spent together as a family can be less than ideal, often the site of conflict, tension, competing demands and often occurs when family members are most fatigued from school or work responsibilities. Moreover, family time is not enjoyed equally by all family members but rather is used in the service of children, at the expense of parents' time for self or time spent as a couple. As Daly explains, family time, like purposive leisure, 'is often cast as a unidirectional construction consisting of what parents do for the sake of their children' (ibid.: 291).

'Family time' like 'family leisure' idealizes family togetherness and the disparity between cultural expectations and experience may leave parents feeling dissatisfied, disillusioned and guilt-ridden (Daly, 2001a). Another idealizing concept is the notion of 'quality time', which 'parents spend with their children doing leisure activities that communicate and support their mutual affection and enjoyment' (Christensen, 2002: 79). Parents create quality time not by working less, but by spending less personal time on themselves. From ethnographic work with 10–11-

year-old children, Christensen found that they value time spent with their families, but taking the perspective of the child as actor, it is 'qualities of time' rather than 'quality time' that they value most. Five qualities of time spent at home with family that children value most are: 'ordinariness and routine; ... someone being there for you; ... having a say over one's time ... having peace and quiet [and] ... being able to plan one's own time' (ibid.: 81). Here we have moved away from parents' perspectives to taking account the meaning of time for children. This would be a positive direction for family leisure research to move in as well.

As a way of unpacking further the meaning of family leisure as 'purposive leisure' it might be useful to introduce the terms 'concerted cultivation' and 'the accomplishment of natural growth' conceptualized by Lareau (2002: 748; see also Lareau, 2003) to identify different cultural logics of childrearing among middle- and working-class black and white families.

According to Lareau, parents' perceptions of the nature of childhood and the parenting role differ by class. Middle-class parents regardless of 'race' provide a variety of organized leisure and sport activities for their children, 'that dominate family life and create enormous labor, particularly for mothers' (Lareau, 2002: 748). These activities are seen as developing lifelong skills. Concerted cultivation emphasizes children's academic performance and the development of individual interests and talents through organized sport and leisure activities, producing a 'cult of individualism in the family' (ibid.). In working-class and poor families the accomplishment of natural growth entails children having fewer organized activities, more free time for informal play and 'deeper, richer ties' with extended family (ibid.: 749). Middle-class children gain an 'emerging sense of entitlement' to material and social privilege from concerted cultivation, while accomplishing natural growth tends to produce an 'emerging sense of constraint' with divergent long-term consequences for children's identities and life paths (ibid.). Shared family leisure is not part of Lareau's study, but her conceptual framework may aid in our understanding of class differences in family leisure – what parents are trying to accomplish and the values they are trying to transmit to children through shared family leisure and children's leisure activities. Unlike family leisure or purposive leisure, Lareau's concepts orient us to children's divergent futures.

Another US study based on interviews with children (Outley and Floyd, 2002) that has implications for understanding family leisure examined the strategies used by black parents living in inner-city areas to arrange and monitor children's leisure experiences. Parents used kinship networks and chaperonage to both facilitate and contain their children's leisure experiences; involved children in out-of-school recreation and church-run programmes to shield then from unsafe and deviant 'street' activities; placed travel and time restrictions on their children, and in some cases 'confined their children to the home' (ibid.: 172). In this study, the 'socially isolated neighbourhood was critical to parents setting boundaries for their children's leisure and parental efforts to promote positive development' (ibid.: 176). This is an important point for understanding family leisure too. Family or purposive leisure is not just a family process, but rather takes place within the structural context of place.

Conclusions

The literature that bears on the study of family leisure suggests six ways in which approaches to family leisure can be enhanced. First, Daly's work tells us that family time is all about 'the social production of memories' (Daly, 2001a: 288), which strengthens family identity. These memories are meant to last beyond the living memories of individual family members to bridge the past and present and extend into the future. Purposive leisure can incorporate this aspect of family time. Second, if purposive leisure could be broadened to include not just what parents are trying to do during shared family leisure but also the other leisure activities they provide that are 'good' for their children, and for which shared family leisure may be sacrificed, then we would have a fuller picture of parents' agendas for their children. Third, the study of family leisure could be broadened to examine shared family leisure within the context of all leisure involvements of family members. Fourth, Lareau's work on cultural logics of childrearing in middle- and working-class families could be a valuable contribution to studying family leisure. My own work with middle- and lower-income Australian families and their leisure uncovered similar patterns in what parents wanted for their children and whether or not they were willing to give up family leisure for children's individual sport activities (Harrington, 2003). Fifth, we could give more attention to studying family leisure from the child's perspective as a social actor, as Christensen et al. (2000) and Christensen (2002) in the field of Sociology of Childhood are doing (Scott, 2004; but see also Delamere and Shaw, 2002). Taking children's perceptions of qualities of time may help us know more about the ways in which children value family leisure (Kelly, 1995), and what they derive from it along with time alone or with others in their individual leisure pursuits. Finally, we might take Kelly's suggestion seriously that we frame our questions around intimacy and leisure, so that the family becomes only one of many contexts for intimate communities. This might lead to examining the particular forms and settings for leisure among more marginalized but intimate social groups. It would also invite a more inclusive approach to studying a diversity of family forms and structures in Leisure Studies.

Bibliography

Allan, G. and Crow, G. (1989) *Home and Family Creating the Domestic Sphere*, London, Macmillan.

Allan, G. and Crow, G. (1991) 'Privatization, Home-centredness and Leisure', *Leisure Studies* 10(1): 19–32.

Ariés, P. (1962) *Centuries of Childhood: A Social History of Family Life*, New York, Random House.

Baldwin, P. (2002) '"Nocturnal Habits and Dark Wisdom": The American Response to Children in the Streets at Night, 1880–1930', *Journal of Social History* 35(3) Spring: 593–611.

Bella, L. (1989) 'Women and Leisure: Beyond Androcentrism', in E. L. Jackson and T. L. Burton (eds) *Understanding Leisure and Recreation: Mapping the Past, Charting the Future*, State College, PA, Venture Publishing, pp. 157–79.

Bella, L. (1992) *The Christmas Imperative: Leisure, Family and Women's Work*, Halifax, Fernwood Press.

Bhatti, M. and Church, A. (2000) '"I Never Promised You a Rose Garden": Gender, Leisure and Home-making', *Leisure Studies* 19: 183–97.

Christensen, P. H. (2002) 'Why More "Quality Time" is Not on the Top of Children's Lists: "The Qualities of Time" for Children', *Children and Society* 16: 77–88.

Christensen, P. H., James, A. and Jenks, C. (2000) 'Home and Movement: Children Constructing "Family Time"', in S. L. Holloway and G. Valentine (eds) *Children's Geographies: Playing, Living, Learning*, London, Routledge, pp. 139–55.

Clarke, J. and Critcher, C. (1985) *The Devil Makes Work: Leisure in Capitalist Britain*, Urbana, University of Illinois Press.

Clarke, J. and Critcher, C. (1995) 'Coming Home to Roost', in C. Critcher, P. Bramham and A. Tomlinson (eds) *Sociology of Leisure: A Reader*, London, E. & F. N. Spon, pp. 55–64.

Couchman, R. (1982) 'Family Recreation: A New Dynamic in Family Life', *Leisurability* 9(4): 4–8.

Crawford, D. W. and Godbey, G. (1987) 'Reconceptualizing Barriers to Family Leisure', *Leisure Sciences* 9: 119–27.

Cross, G. (1990) *A Social History of Leisure Since 1600*, State College, PA, Venture Publishing.

Daly, K. J. (2001a) 'Deconstructing Family Time: From Ideology to Lived Experience', *Journal of Marriage and Family* 63(2): 283–94.

Daly, K. J. (2001b) *Minding the Time in Family Experience: Emerging Perspectives and Issues*, London, JAI.

Dawson, D. (2000) 'Social Class and Leisure Provision', in M. T. Allison and I. E. Schneider (eds) *Diversity and the Recreation Profession: Organizational Perspectives*, State College, PA, Venture Publishing, pp. 99–114.

Deem, R. (1986) *All Work and No Play? The Sociology of Women and Leisure*, Milton Keynes, Open University Press.

Delamere, F. and Shaw, S. (2002) 'Doing Leisure, Doing Gender: Children's Perspectives on Leisure Within the Family Context', in *Celebrating the Past and Future of Canadian Leisure Studies Book of Abstracts*, Tenth Canadian Congress on Leisure Research, University of Alberta, 22–25 May, pp. 86–8.

Freysinger, V. (1997) 'Redefining Family, Redefining Leisure: Progress Made and Challenges Ahead in Research on Leisure and Families', introduction to special issue of *Journal of Leisure Research* 29(1): 1–4.

Gilligan, C. (1982) *In a Different Voice*, Cambridge, MA, Harvard University Press.

Gillis, J. (1996) 'Making Time for Family: The Invention of Family Times and the Reinvention of Family History', *Journal of Family History* 21: 4–21.

Gillis, J. (2003) 'Childhood and Family Time: A Changing Historical Relationship', in A. Jensen and L. McKee (eds) *Children and the Changing Family: Between Transformation and Negotiation*, London, RoutledgeFalmer, pp. 149–66.

Gittens, D. (1985) *The Family in Question: Changing Households and Familiar Ideologies*, London, Macmillan Education.

Glyptis, S. and Chambers, D. (1982) 'No Place Like Home', *Leisure Studies* 1(3): 247–62.

Godbey, G. (1999) *Leisure in Your Life: An Exploration*, 5th edn, State College, PA, Venture Publishing.

Green, E., Hebron, S. and Woodward, D. (1990) *Women's Leisure: What Leisure?* Basingstoke, Macmillan.

Hantrais, L. (1983) *Leisure and the Family in Contemporary France*. Papers in Leisure Studies, No. 7. London, Polytechnic of North London.

Harrington, M. (2003) 'Leisure Patterns and Purposive Leisure in Middle and Lower Income Families', paper presented at the 8th Australian Institute of Family Studies Conference, Melbourne, Victoria.

Harvey, D. (1989) *The Condition of Postmodernity*, Oxford, Blackwell.

Henderson, K. A. (1990) 'The Meaning of Leisure for Women: An Integrative Review of the Research', *Journal of Leisure Research* 22(3): 228–43.

Henderson, K. A., Bialeschki, M. D., Shaw, S. and Freysinger, V. J. (1989) *A Leisure of One's Own: A Feminist Perspective on Women's Leisure*, State College, PA, Venture Publishing.

Henderson, K. A., Bialeschki, M. D., Shaw, S. and Freysinger, V. J. (1996) *Both Gains and Gaps: Feminist Perspectives on Women's Leisure*, State College, PA, Venture Publishing.

Hill, M. S. (1988) 'Marital Stability and Spouses' Shared Time', *Journal of Family Issues* 9: 427–51.

Holman, T. B. and Epperson, A. (1984) 'Family and Leisure: A Review of the Literature with Research Recommendations', *Journal of Leisure Research* 16: 277–94.

Horna, J. (1994) *The Study of Leisure: An Introduction*, Toronto, Oxford University Press.

Iso-Ahola, S. E. (1980) *The Social Psychology of Leisure and Recreation*, Dubuque, IA, Wm. C. Brown.

Jamison, B. (1999) 'Making "Honest, Truthful and Industrious Men": Newsboys, Rational Recreation and the Construction of the "Citizen" in Late Victorian and Edwardian Brisbane', *Journal of Popular Culture* 33(1): 61–75.

Kelly, J. R. (1983) *Leisure Identities and Interactions*, London, Allen & Unwin.

Kelly, J. R. (1995) 'Leisure and the Family', in C. Critcher, P. Bramham and A. Tomlinson (eds) *Sociology of Leisure: A Reader*, London, E. & F. N. Spon, pp. 44–54.

Kelly, J. R. (1997) 'Changing Issues in Leisure–Family Research', *Journal of Leisure Research* 29(1): 132–4.

Lareau, A. (2002) 'Invisible Inequality: Social Class and Childrearing in Black Families and White Families', *American Sociological Review* 67: 747–76.

Lareau, A. (2003) *Unequal Childhoods: Class, Race and Family Life*, Berkeley, University of California Press.

Lasch, C. (1977) *Haven in a Heartless World: The Family Besieged*, New York, Basic Books.

Lenskyj, H. (1988) 'Measured Time: Women, Sport, and Leisure', *Leisure Studies* 7: 233–40.

Luxton, M. (1988) 'Thinking About the Future', in K. L. Anderson et al. (eds) *Family Matters: Sociology and Contemporary Canadian Families*, Scarborough, Ontario, Nelson Canada, pp. 237–60.

Mannell, R. C. and Kleiber, D. A. (1997) *A Social Psychology of Leisure*, State College, PA, Venture Publishing.

Orthner, D. K. (1975) 'Leisure Activity Patterns and Marital Satisfaction Over the Marital Career', *Journal of Marriage and the Family* 37: 91–103.

Orthner, D. K. (1985) 'Conflict and Leisure Interaction in Families', in B. G. Gunter, J. Stanley and R. St Clair (eds) *Transitions to Leisure: Conceptual and Human Issues*, New York, New York University Press, pp. 133–9.

Orthner, D. K. and Mancini, J. A. (1980) 'Leisure Behavior and Group Dynamics: The Case of the Family', in S. E. Iso-Ahola (ed.) *Social Psychological Perspectives on Leisure and Recreation*, Springfield, IL, Thomas, pp. 307–28.

Orthner, D. K. and Mancini, J. A. (1991) 'Benefits of Leisure for Family Bonding', in B. L. Driver, P. J. Brown and G. L. Peterson (eds) *Benefits of Leisure*, State College, PA, Venture Publishing, pp. 289–301.

Outley, C. W. and Floyd, M. F. (2002) 'The Home They Live In: Inner City Children's Views on the Influence of Parenting Strategies on their Leisure Behavior', *Leisure Sciences* 24: 161–79.

Rapoport, R. and Rapoport, R. N. (1975) *Leisure and the Family Life Cycle*, London, Routledge.

Rehman, L. A. (2001) 'Using Eichler to Inform Family Leisure Research', in S. Clough and J. White (eds) *Women's Leisure Experiences: Ages, Stages and Roles*, Eastbourne, Leisure Studies Association.

Rojek, C. (1985) *Capitalism and Leisure Theory*, London, Tavistock.

Rojek, C. (1993) *Ways of Escape: Modern Transformations in Leisure and Travel*, London, Macmillan.

Rojek, C. (2000) *Leisure and Culture*, London, Macmillan.

Rybczynski, W. (1991) *Waiting for the Weekend*, New York, Penguin.

Samdahl, D. M. (1988) 'A Symbolic Interactionist Model of Leisure: Theory and Empirical Support', *Leisure Sciences* 10(1): 27–39.

Samdahl, D. M. and Jekubovich, N. J. (1997) 'A Critique of Leisure Constraints: Comparative Analyses and Understandings', *Journal of Leisure Research* 29(4): 430–52.

Scott, J. L. (2004) 'Children's Families', in J. L. Scott, J. K. Treas and M. Richards (eds) *The Blackwell Companion to the Sociology of Families*, Carlton, Victoria, Blackwell, pp. 109–25.

Seabrook, J. (1973) *The Unprivileged: A Hundred Years of Family Life and Tradition in a Working Class Street*, Harmondsworth, Penguin.

Shaw, S. M. (1985) 'Gender and Leisure: An Examination of Women's and Men's Everyday Experience and Perception of Family Time', *Journal of Leisure Research* 17(4): 266–82.

Shaw, S. M. (1992) 'Dereifying Family Leisure: An Examination of Women's and Men's Everyday Experiences and Perceptions of Family Leisure', *Leisure Sciences* 14(4): 271–86.

Shaw, S. M. (1997) 'Controversies and Contradictions in Family Leisure: An Analysis of Conflicting Paradigms', *Journal of Leisure Research* 29(1): 98–112.

Shaw, S. M. and Dawson, D. J. (2001) 'Purposive Leisure: Examining Parental Discourses on Family Activities', *Leisure Sciences* 23(4): 217–31.

Strauss, M., Gelles, R. and Steinmetz, S. (1980) *Behind Closed Doors*, New York, Doubleday.

Veal, A. J. and Lynch, R. (2001) *Australian Leisure*, 2nd edn, South Melbourne, Addison Wesley Longman.

Wearing, B. M. (1996) *Gender: The Pain and Pleasure of Difference*, Melbourne, Addison Wesley Longman.

Wearing, B. M. (1998) *Leisure and Feminist Theory*, London, Sage.

Wearing, B. M. and McArthur, M. (1988) 'The Family that Plays Together Stays Together: Or Does It?' *Australian and New Zealand Journal of Sex, Marriage and Family* 9: 150–8.

Wimbush, E. and Talbot, M. (1988) *Relative Freedoms: Women and Leisure*, Milton Keynes, Open University Press.

Witt, P. and Goodale, T. (1981) 'The Relationship between Barriers to Leisure Enjoyment and Family Stages', *Leisure Sciences* 4: 29–49.

Zaretsky, E. (1976) *Capitalism, the Family and Personal Life*, New York, Harper & Row.

26
Leisure and Education

Atara Sivan

Education and leisure are significant domains in people's lives. At first glance, they may be seen as contradictory; whereas leisure is associated with freedom and relaxation, education is associated with learning and may not be perceived as related to freedom. This is especially due to the tendency to associate education with a formal way of studying in school as illustrated in the following definition: '[education is] social process in which one achieves social competence and individual growth, carried in a selected controlled setting which can be institutionalised as a school or college' (Page and Thomas, 1977: 113).

The perceived contradiction between leisure and education may also derive from the fact that for many generations schools have been mostly concerned with roles related to work life. However, it is important to note that education can be formal and informal and can be undertaken anywhere. Recent definition of education indicates that 'education does not have to take place in schools', and furthermore, 'it is not a name of a particular activity or process. It is a name applied generically to a number of different activities and processes' (Barrow and Milburn, 1990: 105). This implies that education can be also undertaken within the leisure domain.

The relationships between leisure and education have been highlighted by leisure scholars over the past several decades, indicating that these two domains are interrelated. Parker (1979) has indicated two types of link between education and leisure. The first lies in the educational philosophy which regards preparation for full and satisfying leisure life as part of the aims of education. When translated into practice it implies preparation of 'young people in the schools for the kind of leisure experience which are presently available to them and will be available in later life' (ibid.: 91). The second link lies in ensuring that the learning activities undertaken by students are enjoyable and thus contain the leisure elements. This link Parker names 'education as leisure', where 'the learning process itself can take on some characteristics of leisure' (ibid.: 97). Leisure and education are linked in their common function of developing the personality, and since education is not bounded to schooling but is rather a life-long process, leisure can be infused into education at various forms of adult education.

The strong connection between leisure and education has been further described by Bender et al. as follows: 'education should prepare students for all major life functions, including use of leisure time. Since leisure is central to one's life experience, it rightfully deserves increased educational attention' (1984: 3).

A further examination of the way leisure education has been defined suggests that learning is one of the common threads running through leisure and education. For example, Brightbill and Mobley have perceived leisure as part of learning. Emphasizing the need for education for full life, they highlighted the many potentials that leisure has for learning, asserting that 'In leisure we can, if we choose, add the how to the why of learning' (1977: 28). Roberts's definition of leisure relates it to the process of learning as follows:

> leisure is not precisely bounded. It is more akin to learning than schooling. The beginning and end of a school day may be punctuated with a bell. By contrast, learning is ubiquitous, like work and play. Any sharp definition which clearly separated leisure from the rest of life would distort its own subject-matter. (Roberts, 1983: 44–5)

Recent study on leisure and learning of higher education students provides some data to support the link between leisure and learning. Students' accounts of their leisure and learning experiences have demonstrated that the role of leisure spreads over a wide spectrum of areas. While learning is an activity that occupies the lives of those young people, leisure was found to be related to learning not only by its definition, but also because of its important role of setting the social context for enhancing coherent student study groups (Sivan, 2003).

Kelly (1996) has defined the relationship between leisure and education as complementing. Education provides opportunities for leisure socialization and exposure to leisure experiences. If it is not confined to acquisition of knowledge but rather as a lifelong process aiming for personal growth and development, education could further be viewed as an enriching form of leisure.

One of the ways in which the relationship between leisure and education has been illustrated the most is in leisure education. The following sections examine the concept of leisure education and the way it has been studied and implemented and draw some implications for its future development within the fields of leisure and education.

From leisure and education to leisure education

There is no one definition of leisure education. Historically, leisure education was originated by the educational community by setting it as one of the goals of the education system in US. In 1918, the US National Education Association set forth its well-known Cardinal Principles of Secondary Education, listing the Worthy Use of Leisure as one of the seven objectives of education. With the development of the leisure and recreation movement in North America, more and more documents are to be found in this area. The increase of free time and in the awareness of the benefits of leisure have led to a growing recognition of the need to educate for leisure in other countries as well. As a result, leisure education became part of statements of educational objectives and policies.

In the late 1970s, the need to educate for leisure was explored by Brightbill and Mobley (1977), arguing that while entering the leisure-centred society, it is essential to prepare individuals to live a satisfying and meaningful life in leisure. In their views, leisure education includes values, interests, appreciations and skills, and it is aimed at different needs of the individual. Through this process people get to know themselves better, their abilities, talents and interests and they become more directed in their learning and behaviour towards the society. Besides its individual goal, leisure education aims at shaping the environment so as to enable people to use their leisure in a creative and rewarding way without depending on organized resources.

Another definition of leisure education was put forward in 1977 by the National Recreation and Park Association in the Leisure Education Advancement Project. There, leisure education has been defined as a process which enables people to

recognize the use of leisure (discretionary) time as an avenue for personal satisfaction and enrichment; know the array of valuable opportunities available in leisure time; understand the significant impact that leisure time has and will have on society; appreciate the natural resources and their relationships to discretionary time and the quality of life: and are able to make decisions regarding their own leisure behaviour. (Zeyen et al., 1977: 19)

Similar concepts appear in the work by Mundy and Odum (1979) and Mundy (1998), which regards leisure education as a developmental process which aims at enhancing the individual's quality of life. In their view leisure education is 'a total developmental process through which individuals develop an understanding of leisure, of self in relation to leisure, and of the relationship among leisure, their own lifestyles, and society' (Mundy, 1998: 5).

The perception of leisure education as a developmental process has been further emphasized by Kleiber (2001) who offers a framework for using leisure during the lifespan. Leisure education is to be shaped by the developmental tasks of different periods of people's life and the social context in which those tasks are defined.

In a resource for educators created by Cherry and Woodburn (1978), leisure education has been defined as an ongoing process that can enable people to discover the meaning of leisure, their leisure potential, the way of making leisure part of their lifestyles and the development of skills necessary for their own leisure fulfilment. Through the process of leisure education, individuals increase their knowledge and understanding of the nature and significance of leisure in their lives, they develop their personal resources and skills, and become more aware of their personal values and attitudes towards different dimensions of leisure.

Hayes (1977) has discussed models for leisure education from a leisure counselling point of view. According to this approach, leisure education is a developmental, remedial, preventive and therapeutic process. It includes a variety of aspects such as: personal values, individual goals and objectives, self-confidence and self-esteem skills, knowledge and competencies and successful experiences.

Chinn and Joswiak characterized leisure education as a process that focuses on acquisition of leisure knowledge and skills which employed educational techniques such as behavioural management, task analysis, a learning-centred approach and individualized prescription (1981: 5).

Bender et al. (1984) maintained that leisure education 'is concerned with the leisure experience both as an end and as one means of developing a sense of self-worth, fostering creative and expressive behavior, and facilitating personal growth and realization of unique talents and potential' (1984: 13). Dattilo and Williams (1991) have presented leisure education as a dynamic and multifaceted process, which includes the aspects of human right and self-determination and involves a combination of core and balance approach.

Ruskin has defined leisure education as 'a conscious and systematic education for and/or in leisure which aims to bring certain desirable changes in the use of leisure. These changes may be stated in terms of beliefs, feelings, attitudes, knowledge, skills and behaviour' (1995a: 147).

Additional aims for leisure education were suggested by Faché (1995). These are: the encouragement of social contact and integration in networks of friends, to increase people's awareness of leisure constraints and to improve their ability to overcome these constraints for their participation in their chosen leisure activities, the enhancement of self-initiative and self-reliance and the increase of the ability and responsibility in time planning.

In an international position statement on leisure education, it has been defined as a lifelong process which involves the development of attitudes, values, knowledge, skills and resources related to leisure. It was further stated that 'leisure education has long been recognized as part of the field of education, but not been broadly implemented. It has been perceived as important part of the socialization process within which a variety of agents play a major role' (World Leisure Commission on Education, 2000: 9).

It can be concluded that leisure education is a developmental process by which individuals learn to deal with important aspects of their leisure. Most definitions of leisure education have the common aim of fostering the development of values, attitudes, skills and knowledge relevant to leisure so as to enhance people's quality of life. It is part of the socialization process within which a variety of agents play a major role. Identified as a multifaceted process, leisure education was suggested to be employed in various formal and informal educational and recreational settings. Two of the contexts which were highly advocated were the community and the schools.

Leisure education within the community

An examination of the community role in educating for leisure indicates a growing number of publications in this area. These focus mainly on the link between leisure education and community development and further offer ways in which leisure education can be undertaken within the community. Leisure education and community development have been recognized as educational processes which are concerned with human rights, self-determination and empowerment (Sivan, 2000). Various strategies and processes have been suggested to help community members in achieving their rights to leisure education and recreation opportunities. These include empowerment, advocacy, mobilization integration, linkages, facilitation, social intervention, effective involvement, action learning and networking (World Leisure Commission on Education, 2000; Grossman, 2000).

Leisure education in schools

Schools have been regarded as the major socializing agents for leisure. Underlying the responsibility given to schools to educate for leisure are their important role in the socialization process and the perception of leisure education as part of this process (Kraus, 1964; Corbin and Tait, 1973; Brightbill and Mobley, 1977; Mundy and Odum, 1979; Parker, 1979; Ruskin, 1984; Roberts, 1983; Heyne and Schleien, 1996; Kelly, 1996; Sivan, 1996). Moreover, schools are the primary and the most common institutions of education and many school experiences have potential for imparting leisure knowledge and developing leisure attitudes, values and skills.

To best utilize their potential for leisure education, schools were called to undergo changes in their educational systems to include aspects of enjoyment and intrinsic reward of students (Roberts, 1983; Ruskin, 1984; Kelly, 1996), to place more emphasis on equipping students with attitudes and social skills for their own selection and participation in leisure, to move away from providing short-term recreational skills only and to provide sufficient balance between academic aspects and social, emotional and personal needs satisfaction (Feldman and Gaier, 1980; Hendry and Marr, 1985).

A wide range of channels and areas were suggested for best implementation of leisure education in schools. They vary from academic subjects to extracurricular activities suggesting a multidisciplinary integration which would involve the community. In addition, student-centred and active learning approaches were suggested to be employed in leisure education. Pedagogies such as facilitation, experiential and creative learning, personal experimentation and counselling were advocated (Sivan, 1996).

Whereas the call for schools to undertake leisure education mainly occurred in the US 20 or so years ago, the last decade has seen a growing international recognition of the school as a socializing agent for leisure. This can be attributed to the growing recognition of the significant role of leisure and of the need for schools to provide an all-round education. Apart from appearing in official governments' educational statements of school aims, the role of school in educating for leisure has been highlighted by leisure scholars and professionals (Sivan and Ruskin, 2000).

Leisure education initiatives

So far, the majority of leisure education literature in US has been associated with people with special needs or provision of services to people with disabilities (Dattilo,

2000; Kleiber, 2001). The growing recognition of leisure education internationally has led to an increase in scholarly and professional initiatives which have been extended to varying populations (for example, Bramante, 1997; Faché, 1997; Sivan, 1997; Sivan and Ruskin, 1997). The following section reviews some of the main initiatives undertaken in this area, including position statements, models, programmes and curricula.

Position statements

Recent initiatives undertaken by the Education Commission of the World Leisure Association resulted in a series of position statements on leisure education. The aim of those statements was to arouse international interest and actions in terms of expanding the development of leisure education programmes. These position papers include the international charter for leisure education (World Leisure Commission on Education, 2000), which highlights the role of leisure education and offers strategies for its implementation in schools and within the community. It also suggests principles and strategies for preparation and training of personnel in leisure education.

This initiative followed with numerous position papers on leisure education and community development, populations with special needs, youth at risk and educating for serious leisure (World Leisure Commission on Education, 2000), physical fitness and activity in the context of leisure education (Fu and Ruskin, 2001) and the promotion of health, well-being and leisure: major components of quality of life (Fu and Leung, 2003).

Models

The majority of leisure education models aim at populations with special needs. (Hayes 1977; Joswiak, 1979; Mundy and Odum, 1979; Fine et al., 1985; Dattilo and St Peter, 1991). The development of those models demonstrated a move from the traditional offer of recreational skills towards inclusion of leisure education components in working with people with varying needs. Those models were proposed for application within the therapeutic recreation services with a wide range of aims related to leisure education components. They include systematic models for increasing individuals' awareness of significant aspects of leisure, such as the meaning of leisure, and leisure resources at home and in the community (Joswiak, 1989), leisure strategies for facilitation of increased leisure independence (Dunn, 1981), leisure involvement (Wuerch and Voeltz, 1982) and leisure skills (Fine et al., 1985). Additional components included self-awareness and leisure, decision making, social interaction and leisure and related skills (Dattilo and St Peter, 1991; Dattilo and Williams, 1991), provision of opportunities for development of leisure understanding (Peterson and Gunn, 1984), facilitation of individuals' control and enhancement of their competence in their leisure experiences (Witt et al., 1984).

One model which was developed to facilitate the contextual learning for school-aged students with disabilities focused on individualized, community-based leisure education which involved the family. The model facilitates students' self-determined leisure choices based on their individual interests and it was employed within the context of the family and the community (Johnson et al., 1997).

Some models have been suggested for inclusion in the school systems within the therapeutic recreation service. They suggest the employment of interdisciplinary and co-operative approaches involving practitioners from the recreation and education fields as well as other community resources (Collard, 1981; Bedini and Bullock, 1988).

During the last decade, several resources were offered for undertaking leisure education using a systematic approach. They include a wide range of activities which address the major components of leisure education including leisure appreciation, self-awareness in leisure, self-determination, social interaction, leisure resources, decision-making and recreation skill development (Stumbo and Thompson, 1988; Stumbo, 1992, 1997, 1998, 1999, 2000; Dattilo, 2000).

Curricula

To best facilitate the role of schools as socializing agents for leisure, several leisure education curricula and models were developed. Below is a brief description of some major curricula. The first one, entitled 'The Scope and Sequence of Leisure Education', was developed by leisure service faculty and graduate students at Florida State Department of Education personnel. The model comprises objectives arranged in six categories: self-awareness, leisure awareness, attitudes, decision-making, social interaction and leisure activity skills (Mundy, 1998).

Another leisure education curriculum was developed in 1977 as part of the Leisure Education Advancement Project (LEAP) of the National Recreation and Park Association (Zeyen et al., 1977). The curriculum was developed to assist public schools in developing students' understanding of the role of leisure in people's lives and the wide range of meanings of leisure experiences. It further aimed to help students to appreciate natural resources and their relationship to leisure and the quality of life and to be able to make decisions concerning their own leisure.

Another leisure education curriculum resource was developed by Cherry and Woodburn (1978) from the Canadian Ministry of Culture and Recreation. The resource aims to facilitate teachers' implementation of leisure education in their classes. It offers five strategies to be employed by teachers while implementing leisure education in their classes. These are: teachable moments, leisure incorporated, learning through recreational activity, leisure: a topic in itself, learning: a leisure experience, and the helping relationship. Underlying these strategies are the four key concepts: knowledge and understanding about leisure, personal resources and skills for leisure, personal values about leisure, and positive attitudes towards leisure.

The most recent school-wide leisure education curriculum was developed by the Ministry of Education, Culture and Sports of the state of Israel. The curriculum suggests a framework for schools to undertake leisure education. The target population ranges from kindergarten to twelfth grade students. The curriculum aims

to help the individual, the family, the community and the society to achieve a suitable quality of life and good health by using leisure time intelligently, by developing and cultivating, physical, emotional-spiritual, mental and social aspects, each individually or combined, as they relate to the aims of education in the country and its cultural heritage. (Ruskin, 1995b: 13)

To best achieve this aim the curriculum sets a list of operational objectives divided into three areas: knowledge, understanding and awareness; behaviour, habits and skills; and emotions and values. The strategies offered refer to both formal and informal frameworks with the rationale that leisure education should be infused into the learning of students both inside and outside the classroom (Ruskin and Sivan, 2002).

A recently developed curriculum-based intervention entitled TimeWise: Learning Lifelong Leisure Skills, was implemented and evaluated among middle school adolescents in the eastern US. The aim of this intervention was 'to promote personal development through healthy leisure engagement and prevent the onset of substance abuse and other unhealthy behaviour' (Caldwell and Baldwin, 2004: 311). The curriculum includes six components: self-awareness of time use and the benefits associated with leisure activities; reasons for participating in free time activities; recognizing personal interests and managing boredom; the active pursuit of meaningful activity; managing free time for balance and variety; and integration of concepts.

In addition to the above school-wide curricula, various curricula components were developed for implementation by leisure educators for students with disabilities. A curriculum entitled School–Community Link was developed for facilitation of certified therapeutic recreation specialist for school, community and family use. The curriculum includes six units: leisure awareness; leisure resources; leisure communication skills; making decisions independently; leisure planning; and activity skill instruction (Bullock et al., 1992).

Another curriculum of a similar type was designed to facilitate the transition of young mentally retarded people from school to active participation in the community. It included five components: leisure education to facilitate choice-making and independent recreation participation; leisure coaching; family and friend support; follow-up services to maintain participation in community recreation programmes; and independent community leisure participation (Dattilo and Hoge, 1995).

A third curriculum offers a wide range of strategies for the promotion of lifelong participation in leisure activities for people with developmental disabilities. It includes six components: philosophy of leisure education; appropriate selection of leisure activities for instruction; instruction for skills acquisition; instruction for preference and generalization; inclusive community leisure services; and home involvement in leisure education (Schleien et al., 1995).

Studies on leisure education

Studies undertaken on leisure education have focused on evaluating the impact of leisure education programmes. Fewer than those were studies which surveyed the existence of leisure education and solicited populations' views of this process and its implementation.

Studies undertaken on the effect of leisure education were mainly related to people with disabilities and populations with special needs, and included examining the effectiveness of leisure education programmes with young delinquents (Munson et al., 1985; Aguilar, 1987), youth at risk (Andreano, 2001), youth with behavioural disorders (Munson, 1988), young people with spina bifida (Zoerink, 1988), child abuse victims (McDonald and Howe, 1989), sexual assault victims (Sheffield et al., 1986), people with mental retardation (Anderson and Allen, 1985; Lanagan and Dattilo, 1989; Mahon and Bullock, 1992; Dattilo and Hoge, 1999) and individuals with depression in a long-term care facility (Ochi, 2000).

The effects of leisure education programmes were also examined among the elderly (Backman and Mannel, 1986; Searle and Mahon, 1991, 1992; Mahon and Searle, 1994; Searle et al., 1995; Dunn and Wilhite, 1997; Searle et al., 1998).

These studies have indicated the impact of leisure education on a wide range of variables, such as leisure participation and satisfaction, leisure attitudes, perceived competence, social interaction, self-control, relaxation, locus of control and self-esteem, and further confirmed the significant role that leisure education plays in the rehabilitation process of people with varying needs.

A recent study has investigated the effect of the leisure education curriculum implemented in middle schools (Caldwell and Baldwin, 2004). Results indicated that students who participated in the curriculum were better able to restructure boring situations into something more interesting. Those students further reported higher levels of decision-making, initiative and community awareness as well as participation in new interests.

Surveys

Surveys on leisure education aimed to find out the existence of its instruction and curricula. Using a postal questionnaire, Bedini (1990) examined the extent to which leisure education exists in higher education and in therapeutic recreation. He found that there has been an increase in the instruction of leisure education in recreation and leisure curricula in higher education as well as in its implementation in therapeutic recreation.

An international survey was undertaken to solicit information on the way leisure education has been defined and implemented within educational frameworks. Postal questionnaires were sent to 35 country representatives who were holding positions in the field of education. Results indicated that in most of the countries there is a reference to leisure education in some kind of document, such as a statement of aims. Leisure education is integrated into the curriculum in a variety of ways, but especially during break times, special events and outings and other extracurricular activities (Ruskin and Sivan, 2002).

Attitudinal studies

Two studies were undertaken to gauge the views of people towards leisure education and its implementation. Sivan (1991, 1995) examined the views of secondary school students and teachers in Hong Kong towards leisure education and its relevancy to their schools. Results showed the different perceptions of leisure education and indicated the need for implementation of leisure education in schools, and suggested a range of ways in which it could be integrated into the school curricula.

Robertson (2001) solicited the views of youths who were serving time in detention centres about the extent to which they had been educated for leisure and the potential of leisure education to affect their involvement in delinquent activities. Results indicated that a higher degree of participation in leisure education could help in preventing youth from participation in delinquent behaviours. The results led to a series of principles for leisure education programmes being implemented with these young people.

Both studies are significant in that they provided a voice for those for whom leisure education is intended. The results from both studies served as guidelines for the implementation of leisure education in the different contexts.

Conclusion and implications

Leisure scholars have examined the relationships between leisure and education over the past few decades, highlighting the theoretical and practical links between the two domains. Leisure has been identified as a significant domain through which education can be best pursued, and education as a lifelong process through which leisure components could be instilled. The strong relationship between leisure and education has been mostly illustrated in the development of leisure education.

The need to educate for leisure has gained momentum with the increase of free time and the growing awareness of the benefits of leisure. Even though the role of undertaking this process was assigned to schools, it has been adopted in the US mainly in working with people with special needs and as part of therapeutic recreation.

As fields of study, leisure and education are interdisciplinary, and as such they allow examinations of a wide range of areas and themes. It can be argued that in comparison with educational platforms, leisure education has gained more attention within leisure studies. However, there is still a need to further establish its position as an area of study.

Compared with the number of theoretical arguments and position statements related to leisure education, studies undertaken on this area are relatively few. Those studies were conducted with special needs populations with the aim of examining the effect of leisure education programmes on leisure participation and various psychological variables which could enhance their quality of life. Further investigations could be undertaken to establish the long-term effect of such programmes. Along the same lines, with the development of new leisure education curricula, it would be beneficial to study the ways in which these curricula are implemented and their short- and long-term impact on students' development. An important question to be addressed is: which learning experiences and pedagogies are the most effective in terms of enhancement of students' awareness of leisure and their development of leisure knowledge, skills, attitudes and values?

Since leisure education is best implemented in a multidisciplinary and co-operative approach, it would be also useful to investigate the ways through which it is applied within various community settings and to determine the role of different socializing agents in this process, including the family as a core unit.

With the international trend towards lifelong learning and the growing number of countries which include the need to educate for leisure in their statement of educational aims, cross-cultural studies could further shed light on the ways in which leisure education is implemented and its impact in different contexts and cultures. To better utilize its developmental nature, more initiatives could be undertaken in examining the ways in which leisure education is infused into different adult education programmes and the family lifecycle.

When examining the ways of implementing leisure education, it is useful to refer to the social and cultural contexts for which it is intended. Cultural differences may lead to different perceptions of leisure education and to varying ways of utilizing its potential. Brightbill and Mobley have stated that 'Educational planning that does not involve the voice of those for whom the planning is done is not likely to be either effective or "long-lived"' (1977: 115). Examination of people's views of leisure education in relation to their social and cultural contexts could lay a solid foundation for implementing this process to enhance their quality of life.

Bibliography

Aguilar, T. E. (1987) 'Effects of a Leisure Education Program Development and Evaluation', *Journal of Expanding Horizons in Therapeutic Recreation* 1: 14–20.

Anderson, S. C. and Allen, L. R. (1985) 'Effects of a Leisure Education Program on Activity Involvement and Social Interaction of Mentally Retarded Persons', *Adapted Physical Activity Quarterly* 2(2): 107–16.

Andreano, M. (2001) 'A Leisure Education Program to Develop Skills in Youth at Risk', Master's thesis, University of Florida.

Backman, S. J. and Mannel, R. C. (1986) 'Removing Attitudinal Barriers to Leisure Behavior and Satisfaction: A Filed Experiment Among the Institutionalized Elderly', *Therapeutic Recreation Journal* 20(3): 46–53.

Barrow, R. and Milburn, G. (1990) *A Critical Dictionary of Educational Concepts* (2nd edn), New York, Teachers College Press.

Beck-Ford, V. and Brown, R. (1984) *Leisure Training and Rehabilitation*, Springfield, IL, Charles C. Thomas.

Bedini, L. A. (1990) 'The Status of Leisure Education: Implications for Instruction and Practice', *Therapeutic Recreation Journal* 24(1): 40–9.

Bedini, L. A. and Bullock, C. C. (1988) 'Leisure Education in the Public Schools: A Model of Cooperation in Transition Programming for Mentally Handicapped Youth', *Journal of Expanding Horizons in Therapeutic Recreation* 3: 5–11.

Bender, M., Brannan, S. A. and Verhoven, P. J. (1984) *Leisure Education for the Handicapped: Curriculum Goals, Activities and Resources*, San Diego, CA, College-Hill Press.

Bramante, A. C. (1997) 'The Right to Have Leisure Education', *World Leisure and Recreation* 39(2): 12–14.

Brightbill, C. K. and Mobley, T. (1977) *Educating for Leisure-centered Living* (2nd edn), New York, John Wiley & Sons.

Bullock, C., Morris L., Mahon, M. and Jones, B. (1992) *School–Community Leisure Link: Leisure Education Program Curriculum Guide*, Chapel Hill, NC, Center for Recreation and Disability Studies.

Caldwell, L. L. and Baldwin, C. K. (2004) 'Preliminary Effects of a Leisure Education Program to Promote Healthy Use of Free Time Among Middle School Adolescents', *Journal of Leisure Research* 36(3): 310–35.

Cherry, C. and Woodburn, B. (1978) *Leisure: A Resource for Educators*, Toronto, Ontario, Ministry of Culture and Recreation, Leisure Education Programme.

Chinn, K. A. and Joswiak, K. F. (1981) 'Leisure Education and Leisure Counseling', *Therapeutic Recreation Journal* 15(4): 4–7.

Collard, K. M. (1981) 'Leisure Education in Schools: Why, Who and the Need for Advocacy', *Therapeutic Recreation Journal* 15(4): 8–16.

Corbin, H. D. and Tait, W. J. (1973) *Education for Leisure*, Englewood Cliffs, NJ, Prentice Hall.

Dattilo, J. (2000) *Leisure Education Specific Programs*, State College, PA, Venture Publishing.

Dattilo, J. and Hoge, G. (1995) *Project TRAIL: Transition Through Recreation and Integration for Life*, Athens, GA, University of Georgia.

Dattilo, J. and Hoge, G. (1999) 'Effects of a Leisure Education Program on Youth with Mental Retardation', *Education and Training in Mental Health and Developmental Disabilities* 34(1): 20–34.

Dattilo, J. and St Peter, S. (1991) 'A Model for Including Leisure Education in Transition Services for Young Adults with Mental Retardation', *Education and Training in Mental Retardation* 26.

Dattilo, J. and Williams, D. M. (1991) *Leisure Education: Program Planning, a Systematic Approach*, State College, PA, Venture Publishing.

Dunn, N. J. (1981) 'Leisure Education: Meeting the Challenge of Increasing Leisure Independence of Residents in Psychiatric Facilities', *Therapeutic Recreation Journal* 15(3): 17–23.

Dunn, N. J. and Wilhite, B. (1997) 'The Effects of a Leisure Education Program on Participation and Psychosocial Well-being of Two Older Women Who are Home-centred', *Therapeutic Recreation Journal* 31(1): 53–71.

Faché, W. (1995) 'Leisure Education in Community Systems', in H. Ruskin and A. Sivan (eds) *Leisure Education Towards the 21st Century*, Provo, Utah, BYU, pp. 51–78.

Faché, W. (1997) 'Developing Leisure Education in Primary Schools', *World Leisure and Recreation* 39(2): 34–8.

Feldman, M. J. and Gaier, E. L. (1980) 'Correlates of Adolescent Life Satisfaction', *Youth and Society* 12(12): 131–44.

Fine, A. H., Welch-Bruke, C. S. and Fondario, L. J. (1985) 'A Developmental Model for Integration of Leisure Programming in the Education of Individuals with Mental Retardation', *Mental Retardation* 23: 289–96.

Fu, F. H. and Leung, M. (eds) (2003) *Health Promotion, Wellness and Leisure: Major Components of Quality of Life*, Hong Kong, Stephen Hui Research Centre for Physical Recreation and Wellness, Hong Kong Baptist University.

Fu, F. H. and Ruskin, H. (eds) (2001) *Physical Fitness and Activity in the Context of Leisure Education*, Hong Kong, Stephen Hui Research Centre for Physical Recreation and Wellness, Hong Kong Baptist University.

Grossman, A. H. (2000) 'Mobility for Action: Advocacy and Empowerment for the Right of Leisure, Play and Recreation', in A. Sivan and H. Ruskin (eds) *Leisure Education, Community Development and Populations with Special Needs*, Oxford and New York, CABI Publishing, pp. 55–64.

Hayes, G. A. (1977) 'Leisure Education and Recreation Counselling', in A. Epperson, P. Witt and G. Hitzhusen (eds) *Leisure Counseling: As Aspect of Leisure Education*, Springfield, IL, Charles C. Thomas.

Heyne, L. A. and Schleien, S. J. (1996) 'Leisure Education in the Schools: A Call to Action', *Journal of Leisurability* 23(3).

Hendry, L. and Marr, D. (1985) 'Leisure Education and Young People's Leisure', *Scottish Educational Review* 17: 116–27.

Johnson, D. E., Bullock, C. C. and Ashton-Shaeffer, C. (1997) 'Families and Leisure: A Context for Learning', *Teaching Exceptional Children* (November): 30–4.

Joswiak, K. F. (1979) *Leisure Counselling Program Materials for the Developmentally Disabled*, Washington, DC, Hawkins and Associates.

Joswiak, K. F. (1989) *Leisure Education: Program Materials for Persons with Developmental Disabilities*, State College, PA, Venture Publishing.

Kelly, J. R. (1996) *Leisure* (3rd edn), Boston, Allyn & Bacon.

Kleiber, D. A. (2001) 'Developmental Intervention and Leisure Education: A Life Span Perspective', *World Leisure Journal* 43(1): 4–10.

Kraus, R. G. (1964) *Recreation and the Schools*, New York, Macmillan.

Lanagan, D. and Dattilo, J. (1989) 'The Effects of a Leisure Education Program on Individuals with Mental Retardation', *Therapeutic Recreation Journal* 23(4): 62–72.

Mahon, M. J. and Bullock, C. C. (1992) 'Teaching Adolescents with Mental Retardation to Make Decisions in Leisure Through the Use of Self-control Techniques', *Therapeutic Recreation Journal* 26(1): 9–26.

Mahon, M. J. and Searle, M. S. (1994) 'Leisure Education: Its Effect on Older Adults', *Journal of Physical Education, Recreation & Dance* 65(4): 36–41.

McDonald, R. G. and Howe, C. Z. (1989) 'Challenge/Initiative Recreation Programs as a Treatment for Low Self-concept Children', *Journal of Leisure Research* 21(3): 242–53.

Mundy, J. (1998) *Leisure Education: Theory and Practice*, (2nd edn) Champaign, IL, Sagmore Publishing.

Mundy, J. and Odum, L. (1979) *Leisure Education: Theory and Practice*, Champaign, IL, Sagmore Publishing.

Munson, W. (1988) 'Effects of Leisure Education versus Physical Activity or Informal Discussion on Behaviorally Disordered Youth Offenders', *Adapted Physical Activity Quarterly* 5(4): 305–17.

Munson, W. W., Baker, S. B. and Lundegren, H. M. (1985) 'Strength Training and Leisure Counseling as Treatments for Institutionalized Juvenile Delinquents', *Adapted Physical Activity Quarterly* 2(1): 65–75.

Ochi, S. (2000) 'The Effects of Leisure Education on the Perceived Freedom and Leisure Participation of Individuals with Depression in Long Care Facilities', Master's thesis, Springfield College, Massachusetts.

Page, T. G. and Thomas, J. B. (1977) *International Dictionary of Education*, London, Kogan Page Limited.

Parker, S. (1979) *The Sociology of Leisure*, London, George Allen & Unwin.

Peterson, C. A. and Gunn, S. L. (1984) *Therapeutic Recreation Program and Design: Principles and Procedures* (2nd edn), Englewood Cliffs, NJ, Prentice-Hall.

Roberts, K. (1983) *Youth and Leisure*, London, George Allen & Unwin.

Robertson, B. J. (2001) 'Leisure Education of Incarceration Youth', *World Leisure Journal* 43(1): 20–9.

Ruskin, H. (1984) 'Formal and Informal Education for Leisure-centered Living: Implications for Educational Frameworks', in H. Ruskin (ed.) *Leisure: Towards a Theory and a Policy*, New Jersey, Associated University Presses, pp. 64–79.

Ruskin, H. (1995a) 'Conceptual Approaches in Policy Development on Leisure Education', in H. Ruskin and A. Sivan (eds) *Leisure Education Towards the 21st Century*, Provo, Utah, BYU, pp. 137–58.

Ruskin, H. (1995b) *Leisure Education Curricula: A Framework for Kindergarten to Grade 12*, Jerusalem: Ministry of Education, Culture and Sport.

Ruskin, H. and Sivan, A. (eds) (1995) *Leisure Education Towards the 21st Century*, Provo, Utah, BYU.

Ruskin, H. and Sivan, A. (2002) *Leisure Education in School Systems*, Cosell Center for Physical Education, Leisure and Health Promotion, Magness Press, Hebrew University of Jerusalem.

Schleien, S., Meyer, L., Heyne, L. and Biel Brandt, B. (1995) *Lifelong Leisure Skills and Lifestyles for Persons with Developmental Disabilities*, Baltimore, Paul H. Brookes.

Searle, M. S. and Mahon, M. J. (1991) 'Leisure Education in a Day Hospital: The Effect of Selected Social-psychological Variables Among Older Adults', *Canadian Journal of Community Mental Health* 10(2): 95–109.

Searle, M. S. and Mahon, M. J. (1992) 'The Effect of Leisure Education Program on Selected Social-psychological Variables: A Three Months Follow-up Study', *Terapeutic Recreational Journal* 27(1): 9–21.

Searle, M. S., Mahon, M. J., Iso-Ahola, S., Sdrolias, H. A. and van Dyke, J. (1995) 'Examining the Long Term Effects of Leisure Education on a Sense of Independence and Psychological Well-being Among the Elderly', *Journal of Leisure Research* 27(3): 331–40.

Searle, M. S., Mahon, M. J., Iso-Ahola, S., Sdrolias, H. A. and van Dyke, J. (1998) 'Enhancing a Sense of Independence and Psychological Well-being Among the Elderly: A Field Experiment', *Journal of Leisure Research* 30(1): 107–24.

Sheffield, E. A., Waigandt, A. C. and Miller, D. A. (1986) 'Post-assault Leisure Counseling for Sexual Assault Victims', *Journal of Expanding Horizons in Therapeutic Recreation* 1: 56–63.

Sivan, A. (1991) 'Attitudes of Secondary School Students and Teachers Towards the Aim of School as a Socialising Agent for Leisure', PhD thesis, Hong Kong University, Hong Kong.

Sivan, A. (1995) 'Schools as Socializing Agents for Leisure: The Case of Hong Kong', in H. Ruskin and A. Sivan (eds) *Leisure Education Towards the 21st Century*, Provo, Utah, BYU, pp. 167–75.

Sivan, A. (1996) 'Current Model for Leisure Education in Educational Frameworks', in F. Fu and P. C. Chan (eds) *Recreation, Sport, Culture & Tourism for the 21st Century*, Department of Physical Education, Hong Kong Baptist University, Hong Kong, pp. 192–202.

Sivan, A. (1997) 'Recent Developments in Leisure Education Research and Implementation', *World Leisure & Recreation* 39(2): 41–4.

Sivan, A. (2000) 'Community Development Through Leisure Education – Conceptual Approaches', in A. Sivan and H. Ruskin (eds) *Leisure Education, Community Development and Populations with Special Needs*, Oxford and New York, CABI Publishing, pp. 31–42.

Sivan, A. (2003) 'Has Leisure Got Anything to Do with Learning? An Exploratory Study of the Lifestyles of Young People in Hong Kong Universities', *Journal of Leisure Studies* 22(2), 129–46.

Sivan, A. and Ruskin, H. (1997) 'Successful Models for Leisure Education in Israel', *World Leisure & Recreation* 39(2): 39–40.

Sivan, A. and Ruskin, H. (eds) (2000) *Leisure Education, Community Development and Populations with Special Needs*, Oxford and New York, CABI Publishing.

Stumbo, N. J. (1992) *Leisure Activities II: More Activities and Resources*, State College, PA, Venture Publishing.

Stumbo, N. J. (1997) *Leisure Education III: More Goal-oriented Activities*, State College, PA, Venture Publishing.

Stumbo, N. J. (1998) *Leisure Education IV: Activities for Individuals with Substance Addictions.* State College, PA, Venture Publishing.

Stumbo, N. J. (1999) *Intervention Activities for At-Risk Youth*, State College, PA, Venture Publishing.

Stumbo, N. J. (2000) *Leisure Education Specific Programs*, State College, PA, Venture Publishing.

Stumbo, N. J. and Thompson, S. (1988) *Leisure Education: A Manual of Activities and Resources*, State College, PA, Venture Publishing.

Witt, P. A., Ellis, G. and Niles, S. H. (1984) 'Leisure Counseling with Special Populations', in T. E. Dowd (ed.) *Leisure Counseling: Concepts and Applications*, Springfield, IL, Charles C. Thomas.

World Leisure Commission on Education (2000) *International Position Statements on Leisure Education*, Jerusalem, Hebrew University of Jerusalem, Cosell Center for Physical Education, Leisure and Health Promotion.

Wuerch, B. B. and Voeltz, L. M. (1982) *Longitudinal Leisure Skills for Severely Handicapped Learners: The Ho'onanea Curriculum Component*, Baltimore, Paul H. Brookes.

Zeyen, D., Odum, L. L., Lancaster, R. A., Fernandez, A., Tinker, S. and Verhoven, P. J. (1977) *Kangaroo Kit: Leisure Education Curriculum*, Washington, DC National Recreation and Park Association.

Zoerink, D. A. (1988) 'Effects of a Short-term Leisure Education Program Upon the Leisure Functioning of Young People with Spina Bifida', *Therapeutic Recreation Journal* 22(3): 44–52.

27

Serious Leisure

Robert A. Stebbins

The term 'serious leisure' made its debut in social science circles in 1982. The initial statement (Stebbins, 1982) and several more recent ones bearing on the nature of serious leisure, are now reasonably well expressed in what seems to have become the standard abbreviated definition of this type of activity. Serious leisure is systematic pursuit of an amateur, hobbyist, or volunteer activity that participants find so substantial and interesting that, in the typical case, they launch themselves on a career centred on acquiring and expressing its special skills, knowledge and experience (Stebbins, 1992: 3). Contrary to a widespread tendency to see the idea of career as applying only to occupations, the term, in this definition, is used more broadly, following Goffman's (1961: 127–8) conceptualization of 'moral career'. Broadly considered, careers are available in all substantial, complicated roles, including especially those in work, leisure, deviance, politics, religion and interpersonal relationships (see also Lindesmith et al., 1999: 315–16; Hewitt, 1991: 246).

Note, too, that here the adjective 'serious' embodies such qualities as earnestness, sincerity, importance and carefulness, rather than those of gravity, solemnity, joylessness, distress and anxiety. Although the second set of terms occasionally describes serious leisure in practice, they are uncharacteristic of it, failing to nullify, or, in many instances, even dilute, the overall fulfilment gained by participants. Here, 'serious' is fundamentally a folk term, an adjective the people I interviewed frequently used to distinguish their kind of leisure from casual leisure. For a summary of research on serious leisure, see Stebbins (2001a: chapter 8).

To sharpen our understanding of serious leisure, it is commonly contrasted with 'casual' or unserious leisure: the immediately intrinsically rewarding, relatively short-lived pleasurable activity requiring little or no special training to enjoy it (Stebbins, 1997a). Among its types are play (including dabbling), relaxation (for example, sitting, napping, strolling), passive entertainment (such as TV, books, recorded music), active entertainment (games of chance, party games, and so on), sociable conversation, and sensory stimulation (for example, sex, eating, drinking). It is considerably less substantial, and offers no career of the sort just described for serious leisure. In broad, colloquial language, casual leisure, hedonic as it is, could serve as the scientific term for doing what comes naturally. Yet despite the seemingly trivial nature of most casual leisure, I argue elsewhere that it is nonetheless important in personal and social life (Stebbins, 2001b).

Nature of serious leisure

To gain a more complete understanding of serious leisure, we must go beyond our handy but nonetheless limited one-sentence definition to look more closely at its basic types. Amateurs are found in art, science, sport, and entertainment, where they are inevitably linked in several ways with professional counterparts. For their part, the professionals are identified and defined according to theory developed in the social scientific study of professions, a substantially more exact procedure than the ones relying on simplistic and not infrequently commercially shaped common-sense images of these workers. In other words, when studying amateurs and professionals, descriptive definitions turn out to be superficial, such as observing that the activity in question constitutes a livelihood for the second but not the first, or that the second works full time at it whereas the first pursues it part time. Rather, we get much closer to the essence of both roles by noting, for example, that the two are locked in and therefore defined by a system of relations linking professionals, amateurs and their publics ('the P-A-P system'). (This definition and one based on attitudinal differences are discussed in greater detail in Stebbins, 1979; 1992, chapter 3.)

Hobbyists lack this professional alter-ego, even if they sometimes have commercial equivalents, and often have small publics interested in what they do. Hobbyists can be classified in one of five categories: collectors, makers and tinkerers, activity participants (in non-competitive, rule-based pursuits), players of sports and games (where no professional counterparts exist), and enthusiasts in one of the liberal arts. Fishing (Yoder, 1997), bushwalking (Hamilton-Smith, 1993) and barbershop singing (Stebbins, 1996a) exemplify the third, bound as they are by certain cultural and regulatory norms, while curling (Apostle, 1992), long-distance running (Yair, 1990) and competitive swimming (Hastings et al., 1995) exemplify the fourth, which are bound by rules of the game. Liberal arts hobbyists are enamoured of the systematic quest of knowledge for its own sake (Stebbins, 1994). This is typically accomplished by reading voraciously in the field of art, sport, cuisine, language, culture, history, science, philosophy, politics or literature.

Volunteers, the third basic type, engage in volunteering, defined here as uncoerced help offered either formally or informally with no or, at most, token pay for the benefit of both other people and the volunteer. Concerning the free choice dimension, the language of (lack of) 'coercion' is preferred, since that of 'free choice' is hedged about with numerous problems (see Stebbins, 2002). The logical difficulties of including obligation in definitions of volunteering (it is voluntary activity) militate against including this condition in our definition. As for remuneration, volunteers retain their voluntary spirit providing they avoid becoming dependent on any money received from their volunteering. Structurally, volunteers may serve formally in collaboration with legally chartered organizations or informally in situations involving small numbers of relatives, friends, neighbours and the like, with no such legal basis. Finally, it follows from what has been said elsewhere about altruism and self-interest in volunteering (Stebbins, 1996b) that both the volunteers and those who they help find benefits in such activity.

It should be noted, however, that the field of career volunteering is narrower, even if it does encompass considerable ground. One taxonomy, consisting of 16 types of formal organizational volunteering, shows the wide scope of career volunteering. Career volunteers provide a great variety of services in education, science, civic affairs (advocacy projects, professional and labour organizations), spiritual development, health, economic development, religion, politics, government (programmes and services), human relationships, recreation and the arts. Some of these volunteers work in the fields of safety or the physical environment, while others prefer to provide necessities (for example, food, clothing, shelter) or support services. Although much of career volunteering is connected in some way with an organization of some sort, the scope of this leisure is still broader, including the kinds of helping (informal volunteering) devoted individuals do for social movements or for neighbours and family. Still, the definition of serious leisure restricts attention everywhere to volunteering in which participants find a career, in which they find more or less continuous and substantial involvement, rather than making one-time or occasional donations of money, blood, services, and the like (Stebbins, 1996b).

Making a case for volunteering as leisure – as opposed to unpaid work or unpaid productive activity – poses little logical difficulty. For the word to remain etymologically consistent with its Latin roots, it must be seen, as all leisure is, as uncoerced activity. Moreover, as all leisure, leisure volunteering must be seen as basically either fulfilling or enjoyable experience (if not both), for otherwise we are forced to posit that volunteers are somehow pushed into performing their roles by circumstances they would prefer to avoid, a contradiction of terms.

Six qualities

Serious leisure is further defined by six distinctive qualities. One is the occasional need to *persevere*, as seen in confronting danger (for example, in eating wild mushrooms and climbing mountains: Fine and Holyfield, 1996), managing stage fright (such as when participating in theatre and sport: Stebbins, 1981) or suffering embarrassment (while doing volunteer work, for instance: Floro, 1978: 198). Yet it is clear that positive feelings about the activity come, to some extent, from sticking with it through thick and thin, from conquering adversity. A second quality is, as indicated earlier, that of finding a *career* in the endeavour, shaped as it is by its own peculiar contingencies, turning points and stages of achievement and involvement.

Most, if not all, careers in serious leisure owe their existence to its third quality: serious leisure participants make a significant personal *effort* based on specially acquired *knowledge, training or skill*, and, indeed at times, all three. Examples include such achievements as showmanship, athletic prowess, scientific knowledge and long experience in a role. Fourth, a number of *durable benefits, or outcomes*, of serious leisure have so far been identified, mostly from research on amateurs and hobbyists. They include self-actualization, self-enrichment, self-expression, regeneration or renewal of self, feelings of accomplishment, enhancement of self-image, social interaction and belongingness and lasting physical products of the activity (for example, a painting, scientific paper, piece of furniture). A further benefit – self-gratification, or the combination of superficial enjoyment and deep fulfilment – is to the extent that the component of enjoyment dominates, also one main benefit of casual leisure.

The fifth quality, that participants in serious leisure tend to *identify* strongly with their chosen pursuits, springs from the presence of the other five. In contrast, casual leisure, although hardly humiliating or despicable, is nonetheless usually too fleeting, mundane, and commonplace for most people to find a distinctive identity there. I imagine that this was the quality Cicero had in mind when he coined his famous slogan '*Otium cum dignitate*', 'Leisure with Dignity'.

The sixth quality of serious leisure is the *unique ethos* that grows up around each expression of it. The central component of this ethos is the special social world that develops when enthusiasts in a particular field pursue over many years their interests in it. Unruh defines the social world as:

> a unit of social organization which is diffuse and amorphous … Generally larger than groups or organizations, social worlds are not necessarily defined by formal boundaries, membership lists, or spatial territory … A social world must be seen as an internally recognizable constellation of actors, organizations, events, and practices which have coalesced into a perceived sphere of interest and involvement for participants. Characteristically, a social world lacks a powerful centralized authority structure and is delimited by … effective communication and not territory nor formal group membership. (Unruh, 1979: 115)

Later, Unruh (1980) added that social worlds are characterized by voluntary identification, by freedom to enter into and depart from them. Moreover, because they are diffuse, it is common for members to be only partly involved in all the activities they offer. After all, social worlds vary in size from local to international. Third, people in complex societies are often members of several social worlds, only some being related to leisure. Finally, social worlds are held together, to an important degree, by semiformal or 'mediated communication'. They are rarely heavily bureaucratized, yet because of diffuseness, they are rarely characterized by intense face-to-face interaction. Rather, communication is typically mediated by newsletters, posted notices, telephone messages and mass mailings, as well as by internet communications, radio and television announcements and similar means. And there is the growing possibility that the internet will, in future, become the most popular of these.

Every social world contains four types of members: strangers, tourists, regulars and insiders (Unruh, 1979, 1980). Strangers are intermediaries who normally participate little in the leisure activity itself, but who nonetheless do something important to make it possible by, for example, managing municipal parks (in amateur baseball), minting coins (in hobbyist coin collecting), or organizing the work of teachers' aids (in career volunteering). Tourists are temporary participants in a social world; they have come on the scene momentarily for entertainment, diversion or profit. Most amateur and hobbyist activities have publics of some kind, which are, in this conceptualization, constituted of tourists. The clients of many volunteers can be similarly classified. Regulars routinely participate in the social world; in serious leisure, they are the amateurs, hobbyists and volunteers themselves. Insiders are those among them who show exceptional devotion to the social world they share, to maintaining it, advancing it, and displaying excellence there. In the studies of amateurs, such people were analysed as 'devotees', people highly dedicated to their pursuit, and contrasted with 'participants', or regulars, people moderately dedicated to it (Stebbins, 1992: 46–8).

Missing from Unruh's conceptualization of social world, but nonetheless vitally important for the study of serious leisure, is the observation that an evolved subculture is also to be found there, one function of which is to interrelate the 'diffuse and amorphous constellations'. Consequently, it should be noted that members find associated with each social world a unique set of special norms, values, beliefs, lifestyles, moral principles, performance standards and similar shared representations. Only by taking these elements into account can we logically speak about, for example, social stratification in social worlds. This Unruh does when differentiating insiders from regulars, and was just done here for serious leisure by differentiating devotees from participants.

In addition to the author's work, empirical validation of these six distinctive qualities comes from several studies (for example, Parker, 1996; McQuarrie and Jackson, 1996; Siegenthaler and Gonsalez, 1997; Nichols and King, 1999; Arai, 2000).

Rewards, costs and motivation

In addition, research on serious leisure has led to the discovery of a distinctive set of rewards for each activity examined (Stebbins, 2001a: 13). In these studies the participant's leisure fulfilment has been found to stem from a constellation of particular rewards gained from the activity, be it boxing, ice climbing, or giving dance lessons to the elderly. Furthermore, the rewards are not only fulfilling in themselves, but also fulfilling as counterweights to the costs encountered in the activity. That is, every serious leisure activity contains its own combination of tensions, dislikes and disappointments, which each participant must confront in some way. For instance, an amateur football player may not always like attending daily practices, being bested occasionally by more junior players when there, and being required to sit on the sidelines from time to time while others get experience at his position. Yet he may still regard this activity as highly fulfilling – as (serious) leisure – because it also offers certain powerful rewards.

Put more precisely, then, the drive for fulfilment in serious leisure is the drive to experience the rewards of a given leisure activity, such that its costs are seen by the participant as more or less insignificant by comparison. This is at once the meaning of the activity for the participant and that person's motivation for engaging in it. It is this motivational sense of the concept of reward that distinguishes it from the idea of durable benefit set out earlier, an idea that emphasizes outcomes rather than antecedent conditions. Nonetheless, the two ideas constitute two sides of the same social psychological coin.

The rewards of a serious leisure pursuit are the more or less routine values that attract and hold its enthusiasts. Every serious leisure career both frames and is framed by the continuous search for these rewards; a search that takes months, often years, before the participant consistently finds deep fulfilment in an amateur, hobbyist or volunteer role. The ten rewards presented below emerged in the course of various exploratory studies of amateurs, hobbyists and career volunteers (for summary of these studies, see Stebbins, 2001a). As the following list shows, the rewards of serious leisure are predominantly personal.

Personal rewards:
1. Personal enrichment (cherished experiences)
2. Self-actualization (developing skills, abilities, knowledge)
3. Self-expression (expressing skills, abilities, knowledge already developed)
4. Self-image (known to others as a particular kind of serious leisure participant)
5. Self-gratification (combination of superficial enjoyment and deep fulfilment)
6. Re-creation (regeneration) of oneself through serious leisure after a stint of work
7. Financial return (from a serious leisure activity)

Social rewards:
8. Social attraction (associating with other serious leisure participants, with clients as a volunteer, participating in the social world of the activity)
9. Goup accomplishment (group effort in accomplishing a serious leisure project; senses of helping, being needed, being altruistic)
10. Contribution to the maintenance and development of the group (including senses of helping, being needed, being altruistic in making the contribution).

In the various studies on amateurs, hobbyists, and volunteers, these rewards, depending on the activity, were often given different weightings by the interviewees to reflect their importance relative to each other. Nonetheless, some common ground exists, for the studies do show that, in terms of their personal importance, most serious leisure participants rank first and second self-enrichment and self-gratification. Moreover, to find either reward, participants must have acquired sufficient levels of relevant skill, knowledge, and experience (Stebbins, 1979, 1993). In other words, self-actualization, which was often ranked third in importance, is also highly rewarding in serious leisure.

Finally, it has been argued over the years that amateurs and sometimes even the activities they pursue are marginal in society, for amateurs are neither dabblers nor professionals (see Stebbins, 1979). Moreover, the studies of hobbyists and career volunteers show that they and some of their activities are just as marginal and for many of the same reasons (Stebbins, 1996b, 1998). Several properties of serious leisure give substance to these observations. One, although seemingly illogical according to common sense, is that serious leisure is characterized in practice by an important degree of positive commitment to a pursuit (Stebbins, 1992: 51–2). This commitment is measured, among other ways, by the sizeable investment of time and energy in the leisure made by devotees and participants. A second is that serious leisure is pursued with noticeable intentness, with such passion that Goffman (1963: 144–5) once qualified amateurs and hobbyists as 'quietly disaffiliated'. People with such an orientation toward their leisure are marginal compared with people who go in for the ever popular forms of casual leisure.

Identity, lifestyle and central life interest

Not only do serious leisure activities generate their own lifestyles, they also generate their own identities, both centred on a particular form of leisure regarded by participants as a central life interest. Dictionary definitions, which tend to conceive of lifestyle simply as a way of living, are for the most part circular and hence of little use in the present discussion. Social science definitions have advanced well beyond this truism. Thus

> a lifestyle is a distinctive set of shared patterns of tangible behavior that is organized around a set of coherent interests or social conditions or both, that is explained and justified by a set of related values, attitudes, and orientations and that, under certain conditions, becomes the basis for a separate, common social identity for its participants. (Stebbins, 1997b: 350)

Note that this definition refers exclusively to collective lifestyles. This restriction recognizes that, to this point, the study of lifestyles has concentrated almost entirely on shared patterns of tangible behaviour, leaving us with little information about individual lifestyles (Veal, 1993).

According to the foregoing definition, some lifestyles offer their participants a special social identity. In other words, the participants are members of a category of humankind who recognize themselves and, in some measure, are recognized by the larger community for their distinctive mode of life. Thus a profound lifestyle awaits anyone routinely pursuing a serious leisure career in, say, amateur theatre, volunteer work with the mentally handicapped, or the hobby of model railroading or mountain climbing.

To the extent that lifestyles form around complicated, absorbing, fulfilling activities, as they invariably do in serious leisure, they can also be viewed as behavioural expressions of participants' central life interests in those activities. Dubin (1992: 37) defines this interest as 'that portion of a person's total life in which energies are invested in both physical/intellectual activities and in positive emotional states'. Sociologically, a central life interest is often associated with a major role in life. And since they can only emerge from positive emotional states, obsessive and compulsive activities can never become central life interests.

Dubin's (ibid.: 41–2) examples clearly establish that either a work or a serious leisure activity can become a central life interest. As happens with leisure lifestyle, a leisure identity also arises in parallel with a person's leisure-based central life interest. In other words, that person's lifestyle in a given serious leisure activity gives expression to his or her central life interest there, while forming the basis for a personal and community identity as some one who goes in for that activity.

Conclusions

In broadest perspective, serious leisure can be viewed as both a type of leisure and a form of leisure experience. Leisure can be studied from many angles, however, with experience being but one of them. So analysis of leisure, in general, and serious leisure, in particular, as distinctive experiences helps us understand only one facet, albeit an important facet, of this institution and the set of activities known by this name.

Bibliography

Apostle, R. (1992) 'Curling for Cash: The "Professionalization" of a Popular Canadian Sport', *Culture* 12(2): 17–28.

Arai, S. M. (2000) 'A Typology of Volunteers for a Changing Sociopolitical Context: The Impact on Social Capital, Citizenship, and Civil Society', *Loisir et Société/Society and Leisure* 23: 327–52.

Dubin, R. (1992) *Central Life Interests: Creative Individualism in a Complex World*, New Brunswick, NJ, Transaction.

Fine, G. A. and Holyfield, L. (1996) 'Trusting Fellows: Secrecy, Trust, and Voluntary Allegiance in Leisure Spheres', *Social Psychological Quarterly* 59: 22–38.

Floro, G. K. (1978) 'What to Look For in a Study of the Volunteer in the Work World', in R. P. Wolensky and E. J. Miller (eds) *The Small City and Regional Community*, Stevens Point, WI, Foundation Press, pp. 194–202.

Goffman, E. (1961) *Asylums: Essays on the Social Situation of Mental Patients and Other Inmates*, Garden City, NY, Doubleday.

Goffman, E. (1963) *Stigma: Notes on the Management of Spoiled Identity*, Englewood Cliffs, NJ, Prentice-Hall.

Hamilton-Smith, E. (1993) 'In the Australian Bush: Some Reflections on Serious Leisure', *World Leisure & Recreation* 35(1): 10–13.

Hastings, D. W., Kurth, S. B., Schloder, M. and Cyr, D. (1995) 'Reasons for Participating in a Serious Leisure: Comparison of Canadian and U.S. Masters Swimmers', *International Review for Sociology of Sport* 30: 101–19.

Hewitt, J. P. (1991) *Self and Society* (5th edn), Boston, MA, Allyn & Bacon.

Lindesmith, A. R., Strauss, A. L. and Denzin, N. K. (1999) *Social Psychology* (8th edn), Thousand Oaks, CA, Sage.

McQuarrie, F. and Jackson, E. L. (1996) 'Connections between Negotiation of Leisure Constraints and Serious Leisure: An Exploratory Study of Adult Amateur Ice Skaters', *Loisir et Société/ Society and Leisure* 19: 459–83.

Nichols, G. and King, L. (1999) 'Redefining the Recruitment Niche for the Guide Association in the United Kingdom', *Leisure Sciences* 21: 307–20.

Parker, S. R. (1996) 'Serious Leisure – A Middle-class Phenomenon?' in M. Collins (ed.) *Leisure in Industrial and Post-industrial Societies*, Eastbourne, Leisure Studies Association, pp. 327–32.

Siegenthaler, K. L. and Gonsalez, G. L. (1997) 'Youth Sports as Serious Leisure: A Critique', *Journal of Sport and Social Issues* 21: 298–314.

Stebbins, R. A. (1979) *Amateurs: On the Margin between Work and Leisure*, Beverly Hills, CA, Sage.

Stebbins, R. A. (1981) 'Toward a Social Psychology of Stage Fright', in M. Hart and S. Birrell (eds) *Sport in the Sociocultural Process*, Dubuque, IA, W. C. Brown, pp. 156–63.

Stebbins, R. A. (1982) 'Serious Leisure: A Conceptual Statement', *Pacific Sociological Review* 25: 251–72.

Stebbins, R. A. (1992) *Amateurs, Professionals, and Serious Leisure*, Montreal, QC, and Kingston, Ontario, McGill-Queen's University Press.

Stebbins, R. A. (1993) *Canadian Football. A View from the Helmet*, (reprinted edn), Toronto, Ontario, Canadian Scholars Press.

Stebbins, R. A. (1994) 'The Liberal Arts Hobbies: A Neglected Subtype of Serious Leisure', *Loisir et Société/Society and Leisure* 16: 173–86.

Stebbins, R. A. (1996a) *The Barbershop Singer: Inside the Social World of a Musical Hobby*, Toronto, Ontario, University of Toronto Press.

Stebbins, R. A. (1996b) 'Volunteering: A Serious Leisure Perspective', *Nonprofit and Voluntary Action Quarterly* 25: 211–24.

Stebbins, R. A. (1997a) 'Casual Leisure: A Conceptual Statement', *Leisure Studies* 16: 17–25.

Stebbins, R. A. (1997b) 'Lifestyle as a Generic Concept in Ethnographic Research', *Quality and Quantity* 31: 347–60.

Stebbins, R. A. (1998) *The Urban Francophone Volunteer: Searching for Personal Meaning and Community Growth in a Linguistic Minority*, Vol. 3, No. 2 (New Scholars-New Visions in Canadian Studies quarterly monographs series), Seattle, WA, University of Washington, Canadian Studies Centre.

Stebbins, R. A. (2001a) *New Directions in the Theory and Research of Serious Leisure*, Mellen Studies in Sociology, Vol. 28, Lewiston, NY, Edwin Mellen.

Stebbins, R. A. (2001b) 'The Costs and Benefits of Hedonism: Some Consequences of Taking Casual Leisure Seriously', *Leisure Studies* 20: 305–9.

Stebbins, R. A. (2002) 'Choice in Experiential Definitions of Leisure', *Leisure Studies Association Newsletter* 63 (November): 18–20.

Unruh, D. R. (1979) 'Characteristics and Types of Participation in Social Worlds', *Symbolic Interaction* 2: 115–30.

Unruh, D. R. (1980) 'The Nature of Social Worlds', *Pacific Sociological Review* 23: 271–96.

Veal, A. J. (1993) 'The Concept of Lifestyle: A Review', *Leisure Studies* 12: 233–52.

Yair, G. (1990) 'The Commitment to Long-distance Running and Level of Activities', *Journal of Leisure Research* 22: 213–27.

Yoder, D. G. (1997) 'A Model for Commodity Intensive Serious Leisure', *Journal of Leisure Research* 29: 407–29.

Part 5
Indexical Themes

28
Representation

Chris Rojek

What does it mean to propose that it is unacceptable to study leisure merely as an activity or an institution and that it must also be investigated as a system of representation? Above all, it means committing to a perspective that recognizes that leisure practice is the expression of power relations. This is quite different from those psychologistic approaches that portray leisure as a state of mind. These positions treat human beings as abstract and essentially uniform elements in the social system. For example, Csikszentmihalyi's (1975) concept of 'flow experience' and Neulinger's (1981) insistence on the paramount importance of leisure motivation, rely upon models of leisure that privilege individual experience. They assume that individual experience can be aggregated around a model of common human drives. Flow is portrayed as an equilibrium between intrinsic motivations and extrinsic variables. Equilibrium is understood normatively, to reinforce social values rather than to challenge or oppose them. The sociological counterpart to this is provided by the systems approach in Leisure Studies (Cheek and Burch, 1976).[1] This contends that intrinsic motivation is the expression of the core social values that underpin the social system. It holds that individual preferences in leisure conduct respond strongly to normative pressures. In the words of Cheek and Burch (1976: 156), 'leisure activities serve as an expression of social solidarity and norms to reaffirm the larger social order'.

Such views are ahistorical, that is, they do not incorporate an historical perspective into their analytical arsenal. Nor do they pay sufficient heed to the role of culture and politics in constructing and applying what Bourdieu (1984) called the *habitus* of normative behaviour. By the term, *habitus* Bourdieu meant the generative principles, classificatory schemes and ultimate values inscribed upon individuals as an ordinary part of the socialization process and the various rituals of social membership. Crucially, his discussion connects habitus to *space* and *stratification* so that, for example, within any nation-state considerable variation in principles, schemes and values is envisaged. This is separate from both the psychologistic and Systems approaches to leisure. Both of them operate with a harmonistic model of social order in which leisure practice is assumed to reinforce social integration. Bourdieu's perspective of social order suggests a type of provisional stability organized around conflicting principles, schemes and values. It allows that social order is a product of cultural reproduction which is itself elicited by the ideological representation of interests, responsibilities and needs. But it also maintains that order always involves a struggle and truce between strata over principles, schemes, values and other resources. The process of struggle has the capacity to reconfigure social order, sometimes to the manifest disadvantage of ascendant groups. At such junctures, change in the entire system becomes a possibility.

The value of a comparative and historical perspective

Considered from a comparative and historical perspective, it is evident that it is wrong to regard leisure as a *natural* adjunct of society. A comparative and historical approach encourages students to examine conditions in a given society along synchronic and diachronic dimensions. By the term synchronic is meant the contemporaneous set of divisions that exist between different societies. The diachronic refers to the path of historical change. It encourages students to scrutinize how human data have altered over time. Investigating each dimension makes it incumbent upon students to establish causal models to explain current differences and social and economic transformations. The main value of a comparative and historical perspective is that it helps us avoid the fallacy of ethnocentrism. Ethnocentrism is literally the universal and dogmatic extrapolation of local conditions and values. Comparative and historical analysis helps us realize that our own conditions of life do not apply everywhere and that what we take to be unique about our own time can only be confirmed by examining the past and conditions of life elsewhere. Through it, commonalities and differences in human societies can be more accurately apprehended and calibrated.

For example, anthropologists have established that play forms are so common in human societies as to be legitimately considered to belong to the category of cultural universals (Chick 1991, 2000, 2002). But universality in this case, refers to a set of meta-themes or principles that facilitate cross-cultural classification and research. Within these meta-themes or principles, the meaning of play is understood to vary according to the spatial, social, economic and cultural contexts in which it is institutionalized and practised. For example, the play forms of the 450-strong Gebusi of south-central New Guinea emphasize inclusive conviviality, humour, reciprocity and co-operation. *Gof,* which connotes anger and violence, is condemned. To be sure, ritualized mock forms figure in tribal rituals. But their ascendancy is strictly curbed. Interestingly, the rate of homicide among the Gebusi is 40 times greater than in the US. Why is this? Knauft (1987) suggests that a social structure based upon strong inclusive principles of co-operation in work and play creates an unusually high propensity to censure behaviour that is judged to be transgressive. The main motive for murder among the Gebusi, is the allegation of sorcery, especially when it is made after the occurrence of the sudden illness or death of a fellow tribal member. Emile Durkheim (1965: 427–8) famously maintained that play and leisure excite a state of 'collective effervesence' which contributes to the remaking of moral solidarity. This is clearly visible in the play forms of the Gebusi. But other layers of meaning are also latent. Most notably, play operates as a mechanism for isolating characteristics that test the suspicion of sorcery. This may contribute to the remaking of moral solidarity in that the 'righteous murder' of one erring member of the social unit reinforces the solidarity of the whole. However, it does so in ways most Westerners would meet with disapproval and even revulsion.

It may seem trite to add that even in the West there is considerable variation among leisure customs. For example, the allocation of leisure resources around the siesta in Mediterranean cultures has no parallel in North Western Europe. The relative wealth and development of flexitime patterns may allow some workers in the North West to enjoy a siesta, but the practice is not an integrated feature of the social structure. Similarly, for many Spanish, bull-fighting is a cherished part of national culture. It constitutes a staple in the spectrum of mass leisure events. Yet for most other nation-states in the European Union it is regarded with bemusement or disapproval.

To come now to history, historians have identified significant transformations in play regimes in the West. For example, E. P. Thompson's (1967) classic paper on task and time-driven work orientations maintained that industrialization revolutionized traditional attitudes to work and created entirely new work cultures based upon the contractual principle of limited reciprocal rights and responsibilities between the employer and the labourer.[2] Since human imagination is limitless, the attempt to managerially confine behaviour to a narrow set of ideals or roles provokes resistance, opposition and the hunger for transcendence. For example, Robert Owen's 'new model community' of workers in New Lanark was an experiment in industrial managerial paternalism pioneered against the example of pure capitalism which asserted that the cash nexus is the sole link that binds employers to the workforce. Pure capitalism also provoked reaction from the labour force to time-driven schedules of work organized around the cash nexus. Similarly, trade unionists adopted the doctrine of self-help articulated by muscular Christianity to campaign for the reduction of work hours and the introduction of paid holiday time. Working-class resistance was also evident in the development of leisure and sports forms that challenged the donatory views of leisure advocated by the rational recreation movement (Dunning and Sheard, 1979; Gray, 1981). These forms were used to convey 'the whole way of life' of a social stratum against regimes of power that marginalized, neglected, ignored or consciously belittled them.[3] The representation of leisure and sport here plays an overt political role in the contest between groups over scarce resources.

Some historians contend that leisure had no meaningful existence before industrialization (Bailey, 1987; Cunningham, 1980). By this they mean that the association of leisure with reward for work and programmes of self-improvement were only popularized with the Industrial Revolution. Other commentators maintain that the constituents of contemporary society were laid down between the 1880s and the 1930s. Over this period, a system of mass education was devised and implemented, the conventions of the mass media were instilled into everyday life and the concepts of national and global consumer markets were popularized by corporations (Cross, 1988; Kammen, 1999). Hall et al. (1985), working in a very different tradition of social and cultural theory, argue that it was also at this 'moment' that the regulative mechanisms of the modern state were installed throughout civil society. It was only when the ideas of national-popular systems of regulation, and corresponding national and global markets of interest and behaviour, become generalized, that the concept of leisure, in its modern form, was normalized in the West.

What emerges most trenchantly from this anthropological and historical work is that leisure is socially and culturally *constructed* and communicated through *representation*. The set of desires and needs that allow contemporary social psychologists to speak of 'intrinsic motivation', is historically produced and reveals significant cross-cultural variation. To present leisure as a system of representation therefore implies the subsidiary questions of *what* is being represented, *who* is representing and *how* representations have changed?

The representation of smoking as a leisure pursuit

Before coming to the issue of how representation might be approached theoretically, it will be helpful to review a concrete example of how the representation of a leisure form has been repositioned in popular culture. The case of tobacco smoking provides some fascinating material. In traditional Native American society tobacco was used as a hallucigen in shamanistic rituals. It was first introduced into Europe in the fifteenth and sixteenth centuries by explorers returning home from the New World. Hughes's (2003) incisive and authoritative study demonstrates the astonishing range of representations associated with the practice. For example, it was linked with high fashion, sophistication, modernity, science, individuality and collective solidarity. Remarkably, it was also believed to be a cure for both the plague and cancer.

Yet from the first, it had powerful detractors. In 1604, King James I published a treatise against smoking entitled 'A Counterblast to Tobacco'. In the seventeenth century, Michael Feodorvich, the first Romanov Czar, declared smoking to be a deadly sin and introduced a variety of punishments for the possession of tobacco. During the same period, Pope Clement VIII threatened excommunication for anyone found smoking tobacco in a holy place. However, these measures to restrain the practice proved fruitless. By the twentieth century tobacco smoking had developed into a mass leisure practice in Western society. Its use was regarded to be a matter of individual conscience. Risks associated with smoking and secondary or 'passive' smoke inhalation were scarcely understood.

Following the US Surgeon General's Report in 1964, which reported that an irrefutable causal link exists between tobacco smoking and many avoidable diseases, such as lung cancer, cardiovascular degeneration and respiratory disease, the status of smoking as a leisure activity was redefined. Gradually, it became subject to progressive layers of stigmatization, at first from anti-smoking consumer groups, and then the medical profession and officials of the state. Although there are significant eddies and flows in the process, the current of change is strikingly consistent. In 1965 the Federal Cigarette Labelling and Advertising Act required the Surgeon

General to print health warning's on cigarette packets. In the same year the UK banned cigarette advertising on television. The US took the same course of action in 1970. In 1971 the UK government achieved a voluntary agreement for tobacco companies to print health warnings on cigarette packets. In 1973 US federal law introduced mandatory nonsmoking compartments on domestic flights. In 1987, the law was extended to apply a complete ban on airline flights of less than two hours. In 1990 US law went further by banning tobacco smoking on interstate buses and all domestic flights with a duration of less than six hours. In 1992 the US Supreme Court ruled that warning labels on cigarette packets do not protect US companies from lawsuits. In 1999 the UK hospitality industry introduced a Voluntary Charter on Smoking in Public Places which advised pubs and restaurants to introduce signs informing customers of the health risks associated with smoking. In 2000 a US jury awarded punitive damages of nearly US$145 billion against five US tobacco companies after a class action in the state of Florida. In 2003 the advertising and promotion of tobacco was banned in the UK, and New York followed Delaware and California in introducing a state-wide ban in smoking in public places. In 2004, Ireland followed suit. At the time of writing, the majority of US states and member nations of the European Community have not followed the states of Delaware, California and New York in the US, and Ireland in the EC, in introducing a ban on smoking in public places. However, given the historical trend, the probability is that most will follow suit in the near future.

The shifts in the status of smoking as a leisure pursuit reflect a complex process of representational positioning and repositioning that has occurred over several decades. For most of the twentieth century, the cachet given to smoking as a leisure practice was reinforced by cigarette manufacturers who used advertising to weave a web of positive connotations ranging from personal sophistication to subcultural or class solidarity. This was gradually challenged by anti-smoking groups that labelled smoking as an anti-social activity, the medical profession who identified causal links between smoking and illness, and state officials who became persuaded that the financial and social costs of smoking-related illness were no longer acceptable. The traditional defence of the practice is that smoking is a matter of individual conscience. This has been attacked on two fronts by a series of cogent moral arguments having to do with the hazards of tobacco use. In the first place, it is contested that a primary condition of mature citizenship is *care for the self*. Smokers are represented as infringing this prime responsibility by engaging in a leisure practice that poses serious risks to their health. The second series of moral representations is more subtle. It addresses the citizen's responsibilities in respect of *care for the other*. Medical professionals, progressive journalists and moralists have represented smoking as a risk to the unborn child. Similarly, passive smoking is held to expose the smoker's family and social networks to peril. By representing the threats to health faced by others who associate with smokers, the traditional defence of smoking as a leisure practice is seriously compromised. The argument redefines the practice from being viewed as a mere matter of individual conscience, to the moral responsibility of individual conscience with respect to others.

Interpellation, ideology and hegemony

What does it mean to claim that a leisure practice has been *repositioned* so that its significance and value exchanges a positive connotation for a negative one? Plainly this has occurred in the case of tobacco smoking. The question is *how* has it occurred? Or, more precisely, what are the structural stimuli that transform leisure practice from overwhelmingly positive to largely negative connotations? To answer this question it is necessary to begin with a consideration of the mechanisms that led to the representation of the practice as positive in the first place.

A useful entrée into the subject of representation is the work of Stuart Hall. Although I have reservations about some aspects of Hall's approach, it constitutes a very cogent model of how representation functions to allocate social, economic and cultural resources and position behaviour (Rojek, 2003). The fulcrum of Hall's work is problems of culture. However, several of his former students have extended his perspective by focusing upon leisure as an element of culture in their investigations of youth subcultural play forms, feminist identities and class and leisure (Hebdige, 1979; McRobbie, 1993a, 1993b; Clarke and Critcher, 1985). In all of this work, representation is central.

To understand why, it is necessary to examine the concepts of interpellation, ideology and hegemony. Hall (1985, 1986) borrows the concept of interpellation from the French structuralist philosopher Louis Althusser. The concept refers to the process by which subjectivity is 'hailed' or 'summoned' by the ideological and repressive state apparatus in society. Through schools, welfare organizations, hospitals, the police, the judiciary and the mass media, particular constructions of normality and respectability are assembled. This is partly a *directed* process in the sense that it is designed to fulfil the political objectives of ascendant groups to reinforce their privileged position. Crucially, it also reflects the naturalistic fallacy that what is good for the goose is good for the gander. In other words, the values and pack-drill that have proved their worth for ascendant groups are judged to have a corresponding beneficial effect when applied to other strata, providing the economic, racial, religious and cultural preconditions of being deserving obtain. Interpellation therefore often conflates control with progress. A good example in leisure studies is the rational recreation movement which, after the 1870s, sought to model the leisure practice of subordinate strata as part of a wider project of social improvement.

Interpellation is crucial in formatting identity. It uses various materials drawn from folklore, myth, custom, historical events, religion and political fiat to establish lines of social inclusion and exclusion. In positioning people in relation to other resources, including other people, interpellation establishes privileges in the struggle with scarcity. A common error in using the concept is that it is portrayed as erasing differences. Actually, interpellation *establishes* differences by constructing a hierarchy of rights with respect to scarce resources.

The representation of privileges is always bound up with an ideology. An ideology may be defined as a regime of representations that justify the ladder of privileges and the distribution of resources within the human group. Ideology operates most effectively when the values and principles that it perpetuates are treated naturalistically as 'common sense'. Since some groups occupy disadvantaged positions with respect to scarce resources, they will seek to rectify the situation by resisting ideology. This involves the use of strategies of counter-interpellation that challenge 'common sense' views of privilege and natural order. For example, the right of the richest social strata to have greater access to leisure resources may be opposed by the proposition that it is unjust because it ultimately depends upon forcibly limiting less advantaged strata from having access to the same resources. The concept of hegemony is designed to capture the process of reproducing ideology as the paramount social reality over a given territory. Hegemony involves the 'voluntary' engineering of popular consent. It frames the terrain in which the power contest over scarce resources is fought. Hegemony ultimately rests on the legitimate use of forces of physical coercion most notably through the mobilization of the police and armed forces. However, typically this is implemented only as a last resort. The habitual engineering of consent is conducted by predisposing debate and struggle to follow particular trajectories which do not destabilize the system. Hall's (1982, 1984, 1989) work concentrated mainly on the role of what he termed 'the repressive/interventionist state' and the mass media in hailing or summoning specific types of civil subjectivity to achieve hegemonic control. Notwithstanding the focus on British experience, most of the analytical principles and processes of interpellation that he outlines are transferable to other Western societies.

He identified the period between the 1880s and the 1920s as the time-span in which the modern nation-state in Britain was formed.[4] At this 'moment', the pivotal modern institutions of the state were created, notably the three party system, the commitment to public welfare provision and the development of a corporatist partnership between the state, industry and organized labour. Drawing freely on the terminology coined by Antonio Gramsci, Hall referred to this formation as 'a complex unity'. By this term he meant an enduring hegemonic compact that, by and large, was successful in assimilating conflict and dissent. It did so by applying devices like patriotism and welfarism to instil pride and a sense of family among civil subjects of the Nation and Empire. Although Hall does not refer to it in detail, sport and leisure performed a significant role in galvanizing emotions of National and Imperial pride and belonging. National sporting contests, parades, youth gymnastics and drill, processions, exhibitions and festivals were organized to solidify consensus (Springhall, 1977; Mangan, 1992). Indeed, the growth of paid holiday time and the shortening of the working week were enunciated by the central corporate players of business, the state and organized labour, as unequivocal evidence of the progressive character of the social and political system. A distinctive feature of this system was held to be the 'automatic' delivery of unprecedented levels of prosperity and more free time than had been known in the days of previous generations in industrial society. Between the 1880s and 1920s, the expansion of publicly funded leisure at the levels of both the municipality and the nation-state, was portrayed not as the outcome of a struggle between groups over scarce resources, notably employers, the state and labour, but as technical proof of the superiority of the corporatist version of capitalism over the unreformed market and of course, fascism and communism. Corporate parlance in Britain during most of the 1920s represented the system as progressively delivering the goods. *Ipso facto*, projects designed to change the system by introducing new regimes of resource allocation and distribution of prestige were tacitly bracketed with unrest and sedition.

The 1928 stock market collapse modified this situation, most notably by demonstrating the transparent failure of the system to deliver the good life. This catastrophe produced an eruption of pressures to reform corporatism, the most radical of which was the modern communist movement. Among its aims was the utopian commitment articulated by Marx (1969) in his discussion of the distinction between the realm of necessity and the realm of freedom by abolishing the division between work and leisure and constructing a society of mutuality and reciprocity capable of supporting the free and full development of all individuals. The war against fascism diverted these energies from the attempt to seize control of the state. However, their consequences were palpable in the post-war settlement of the welfare state. All citizens were recognized as possessing entitlements for education, health care and pensions. But underlying this provision was the notion of the respectable citizen. Post-war respectability was understood to be represented by a number of characteristics, the most notable of which were commitment to paid employment, civil obedience, heterosexual marriage, the nuclear family and leisure and recreation pursuits that enhanced community integration and self-improvement.

According to Hall et al. (1978), by the early 1960s a number of factors combined to destabilize this long-standing compact in British life. A succession of balance of payments crises exposed the underlying weaknesses in the economy and created demands for modernization. To this was added a major influx of Asian and Afro-Caribbean migrants from the former British Empire who challenged the aspect of white monocultural prominence in hegemony. In addition, emerging youth subcultures and the permissive society flagrantly attacked the notion of respectability that underpinned the welfare state. This was evident in many areas of ordinary everyday life, most notably in the development of more relaxed attitudes to homosexuality and heterosexual relationships outside marriage, greater tolerance for lifestyles built around hedonism and self-expression over the work ethic and docile compliance and expansion of subterranean drug cultures which opposed the values of straight society. In Hall's view, the threat of dissensus precipitated the drift towards 'the law and order society' that climaxed in Margaret Thatcher's version of 'authoritarian populism'. The latter is investigated as a type of reactionary politics which is anti-permissive, attempts to reassert patriotic dogma, deplores welfare dependence and sanctifies self-reliance. In Hall's analysis, this idealization of the civil subject was prosecuted along many fronts including legal measures like Clause 28 that attacked homosexual rights, the extension of police powers, the introduction of a core curriculum and audit trail in schooling and universities, the intensification of means testing in the allocation of resources from the welfare state and, of course, the manipulation of the mass media.

Encoding and decoding

Hall's (1973, 1982, 1993) work identifies the mass media in contemporary society as pivotal in public opinion formation. It is the decisive means of representation in public life, and as such, establishes the parameters of public paramount reality. His encoding/decoding model challenged the prosaic assumptions of mass communications theory by insisting that the media do not *reflect* social reality rather they *construct* representations of it in particular directions. The news and entertainment broadcasts of television and radio are coded to elicit 'preferred readings' among the populace. Encoding has powerful tendencies to represent social reality in ways that confirm hegemony. Hall suggests that this is a deliberate objective of ascendant groups, but he also holds that it is the naturalistic reflection of their *habitus*. This articulation carries greater cultural weight because the media has a sympathetic relationship to power. It tends to favour a 'consensus' view of society and the news, and it overwhelmingly reflects the values of the centre-ground.

Hall does not pose the question, but it is evident from his discussion that subjects are especially susceptible to media interpellation in leisure time, since it is here that individuals think of voluntarism as being most concentrated. Watching the morning or evening news, reading newspapers or listening to the radio in the home, are crucial junctures in which our common understanding of social reality is consciously and subconsciously formatted. Mass society theorists argued a similar case in the 1950s, especially with respect to the alleged manipulative effects of advertising and television (Packard, 1957; Stein et al. 1960). However, where these theorists end up positing a type of conspiracy theory involving avaricious corporations, Hall sees political manipulation as an ordinary feature of creating civil subjectivity that has its roots in the formation of the modern nation-state.

While the weight of his analysis is on the power of the media to put a particular ideological gloss on social reality, his concept of decoding is designed to demonstrate that the grip of ideology can be broken and, by extension, that a form of emancipatory politics is viable. As Hall puts it:

> I used ideology as that which cuts into the infinite semiosis of language. Language is pure textuality, but ideology wants to make a particular meaning ... it's the point where power cuts into discourse, where power overcuts knowledge and discourse; at that point you get a cut, you get a stoppage, you get a suture, you get an overdetermination. The meaning constructed by that cut into language is never permanent, because the next sentence will take it back, will open the semiosis again. And it can't fix it, but ideology is an attempt to fix it. (Hall, 1993: 263–4)

Hall's approach may be criticized for overstating the role of the media in constructing a public perspective on paramount reality that favours consensus. Ethnographic studies of working-class leisure practice richly illustrates mass scepticism about the impartiality of the media, and the importance of irony and ridicule in creating cultures of resistance (Willis, 1977, 1978; Blackshaw 2003). Similarly, Steedman (1986: 6) and Johnson (1996: 103–4) both warn of the danger of allowing structuralist approaches to culture to erase subjective aspects of practice. Hall's (1992, 1995) own work on race in the 1990s exists in some tension with the position that he established on the media in the 1970s and 1980s. For it demonstrates the vitality and inventiveness of marginalized cultures in challenging the codes of paramount reality.

As with Althusser and Gramsci, his work also shows a bias toward over-egging the significance of the state apparatus in interpellation. Perhaps this is a general fault of Western European approaches to leisure and culture. Certainly, North American commentators have been more alive to the role of multinational corporations in 'hailing' or 'summoning forth' particular types of subjectivity. Here the connection between advertising, marketing, branding and the construction of identity in consumer culture has been more vigorously explored (Ewen, 1976; Goffman, 1967; Ritzer, 1992). The result is a better appreciation of the role of multinational corporations in the regulation of leisure choice and practice.

In general, Hall's work is more tenable as a social critique of the repressive/ interventionist state in capitalist society. His view of a feasible alternative is somewhat woolly. In so far as it exists at all, it seems to point to the *strengthening* of state powers in respect of market regulation, policies of anti-racism, the creation of genuine gender equality and the expansion of public investment (Giddens, 2000: 28). The failure of Hall to articulate a feasible social and economic alternative to capitalism greatly weakens the force of his argument. It is one thing to maintain that choice, freedom and self determination in culture and leisure always occur in a context in which dominant groups encode public notions of paramount reality. This is the context in which our struggles for subjectivity and resistance occur. But the resultant question is how can encoding processes be rendered more transparent and amenable to popular interest in a context dominated by multiculturalism and globalization? Beyond suggesting the extension of state powers based upon the revival of a version of socialist humanism, Hall has little to say on this crucial matter.

Markers and theming

Under globalization the complexities of encoding and decoding are compounded. Leisure forms might be thought of as being represented by markers. MacCannell (1989) pioneered the analysis of markers in his study of tourism. Drawing on symbolic interactionism and semiotics, he argued that tourist sights are represented to us through a system of signs. Usually the first contact a tourist has with a sight is not the object or space itself, but representations thereof. A marker signifies the tourist sight to sightseers. It is culturally mediated through various channels of the mass media such as film, television, literature and tourist brochures and also through everyday visual/oral culture (travellers' tales, lectures, personal photographs/videos). The relationship between a marker and a sight may seem to be a very simple thing. For example, a photograph of Nelson's column in Trafalgar Square automatically represents London to the sightseer. However, a moment's reflection reveals the relationship between a marker and a sight to be more complex, abounding in interpretive difficulties. For markers, like signs, do not carry unitary meanings. For some viewers a photo of Nelson's column may signify British heroism, historical pageantry and national resolve. Others might see in the same photo, British imperialism, a perfidious history of violence, intrigue and plunder and national arrogance. This raises many analytical challenges in the study of the meaning of leisure/tourist space and practice.

To begin with, decoding requires us to empathize with cultural, subcultural and racial data that may be quite alien and, at first acquaintance, indecipherable. Nor is it merely a matter of sifting through multiple and often contrary meanings, trying to put ourselves in the shoes of others who have a different orientation and set of values, and trying to crack conventions and systems of encoding with which we are unfamiliar. Under the condition of globalization, markers *condense* meanings so that representation is overdetermined, making it tricky to affirm an authoritative reading to the sight or practice.

The context of multiculturalism and globalization presents special challenges to the architecture of tourist and leisure space. Authoritative meanings can no longer be asserted or counted upon.

Gottdiener's (1997) concept of theming demonstrates how leisure and tourist spaces are endowed with symbolic narrative content that predisposes inhabitants to pursue preferred scripts of behaviour. His work illustrates the limits of linear narratives and the tendency for overdetermination to destabilize authoritative meaning. In the nineteenth century, lavish ornamentation was used in the design and construction of shopping arcades to symbolize consumer refinement and luxury. Similarly, in the years following the Second World War, theme parks were equipped with motifs designed to make certain preferences of leisure choice idiomatic in consumer culture. A case in point, analysed by Gottdiener (1997: 111–14), is Disneyland. This space carries the overwhelming message that leisure is freedom. But the motifs that it deploys to articulate this message are almost exclusively chauvinistic. From the sanitized, sentimental version of Main Street USA that the visitor first encounters in the park, to the themed fantasy spaces of Adventureland replete with references to Tom Sawyer and Huckleberry Finn; Fantasyland with its constant, knowing nods to characters and narratives in the Disney animation films; Frontierland with echoes of the life and times of Davy Crockett, Jim Bowie, Buffalo Bill and the myths of the Wild West; and Tomorrowland, with its crime-free, death-proof vision of the future, Disneyland offers a commercially cauterized version of the American dream as the template for world society.

Much of Gottdiener's (1997) discussion is devoted to demonstrating the tendency of boldly themed leisure and tourist environments to deconstruct into a mélange of meanings through successive consumer use and rivalry between leisure/tourist providers. For example, he analyses the Las Vegas strip as a cornucopia of representation mixing architectural motifs of high culture with low culture references to tropical paradise, the Wild West, Piratical formations (1997: 144–7). Nostalgia and Arabian Fantasy. For Gottdiener, the abundance of these motifs on the strip indeed make it difficult to attribute a dominant code or meaning. But perhaps this ignores the one authoritative function behind all of the attractions on the Las Vegas strip: making money. The strip is an allotment of calculated fantasies designed to induce conspicuous consumption. The rather glittery representation of the Egyptian sphinx and pyramids at the Luxor Hotel and feudal fairyland of the Excalibur Casino are designed to promote pharonical and Monarchical impulses of financial extravagance in the day-trippers, long-weekenders and vacation-break visitors.

Ritzer (2004), reflecting a similar conviction that ersatz architectural styles, designer values and consumer experiences are becoming normalized, submits that the unintentional effect of these endeavours is to neutralize processes of encoding and decoding. Leisure and consumer cultures that used to acknowledge and represent discretion and variety are being replaced by *the globalization of nothing*. Spaces of shopping, recreation and civic communal virtue such as metropolitan squares, are becoming indistinguishable. Echoing Auge's (1995) analysis of the proliferation of 'nonplaces' under 'supermodernity', Ritzer points to the standardization of representation around the themes of money and multinational control.

Conclusion

Questions of coding and theming have focused on the commodification and standardization of leisure. These issues have also posed the subject of resistance, but it has usually been examined in the context of the study of culture rather than Leisure Studies (Hall and Jefferson, 1976; Hall et al., 1978). By and large, students of leisure have tended to treat resistance and opposition in leisure as epiphenomena. Stebbins's (1992) celebrated distinction between serious and causal leisure provides a case in point. Serious leisure refers to activities that contain the notion of career development and usually involve the transfer of social capital to the community. Casual leisure practices are opportunistic, unplanned and pursue a desultory, unsystematic set of aims. Although Stebbins recognizes that causal forms are unavoidable in contemporary society, given the liquid nature of roles and norms, his preference is to encourage the proliferation of serious forms. Yet what this neglects is the solidification of casual forms into what might be called *alter-identities*. That is, the development of consistent leisure identities that cluster around values which oppose or invert serious types of leisure. Representations of casual forms in literature, film, popular music and other branches of the media often depict them as exciting, enlarging, and pointedly contrast them with the worthiness of serious forms.

The political dilemma of modern society is that it is attached to models and programmes of life that are binding and solid, but it produces conditions of experience that are plural and liquid. Liberal democracy and its alternatives face the difficulty of articulating ways of being in leisure practice that are not experienced by some sections of societies as traps from which they seek to escape (Rojek, 1993, 1995; Blackshaw and Crabbe, 2004). This should not be taken as a comment on the poverty of these political programmes. For many people they offer stability and direction. The trouble is that in conditions where diverse lifestyle options and opportunities are produced prolifically, they are unable to be universal.

Representations of leisure practice as fulfilling, satisfying and harmonistic generate counter identities. They are, so to speak, double-coded so that the very attributes that signify integration for some are defined by differently positioned individuals and groups to signify reaction. This is obscured in Stebbins's (1992) account, because it treats serious and casual forms as polarized forms and implies they go with contrasting identity types. What this ignores is the multiplicity of representations of leisure that proliferate in culture and the associated issue of double-coding. Viewed historically, it is quite clear that some leisure practices that are coded in a positive way are redefined negatively so that the original 'natural', 'common sense' associations are inverted. The case of tobacco smoking examined above, provides a good example. By the same token, leisure practices that are generally represented negatively often persist despite representations designed to reduce or eliminate them. Among individuals and groups positioned in reaction to these representations, these leisure practices may become normalized and symbolize calculated detachment from the values of the straight leisure society. The recreational use of illegal drugs, and the subcultures attached to them, provide a good example.

Most research suggests that adolescent illicit drug use in Europe, and especially the UK, peaked in the 1990s (ESPAD, 1997, 2001). Despite some recent evidence of a small contraction in drug use, the percentage of regular users remains high. Goddard and Higgins (1999) estimate that around 20 per cent of mid-adolescents in the UK are regular users of Class A drugs, with higher rates of 28 per cent in the North of England. Research among British university students suggests that up to 60 per cent have some drug experience (Makhoul et al., 1998; Webb et al., 1996; Ashton and Kamali, 1995). Rates of use among British adolescents are now comparable with rates among American high school students (NHSDA, 1999). Despite the attempts by state medical and police authorities to stigmatize Class A drugs like cocaine, ecstacy and heroin as addictive and life-threatening, the evidence is that they continue to be consumed widely, especially among participants in the club scene.

'Regular use' is to some extent, an elastic concept. Among the 60 per cent of British university students who have tried Class A drugs, many do so only as part of the weekend or midweek clubbing scene. Generally speaking, young people seem to have strong anti-drug use beliefs in early adolescence, but this does not prevent them from using drugs recreationally with their peers in mid-adolescence and in the often difficult years, before securing stable paid employment (Parker et al., 1998).

Researchers submit that there has been considerable cultural accommodation to drug use among young people in the last 30 years, especially with respect to cannabis. The use of drugs among social networks is widespread. Even where members of networks are not regular users, levels of condemnation and disapproval of so-called 'sensible' drug use are negligible. Parker et al. (2002) propose that it is legitimate to apply a 'normalization' thesis in relation to sensible drug-use. Their work concludes that many young people are able to combine participation in higher education and the labour market with significant drug use in leisure. The normalization of the recreational use of drugs suggests high levels of calculation and flexibility among young people in relation to the representation of illegal leisure practice. Instead of a polarized model between users and non-users, patterns of *strategic use* are probably closer to reality.

The example of the recreational use of illicit drugs illustrates how double-coding operates in the strategic application of leisure practice and lends support to commentators who reject the proposition of unity of identity in leisure practice

(Blackshaw and Crabbe, 2004; Rojek, 2000, 2005). Individuals are quite capable of stigmatizing drug use in public in the morning, while buying and taking illicit drugs in the afternoon. To reemphasize one of the central points made by labelling theory in cultural criminology, the practice of individuals is heavily conditioned by the perception of the social reaction to given trajectories of behaviour. In examining the question of representation in leisure practice therefore, care should be taken to establish accurately the position of the individual not only in relation to access of scarce economic resources but also in respect of regulative cultures. We do not act freely in our leisure according to our own lights of choice and self-determination. Rather we are positioned in economic and cultural fields which influence our access to scarce resources. Our trajectories of leisure practice are conditioned not only by the distribution of these resources, but also by their representation, theming and coding.

Notes

1. Cheek and Burch draw heavily on the social systems approach developed by Talcott Parsons.
2. E. P. Thompson applies a Marxist perspective to the question of industrialization and leisure. This can be contrasted with Durkheimian and Weberian approaches (see Rojek, 1985: 34–74).
3. The emphasis upon leisure as 'a whole way of life' is associated with the work of Raymond Williams (1958, 1961). This 'culturalist' approach was criticized by Hall (1980) who argued that it was too ethnocentric and atheoretical.
4. Contrasting views of the origins of the modern British nation-state can be found in Colley (1992) and Kumar (2003).

Bibliography

Ashton, C. and Kamali, F. (1995) 'Personality, Lifestyles, Alcohol and Drug Consumption in a Sample of British Medical Students', *Medical Education*, 29: 187–92.
Auge, M. (1995) *Non-places*, London, Lawrence & Wishart.
Bailey, P. (1987) *Leisure and Class in Victorian England*, London, Methuen.
Blackshaw, T. (2003) *Leisurelife*, London, Routledge.
Blackshaw, T. and Crabbe, T. (2004) *New Perspectives on Sport and 'Deviance'*, London, Routledge.
Bourdieu, P. (1984) *Distinction*, London, Routledge.
Cheek, N. and Burch, W. (1976) *The Social Organization of Leisure in Human Society*, New York, Harper & Row.
Chick, G. (ed.) (1991) *Play and Culture*, Champaign, IL, Human Kinetics.
Chick, G. (2000) 'Opportunities for Cross-Cultural Comparative Research on Leisure', *Leisure Science* 22: 79–91.
Chick, G. (2002) 'Cultural Consonance in a Mexican Festival System', *Field Methods* 14: 26–45.
Clarke, J. and Critcher, C. (1985) *The Devil Makes Work*, London, Macmillan.
Colley, L. (1992) *Britons: Forging the Nation 1707–1837*, London, Pimlico.
Csikszentmihalyi, M. (1975) *Beyond Boredom and Anxiety*, San Francisco, Jossey Bass.
Cross, G. (1988) *Time and Money*, London, Routledge.
Cunningham, H. (1980) *Leisure in the Industrial Revolution*, London, Croom Helm.

Dunning, E. and Sheard, K. (1979) *Barbarians, Gentlemen and Players*, Oxford, Martin Robertson.

Durkheim, E. (1965) *The Elementary Forms of Religious Life*, New York, Free Press.

ESPAD (1997) *Alcohol and Other Drug Use Among Students in 26 European Countries*, Stockholm: Swedish Council on Alcohol and Other Drugs.

ESPAD (2001) *Alcohol and Other Drug Use Among Students in 30 European Countries*, Stockholm: Swedish Council on Alcohol and Drugs.

Ewen, S. (1976) *The Captains of Consciousness*, New York, McGraw-Hill.

Giddens, A. (2000) *The Third Way and Its Critics*, Cambridge, Polity Press.

Goddard, E. and Higgins, V. (1999) *Smoking, Drinking and Drug Use Among Young Teenagers in 1998*, London, Office of National Statistics.

Goffman, E. (1967) *Interaction Ritual*, New York, Pantheon.

Gottdiener, M. (1997) *The Theming of America*, Boulder, CO, Westview.

Gray, R. (1981) *The Aristocracy of Labour in Nineteenth Century Britain*, London, Macmillan.

Hall, S. (1973) 'Encoding and Decoding in Television Discourse', Stencilled Occasional Paper, Birmingham Centre for Contemporary Cultural Studies.

Hall, S. (1980) 'Cultural Studies: Two Paradigms', *Media, Culture & Society* 2: 57–92.

Hall, S. (1982) 'The Rediscovery of "Ideology"', in M. Gurevitch, T. Curran and J. Woollacott (eds) *Culture, Society and the Media*, London, Methuen, pp. 56–90.

Hall, S. (1984) 'The Rise of the Representative/Interventionist State', in G. McLennan, D. Held and S. Hall (eds) *State and Society in Contemporary Britain*, Cambridge, Polity Press, pp. 7–49.

Hall, S. (1985) 'Signification, Representation, Ideology: Althusser and the Post-structuralist Debates', *Critical Studies in Mass Communication* 2(2): 91–114.

Hall, S. (1986) 'The Problem of Ideology: Marxism Without Guarantees', *Journal of Communication Inquiry* 10(2): 5–27.

Hall, S. (1989) 'Authoritarian Populism', in B. Jessop et al. (eds) *Thatcherism: A Tale of Two Nations*, Cambridge, Polity Press, pp. 97–107.

Hall, S. (1992) 'The West and the Rest: Discourses and Power', in S. Hall and B. Gieben (eds) *Formations of Modernity*, Cambridge, Polity Press, pp. 275–332.

Hall, S. (1993) 'Reflections Upon the Encoding/Decoding Model: An Interview with Stuart Hall', in J. Cruz and J. Lewis (eds) *Viewing, Reading, Listening: Audiences and Cultural Reception*, Boulder, CO, Westview, pp. 253–74.

Hall, S. (1995) 'Fantasy, Identity, Politics', in E. Carter, J. Donald and J. Squires (eds) *Cultural Remix*, London, Lawrence & Wishart, pp. 63–9.

Hall, S. and Jefferson, T. (eds) (1976) *Resistance Through Rituals*, London, Hutchinson.

Hall, S., Critcher, C., Jefferson, T. and Roberts, B. (1978) *Policing the Crisis*, London, Macmillan.

Hall, S., Langan, M. and Schwarz, B. (eds) (1985) *Crises in the British State 1880–1930*, London, Hutchinson.

Hebdige, D. (1979) *Subculture*, London, Routledge.

Hughes, J. (2003) *Learning to Smoke*, Cambridge, Cambridge University Press.

Johnson, R. (1996) 'What is Cultural Studies Anyway?' in J. Storey (ed.), *What Is Cultural Studies*, London, Edward Arnold.

Kammen, M. (1999) *American Culture, American Tastes*, New York, Basic Books.

Katz, J. (1988) *Seductions of Crime*, New York, Basic Books.

Knauft, B. (1987) 'Reconsidering Violence in Simple Human Societies', *Current Anthropology* 28(4): 457–82.

Kumar, K. (2003) *The Making of English National Identity*, Cambridge, Cambridge University Press.

MacCannell, D. (1989) *The Tourist* (2nd edn), London, Macmillan.

McRobbie, A. (1993a) 'Feminism, Postmodernism and the Real Me', *Theory, Culture & Society* 11(4): 127–42.

McRobbie, A. (1993b) 'Shut Up and Dance: Youth, Culture and Changing Modes of Femininity', *Cultural Studies* 7(3): 406–26.

Makhoul, M., Yates, W. and Wolfson, S. (1998) 'A Survey of Substance Use at a UK University: Prevalence of Use and Views of Students', *Journal of Substance Misuse* 3: 119–24.

Mangan, J. (1992) 'Britain's Chief Spiritual Export', in J. Mangan (ed.) *The Cultural Bond: Sport, Empire, Society*, London, Frank Cass.

Marx, K. (1969) *Capital* Volume 1, London, Lawrence & Wishart.

Neulinger, J. (1981) *To Leisure: An Introduction*, Boston, Allyn & Bacon.

NHSDA (1999) *The 1998 National Household Survey on Drug Abuse*, Department of Health and Human Services.

Packard, V. (1957) *The Hidden Persuaders*, New York, Mackay & Co.

Parker, H., Aldridge, J. and Measham, F. (1998) *Illegal Leisure: The Normalization of Adolescent Drug Use*, London, Routledge.

Parker, H., Williams, L. and Aldridge, J. (2002) 'The Normalization of "Sensible" Recreational Drug Use', *Sociology* 36(4): 941–64.

Ritzer, G. (1992) *The McDonaldization of Society*, Thousand Oaks, Pine Forge.

Ritzer, G. (2004) *The Globalization of Nothing*, Thousand Oaks, Pine Forge.

Rojek, C. (1985) *Capitalism and Leisure Theory*, London, Tavistock.

Rojek, C. (1993) *Ways of Escape*, Basingstoke, Macmillan.

Rojek, C. (1995) *Decentring Leisure*, London, Sage.

Rojek, C. (2000) *Leisure and Culture*, Basingstoke, Macmillan.

Rojek, C. (2003) *Stuart Hall*, Cambridge, Polity Press.

Rojek, C. (2005) *Leisure Theory*, Basingstoke, Palgrave Macmillan.

Springhall, J. (1977) *Youth, Empire and Society*, London, Croom Helm.

Stebbins, R. (1992) *Amateurs, Professionals and Serious Leisure*, Montreal, McGill University Press.

Steedman, C. (1986) *Landscape for a Good Woman*, London, Virago.

Stein, M., Vidich, A. and White, D. (1960) *Identity and Crisis*, Glencoe, Free Press.

Thompson, E. P. (1967) 'Time, Work-Discipline and Industrial Capitalism', *Past and Present* 38: 56–97.

Webb, E., Ashton, C., Kelly, D. and Kamali, F. (1996) 'Alcohol and Drug Use in UK University Students', *Lancet* 348: 922–5.

Williams, R. (1958) *Culture and Society*, London, Chatto & Windus.

Williams, R. (1961) *The Long Revolution*, London, Chatto & Windus.

Willis, P. (1977) *Learning to Labour*, London, Saxon House.

Willis, P. (1978) *Profane Culture*, London, Routledge & Kegan Paul.

29
Identity

Chris Rojek

How should we approach the relationship between leisure practice and identity? That the relationship exists is a veritable cliché of Leisure Studies. Those who enter the field for the first time encounter a plethora of descriptive studies which propose that leisure practice crystallizes leisure identity in sport subcultures (Pearson, 1979; McQuarrie and Jackson, 1996), volunteering and mutual aid groups (Bishop and Hoggett, 1986; Cuskelly and Harrington, 1997), amateur hobbyists (Lavanda, 1988; Fine, 1989), celebrity cults (Jenkins, 1992; Barbas, 2001) and much else besides. But when one moves from the level of description to that of explanation, the picture becomes more indefinite. Social psychological approaches portray leisure activity as an expression of individual preference, which presupposes that identity *precedes* choice (Neulinger, 1981; Csikszentmihalyi, 1975). Yet the details of the evolution and dynamics of identity formation are typically unparticularized. These accounts depend upon taken-for-granted assumptions about the uniformity of socialization and the unity of identity that rapidly disintegrate under examination. The questions are: How is identity and choice in leisure related to power? What accounts for differences in leisure trajectories? In what ways is personal choice patterned?

Conversely, sociological approaches typically address individual preference and leisure choice as the reflection of the resources of context. Thus, Gary Fine (1989) in his study of the leisure practices of amateur mycologists (students of fungi) assigns prominence to the *knowledge* and *sociability* provided by Mycological Societies, which rather begs the question of why only *some* people are drawn to mycology in the first place. If the argument is that we are channelled into leisure activities by various social forces, the relationship between choice and structure requires much greater elucidation. Invoking the influences of class, gender, race, status and other structural influences helps us to acknowledge that leisure choice and practice is *relational*. But the dynamics between choice, structure and identity are nuanced and this raises the question of how we might methodologically study them.

The situated actor: embodiment and emplacement

In considering the relationship between identity and leisure practice it is preferable to start from the position of the *situated actor*. This is more realistic than either functionalist approaches that assume individual freedom, choice and self-determination (Parker, 1983) or systems approaches which relate individual behaviour to structural constraint and tradition (Cheek and Burch, 1976). The two most salient features in respect of situation are *embodiment* and *emplacement*.

Embodiment, refers to the obvious but peculiarly neglected fact, that leisure actors are always and already embodied and that the biological fate of the body is to age and die. By insisting on the pivotal importance of the body, social analysis aims to highlight questions of sensuality and vulnerability, partly as a counter to other approaches that fasten upon the state of mind or rational choices of actors. This accent owes much to feminist contributions to identity and power. However, Heidegger's (1962, 1977) philosophy of phenomenology is also important. While it is valid to criticize the masculinist assumptions in Heidegger's approach, his insistence that sensual experience is pivotal in the human experience of being-in-the-world challenges approaches that over-pronounce the significance of state-of-mind and rational-choice theories. Heidegger's perspective portrays being-in-the-world as a condition that is intrinsically frustrating since the satisfaction of our sensual needs are dependent upon others and, as such, are subject to regular conflict, interruption and rejection. The condition of embodiment means that pleasure and satisfaction must have evanescent, fleeting qualities. Leisure itself cannot be regarded as a self-sustaining object in life, since the convergence between desire and satisfaction is transitory. Of course, differentials in power, especially in respect of class, gender, race and status obtain. These differentials position actors unequally in relation to scarcity. By the term scarcity is meant not merely unequal access to economic resources, but also cultural, honorific ones. Vulnerability, sensuality and the decline of the body are all understood to be universal facts of the human condition. However, the positioning of individuals in relation to scarcity is understood to be related to diversity and difference within class, gender, race and status formations.

Emplacement refers to the position that the individual occupies in relation to the conditions of abundance and scarcity. Abundance and scarcity are understood in terms of the relative distribution of economic, cultural and honorific resources. Emplacement focuses upon the positions of actors in relation to these resources and, as such, recognizes inequality in access to be fundamental in the human condition. It reinforces our awareness of the relational character of individual action with respect to leisure identity. In many accounts of leisure identity, the environment is understood to be external, stable and independent from the individual (Neulinger, 1981; Csikszentmihalyi, 1975; Cheek and Burch, 1976). In contrast, emplacement insists that environments both condition leisure practice and are conditioned by individual action. This is most apparent in leisure institutions. These predominate in the organized distribution of leisure resources. Examples include recreation centres, national parks, cinemas, theatres and concert halls, sporting arenas, swimming pools, bars, pubs and restaurants. Leisure institutions require actors to adopt positions that situate them in relation to the consumption of leisure resources. To put it differently, a corollary of emplacement is that actors must be conscious of institutionalized scripts that legitimate behaviour. Every society produces institutionalized scripts to regulate the behaviour of individuals in relation to the question of access to scarce resources.

Of course, these scripts do not determine behaviour. Around every role and every identity, *edgework* occurs. The concept of edgework was developed by Lyng (1990) to refer to the quest for self-actualization that motivates adventure leisure activities. Leisure forms like sky-diving, mountain climbing, motor racing and skiing test identity in potentially hazardous situations in order to extend experience beyond the conventional boundaries of everyday life. However, the concept can be applied more prosaically to refer to subjective boundary exploration at the edge of conventional roles and forms of identity. By testing our identities as fathers, mothers, responsible professionals, students and the like, we acquire the sense of moving into zones of excitement and sensual gratification that are suppressed in normal everyday life (Ferrell and Hamm, 1998).

A case in point is examined by Vaaranen and Wieloch (2002) in their study of adolescent male subcultures organized around speed racing in Finland. These subcultures powerfully express the organization of identity around motor cars, the quality of engines, music and heavy drinking. 'The Cruising Club' subculture in Helsinki consists of working-class males who mess around with reconditioned automobiles and engage in illegal street races. Drag Racers and Amcar devotees in Finland adopt a style of dress associated with 1950s music, oily jeans, leather jackets, metal key chains and letting both the hair and beard grow. The working-class adolescent male subcultures organized around speed racing are poorer and adopt a style of dress that symbolizes distance and their emplacement at the margin of social and economic resources. Typically, they wear sweat pants, white sports socks, modest leather shoes, a light cotton jacket and a baseball cap. Paul Willis (1977) famously agued that working-class schools produce an adolescent labour force destined for working-class jobs. Having a laugh, mocking teachers, being disruptive in class are analysed as forms of edgework resistance against a system that is understood to be heavily weighted against them. Vaaranen and Wieloch's (2002) study presents the subculture of the Cruising Club as an extension in leisure of the pattern of working-class school and domestic subcultures. Speed racing and breaking the law provides temporary excitement and a counter-identity to dead-end jobs. But they do not offer genuine respite from the destiny of the great majority of working-class children. They are temporary solutions that sometimes culminate in the death of street racers, but more typically end in capitulation to the inexorable regime of working-class reproduction.

Blackshaw's (2003) study of a male working-class leisure subculture in Leeds presents similar findings. Leisure practice in his 'lads' culture based in the pub and the nightclub, revolves around the celebration of autonomy, control and resistance by various rituals of excess including the consumption of alcohol and narcotics, unbuttoned language, flagrant sexual stereotyping, lewd gestures and acts of aggression. Leisure practice invests the world of work and class dependency with a momentary carnivalesque quality that reinforces subcultural solidarity. However, the sense of freedom that it generates is pulled back by the undertow of being unable to escape from wage labour and all of the dependencies on personal aspiration, time use and mobility that go with it. The leisure of the lads may appear to be selfish and purposeless, but this is anything but the case. The counter-identities it erects celebrate excess and conspicuous consumption to ritually impugn an unbreakable subordination to the treadmill of wage labour and obstructed life chances. Interestingly, Blackshaw's (2003) work demonstrates how the Friday night drink settles into a regular slot of nostalgia for the lads, as they progress through the lifecycle, and accept their fate by taking humdrum jobs and becoming responsible breadwinners. Solidarity persists, but excess is now celebrated through ritualized recapitulations of the young days when the lads were sowing their wild oats. The dominant motif in Blackshaw's (2003) ethnography is that of the fatal engulfment of excess, excitement and colour in leisure practice by the density of time-worn patterns of working-class reproduction and the drift towards respectability.

Embodiment and emplacement compel the student of leisure to explore identity in relation to *context* and *change*. While studies of working-class leisure practice point to general patterns of identity formation, within these patterns there is a constant struggle for subjectivity. For example, Goffman's (1967) work on gambling casinos, while not strictly speaking a study of leisure identities, nevertheless powerfully expresses how the dynamics of leisure practice provide opportunities for styling identity in ways that dramatically contrast with the responsibilities of serious life. Gambling casinos can be thought of as escape zones in which adults engage in institutionalized risk-taking and coquetry, but always in ways that seek to confer personal distinction. Play forms are calculated to dice with risk but also to represent competence. Gamblers who constantly hedge their bets, no less than those who lavishly throw caution to the wind, participate in fields of action that involve judgements about primary capacities and qualities of character. Participation is heavily gendered, with men having many more opportunities to play the field than women. Yet even within gender distinctions, Goffman is deeply sensitive to the play and variety of identity positions in relation to context and change. What emerges most powerfully from his discussion is that the self and its experiences provide no simple unity.

Post-structuralism

This idea that identity consists of no simple unity is central to the influential tradition of post-structuralism (Foucault, 1978, 1985, 1986, 1988; Probyn, 1993). Our intuitive view is that identity is independent and unique. The Cartesian view of 'Man' presents an independent, stable, integrated mind and body. The post-structuralist perspective breaks sharply with this position and offers a post-Cartesian model of human subjectivity. To begin with, it presents the concepts of independence and uniqueness as effects of historically shifting discourses, practices and technologies. Take the idea of leisure. From historical studies we know that leisure forms and practices have not been *constant* in human history. All human societies appear to have evolved play forms. But the concept of leisure as specialized time and space in which the individual experiences greater levels of freedom, choice and flexibility than elsewhere depends upon historical and social conditions in which philosophical and practical ideas of freedom, choice, personhood and flexibility emerge as meaningful ideas in respect of the human condition. This approach urges us to consider leisure as the 'effect' of multiple practices and linkages in society and history. By the same token, post-structuralism conflates the concept of the human subject with polysemy. The linearity and unity of self, proclaimed by the Cartesian tradition, is rejected in favour of a position that treats identity as liquid and accounts for this liquidity in terms of the context and change of discourse.

But if identity is simply the effect of discourse, how can we explain subjective difference, particularity and causality? Post-structuralism correctly noted that the impasse of structuralism is precisely its habit of tackling issues of change and diversity with deterministic propositions. For example, the accent on the concept of patriarchy in feminist contributions to the study of leisure in the 1980s exaggerated the unity of women's subordination. Even when confined to the condition of working-class women, it permitted the force of the concept to override issues of difference and opposition within 'the common world of women' (Deem, 1986; Green et al., 1991).

To begin with, the post-structuralist perspective appears to offer liberation from both arid individualism, that emphasizes the autonomy of individuals, and cod structuralism with its no less infertile stress upon the uniformity of identity. It does so by recognizing the multiplicity of discourses that shape identity and the liquidity of change. These discourses are presented as pre-empting notions of stable identity. Yet if identity is writ in water, with, as such, all of the eddies, shifting flows and sheer porosity implied in grasping it analytically, how can anything interesting be said about the history or future of leisure forms and practice? Post-structuralism, as it were, 'writes over' the issue of *accumulation* in identity. Putting it at its simplest, the ideas that some things change, and that change makes a difference, cannot be perpetually destructed by referring to discourse. In doing so, post-structuralism dissolves biography and history and begs a number of ethical questions in relation to identity. Not everything in the form and practice of leisure identity is relative to context and change. Some identity forms and practice leave traces that are coherent, continuous and require actors to collectively reposition themselves in relation to issues of abundance and scarcity and to acknowledge a *causal* transformation behind their decisions. These actions frequently accompany ethical questions having to do with distributive justice and imperatives of care for the self and care for the other. Moreover, this repositioning may shift the balance of power in society, thus transforming the situation of strata in the struggle over accumulating scarce resources.

Identities: subjective and commodity

The positioning of individuals in relation to scarce resources, poses the independent question of how identity is constructed and resources distributed. Class, gender, race and status distinctions are typically cited as the key structural influences canalizing resources and formatting identity. The study of embodiment and emplacement demonstrates that it is essential to distinguish between the rhetoric and relations of structural influences in the formatting of identity. It is one thing to claim that class constructs identity, but quite another to examine how different individuals relate to class inequalities and struggle to create distinctive forms of subjectivity in a situation that has many commonalities. We must remember that not only individuals, but also the structural forces in which they are situated, possess identities.

Consider the case of class. Various studies demonstrate that class distinctions in leisure relate to differences in income, education, social networks, access to mobility, domestic space, values, myths and beliefs and that these translate into palpable class divisions in leisure activities (Clarke and Critcher, 1985). Class influences not merely the issue of leisure choice, but the *ontology* of leisure practice. That is the experience of being, which is the nucleus of identity. We can illustrate this in two ways by referring briefly to the classical work of Marx.

In the *Economic and Philosophic Manuscripts of 1844*, Marx proposes that freedom and choice are meaningless under capitalism. This is because individuals can create nothing and be nothing without engagement with the *sensuous external world* (Marx 1844: 109). Under capitalism this engagement is regimented by the requirements of the labour contract and the need to generate economic wealth. Not only wage labourers, but also capitalist employers are positioned in relation to the sensuous external world in ways that squeeze and obstruct their capacity to engage in self realization. The forms of identity they can achieve then, are impaired by the economic requirements of the system. As Marx puts it:

> Just as in religion the spontaneous activity of the human imagination of the human brain and the human heart operates independently of the individual – that is, operates on him as alien, divine or diabolical activity – so that the worker's activity is not his spontaneous activity. It belongs to another; it is the loss of self.
>
> As a result therefore, man (the worker) only feels himself freely active in his animal functions – eating, drinking, procreating, or at his most in his dwelling and in dressing-up, etc. and in his human functions he no longer feels himself to be anything but an animal. What is animal becomes human and what is human becomes animal. (Marx, 1844: 111)

Patently, Marx holds that identity is *imposed* upon wage-labourers and capitalists by an economic and political system that they have created, but which has grown to elude their control. Marx refers to labour which 'belongs to another', 'the loss of self' and the reduction of working-class leisure to 'animal functions' (the only activity in which 'Man' feels himself to be freely active).

In later works, Marx (1954, 1956, 1959) develops the argument that under capitalism we cannot achieve free engagement with the sensuous external world, and hence cannot achieve identities that provide ontological security, by turning to examine the commodity. In the first place, he notes that the labour contract positions us in relation to scarce resources. Capitalist and wage-labourer are divided from nature by the requirement to generate economic wealth. Not only this, but the capitalist is divided from the worker and the worker is divided from the capitalist, by different interests. The capitalist seeks to maximize the revenue produced through the labour process, and the worker seeks to maximize an economic return, and whatever limited control that remains in the act of production. What each produces is commodities. Under conditions in which ontological security is obstructed by the economic and political requirements of the system, identity formatting is attached 'naturally' to the commodity. What we buy is an index of who we are, not least because having and wanting commodities prevents us from asking deeper questions about the nature of our relation to happiness with respect to our self, others and Nature. In the Marxian account, class is not simply an aspect of identity, it establishes the boundaries of identity.

Of course, commodities are not the only mechanism for formatting identity. Within the Marxist tradition, a powerful case has been made that the state plays a crucial role in organizing subjects (Gramsci, 1971; Althusser, 1971, 1977). Hall's (1982, 1984, 1988) work on the 'the repressive/interventionist state' and 'authoritarian populism' argues that the state constructs and positions identities in complex ways so as to maintain hegemony.[1] Moreover, this tradition has been extended into leisure studies by Clarke and Critcher (1985), who argue that identity and choice in leisure forms is deeply inscribed by the action of the state. Be that as it may, commodities are evidently a very significant means around which identities are clustered and developed.

We can illustrate this with two examples from consumer culture in which new types of leisure identity were rapidly constructed and new formations emerged in relation to scarce resources: the industry-wide identity subcultures organized around the automobile and the specific brand identity of the Apple Mac computer. In both examples, pronounced significance is assigned to the role of discourse (through advertising, marketing and branding) in formatting identity. This approach is a departure from most of the recent literature on identity which, following Althusser (1971, 1977), Gramsci (1971) and Foucault (1975), emphasizes the role of the state in constructing identity. This has been particularly emphasized in the recent work on national identity (Hall, 1984, 1988; Kumar, 2003). While this work has contributed much to our understanding of how identity is formed it has also obstructed the part played by corporations in consumer culture in forging subjective recognition and difference.

The automobile as consumer 'dream machine'

The advent of the automobile as a staple in consumer culture dramatically repositioned individuals with respect to speed, distance and flexibility. It elicited new forms of leisure and correlative identity types in society. It did so very rapidly. For example, in 1900 there were 300 automobiles in France. By 1913 there were 100,000. Between 1896 and 1900, at least ten journals devoted to 'automobilism' were founded. They concentrated on the ever-breaking speed records that, by 1906, exceeded 200 kilometres an hour (Kern, 1983: 113). From the outset the automobile was associated with strong escapist and ludic associations. We should note that, at this time, motorized vehicles were beyond the reach of middle- and working-class pockets. Their purchase and use conformed to the style of conspicuous consumption that Veblen (1899) beheld in the leisure practice of the leisure class. For example, William K. Vanderbilt's Long Island villa had a 100-car garage, wherein he stored a fleet including some of the most expensive makes in the world. The development of motor clubs, like the New York-based Automobile Club of America, was founded and dominated by wealthy enthusiasts. The first automobile shows were patronized as important social events for the *haute monde* (Gartman, 1994: 33–4). With astonishing rapidity, they became a focal part of the social calendar of the leisure class. Western Europe followed suit. In the UK the Automobile Club of Great Britain and Ireland was founded in 1897. King Edward VII's interest conferred royal patronage upon motoring as a leisure pursuit.[2] The first British Grand Prix was held at Brooklands in 1926 and became an annual gathering for wealthy enthusiasts. The first identity characteristics associated with the automobile, then, were luxury, style, wealth and social cachet. At this time, the brand of identity that motor car manufacturers were intent upon burnishing upon public consciousness accentuated social *distance* and freedom from the obligation to engage in paid labour.

However, the sheer lifestyle revolution that the motor car presented to society, and the profits that could be made by making consumers buy into it, ensured that the automobile industry would pioneer the principles of mass production and extend the image of the car in styling personality. The process accelerated after the assembly line system developed by Henry Ford brought the automobile into the hands of lower social strata. The corollaries of this were ever more sophisticated ways of advertising, marketing and branding the automobile as a desired lifestyle accessory and focus of identity. The middle class embraced the car as a means of practising 'therapeutic leisure' because it allowed them to escape the city and enjoy country air. As Rybczynski (1991: 182–4) notes, new leisure forms like the day trip and auto-touring were born, almost overnight.

From the first then, the automobile was not simply a means of accelerated transport, it was a basis for representing prestige, rank and achievement. As a plaything of the leisure class, it was initially, deeply resented by the working class. In the first place, they were too poor to buy a car. What is more, their inner-city neighbourhoods suffered most of the environmental blight caused by the pollution of the horseless carriage. However, as mass production techniques brought the car within the reach of working-class budgets, the situation was transformed. By 1939 there was one car for every four inhabitants in the US; one for every eight in Canada; one for every 18 in Britain and France; and one for every 42 in Nazi Germany (Rybczynski, 1991: 182–3). Even then, distinctions in price, styling and luxury components, made the automobile a symbol of class antagonism. The brand of car purchased, became a lifestyle statement. The difference between a Jaguar and a Fiat reflected not merely separate income brackets, but also *personality*. This was especially important in consumer society where performativity was becoming paramount. Performativity refers to the construction of identity for the purpose of *impression management* rather than the expression of *character*. Several studies argue that the rise of consumer culture undermined the character type of the inner-directed rugged individual assembled through tradition and experience and replaced it with that of the outer-directed individual for whom appearance and style of were the keys to self-worth (Riesman, 1950; Lowenthal, 1968). Performative cultures assign great importance to appearance, fashion and style in identity and devise various ways of auditing social impact and monitoring personal performance. Samantha Barbas (2001) seizes on a powerful motif of this transformation in her analysis of the rise of the movie industry and the cult of celebrity that quickly surrounded stars. She demonstrates how fans quickly adopted the mannerisms, gestures, speech styles and philosophy of movie stars. By the 1920s, the celebrity entertainment class had replaced the leisure class as the standard for emulation in consumer culture.

The automobile provided an extension of the Hollywood dream machine. Gartman's (1994: 136–81) brilliant study of the automobile in consumer culture demonstrates that in the late 1940s and 1950s auto-manufacturers adopted patterns of advertising, marketing, branding and design that sought to make the automobile a symbol of achievement and impression management. The form of fantastic styling drew heavily on futuristic design idioms which conflated the connotations of aeroplane and rocket travel with the motor car. Examples include the wraparound windshield inspired by the canopies of the jet engine and rising fins on each rear fender simulating the vertical stabilizers on jets. The dashboard was expanded to include an unparalleled range of gadgetry. The design focus was on escape and entertainment. The car was explicitly redefined as a mobile temple of amusement. The Detroit dream machine mirrored the Hollywood dream factory in manufacturing commodities that immediately radiated power, style and attraction and excitement. Leisure identities formed around auto luxury and speed became stressed in consumer culture.

The auto-industry provides a rich set of examples of how the branding of auto luxury and speed was and is used to construct cultural and personal identity. Automobiles are not simply machines, they are coded with cultural representations that say something about personality. To redeploy a model first used in the analysis of the social construction of tourist sites, we can think of advertising, branding and marketing in the auto-industry as perpetuating a flexible index of personal lifestyle values to which consumers are 'dragged' (Rojek, 1997). The desire of consumers is stimulated and 'dragged' to brands by the personal lifestyle values devised by the industry. Key features of these values are attraction, fashion and flexibility since it is not in the interest of the industry to perpetuate the idea of 'a car for life' in consumer culture. Replaceability and reinvention are central to the industry's financial momentum. As such, they figure prominently in the advertising, branding and marketing idiom of the industry that define the index of values to which consumers are 'dragged'. In performative cultures, individuals do not merely buy a product, they buy an index of lifestyle images through which personality and social standing are articulated. Of course, they can choose not to play the game. But in a condition in which so much about personal worth is expressed by ownership and style, the odds are very much against doing so. The example, raises scepticism about how free consumers are to make lifestyle choices. The formatting of identity is much more than a matter of personal will. It involves shifting and interlocking discourses produced by multinationals, the state, the media and other institutions, which position actors to make preferred choices in leisure and lifestyle.

'Think different': the Apple Mac

The Apple Macintosh may have less than a 7 per cent share of the computer market, but the brand is associated with exceptionally high levels of loyalty (Vincent, 2002: 43–52). From the first Apple machine, produced in 1975, the brand has been strongly linked with technical wizardry, consumer freedom and a rock 'n' roll attitude. Prior to Apple, industry leaders like IBM were sceptical about the market potential for personal computers. Apple's branding strategy always emphasized innovation, ease of use, flexibility and daring. The machine that embodied these values was the Macintosh, launched in 1984. Among many revolutionary features, this computer introduced the mouse with a desktop range of features that could be quickly understood at an intuitive level. The campaign launch for the product has become a legend in the advertising industry. Apple chose to unveil the machine at the Super Bowl. Harnessing popular anxieties about George Orwell's *1984*, the ad portrayed a grey, docile, regimented world dominated by Big Brother. The latter was a metaphor for IBM. Inside an auditorium hundreds of drones are watching and listening to corporate spin about 'the information purification drive'. Suddenly a woman wearing brightly coloured clothing tears down a hallway, pursued by security men. She flees her restrainers and hurls a sledgehammer at the screen. The image of Big Brother explodes, and the audience is bathed in liberating electricity and light. The tag line at the end of the ad reads: 'On January 24th Apple Computer will introduce Macintosh. And you will see why 1984 won't be like 1984.' The ad established the idea of Apple as a heroic David working in a marketplace dominated by huge, impersonal Goliaths. This brand identity has been consistently reinforced in subsequent advertising campaigns for new products.

For example, the 'Think Different' campaign of the mid-1990s prominently featured photographs of legendary maverick celebrities like Alfred Hitchcock, Mohammed Ali, Martha Graham, Thomas Edison, Pablo Picasso, Albert Einstein, and John Lennon and Yoko Ono. It deliberately sought to exploit and develop a product identity around creativity, boldness and style. In the words of the ad campaign:

Here's to the crazy ones.
The Misfits.
The Rebels.
The troublemakers.
The round pegs in square holes.
The ones who see things differently.

They're not fond of rules. And they have no respect for the status quo.
You can praise them, disagree with them,
quote them, disbelieve them, glorify or vilify them.

About the only thing you can't do is ignore them. Because they change things.
They invent. They imagine. They heal.
They explore. They create. They inspire.
They push the human race forward.

Maybe they have to be crazy. How else can you stare at an empty canvas and
see a work of art? Or sit in silence and hear a song that's never been written? Or
gaze at a red planet and see a laboratory on wheels?

We make tools for these kind of people.
While some see them as the crazy ones, we
see genius. Because the people who are
crazy enough to think they can change the
world, are the ones who do.

The success of the Macintosh and the subsequent line of Apple II computers
vindicated the company's branding strategy. But it also paved the way for PC
manufacturers to emulate what had succeeded for Apple. Although IBM's market
dominance declined, new PC companies like Dell and Compaq emerged to challenge
Apple's position. Simultaneously, Microsoft introduced a new operating system
Windows, which adapted many of the features pioneered in the Mac OS system.
Windows was more price-competitive and offered a larger software library.

Apple's response was to return to the values that paid such dividends when the
company was launched in 1984. Innovation, flexibility and daring were encapsulated
in the new iMac design which used colour in machine casing and introduced new
features such as built-in DVD drives, internet connectivity, iPhoto, iMovie and
iTunes. The company also exploited and developed the association of Mac with
lifestyle choice and personality by opening a chain of Apple stores in cities like
New York, Los Angeles, Tokyo and London. The stores don't just sell retail products.
They offer workshops, a lecture series on how to get the most out of your Mac and a
resident team of 'Geniuses' on hand to supply technical solutions to hardware and
software operating problems. In other words, an entire lifestyle is on offer.

The branding of Apple Macs and the various advertising campaigns sponsored
by the company has consistently sought to create a strong index of identity traits
in order to attract consumers. As with the case of automobile branding, Apple has
sought to portray their range of computers not simply as machines but as leisure
and lifestyle accessories. The stress on thinking different, innovation, flexibility and
daring are designed to appeal to a particular kind of individual, usually based in
the creative industries and education. It might be said that individuals cultivated
these values prior to Apple's branding campaign. But the company clearly redefined

them in relation to the Mac product range, making the consumption of Macs a transparent statement about personality and leisure and lifestyle choice.

Conclusion: identity – the chicken or the egg?

Some years ago, Ernest Gellner (1997: 90) asked the witty and pertinent question: do nations have navels? This was a question having to do with the nature of national identity. He argued that there are two ways in which the question can be answered: from the perspective of a primordialist or a modernizer. A primordialist believes that nations were born in ancient times and that there is a direct line of continuity between then and now. Such thinking lends itself to picture nations in terms of common 'bloodline' and a 'family' of interests. Conversely, a modernist considers the nation to be composed not merely of one factor, such as 'history', but by many overlapping factors having to do with discourse and imagination. Indeed a dyed-in-the-wool modernist regards history itself to be inflected by discourse and imagination and allows at best, that nations should be thought of as 'imagined communities' (Anderson, 1991).

In asking his question, Gellner (1997: 95) concludes that there is evidence for both sides. Some 'continuous', 'timeless' traditions are of recent date and have been invented, to supply a sort of symbolic shorthand for the idea of national identity.[3] The reinvention of nations has been tried in the twentieth-century revolutions around communism and fascism. In Europe, while these experiments have largely disintegrated, this is not true in the rest of the world, where communist China, for example, may become a superpower with the capacity to rival the United States in the twenty-first century. Even in Europe where the experiments in reinvention have mainly collapsed, their consequences have not vanished and, in this sense, visible continuities persist. Gellner (ibid.: 96) himself concluded that, 'my own view is that some nations possess genuinely ancient navels, some have navels invented for them by their own nationalist propaganda, and some are altogether navel-less'.

This is a good way of looking at the question of the relationship between identity and structure in leisure practice. It applies not only to the relationship between class and subjectivity, but to the relationships between the other main structural influences in leisure practice namely gender, race and status in relation to subjectivity, to say nothing of how the structural relationships interrelate with one another. These questions often end up being presented in chicken-and-egg terms. Does subjective leisure identity precede structure, in the way that some social psychologists believe with their emphasis on motivation and inner drives? Or is structure the egg from which personal leisure identity is hatched? The two examples considered above lean heavily towards the latter view. The auto-industry and Apple computers constructed visible forms of leisure identity organized around commodities and sought to drag or insert individuals into the parameters of these identity types. But this way of arguing might easily be overturned by showing that the attraction of consumers to automobiles and Apple computers harnessed cultural traits that preceded the commodity form. For example, the cultural interest in speed, performance and fashion existed long before the first automobile and clearly was a focus for identity clustering. The question of how leisure identities emerge is seldom one of a simple relationship between structure and subjectivity. For both are implicated in much wider social, cultural, economic and political processes. This is the burden of the post-structuralist approach to identity and, as we have seen, it has a good deal to commend it. But in as much as it results in dissolving biography and history into discourse it is not helpful.

Today, many nourish the hope that those forms of identity organized around national intolerance or claims of national superiority are falling away to be replaced by a new form of cosmopolitan identity (Held, 1995; Archibugi, 2000; Dharwadker, 2001). *Prima facie*, leisure practice lends much support for this argument for the practices of mass communication, world music, world film, tourism, net surfing and the like, broaden our knowledge of other cultures and expose the limitations of our own national identities. The cosmopolitan looks forward to a condition in which individuals enjoy multiple citizenships – citizens of their immediate communities and the wider regional and global networks that impact upon their lives (Held, 1995: 233).[4]

But there are difficulties with this argument. To begin with, the geopolitical mechanisms for making practising cosmopolitan citizenship are undertheorized. In a climate where the interests of nation-states still prevail, it is difficult to envisage what catalyst, other than natural disaster, would bring them together to form binding transnational organizations. One might say that the institutions of the European Community, the United Nations and the World Heritage Committee clearly falsify this argument since they do exert transnational power in shaping civil society within nation-states. While it is fair to make this point, we should remember that these institutions function in a context wherein national diversity is still recognized and supported. It might be objected that the Allied invasions of Afghanistan and Iraq after 9/11 suggest that respect for national diversity is rapidly declining. Although the Allies are committed to creating long-term self-rule in both countries, they are doing so by imposing Western institutions upon national structures and sponsoring a nationalist political elite that will identify its interests with those of the West. This policy has already provoked various forms of reactionary nationalism, since no nation is composed of homogeneity. More is likely, since the attempts of governments to ignore diversity will be experienced as oppression by those who wish to retain local and regional claims of difference. Achieving standardization and regimentation in social and cultural conditions is more difficult than many accounts of globalization allow (Ritzer, 2004).

The argument about the spread of cosmopolitanism and globalization needs to be handled with care. The presence of forms of consumerist cosmopolitanism, such as the presence of Kentucky Fried Chicken outlets in Beijing or the rise of a niche market of US soccer fans that regularly follow English Premiership Football on satellite television, is not, in itself, evidence that national boundaries are melting. Nor does it suggest that a 'one world' model of leisure is rapidly emerging. Privilege remains the main feature of access to cosmopolitan experience. Those who regularly travel the world do so because they have independent means or because the organizations that employ them send them, or because they have decided to opt out of conventional career structures. The overwhelming majority of the world's population do not have these opportunities and therefore have much lower chances of developing cosmopolitan attachments.

Moreover, despite the democratizing aspects of political cosmopolitanism, in respect of, for example environmental protection and the preservation of heritage, the main incentive behind the development is the conventional capitalist goal of profit maximization. Multinational corporations and capitalist states oil the wheels of cosmopolitanism through business strategies and trade arrangements in pursuit of the orthodox goal of wealth creation. While there is some evidence that these activities distribute a degree of wealth to metropolitan centres in the developing world, the bulk of new wealth has been concentrated in the hands of the developed Western industrial countries. On key criteria, the development gap between the developed and developing world has *increased* during the last 20 years, when the case of cosmopolitan democracy has been made most loudly. In addition, one should note that as consumerist cosmopolitanism has developed and the leading capitalist countries have forged new business and trade relations globally, it has unintentionally created opportunities for the illegal globalization of drugs and prostitution.

The idea then, that cosmopolitanism can create new forms of identity which are more inclusive, tolerant and reciprocal, must be handled with caution. Identity interests bite hardest when they address the issue to the relation of the individual and the community in relation to the distribution of scarce resources. Scarcity here, may be considered in economic terms, but crucially it also embraces political, honorific and cultural dimensions. Until the nations of the world develop strategies to deal effectively with global inequalities, various problems of scarcity will remain. As such, it is too early to declare the death of the politics of identity.

Notes

1. The concept of hegemony refers to the legitimation of the struggle for domination. However, in Hall's work there is significant slippage in the meaning of the concept. Six meanings can be distinguished: (1) The engineering of voluntary, popular 'consent'. It operates at multiple levels in the social formation, the most significant of which are the economic, political and cultural; (2) the horizon for agency and practice within which conflicts are fought out, appropriated, obscured or contained; (3) the terrain that ideas and conflicts occupy. It predisposes debate to occur in particular directions via persuasion and consent; (4) the positioning of difference, so that some points of view are accentuated or pronounced and others are marginalized or erased; (5) the form of political, intellectual and moral leadership; (6) the representation of mastering a determinate field of force. It is inherently contradictory and therefore publicly contested (see Rojek, 2003: 114–15).
2. King Edward VII's interest in motoring led to the club being renamed the Royal Automobile Club (RAC).
3. For a discussion of the invention of 'ancient' traditions and its purpose in maintaining hegemony see Hobsbawm and Ranger (1983).
4. One weakness of the literature on cosmopolitan citizenship is the failure to articulate effective global institutions of regulation.

Bibliography

Althusser, L. (1971) *Lenin, Philosophy and Other Essays*, London, New Left Books.

Althusser, L. (1977) *For Marx*, Harmondsworth, Penguin.

Anderson, B. (1991) *Imagined Communities: Reflections on the Origin and Spread of Nationalism*, 2nd edn, London, Verso.

Archibugi, D. (2000) 'Cosmopolitan Democracy', *New Left Review* (July–August): 137–50.

Barbas, S. (2001) *Movie Crazy*, New York, Palgrave Macmillan.

Bishop, J. and Hoggett, P. (1986) *Organizing Around Enthusiasms*, London, Comedia.

Blackshaw, T. (2003) *Leisurelife*, London, Routledge.

Cheek, N. and Burch, W. (1976) *The Social Organization of Leisure in Human Society*, New York, Harper & Row.

Clarke, J. and Critcher, C. (1985) *The Devil Makes Work*, London, Macmillan.

Csikszentmihalyi, M. (1975) *Beyond Boredom and Anxiety*, San Francisco, Jossey Bass.

Cuskelly, G. and Harrington, M. (1997) 'Volunteers and Leisure', *World Leisure & Recreation* 39(3): 11–18.

Deem, R. (1986) *All Work and No Play?*, Milton Keynes, Open University Press.

Dharwadker, V. (ed.) (2001) *Cosmopolitan Geographies*, New York, Routledge.

Ferrell, J. and Hamm, M. (eds) (1998) *Ethnography at the Edge*, Boston, North Eastern University Press.

Fine, G. (1989) 'Mobilizing Fun', *Sociology of Sport Journal* 6(4): 319–34.

Foucualt, M. (1975) *Discipline and Punish*, Penguin, Harmondsworth.

Foucault, M. (1978) *The History of Sexuality, Vol. 1: Introduction*, Harmondsworth, Penguin.

Foucault, M. (1985) *The History of Sexuality, Vol. 2: The Use of Pleasure*, New York, Random House.

Foucault, M. (1986) *The History of Sexuality, Vol. 3: The Care for the Self*, New York, Random House.

Foucault, M. (1988) 'Social Security', in L. Kritzman (ed.) *Michel Foucault, Politics, Philosophy and Culture*, London, Routledge, pp. 159–77.

Gartman, D. (1994) *Auto-Opium*, London, Routledge.

Gellner, E. (1997) *Nationalism*, London, Phoenix.

Goffman, E. (1967) *Interaction Ritual*, New York, Pantheon.

Gramsci, A. (1971) *Selections from Prison Notebooks*, London, Lawrence & Wishart

Green, E., Hebron, S. and Woodward, D. (1991) *Women's Leisure, What Leisure?* London, Macmillan.

Hall, S. (1982) 'The Rediscovery of "Ideology": Return of the Repressed in Media Studies', in M. Gurevitch, T. Curran and J. Wollacott (eds) *Culture, Society and the Media*, London, Methuen, pp. 56–90.

Hall, S. (1984) 'The Rise of the Representative/Interventionist State 1880s–1920s', in G. McLennan, D. Held and S. Hall (eds) *State and Society in Contemporary Britain*, Cambridge, Polity Press, pp. 7–49.

Hall, S. (1988) *The Hard Road to Renewal: Thatcherism and the Crisis of the Left*, London: Verso.

Heidegger, M. (1962) *Being and Time*, Oxford, Blackwell.

Heidegger, M. (1977) *The Question Concerning Technology and Other Essays*, New York, Harper & Row.

Held, D. (1995) *Democracy and the Global Order*, Cambridge, Polity Press.

Hobsbawm, T. and Ranger, T. (eds) (1983) *The Invention of Tradition*, Cambridge, Cambridge University Press.

Jenkins, H. (1992) *Textual Poachers*, London, Routledge.

Kern, S. (1983) *The Culture of Time and Space 1880–1918*, London, Weidenfeld & Nicolson.

Kumar, K. (2003) *The Making of English National Identity*, Cambridge, Cambridge University Press.

Lavanda, R. (1988) 'Minnesota Pageant Queens', *Journal of American Folklore* 101: 168–75.

Lowenthal, L. (1968) 'The Triumph of Mass idols', in L. Lowenthal, *Literature, Popular Culture, and Society*, Palo Alto, Pacific Books.

Lyng, S. (1990) 'Edgework: A Social Psychological Analysis of Voluntary Risk Taking', *American Journal of Sociology* 95: 887–921.

Marx, K. (1844) *Economic and Philosophic Manuscripts 1844*, New York, International Publishers, 1964.

Marx, K. (1954) *Capital, Volume 1*, London, Lawrence & Wishart.

Marx, K. (1956) *Capital, Volume 2*, London, Lawrence & Wishart.

Marx, K. (1959) *Capital, Volume 3*, London, Lawrence & Wishart.

McQuarrie, F. and Jackson, E. (1996) 'Connections between Negotiation of Leisure Constraints and Serious Leisure', *Society and Leisure* 19: 459–83.

Neulinger, J. (1981) *To Leisure: An Introduction*, Boston, Allyn & Bacon.

Parker, S. (1983) *Leisure and Work*, London, Allen & Unwin.

Pearson, K. (1979) *Sporting Subcultures of Australia and New Zealand*, Brisbane, University of Queensland Press.

Probyn, E. (1993) *Sexing the Self*, London, Routledge.

Riesman, D. (1950) *The Lonely Crowd*, New York, Doubleday.

Ritzer, G. (2004) *The Globalization of Nothing*, Thousand Oaks, Pine Forge.

Rojek, C. (1997) 'Indexing, Dragging and the Social Construction of Tourist Sights', in C. Rojek and J. Urry (eds) *Touring Cultures*, London, Routledge, pp. 23–51.

Rojek, C. (2003) *Stuart Hall*, Cambridge, Polity Press.

Rybczynski, W. (1991) *Waiting for the Weekend*, New York, Penguin.

Vaaranen, H. and Wieloch, N. (2002) 'Car Crashes and Dead End Careers', *YOUNG: Nordic Journal of Youth Research* 10(1): 42–58.

Veblen, T. (1899) *The Theory of the Leisure Class*, London, Allen & Unwin.

Vincent, L. (2002) *Legendary Brands*, Chicago, Dearborn.

Willis, P. (1977) *Learning to Labour*, London, Saxon House.

30

The Concept of Praxis: Cultural Studies and the Leisure Industries

Chris Barker

In this chapter I shall be exploring the concept of praxis and its applications in the context of selected leisure activities as understood by writers and researchers in the domain of cultural studies. I first sketch out the meaning of the concept of praxis in general terms before settling on the notion that it can be understood not only as an overcoming of theory and practice but also as a kind of 'situated creative doing'. Subsequently, I seek to illustrate this process through a somewhat whirlwind tour of the debates in cultural studies about watching television, consuming commodities and developing youth subcultural style.

The concept of praxis

We commonly think of a practice as a way of doing things, an action, application or performance that is contrasted to theory or abstract thinking. This counterpoising of theory to the practical is a legacy of Aristotle's classification of disciplines as theoretical, productive or practical. However, Aristotle also introduced the idea of 'praxis' which is not merely a mechanical making but a *conceptually inspired* 'creative doing'. Thus the concept of praxis, which derives from the Greek word for 'action that shapes the world', seeks to dissolve the distinction between theory and practice.

The concept of praxis involves a deconstruction of the binary pair of theory and practice, involving recognition that each belongs to and in the other. For example, theory is not an unproblematic reflection or discovery of objective truth about an independent object world. This is so because there is no archimedian vantage point from which one could verify any claimed correspondence between the world and language (Rorty, 1980). Instead, theory involves justifying statements in the context of intersubjectively formed constitutive rules regarding what establishes legitimate forms of reasoning. Here language and thus theory is conceived of as a *tool* for action rather than a mirror for representing the world. Hence, theory construction is a self-reflexive discursive endeavour that seeks to interpret and intercede in the world. Theory is grasped as a tool, instrument or logic for intervening in the world. That is to say, theory is a practice.

Equally, the meaning of a practice does not inhere within the action itself and no amount of the stacking up of empirical data about practice can produce a meaningful story outside of the structures of language. Language is the means and medium through which we form knowledge about ourselves and the social world, it forms the network by which we classify the world and make it meaningful. That is, language gives meaning to material objects and social practices that are brought into view and made intelligible to us in terms which language delimits. The meaning of a given practice – to kick, to sing, to theorize, to dance, and so on – does not derive from an essence of 'kick' or 'dance' but from the way the word is used in the context of a specific language-game (Wittgenstein, 1957). That is, a practice only makes sense within the context of a theory or narrative about our lives. In sum, theory is a practice and a practice makes sense only through theory – this is the initial meaning of the concept of praxis.

The development of Marxism proved to be a significant moment in the modern extension of the use of the concept of praxis into the social and cultural domain. Marx set out to demonstrate the validity of historical materialism by arguing that 'It is not the consciousness of men that determines their being, but, on the contrary, their social being determines their consciousness' (Marx, in Bottomore and Rubel, 1961: 67). That is, the historical specificity of human affairs is a consequence of the material conditions of existence. As humans produce food, clothes, and all manner of tools with which to shape their environment, so they also create themselves. However, in his famous 'Thesis on Feuerbach' he is critical of all previous forms of materialism for conceiving of 'reality' *only* as an object of contemplation rather than as a practice. Indeed, in the most widely quoted of the 'Thesis on Feuerbach' Marx argues that 'The philosophers have only *interpreted* the world in various ways; the point is to *change* it' (Marx, in ibid.: 84).

However, as Marx argued, while humans are practical beings the ground on which they act has already been determined for them. Thus 'men [sic] make their own history, but they do not make it just as they please; they do not make it under circumstances chosen by themselves, but under circumstances directly encountered, given and transmitted' (Marx, in ibid.: 53). For Marx this is understood to be praxis in play; that is, on the one hand the consciousness of human beings is the product of particular historical material conditions, but on the other hand we are able to change those conditions, which by implication, leads to further alterations in human thinking. Thus the very knowledge produced by people under specific historical conditions enables them to bring about material change and as a consequence to change themselves. Thus does the circle of praxis keep turning.

Agency and determination

We can see in the above discussion of Marx that as well as dissolving the distinction between 'theory' and 'practice', the notion of praxis can also be understood as overcoming the binary divide between 'thought' and 'action' as well as between 'agency' and 'determination'. This is of particular significance and relevance to an understanding of leisure practices since many theoretical approaches to leisure, along with contemporary common sense, conceive of it as an area of free choice springing from the actions of the self-determining actor. The problem of agency and determination asks whether our actions and choices are freely made based on independent knowledge (thought/*theory*) or whether they have already been determined for us by pre-existing social and cultural *practices*. The concept of praxis helps us to grasp the actor as simultaneously culturally situated – that is, determined – and as a choice-making actor. That is, praxis describes a kind of 'situated creative doing'.

The idea of agency has commonly been associated with notions of freedom, action, creativity, originality and the possibility of change brought about through the actions of free agents. By contrast, to say that an act has been determined, for example by the structures of class or gender, involves the attribution of a chain of cause and effect that denies human beings 'free will' or agency. That is, human actions are understood to be the consequence of the structures of society. However, the binary of structure and action or of agency and determination upon which this dilemma hangs needs to be overcome.

As Giddens argues (1984), individual actors do not bring regularized human activity, or structure, into being. However, that structure is continually re-created by them via the very means whereby they express themselves as actors. That is, in and through their activities agents reproduce the structural conditions that make those activities possible. This involves what Giddens calls the 'duality of structure', whereby structures are not only constraining but also enabling. While individual actors are constrained and determined by social forces that lie beyond them as individual subjects, it is those very same social structures that enable subjects to act. For example, the expectations and practices associated with gender construct men and women differently as subjects. Having been constituted as a man or a woman by the structures of gender – for example, having learned to be a culturally sanctioned father or mother – we then act in accordance with those rules reproducing them once again.

In order to grasp the way in which the divide between agency and structural determination can be overcome we need to make an important conceptual distinction between agents who are held to be free in the sense of 'not determined' and agency as the socially constituted capacity to act. While the former notion makes no sense, for there can be no uncaused human acts, the latter asks us to consider agency as consisting of acts which make a pragmatic difference. Here, agency means the enactment of X rather than Y course of action. Of course, precisely because socially constructed agency involves differentially distributed social resources that give rise to various degrees of the ability to act in specific spaces, so some actors have more scope for action than do others.

To undertake a course of action that makes a difference does not mean that we have engaged in an undetermined activity. Rather, the basis for our 'choice' has been determined or caused by the very way we have been constituted as subjects;

that is, by the where, when and how of our coming to be who we are. In that sense agency is determined by the social structures of language, the routine character of modern life and by psychic and emotional narratives that we cannot bring wholly to consciousness. Neither human freedom nor human action can consist of an escape from social determinants and as such it is a rather pointless metaphysical question to ask whether people are 'really' free or 'really' determined in any absolute sense.

It is useful to consider agency and determination as different modes of discourse or different languages for different purposes. Thus, the language of agency celebrates the cultural power and capacities of persons, encourages us to act and to seek improvement of the human condition as well as persuading us to take responsibility for our actions. It also enables institutions, for example, the courts, to hold persons accountable for specific acts. By contrast the language of determination helps to trace causality home and points to the contours of cultural life that enable some courses of action while disempowering others. Here the purposes are solidarity, the alleviation of individual responsibility and acceptance that there are limits to the plasticity of the human condition.

We are dealing then with the language of the dance in which we actively and creatively perform ourselves through a cosmic choreography that has no author. The notion of praxis is pertinent here in two ways; first, that 'agency' and 'structure' or 'freedom' and 'determination' are but two sides of the same coin, and second, that human theory about such matters is itself a form of practice.

Watching television: ideology and the active audience

At this point it will be useful to see how the concept of praxis can be related to the central leisure activity of the Western world, namely, watching television. As Raymond Williams (1974) commented, not only do we watch more drama on TV than might have been seen in a year or even a lifetime in other historical periods, but also we spend more time doing so than on preparing and eating food. The concern of course has been that the media have acted as vehicles for corporate marketing, manipulating audiences to deliver them to advertisers. This is allied to the assertion of a general ideological effect by which media messages create and reinforce audience attachment to the status quo. Thus, in the context of Western liberal democracies, the concept of ideology was used by neo-Marxists to explain the maintenance of Bourgeois class control and the failure of proletarian revolution to materialize in the context of class divided and exploitative capitalist social formations.

The ideological effect

The concept of ideology has referred to the way structures of signification are used to justify the power of ascendant groups. Here ideology has a double character, both of which function to legitimate the sectional interests of powerful classes. Namely, (a) ideas as coherent statements about the world that maintain the dominance of capitalism, and (b) worldviews which are the systematic outcome of the structures of capitalism which lead us to inadequate understandings of the social world.[1]

Significantly, for many writers exploring the relationship of television and ideology, the meanings of texts are held to have been 'injected' directly into the minds of television viewers without modification in the manner of a hypodermic needle. Ironically, this kind of thinking has something in common with other more mainstream media research paradigms that seek out the behavioural effects of the media. These include early studies in TV and violence (Halloran, 1970) and more contemporary 'cultivation analysis' (Signorelli and Morgan, 1990) that produces statistical correlation between the volume of television consumed and attitudes such as pessimism. Further, both Marxism and 'effects' research share a sense that the overall consequence of television on attitudes is to reinforce the views that one already holds. Here television is understood to be a determinist and essentially conservative force.

In terms of the balance between structure and agency, both ideological analysis and functional/behavioural analysis tend towards the structural and determinist end of the spectrum. Thus for Althusser (1971), 'ideology hails or interpellates concrete individuals as concrete subjects' and 'has the function of constituting concrete individuals as subjects'. Indeed, subjects are the effects of ideology because subjectivity is constituted by the positions which ideological discourse obliges us to take up. For Althusser television is an aspect of 'Ideological State Apparatuses' (ISA) that not only transmits a general ruling class ideology that justifies and legitimates capitalism, but also reproduces the attitudes and behaviour required by major class groups within the division of labour.

A central problem with Althusser's argument is that ideology appears to function behind people's backs in terms of the 'needs' of an agentless system. That is, Althusser's views are too determinist and functionalist in orientation ignoring the place of human agency. The popularity of Gramsci's writing within cultural studies was in partial response to this problem. Within Gramscian analysis, ideology provides people with rules of practical conduct and moral behaviour equivalent 'to a religion understood in the secular sense of a unity of faith between a conception of the world and a corresponding norm of conduct (Gramsci, 1971: 349).

In effect, Gramsci makes ideological struggle and conflict within civil society the central arena of cultural politics so that exploring the functions of ideology within popular texts such as television became the central practice of cultural studies. For example, early work on advertising understood the promotion of commodities to involve the creation of an 'identity' for a product so that in buying the products we buy into the image and so contribute to the construction of our identities through consumption. For Williamson (1978), advertising is ideological in its obscuring of economic inequality at the level of production by images of free and equal consumption.

Gramscian themes of ideology are also apparent in that seminal cultural studies text *Policing the Crisis* (Hall et al., 1978). This book explored the 1970s moral panic in the British media surrounding street robbery giving an account of the political, economic, ideological and racial crisis which formed its context. It sought to demonstrate the ideological work done by the media in constructing 'mugging' and connecting it with concerns about racial disorder while illustrating the popularization of hegemonic 'ideology' through the professional working practices of the media.

The active audience

While the concept of ideology as filtered through the work of Gramsci was less functionalist and determinist than that of Althusser, there is still a sense of 'ideological effect' by which audiences are subject to ideology. In response, proponents of the so-called 'active audience' approach argued that one could not legitimately 'read off' audience understandings from textual analysis either in terms of behavioural or ideological effects. It was argued that television audiences are not an undifferentiated mass of aggregated but isolated individuals, but rather that watching television is a socially and culturally informed activity which is centrally concerned with the negotiation of *meaning*. That is, audiences are active creators of meaning in relation to television and they do so on the basis of previously acquired cultural competencies forged in the context of language and social relationships.

Specifically, the encoding–decoding model of communication as developed by Stuart Hall (1981) – himself the prime mover behind the adoption of Gramscian theory inside cultural studies – suggests that whatever analysis of textual meanings a critic may undertake, it is far from certain which of the identified meanings, if any, will be activated by actual readers/audiences/consumers. In particular, the production of meaning does not ensure consumption of that meaning as the encoders might have intended. Subsequently, David Morley's (1980) research into the audience for the British news 'magazine' programme *Nationwide* was said to have provided empirical support for Hall's model.

Also significant in the development of 'active audience' theory was the reader-reception tradition of hermeneutics that challenges the idea that there is one textual meaning associated with authorial intent. It contests the notion that textual meanings are able to police meanings created by readers/audiences but instead stresses the interactive relationship between the text and the audience. Thus the reader approaches the text with certain expectations and anticipations which are modified in the course of reading to be replaced by new 'projections'. Thus reading involves not merely reproduction of textual meaning but the production of new meaning by the readers. The text may structure aspects of meaning by guiding the reader but it cannot fix meanings that are the outcome of the oscillations between the text and the imagination of the reader.

That television is more uneven and contradictory in its impact than the notion of 'ideological effect' suggests is illustrated by Lull's research in China. According to Lull (1997), television was introduced into China by a government hoping to deploy it as a form of social control and cultural homogenization. However, it has turned out to play quite the opposite role. Although the Chinese government has attempted to use television to re-establish social stability after Tiananmen Square it has instead become a central agent of popular resistance. Television has amplified and intensified the diversity of cultural and political sentiments in China by presenting alternative views of life. Driven by the need to attract larger audiences, television has become a cultural and ideological forum of competing ideas as commercial and imported dramas have been juxtaposed to China's own economic difficulties. Further, not only are programmes themselves polysemic, but audiences have become adept at reading between the lines of official pronouncements.

Praxis and the hermeneutic circle

There is now a good deal of mutually supporting work on television audiences within the cultural studies tradition from which one can conclude that audiences are active and knowledgeable producers of meaning not products of a structured text. However, meanings *are* bounded by the way the text is structured and by the domestic and cultural context of viewing. Thus watching television involves the interplay and mutual constitution of meaning by texts and audiences that constitutes a moment of praxis sometimes called the 'hermeneutic circle'.

It has often been assumed that the active nature of the audience undercuts the role of ideology, whose reproduction was associated with passive audiences. Thus many writers have linked the active audience with resistance to ideology. However, to simply associate the active audience with an inevitable 'resistance' to ideology or cultural homogenization is as mistaken as the previous reliance on the hypodermic model of audience response. Audiences are *always active* in relation to decoding texts whose meanings are continually unstable and in flux. In this context, watching television is both constitutive of and constituted by forms of cultural identity. In other words, television forms a symbolic resource for the construction of cultural identity just as audiences draw from their own sedimented cultural identities and cultural competencies to decode programmes in their own specific ways. Whether audience decodings constitute 'resistance' to ideology or cultural homogenization is a case by case empirical question.

Audience activity can deconstruct ideology only when alternative discourses are available so that the self becomes a site of ideological struggle. For example, Liebes and Katz (1990) argue that their study provides evidence of divergent readings of television narratives founded in different cultural backgrounds. They draw the conclusion that audiences use their own sense of national and ethnic identity as a position from which to decode programmes so that American television is not uncritically consumed by audiences with the destruction of 'indigenous' cultural identities as the inevitable outcome. However, the very deployment of their own cultural identifications as a point of resistance also helps to constitute that very cultural identity through its enunciation.

In other words, an act of 'resistance' is also an act of reinforcement. As they perform as active agents so they are simultaneously being structured by a different set of discourses of ethnicity and nationality. Indeed, my own research carried out amongst British Asian teenage viewers of soap opera in the UK (Barker, 1999) suggested that they were both active *and* implicated in the reproduction of ideology about the family, relationships and gender. Indeed, audience activity is a *requirement* for the engagement with and reproduction of ideology. Here the concept of praxis helps us to understand that an audience is always both 'situationally determined' and 'active' where activity can involve both 'acceptance' and 'resistance'. It is not so much a question of whether audiences are structured by texts or generate their own meanings, or even of the interplay between texts and readers, but rather the moment of praxis by which subjects are simultaneously active and structured.

Production and consumption

The expansion of television into our central leisure activity is an aspect of the wider post-war rise of consumer culture so that the surface of Western culture is now constituted by visual-based consumer images and meanings. This is a promotional culture plastered with the signs of Coca-Cola, Nike, Marlboro, Microsoft, and so on, and consumption is core to our leisure time. The question remains, what does this all mean for individuals and for our culture in general?

- On the one hand, cultural studies writers have expressed the fear that consumer culture generates meanings that serve to justify and reproduce the power of capitalist domination.
- On the other hand, a series of studies of consumption have stressed the productive role played by commodities as resources for the creative generation of new identities and lifestyles.

Poisonous consumption

There has long been a strand of thinking about culture that has been critical of the consumption practices of capitalist societies. A contemporary manifestation of this stream of thought is the work of Baudrillard (1983) who suggests that consumerism is at the heart of a postmodern culture that is constituted through a continual flow of images that establishes no connotational hierarchy and thus no sense of value. Postmodern culture is argued to be literally and metaphorically 'superficial'. This a culture in which no objects have an 'essential' or 'deep' value and where worth is determined through the exchange of symbolic meanings. For Baudrillard, postmodern culture is marked by an all-encompassing flow of fascinating simulations and images, a hyperreality in which we are overloaded with images and information.

For Jameson (1984), who draws on the work of Baudrillard, postmodernism is implicated in a depthless sense of the present and a loss of historical understanding. We live in a postmodern hyperspace, in which we are unable to place ourselves, that involves the loss of authentic artistic style in favour of pastiche and the transformation of representations of the world into images and spectacles. This is a culture of simulacrum (or copy for which no original existed) that transcends the capacities of the individual to locate themselves perceptually or cognitively and in which history has been reduced to stylistic connotation. For Jameson, this represents the cultural style of late capitalism operating in a new global space and which, by extending commodification to all realms of personal and social life, transforms the real into the image and simulacrum.

For example, Disney World provides a multimedia experience representing a tourist attraction and a symbolically desirable lifestyle that critics influenced by Baudrillard have attacked for its hyperreality, its collapsing of the real and the fake (and indeed its celebration of the fake). This is a 'public' culture where civility and social interaction occur in the context of a security regime in which there are no guns, no homeless people and no drugs. Disney's idealized and fantasized

Main Street USA presents to us in symbolic and imaginary form the pleasurable aspects of urban life while removing the fear. It is a far cry from the experience of New York City. Through its private management, spatial control and stimulating/ simulated visual culture, Disney World is the new model for public space that is being reproduced in an endless stream of shopping malls (Zukin, 1996).

Transgressive commodities

The arguments reviewed above have all implied that in various ways commodities are inherently 'unsound'. However, a number of cultural critics have increasingly identified the propagation of creative, oppositional and resistant meanings in relation to the commodities produced by consumer culture. Thus Kaplan (1987) claims a transgressive and progressive role for postmodern music videos that, she argues, offer no assured narrative position for the viewer thereby undermining the status of representation as real or true. In particular, she explores the ambiguity of Madonna as a commodity sign that deconstructs gender norms. For Kaplan, Madonna is able to 'alter gender relations and to destabilize gender altogether' (Kaplan, 1992: 273). This is achieved she suggests because Madonna's videos are implicated in the continual shifting of subject positions involving stylized and mixed gender signs that question the boundaries of gender constructs.

Creative consumption

Consumption oriented cultural studies has argued that while the production of popular music, film, television and fashion is in the hands of transnational capitalist corporations, meanings are produced, altered and managed at the level of consumption. For example, Fiske argues that popular culture is constituted by the meanings that people construct rather than those identifiable within texts. While he is clear that popular culture is very largely produced by capitalist corporations, he 'focuses rather upon the popular tactics by which these forces are coped with, are evaded or are resisted' (Fiske, 1989: 8).

The work of McRobbie (1991) illustrates the transformation in thinking that has taken place within cultural studies. In her early work, McRobbie is suspicious of the consumer culture from which 'girl-culture' stems. For example, the teenage girl-oriented magazine *Jackie* is held to operate through the codes of romance, domesticity, beauty and fashion, thereby defining the world of the personal sphere as the prime domain of females. Later, McRobbie critiques her own reliance on the analysis of *documents* and suggests that girls are more active and creative in relation to magazines and other forms of consumer culture than she had given them credit for. For example, she points to the productive, validating and inventive bricolage of fashion style that women originate as well as to the dynamic character of shopping as an enabling activity.

Similarly, Willis (1990) argues that rather than being inherent in the commodity, meaning and value are constructed through actual usage so that contemporary culture is not meaningless or superficial surface but involves the active creation of meaning by all people as cultural producers. Here young consumers assert their personal competencies through dancing and the customization of fashion, and in doing so transform and recode the meanings of everyday objects. Willis argues that it is, ironically, capitalism and the expansion of consumerism that have provided the increased supply of symbolic resources for young people's creative work. Capitalism (in the world of work) may be that from which escape is sought, but it also provides the means and medium (in the domain of consumption) by which to do so. Thus consumption practices are able to offer resistance to the apparent passivity and conformity of consumer culture.

Here we face the paradox that consumer culture is both constraining and enabling. On the one hand, this is a wasteland culture with a black hole of meaninglessness at its heart. On the other hand, this is also a moment in which identity construction is an active project involving the appropriation of signs and commodities. Where 'resistance' is taking place it is commonly happening 'inside' consumer lifestyles, transforming commodities and using the mass media, since there is no 'outside' to consumer culture from which external resistance can be mounted.

In general, it is argued that people range across a series of terrains and sites of meaning which, though not of their own making, are ones within which they can actively produce sense. Thus we may come to understand that the consumption-based identities of contemporary life are culturally situated and determined even as they are a consequence of agency and 'creative doing'. This is the 'situated creative doing' of praxis by which identities are constituted by an embodied performativity that is both derivative and original. This argument will be further illustrated through the performativity of identity in the context of youth cultures.

Identity, performativity and style

The concept of identity pertains to cultural descriptions of persons with which we emotionally identify and which concern sameness and difference. Within cultural studies, identities are understood to be discursive productions representing the processes by which discursively constructed subject positions are taken up (or otherwise) by concrete persons (Hall, 1992). And yet, just as identity has come to be understood as a contingent cultural production, so we have also come to understand it in the context of contemporary culture as an individual project. The idea of identity as a project refers to the ongoing creation of narratives of self-identity relating to our perceptions of the past, present and hoped-for future. As modernity not only breaks down the traditional forms of identity but also increases the levels of resources for identity construction, so we are all faced with the task of constructing our identities as a project (Giddens, 1991).

In understanding identity as both a *product* of a given culture and a *self-project* we are reprising in some respects the themes of structural determination and agency discussed above and arrive at a similar point, namely, that identity production can be grasped as a moment of praxis. This argument is strengthened when we explore it also as a performance. A 'performative' is a linguistic statement that puts into effect the relation that it names; for example, within a marriage ceremony 'I pronounce you ...' is a performative statement. As described by Judith Butler (1993), performativity is not a singular act but rather is always a citation and reiteration of a set of existent norms and conventions. For example, judges in criminal and civil law do not originate the law or its authority but cite the conventions of the law that is simultaneously consulted and invoked.

Though deployed by Butler in relation to sex and gender, this argument can also be applied to the category of youth. Thus youth is not a universal of biology but a changing social and cultural construct that appeared at a particular moment of time under definitive conditions and which is performed. As Hebdige (1988) argued, youth subcultures respond to surveillance by making a 'spectacle' of themselves for the admiring glances of strangers (and the media in particular). Thus the politics of youth culture is a politics of gesture, symbol and metaphor that deals in the currency of signs.

The performativity of style

In its formative days cultural studies explored the performativity of youth cultural identity through the notion of style. In this context, style was constituted by the signifying practices of youth subcultures including the display of codes of meaning achieved via the transformation of commodities as cultural signs. Thus, according to Hebdige (1979), British punk was a 'revolting style' that was not simply responding to the crisis of British decline manifested in joblessness, poverty and changing moral standards, but was performed and dramatized in an angry, dislocated, but self-aware and ironic mode of signification.

Indeed, for many cultural studies writers the cultural symbols and styles by which subcultures expressed themselves represent a 'fit' (or homology) between the groups' structural position in the social order and the social values of the subcultures' participants (for example, Willis 1978). Thus particular subcultural items parallel and reflect the structure, style, typical concerns, attitudes and feelings of the group. Consequently, the creativity and cultural responses of subcultures are not random but expressive of the contradictions of social structure. Thus we have the sense that the creative, expressive and symbolic work of subcultural style and indeed the very categories of youth and Punk (above) are constituted by a situated creative doing – the praxis of performativity.

Contemporary theorists of youth culture (see Redhead et al., 1997) have suggested that subcultures are not formed outside and opposed to the mainstream culture, but rather they are formed within and through the media. For example, the notion of the 'underground' is defined against the mass media and delights in 'negative' media coverage. Indeed, radio or TV bans and/or ironic mocking performances are the highlights of subcultural lifestyles so that 'derogatory media coverage is not the verdict but the essence of their resistance' (Thornton, 1995: 137). Further, what Thornton calls 'subcultural capital' involves distinctions between 'us' (alternative, cool, independent, authentic, minority) and 'them' (mainstream, straight, commercial, false, majority) which are in part the consequence of moral panics or distinctions of 'hipness' which record companies helped to foster. In both cases, subcultural style can be understood to be the product of both the situated/structural forces of consumer/media culture and of the 'creative doing' of young people in a moment of praxis.

Conclusion

The concept of praxis suggests a uniting of consciousness and action that shapes the world in a moment that simultaneously alters the conditions for the next such instance. Praxis is a way to understand the 'doubleness' of theory/practice and structure/agency so that they are not best grasped as binary pairs or opposites but as 'One'. For example, praxis is a way to think about the 'situated creative doing' of leisure activities that enact original but derivative performances staged under conditions not of our own making. Thus watching television involves both audience activity and the circulation of ideology. Likewise, the commodities of consumer culture are the grounds of cultural emptyness yet may also be the basis of meaningful action; for example, in and through the performative and style-based identities of youth cultures.

Note

1. Ideology as deployed by Althusser and many other Marxists involves misrecognition of the real conditions of existence. That is, ideology is false. I do not accept this argument myself and think that at best the concept of ideology entails 'binding and justifying' ideas or 'power/knowledge'. However, in order to maintain some consistency of terminology I continue to use the word 'ideology' throughout this chapter even though in other contexts I might prefer not to do so. For elaboration of this argument, see Barker (2002).

Bibliography

Althusser, L. (1971) *Lenin and Philosophy and Other Essays*, London, New Left Books.
Barker, C. (1999) *Television, Globalization and Cultural Identities*, Milton Keynes, Open University Press.
Barker, C. (2002) *Making Sense of Cultural Studies: Central Problems and Critical Debates*, London, Sage.
Baudrillard, J. (1983) *Simulations*, New York, Semiotext(e).
Bottomore, T. and Rubel, M. (eds) (1961) *Karl Marx: Selected Writings in Sociology and Social Philosophy*, London, Pelican.
Butler, J. (1993) *Bodies That Matter*, London and New York, Routledge.
Fiske, J. (1989) *Understanding Popular Culture*, London, Unwin Hyman.
Giddens, A. (1984) *The Constitution of Society*, Cambridge, Polity Press.
Giddens, A. (1991) *Modernity and Self-Identity*, Cambridge, Polity Press.
Gramsci, A. (1971) *Selections from the Prison Notebooks*, ed. Q. Hoare and G. Nowell-Smith, London, Lawrence & Wishart.
Hall, S. (1981) 'Encoding/Decoding', in S. Hall et al. (eds) *Culture, Media, Language*, London, Hutchinson.
Hall, S. (1992) 'The Question of Cultural Identity', in S. Hall, D. Held and T. McGrew (eds) *Modernity and its Futures*, Cambridge, Polity Press.
Hall, S., Critcher, C., Jefferson, T., Clarke, J. and Roberts, B. (1978) *Policing the Crisis: Mugging, the State and Law and Order*, London, Macmillan.
Halloran, J. (1970) 'The Effects of the Media Portrayal of Violence', in J. Tunstall (ed.) *Media Sociology*, London, Constable.
Hebdige, D. (1979) *Subculture: The Meaning of Style*, London and New York, Routledge.
Hebdige, D. (1988) *Hiding in the Light*, London, Comedia.
Jameson, F. (1984) 'Postmodernism or the Cultural Logic of Late Capitalism', *New Left Review* 46.

Kaplan, E. (1987) *Rocking Around the Clock: Music Television, Postmodernism and Consumer Culture*, Boulder, CO, Westview Press.

Kaplan, E. (1992) 'Feminist Criticism and Television', in R. Allen (ed.) *Channels of Discourse, Reassembled*, London and New York, Routledge.

Liebes, T. and Katz, E. (1990) *The Export of Meaning*, Oxford, Oxford University Press.

Lull, J. (1997) 'China Turned On (Revisited): Television, Reform and Resistance', in A. Sreberny-Mohammadi, D. Winseck, J. McKenna and O. Boyd-Barrett (eds) *Media in a Global Context*, London, Edward Arnold.

McRobbie, A. (1991) *Feminism and Youth Culture*, London, Macmillan.

Morley, D. (1980) *The Nationwide Audience*, London, British Film Institute.

Redhead, S., Wynne, D. and O'Connor, J. (1997) *The Clubcultures Reader*, Oxford, Blackwell.

Rorty, R. (1980) *Philosophy and the Mirror of Nature*, Cambridge, Cambridge University Press.

Signorielli, N. and Morgan, R. (1990) *Cultivation Analysis: New Directions in Media Effects Research*, Newbury Park, Sage.

Thornton, S. (1995) *Club Cultures: Music, Media and Subcultural Capital*, Cambridge, Polity Press.

Williams, R. (1974) *Television: Technology and Cultural Form*, London, Fontana.

Williamson, J. (1978) *Decoding Advertisements*, London, Marion Boyers.

Willis, P. (1978) *Profane Culture*, London, Routledge & Kegan Paul.

Willis, P. (1990) *Common Culture*, Milton Keynes, Open University Press.

Wittgenstein, L. (1957) *Philosophical Investigations*, Oxford, Blackwell.

Zukin, S. (1996) *The Culture of Cities*, Oxford, Blackwell.

31
Articulation

David Harris

The concept 'articulation' appears in one of the famous early collections of papers published by members of the Birmingham Centre for Contemporary Cultural Studies (CCCS). Members of that Centre produced several such collections, separate publications by some of the better-known alumni, including Hall (often with colleagues), Clarke, Critcher, Hebdige, McRobbie and Willis. When leading members gravitated to the UK Open University in the 1980s, they also produced a definitive undergraduate course on cultural studies (Open University, 1982) that spawned a number of similar materials and degree programmes throughout the UK, not only in British Cultural Studies (BCS), but also in Media and Sociology. In Leisure Studies too, a Cultural Studies approach became prominent, especially in the work of Clarke and Critcher (1985), Hargreaves (1986) or Tomlinson (1989).

'Articulation' was one of a cluster of innovative concepts developed in that approach. British Cultural Studies had emerged from some critical pioneering work on working-class culture in Britain (Thompson, 1968; Hoggart, 1981). The 'founding fathers' had been based at several UK universities, but the end of the 1960s saw a successful attempt to found a definite centre for cultural studies at Birmingham University (UK). As Hall's account reveals (in Hall et al., 1980), though, there had been some early scepticism from other well-established academic disciplines at Birmingham, especially from Sociology and from English Literature. It became necessary theoretically, and in terms of institutional politics, to clarify the relationship of BCS to those rival academic approaches. As I shall argue below, this attempt to separate from, or 'break' with, academic work in Sociology in particular, has produced some noticeable problems with BCS, notably a failure to theorize adequately the social processes involved in the formation of popular culture and a consequent lapse into idealism (see Harris, 1992; Wood, 1998).

One appealing theoretical route towards distinctiveness involved attempting to incorporate many of the recent insights of European Marxism, part of the more general project of the British New Left to radicalize British scholarship and political thinking. The apparent popularity of political and cultural radicalism, focused in the student revolts of the period, seemed to provide some immediate political context as well.

A number of theoretical works were scoured for suitably radicalizing concepts to understand popular culture in Britain. For various reasons, partly theoretical and partly political, the main interest came to settle on the works of Gramsci, and later Althusser, rather than, say, Critical Theory. Gramsci supplied the way forward for a complex analysis of the role of culture in modern, especially Western, states, where cultural and political institutions clearly occupied an important role in the formation of ideology, yet where they also seem to enjoy a certain independence both from a ruling class, and from a central state. Gramsci's ideas also provide another pay-off, this time in much more parochial academic circumstances – the central concepts can also be seen to offer a radicalized version of some of the classic debates in Sociology (such as the tension between 'structure' and 'agency'). The necessarily rather vague discussions of central concepts (Gramsci did much of his work in prison) have the considerable benefit of promising a theoretically rich research programme with the potential to yield an almost endless stream of concrete investigations of various popular cultural phenomena. In this way, to borrow a Gramscian phrase, the approach was able to 'win consent'.

The concepts concerned include the notion of 'hegemony', for example. Gramsci's own work, especially the *Prison Notebooks* (see Smith and Hoare, 1971) provide examples of the use of this term in analysing the particular political struggles going on in Italy of the 1930s and 1940s. Briefly, competing factions, by no means all of them based on the fundamental social classes of classic Marxism, were struggling for dominance in the ideological field as well as in attempts to monopolize the state and its organs. The ideological struggle involved efforts to connect a number of popular concerns and practices into an overall political ideology. To be specific, various bourgeois and social reformist ideologies had to be challenged, and the everyday struggles and concerns of workers and peasants, Protestants and Catholics, Piedmontese and Sicilians had to be integrated into an overall support for the emerging Communist Party. Hegemony therefore refers to a kind of cultural domination or leadership at the level of ideas and practices: a successful or hegemonic class will be able to demonstrate the superiority of its own organizing political ideas, its own right to come to power, its own ability to manage and overcome the rival ideas of other competing groups. Full integration of all the competing options, thrown up in all their complexity by varieties of social and political experience, may well be rare, and there will be constant work involved in managing those beliefs and practices that remain as forms of resistance to full integration. The real struggle to manage competing beliefs will lie at a rather sophisticated level. CCCS writers referred here to the influential work of Lukes (1974) on levels of power, the most subtle of which involves making opposition unthinkable, something beyond the pale of acceptable thought, something that cannot even be put on the agenda. Articulation refers to this general process of managing different political beliefs and practices.

Youth cultures

However, in the early stages of the entire project, the concept 'articulation' seems to take on a more sociological aspect. It appears in the famous discussion of the rise of youth cultures in Britain in the 1970s and 1980s (Hall and Jefferson, 1976). Typically, the editorial team set out to establish a new and innovative path towards understanding youth subcultures, separating itself clearly from existing sociological and psychological work. Thus early American work had used the term 'subculture' to describe the peculiar combination of conventional and deviant beliefs expressed in some criminal groups (see especially Cohen, 1955). Very briefly, juvenile delinquents had reacted to the core values of respectable American society by 'inverting' them. However, this argument had to be subject to Marxist scrutiny, and the obvious objection was that there were no core values integrating the whole of society in the first place, but rather competing class values. The underlying class struggle, which we can now see in terms of a hegemonic struggle to incorporate working-class resistance, would provide a particular agenda or organizing framework. Terms could be borrowed from Marxist theory to explain the dimensions of the ideological and political space within which working-class culture located itself: some aspects of this culture would clearly involve rejections of and alternatives to dominant conceptions of a range of cultural options and behaviour.

Working-class youth would inherit this cultural problematic, and would be able to find its own ways to perform cultural resistance. Younger members also stand in a problematic relationship to the cultures of their parents. In other words, there is an age dimension to youth cultures, involving both acceptance and rejection of the specific values of the working-class older generation. This is seen most obviously in the different clothes, musical tastes and drugs of choice displayed in youth cultures of the time. In this way Gramscian analysts could radicalize the popular psychology of adolescence which was prominent in the mainstream commentary on youth at the time.

The new approach could be summarized by the formulation of a 'double articulation' – a series of connections between youth cultures, 'first to their "parent" culture (e.g. working class culture), second to the dominant culture' (Hall and Jefferson, 1976: 15). It might also be clear from the above description that there had been a very promising academic articulation of the work in different traditions to produce a ground-breaking series of specific analyses, of teddy boys, mods, hippies and bikers, for which the Hall and Jefferson (1976) collection is famous.

However, a specific problem also appeared in that collection. Put simply, was gender a factor in the formation of youth cultures as well as age and social class? McRobbie's own dissatisfaction (in Hall and Jefferson, 1976) with the omission of gender and the similar criticism of later generations of CCCS students were to lead to major efforts to rethink the core concepts of Gramscian analysis altogether (Women's Study Group, 1978), but one response to this early criticism is also revealing – perhaps gender was also 'articulated' in youth cultures, and not just class and generation (Powell and Clarke, in Hall and Jefferson, 1976). This seems to overcome the immediate problem, but only by raising a more general one: what else might be articulated?

Hebdige's subsequent work was to argue for a profound structuring influence on white British youth cultures emanating from various relationships with the cultures of ethnic minorities (for example, Hebdige, 1979). No doubt others could have made similar claims for the influences of other cultural, social and geographical dimensions. Indeed, the number of dimensions involved in articulation seemed to be much larger than the original analysis had suggested, unless some claim was being made that class and generation were somehow more fundamental – this claim in particular has become more and more difficult to sustain.

Another early doubt suggested that the whole analysis of articulation was 'asymmetric' (Murdoch and McCron, in Hall and Jefferson, 1976). That is to say that articulation can only be studied in the past, that we can see from current complexities how elements have been articulated together, but it becomes much more difficult to work the other way around, and use a general theory of articulation to predict future combinations. There is a clear challenge to the validity of the entire analysis since it becomes difficult to separate mere contingency from theoretical reasoning.

There was also a comment about methodology (Butters, in Hall and Jefferson, 1976) – CCCS work was to break with the old problems of oscillation between induction and deduction that had haunted much social theorizing. Instead, they were to explore nothing less than a Sartrean dialectic, moving beyond this stale opposition and permitting a radical new link between concrete and general analysis: 'a round-trip passage from a presumptive theory of the whole social order, to the level of negotiated cultural nexus in which individuals make and live their experience, and back to the totality, carrying now some means to criticise the original account' (Hall and Jefferson, 1976: 270–1). Doubts about whether this theoretical transcendence ever came to pass will be discussed as we proceed.

Wood (1998) makes an important general criticism here. The approach overemphasizes the political aspects of culture and leisure to the neglect of those aspects that are not implicated in the struggle for hegemony: it reduces culture to ideology, as he puts it.

To take another example of neglected social and cultural processes, Hebdige (1979) points out that the role of the mass media in offering already articulated styles was not discussed. Instead, a rather obscure mechanism was invoked, whereby collective experience just gets transformed into the sudden nationwide emergence of a penchant for velvet jackets, crepe-soled shoes, long haircuts, and the like. The problems involved here concern the actual mechanisms of articulation, and in particular the agents at work in producing concrete and specific articulations of such detailed matters as hairstyles.

One early answer involved the process of 'homology' as a possible solution. In the Introduction to Hall and Jefferson, the concept is used to think out the relations between 'aspects of group life' and the ways in which 'appropriated objects and things were made to reflect, express and resonate' (Hall and Jefferson, 1976: 56), to become distinctive youth styles. The approach was developed much more extensively in Clarke's chapter on style, which does attempt a sustained analysis of the connections between concrete agents responsible for stylistic innovations (seen in terms of Levi-Straussian bricolage) who mediated the contacts between subordinate and hegemonic cultures. To trace some of these steps in slightly more detail, Clarke argues that the activities of bricoleurs are constrained by the existing cultural material. This limits bricolage to '*transformation and rearrangement* of what is given (and "borrowed") ... its *translation* to a new context and its *adaption* [*sic*]' (ibid.: 178, original emphasis). Culturally, youth groups choose material which provide a structure of recognition or similarity already and immediately – (citing Willis) 'there is a clear homology or *fit* between the intense activism, physicality, externalisation of attitudes in behaviour, taboo on introspection, and love of speed and machines of his "Motor-Bike Boys" and the early Rock'n'Roll music to which they were exclusively attached' (ibid.: 179).

Yet there are also discussions of social processes involved. At one level, Clarke points to processes of solidarity and distanciation between the stylistic groups, the processes of drawing and maintaining social boundaries to include insiders and exclude and demonize outsiders. Then there are social reactions, including relations with the mass media and the police. Finally, there are the contradictory and variable relations with commerce, which threatens to both diffuse and defuse youth style, and which find considerable success with some groups (mods especially), and resistance from others (hippies with their notion of fully alternative societies). Overall, youth cultures are vulnerable to hegemonic reincorporation because they offer only 'magical resolutions' of the real contradictions of capitalism.

There is an argument throughout that the real problem is that youth cultures are located predominantly in the vulnerable sphere of leisure. Youth cultures are concentrated in that sphere because leisure represents an area of relative freedom and some genuine power over lifestyles, and thus it is that leisure has been central for the shaping of subordinate working-class culture 'since the mid-nineteenth century' (ibid.: 176). However, this has 'displaced' concerns from the area of work, the site of proper forms of class struggle. As a result, unreformed work relations tend to exert a powerful effect on working-class leisure, as in the cult of masculinity. Work (and marriage) finally act to domesticate oppositional culture.

Clarke's work is more concrete than critics like Wood suggest, but there is still a major problem in his approach. It is eclectic, and much of it seems little different from structural anthropology or from 'bourgeois' accounts of subcultures, especially those in Downes (1966). The main articulating mechanisms are described in more detail, but the 'levels' model with its expanding 'constraints' still fails to offer a consistent dynamic process of articulation.

Willis's work offers another option, actually based on some early doubt about the concept of hegemony (Willis, 1977: 170). The famous (1977) work on school subcultures operates with a group of 'lads' who ably articulate their perceptions and understandings, and there are two concrete agents which articulate the culture of working-class 'lads' with ideological themes about manual labour and masculinity: schools themselves, and more specifically careers education within schools. It is these agents who manage the clever trick described in Willis's book: despite the oppositional culture 'the lads' develop, and the problems this causes teachers and schools, they end up in manual labour which has been their assigned destination all along. However, the other theme in the book became important in BCS as well

– the use of ethnographic data to accompany abstract theorizing about ideology and its mechanisms.

Willis shares the common reservation about ethnographic data used in bourgeois studies, of course – that it describes only surface forms and misses out the most important structuring forces of hegemony, which, sometimes by definition, cannot be grasped in the everyday knowledge of members of the working class. Butters, in Hall and Jefferson (1976), outlines some excellent criticisms about the methodological principles of ethnography and its inherent incoherence. Nevertheless, working-class experience can not be simply written off as ideologically corrupted since it must be the fundamental origin of resistance (see Coward, 1977, for an excellent critique of this 'ascribed role' for working-class agents). Ethnography would permit some kind of study of actual articulating agents. An uneasy use of ethnographic data ensued, much of it based upon the Willis claim (in Hall et al., 1980; and see Willis and Trondman, 2000) that ethnographic data could at least be used to generate 'surprise'. This would help check theory and limit its abstractions. However, strictly speaking, this could only happen if ethnographic data were granted some validity, which involves some retraction of the strict Gramscian position, while permitting the analysis of hegemonic structures to have the last word.

Mass media

Hall (in Curran et al., 1977) has written a thought-provoking account of the general 'ideological effect' of the mass media in Britain, part of a more general cluster of CCCS analyses involving how the concept of 'the nation' is constructed and represented. This particular account involves seeing the role of the media as offering both an analytic and a synthetic dimension. In the first phase, the British nation is seen as a collectivity comprising various separate elements, such as the different regions, different generations, ethnic minorities, the genders, and so on. Dividing up the nation in this way is already ideological, for Marxists, in a particularly strong sense. Drawing upon Marx's own work on methodology in the *Grundrisse* (Marx, 1877), we can see these categories as phenomenal forms, representing only too well a misleading surface reality. The real analytic categories which explain these surface elements and their apparent separation turn on the notion of the capitalist mode of production, specifically its class structure, of course, but Marxist conceptions of social class are conspicuously missing from popular media discourses. Having divided up the social totality in this plausible but misleading manner, the media then classically offer misleading articulations of the elements to reconstruct 'the nation'.

Perhaps the best concrete illustration of this particular approach is provided by a critique of the popular British television light current affairs programme *Nationwide* in the famous Open University course on popular culture (Open University, 1982). The Christmas special edition depicts Britain as a collection of social groups which can be represented by visiting the various BBC regions, and showing how various community activities are taking place: in the northern region, the Salvation Army is delivering Christmas parcels to the elderly poor; in Bristol, black and white families are getting together to have a Christmas party; in the eastern region, Father Christmas is seen parachuting into green fields and being welcomed by local children. The regional focus then merges into a *Nationwide* Christmas party held at the Guildhall in London, the ideological heart of the nation, according to (Bennett's) commentary. The hegemonic work is clear – Britain has its social divisions, but these are natural, or inevitable, and they can be overcome by the sort of special social and spiritual effort made at Christmas.

Another famous piece (Hall, in Hall et al., 1980) concerns an attempt to deploy the mechanisms of 'coding' and 'decoding'. The idea is to show how the constructive cultural processes deployed by the media can come to take on ideological or hegemonic functions. Coding is essential to the business of representation undertaken by the media, as 'reality' is expressed and made to make sense through the conventions of television. Although he is cited there is very little exploration of the actual work on specific codes undertaken by Barthes (see Barthes, 1975), however. Instead, Hall wants to argue that some codings are 'dominant' in the sense that they represent and re-present 'common sense' (really ideological) conceptions of the world.

However, it is also necessary to attend to 'decodings'. Hall enters a strong reservation against the view that the ideological messages in mass media simply enter uncritically the consciousness of the viewers. This view would infringe the Gramscian notion that there must always be cultural resistance and struggle, based on the oppressive experiences of the victims of capitalism. Therefore, the possibility of critical decoding must exist. It is worth pointing out that this particular 'must' is not based on any concrete analysis of actual alternative decodings.

Further speculation sketches out some of the abstract possibilities for such decodings, borrowing from more sociological work on the dimensions of class consciousness. Parkin (1971) suggested that those already possessing some critical radical political resources would be likely to see mainstream culture quite differently – as distorted, partisan and limited. This could well inform a critical reaction to the coverage on television of industrial disputes or other news items. Parkin did not think that this oppositional stance would be spread beyond the ranks of trade union militants or active socialists. For the rest of the population, acquiescence in dominant codings was probably more likely, although a third group might be able to express some partial opposition or at least suspicion.

This theoretical model is closely associated with the attempts by Morley to investigate the audience for current affairs: again *Nationwide* was chosen (Morley, in Hall et al., 1980; and in Open University, 1982). The research showed that different segments of the audience did indeed respond in different ways to the contents of *Nationwide* broadcasts. The segments were defined rather oddly, in fact, yet some were able to resist being involved in the ideological notions of national unity. This is a turning point in Gramscian studies of the television audience, and has led to some further exploration along similar lines, including the study of different perceptions of racism in television sports commentary between white and black viewers (McCarthy et al., 2003).

To take another well-known example, Hall et al. (1978) explored media articulations in analysing a 'moral panic' about British street crime. 'Moral panic' is another borrowed term and it is duly politicized by arguing, speculatively, that the police and the state have particular vested interests in moral panics about street crime. These organizations can claim more resources for policing: extra policing can then be used to defend the state against more politicized struggle such as industrial militancy or street demonstrations. However, another focus concerns the role of the media in working up isolated cases of street crime involving black youth into a whole moral panic about 'race' and 'mugging'. The media are involved in the cycle of representation and re-presentation mentioned above, amplifying and shaping fears about social change, nationalism and immigration into a specific fear of black people. Just when we think we might have a description of an actual articulating agent, though, Hall et al. deny they are offering a simple conspiracy theory. Hegemony works in subtler ways, and the media professionals think they are acting autonomously or even critically towards the state. However, this only adds to their credibility which deepens the ideological effect of their articulations. News values (happen to? must?) lie nested inside hegemonic agendas in the way we have described above.

The argument remains controversial and oddly constructed, however. For one thing, only press articles were scrutinized and not television programmes. For another, the authors gloss the issue of moving from specific levels to more theoretical levels of analysis, from outlining professional news values to notions of hegemony, by a rather disingenuous claim that they are somehow forced to proceed towards the general level: 'our analysis can no longer remain at the [more specific levels] ...The "problem of authority" directs us to a different level of analysis' (Hall et al., 1978: 177). This is almost an empiricist argument that 'the facts' have pointed to the issue of hegemony all by themselves, and it is of course purely rhetorical, since the attempt to connect specific discourse to hegemonic ones had been in place from the very beginning. It is particularly informative to compare this manoeuvre with the ambitious claim to methodological innovation in Butters (Hall and Jefferson, 1976), which was mentioned above.

Bond and hegemony

However, the work that best demonstrates a move into more concrete analysis of leisure interests, especially popular media, is provided by the different efforts of Bennett on the Bond movie (Open University, 1982; Bennett and Woollacott, 1987). The earlier piece operates quite closely within the overall model of hegemony and articulation that was characteristic of the approach to popular culture in the Open University course of the time.

The more orthodox Gramscian analysis read the Bond movie as an example of hegemonic articulation. There were three dominant political codes identified, all of which produced an ideological effect. Borrowing upon the earlier work of Eco on the codes at work in the Bond novels, Bennett argued, for example, that the 'Imperialist code' brought together representations of other nations and 'races' and allowed the character of Bond to assert superiority over them. The allegedly characteristic British qualities of improvisation and moral fibre permitted Bond to overcome Russians, outperform Americans (despite their superior resources), and stand up to a variety of exotics, from Korean martial arts experts to Afro-Caribbean exponents of voodoo. The 'sexist code' also performed important ideological work, showing how Bond was able to overcome women, especially those who were 'out of place', typically both sexually and politically. Not to put too fine a point on it, Bond was able to sexually conquer asexual celibates such as Honeychile Ryder, or lesbians such as Pussy Galore, which restored them to 'normal' heterosexual identities and also enlisted their support in the struggle against the villain. In his 1982 work, Bennett pointed to the wider ideological significance of these dramas, in reasserting Britain's claim to be an international power and in offering resistance to a threatening increase in feminist demands, respectively.

The subsequent analysis (Bennett and Woollacott, 1987) is significantly different, however, although other critics see the changes more as an elaboration (Barker and Beezer Barker, 1992). Bennett and Woollacott discover far more about the concrete mechanisms of actually making films, pursuing, via ethnographic analysis, the coding and representational work that actually goes on. For example, they note that it is much more useful to visually represent Bond's ingenuity by having him use various gadgets rather than pursue the literary devices in the novels (internal dialogue as Bond plays games of cards, for example). Conventional film techniques are used to raise excitement, such as car chases or stunts. The films themselves begin to relate to each other, with the later ones quoting or citing scenes in the earlier ones. Bond characters even quote bits of academic criticism of Bond films, as when Octopussy mocks Bond for thinking that he can sexually dominate her and thus put her back into place. This development of cultural autonomy, and the commercial pressures to tone down the celebration of Britishness in order to achieve global sales, mean that the Bond films can no longer be seen simply as containers of hegemony. Indeed, their hegemonic role remains as a mere possibility rather than as a central reading.

The audience is conceived rather differently too. There is more than a hint here of the substantial change of mind that Barthes's later work reveals. Briefly, in arguing for a 'new semiology', Barthes suggests that analysis should shift from trying to uncover ideological levels towards looking at how signs themselves actually relate to each other. This self-referential quality has been noticed in analyses of popular music, for example (Chambers, 1985) and in youth cultures like punk (Hebdige, 1979). The 'new semiology' also implies a break with Gramscianism though, in that the reference to social conditions and hegemonic struggle ceases to be crucial: it may serve as an originating moment, but its significance is soon lost in the rapidly developing chain of self-reference in all its rich forms (the parodies, *hommages*, citations and quotations, inversions and pastiches mentioned above).

The same collection also argues for the 'death of the author' and subsequently the death of the reader, a theme developed specifically in Bennett and Woollacott (1987). The audience is now seen as consisting of a set of 'reading formations' who bring resources based on their own readings of other texts, and their own interests and intentions. These formations are much more abstract cultural entities than the old human agents formed from resisting social fragments. They see a specific version of the Bond film, which may not be similar to specific versions viewed by other formations. Indeed, Bennett and Woollacott go all the way with Barthes and agree that there is no longer a single text associated with a single Bond movie: instead, a constellation of readings are on offer, found not only in the movies but in the reviews, film posters and critics' comments as well. The concept of 'reading formation' is still not specific and concrete enough for some critics (see Seiter, in Seiter et al., 1989), but we have developed a long way from the simple three-part model of Parkin and Hall.

Discourse and discipline

We can find similar developments in other work by Bennett as well. In his discussion of cultural policy, for example, Bennett (1998) wants to suggest that the Gramscian notion of the state and its hegemonic functioning is too limited. Instead, a Foucauldian notion of discourses is developed as an alternative. To put this in terms of our main theme, elements are articulated together into discourses through a number of specific effects, rather than through the overall articulating mechanisms of the state and its organs. These discourses coalesce around the familiar Foucauldian attractors, both linguistic (enunciations and various kinds of systematic discourses including scientific ones), and institutional (specific organizations combining knowledge and power).

Of course, some Gramscians once believed that Foucault and Gramsci were in the same camp. Hargreaves (1986) is perhaps the best example here, arguing that Foucault's more specific analyses could be simply used to round out, or 'elaborate' Gramscian work. His example of the health and fitness craze as a 'disciplinary apparatus' suggests that the craze integrates together a number of discourses, including athletic, beautician, health and cosmetic themes, but it is clear that the overall significance is that subjects will be produced that are disciplined both to produce and to consume in modern capitalism. The modern 'disciplinary apparatus' is an extension of the earlier attempt by the state to introduce 'rational recreation'. Bennett is much less certain that the themes can be combined, however, and sees the work of Foucault as departing radically from the conception of the state as the main source of power and ideology held by Gramscians.

A philosophy of articulation

Hall and his colleagues (for example, Hall and Jacques, 1983) engaged in some analysis of mainstream British politics too, which I cannot summarize here. A general theoretical dilemma emerged, however, in the discussions about the future of socialist politics. One option was the 'post-Marxist' position, especially associated with the work of Laclau and Mouffe (see Torfing, 1999, or Townshend, 2004, for some excellent commentaries). This took the view that the workings of the economic or social system would not deliver a reliable base for socialist political belief.

Behind this specific point lay a more general 'philosophical' argument, however. Briefly, to claim that class interests lay behind articulation was 'essentialist' (or 'foundational'), and involved some dubious assumptions. To reject this position, led to one pure possibility only – that there were no essential generating interests at all, but that coalitions or articulations depended on a process of articulation itself. Whatever emerged as important did so because of these articulations, not because of some underlying logic of history, tendencies towards class warfare, laws of economic development and the like. This typically philosophical concern for 'pure' concepts and for logically discrete categories leads, rather ironically for a Marxist project, away from concrete analysis altogether, though. There is a neglect of actual social formations and processes that have generated the necessary collective and solidaristic response found in cultures, including some concrete work on the social formation of class consciousness or racism.

There seemed to be a new and much more widespread kind of oppositional politics on offer at first, but also problems for Gramscians (see Hall, in Grossberg, 1986). Basically, it made politics too flexible and free-floating, so that more or less any kind of dispute could be seen as 'political', and as no less important than any other. The approach also opened the possibility that effective articulators might be able to build political blocs by the sheer force of discourse alone. There were some unfortunate examples to be noted, in Italian fascism, and, closer to home, in the short-lived Social Democratic Party (SDP) in Britain. This party did enjoy some electoral success and might have emerged as the major form of challenge to Thatcherism, but the Gramscians had serious reservations, seeing social democracy as an opportunist matter of marshalling local and temporary dissent, using vague political slogans and formulae such as being both 'tough' and 'tender' towards crime. Something of this critique seems to have been revived in Hall's recent attempt to criticize New Labour (Hall, 2003) and to propose instead an option of uniting all those who have suffered under advanced capitalism into a kind of socialist popular front. Would this front be united by a genuine common interest, though, or merely because some fiery orator had articulated various groups?

Articulation revisited

Some of the latest work in the BCS tradition offers a slightly different take on the old dilemmas. A textbook, written by duGay and others (1997) for a new version of the Cultural Studies course at the UK Open University, discusses the constellations of meanings centred on objects and their uses, specifically the Sony Walkman. The analytic effort involves connecting the specific object back into some sort of social and political totality again. This time, the totality is represented by words like globalization and consumerism, however. These now serve as the ideological articulating mechanisms which bring together the necessary aspects of the Sony Walkman – its engineering, technology and production, the whole apparatus of marketing and advertising, and the feedback loops connecting consumption back to design and production. The term 'articulation' is used specifically to describe the key integrating role of the product designers. For example, designers were able to articulate together specific leisure uses and design features when they noticed that young people were using the Walkman to accompany their health and fitness activities: the result was a lightweight Walkman with an anti-roll mechanism. If market research discovered that people were using the Walkman to isolate themselves from their surroundings, advertising themes would develop this idea, and the product engineers would do so as well, principally by removing the socket that permitted joint listening from the early products. DuGay et al. argue that this is not merely 'adding value' to the product, but articulating culture and engineering.

Yet this analysis reveals at its clearest the old dilemmas all over again. There is no coherent and agreed content to the term 'articulation'. We have a two-level analysis featuring both the specific activities of definite human agents (the designers), and the more general mechanisms of commercialization and globalization that evidently structure and constrain those activities as well. The piece is actually rather incurious about the activities of designers themselves, for example, who are permitted just to be 'creative' in some free-floating way, a rather uncritical stance also found in Gardner and Shepherd Gardner (1989), from whom much of the analysis derives. Classically asymmetric, the analysis also failed to predict the collapse of the Walkman, despite all the infernal arts of the articulators, as the iPod swept the market.

Without the insistence on the special importance of 'articulation' the duGay et al. analysis looks less original, which invites in turn comparison with other well-known examples of critical analyses of consumerism. Jameson (1991) proposes, in effect, to expand the notion of capitalist commodification to reclaim the apparently separate and cultural moments of duGay et al.'s analysis. However, this would involve more retreat than would be congenial from the idea some kind of 'political' role by the 'active consumer' (see Willis, 1990). Oddly though, there is little on the active consumer directly in duGay et al., certainly compared to Goldman and Papson (1998), say, on the Nike phenomenon. Ritzer's (1999) work on 're-enchantment' also opens more possibilities: it is theoretically more open to conflicting analyses drawn from Weber and Baudrillard as much as from Marxism, and it is more dynamic and informative on the cycle of resistance and reincorporation described in terms of dis- and re-enchantment.

Articulation and its inarticulacies

It is possible to see the notion of 'articulation' as involving considerable ambiguity and contradiction. Advocates of Gramscian approaches set themselves up for difficulties by insisting on two levels of analysis: one more concrete, specific and autonomous; the other more general, theoretical and determining. This can never be a coherent formulation. The earlier variant ran into the sort of difficulties expressed by post-structuralist critiques of essentialism. Hirst was to argue this as a problem against Hall (actually when they were discussing the term 'relative autonomy' – in Hunt, 1977). Hirst was to insist that any coherence could only be the result of dogmatism – the insistence that youth culture, news values, Bond movies or leisure goods must be enmeshed in hegemonic struggle.

The argument that there 'must' be articulation at work in all the areas we have discussed has different inflections – sometimes it is a political imperative, an appeal for coherence in order to marshal political action; at other times it is a theoretical 'must', an attempt to 'map' specific work on to a particular theoretical research programme to gain an edge over rivals. In many cases, it is actually the rivals that have provided the substantive work in the first place, and Gramscianism contents itself with radicalizing and systematizing the results. Given the important institutional university context for the work, it seems that the most successful example of articulation is provided by Gramscianism itself in its long and tortuous attempts to establish itself as an academic research, publication and teaching programme against rival Marxisms and bourgeois academic disciplines alike.

Bibliography

Barker, M. and Beezer Barker, A. (eds) (1992) *Reading into Cultural Studies*, London, Routledge.

Barthes, R. (1975) *S/Z*, London, Jonathan Cape.

Barthes, R. (1977) *Image-Music-Text*, London, Fontana/Collins.

Bennett, T. (1998) *Culture: A Reformer's Science*, London, Sage.

Bennett, T. and Woollacott, J. (1987) *Bond and Beyond the Political Career of a Popular Hero*, London, Macmillan Education.

Chambers, I. (1985) *Urban Rhythms: Popular Music and Popular Culture*, London, Macmillan.

Clarke, J. and Critcher, C. (1985) *The Devil Makes Work: Leisure in Capitalist Britain*, London, Macmillan.

Cohen, A. (1955) *Delinquent Boys: The Culture of the Gang*, Glencoe, IL, Free Press.

Coward, R. (1977) 'Class, Culture and the Social Formation', *Screen* 18(1): 75–105.

Curran, J., Gurevitch, M. and Woollacott, J. (eds) (1977) *Mass Communication and Society*, London, Edward Arnold in association with the Open University Press.

Downes, D. (1966) *The Delinquent Solution: A Study in Subcultural Theory*, London, Routledge.

duGay, P., Hall, S., James, L., Mackay, H. and Negus, K. (1997) *Doing Cultural Studies: The Story of the Sony Walkman*, London, Sage in association with the Open University Press.

Gardner, C. and Shepherd Gardner, J. (1989) *Consuming Passion: The Rise of Retail Culture*, London, Unwin Hyman.

Goldman, R. and Papson, S. (1998) *Nike Culture*, London, Sage.

Grossberg, L. (ed.) (1986) 'On Postmodernism and Articulation: An Interview with Stuart Hall', *Journal of Communications Inquiry* 10(2): 45–61.

Hall, S. (2003) 'New Labour has Picked Up Where Thatcherism Left Off', *Guardian*, 6 August, and online at <http://www.guardian.co.uk/comment/story/0,3604,1012982,00.html>.

Hall, S., Critcher, C., Jefferson, T., Clarke, J. and Roberts, B. (1978) *Policing the Crisis: Mugging, the State, and Law and Order*, London, Macmillan.

Hall, S., Hobson, D., Lowe, A. and Willis, P. (eds) (1980) *Culture, Media and Language*, London, Hutchinson.

Hall, S. and Jacques, M. (eds) (1983) *The Politics of Thatcherism*, London, Lawrence & Wishart and *Marxism Today*.

Hall, S. and Jefferson, T. (eds) (1976) *Resistance Through Rituals*, London, Hutchinson.

Hargreaves, J. (1986) *Sport, Power and Culture*, Cambridge, Polity Press.

Harris, D. (1992) *From Class Struggle to the Politics of Pleasure: The Effects of Gramscianism on Cultural Studies*, London, Routledge.

Hebdige, D. (1979) *Subcultures – The Meaning of Style*, London, Methuen.

Hoggart, R. (1981) *The Uses of Literacy*, Harmondsworth, Penguin.

Hunt, A. (ed.) (1977) *Class and Class Structure*, London, Lawrence & Wishart.

Jameson, F. (1991) *Postmodernism or the Cultural Logic of Late Capitalism*, London, Verso.

Lukes, S. (1974) *Power: A Radical View*, London, Macmillan.

McCarthy, D., Jones, R. and Potrac, P. (2003) 'Constructing Images and Interpreting Realities', *International Review for the Sociology of Sport* 38(2): 217–38.

Marx, K. (1877) *Grundrisse*, London, Pelican Books, 1977.

Morris, M. (1988) 'Banality in Cultural Studies', *Discourse* 10: 3–29.

Open University (1982) *Popular Culture (E812)*, Milton Keynes, Open University Press.

Parkin, F. (1971) *Class, Inequality and Political Order*, London, MacGibbon & Kee Ltd.

Ritzer, G. (1999) *Enchanting a Disenchanted World: Revolutionizing the Means of Consumption*, Thousand Oaks, CA, Pine Forge Press.

Seiter, E., Borchers, H., Kreutzner, G. and Warth, E-M. (eds) (1989) *Remote Control: Television, Audiences and Cultural Power*, London, Routledge.

Smith, G. and Hoare, Q. (1971) *Selections from the Prison Notebooks of A. Gramsci*, London, Lawrence & Wishart.

Thompson, E. (1968) *The Making of the English Working Class*, London, Pelican.

Tomlinson, A. (1989) 'Whose Side Are They On? Leisure Studies and Cultural Studies in Britain', *Leisure Studies* 8(2): 97–106.

Torfing, J. (1999) *New Theories of Discourse: Laclau, Mouffe and Zizek*, Oxford, Blackwell.

Townshend, J. (2004) 'Laclau and Mouffe's Hegemonic Project: The Story So Far', *Political Studies* 52: 269–88

Willis, P. (1977) *Learning to Labour: How Working Class Kids Get Working Class Jobs*, Farnborough, Saxon House.

Willis, P. (1990) *Common Culture*, Milton Keynes, Open University Press.

Willis, P. and Trondman, M. (2000) 'Manifesto for Ethnography', *Ethnography* 1(1): 5–16.

Women's Study Group (1978) *Women Take Issue*, London, Hutchinson.

Wood, B. (1998) 'Stuart Hall's Cultural Studies and the Problems of Hegemony', *British Journal of Sociology* 49(3): 399–414.

32
Community

Alison Pedlar and Lawrence Haworth

'Community', one of the most frequently used words in our vocabulary, is a highly honorific term. We deplore the 'loss of community' and search for ways to 'rebuild community'. But at the same time we have difficulty saying precisely what it means to be a community, or, alternatively, deciding which among various proposed but mutually incompatible definitions of community should be preferred. This chapter seeks to enhance our understanding of community, and of the conditions under which it deserves its honorific connotation, by looking at some ways researchers have connected the idea of community with that of leisure. Leisure research itself, with some significant exceptions to be noted below, has paid scant attention to the idea of community. But in the disciplines out of which the interdisciplinary study of leisure has arisen – for example, sociology, social psychology and political theory – leisure and community are frequently interrelated themes.

Elemental understandings of the meaning of community

Among the sources of confusion surrounding the meaning of community is that there are many different kinds of community. We have physical, emotional, psychological, social and economic communities of interest. Most of us are members of a large number of communities, some of which overlap one another, thus giving rise to multithreaded communities. Other communities may be quite distinct and isolated – a cloistered nunnery, say, to cite an extreme example. And it is possible that we are members of some communities without even being aware of the fact.

Indeed, one may ask how we know when we are in community. Wood and Judikis (2002) have suggested an approach to dealing with this question by separating communities according to their fundamental differences. They suggest five community categories: (1) nuclear, such as family or a group that functions as family, characterized by intimacy and bonding; (2) tribal, which includes identification by gender or social class grouping; (3) collaborative, such as special interest groups which have common, agreed upon purposes; (4) geopolitical, which may be political, educational, social or economic, contained by geographic boundaries; (5) life communities, which encompass the sum of family, acquaintances, and other significant people who impinge on the whole of one's life. As well, of course, modern community is fluid inasmuch as global forms of communication provide the opportunity for greater connectivity between people than ever before (Delanty, 2003). In this discussion, we shall not limit the exploration to any particular category of community, but will seek to bring as broad an understanding to the concept as is feasible within the confines of a necessarily short chapter.

Community is studied by scholars and researchers from the widely differing perspectives of numerous disciplines, from anthropology, sociology, psychology, planning, architecture, social work and geography, to philosophy, history and literature – and the list could be considerably expanded. One of the challenges in studying community therefore is to gain an understanding that allows for a multiplicity of possible interpretations in relation to form, content and structure of the concept.

For the purposes of this exploration we find the following conceptualization of community to be helpful:

> In any genuine community there are shared values: the members are united through the fact that they fix on some object as pre-eminently valuable. And there is a joint effort, involving all members of the community, by which they give overt expression to their mutual regard for that object. (Haworth, 1963: 86)

The emphasis here is on shared values, joint effort, and the involvement of all members in an activity or way of life, with the understanding that the activity or way of life may or may not be admirable. This establishes the idea that whether a community is desirable depends on our estimate of the shared values that form the members into a community and of the legitimacy of their ways of pursuing or seeking to preserve those values. Where the shared value is a way of life we have or may have a so-called 'traditional community', for example a medieval manorial village, community as *place*. Where the shared value is an activity or project we have a purposive community, for example an orchestra or choir who share an appreciation for the music they are performing.

In the discussion that follows, when we talk of community we shall be approaching it from a broadly spatial and social perspective, so that community refers to a city, a neighbourhood, or a collectivity of people with a common interest. But in the background will be the understanding that the community deserves to be called a community by virtue of the fact that in their life together there are shared values among the members.

Our other key term is 'leisure', which is generally understood in either (or both) of two distinct but related ways. Of course, elsewhere in the text, leisure is explored more centrally than the meanings we present here. For the purposes of this chapter, leisure suggests free time, those phases of our life when we act not from necessity – for example, to earn a living – but on the basis of an unforced choice. But also leisure has a primarily adverbial use: we are sometimes said to act in a leisurely fashion. That is, the activity is experienced as having a character of finality. The contrast is with instrumentality. In leisure we sense that the rationale for what we are doing lies in the activity itself and not or not simply in the results achieved. The musicians cited in the preceding paragraph may be imagined to be 'at leisure' in this sense, regardless of how much they may also need the work. The two senses of leisure are of course compatible: one who enjoys free time, and so is in that sense at leisure, may choose to occupy that time doing things that are felt to be intrinsically worth doing, and so be at leisure in the second-mentioned sense.

As suggested above, within Leisure Studies, community research has not been particularly prominent, especially among North American researchers. More recently, however, community has achieved some attention in leisure research and several enquiries have been directed toward developing an understanding of community. As well, among British scholars there have been some landmark studies of communities. Many of these works have come from sociology of leisure scholars. Within sociology, in seeking to further our understanding of class and class systems, researchers have considered social structures and organization which has led them to examine specific communities. An example is Derek Wynne's (1998) study of life in the housing estate he calls 'The Heath'. Leisure, class and community are prominent aspects of Wynne's work. In some earlier foundational works, such as Smith et al.'s *Leisure and Society in Britain* (1973), scholars addressed a range of aspects of everyday life which interface with leisure, but again, class is noted as a pervasive influence on people's leisure. Similarly, discussion of community has often been tied to understanding the influence of class in relation to where and how people live, work and spend their free time.

Working from a North American perspective, the Chicago School, including notably studies by Park et al. (1925), reinforced this attention to the relationship between class, community and leisure. The life ways of people in the new suburbs as well as the older inner-city neighbourhoods were delineated by socioeconomic status, which in turn shaped social relations in work and in leisure. White (1955), Gans (1966) and Havighurst and Feigenbaum (1959) all brought attention to the relationship between leisure and class interests, identifying the ways in which different tastes and values varied by class and, in turn, community. Similarly, significant works which focused attention on leisure, class and community appeared during the 1980s and 1990s, including especially the widely read *Habits of the Heart* by Bellah et al. (1985), and the equally widely read *Bowling Alone* by Putnam (2001). More recently, works such as Florida's *Rise of the Creative Class* (2002) and a book by Putnam et al. that serves as a follow-up to *Bowling Alone*, entitled *Better Together* (2003), have deepened our understanding of community and leisure. We shall discuss these works later. But before proceeding further with an exploration of the relationship between leisure and community as articulated by these and other scholars, it is important to consider two main ideas, introduced over a century ago, that are foundational to community theory – *Gemeinschaft* and *Gesellschaft*.

In speaking of *Gemeinschaft*, Tönnies (1964) had in mind what we now call 'intentional communities', such as are found in folk societies. *Gemeinschaft* refers to communities that are all-encompassing. More or less the entirety of each member's life is spent in interactions with the other members, there is extensive mutual dependence or interdependence, and affective relationships run deep. The community is largely self-sufficient and self-contained. An approximate contemporary example would be a kibbutz or a closely-knit Amish community. Intentional communities may be political, economic, social, demographic or religious in purpose. Typically they are closed communities that do not welcome outsiders and are tradition-bound. Feminist theory has been particularly influential in challenging the honorific connotations associated with community, especially community of the intense sort that *Gemeinschaft* points to. Membership in such communities is by ascription, expectations preclude experimentation and individual freedom and choice are largely absent. As well, it was [and is] in the comprehensive, intentional community that inequities and diminution of women's roles were most pronounced (cf. Friedman, 1992; Young, 1995; Kingdom, 1996).

Gesellschaft, in Tönnies' account, is the polar opposite of *Gemeinschaft*. The contrast is that between a community and a 'mere' association. In *Gesellschaft*, individualism, independence and an absence of meaningful social or reciprocal arrangements and ties are prominent features of daily life.

The *Gemeinschaft/Gesellschaft* distinction is placed in historical context by relating it to a parallel distinction also made over a century ago by the jurist, Sir Henry Maine. Maine's (1931) slogan was 'from status to contract'. At an earlier time, people's life prospects were fixed by a status which they acquired at birth as a birthright. This birthright gave one one's role in society; there was little chance that this would change during one's lifetime. As we say now, there was minimal social mobility. Gradually, especially as Europe moved out of the medieval and into the modern era, status was replaced by contract. Now and increasingly the roles and engagements that define a person's life are not so much fixed at birth as they are outcomes of freely entered into arrangements with others, contracts. So, instead of being condemned by an accident of birth to devote one's life to a specific trade, one is free to move from one occupation to another as one's talents and opportunities allow.

The *Gemeinschaft/Gesellschaft* distinction is deepened by associating it with Maine's idea of an historical movement from status to contract. In *Gemeinschaften*, intentional communities, people's life circumstances are typically fixed by status. By contrast, the growth of *Gesellschaft* both marks the replacement of status by contract and is motivated by the emerging importance of contract in determining people's life prospects.

With these distinctions before us we are in a position to identify a major issue posed by the standard assumption that community and leisure are both 'good things'. Community, most prominently in its *Gemeinschaft* guise, presents to the modern sensibility two problems. First, it tends to be closed and exclusive. By contrast, *Gesellschaften* are, or at least hold the promise of being, open and inclusive. Second, communities, especially intentional communities, are often and with some reason thought to be non-conducive to both individual growth and flourishing and to recognition of individual rights. *Gesellschaften*, or, in general, looser forms of association, by contrast, appear to offer the sort of open environment that enables people to flourish and in which individual rights are likely to be recognized.

Community is thus thought to put at risk two prime modern values, diversity and individuality. And we tend to suppose that environments that nurture diversity and individuality are also natural and conducive sites for leisure, in both senses of the term, leisure as free time and leisure as intrinsically rewarding activity. Worth noting here is that these conceptualizations of leisure and the values of modern society, namely diversity and individuality, may or may not be relevant in the context of less modern and more collectively organized societies. For the purposes of this chapter, however, we shall speak in the context of cultural values that are familiar to Western industrial society.

   The issue then is this: how can we realize the obvious benefits that community brings, for example, its role in the formation of identity, without sacrificing our commitment to diversity and individuality, individual flourishing? Or, from another perspective, how can we fit meaningful leisure into our lives without thereby undermining community? With these questions at the back of our minds, we may now review some of the literature in which the modern problem of community is addressed.

The embrace of ruralism

The idea of social renewal through community was part of the garden city movement of the late nineteenth century. Ebenezer Howard's (1945) social revolution sought to resist the pressures of urban specialization, impersonality and anonymity that had come to characterize urbanism. Thus, the garden city movement embraced ruralism in an effort to substitute co-operative relations for selfishness, and although Howard did not reject all things urban, he sought to bring more people closer to the countryside in compactly built towns, surrounded by pastoral landscape. In examining the growth of the modern-day residential suburb, certain antecedent conditions are identifiable. Among the factors more frequently associated with the movement of people to residential environments on the outer edges of the city is the ancient belief that a holiday in the countryside is the antidote for the maladies of city life. There can be little doubt that the value of life in the country was reflected in Howard's design for the ideal community. Subsequent to the garden city movement we have witnessed mass development of suburban housing, but the newer developments incorporate few of the diverse characteristics which rendered Howard's plan a viable alternative to exploding and sprawling cities. However, through the twentieth century and continuing today, we have witnessed unabated movement of people into the suburbs and away from the 'ills' of inner-city life. The image of the city as an unsatisfactory environment in which to live was reinforced by the idealization of the suburban alternative. It was in the suburb that Bellah et al. found the lifestyle enclave:

> Members of a lifestyle enclave express their identity through shared patterns of appearance, consumption, and leisure activities, which often serve to differentiate them sharply from those with other lifestyles. They are not interdependent, do not act together politically, and do not share a history. If these things begin

to appear, the enclave is on the way to becoming a community. (Bellah et al., 1985: 335)

While the suburbs were growing, after decades of neglect many inner cities were struggling to survive. It would be difficult to envisage any kind of community surviving in the sterile buildings housing corporate head offices, or dilapidated, boarded-up doorways to former shops that became 'homes to the homeless'. In this environment, community virtually disappeared. Indeed, the flight from the inner city can be explained by many factors, including the post-war developments of home mortgage insurance for veterans, the desire to own one's home, the idealization of the countryside, and new expressways. Land developers and planners responded to these factors by ensuring availability of suburban housing to meet the demand. This gradual dispersal of people to suburbia left many inner-city areas hugely disadvantaged. Those who did not move out but remained in those areas were similarly disadvantaged, indeed, didn't move out *because* of their disadvantages, including especially poverty and, for many, the accident of being a member of a group, a visible minority, which suburbia rejected.

Suburbanization of the landscape in and around cities dramatically changed the nature of community connectedness and city life. The work of Jane Jacobs (1961) and Lewis Mumford (1961) has been widely acknowledged as insightful but more importantly *right* in terms of the tragedy of neglect of our inner cities, the devastation done by suburban sprawl and the attendant dependence on the motor car that has furthered the diminution of community.

As cities declined, vast areas were torn down and large postmodern office buildings were erected as part of an effort to rejuvenate downtowns. Some developments within cities have included refurbishing central areas and a push to encourage people to 'come back to the city'. Recently we have witnessed a slight resurgence of interest in inner cities, or at least in those that have maintained or managed to create the vibrant neighbourhoods that Jane Jacobs talked about in the *Death and Life of Great American Cities* (1961). This encouraging development is attributable, perhaps, to the leisure preferences of those talented and technologically-savvy individuals identified by Florida (2002) as forming the new 'creative class'. According to Florida's analysis, the creative class has redefined many of the expectations people have held around work, leisure and community. We shall return to the discussion of Florida's views in the context of revisionist thought around leisure, individualism and social relations.

Communitarianism: the individual and the collective interest

Some would claim that openness and diversity are essential if a community is to be healthy (Wood and Judikis, 2002). This is a view that is held by those communitarians who seek to democratize our community structures. For instance, Dewey's (1954) contribution to community education and political democracy pointed to the centrality of commitment and mutual respect for the well-being and flourishing of every member of the community, and Dewey realized the importance of public institutions and political action for achieving these ends. Reflected here are some of the major tenets of that strand of communitarian thought which speaks of collective responsibility, co-operation, reciprocity and mutual aid in social relations, in contrast to liberalism with its narrow focus on individualism and individual rights (Kingdom, 1996). It would be a mistake, however, to suggest that communitarianism is unable to incorporate individual interests and is insensitive to individual rights.

There is to be sure a communitarian right-wing, which single-mindedly emphasizes the primacy of overall community traditions and values at the expense of minority rights. But this right-wing forms a small faction. The larger thrust of communitarianism is to stress the importance of community *for* personal development and fulfilment. The point is not that we should ignore the values of individual rights and human flourishing, but that we should reject the naive supposition that these can be protected outside community and in the absence of state action to promote public goods. Among the several strands of communitarian thought, there are three that serve as useful illustrations of the ways in which communitarians are sensitive to the importance of individual rights and personal fulfilment. These perspectives are value communitarianism (Frazer and Lacey, 1993), democratic communitarianism (Bellah, 1998), and radical communitarianism (Hughes, 1997). Frazer and Lacey note that value communitarianism emphasizes the values which express mutually supportive endeavours. This then leads them to place political priority on cultural practices and institutions which recognize and reaffirm communal and mutually supportive aspects of human life. Importantly, on this view self-fulfilment and the social good are seen as working in tandem.

Bellah's democratic communitarianism posits that individuals flourish only in and through communities. We do not exist in a vacuum, and healthy communities are a prerequisite for strong, healthy and vigorous individuals. For democratic communitarians solidarity is a central value, for we become who we are through our relationships, wherein we find reciprocity, loyalty and a shared commitment to the good. Equally, participation is both a right and a duty, and communities are positive goods only when they provide the opportunity and support to participate in them. In these respects, at least, modern communitarianism echoes Aristotle's central political thesis, that 'man' (and, we must add here, woman) is a political animal: in the same way that the growth of any living thing depends on its finding itself in a suitable, nurturing environment, we humans are able to flourish only in a politically organized community. And it should be mentioned that one of the major reasons Aristotle thought this was that in his view such a community established the conditions for people (alas, for Aristotle, only *some* people, adult male citizens) to lead leisurely lives.

A more radical communitarianism that has emerged among European scholars suggests that the North American communitarianism of people like Etzioni (1991, 1998) tends toward moral authoritarianism in that it fails to recognize the importance of balance between rights and duties (Hughes, 1997). In addition, radical communitarians see the new social movements as being at the forefront of rekindling active citizenship, where the primary object is the well-being of those most in need (de Leonardis, 1993).

Not unlike the debates that have linked social cohesion to the health of communities, radical communitarianism recognizes that the very idea of community involving bonds and loyalties becomes increasingly untenable in late modern society without some means of counteracting the forces of social exclusion. Social cohesion is seen as critical to the establishment of a civil society. It was described by the 1999 report on Education for Democratic Citizenship and Social Cohesion from the Council of Europe as follows:

> Social cohesion comprises a sense of belonging – to a family, a social group, a neighbourhood, a workplace, or a country. Yet this sense of belonging must not be exclusive. Instead, multiple identities and belonging must be encouraged. Social cohesion also implies the well-being of individuals and of the community, founded on tenets such as the quality, health and permanence of society. In addition to social ties, cohesion must be built upon social justice. (Council of Europe, 1999)

The report goes on to say that 'Social ties are built less upon employment than upon active participation – whether paid or not'.

Accordingly, as a growing body of literature suggests, leisure can be a site for the development of social cohesion and its corollaries, social ties and social capital (Arai and Pedlar, 2003; Glover, 2004). The ties that are associated with social capital are often referred to as weak or strong ties, and function in ways that bridge to other individuals and communities, or bond people within a community (Coleman, 1988; Putnam, 2001). It is generally assumed that a healthier, open community will be one that has bridging social capital and hence connections with a number of other sources of social capital outside the community. Thus the ripple effect of bridging ties means that social relations are characterized by reciprocity and mutuality, not unfamiliar concepts within communitarian thought. An outcome of this sort of connectivity is that people have greater opportunity to exercise their citizen rights, to participate in the life of their community.

Over the past several years an emerging literature in leisure studies has focused attention on civil society and leisure. For instance, Hemingway (1999) has explored the relevance of leisure to participatory democracy and active citizenship. Important to note here is the association between democracy and *certain forms* of leisure activity – as Hemingway argues, leisure that includes participation, communication, autonomy and development is necessary for the creation of social capital which contributes to strong citizenship. He goes on to say:

> Thus, (1) the more the individual participates actively in social structures, (2) the more autonomy the individual experiences, and (3) the more her/his individual capacities develop, then (4) the greater the accumulation of social capital that may be transferred not only to other leisure activities, but to other social roles, relations, and structures generally. (Hemingway, 1999: 157)

The centrality of social roles and connectivity in leisure is an important aspect of the democratic processes which Hemingway addresses. So too, of course, is the way in which leisure is provided, in terms of the role afforded the individual: is it that of a client or a citizen? 'Citizens participate more or less directly in decisions that shape their communities; clients receive benefits and entitlements dispensed by an administrative or professional hierarchy' (ibid.: 162).

Scholars have further argued for the connection between politics and leisure, particularly in terms of a conceptualization of leisure that goes beyond the idea that leisure necessarily involves activity that serves no public purpose, meets no social need (Haworth, 1984; Rojek, 2001). In this regard Rojek refers to civil labour as 'voluntarily chosen socially necessary labour, designed to sustain the commons and reaffirm the individual's responsibilities and obligations to society' (2001: 122). This is congruent with a communitarian worldview which seeks to balance rights, responsibilities and obligations.

Evidence from Putnam et al. in *Better Together* (2003) demonstrates the roles that active citizens can and do take to address community problems. Whereas Putnam's earlier work, *Bowling Alone* (2001), supported the thesis that over the past 50 years or so there has been a sharp decline in social connectedness and therefore of social capital, *Better Together*, based on case studies situated in a variety of social settings, from major urban cities to smaller rural places, offers plenty of grounds for hope. This more recent work illuminates the ways in which citizens are connecting and beginning the process of improving both the quality of community life and, albeit perhaps unconsciously, their personal situations, through what Rojek might describe as civil labour. The people Putnam et al. studied were involved in creating social capital, which as the authors describe it entails 'developing networks of relationships that weave individuals into groups and communities' (2003: 1). In these processes they were engaged in a whole host of activities, ranging from a public arts project which used dance to interpret stories of a local shipyard's history, to children organizing to improve railroad crossing safety. In all of the cases studied, the researchers suggested alternative strategies which might have been invoked to bring about immediate solutions, but which, because they were incongruent with the needs and strengths of the people whose lives were affected, may not have been sustainable. In line with good community development work, the solutions that were identified and implemented by the members themselves were ultimately the most effective and satisfying (Pedlar, 1996). They all involved community members' time, they grew from social networks, and they were intricately tied to social capital which can be applied to solving other local issues that may arise in future. The benefits of such involvement in what we may think of as civil labour are considerable and may well extend to others beyond those immediately concerned with the issue.

None of this is to suggest that communities have no need of public or government involvement. In fact, just the opposite is the case. As Putnam et al. point out, in the situations they studied participatory strategies required government support and politicians who were ready to stand firm with the constituents, realizing that return on public investment may be slower with collective citizen action than with essentially politically or economically expedient solutions.

The relationship between citizens and politics in many ways echoes Borgmann's (1992) concern for communal politics. In his seminal work on postmodernism, community and leisure, he deplores the privatization of life and the conversion of public space into instrumentalities. Once, public squares and markets, even sidewalks, were sites for community, in which people engaged with one another in pursuits they experienced as intrinsically meaningful. This is to say as well that these spaces functioned as sites for leisure, and an expression of leisure that solidified community in public settings. Now the same spaces have been largely instrumentalized. The street enables us to reach the market where we buy the goods that we will consume at home or in some other private setting. It is in that setting, cut off from the public sphere and the life of the city, that leisure, such as it is, is found. Leisure is not only privatized but commodified.

These fairly familiar observations are given depth and freshness by Borgmann's embedding the ideas of privatization and commodification in a construct, the device paradigm, which he introduced in an earlier work, *Technology and the Character of Contemporary Life* (1984). In terms of this construct, the defining feature of modern technology is that it converts things into devices. The *device paradigm* suggests that with technological advance, the tools people use both in their work and while enjoying leisure increasingly become 'machinery' that procures benefits (commodities) at, say, the push of a button or a voice-actuating command. The result is a commodity handed forth by the machinery without the need for engagement by the person who is to consume the commodity. Insofar as our leisure and work life are taken up with devices, we become less engaged with one another and more passive in our relationship with the world. A result is that commodified leisure in private spheres disengages us from one another and from the world we inhabit, thus weakening our grip on its reality.

Borgmann stresses the importance of communal celebrations, more broadly, a festive city, as corrective steps to overcome the device paradigm's corrosive impact on community and leisure. He is clear that in coming together around communal celebrations, such as are possible when singing in a choir for the joy of singing, when experiencing ethnic and cultural richness in food and music festivals, playing baseball for the sake of the game itself, communities cannot divorce themselves from the role that governments can play in shaping the common arena or festive city.

> Through political action we must see to it that arts and athletics are given central and festive structures and locations in our communities, that they have the staff they need to set the stage for communal celebration. (Borgmann, 1992: 138)

The vitality and connectivity that Borgmann has described as foundational to the festive city remind us of the significance of an environment that encourages leisurely exchanges, where people can meet, talk, sit, in public spaces that welcome rather than deter their presence. For a number of decades it seems we lost sight of that entirely in the mammoth removal of congenial urban landscapes following the promptings of misguided 'urban renewal'. Disregard for the human and social fabric of our cities did enormous damage and caused immense displacement of people and communities with minimal resources and no real alternatives.

Communal politics may serve to temper these tendencies of modernism, but it requires a committed and energetic citizenry with an ability to make their voices known and heard. They need to be not just knowledgeable, but must have the ability to act on that knowledge. Some examples of success in this regard are found in a recent published special issue of *Leisure/Loisir* Vol. 27 (2002/03). Connolly's account of women who worked collectively to ensure their neighbourhood remained liveable and Mair's report of citizens engaged in civil leisure as they sought to protest the actions of international trade organizations are two good examples of communal politics (the reader will find other relevant examples in the special issue). Volunteerism and its relationship to serious leisure (Stebbins, 2002) have also received increasing attention in the literature over the past decade (Arai, 2000; Arai and Pedlar, 1997; Parker, 1997; Reid and van Dreunen, 1997). In most instances, while engaging in the initiative, people likely would not make the connection between leisure and politics, but instead would think of their involvement as being generally feasible outside of time that was otherwise obligated. In addition, it has been suggested that when engaged in civil labour or collective action aimed at some overall improvement in community life, there are also personal benefits that accrue to the individual, so that the separation between the collective interest and the individual interest becomes at best tenuous. Again, this would be congruent with a communitarian worldview that does not see self-sacrifice as an inevitable consequence of contribution to the betterment of the community.

Community and leisure revisited

An ongoing area of concern among community and urban studies researchers has to do with diversity and openness – openness to new ideas, new people, new life ways; more broadly, the openness of the community generally so that it is accessible to all, especially to visible minorities and marginalized people. Similarly, diversity is an area of research and scholarship that has not received as much attention as it ought within leisure studies. Florida's work, *The Rise of the Creative Class* (2002), presents a revisionist perspective on community life and leisure that draws attention to this neglect. In his exploration of the changing face of cities, he has taken the analysis of community back to one based in economics and class. He identifies a new 'creative class' of people who are actively engaged in redefining community and leisure in our cities and towns. People who are identified as belonging to the creative class live in cities that are characterized by lively economies. These cities are distinct in that they have a highly talented workforce on the cutting edge of technology. In addition, members of the creative class are not only tolerant but welcome uniqueness and differences in the physical, social and cultural fabric of the community. Florida sums up the defining characteristics of the creative class by referring to the three 'T's: talent, technology and tolerance.

The creative class are, according to Florida, a world away from Veblen's (2001) leisure class of the early twentieth century. Unlike the class of conspicuous consumers Veblen identified, members of the creative class consume *experience*. Their life ways are characterized by living and experiencing life to the full, with every moment finding them absorbed in work or leisure which is active and engaging. They gravitate to communities, described by Florida as Creative Centres, which are open to this level and variety of engagement. Florida describes these centres as providing 'the integrated eco-system or habitat where all forms of creativity – artistic and cultural, technological and economic – can take root and flourish' (Florida, 2002: 218). They choose to live and work in these centres because they find there a variety of 'scenes'; for instance, 'a music scene, art scene, technology scene, outdoor sports scene and so on' (ibid.: 224), all critical considerations in the expression of their preference for what they describe as real and authentic (an independent Fair Trade coffee shop, say), in contrast to generic (Starbucks is the most obvious contrast here); 'authentic' places are felt to offer unique and original experiences.

Florida further suggests a theory of creative capital: 'regional economic growth is driven by the location choices of creative people – the holders of creative capital – who prefer places that are diverse, tolerant and open to new ideas' (ibid.: 223). In a sense this begs the question as to whether these centres would indeed function as open communities – for the creative class are highly educated and highly talented and no doubt highly paid. They apparently care hugely about the quality of the places where they have chosen to live. They become engaged in seeking to ensure that historic buildings are preserved, that ethnic neighbourhoods are encouraged, and that their workplaces and neighbourhoods are vibrant and offer the depth and range of authentic experiences they require. What is less clear is how they respond to the displacement of people which must inevitably accompany the sorts of urban changes their tastes and enthusiasms give rise to. One cannot but question whether there isn't an aspect of consumption here that would bring the life ways of the creative class into the realm of the sort of hypermodernism that Borgmann (1984) has cautioned against in his account of leisure and advanced technological society.

Future possibilities?

What does our exploration of community and leisure suggest with respect to possible futures? What, under modern conditions, might be the relationship between leisure and community? Is it reasonable to speak of a future where this relationship enables our cities and towns to be both welcoming of diversity and fully open and accessible to all, including especially visible minorities and those who are marginalized in one way or another? And, parallel to this, how can we bring to these communities forms of leisure that do not trivialize our lives?

One might think that Florida has the answers. But, in our view, the leisure of the creative class has the potential to become frenetic and distracted in its continuing search for ever more intense *experience*. As well, despite the absence of 'passivity', the leisure lifestyle of the creative class may not ultimately be that much different from the stultifying world of absorption with television and the like that so concerns such critics of technology as Putnam and Borgmann. For underneath the sharp contrast with respect to activity and passivity there appears to be a common feature of self-absorption and a turning away from public goods.

It is more hopeful to reflect that we may be entering an age when citizens are increasingly cognizant of the relevance of agency, the importance of knowing and the ability to act on that knowledge in the interest of securing public goods. For instance, the pressures of globalization may be resisted in ways which bring people together in civil leisure (Mair, 2002/03). Similarly, civil leisure can function to build stronger communities – citizen efforts to restore and rejuvenate libraries in our cities and towns are bringing life back to parts of cities that had been stagnant and isolated. These revitalized spaces serve as 'a kind of community center, a place where people get to know one another, where communities find themselves' (Putnam and Feldstein, 2003: 49). One who is looking for evidence of the openness of a community might well check out the local library – truly a public good. In addition, people are celebrating their communities in leisure through, for instance, communal festivals, community gardens and neighbourhood art projects (Borgmann, 1992; Glover, 2003; Putnam and Feldstein, 2003; Wynne, 1998).

These reflections point to a future in which the focus of life is more outward-looking than it has been in the recent past. Leisure research and practice might reinforce this prospect by attending to the ways people at leisure are able to find meaningful community with one another in energetic activity devoted to enriching the public sphere and in that sphere celebrating the goods they have in common. The construct that informs such research would be that of a community set in a habitat that is genuinely open, inclusive, appreciative of diversity and encouraging of human flourishing.

Bibliography

Arai, S. (2000) 'Typologies of Volunteers for a Changing Socio-political Context: The Impact on Social Capital, Citizenship, and Civil Society', *Loisir et Société/Society and Leisure* 23: 327–52.

Arai, S. and Pedlar, A. (1997) 'Building Communities through Leisure: Citizen Participation in a Healthy Communities Initiative', *Journal of Leisure Research* 29(2): 167–82.

Arai, S. and Pedlar, A. (2003) 'Moving Beyond Individualism in Leisure Theory: A Critical Analysis of Concepts of Community and Social Engagement', *Leisure Studies* 22: 185–202.

Bellah, R. N. (1998) 'Community Properly Understood: A Defense of "Democratic Communitarianism"', in A. Etzioni (ed.) *The Essential Communitarian Reader*, Lanham, MD, Rowman & Littlefield, pp. 15–20.

Bellah, R. N., Madsen, R., Sullivan, W. M., Swidler, A. and Tipton, S. M. (1985) *Habits of the Heart: Individualism and Commitment in American Life*, New York, Harper & Row.

Borgmann, A. (1984) *Technology and the Character of Contemporary Life: A Philosophical Inquiry*, Chicago, IL, University of Chicago Press.

Borgmann, A. (1992) *Crossing the Post-modern Divide*, Chicago, IL, University of Chicago Press.

Coleman, J. S. (1988) 'Social Capital in the Creation of Human Capital', *American Journal of Sociology* 94: S95–120.

Connolly, K. (2002/03) 'Do Women's Leadership Approaches Support the Development of Social Capital? Relationship Building in a Voluntary Neighbourhood Initiative', *Leisure/Loisir* 27(3/4): 239–64.

Council of Europe (1999) *Education for Democratic Citizenship and Social Cohesion*, Strasbourg, Council of Europe. Online: <http://culture.coe.int/postsummit/citizenship/concepts/erap99_60.htm>.

Delanty, G. (2003) *Community*, London, Routledge.

de Leonardis, O. (1993) 'New Patterns of Collective Action in a "Post-Welfare" Society: The Italian Case', in G. Drover and P. Kerans (eds) *New Approaches to Welfare Theory*, Aldershot, Edward Elgar, pp. 177–89.

Dewey, J. (1954) *The Public and its Problems*, Chicago, IL, Swallow Press.

Etzioni, A. (1991) *A Responsive Society: Collected Essays on Guiding Deliberate Social Change*, San Francisco, CA, Jossey-Bass.

Etzioni, A. (1998) 'The Responsive Communitarian Platform', in A. Etzioni (ed.) *The Essential Communitarian Reader*, New York, Rowman & Littlefield, pp. xxv–xxxix.

Florida, R. (2002) *The Rise of the Creative Class: And How it's Transforming Work, Leisure, Community and Everyday Life*, New York, Basic Books.

Frazer, E. and Lacey, N. (1993) *The Politics of Community: A Feminist Critique of the Liberal–Communitarian Debate*, Toronto, Ontario, University of Toronto Press.

Friedman, M. (1992) 'Feminism and Modern Friendship: Dislocating the Community', in S. Avineri and A. de-Shalit (eds) *Communitarianism and Individualism*, Toronto, Ontario, Oxford University Press, pp. 101–19.

Gans, H. (1966) *The Levittowners: How People Live and Politic in Suburbia*, New York, Pantheon Books.

Glover, T. (2003) 'The Story of the Queen Anne Memorial Garden: Resisting a Dominant Culture Narrative', *Journal of Leisure Research* 35(2): 190–212.

Glover, T. (2004) 'The "Community" Center and the Social Construction of Citizenship', *Leisure Sciences* 26: 63–83.

Havighurst, R. J. and Feigenbaum, K. (1959) 'Leisure and Life Styles', *American Journal of Sociology* 63: 152–62.

Haworth, L. (1963) *The Good City*, Bloomington, IN, Indiana University Press.

Haworth, L. (1984) 'Leisure, Work and Profession', *Leisure Studies* 3: 319–34.

Hemingway, J. (1999) 'Leisure, Social Capital, and Democratic Citizenship', *Journal of Leisure Research* 31: 150–65.

Howard, E. (1945) *Garden Cities of Tomorrow*, London, Faber & Faber.

Hughes, G. (1997) *Communitarianism and the Future of Social Policy*, Milton Keynes, Open University. Available online at <http://www.psa.ac.uk/cps.1997/hugh.pdf>.

Jacobs, J. (1961) *The Death and Life of Great American Cities*, New York, Random House.

Kingdom, E. (1996) 'Transforming Rights: Feminist Political Heuristics', *Res Publica II*(1): 63–75.

Leisure/Loisir (2002/03) Special issue: 'Volunteerism and Leisure', 27(3/4).

Maine, H. (1931) *Ancient Law*, New York, E. P. Dutton.

Mair, H. (2002/03) 'Civil Leisure? Exploring the Relationship between Leisure, Activism and Social Change', *Leisure/Loisir* 27(3/4): 213–38.

Mumford, L. (1961) *The City in History*, New York, Harcourt, Brace & World, Inc.

Park, R., Burgess, E. and McKenzie, R. (1925) *The City*, Chicago, IL, University of Chicago Press.

Parker, S. (1997) 'Volunteering – Altruism, Markets, Causes and Leisure', *World Leisure and Recreation* 39(3): 4–5.

Pedlar, A. (1996) 'Community Development: What Does it Mean for Recreation and Leisure?' *Journal of Applied Recreation Research* 21(1): 5–23.

Putnam, R. D. (2001) *Bowling Alone: The Collapse and Revival of American Community*, New York, Simon & Schuster.

Putnam, R. D. and Feldstein, L. M., with Cohen, D. (2003) *Better Together: Restoring the American Community*, New York, Simon & Schuster.

Reid, D. G. and van Dreunen, E. (1997) 'Leisure as a Social Transformation Mechanism in Community Development Practice', *Journal of Applied Recreation Research* 23(1): 45–65.

Rojek, C. (2001) 'Leisure and Life Politics', *Leisure Sciences* 23: 115–25.

Smith, M., Parker, S. and Smith, C. (eds) (1973) *Leisure and Society in Britain*, London, Allen Lane.

Stebbins, R. (2002) *The Organizational Basis of Leisure Participation: A Motivational Exploration*, State College, PA, Venture Publishing.

Tönnies, F. (1964) *Community & Society (Gemeinschaft und Gesellschaft)*, East Lansing, MI, Michigan State University.

Veblen, T. (2001) *The Theory of the Leisure Class* (originally published in 1899), New York, Modern Library.

White, R. C. (1955) 'Social Class Differences in the Use of Leisure', *American Journal of Sociology* 61(2): 145–50.

Wood, G. S. and Judikis, J. C. (2002) *Conversations on Community Theory*, West Lafayette, IN, Purdue University Press.

Wynne, D. (1998) *Leisure, Lifestyle and the New Middle Class: A Case Study*, London, Routledge.

Young, I. M. (1995) 'The Ideal of Community and the Politics of Difference', in P. A. Weiss and M. Friedman (eds) *Feminism and Community*, Philadelphia, PA, Temple University Press, pp. 233–58.

33
Resistance

Susan M. Shaw

The idea of leisure as resistance raises questions about the political nature of leisure, and particularly about human agency, power, and social and cultural change. In this sense, resistance is not a neutral term that can be easily added to or dropped from the analysis of leisure at will (as in 'add resistance and stir'). Rather, it forces researchers to address not only theoretical questions about paradigmatic assumptions, but also political questions about the purpose and role of social research, about social action, and about praxis.

Until recently the concept of resistance had received scant attention in the leisure literature. This may reflect a disinclination on the part of researchers to become embroiled in political issues. It also may reflect a strong belief among many researchers that leisure has an important beneficial role to play in people's lives, and that we should be promoting the benefits of leisure rather than addressing more 'political' and potentially negative aspects. In addition, perhaps the need and desire for academic respectability for leisure research, particularly in North America, has encouraged researchers to focus on positivist and post-positivist approaches to research, and the acquisition of 'objective' knowledge and understanding, rather than social activism or social critique (see Hemingway, 1999, for a discussion of these issues).

In some ways, the failure to address the politics of leisure is an ironic situation for leisure scholars, since much of the early impetus for the study of leisure arose out of political or quasi-political concerns. For example, the early playground movement represented a desire from some sectors of society for the provision of 'wholesome' leisure, especially for those children and youth who might otherwise get involved in anti-social or criminal activities (Markham, 1991). Another political issue that also provided a major impetus for the academic study of leisure in the Western world was the expectation in the 1950s and 1960s that an 'Age of Leisure' was soon to become a reality (for example, see Dumazedier, 1967; Larrabee and Meyersohn, 1958). Rapid technological advancements following the Second World War seemed to augur the promise of a new life of freedom, devoid of the drudgery and long hours of work that had characterized the early years of the Industrial Revolution. Concerns were expressed about the potential danger of the misuse of the newfound freedoms (de Grazia, 1964), as well as possible negative repercussions related to the loss of work (Jenkins and Sherman, 1979). This led to the promotion of recreation as a solution and to calls for better leisure service delivery systems.

The political heritage underlying leisure research, though, did not lead to any systematic study of the political nature of leisure. In recent years researchers have continued to document some of the benefits of leisure, including the benefits associated with risk reduction, such as crime delinquency and drug taking, especially among 'at-risk youth' (for example, Witt and Crompton, 2001). Nevertheless, the broader political ramifications of leisure practice and the link between leisure and power have not been widely discussed.

The dominance of the social psychological paradigm in much of the leisure literature has also led scholars to focus most of their attention on issues of individual experience, meaning and behaviour, and away from issues of structural power relations or social control. The notion of leisure as a state of mind, or set of perceptions (such as freedom of choice and lack of obligation), was a major focus for a number of leisure scholars in the 1980s, leading to enhanced understanding of leisure meanings for individuals (Mannell and Kleiber, 1997). In addition, the social and interpersonal nature of leisure has been widely explored (Kelly, 1983), as has the range of constraints that interfere with or limit access to desired leisure (Jackson and Scott, 1999; Jackson, 2005). This area of leisure scholarship, then, has focused on the individual and his or her perceptions and behaviours, with considerably less attention being given to macro-sociological or cultural issues. And, while labour market activity and civic participation are both recognized as political, with implications for maintaining or challenging societal power relations and for understanding hegemonic processes in general, leisure is often thought of as 'innocent' (Green et al., 1990). Thus leisure has come to be seen, both by academics and in popular ideological constructions, as marginal or inconsequential to more significant political issues or concerns.

The idea of leisure as resistance overcomes these problems by bringing together the notion of leisure as freedom of choice with macro concerns about political issues and the distribution of power. Resistance can be seen as an act or series of actions that enhance freedom of choice and personal control. This agenic action can occur through challenging social and cultural impositions or constraints, including constraints on leisure participation (constraints on opportunities for or the availability of leisure), as well as through challenging constraints that emerge through various forms of leisure practice (Shaw, 1994). The latter might include resisting the role of leisure facilitator or leisure enabler for other people's free time activities (Thompson, 1999). For many theorists, though, the concept of resistance is also closely tied to the idea of challenging hegemonic processes through the critique of dominant ideologies and of the political ideas, beliefs and practices of the dominant hegemonic group or class (Clarke and Critcher, 1985; Tomlinson, 1998). Thus resistance could include refusing to conform to dominant groups' notions of appropriate leisure activities, and/or it could imply using leisure time or leisure activities to resist other aspects of the hegemonic order.

The social interactional nature of leisure is essential to the idea of resistance as well. Although individual action could be seen as an act of resistance or an attempt to enhance personal power, the political significance of resistance lies in the process of communication and the impact such acts may have on other people and on the potential for influencing political beliefs and ideologies. For example, beliefs about appropriate class-related or gender-related behaviours can be perpetuated and/or challenged through different forms of leisure practice, and through social interaction in leisure settings (Shaw, 1999). These behaviours can influence other participants, spectators, or casual observers, thus becoming part of the process in which meanings and beliefs are contested, negotiated, constructed and reconstructed.

The tie between this process of resistance and the idea of leisure as a site of relative freedom of choice is again evident. While resistance can occur in all settings and circumstances, it has been argued that leisure provides enhanced opportunities for resistant acts because of the greater opportunities for self-expression and self-determination (Wearing, 1998). Leisure as entertainment also provides opportunities to influence spectators as well as participants. Moreover, the belief in the innocence or marginality of leisure with respect to important and consequential social processes may mean that resistance through leisure could be particularly effective. Its potential role in challenging dominant power relations may go unrecognized, allowing for greater opportunities to effect change in circumstances relatively free of social control.

Although these arguments suggest the significance of leisure as a site of resistance, the conceptual framework for understanding resistance in and through leisure remains underdeveloped. The intellectual roots or theorizations about resistance lie in other bodies of literature. It is this literature that can potentially help in the development of conceptualizations for understanding leisure as resistance, while at the same time broadening the discussion of the politics of resistance in general.

Paradigmatic roots and issues

Current thinking about resistance is often attributed to Foucault's writings, particularly as they relate to his notion of power (for example, see Foucault, 1978, 1980; Dreyfus and Rabinow, 1983). Foucault's contention that power is constituted and transmitted through discourse (Foucault, 1978), suggests a close relationship between power and knowledge. Since discourses are ways of talking abut knowledge and truth, they create and reflect rules for what it is possible to talk about and how that talk can proceed (Ramazanoghu, 1993).

For Foucault, power is seen not only as pervasive, but also as personal rather than structural and institutional, making it unstable and subject to challenge. Because his conceptualization of power is personal and individual, produced and displayed through discourse, this implies the ever-present possibility of resistance through counter-discourses. Thus resistance is seen to be always possible: that is, power is everywhere, and where there is power there is also resistance (Dreyfus and Rabinow, 1983). Resistance, then, is something that is available to everyone and can be used to challenge knowledge, beliefs and constraints arising out of the imposition of the discourses of powerful others. Further, this suggests that there are many different forms of resistance. According to Foucault,

> There is a plurality of resistances, each of them a special case: resistances that are possible, necessary, improbable; others that are spontaneous, savage, solitary, concerted, rampant, or violent: still others that are quick to compromise, interested or sacrificial; by definition, they can only exist in a strategic field of power relations. (Foucault, 1978: 96)

Foucault's ideas on resistance and the notion of counter-discourses producing new knowledge and new powers are consistent with the postmodernist emphasis on identity as well. That is, resistance leads to the creation of new and alternate personal identities, and allows individuals to challenge imposed conceptualizations of self (Wearing, 1998). Multiple identities and multiple subjectivities are possible, reflecting varieties of meanings, experiences, perceptions and constructions of self.

Foucault's work has had a major influence on the theorization of power and resistance. It has created awareness of the many different sources of power that are available and on the multiple ways in which resistant acts can precede. In particular, the idea of personal power and the ever-present possibility of resistance places human agency at the centre of understanding, and rejects the notion of humans as passive victims of oppression. Nevertheless, and in part because of the focus on agency, Foucault's work has also been subject to criticism.

One group of critics is made up of theorists with a more structuralist orientation, particularly feminists and cultural theorists (for example, Ramazanoghu, 1993; Kellner, 2001). The idea of resistance is not unique to postmodernist thinking, but has long been a part of structuralist theorizing wherein the hegemonic process and dominant relations of power and oppression are never complete, but are always subject to contestation (Clarke and Critcher, 1985). Early Marxist and neo-Marxist ideas about praxis and empowerment have continued to inform researchers interested in social change for marginalized and powerless groups in society, and in finding ways to challenge dominant relations of power, whether these are related to class, race, ethnicity, sexuality, gender or other social dimensions.

The structuralist critique does not focus so much on the many different types of power or power enactment discussed by Foucault, nor about the idea of varieties of resistance, but rather about whether power is generally available to all, or whether it tends to be located in particular identifiable pockets or groups of society. According to Ramazanoghu and Holland (1993), Foucault rejected the idea that power was in the hands of particular groups or categories while other groups remained, despite the possibility of resistance, relatively powerless. For example, Ramazanoghu has argued that Foucault's theory of power

> does not allow us to ask where men's sexual power comes from, nor why it is so powerfully consolidated, institutionalised and reproduced ... The question of *why* men have power over women cannot be entirely reduced to analyses of discourse,

since the links between individual relationships and the institutionalised power of heterosexuality and masculinity cannot then clearly be traced. (Ramazanoghu and Holland, 1993: 256, emphasis in the original)

In fact, in some of his writings Foucault did recognize that networks of power occur, and that individual acts of resistance can be strategically aligned. For example, in 1978 he wrote:

> Just as the network of power relations ends by forming a dense web that passes through apparatuses and institutions, without being exactly localized in them, so too the swarm of points of resistance traverses social stratifications and individual unities. And it is doubtless the strategic codification of these points of resistance that makes a revolution possible, somewhat similar to the way in which the state relies on the institution integration of power relations. (Foucault, 1978: 96)

Nevertheless, Foucault paid relatively little attention to these networks or alliances. For some, then, his work is seen to undermine, or at least to not be particularly helpful to the emancipatory task of scholars concerned about racism, patriarchy or class-related oppression. Criticisms range from claims that Foucault is advocating an individualistic and even narcissistic concept of liberation (for example, see Soper, 1983) to concerns that if resistance is everywhere, there is no need for people in oppressed groups to unite (Ramazanoghu and Holland, 1993). In other words, the collectivist aspect of resistance, so central to critical and structural theorists, is downplayed by Foucault.

Related to this issue of individual or collective power and resistance is the question of ideology. For many theorists the targets of resistance are the ideologies which function to maintain the power of dominant or hegemonic groups, but Foucault's analysis suggests that targets are much more diverse, and could include anyone (and potentially everyone) who gains or maintains power through discourse. Foucault's conceptualization of resistance, therefore, is broader, but more difficult to specify or pinpoint compared to the structuralist perspective.

This leads to the second area of criticism of Foucault's work on resistance, which is that the concept remains too vague and inadequately defined. This criticism expands to incorporate other postmodernist views of resistance as well. Some critics maintain that there has been a somewhat naive or 'simple' celebration of resistance in postmodernist thinking (for example, see Ramazanoghu and Holland, 1993), without an adequate theoretical underpinning (Crook, 2001). Others argue that there has been a fetishism of the concept in some academic writings (Kellner, 2001) that relates to the valuation of resistance as personal power or empowerment without distinguishing different types of power (such as individual versus group power, or oppressive versus benign power). This critique raises the fundamental question of exactly what is being resisted (Lemert, 1997). Can all forms of agenic behaviour be interpreted as resistance? If this is the case, does the idea of resistance not become too broad to be useful? And has it thus lost some of its analytical and explanatory potential?

These issues, of course, are not unique to postmodernist views of resistance, but are indicative of more general definitional problems associated with this concept (Shaw, 2001). The issues raised lead to a series of as yet unanswered questions, including: can resistance be both individual and collective, and, if so, is there a need to distinguish between these different types of resistance? Is resistance an act that is directed against dominant relations of power, ideologies and/or discourses, or can it also be directed against personal or individual objects of constraint? Again, is there a need to distinguish between different types of targets? Is there a need to clarify what is successful or effective versus ineffective acts of resistance? And/or is resistance, like hegemony, always incomplete and contradictory? If so, how can acts of resistance be conceptualized, characterized, uncovered, or determined?

Despite these problems and questions, the concept of resistance, with its focus on agency and its potential to link agency and structure, seems to be increasingly utilized by social researchers. In particular, the concept has gained some ascendancy in the field of leisure studies in recent years, perhaps as a reflection of other social research, and perhaps because, as indicated earlier, leisure may be a particularly significant, if largely unrecognized, site for many forms of resistant behaviours.

Applications to leisure

Applications of the concept of resistance to leisure have most frequently revolved around the issue of gender. These applications, therefore, are typically based on an assumption of structured gender relations and resistance to gender-related ideologies such as hegemonic notions of femininity and/or masculinity, or ideologies associated with motherhood, familism or caregiving. Most of this research has focused on women's resistant leisure and the different ways that this can occur.

The relative lack of leisure availability for women led researchers to note that simply claiming entitlement to leisure is an act of resistance. For example, Freysinger and Flannery (1992) argued that women's claim of entitlement to self-determined leisure represented a form of resistance against the socially constrained roles of wife and mother. Similarly, mothers of first babies in Wearing's study (1990) were seen to be resisting the dominant discourse of motherhood by giving themselves 'permission' to take time and space for their own leisure. Bedini and Guinan's (1996) study revealed how difficult it was for women who are caregivers to claim entitlement to leisure, though some were better able to do this than others. A more recent study (Herridge et al., 2003) also showed that some young women in heterosexual relationships resist the constraints that these relationships place on their own independent leisure (although accommodation to partners' wishes is a more typical response). Together these studies indicate that the notion of resistance may be important for understanding women's access to leisure, although exactly what they are resisting and how they are resisting this may vary.

Other research has explored how leisure practice and the conduct and contest of leisure can be used to resist discourses or beliefs about femininity and appropriate feminine behaviour. Sport is one avenue that is available to women for resistance to masculine hegemony (Bryson, 1987). Sport involvement, as well as other forms of leisure participation such as motorcycle riding (Auster, 2001), can provide the opportunities to create autonomous and resistant identities (Wearing, 1992). Women's friendships also provide means of resistance through the sharing of experiences and through the use of humour to subvert sexist imagery (Green, 1998).

Again, the relevance of the idea of resistance is compelling, but the process is varied and complex and this is particularly evident from research that has revealed the contradictory nature of resistance. In a study of women ice hockey players in Canada, Theberge (2000) discusses how women's participation in this male-dominated sport refutes the myth of female frailty, while simultaneously offering apparent confirmation of categorical gender distinctions through the naturalization of difference. Similarly, a study of female body-builders revealed how this apparently non-compliant activity for women fosters compliance to some traditional versions of femininity (for example, sexual objectification) as well as resistance to other components, such as physical passivity (Guthrie and Castelnuovo, 1992). In addition, in a recent study of Masters athletes (55 years of age and older) in Australia (Dionigi, 2004), a conflicting interplay of resistance and conformity was revealed. For these master athletes, resistance was primarily directed against the negative stereotypes of old age through proving that older adults are capable of competing in physically intense sports. At the same time, though, this type of resistance was linked to acceptance of orthodoxies associated with competitive sports and youthfulness, and with the denial of aging.

Moving beyond sports activities, a study of bachelorette parties (a recent alternative to the North American tradition of the bridal shower) concludes that these events can be seen to reinforce the narrow image of the sexualized female or can be understood as resistance to culturally constructed values such as female submissiveness (Tye and Powers, 1998). Even participation in violent and sexist video games play can sometimes represent resistant behaviours. In a study of avid male and female players (Delamere, 2004), the games' images and actions, as well as the cultural environment of video game play, clearly reinforced female sexualization and 'emphasized femininity' (Connell, 1987) as well as male violence against women. Nevertheless, the female game players deliberately resisted the misogynistic aspect of the gaming culture and claimed their right to participate in this male dominated activity on equal terms with the male gamers. This is consistent with the conclusions of Bryce and Rutter (2003) about the gender dynamics of computer gaming and some women players' determination not to be excluded from this form of leisure practice.

Discussions of the contradictory nature of resistance is not unexpected since it can be argued that, like hegemony, resistance is never going to be fully complete, but continuously subject to change, interpretation, revision and ambiguity. This does not deny or invalidate the usefulness of the concept, but it does reinforce the need for further theorization, including closer attention to the processes, nuances, and individual and collective meanings, reflections, and interpretations. The research on women's leisure and resistance has indicated some ways in which the idea of resistance resonates with and informs questions related to gender equity and women's empowerment, and suggests that this framework of analysis may be relevant to other areas of leisure scholarship as well.

Most of the research on men, sport and gender relations (for example, Messner and Sabo, 1990; McKay et al., 2000) has focused on ways in which male sport and the sports culture reinforce and reproduce masculine hegemony. For example, the McKay et al. book, utilizing a pro-feminist framework, has demonstrated the importance of gender as a focus of analysis for understanding male sport. In particular, this work provides an extensive analysis of the ways in which sports typically reproduce and ideologically naturalize existing gender hierarchies as well as hierarchies related to race, ethnicity, sexuality and class. Yet the issue of resistance is not absent from this body of scholarship, and this attention to resistance reflects the variations in behaviours, experiences and forms of male sport. The growth of gay sports cultures, such as the Gay Games, and the increasing number of openly gay male professional athletes suggests some progress in resistance to the homophobic environment of many sports contexts (Pronger, 2000). Nevertheless, Pronger argues that these changes do not represent a fundamental challenge to sociocultural structures, but have given lesbians and gay men 'the opportunity to conform to those structures' (ibid.: 242). Similarly, Dunbar's (2000) analysis of black masculinity addresses the complex question of professional sport as a potential site of resistance, as well as a site for the reproduction of racism and sexism.

These analyses resonate with Laberge and Albert's extensive work on gender transgressions of adolescent boys (2000). While this study showed social class to be a confounding factor, gender transgressions within sport were typically seen by male adolescents to threaten masculinity, and resistance to male norms of behaviour was muted. These findings of the muted, hesitant or ambivalent resistance in the sports environment are, perhaps, to be expected because of the dominant male sports culture. Resistance to male hegemony may be more likely to occur in other areas of male leisure practice – a topic that has received little academic attention to date.

Apart from questions of gender, though, the idea of resistance may have considerably more potential than currently realized for understanding the meanings and significance of a range of different forms of leisure and different types of resistance. In a recent paper by Shinew et al. (2004) on race and leisure, the argument is made that two different types of resistance may be of significance in understanding race-related constraints. First, resistance could be directed towards breaking down barriers and gaining opportunities to participate in a wide range of leisure activities. This would be consistent with arguments about women gaining access to male dominated activities such as sports or computer games. Second, resistance could be manifested through the choice of pursuits that reinforce the individual's unique subculture, thus helping to maintain cultural identity. These are ideas that are clearly worthy of further exploration. They are also ideas that could be applied to issues of class and ethnicity, placing emphasis on resistance to the values that demean, subjugate or devalue certain types of activities, and instead celebrating difference and diversity.

Resistance to the impact and fallout of various aspects of globalization may also be evident in leisure. The notion of civil leisure, as discussed by Mair (2002/03), refers to the use of leisure and social activism as a form of resistance through the creation of public discursive space. The significance of this idea is that it places emphasis on the political nature of leisure and how leisure can become a public realm for discussions about local and global society. Resistance to Western domination can also take the form of the rejection of American (and other Western) media, such as movies, television programmes, music, books and magazines. Evidence for this can be seen in support for multiculturalism, for cultural maintenance and for increased understanding of non-Western traditions of leisure. Evidence can also be seen in emerging pockets of resistance to 'reality TV' and to other forms of hyperreality in leisure. Other potential areas of interest that relate to the idea of resistance include the voluntary simplicity movement (for example, Elgin, 1993), with its focus on leisure as an area of life that may be becoming increasingly complex, as well as the growing movement to fight overwork and time poverty through a stronger focus on leisure, culture and work reduction (for example, de Graaf, 2003; Hayden, 1999). These examples of challenges to dominant cultural patterns have not been systematically examined in terms of resistance. Greater attention to these issues and trends may enhance our understanding of the political nature of leisure practice, and may help to develop a more inclusive framework for future analyses.

Incorporating resistance

It is argued here that, in many ways, the concept of resistance has the potential to contribute to and enhance our understanding of leisure. The notion of resistance is relevant to many different subareas of leisure scholarship, including analysis of gender, race, ethnicity, class, family, sexuality, disability and caregiving, and it could provide a bridge for theory development and for connections to other areas of cultural analysis. With its roots in both structuralist and postmodernist camps, resistance addresses the balance of agency and structure. It also addresses issues of subjectivities, diversities and individual action, while at the same time illustrating the need to incorporate questions related to material conditions and the distribution of power among population subgroups and subcultures. The central contributions of the idea of resistance can be characterized as recognition of the political nature of leisure, of the importance of relative freedom and self-determination in leisure settings, and of the potential, although contradictory and ambiguous, for challenging relations of power. Resistance emphasizes the significance of leisure as a site where the personal is closely tied to the political.

Nevertheless, the concept of resistance remains problematic. It is not clearly defined in the literature, but remains a slippery and imprecise notion in a number of ways. First, there is a lack of agreement with regard to the issue of individual or collective resistance. Foucault's theorizing focuses primarily on individual gains in personal power through counter-discourses. Others have argued that resistance is inherently collective because, by definition, an individual act of resistance has implications for others. This latter argument is more consistent with the idea of structured power relations and the unequal distribution of power and resources. These differences in theoretical underpinnings suggest not only the need for theoretical refinement, but also that such refinement should recognize and differentiate between all types of resistance (that is, individual, collective, or both).

Related to the debate over individual versus collective action is the question, raised earlier, of what or who is being resisted. The idea of individual resistance suggests personal empowerment through resistance to constraints and impediments in individual and unique environments or situations. Despite very different theoretical underpinnings, there are some similarities here to the literature on leisure constraints (Jackson and Scott, 1999; Jackson, 2005), where the impetus is not empowerment *per se*, but seeking opportunities for leisure involvement through overcoming specific types of constraint. On the other hand, the notion of collective resistance suggests that some acts of rebellion that are personal or individual would not be seen as 'resistance' if they do not represent a challenge to existing structured relations of power within a given society. That is, overcoming constraints or barriers and enhancing personal power would also have to be acts that challenge patterned relations of power to be recognized as resistance.

This issue is extensively addressed by Dunbar (2000) in her discussion of Dennis Rodman, the African American basketball player who gained considerable media attention in the 1990s through declaring himself 'bad', dressing in female attire, wearing make-up and flirting with homosexuality. According to Dunbar, Rodman was exhibiting 'reproductive agency' rather than resistance:

> Reproductive agency such as Rodman's exists within a consumer context and merely offers an individualized rebellious style that appeals to some consumers. Resistant agency takes the form of action against corporate consumer culture to disrupt oppressive institutions. Rather than constitute resistance, individualized agency such as Rodman's is part of the process of hegemony whereby dominant norms and relations become accepted by a mass society through consent backed by the threat of force or sanction. (Dunbar, 2000: 284–5)

Dunbar's analysis focuses essentially on the outcomes and implications for oppressive institutional relations. Because of this she also looks at audience reactions, arguing that Rodman's rebellious actions could potentially leave room for 'resistant agency' by audiences, depending on how audiences interpret and respond to Rodman's image and behaviours. Thus this raises the issue of the outcomes of resistance as well. Whether resistance should be characterized according to outcome (effective or ineffective in removing constraints or counteracting dominant relations of power), or by intent (a deliberate challenge to power relations or an unintended or 'accidental' consequence of action), or both, is a question that needs further consideration. Attention to this issue might help to bring greater definitional clarity to the concept and/or result in distinguishing different modes of resistance.

To reiterate, the complexity of issues surrounding the idea of resistance indicates a need for better theorization. One way to help the process of clarification would be to conceptualize resistance as a process rather than as an act or specific incidence of agency. The processual nature of resistance would include consideration of the initializing act or actions (including the aspects of intent and deliberation as well as social context), the meanings, experiences and interpretations associated with the process (including individual meanings as well as collective meanings and audience reactions), and the outcomes or implications for individuals, for social/subcultural groupings and for societal power relations. In addition, as illustrated by Auster's (2001) research, resisting through non-traditional leisure choices is clearly facilitated by certain environmental, situational or interactional conditions that, for example, might include support for and awareness of such opportunities.

The many components of resistance that need to be factored into an understanding or clarification of the process illustrate the dangers of an oversimplified definition of the concept. A naive celebration of resistance has to be avoided, since resistance is not simply another 'benefit' or positive outcome of leisure to be added to the existing list. Rather, any discussion of resistance needs to be grounded within a broader understanding of the different components and contexts of particular leisure environments, practices, or settings. At the same time, the danger of simple dichotomization, which assumes that specific acts, practices or processes can be determined to be resistance or not, also needs to be avoided. Not only are specific situations complex and ongoing, but the contradictory nature of resistance defies simple categorization. The co-existence of resistance and reproduction is related to the instability and ongoing construction, reconstruction and contestation of hegemony, and, in postmodern society, to changing social conditions and social consciousness as well (Rojek, 1995). Greater clarification of the idea of resistance needs to be tempered with awareness of its complexities, ambiguities and contradictions.

Despite these complications, the argument can be made that resistance is not only a relevant concept for understanding leisure, but also an optimistic concept (Wearing, 1998). It focuses attention on social change, equity and the possibilities of empowerment. While leisure is clearly not a simple tool that can be used or manipulated to bring about social change, different forms of resistance are possible through claiming the right to leisure and through involvement in specific and potentially empowering types of leisure practice. Greater attention to the idea of resistance can thus enhance our understanding of the ways in which leisure may be an important component of social change and social transformation.

Bibliography

Auster, C. J. (2001) 'Transcending Potential Antecedent Leisure Constraints: The Case of Women Motorcycle Operators', *Journal of Leisure Research*, 33: 272–98.

Bedini, L. A. and Guinan, D. M. (1996) '"If I Could Just be Selfish ...": Caregivers' Perceptions of Their Entitlement to Leisure', *Leisure Sciences* 18: 227–39.

Bryce, J. and Rutter, J. (2003) 'Gender Dynamics and the Social and Spatial Organization of Computer Gaming', *Leisure Studies* 22: 1–15.

Bryson, L. (1987) 'Sport and the Maintenance of Masculine Hegemony', *Women's Studies International Forum* 10: 349–60.

Clarke, J. and Critcher, C. (1985) *The Devil Makes Work*, London, Macmillan.

Connell, R. W. (1987) *Gender and Power: Society, the Person, and Sexual Politics*, Stanford, CA, Stanford University Press.

Crook, S. (2001) 'Social Theory and the Postmodern', in G. Ritzer and B. Smart (eds) *Handbook of Social Theory*, London, Sage, pp. 308–23.

de Graaf, J. (ed.) (2003) *Take Back Your Time: Fighting Overwork and Time Poverty in America*, San Francisco, CA, Berrett-Koehler Publishers.

de Grazia, S. (1964) *Of Time, Work, and Leisure*, Garden City, NY, Anchor Books.

Delamere, F. M. (2004) '"It's Just Really Fun to Play"! A Constructionist Perspective of Violence and Gender Representations in Violent Video Games', PhD thesis, Department of Recreation and Leisure Studies, University of Waterloo, Ontario.

Dionigi, R. A. (2004) 'Competing for Life: Older People and Competitive Sport', PhD thesis, Department of Recreation and Tourism Studies, University of Newcastle, Australia.

Dreyfus, H. L. and Rabinow, P. (1983) (eds) *Michel Foucault: Beyond Structuralism and Hermeneutics*, Chicago, IL, University of Chicago Press.

Dumazedier, J. (1967) *Toward a Society of Leisure*, New York, Macmillan.

Dunbar, M. (2000) 'Dennis Rodman – Do You Feel Feminine Yet? Black Masculinity, Gender Transgression, and Reproductive Rebellion on MTV', in J. McKay, M. A. Messner and D. F. Sabo (eds) *Masculinities, Gender Relations, and Sport*, Thousand Oaks, CA, Sage, pp. 263–85.

Elgin, D. (1993) *Voluntary Simplicity: Toward a Way of Life that is Outwardly Simple, Inwardly Rich*, New York, William Morrow & Co.

Foucault, M. (1978) *The History of Sexuality*, New York, Vintage Books.

Foucault, M. (1980) *Power-Knowledge: Selected Interviews and Other Writings 1972–1977*, New York, Pantheon Books.

Freysinger, V. and Flannery, D. (1992) 'Women's Leisure: Affiliation, Self-determination, Empowerment and Resistance?' *Loisir et Société (Society and Leisure)* 15: 303–21.

Green, E., (1998) '"Women Doing Friendship": An Analysis of Women's Leisure as a Site of Identity Construction, Empowerment and Resistance', *Leisure Studies* 17: 171–85.

Green, E., Hebron, S. and Woodward, D. (1990) *Women's Leisure: What Leisure?* Basingstoke, Macmillan.

Guthrie, S. R. and Castelnuovo, S. (1992) 'Elite Women Bodybuilders: Models of Resistance or Compliance?', *Play and Culture* 5: 401–8.

Hayden, A. (1999) *Sharing the Work, Sparing the Planet: Work Time, Consumption, & Ecology*, Toronto, Ontario, Between the Lines.

Hemingway, J. L. (1999) 'Critique and Emancipation: Toward a Critical Theory of Leisure', in E. L. Jackson and T. L. Burton (eds) *Leisure Studies: Prospects for the Twenty-first Century*, State College, PA, Venture Publishing, pp. 487–506.

Herridge, K. L., Shaw, S. M. and Mannell, R. C. (2003) 'An Exploration of Women's Leisure within Heterosexual Romantic Relationships', *Journal of Leisure Research* 35: 274–91.

Jackson, E. L. (ed.) (2005) *Constraints to Leisure*, State College, PA, Venture Publishing.

Jackson, E. L. and Scott, D. (1999) 'Constraints to Leisure', in E. L. Jackson and T. L. Burton (eds) *Leisure Studies: Prospects for the Twenty-first Century*, State College, PA, Venture Publishing, pp. 299–321.

Jenkins, C. and Sherman, B. (1979) *The Collapse of Work*, London, Eyre Methuen.

Kellner, D. (2001) 'Cultural Studies and Social Theory: A Critical Intervention', in G. Ritzer and B. Smart (eds) *Handbook of Social Theory*, London, Sage, pp. 395–409.

Kelly, J. R. (1993) *Leisure Identities and Interactions*, London, Allen & Unwin.

Laberge, S. and Albert, M. (2000) 'Conceptions of Masculinity and Gender Transgressions among Adolescent Boys: Hegemony, Contestation, and the Social Class Dynamic', in J. McKay, M. A. Messner and D. F. Sabo (eds) *Masculinities, Gender Relations, and Sport*, Thousand Oaks, CA, Sage, pp. 195–221.

Larrabee, E. and Meyersohn, R. (1958) *Mass Leisure*, New York, The Free Press.

Lemert, C. (1997) *Postmodernism is Not what you Think*, Malden, MA, Blackwell.

Mair, H. (2002/03) 'Civil Leisure? Exploring the Relationship between Leisure, Activism and Social Change', *Leisure/Loisir* 27: 213–37.

Mannell, R. C. and Kleiber, D. A. (1997) *A Social Psychology of Leisure*, State College, PA, Venture Publishing.

Markham, S. E. (1991) 'The Impact of Prairie and Maritime Reformers and Boosters on the Development of Parks and Playgrounds, 1880–1930', *Loisir et Société (Society and Leisure)*, 14: 219–33.

McKay, J., Messner, M. A. and Sabo, D. F. (eds) (2000) *Masculinities, Gender Relations, and Sport*, Thousand Oaks, CA, Sage.

Messner, M. A. and Sabo, D. F. (eds) (1990) *Sport, Men, and the Gender Order: Critical Feminist Perspectives*, Champaign, IL, Human Kinetics.

Pronger, B. (2000) 'Homosexuality and Sport: Who's Winning?' in J. McKay, M. A. Messner and D. F. Sabo (eds) *Masculinities, Gender Relations, and Sport*, Thousand Oaks, CA, Sage, pp. 222–44.

Ramazanoghu, C. (ed.) (1993) *Up Against Foucault: Explorations of Some Tensions between Foucault and Feminism*, London, Routlege, London.

Ramazanoghu, C. and Holland, J. (1993) 'Women's Sexuality and Men's Appropriation of Desire', in C. Ramazanoghu (ed.) *Up Against Foucault: Explorations of Some Tensions between Foucault and Feminism*, London, Routledge, pp. 239–64.

Rojek, C. (1995) *Decentring Leisure: Rethinking Leisure Theory*, London, Sage.

Shaw, S. M. (1994) 'Gender, Leisure and Constraint: Towards a Framework for the Analysis of Women's Leisure', *Journal of Leisure Research* 26: 8–22.

Shaw, S. M. (1999) 'Gender and Leisure', in T. L. Burton and E. L. Jackson (eds) *Leisure Studies at the Millennium*, State College, PA, Venture Publishing, pp. 271–81.

Shaw, S. M. (2001) 'Conceptualizing Resistance: Women's Leisure as Political Practice', *Journal of Leisure Research* 33: 186–201.

Shinew, K. J., Floyd, M. F. and Parry, D. (2004) 'Understanding the Relationship between Race and Leisure Activities and Constraints: Exploring an Alternative Framework', *Leisure Sciences* 26: 181–99.

Soper, K. (1983) 'Productive Contradictions', in C. Ramazanoghu (ed.) *Up Against Foucault: Explorations of Some Tensions between Foucault and Feminism*, London, Routledge, pp. 29–50.

Theberge, N. (2000) *Higher Goals: Women's Ice Hockey and the Politics of Gender*, Albany, NY, SUNY Press.

Thompson, S. M. (1999) *Mother's Taxi: Sport and Women's Labour*, Albany, NY, SUNY Press.

Tomlinson, A. (1998) 'Power: Domination, Negotiation and Resistance in Sport Cultures', *Journal of Sport and Social Issues* 33: 235–40.

Tye, D. and Powers, A. M. (1998) 'Gender, Resistance and Play: Bachelorette Parties in Atlantic Canada', *Women's Studies International Forum* 21: 551–61.

Wearing, B. (1998) *Leisure and Feminist Theory*, London, Sage.

Wearing, B. M. (1990) 'Beyond the Ideology of Motherhood: Leisure as Resistance', *Australian and New Zealand Journal of Sociology* 26: 36–58.

Wearing, B. M. (1992) 'Leisure and Women's Identity in Late Adolescence', *Loisir et Société (Society and Leisure)* 13: 323–42.

Witt, P. A. and Crompton, J. L. (eds) (2001) *Recreation Programs that Work for At-risk Youth: The Challenge of Shaping the Future*, State College, PA, Venture Publishing.

Index